M. Wesley Roper
Muskingum 1960

Modern Society

Contributing Authors

Henry Bush, *Chs. 27, 28*

Thomas Hoult, *Ch. 14*

Roger Marz, *Chs. 23, 26*

Murray Seidler, *Chs. 1, 18, 22*
Wayne State University

James Burkhart, *Chs. 24, 25*
Stephens College

Raymond Lee, *Chs. 20, 21*
State Teachers College,
Indiana, Pennsylvania

Vera Kohn and Stephen Sarasohn,
Ch. 17

C. DeLisle Crawford, *Study Aids*
Hillsdale College

John Biesanz, *Wayne State University*

and Mavis Biesanz

odern Society

AN INTRODUCTION
TO SOCIAL SCIENCE

Second Edition

Prentice-Hall, Inc. *Englewood Cliffs, New Jersey*

1959

Modern Society, *Second Edition*

Biesanz and Biesanz

**Prentice-Hall
Sociology Series**

Herbert Blumer, *Editor*

Typographical Design by Walter Behnke

Second printing, August, 1959

59769

Preface

The authors of *Modern Society* have been highly gratified with its reception throughout the country, and with its translation into Spanish. In this new edition we have tried to come even closer to achieving our primary aim—"to present certain basic understandings that a person must possess if he is to approach the issues and problems of modern society rationally and constructively." We have emphasized these understandings rather than the problems to which they may be applied, which is in keeping with the approach used in integrated social science programs in every section of the country. We have sought to preserve the features of the first edition which have led to its wide adoption: a clear, simple writing style; cross-cultural comparisons; an integrative theme, "freedom and control in a complex society"; and the cumulative use of concepts and methods from several of the social sciences.

This edition is a thoroughgoing revision. In response to many requests we have added chapters on The Farmer and on State and Local Government. Chapters completely rewritten include: Education, Religion as a Social Institution, Prosperity Without Inflation, and the entire section on the Governing of Man. A new and unique feature of this edition is a carefully prepared set of Study Aids accompanying the discussion questions for each chapter. Of special value for the development of critical thinking and communications skills, these Study Aids also help the teacher or student to relate meaningfully the characteristic experiences and insights of the several social sciences to each other and to his own field of interest. Also new is an annotated list of relevant film strips that are available for classroom use. As in the first edition, the discussion questions for the various chapters have been phrased to encourage the reader to relate the new material to that which has gone before.

Wilbur Mangas, of the Project Planning Department of Prentice-Hall, helped immeasurably to prepare the manuscript for publication by working closely with us from the planning stage until bound books were received. We also owe thanks to Richard Hansen, Editor of the College Division, for his help and advice. During the long period of planning and writing we were encouraged by Wayne State University administrators Don Hecock, Victor Rapport, and Edgar Schuler.

We are very grateful to those who helped us on the first edition, both for their excellent chapters and for suggestions. At the time of writing the second edition, however, promotions, transfers, Fulbrights, and retirements had taken their toll. With but one exception, the contributors to this edition used the earlier book in their classes; and from this day-to-day experience, from their own specialized knowledge, and from their intimate connection with the general education movement, had developed excellent ideas on how to write an improved second edition. With but one exception we have worked very closely with the contributors during the planning and writing. This is not a book of readings but a unified text.

On the present edition we have been helped by many more than we could possibly mention. These include John Payne, Houston Robison, Luke Smith, Norman Allen, David Stout, J. Richard Wilmeth, Chester Hunt, Donald Ackerman, Fred Terrien, Charles Chapman, Paul Weidner, Edgar McKay, Charles Schutz, Paul Drost, H. P. Lohrman, Melvin Williams, I. Roger Yoshino, W. Gregor Macfarland, and J. E. Griner. Wayne State University colleagues, most of whom were also helpful in the first edition, include Leonard Moss, Alvin Rose, Thomas McEnroe, Theodore Fleming, Meyer Barash, Eleanor Wolf, Maude Fiero, Mel Ravitz, Helen Hause, and Roberta Sigel. We would especially like to express our appreciation to Professor Theodore Morgan of the University of Wisconsin, who generously permitted us to adapt Chapter 16 "Laissez Faire, the Mixed Economy, Socialism" from his *Introduction to Economics*, 2nd ed. (Prentice-Hall, 1956). Our thanks also to Lee W. Cochran and Russell M. Ross of the State University of Iowa for their help in preparing the film list. The generous help of Mrs. Peter Hiltunen and Elizabeth Hiltunen made it possible for a mother of three children to play an active part in preparing the book. We dedicate this edition, as we did the first, to our mothers: Maude Berry Biesanz and Hilja Lempia Hiltunen.

J. B.
M. B.

Contents

Science and
Social Science

This is an age of worship at the altar of science. There are very few among us who know what science is, but almost all of us are in favor of it. The word evokes reassuring visions of men in white coats, men who industriously go about their laboratories keeping watch over the marvelously colored liquids in their test tubes. Indeed the word "science" has magical qualities. One of the surest ways of gaining support

1

and widespread approval for almost any project is to suggest that it is a *scientific* attempt to do something or other. And what that "something or other" is often seems unimportant so long as the project is associated with science. "Science" is one of the key virtue words of twentieth-century American society. One might well wonder whether even religion has greater influence and power over Americans.

But we are inclined to forget that science has not always been looked upon as good, and that even today it is not held in esteem everywhere. This attitude was once charmingly expressed by a Turkish official in reply to the request of an English traveler for information about Turkey:

My Illustrious friend, and Joy of my Liver! The thing you ask me is both difficult and useless. . . . I have neither counted the houses nor inquired into the number of inhabitants of [this place]; as to what one person loads on his mules and another stows away on the bottom of his ship, that is no business of mine. . . .

Listen O my son! There is no wisdom unto the belief in God! He created the world, and shall we liken ourselves unto Him in seeking to penetrate into the mysteries of His creation? Shall we say, Behold this star spinneth round that star, and this other star with a tail goeth and cometh in so many years? Let it go! He from whose hand it came will guide it and direct it.

. . . I praise God that I seek not that which I require not. Thou art learned in things I care not for; and as for that which thou hast seen, I spit upon it. Will much knowledge create thee a double belly . . . ? O my friend! If thou wilt be happy, say, There is no God but God! [1]

It is clear that the author of the letter did not assume, as apparently did his English friend, that knowledge was to be sought for its own sake. To this Turkish official the outlook that we associate with science would certainly have appeared nonsensical. He viewed the world in a way that seems strange to most Americans at mid-century. Science, which was foreign to his scheme of thinking, may be highly praised or frowned upon depending on the time and place in which a person lives. It is true that scientists attempt to exclude bias from their observations and findings, but this does not alter the fact that the kind of evaluation given to science rises out of group attitudes and preferences. The desire to be impartial or objective is not inborn in man!

No doubt some of you who are now reading this chapter are surprised to find a discussion of science in a text of this sort. You perhaps believe that science is something that can be written about authoritatively only by the chemist, the physicist, or the mathematician. Even though you are enrolled in a course in social science, you may be wondering where science fits into the picture. The major purpose of this chapter is to shed more light on the nature of science and on its relationship to social investigation.

The Scientific • Many scientists themselves would un-
Method doubtedly find it very difficult to explain what science is. Scientific workers
often become so involved in *what* they
are investigating that they forget that, insofar as science is concerned, it is *how* and in what spirit they are investigating that is important. In other words it is approach rather than content that is the test of science. Chemistry, physics, and biology are considered sciences not because of their subject matter, but because of the *way* in which they are studied. Both astronomy and astrology, for example, are concerned with the position of the stars, but of the two only astronomy can properly be called a science because it is based upon the scientific approach, whereas astrology is not.

Science has been variously defined. Interestingly enough, not even scientists themselves agree on the essential nature of science. Many have regarded it as an "organized body of knowledge," others, more accurately, as an "organized way of obtaining knowledge." [2] Two thoughtful students have arrived at a definition that is best for our purposes. "*Science is efficient inquiry.*" [3] Similarly, an eminent anthropologist simply suggests that, "Science is sciencing." [4] The essence of his definition and the essence of what we have been trying to say is that science is a method.

There is no one road to scientific knowledge, but certain fruitful procedures of investigation are basic to the scientific method. And it is well to be familiar with them, provided they are not thought of as a rigid or unalterable plan for scientific work. It is customary to think of scientific investigation as involving four steps:

(1) *Making an hypothesis.* It is necessary for an investigator to define clearly, at least in his own mind, the thing that he is trying to prove or disprove. An hypothesis in its most basic sense is a statement of the problem to be tackled, and it may often arise out of the researcher's hunch or guess about what is true. It is what is assumed to be correct by the researcher as he begins his study; and depending on the evidence uncovered as he proceeds, he may alter, abandon, or verify his hypothesis. The formulation of an hypothesis helps scientific workers direct their energies to the task at hand instead of dispersing them in many directions.

It sets the stage for a planned voyage of discovery rather than a wandering and wasteful one.

(2) *Observing and recording.* This step involves very careful scrutiny of the data being studied. It entails using the human senses to their fullest, aided if possible by precision instruments, so that the matter being viewed is revealed in all its aspects. Such careful inspection must be matched by the precise description and recording of what is observed.

(3) *Classifying and organizing.* It is only when observed data have been classified and organized—that is, arranged in logical groupings—that relationships and patterns emerge. To note such phenomena is the main business of science. Science is concerned not with things but with the relationships among them.

(4) *Generalizing.* This is essentially the step wherein the scientific theory or law is formulated. That is, a formalized statement is made that describes the behavior of the data *under certain specified conditions.* It should be remembered that, contrary to popular impression, laws do not remain fixed. Once stated they are constantly subjected to qualification and revision.

The Scientific •   As it is generally and properly under-
      Spirit   stood, however, science involves some-
                      thing more than method and the related
                      procedures we have just described.
There is also, as we suggested above, what might be called a scientific spirit or attitude. This attitude is largely a matter of the state of mind of the investigator toward his subject. The notion of a scientific spirit becomes clearer if we think of it as a complex of attitudes, which may be broken down in the following way:

(1) *Curiosity.* This is simply the disposition to inquire. It is, however, different from curiosity in the ordinary sense. There are many curious people among us, but most of them are not scientists. Scientific advancement depends on curiosity of a highly disciplined and ordered sort.

(2) *Objectivity.* Objectivity refers to the way in which the researcher approaches the matter he intends to investigate. It is to be hoped that he will be able to examine his own preconceived notions regarding his research subject and that he will be able to control them. At all times he must be alert to the dangers of distorting his investigation because of his initial bias. He must be willing to consider all relevant facts in dispassionate fashion.

(3) *Patience.* The scientist must be disposed to take infinite pains. His work should be cautious, careful, and precise.

(4) *Courage.* The scientific worker must be prepared to state his findings no matter what they are or whom they might displease.

This scientific spirit is not easily or often achieved. The advice of one renowned scientist to "sit down before the facts as a little child, and let them lead you where they will" [5] is a beautiful ideal that scientists have not often attained. Yet it is well for the scientists to set their sights high, for high ideals often lead to high achievement.

The Position   •   With these remarks on the nature of
of Social Science   science in general as background, let
                            us consider the position of the social
                            sciences in the realm of science. Not
all students of the scientific method, nor even all social scientists, are convinced that the various social sciences such as history, political science, sociology, anthropology, and economics qualify as full-fledged sciences. Certainly, the general public does not accord the social scientist the same kind of hearing that it gives to those who work in the field of the natural sciences. For example, Albert Einstein, the world's most renowned mathematician, was listened to eagerly and reverently when he spoke on international affairs, something about which he may have known no more than you or I. But the remarks of a trained international relations specialist will often go unnoticed. The prevalent view in America seems to be that specific training counts for little in understanding social affairs. "The man in the street," who would not dare to venture an opinion on atomic fission, glibly expounds on international relations. The attitude of many Americans toward the expert in social affairs was reflected in the hostility that was directed at the New Deal's "Brain Trust," which was basically composed of university social scientists.

Indicative of the superior status allotted to such fields as mathematics, chemistry, and physics is the fact that they are usually referred to as the "exact" or "natural" sciences. It would seem that the social sciences have barely escaped becoming known as the inexact or unnatural sciences.

The difference between the "natural sciences" and the "social sciences" perhaps becomes clear if we remember that human nature is acquired by men through group living. All the social sciences study, with different emphases, the same reality—man in terms of his relationships with other men. This is the justification for the word "social." Some of the natural sciences, such as biology and its many allied fields, also study man. These branches of knowledge, however, are concerned primarily with man as an individual physical organism. Their basic stress is not upon man as a social being. The physical or natural sciences investigate the physical universe, which man did not make, but of which, as a biological organism, he is a part. The social sciences, on the other hand, deal with the social universe, the network of human relationships that is a product of man's group life. The social universe is just as real as the physical universe despite the fact that it appears more intangible.

Briefly, the natural sciences attempt to examine the physical universe by the scientific method, and the social sciences attempt to examine the social universe by the same method.

During the present and past century man has made remarkable strides toward bending the physical universe to his will; yet his control over the social universe has not increased proportionately. Throughout the ages philosophers have repeatedly told man "know thyself." Despite this good advice, man has learned more about external things than about himself. We know more about the air we breathe, the water we drink, and the sand we walk on than we do about ourselves.

Although the ultimate end of any science is control of the phenomena being studied, the social scientist is not a reformer. He deals with problems of knowledge—i.e., scientific problems—rather than problems of action or social problems. His findings can, of course, be intelligently used in dealing with social problems, but this is the task of policy-makers and administrators rather than social scientists. In his role as a citizen the social scientist may, of course, deal with the solution of social problems, but as a scientist his first concern is with knowledge rather than action or reform.

Obstacles to the Scientific Study of Human Behavior

• *Difficulty of attaining objectivity.* The achievement of a particular state of mind on the part of investigators has had an important bearing upon all scientific progress. A basic tenet of scientific inquiry, as we have already pointed out, is that insofar as possible an objective and dispassionate attitude must be maintained in regard to the materials being studied. Perfect objectivity is probably never obtained in any science. Yet in the fields of mathematics, chemistry, and physics notable advances have been made in that direction. The social sciences, however, have not known comparable success in this area.

This disparity in impartiality stems from the fact that the emotional stake is inevitably larger in the social sciences than in those fields that do not deal with man as a social being. No man is able to study about his fellow human beings without the process of identification affecting, to some extent, his methods of inquiry and his findings. Everyone harbors feelings, and often strong feelings, concerning the various aspects of human affairs. One person views another in terms of a whole complex of preconceived notions or stereotypes that are colored by feelings of love and hate and various shades and combinations of these emotions. But, it may be asked, should a change be sought in this situation? "An individual attaining this ideal of an entirely emotionless being, devoid of all human passions and prejudices, probably would present," writes one social scientist, "a well-nigh classical case of pseudo-feeble-mindedness." [6]

Nevertheless, few would deny that it is much easier for individuals to remain neutral when examining the subject matter of the natural sciences than when examining the subject matter of the social sciences. For example, most persons are not inclined to view chemical and physical relationships in partisan fashion. We do not feel that it is immoral for sulphur and mercury to intermix. We do not worry about the fact that atoms are imprisoned within molecules. We do not love one chemical element and hate another. But in the realm of human affairs many of us do frown upon the intermingling of Negroes and whites. We do worry about slave labor camps in Russia. We do exhibit prejudices with respect to race, religion, and nationality.

Headway in any scientific endeavor depends on distinguishing the "self from the not self." [7] Because men tend to identify themselves with other men this is much harder to do in the field of the social sciences than in the natural sciences. However, it should be pointed out that this very fact of identification constitutes an advantage, at least in one respect. An area of reality not available to the physical scientist is available to the social scientist. When the physical universe is investigated, it is always viewed from the outside. Man did not create the physical universe and cannot identify himself with it. Man, collectively speaking, did create the social universe and is able to identify himself with it. For the social universe is, after all, composed of the behavior patterns of men. Man is able, in short, to achieve certain kinds of understandings about the behavior of other men that are closed to him when he examines the natural world.

Despite this particular advantage, the identification process has been, on the whole, the most serious obstacle to objectivity in social science. Real progress in the physical sciences was made only when man learned to detach himself from what he studied and to explain the universe in terms of its own workings rather than in terms of his own mind. Along these lines, it has been suggested that scientific understanding developed first in those areas where it was easiest for man to distinguish between himself and the matter he was studying—where what he was studying was least vital to man's existence.

According to one student of science, to be more specific, the natural sciences developed in the order of their remoteness as factors influencing the behavior of human beings. Hence astronomy, which concerns itself with the behavior of heavenly bodies, developed before physics, which concerns itself with the behavior of things on earth. Likewise, in the field of medicine, anatomy, which is the study of structure, developed before the more vital physiology, which is the study of function. Thus, in terms of this interpretation of the history of science, the social sciences have not yet reached maturity precisely because they deal with matters that are so significant to mankind. It is suggested, in other words, that the more important the subject to be studied, the harder it is to be objective.[8]

The problem of formulating "laws." Whether or not the fields of social investigation will develop into full-fledged sciences depends, in the view of many persons, on social science's success in formulating laws comparable to those of the physical sciences. If this criterion is to have any meaning or validity, the real nature of physical laws must be kept in mind. Such laws are not in any literal sense discovered by man in nature. They exist in the minds of men rather than in the world of nature. For laws merely describe uniformities that can be observed in behavior; they do not constitute behavior itself. Moreover, it is essential to remember that scientific laws do not apply in all instances. They hold good only under certain specified conditions. For example, the deservedly renowned law of falling bodies applies only to objects that are at sea-level and in a vacuum. Thus a *law is a "generalized description of the behavior of a phenomenon under given conditions."* [9] Not all the problems confronting the physical scientist have been resolved by the formulation of precise and meaningful laws. The precision and the definitiveness of the natural sciences often have been exaggerated by unsophisticated students of science.

The problem of prediction. The matter of prediction or the perception of general patterns, assuming that such patterns do exist, would appear to be more difficult in the social sciences than in the natural sciences. The fact that the social sciences deal with living matter helps to explain this. For the same reason, among the natural sciences, predictions in the field of biology are less certain than in the field of physics.

The method of science, it should be understood, is not particularly fruitful when applied to the study of unique occurrences, for in such study there is no opportunity for making comparisons or for noting uniformities. Social science research lends itself best to prediction when it confines itself to the task of studying recurring patterns, events, or situations as they are related to group life. This statement is substantiated by the fact that social prediction appears to be more successful in the field of demography, which is the statistical study of population.

Use of the experimental method. Any discussion of the general difficulties relating to the development of a more mature and more exact social science must take into consideration the experimental method. This method has been, to a large extent, responsible for the enormous strides made in the physical sciences. "The fundamental rule of the experimental method is to vary only one condition at a time and to maintain all others rigidly constant." [10] This procedure is usually accomplished in physics and in chemistry with the aid of laboratory conditions and precision instruments. Obviously, the laboratory analysis of human beings in group situations is usually not practicable. Happily, our customs do not allow us to treat human beings as mere guinea pigs. Furthermore, the social sciences are still lacking in precision instruments comparable to those that are used in the natural sciences, although it is true that technical aids are being used increasingly in social science research. Yet it is very clear that the experimental method has not found widespread application in the social sciences.

Need for a precise language. Finally, in our attempt to shed light upon the immaturity of social science, we turn to language. It is debatable whether the present state of social science language is a cause of the immaturity of social science or merely a reflection of it. But what is certain is that contemporary social science language is not an adequate medium of scientific communication.

No science can prosper without a precise and universal language, a language that is exact and understood by scientific workers the world over. The progress that has been made in fields like astronomy, physics and chemistry has been in no little way related to the fact that these sciences have utilized mathematics as their language. Mathematics well meets the requirements of precision and universality. It facilitates meaningful communication between scientists everywhere. The most notable scientific achievement of our time, the release of atomic energy, was made possible through an international exchange of scientific information and ideas.

Some less than friendly critics have suggested that the social sciences tell us about things that every person knows in language that nobody can understand. This is hardly an accurate statement. But unfortunately it cannot be denied that social scientists do have real difficulty in communicating with laymen and even with one another. They are confronted by serious semantic problems—that is, problems relating to the meaning of words. Many words used in social science are also in wide use among laymen. Moreover, these same words are frequently used in quite different ways. To the layman, for example, the word "culture" merely refers to art, literature, and music. To the social scientist, however, culture includes all the man-made aspects of the environment. There are also some identical words that are used differently by persons working in the various social science fields. To the sociologist the word "socialization" means the process whereby an individual acquires human nature; to the political scientist or economist it means government ownership and control of an industry. Similarly the word "value" means one thing to the economist and another thing to the sociologist.

The inadequacy of contemporary social science language has so discouraged some persons that they have concluded that the social sciences will come of age only if and when and to the degree that they adopt mathematics as their language. Others question whether such an adoption would be possible or desirable. In any case the picture is not hopeless. During recent years much headway has been made toward the development of a more precise and more universal language in the social sciences.

New Developments in Social Science   •   Thus far we have been stressing the difficulties that confront social science. We do not suggest, however, that the present situation of the social sciences justifies only gloom. In addition to progress toward the development of a common language, there are other promising developments in social science.

Theory and research. Every science stands on two legs: theory and research. Some social scientists have made their chief contributions as "armchair theorists," posing the great questions about human behavior within a general framework. Others have concentrated on empirical research—that is, direct observation of specific data. Either contribution alone is fruitless. Theory must be tested against fact and fact fitted into

meaningful patterns by theory. Modern social scientists realize the complementary nature of both approaches. They neither accept untested
generalizations nor aimlessly collect data unrelated to any general theory.
The professional political scientist, for example, is no longer content
simply to study constitutions and various government documents; he
now well realizes that there is always a large gap between adopted rules
and regulations and people's behavior. He is more and more concentrating
his attention on the way in which people really behave with respect to
governmental systems.

Methods. Social scientists are evolving and testing methods appropriate
to empirical research. Among these methods, the two that are perhaps
the most fundamental are the case study and social statistics. Many of the
newer observational research techniques in social science are related to
them.

The *case study* is a form of qualitative analysis involving the very
careful and complete observation of a person, a situation, or an institution. It is a variation of the historical method; it is, in effect, the historical
method being applied to the present. Thoroughness is the keystone of
this method. The case study stresses complete, exhaustive, detailed analysis that enables a person to analyze total situations in comprehensive
fashion. The success of the case method depends on all relationships
being noted and all observations being carefully recorded.

The *statistical method* is, of course, quantitative analysis. "Social
statistics is mathematics applied to human facts. Statistics call for objective data that can be counted or measured in some way. Statistics means
that facts when measured by different observers using the same methods
will always yield the same results." [11] One statistician suggests that statistics is essentially a form of reasoning.

The attempt to measure social data is a basic trend in contemporary
social science. More and more of our university social science departments are including social statistics in their offerings. Yet we should
remember that all sound quantitative analysis rests upon sound qualitative analysis. Most competent social scientists would agree that the case
method and the statistical method are complementary and interdependent. It is largely the case method, for example, which provides the
materials that social statistics attempts to summarize. On the other hand,
it is only when case studies and various aspects of them are summarized
by statistical procedures that the revelation of uniformities—which is the
main business of science—is accomplished. It would not be an exaggera-

tion to suggest that qualitative and quantitative analysis are the Siamese twins of science.

Integration. Another significant and hopeful development in social science is the trend toward integration of the approaches and knowledge of the various fields. This trend appears to be affecting university social science instruction and research in every part of the country. Social science integration is based on the theory that our contemporary social world can be comprehended only in terms of a number of the social sciences. Take, for instance, the phenomenon of war in the twentieth century. In order to gain any basic understanding of this problem, it is necessary to turn to several of the social sciences. To put it briefly and incompletely, political science informs us about the relationship between war and the national state system; economics shows us how war and international trade are intimately related; sociology and social psychology provide us with information concerning the dynamics of group life as they are related to the development of a war mood. All these avenues of explanation, and others as well, must be considered if war in our time is to be understood.

From the point of view just described, the social sciences are like worms in a can; they are all intertwined. But the social world with which the social sciences deal bears little relation to the kind of social science departmental divisions that have grown up in American education. The attempt to distinguish what falls within the province of economics or sociology or political science has often led to dangerous distortions of reality.

Impressive arguments can, of course, be marshaled for a more specialized approach to the social sciences, and it is easier to talk about integration than it is actually to integrate. Nevertheless, an increasing number of social theorists and researchers are convinced that it makes educational sense to view the social world from the vantage points of the several social sciences.

In short, the newer tendencies in social science, as exemplified by the development of theory backed up by empirical research, the progress toward a more universal and precise language, and the trend toward integration, all indicate and contribute to the development of a more mature and exact social science.

PART ONE

Culture, Society, and Personality

The San Blas Cuna of Panama

Before inquiring into what culture is and does, let's make an imaginary flight of a few hours from Miami to visit some Indians we know. They live only minutes away by plane from bustling Panama City and the Canal Zone on some beautiful tropical islands where coconut palms grow gracefully out of white sand. Our guides on the trip will be an anthropologist, Dave Stout, and a Canal Zonian, Fred McKim,

15

both of whom lived among these Indians and studied their way of life.[1]

About 20,000 Cuna Indians live on the Archipelago of San Blas, a string of islands along the eastern coast of Panama, which are protected from the turbulent Caribbean by coral reefs. Their crowded villages occupy about thirty islands, chosen for their nearness to the mouths of streams on the mainland, where all firewood and fresh water are obtained and agriculture is carried on. The islands are better suited for human habitation than the mainland, because they are freer of malarial mosquitoes. Many of the islands are also used for raising coconuts, which are the basis of the Cuna trade with the outside world.

The People   •   The Cuna are unusual among American Indians in several respects. They have maintained their tribal identity and a remarkable degree of independence and of "breed purity" in spite of having been in contact with conquering Spaniards, of having lived under the flags of Colombia and Panama, and of having traded with ships of many nations for over a century. They never submitted as beasts of burden for the Spanish treasure hunters, and only within the last decade or two have they accepted a measure of Panamanian authority. They still maintain zealous watch over their women lest they be violated by visitors. Only rarely, and then with utmost precaution, do they allow non-Cuna men to stay overnight on their islands.

San Blas Indians. *Women and children pose in their colorful native costumes. Note albino woman toward center of group.*

As a result of centuries of close inbreeding, the Cuna are a distinct physical type. Brown-skinned and thickset, with powerful shoulders and backs and deep chests, which make their legs appear thin and short in contrast, they are among the shortest people in the world. Men average 4 feet 8 inches in height, women 4 feet 5 inches. A most striking feature, noticed by visitors since the early Spaniards and buccaneers, is the high percentage of albinos (persons with pale, milky skin, light hair, and pink eyes) among them.

Boys do not bother to wear clothing until they are somewhere between six and nine years old, when they adopt the simple masculine costume of loose shirt and drill trousers, which are often rolled up to the knee. When making a trip to Colon, the nearest large city, about 80 miles away by boat, men wear ready-made suits, white shirts and neckties, felt hats, and sometimes shoes.

Little girls, on the other hand, are replicas of their mothers from early childhood. The female costume is striking and colorful, and a delight to the tourist. With a calf-length skirt of dark blue figured material, the woman wears a *mola,* a gaudy blouse of bright cotton, with blue or red predominating, which she has worked into intricate designs in appliqué. From her nose dangles a gold ring. A red or black streak is painted down the middle of her nose and her cheeks may be reddened. Over her straight black bobbed hair she wears a red and yellow scarf that hangs below her shoulders. Her arms and legs are tightly bound for several inches in colored glass beadwork. Around her neck she wears many necklaces, which indulge her fancy and display her wealth. Some of these necklaces are made of seeds, others of shells, animal teeth and claws, beads, and scented wood. But she takes most pride in her necklace of silver coins. She may also wear heavy gold ear disks.

The Cuna place a high value on personal cleanliness and may take several baths daily, either in the sea or river or in special bathhouses constructed on the shore.

Villages • Some islands are entirely covered with
and Dwellings the thatched-roofed dwellings of the
Cuna, the houses being separated by a
passageway, whose width depends on
the space available. The typical house forms a large rectangle, perhaps 25 to 50 feet long, 15 to 40 feet wide, and 12 to 25 feet high, containing but one room and one story. It is built on a frame of poles driven into the ground and held together with vines and strips of bark. The walls are of bamboo, reeds, or light poles, set upright and lashed to the frame.

There are no windows, but light and air pass through the cracks between the poles, and there is a doorless entrance at each end. The roof is thatched with palm leaves piled a foot thick to keep out sun and rain.

Hammocks are hung for perhaps 12 to 20 persons in such a house. Their belongings hang along the walls, and pushed to the side are one-piece wooden seats, benches, packing-box tables, wooden chests, and storage platforms. The floor is of hard-packed earth. A cookhouse, 15 by 30 feet, adjoins the living quarters. Here a fire burns on the floor, fed by three or four long thick logs radiating like the spokes of a wheel; they are pushed toward the center as they burn, and their ends glow through the night.

Rectangular thatched enclosures built on piles over the water serve as latrines and bathhouses. Each village also has a meeting house.

Village and Family　•　In this large house lives a Cuna family,
Organization　　which may include three or four generations. Casual observers often jump to the conclusion that the San Blas Cuna are under "petticoat government" because when a man marries he moves in with his wife's family, and each large household is united through the female line. The oldest male, however, is head of the household. Besides his wife and unmarried children, the household includes his married daughters and granddaughters and their husbands and unmarried children. Each evening the head of the household decides what tasks each man is to do next day. When they go together to the mainland, they are seated in the canoe in a strict order by age, and walk in that same order on the mainland. The same hierarchy holds true for women, whose status is linked to that of their husbands. The wife of the head man apportions tasks and exercises authority over the other females in the household.

Father and son continue to help each other after the son marries, but only with the permission of the head of the son's new household. Any tyrannical tendencies on the father-in-law's part are checked by public objection and censure by the father of the exploited young man; in extreme cases the young man may divorce his wife without paying any penalty to her family. Upon the death of the head of the household, each of the couples may leave and set up their own household, particularly if they have large families. If they choose to remain together, the oldest son-in-law becomes the new family head, unless the deceased man is survived by his wife's sister's husband, a brother, brother-in-law, or son older than any of the sons-in-law and living in the house at the time. In either case, two or more related households cooperate in work and ceremonies.

Village government has been described as a "socialized democracy based on individual rights and individual responsibilities." It is headed by a chief chosen by majority vote of the married men; he may hold office for life unless some serious failing moves the villagers to depose him. He must possess an extensive knowledge of the myths, folktales, and legendary history of the tribe. He presides over village meetings, which are held three to five times a week and are of two kinds.

One type of meeting is a "talking" meeting attended by married men, where business of interest to the village is discussed. At the "singing" meeting, attended by all, the chief chants allegories based on myths and legends. These allegories contain morals that set the pattern for good behavior. Among the most important rules for conduct are cooperation in the work of the village and household, truthfulness, modesty, chastity, honesty, and neighborliness. A person who violates any rule is called to the council meeting where he can tell his version of what happened and then must listen to the chief reciting or chanting the appropriate myths or folktales. He is not otherwise punished by the village, but the knowledge that violators are shamed before the villagers is sufficient to keep most people in line. An offender may be punished, however, by the family of an offended person.

Besides the chief, village officials include elders, who act as advisors; a treasurer of village funds; policemen, who summon people to meetings, keep order there, and collect food for feasts; and a number of men in charge of various communal enterprises, such as house-building and communal farms. Every community also includes medicine men, ceremonial chanters, grave-diggers, and a marriage-maker. Learning and experience are considered essential requirements for men who fill the more important posts.

Most of the villages belong to one of two main political parties, each headed by a high chief chosen for life by delegations of village chiefs and other officials. He must above all be very learned in tribal history and tradition. These parties date back to 1925, when one faction favored and another opposed revolt against Panama. Apparently there are no longer differences so deep as to disrupt tribal solidarity.

Work and Play • The Cuna regard work as a privilege. When children are allowed to try their hand at adult activities, they feel proud and grown up and develop a cheerful attitude toward necessary tasks. Work is done with zest as a natural outlet for a healthy mind and body; idleness is regarded as a sign of illness. All able-bodied persons are expected to do their share; not even the chief expects to escape manual labor.

The household stirs at cockcrow. After drinking hot chocolate sweetened with sugar cane juice, they leave for the river, silently paddling their dugouts in the growing light. After the sun comes up, they exchange light banter and laughter. The men take the jungle trails to their cultivated plots. If the women have come along, they stay at the stream to wash clothes and fill vessels with fresh water.

Plots of land have been reclaimed from the virgin forest by hacking the growth with a huge, heavy knife called a *machete* and then burning off the vegetation. Plots are marked off by paths and are individually owned, but work is performed cooperatively by groups of relatives or friends. The plantain tree, a cousin to the banana, furnishes the plantain, which is the Cuna staff of life and can be cooked in various ways. Sugar cane, rice, yams, corn, the starchy manioc root, pineapple, and bananas are the other chief food crops. Fruit trees are also tended. Dibbles (iron-tipped planting sticks) and machetes are the chief tools used. Fish, game, and chickens raised on communally owned island farms, which each man tends for ten days in his turn, supplement the diet.

The Cuna have a cash crop, the coconut, that has in many respects changed their way of life. They moved to the islands partly because they are ideal places to raise the palms, and since then their economy has changed from a self-sufficient one to one dependent in part on world markets. Money and private property have become more important; more goods such as cloth and utensils are bought rather than made. From trading schooners the Cuna buy many items such as enameled pots, fishing equipment, guns, cloth, soap, salt, sugar, kerosene, plug tobacco, and glass beads. They usually pay for these things with coconuts, less often with oranges or eggs. For the goldsmith's products they pay with pigs on the installment plan. All barter commodities have a money value, and United States and Panamanian coins and bills, with the exception of pennies, circulate freely. On nearly every island there is a privately owned store that provides the villagers with kerosene, salt, sugar, soap, and matches in return for money, coconuts, or eggs. Trade between individuals is rare, except for buying canoes and the medicine man's cures.

Nearly everyone—man or woman—owns some crop lands and coconut plantations. Other forms of wealth are jewelry, women's clothing, money, and a great variety of hoarded white man's goods. Almost all wealth is derived ultimately from the possession of coconut trees, though younger men earn cash by working in the cities and the Canal Zone, and women sell *molas* and necklaces to tourists.

After working on the mainland till noon, the Cuna bathe in the river or sea and return to the village. They eat a meal from a "table" of banana leaves spread on the floor and set with gourd utensils. Men are served first. The afternoon may be occupied in a variety of pursuits. Women prepare food, sew clothing, weave hammocks. Men weave baskets, often do their own sewing and mending, make fishnets, sails, paddles, and gourd utensils, fashion canoes out of cedar or mahogany logs, or lesser woods if necessary, go fishing, and help each other build houses. Children swim and wade for hours.

There is no fixed dividing line between work and play. While they do their tasks, the Cuna talk, tell folktales, joke, and generally enjoy one another's company. They also enjoy swimming, sailing, visiting other islands, and various ceremonial occasions. Although each man regards the village of his birth as best, men travel freely among the islands, visit Colon, work in Panama and the Canal Zone, and for decades have served as sailors, often on American ships.

The world of the Cuna is timeless insofar as clocks and calendars are concerned. No written record is kept of dates and events. Tribal lore is passed on orally. To recall some past event, the Cuna refer to the seasons—the dry and rainy season, turtle season, tarpon season, mango season (May and June), orange season (November-December)—or to some other and more important event that was concurrent.

Beliefs   •   The Cuna conception of the world and their place in it gives them a strong sense of rightness and security. They believe that God created everything, including His own wife, and it is from their union that everything and everyone has come. The Cuna were the first created and noblest of all peoples. Besides God and His wife there is also an important female deity called Mu, who was delegated by God the task of forming human babies and giving them their individual attributes. God is all-powerful and all-seeing. All His provisions indicate that He wants man to be happy. But He does not tolerate sin. Three times He has destroyed the world, by fire, darkness, and flood, and in addition has visited local catastrophes upon earth to show His displeasure. After the flood, eight hundred years ago, He sent to earth on a plate of gold a superman named Ibeorkun, who explained to the Cuna the name and use of everything and laid down rules of behavior. The most important of these rules is that a person must be a good neighbor.

From this it follows that he must not lie, steal, commit adultery, or bear false witness. If these rules, which are taught orally in chants and folktales, are violated, God will punish the offender, either here or in the afterworld, through the agency of evil spirits.

The Cuna conceive of the world as an earth-plane on which people live, with a heaven of eight invisible layers above and an underworld of eight layers below, on the fourth layer of which live the chiefs of the evil spirits. The sky is hemispherical and is pierced at one point. The sun travels around the world on a ship on which certain evil spirits and demons also ride. The moon and certain stars travel on another ship.

All people and everything in nature are believed to have souls or *purbas* that are invisible, but whose existence is proven by shadows, echoes, and reflections. *Purbas* are believed to have an everlasting existence. After death, which the Cuna believe to be predestined, a person's soul travels first through the fourth layer of the underworld and then to heaven, where he is resurrected and thereafter lives a life similar to his life on earth, except that it is much more splendid. Heaven is lavishly furnished with many of the attributes of American civilization, which returning sailors and Zone workers have described in glowing terms.

These beliefs are not given institutional form in any body of priests, ritual, and the like. They are expressed in traditional chants, in the ceremonies of death and puberty, in the folktales and legends that many Cuna know and relate. They are effective in governing conduct because of the unity of the group and the fact that few are willing to risk being shamed in a public meeting for any transgression.

There are, however, two figures in Cuna society who command special power over evil spirits: the *nele* and the *innatuledi*. The highest status in Cuna society is accorded the *nele*, who is marked for special wisdom and insight by the fact that he is born with a caul. (That is, the placental membrane appears to cover his head at birth.) Through a course of learning covering many years and culminating in a special eight-day chant, a person born with a caul becomes a seer, a supreme worker with the supernatural, a theologian, and a diagnostician of disease. He is not surrounded with an air of holiness or sanctity, but is greatly respected. There are about ten *neles* among the Cuna, four of whom are women.

Most *neles* are also *innatuledis*, or medicine men, but there are many *innatuledis* who are not *neles*. Each island has several *innatuledis*, some as many as seven. They, too, undergo a long period of training during which they learn many medicines and chants. Their function is to try to cure illness, never to use sorcery for harm. The apparatus of an *innatuledi* consists principally of a great variety of powdered medicines prepared from plants, leaves and herbs, grotesquely shaped tree roots, sections of twisted vines and thorny branches, red paint, resins, cacao beans and several varieties of pepper pods, magic stones (believed to be powerful because they either stay cool when others get warm or vice versa), and small carved wooden fetishes, many in human form. Equally important are the words of chants used in connection with these medicines, for otherwise they are powerless to cure.

Full albinos enjoy a special status among the Cuna. Called "moon-children," they are believed to be more intelligent than pigmented persons; but because they cannot tolerate much sunlight, they are not considered good workers. They are, however, believed to be particularly free of sin and to have special favor with God; they will inhabit a special and superior place in heaven. To them is entrusted the task of scaring off the sky dragon who eats the sun and the moon during eclipses.

The Life Cycle • Birth takes place within the house in an improvised enclosure from which men and children are excluded. An *innatuledi* standing outside the enclosure chants and supplies the childbirth medicines as the midwife inside reports progress. The mother lies in a hammock, and the child is born into a waterfilled canoe beneath. The midwife buries the umbilical cord in the earth floor of the house. For three days after birth the father keeps to the house.

Infants are kept in a hammock and occasionally carried astride the hip. They are greatly desired and are cared for attentively by all the women of the household. Children often nurse up to age four or even six, unless the mother becomes pregnant again. They are treated leniently, and seldom struck. Although adults are not demonstrative among themselves, they are affectionate toward children. Boys are given great freedom and learn to swim and paddle canoes while very young. Girls are kept closer to home and spend much of their time caring for younger children. Some children now attend the schools that have been established on a number of the islands where they spend a few years learning to speak, read, and write Spanish.

Boys are considered eligible for marriage and for participation in village government when they are capable of doing a man's work, but no special ceremony celebrates their attainment of adult status. It is different with girls. The high point of the girl's life is reached during two ceremonials, the first of which announces that she has reached puberty, the second that she is eligible for marriage. The girls' ceremonies outshine all other observances in the life cycle. They are made the occasion for feasting, drinking, chanting, dancing; thus they serve as recreation and also bind the community more closely by reiterating the traditions of the tribe.

At her first menstruation, the girl is confined in an enclosure of staves and leaves for four days and frequently bathed with sea water by her female relatives. On the fourth day a woman, who is especially charged with the task, cuts her hair; she is painted black with a fruit juice and then released. Her future is foretold by two men who dig up land crabs on the mainland and see portents in their behavior. Meanwhile, *chicha*, a fermented drink of corn and sugar cane juice, is being prepared. When it is ready, about ten days later, the ceremony is resumed, with the men smoking long cigars, smoldering end in the mouth, and drinking *chicha* all day long. Near the end of the day the girl serves all the participants a cup of *chicha*. At night the *kantule*, or ceremonial chanter, recites the epic poem that incorporates the girl's life from birth to puberty and reiterates many of the teachings of Ibeorkun, who instituted this ceremony, which is called "The Flowering." The mystic numbers 4 and 8 recur throughout. The *kantule's* assistants play flutes and some of those present dance or dramatize sections of the chant.

One to five years later, a four-day ceremony indicating the girl's readiness for marriage is held. It is even more elaborate and expensive than the puberty ceremony. The family accumulates food and fuel for months in advance; the entire village contributes wood, sugar cane, and bananas. When the necessary huge quantities of *chicha* are ready, the ceremony is begun. The *kantule* directs the episodes. The girl is again confined in an enclosure, the long cigars are smoked, and much *chicha* is drunk. To keep evil spirits away, all those present have their faces, the palms of their hands, and the soles of their feet daubed with red paint, and cacao beans are kept continually burning in a number of receptacles.

For three days and nights the *kantule* and his assistants take turns chanting and playing flutes. The chants deal with the origin and history of the ceremony, the story of life from puberty to the grave, the wonders of land and sea, and stories of men and lesser creatures, each with an instructive moral for the education of the girl, who is listening in her enclosure. Again there is dancing; animals mentioned are mimicked and events are dramatized. On the fourth day the girl's hair is cut and she is given a permanent name that her mother has chosen from among those mentioned in the chants. Names are considered very important. There is a taboo against speaking the names of the dead, and the Cuna are circumspect in using personal names, often using kinship terms instead.

When girls are 15 to 17 and boys are 18 to 20, they are considered ready to marry. Marriages are arranged by parents, with the girl's father usually taking the initiative. If the girl or boy is opposed to the marriage it need not go through; but in the closely knit community, such opposition is rare. When a marriage has been arranged, the fathers notify the marriage-maker, who, with several assistants of his own choice, comes and carries the man to the girl's house, calling "Husband!" as they go. There the couple is placed in a hammock together. The young man runs away four times and is brought back again, remaining longer each time. The fifth time he stays all night. (If he is opposed to the marriage, he may refuse to come back the second time.) The two stay awake all night, for it is a bad omen to fall asleep, but no intimacies occur. Next morning he accompanies his father-in-law to the mainland and fetches firewood, an act which serves to seal the marriage. The girl goes to his old home and does some household task. That night the marriage is consummated.

Newlyweds are usually embarrassed for some time after marriage, and the bride, especially, keeps to the house. The Cuna are extremely reticent about sex; not until the marriage does an aunt or older sister instruct the girl in sexual matters. They stress sexual modesty, and exhibit strong feelings of shame concerning the genitals, sexual activity, and excretion. It is considered very improper if not sinful to speak openly of sex. The sexual impulse is regarded as an expression of one's *niga*, a supernatural attribute manifested in potency and strength. Persons are also thought to possess varying degrees of *kurgin*, or inclination to make love.

Marriages, with very few exceptions, are monogamous and are easily dissolved; the children remain with the mother and the father loses all control over them. A person is considered a full adult when he or she has married and had a child. He is thought to be in the prime of life from that point on until he can no longer do a day's work.

When a Cuna villager dies, he is immediately washed and dressed in his best clothes, laid in a hammock, and covered with a sheet. Mourning begins at once and goes on for a full day and night. A death chanter recounts the song of death, which goes on for hours, detailing the long and arduous journey of the dead soul bound for heaven. Relatives review the life and character of the deceased and speculate on what punishments he will suffer on his journey. Many come to give him messages for their dead friends and relatives.

The second morning, the hammock is tied up and carried on a long pole by two gravedigger-pallbearers to a canoe, in which the closest relatives also ride to accompany the body to the mainland cemetery.

There mourning continues while the grave is dug. Near nightfall the hammock is placed in the grave, suspended from two strong stakes that protrude above the ground. Personal articles and models of such things as canoes and bows and arrows are placed in the grave. Over the hammock a platform of staves and leaves is fashioned; then the grave is filled with dirt. Broken furniture and other articles are left on the grave for the use of the dead on his journey. Just before the gravediggers leave, they fasten a string to one of the stakes and lead it down to the river, tying it to a pole on the other side. The first person coming up or down the river must cut the string to prevent evil spirits from harming himself or the dead person and to ensure the departed a less hazardous journey to the afterworld.

The Cuna · What we have described as the Cuna
Way of Life way of life is today an entirely true
picture only where foreign influence
has been most strongly resisted. Some
islands, such as Narganá, have been "modernized" considerably through the influence of returning sailors, American Protestant missionaries, and Panamanian government agencies. These influences have affected the dress habits, marriage patterns, household arrangements, and beliefs of the Cuna, in varying degrees, and we shall be referring to them from time to time in later chapters.

In spite of the encroachments of foreign ways of life, most of the Cuna still live by the old traditions. These stress the importance of cooperation, neighborliness, respect for property, sexual modesty and chastity, truthfulness, cleanliness, and modesty concerning one's own achievements. Respect is accorded those who are considered learned, experienced, industrious, and obedient to the moral code. The Cuna practice political and economic democracy based on a strong community spirit, individual freedom, and individual responsibility. Their way of life impresses a person as peaceful and orderly and apparently satisfies all their needs and wants.

The Nature
of Culture

In Chapter Two we sketched some of the chief
features of the way of life of one group of
people. Nowhere else can a group be found
that lives quite this way. South Sea Islanders,
American Indians, African tribes, even other
Panamanian Indians have very different customs and beliefs. Each of these ways of life
is a *culture*. The group of people that shares
a common culture is called a *society*.

27

In this chapter we shall inquire into the meaning of culture in general, using illustrations from particular cultures. When we use the word *culture* in the general rather than the specific sense, we refer to the *learned portion of human behavior, the man-made part of the environment.* We do not mean only those aspects of human behavior that indicate taste, refinement, and interest in the "fine arts." Methods of garbage disposal are as much a part of culture, in the social scientist's sense of the term, as symphony orchestras. All human beings have culture, a San Blas housewife as much as a bejeweled patroness of the Metropolitan Opera. For a culture is the way of life of a group, and all its members share in it to a greater or lesser degree. Each group defines "human nature" in terms of its own particular culture. Some learned behavior, of course, is not cultural. We are referring here to that portion of learned behavior that is shared with and learned from others in the society.

Nor should culture be confused with the usual meaning of *civilization.* The word *civilized,* commonly used to mean the opposite of *primitive,* comes from the Latin *civis,* or town-dweller, and implies fairly large urban societies with complex economic and political systems. Many anthropologists have abandoned the word *primitive* to describe cultures that lack these elements, because it implies "backwardness" and a belief in a "ladder of progress" along which all peoples stand at one stage or another. They now favor the word *nonliterate,* indicating the absence of written language. *Preliterate* is also used, but because this word, like *primitive,* implies a line of progress, nonliterate is usually preferred. The San Blas Cuna would be classed as nonliterate.

The branch of social science most directly concerned with the study of culture is anthropology. The anthropologist's method has traditionally been to live in a strange society—usually a small nonliterate one—and to compile an organized description of its way of life. He tries to observe, describe, and analyze without judging or trying to influence what he sees. When many anthropological studies are considered together, they illuminate human behavior in many ways. To make this task easier and more systematic, a Cross-Cultural Survey has been compiled at Yale University; thus available data from many societies are filed so that any specific aspect of culture in different manifestations can be readily studied and compared.

One of the fundamental facts that has emerged from anthropological study establishes that most human behavior is learned rather than instinctive. Let us examine first the biological basis for human behavior, and then the characteristics of culture, in order to expand our brief definition of culture.

The Biological • Man is an animal. Like other animals
Basis with which he shares the earth, he is
of Culture a product of hundreds of thousands
of years of evolutionary development.
Scientists believe that the earth is more
than a billion—perhaps even 2 billion—years old. Modern man appeared
only about twenty-five thousand years ago, presumably in Western
Europe and the Mediterranean region.

To show what a latecomer to earth man is, a British scientist has
asked us to imagine that the height of the Empire State Building represents the age of the earth—a scale of about 2 million years to a foot. A
book placed upright on the building's TV tower would represent the
entire existence of *homo sapiens*. The thickness of a dime placed on the
book would correspond to the whole of human civilization back to the
founding of the earliest cities. And the era of modern science and technology would be about as thick as a postage stamp! [1]

Biologists classify animals according to structural characteristics.
Man belongs to the phylum *Chordata*, which is characterized by a group
of cells along the back, which help to stiffen the body and serve as the
central cord of the nervous system. Like other members of the sub-phylum
Vertebrata, man has a bony spinal column. The *Vertebrata* are further
sub-divided into classes, including the *Mammalia*, which embraces man
and other animals that are warm-blooded and bear their young alive.
Of the various orders of mammals, man, like the monkeys and apes, is
placed in the *Primate* order. The sub-order *Anthropoidea* includes the
great apes, such as the chimpanzee and the gorilla, as well as man.

The next sub-division is the family *Hominidae*, or "manlike," which
includes only modern man and his ancestors, the fossil men—Java man,
Neanderthal man, and Cro-Magnon man. Within this family modern man
belongs to the species *sapiens* (wise) of the genus *Homo* (man).

Being an animal, man has much in common with other animals.
Being one species, he also has many unique traits. Let us consider first
some of the things he shares with other animals, besides those structural
characteristics we have already pointed out.

Like all living animals, man is made of sensitive protoplasm and is
continually taking in and discharging matter and energy. His basic
problem is to adjust to his environment and to satisfy his biogenic needs
and drives, which include his need to eat, rest, exercise or engage in
random activity, satisfy thirst, eliminate, maintain his body temperature,
breathe, and discharge sexual tensions. These inborn needs or drives
make themselves felt as states of tension or lack of balance, which the
organism seeks to satisfy or dispel.

Like other mammals, man is bisexual. Like other primates, he knows no special season for mating and procreation. He usually gives birth to single offspring after long pregnancies, and the infant is helpless for a long period after birth. All these biological facts have tremendous implications for human society and culture.

Although man is an animal, we do not imply that he is "nothing but an animal." He differs from all other members of the animal kingdom in his capacity for becoming human.

What traits make *homo sapiens* capable of acquiring and building culture? First of all, two things he does *not* have are highly significant.

(1) He inherits very few patterns of behavior. He is born with a few *reflexes*, or automatic responses, each attached to a given stimulus. His pupils contract in strong light. His salivary glands "water" when he is hungry and when food is placed before him. His muscles contract when he feels pain. His nervous system governs his breathing, heartbeat, digestion, and excretion with relatively little voluntary modification on his part. Aside from these few reflexes he inherits no fixed patterns of response. Although much animal behavior is governed by *instinct*—increasingly so as we go down the developmental levels to the lower orders—man's behavior is not. An *instinct* is an inherited mode of behavior that has a physiological basis, clearly determines behavior, and is universal in expression in the species. Social scientists have abandoned this concept because it has no value in explaining human behavior. The old idea that war stemmed from man's "pugnacious instinct," for example, does not explain why man is not constantly at war. Even the "maternal instinct" is not instinctual. Little girls and childless women act maternal; and surgery and old age, which eradicate or atrophy the child-bearing organs, do not alter a mother's love for her children. Some mothers reject their children, and abortion and infanticide are practiced in many societies.[2]

(2) Man also lacks biological adaptations to specific environmental conditions. The polar bear's heavy coat, the elephant's tusks, the rabbit's protective coloring, and the fish's fins and gills are all extremely useful under certain conditions. But few animals are fitted for more than one kind of climate, food supply, or life situation. Man, on the other hand, is found pretty well distributed over the face of the earth in a wide variety of surroundings.

Thanks to his lack of fixed, inborn patterns of behavior and specific biological adaptations, man is very plastic, flexible, and adaptable. On the positive side, what biological characteristics does he possess that enable him to build and acquire culture, the human means of adapting to the environment?

He has a *prehensile hand,* with a thumb that he can oppose to each of his four long fingers. Thus he can grasp and manipulate and create with his hands. His hands are freed for doing work by his *upright posture.* He can stand on his two long legs because his curved spine and his arched foot cushion the shock of walking and prevent injury to his brain. His *binocular vision* can be focused for different distances. The higher primates, man's distant cousins, share these three attributes with him to some degree, but these traits alone are not sufficient to enable the great apes and monkeys to build culture.

What really sets man apart from the rest of the animal kingdom is his highly *complex nervous system,* including a large *brain,* and his *vocal apparatus.* Man's brain case is about three times as large as the gorilla's and is especially well-developed in the frontal area. This large brain is also very complex; there are perhaps 10 billion nerve endings embedded in the cerebral cortex.

Man's vocal apparatus enables him to speak articulately. Compared to the primates, his jaws are smaller and less protruding, and he has no obstructions (such as the simian plate) to interfere with the free movement of his tongue. His face is comparatively vertical, and his canine teeth are approximately the same size as his other teeth. This apparatus would, of course, be of no value to him if he did not have a highly developed speech area in his brain, which really makes it possible for him to symbolize and communicate, to learn, think, remember, and foresee. Thus he can create culture, acquire it from his fellows, and transmit it to others.

Importance • of the Human Group   In spite of his biological potentialities, no infant would acquire culture if he were not nurtured by a functioning social group. He would never use his prehensile hands to hit a home run or weave a basket, nor his brain and vocal apparatus to learn a language. He would not even be human. The first years of his long childhood are especially crucial for his acquisition of culture and personality.

Cases of extreme isolation from social contacts help to prove that human nature is a product of social life. Sociologist Kingsley Davis has investigated two such cases—Anna and Isabelle.[3]

(1) Anna was an illegitimate child whose stern grandfather kept her isolated in an upstairs room, where she received only enough care to keep her alive and little or no friendly attention or instruction. She was found and removed from the room when she was nearly six years old.

She could not walk, talk, or feed herself. She was extremely emaciated and apathetic, "lying in a limp, supine position and remaining immobile, expressionless, and indifferent to everything. She was believed to be deaf and possibly blind." [4]

For the next four and a half years, until she died, Anna was exposed to socializing influences. Before she died she had learned to walk, to talk in phrases, to practice habits of cleanliness, to follow directions, identify a few colors, string beads, build with blocks—in short, she had the abilities of a normal two- or three-year-old.

(2) Isabelle was also an illegitimate child, kept in seclusion for six and a half years. She spent most of her time in a dark room with her deaf-mute mother, with whom she communicated by means of gestures. When she was found, she exhibited the behavior traits of a six-month-old child. Lack of sunshine and proper diet had left her with rickets, and she was thought to be deaf and feeble-minded.

Nonetheless, those in charge of her began a systematic program of skillful training. After she finally began to respond, she went through the usual stages of socialization that a child experiences from ages one to six in proper succession and far more rapidly than normal, learning in two years what ordinarily takes a child six. After she first began to vocalize, it was only about two months before she was putting sentences together and nine months more before she was reading, writing, counting, and re-telling stories. When she entered school, she took part in all activities normally.

These cases indicate how little purely biological resources contribute to personality and how all-important communicative contact is to the process of becoming human. Anna's comparative slowness might be explained by a lower innate intelligence, but another important factor is that she had lacked any friendly contact such as Isabelle had with her mother, even in seclusion. Isabelle's rapid acquisition of culture invites speculation. Just how long could a person be kept in seclusion before he lost his capacity to acquire culture? Davis speculates that it might be only ten years, and certainly no more than fifteen.

Characteristics of Culture • *Culture is uniform yet variable.* Culture exhibits certain similarities in all societies because *homo sapiens* is all one species, with the same psychological make-up, the same organic needs, and the same essential life experiences the world over. Yet man has as many ways of satisfying the same organic and psychological needs as he has separate groups.

Similarities. Cultural similarities may be summed up in terms of the content of the culture. All cultures include a *technology,* or pattern of behavior that deals with utilizing natural resources to secure food and manufacture artifacts. All have an *economic system,* a set of beliefs and practices that governs the production, distribution, and consumption of goods and services. All have a *social structure,* a web of mutual rights and responsibilities based at least on age and sex, and usually on many other differentiations. A universal element of this social structure is the *family* system, which regulates sex behavior and provides for the care of children. Another is the system of *social control,* which includes *political organization* and *government* and regulates the relationships between individuals and groups within the society and between the society and other societies. All societies have a system of *education,* formal or informal, which trains the infant and child in cultural skills, knowledge, and beliefs.

All societies have some *belief system,* whether mythological, scientific, or philosophical, which explains the nature of the universe and man's place in it and defines good and bad, right and wrong. Prominent in this

SOME UNIVERSAL PATTERNS IN CULTURE

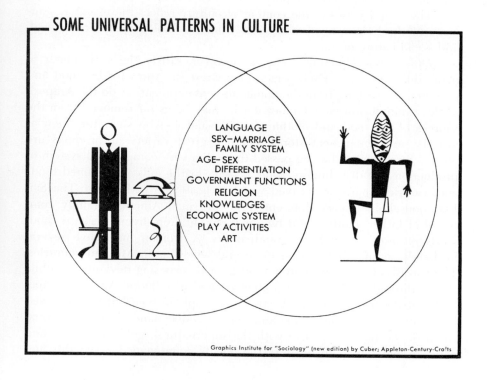

LANGUAGE
SEX–MARRIAGE
FAMILY SYSTEM
AGE–SEX
DIFFERENTIATION
GOVERNMENT FUNCTIONS
RELIGION
KNOWLEDGES
ECONOMIC SYSTEM
PLAY ACTIVITIES
ART

Graphics Institute for "Sociology" (new edition) by Cuber; Appleton-Century-Crofts

system is the universal element of *religion,* a system of beliefs and practices concerned particularly with man's relations to unknown forces.

Language is a universal cultural element because symbolic communication is basic to the existence of culture. It is the chief vehicle for the accumulation and transfer of knowledge and belief. Some form of aesthetic expression is found in every culture; the aesthetic *arts* include painting, sculpture, music, drama, and literature. According to anthropologists, any activity is related to the arts if its performance or product, "over and above its possible efficiency or utility, affords . . . satisfaction to the one who produces it or to those who may view it." [5]

Recreational or *play* activities are also present in all cultures, and some anthropologists believe that war is a universal phenomenon. Other investigators, however, have found peoples to whom warlike activity and the concept of war are completely alien.

As we shall see later, all these cultural elements are more or less closely interwoven. Religion, for example, insofar as it regulates man's relationship to his fellows, is part of the system of social control. In some cultures there is no sharp dividing line between work and play. We separate them here only for purposes of analysis and comparison.

These similarities in the content of culture reflect the essential similarity of the human needs that arise from the biological, psychological, and social nature of man.

Differences. Different societies, however, satisfy the same needs in many different ways. Each person may wrest the yams for his food and grass for his clothing from the immediate environment, as do the Arapesh in the mountains of New Guinea. Or he may be as far removed from the sources of his food and clothing as you and I, who shop for them at grocery and department stores where a great variety of products are offered for sale after having passed through a very complicated system of production and distribution. Some peoples loathe milk and canned foods and eat fried snails or decayed wood or head lice with gusto. The San Blas household is very different from the small American family composed of father, mother, and two or three children, living perhaps thousands of miles away from grandparents. A woman may have several husbands, as in Tibet, or a man several wives, as in Moslem countries. The San Blas Cuna insure proper behavior by exposing deviants to public shame through the chants of a chief trained in folklore. Americans, too, find that the fear of ridicule keeps most people in line; but we also need laws, courts, policemen, jails, and fines. Voodoo dances and the formal ritual of the mass both deal with the supernatural; gold nose rings and pancake make-up both beautify the female countenance; cockfights and

Shakespearean dramas both help people pass leisure time; tom-toms and violins both produce pleasing sounds; the chants and potions of the *innatuledi* and the penicillin and oxygen of a modern physician are means of coping with disease; hundreds of languages and dialects testify to the flexibility of man's tongue.

Why this immense variety in cultural behavior? Two possible answers are that each group's culture is dictated by its biological heredity, or by its geographic environment.

If the first were true, then each culture would be manifested by a different race of mankind. There are now about a thousand cultures distinguishable by anthropologists. There is only one true race—the human race—in which we can distinguish perhaps three "races" by differences in such things as skin color, hair texture, and eye formation. But these racial types are by no means distinct in mental and physical capacity nor in organic drives and are so mixed all over the world that only a minority conforms to the "ideal" type for each racial group. Within each of these racial groups there are great variations in culture, from simple to complex. Over the centuries no one race has displayed a greater capacity for culture-building than any other. While the Europeans were still wearing bearskins, the Chinese were building palaces and had a highly developed art and literature, and the Egyptians had introduced bronze plumbing. There are greater differences among individuals within a "race" than among races as wholes.

Geographic environment—the natural setting or habitat—seems on the face of it to be a more reasonable explanation for the diversity of cultures. It seems obvious, for example, that Eskimo culture could not exist anywhere but in the Arctic. Some observers have gone so far as to say that habitat *determines* the culture. These "environmental determinists" are, however, easily proved wrong by two complementary observations. First, different cultures are found in similar settings. The Eskimos hunt animals and build igloos; the Siberians, in a similar habitat, herd reindeer and build huts of wood and skins. The Pueblo Indians are cultivators; the Navahos, in the same desert setting, are sheep-herders. Second, similar cultures are found in different settings. Essentially similar Polynesian cultures are spread over such varying habitats as the Hawaiian Islands and New Zealand.

What, then, is the real relationship of the habitat to the culture? Habitat is but one of a number of forces that help to shape culture. Its influence is greatest where primitive people cope with a harsh environment, as in the Arctic or the desert. Its impact is greater on some aspects of culture than on others—technology and economics are more closely related to natural resources, for example, than are art, religion, and the family system. The habitat thus exercises a *selective limitation* on behavior.

As man's technology becomes more efficient, he is progressively less limited by habitat; he can even alter his habitat to a great degree. The narrow Isthmus of Panama illustrates both statements. Doctors largely eliminated the hazards of tropical disease by discovering how malaria and yellow fever were caused and how they could be prevented. They thus cleared the way for a gigantic alteration of the natural environment— the canal that joins the Atlantic and Pacific oceans.

We may say, in short, that culture and habitat stand in a reciprocal relationship. Culture is not a passive element that is shaped by habitat. It reacts upon the very environment that serves as its physical setting, and this reaction increases as technology becomes more efficient.[6]

What, then, is the real explanation of the enormous variety of human behavior? First of all, man is highly flexible and adaptable; his basic needs can be satisfied in any number of ways. His digestive system will tolerate an enormous variety of foods; and his need for clothing can be met by grass, bark, animal or vegetable fibers, furs, skins, and synthetics, in a limitless array of patterns. His housing does not even conform necessarily to our mental picture of four walls and a roof, for it may be a lean-to, a round hut, or a cave. He builds strikingly different social arrangements around the needs for reproduction and protection of the group. His original solution to a problem may be a combination of accident and the possibilities afforded by the natural environment. In time, the procedure comes to seem right and natural.

Then, too, once man has solved his basic problems, he has lots of creative energy and intelligence left over. He further selects from the "great arc of potential human purposes and motivations," to use anthropologist Ruth Benedict's phrase, and elaborates certain aspects of his culture at the expense of others. He may elaborate his technology and science, as Americans have, or his religious ceremonials, as do certain Australian tribes, or his art and architecture, as did the Mayas of Central America. Once he has selected an area of special interest and elaboration, he continues to develop it; thus differences pile upon differences. "The bulk of all cultures consists of what are, from the practical point of view, embroideries upon the fabric of existence."[7] It is of these very embroideries that man is proudest, and it is these that make him most distinctly human.

The differences in cultures make anthropology a highly fascinating subject, but in the long run what really impresses the student is the basic similarity of human behavior all over the world. He comes to realize that each culture seems as right to its members as his own appears to him. He sees the universal patterns emerging from the mass of detail. As Ralph Linton, a famous anthropologist, said, "The fact that all societies have some sort of family organization is much more significant in the long run than the fact that Tibetan women of the lower class usually have several husbands." [8]

Culture is socially transmitted—that is, learned from others. As the cases of Anna and Isabelle demonstrate, culture is not inborn or instinctive. Writers who use such expressions as "instinctive good manners" or "instinctively looked both ways as he crossed the street" are being slipshod in their choice of words. Any mother could tell them how much drilling it takes to instill manners and safety precautions into a growing child! Such behavior may finally be so thoroughly learned that it *appears* to be innate, calling for little or no reflection on the part of the person displaying it, but this is quite different from saying that it is inborn. This use of the word "instinctive" is thus a tribute to the thoroughness of learning or conditioning. Even such a basic organic process as sleep is culturally conditioned. We learn to be comfortable on a soft innerspring mattress well up off the floor. The Japanese learn to sleep soundly on mats with wooden headrests. Each would have to learn to sleep all over again in the other's accommodations.

We learn not only actions, but also thoughts and feelings. We learn to respect the flag as well as to salute it; we learn to feel reverence in church as well as to follow the ritual; we learn our culture's standards of what is good, beautiful, disgusting, wrong, and the like.

So much of this cultural behavior is learned in the first few years of life that by the time a Chinese child is four or five he is stamped with the ways of doing, thinking, and feeling of his culture, as is an American child of the same age. If by some circumstance the Chinese boy had been raised in the United States and the American in China, each would reflect the culture in which he was brought up rather than the culture of his parents. This actually happened to a son of American missionaries in China. Orphaned in early childhood, he was brought up by a Chinese family. When he came to the States as a young man, his light hair and blue eyes were all that betrayed his ancestry; his posture, his gait, his language, attitudes, likes, and dislikes were all Chinese. He did not feel at home in the United States and returned to China. Identical twins raised in different cultures offer further proof of the powerful influence of culture.[9]

Language. Language is the chief mechanism of culture transmission. It has been called "mankind's fundamental institution," for without it there would be no truly human behavior. We hinted at its importance when we mentioned that the chief biological basis of culture lies in man's brain and vocal apparatus, and when we discussed the role of the human group in making an infant into a human being. Now let us examine the nature and function of language more closely.

"All living beings," to quote a text in social psychology, "learn to respond to cues in their environment. Inevitably some stimuli come to stand for other stimuli." [10] The process of learning these cues is called *conditioning.* A dog learns to expect food when he hears a certain kind of whistle; a child learns to expect food when his mother says, "Come to breakfast." These learned cues are called *signs;* a sign conveys a *meaning.* "Almost any object, act, occurrence, or quality may function as a sign of something else. The red glow of wood or metal indicates that it is hot; a gesture may reveal anger; a cross is a symbol of religious affiliation or sentiment; a red light is a warning of danger; a falling barometer forecasts a change of weather; a pointer on a dial tells an aviator how high he is flying; and so on endlessly." [11]

Signs may be "natural" or "conventional." A *natural sign* is any kind of stimulus that derives its meaning from a concrete situation—the red glow of wood, the angry gesture, the falling barometer, the reaction of starch to iodine, the click of a Geiger counter in the presence of radioactive material, a child's fever at the onset of measles. A *conventional* sign, or *symbol,* on the other hand, is a word, thing, or action that derives its meaning from usage and mutual agreement; it is arbitrary or movable. The word "hell" means totally different things in German and in English. Nodding the head is an affirmative sign in some cultures, a negative one in others. Americans in Guatemala are confused when Guatemalans wave goodbye with what we interpret as a beckoning motion. The snake is a symbol of evil in some cultures, of fertility in others.

All words are symbols, and languages are systems of vocal or verbal symbols that are voluntarily produced and have a specific and arbitrary meaning in a given society. Language is shared behavior. It involves a speaker or writer and his hearer or reader. Conversation, "the essential and original form of language," is cooperative social action. Even writing, though it may be in an old book, involves communication and interpretation between at least two people.

Language may be used in several ways. Speaking or writing may be almost entirely *expressive* behavior in some situations. "Ouch!" and "Darn!" express pain and annoyance; tea party chitchat about the weather expresses amiability. Commands and sales talks, which are aimed at producing a specific response in the reader, are examples of the *evocative* use of language. The instructions with a do-it-yourself kit or the precise description of a chemical experiment are examples of the *referential* use of language, in which each word is chosen to stand for a specific referent, insofar as possible. Most uses of language, and all good literature, mingle all three of these functions.[12]

In a broad and general sense, as we have seen, language is the basis of culture and civilization and the key to the process of becoming human. In what specific ways does it make culture—and hence human nature—possible?

Although animals are limited to the "here and now," language frees man from the limitations of time and space. He can communicate about things that are not immediate or present. He can go beyond the limits of his senses because words can be made to stand for abstract ideas. No one has ever seen an electron or a soul, nor has anyone seen "culture" or "honesty," which are abstractions derived from behavior. Man can learn and remember far more than animals can, both as an individual and as a society that accumulates and stores culture. This function is im-measurably aided by written language, which is essential to civilization. Man can, thanks to language, communicate with himself—that is, he can think and reason, and solve problems. He can imagine things he has never experienced directly, and he can relate himself to other men, defining these relationships in words such as father, friend, foe, teacher, customer, and priest. The complex web of social relationships is largely built upon these verbal definitions.

Thus we can see that language is the chief key to the three aspects of human behavior we are considering in Part One—culture, society, and personality. It is also essential to understanding any one culture, for "the worlds in which different societies live are distinct worlds, not merely the same world with different labels attached."[13] Each language presents to the learning child a ready-made and distinctive way of looking at things, of perceiving and interpreting reality. The grammar of a language, for example, organizes reality into a pattern. The language of the Yirkala tribe of Australia lacks the subjunctive mood; members of the tribe can-not speculate "If . . . then. . . ." Anthropologists studying their behavior patterns had to describe hypothetical situations in the present tense and notice what happened.[14] Concepts of space and time, which seem so specific and objective to us, so measurable by clocks and meters, are entirely different in some cultures. To the Hopi Indians, for example, time varies with each observer.

Each language is the outcome of the common experiences of the members of a social group, and as such reflects their history and interests. The English, living on their island, have a language rich in expressions for the sea; the Arabs are said to have about 6,000 words that are connected in some way with the camel; the American woman's interest in clothes and furnishings is reflected in her vocabulary, which has many more words to describe color and texture than her husband's. Even within the same society we say that those people who share common interests and attitudes "speak the same language."

In each language, things are organized into systems or categories in terms of their significance for behavior. This grouping is done by means of *concepts,* or verbal symbols. You, for example, are a student. This word "student" isolates one aspect of your personality that you have in common with others, though the members of any student body differ enormously in physiological make-up, appearance, intelligence, and even in national or cultural background. The concept of culture itself is a symbol for something that can only be inferred from the behavior of human beings as it falls into more or less regular patterns. But as a symbol, it is very useful. This book will introduce a number of other concepts that the student will learn and share with the instructor and his fellow students. Your agreement on common meanings for verbal symbols will enable you to use them as tools for discussion and thinking.

Useful as words are, they can also be treacherous. Only a few special languages, like those of mathematics and chemistry, are completely referential, or nearly so. Most words convey not only their precise, objective meanings, their *denotations,* but also are freighted with *connotations* that have an historic and emotional coloring. Consider what the words "home," "mother," and "democracy" mean in our culture. People have a tendency to materialize abstractions—that is, to act as if words were *things* rather than concepts. Social scientists, for example, find that they have to be careful when they are working with the culture concept lest they forget it is only a convenient abstraction, although a highly significant and useful one.

Culture is ideational. Culture is not actual behavior in all its varying manifestations within a society. Rather it is carried in the minds of individual members of the society as a set of ideas, of common understandings about the right and proper thing to think, feel, say, and do in any given situation. These common understandings are called *social norms* or *ideal patterns;* the *real patterns* of actual behavior are statistical norms and deviate from the ideal patterns in varying degrees. Kinsey's reports on sexual behavior, for example, are based on real patterns and present statistical norms. Many people were outraged when these reports appeared because they indicated substantial deviation from the ideal patterns or social norms that traditionally govern this aspect of human behavior in the United States.

Culture lends meaning and attaches values to things and actions and defines their significance for human behavior. Culture is not expressed in *overt* (visible) behavior alone. We may watch a ritual rain dance, but the beliefs and attitudes that motivate it are hidden from us. A foreigner observing an American Christmas or Easter celebration may note the ritual with meticulous detail, but if he interprets its meaning in terms of his own culture, he will inevitably produce a caricature of the complex. On the other hand, a really acute foreign observer may be able to detect covert behavior of which we are quite unaware, or which we take so for granted that we cannot explain it except by saying, "Of course . . . it's natural; it's human nature to feel that way."

Material objects, obviously, are not integral elements of culture; they are products of and adjuncts to cultural behavior, and are given meaning and value by the culture. A child's definition, "A chair is to sit," may illustrate the point. To us a chair has meaning; we associate certain behavior with its production and its use. To someone from a society whose culture lacks these behavior patterns, however, a chair may mean only a curiously shaped piece of wood to use as kindling, or a weapon, or a platform to put things on.

If germ warfare wiped out everyone who was familiar with American culture without damaging material objects—the streets, houses, clothes, books, toys, food, radio and TV sets, and the like, which are so essential to our cultural behavior—and a new group of people took them over, we could not say that American culture still existed. The meanings, the behavior patterns associated with the objects, the skills, attitudes, abilities, ideas, knowledge, and habits of the culture-bearing individuals would be gone with them. Some approximation might be pieced together from surviving literature, but it would be only a rough one. Archeologists digging up the relics of ancient cultures can reconstruct much of the way of life of ancient peoples just from the material survivals, but the meaning such objects held for their original owners must necessarily remain largely a matter of ingenious guesswork.

Culture is socially shared. It consists of customs—the shared habits of a social group. This group may be the whole society, or a smaller group within the society—a social class, an ethnic group, the inhabitants of a region, even a family or a school. A distinctive culture that is shared by a group within a society is called a *sub-culture*. Examples of sub-cultures in the United States are Middle Western culture, Jewish culture, middle-class culture, the distinctive culture of the Harvard campus or of a small-town high school, and the sub-culture of a large family.

Different elements of a society's culture are shared in varying degrees. Theoretically, a child can learn everything that is available to learn about a culture, but he will not learn all of it by any means. Aristotle has often been called the last man to command all the knowledge of his time, but he certainly did not master all the specialized skills of the housewife and mother, the blacksmith, the sailor, the sculptor, or the musician. Even in a simple society such as the San Blas Cuna, the fact of sex limits a person's participation in the culture, as do age and the special training of the *innatuledis* and *neles*.

When measured by the degree to which they are shared by members of a society, cultural elements fall into three categories. These elements are called *universals, specialties,* and *alternatives*. The common customs, understandings, and emotional reactions shared by all normal adult members of a society are *universals*. There are many universals in a simple and unified society, fewer in a large and complex one. The particular language and the ideal patterns for social relationships are universals in any one society. The most important universals are those values that lie far below the level of consciousness or are so taken for granted that they are rarely if ever expressed in language. Monogamy, democracy, and freedom are examples of such values in American culture. In medieval Europe the Christian religion was a universal. Our modern complex society, in contrast, includes many shades of belief and lack of belief.

Specialties are elements that are shared by certain distinct categories of individuals, such as various classes, occupations, localities, or the devotees of some recreational or scientific or academic interest. They involve certain knowledges and skills that are shared only by those who belong to the category, although, as in the case of a doctor or a cook, other members of a society expect certain definite results from the possession and practice of such skills. Specialties among the San Blas Cuna include the functions performed by the *neles, innatuledis,* and *kantule,* the division of labor between the sexes, and a few others. In our complex culture there are innumerable specialties, for even broad categories of occupations are broken down into specialties. Like universals, specialties are accepted by the members of the society, for all share in their benefits.

Alternatives are traits that are shared by certain individuals, but are not common to all members of the society nor even to all the members of any one of its socially recognized categories. Alternatives include a very wide range of elements that represent different reactions to the same situations or different ways of achieving the same ends. The San Blas Cuna culture includes comparatively few alternatives; ours includes a great number. Some alternatives entail free choice at any time. A clerk may write with a fountain pen at one time or with a pencil or a typewriter at another. A man may travel by railroad, airplane, automobile, horse, or bicycle. Other choices are more permanent. Once a person has chosen the Baptist religion he is quite unlikely to change to Catholicism, and vice versa.

A fourth category of habits, ideas, and conditioned emotional responses lies beyond the realm of culture because it is not socially shared. This category embraces *individual peculiarities*. You may be abnormally afraid of thunder because of a harrowing childhood experience that befell you during a storm. You may concoct your own nightly bedtime snack or eat a most unconventional breakfast in the belief that it will see you through a morning of work better than the usual orange juice, cereal, and coffee.

In general, the cultures of simple societies are more uniform and predictable than the cultures of complex societies because simple societies embrace a larger porportion of universals. When a person refers to a middle-aged San Blas Cuna man, for example, almost everything about this man's interests, habits, activities, and beliefs can be inferred. But such is not the case in complex cultures marked by sub-cultures. The statement "He is an American" tells us something, but to say "He is a western American farmer" reveals even more by placing the person in an occupational and regional sub-culture. Additional clues fill in the picture more completely: "He is the son of Swedish immigrants . . . a Republican . . . a prosperous dairy farmer . . . He is twenty-nine . . . a high-school graduate . . . He has three children." As we shall see later, culture and sub-cultures shape a person's personality to such an extent that we already know a great deal about this one man. Of course, we do not know exactly what he looks like or what his individual peculiarities are; but knowing what each of these clues means in American life, we are fairly confident of knowing a great deal about his habits, attitudes, and beliefs.

Culture can be preserved and accumulated; thus it is highly stable and continuous. Culture is not created by any one individual or generation, nor limited to anyone's particular life span. Many of the basic elements of our culture go back to prehistoric times. In fact, the earliest traces of culture—the use of fire and the fashioning of stone tools—developed about a million years before the birth of Christ and represented the bulk of man's cultural equipment for half a million years. Perhaps around 100,000 B.C. man began to make tools of bone. Between 75,000 and 14,000 B.C. he began to live in cave communities, bury his dead, use wood, and draw and paint on the walls of caves. Prehistoric man also invented the wheel, screw, and lever, evolved techniques of hunting and fishing, and used waterways for transport. By 10,000 B.C. the practice of agriculture had begun; plants and animals were domesticated. This last development has been called the first great revolution in the history of the human race, for the shift from hunting and food-gathering to agriculture made possible an assured and abundant food supply and thus laid the basis for more highly developed economic and social systems with greater specialization and security. Metal-smelting, the alphabet, arithmetic, astronomy, and other cultural elements were evolved by Oriental and Near Eastern civilizations long before the birth of Christ. Many of our beliefs and superstitions, ethical and religious systems, and literary and artistic traditions, too, are rooted deeper in the past than most of us realize.

Why does culture continue generation after generation? Because children are taught to follow the ways of their forebears. Their elders teach them some things with particular emphasis because they consider them highly important, other things because they know no alternative. Also, many elements of culture continue because people feel more at ease doing things the customary way and tend to resist change, particularly as they grow older.

Every culture, nonetheless, is subject to a continual process of change. In a "static" society, more or less insulated from outside influences, the rate of change may be exceedingly slow, so that a visitor can return a decade or two later and feel that time has stood still. But in a "dynamic" society such as ours, change is so rapid in many areas that the technology, customs, and attitudes of one generation are strikingly different in many respects from those of their parents. We shall consider the processes of cultural change in some detail in Chapter Five, and in many connections throughout the book.

Culture tends to be organized and integrated. A culture is more than the sum of its parts. A mere listing of customs and the material objects that are associated with them would by no means give a true picture of the culture.

For analytical purposes, anthropologists have developed the concepts of cultural traits, complexes, and patterns. *Traits* are the smallest elements by which a culture can be described—a single custom, such as shaking hands, or a custom plus equipment, such as knotting a necktie. A number of cultural traits fit together into a meaningful whole called a *complex,* and complexes in turn are grouped into *patterns* around a central interest or theme from which they derive their meaning.

Consider the act of slipping a gold band on the finger of a girl who is wearing a long white gown. It is a meaningful part of an American culture complex that also includes throwing rice, wrapping gifts, writing thank-you notes, tying shoes and streamers to a car, and many other traits. Along with other complexes—housekeeping, child-raising, and so on—it is part of the pattern of marriage and family life. Not all actual weddings include all these traits; but they all have meaning to all Americans, who share a common understanding, an ideal mental picture, of the set of behaviors involved in getting married.

A culture also tends to be integrated. *Integration* means mutual adjustment between cultural elements, lack of conflicts and inconsistencies,

A Culture Complex. *Many traits cluster in the culture complex we call a wedding, which in turn is part of our cultural pattern of marriage and family life.*

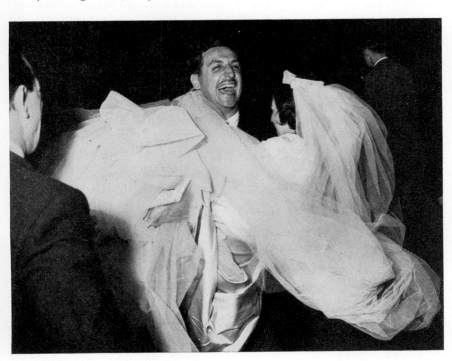

a unity of beliefs and practices. It is always a matter of degree; a culture is *more* or *less* completely integrated, for every culture has some inconsistent elements.

Among the things that hold the various patterns of culture together and shape them into a more or less meaningful whole are (1) the dominant cultural *values*, the standards or principles by which social and individual goals are chosen; (2) the *beliefs* or ideologies that underlie the continuous activity of the society; and (3) the *symbols* and *rituals* that express and help to sustain these values and beliefs.

Definition   •   We shall say more about the nature of
of Culture   culture in subsequent chapters, as we
discuss cultural integration, change, and
functions, and the significance to us of
the culture concept. We have said enough now, however, to shape a more comprehensive definition than we attempted at the beginning of this chapter.

Culture, man's characteristic adaptation to his physical environment, his biological nature and his group life, arises out of language communication within a social group and is a configuration of shared understandings concerning the meaning and value of things, ideas, emotions, and actions.

The Functions
of Culture

Culture serves man in three ways: (1) it
adapts him as a biological species to his environment; (2) it provides the individual with
ready-made adjustments to his natural environment, his fellows, and his own biological
and psychological needs and drives; and (3)
it ensures the unity and survival of the social
group. We have already discussed the first of
these functions in comparing man's flexible

47

adaptation to his environment with the rigid, inborn instincts and biological equipment of animals and insects. Much that can be said about the second function we implied in our treatment of the nature of culture, but certain points bear emphasis.

How Culture   •   *Ready-made definitions of situations.*
Serves   Culture provides the individual with a
the Individual   blueprint for behavior, thought, and feeling in almost any situation. The newborn baby no more analyzes the culture into which he is born than he analyzes the air before he breathes it. The culture is there, and the intimate groups with which the child is associated most closely during his early years—family, play group, school, and church—teach him the ways of the culture as if there were no others. If he questions with a rebellious "Why?" he hears, "Because that's the way it is."

Culture provides the individual with ready-made explanations of the origin of man, the nature of the universe, and man's role in that universe. These may be mystical or superstitious explanations, or they may be in large part scientific. In either case, they answer fundamental questions. Culture determines whether a child asking about a thunderstorm will be told that the god Thor is angry and throwing his hammer across the sky, or that the storm is a natural phenomenon caused by atmospheric pressure and electrical charges.

Culture defines situations for its participants. It provides them with meaning for things and events. The individual's definitions of what is natural and unnatural, logical and illogical, normal and abnormal, moral and immoral, beautiful and ugly, important and unimportant, interesting and uninteresting, and good and bad, are derived from his culture.

Culture gives men a conscience. Conscience is not an inborn, universally similar trait. It may be a still, small, inner voice, but it comes from the group's definitions of right and wrong. It results from the *internalization* of the group's values and standards, their incorporation into the personality. When a person violates these standards, he feels ashamed or guilty, even when there is slight chance of his being found out. Conscience exercises a strong control over his behavior. In some cultures premarital sex relations arouse guilt feelings; in other cultures they do not. A Catholic's conscience will prevent his eating meat on Friday, or trouble him if he does so; but a Protestant does not have to live up to this standard. Both typically find conscience an effective deterrent to rape, theft, murder, and bigamy.

Satisfaction of needs. Culture provides for the satisfaction of the individual's biological needs. He does not have to work out a way to keep warm, to satisfy hunger and thirst, to fulfill his sexual desires, to get his rest. Patterns that regulate and channel these elemental functions are present in the culture and confront the child from infancy on. He is taught how and when and where he may satisfy his needs. He learns the diet pattern of his culture, modesty and hygiene of elimination, proper conduct in sexual affairs, patterns of propriety in dress. In fact, according to social psychologists, these biological needs are so diffuse that the group—the parents usually—must define them for the child, teach him the language in which to express them, and through language teach him how they are to be satisfied. Thus the "gross organic need," the physiological state of tension or disequilibrium we know as "thirst," is defined for the baby and channeled into a habitual pattern by the mother who offers milk and water when she suspects the baby is thirsty and links the feeling to the words "Are you thirsty?" and to the breast or bottle or cup. The role of learning is important not only in knowing how to satisfy, but also in *recognizing* the drive. A mother learns that children often cannot recognize why they are uncomfortable; she sees their irritability fade after she gives them a drink of water and teaches them to recognize the feeling of thirst and to satisfy it by asking for a drink. The process is so woven into busy everyday life that the mother's role of teaching and the child's role of learning are not so readily apparent as they are, say, in training in good manners.

Culture also heightens man's pleasure in satisfying his biological needs by building upon them an enormous superstructure of ritual. In our culture, for example, we make eating more pleasurable by concentrating on the preparation and serving of food; in some cultures people alternately feast and fast to heighten their enjoyment of food. Sexual restrictions also heighten interest in eventual satisfaction. And nowhere is man satisfied merely to cover his nakedness for the sake of warmth and modesty. Style and fashion in dress have been an area of great interest in most cultures.

Culture not only provides patterns for satisfying man's elemental needs, but also *creates* needs. A person's desire for cigarettes or alcohol may be just as compelling as his requirements for food or sleep. His need for aesthetic satisfaction or success or wealth in a culture where these things are highly valued is often stronger than his sexual drives. The present-day American needs many things that his parents got along without, because many items that in the past were unknown or considered luxuries are now defined in our culture as necessary to the good, full life—a new-model car, a TV set, a split-level house, a college degree.

Perception and emotion. As we said in the discussion of language, culture determines what a person's tastes and interests will be and how he will perceive things in general. It even defines and guides the emotions he feels and the way in which he expresses them. Culture, for example, largely determines a person's fears. In one culture, a strong warrior may quail at the sight of a menstruating woman. His culture defines such an occurrence as dangerous and requires that women be isolated at this time. The early settlers of New England feared witchcraft. A generation ago many Americans feared a penniless old age; today many of us fear that we may not reach old age at all because of such threats as intercontinental missiles.

Goals. In a broader sense, culture gives meaning to life, purpose to existence. It provides the individual with values and goals, hopes and aspirations, "something to live for." In one culture, men may strive for material possessions, in another for spiritual salvation, in a third for pleasant enjoyment of the passing moment.

A common culture gives men a sense of belonging or identification. It binds men together into a "we-group" that sets them off from people of another culture. Immigrants to America cluster into colonies because they share a common language and common understandings.

Culture and personality. Culture adapts a person to his place in society. Every culture provides means of training persons for their role and position in the group. Patterns exist for a good housewife, a good farmer, a good president, a good teacher, a good clergyman, and so forth.

Culture is the nourishing milieu for personality. Just as food affects a person's bodily condition and growth, determining whether or not he will reach the potential limit of his stature and strength and good looks, so the culture is food for the personality. If a person is born into a society where food is scarce and limited, he will probably be small and stunted and weak; if he is born into a culture that is meager, he will have a meager personality. No matter how intelligent, how innately capable he is of great achievement, the individual cannot surpass the bounds of the culture with which he comes into contact (though he may build inventions upon its existing elements). As Grey's "Elegy Written in a Country Churchyard" says, "Some mute inglorious Milton here may rest, some Cromwell guiltless of his country's blood." The limited rural culture of the forgotten dead did not give the scope to their innate abilities that the richer life of London would have offered.

A rich and complex culture presents the individual with challenges and opportunities. Just as a person may wisely choose a nutritious and varied and enjoyable diet, or stick to a habitual but poorly planned one, so an individual may wisely and profitably avail himself of the cultural environment or neglect its potentialities and his own.

All that we have been saying impresses us with the profound influence that culture exerts on the individual. Indeed this influence is so great that social scientists find it interesting and profitable to explore "national character," studying the extent to which a common culture tends to produce common personality types. We should not assume, however, that all members of a society are mere rubber stamps produced by cultural patterns. Common sense observation tells us that this is by no means the case. Within the limits imposed by our culture, which dictates, among many other things, a certain proper apparel for campus wear, certain general types of hairdos, a common language, and a daily routine and etiquette, your classmates are definitely individual personalities. It is not necessary to go into this subject more deeply here. Our purpose is simply to point out that the individual is not merely a sponge soaking up culture. In Chapter Eleven, we shall see that because of biological and temperamental differences, unique life experiences, and other factors, one person's version of culture is different from another's, even if both are members of the same family. Furthermore, the individual is the instrument initiating cultural change. Rebellious and unconventional though he may be, the major portion of his personality, nonetheless, reflects the cultural influences we have already mentioned.

Culture as • Culture fulfills its third function—en-
Social Control suring the unity and survival of society
—by (1) providing patterns for the behavior of individuals and groups in the society, (2) providing means of teaching individuals to behave according to these patterns or "rules of the game," and (3) providing means of enforcing correct behavior. The patterns are the customs or norms, the process of teaching them is called *enculturation* or *socialization,* and enforcement is carried out through a system of *sanctions* or rewards and punishments. (You will notice we have not said, "*Culture* teaches the individual to behave and enforces his correct behavior." Culture is the pattern; groups and individuals put the patterns into action.)

All these three very closely related functions of culture are aspects of *social control,* the means by which society establishes and maintains order. Social control can refer to something as elaborate as our system of government, with its vast machinery of law enforcement; but here we

Cultural Symbols of Authority. *The Queen of England personifies British values. St. Peter's in Rome is meaningful to Catholics all over the world.*

shall consider it in a more fundamental and inclusive sense as the network of mutual expectations that create order in a society and the sanctions that keep these expectations in force. Social control boils down
essentially to people who, as individual members of society and as
members of groups, influence one another to behave according to cultural
patterns.

Obviously the system of social control is different from culture to
culture. The patterns vary, the methods of indoctrinating the individual
vary, and the methods of enforcing adherence to the patterns vary. In
some cultures all the life situations are defined for the individual; in
others only crucial ones are defined, and a person is left free to make a
number of choices.

Freedom and control. This situation does not jibe with the classic picture of the great monster, society, crushing the freedom of the puny
individual. Simply because every society has a system of social control it
does not follow that no one living in society is really free. "Freedom" and
"control" are not essentially contradictory terms.

Because a person cannot exist without society, and society cannot
function without controls, a person's very existence depends on social
control. A child growing up alone, provided in some fantastic fashion with
the biological essentials of life—would he be free? Perhaps he would be,
in the sense that an animal is free; but, like Anna and Isabelle, he would
not be free to develop his potentialities as a human being. Culture provides that freedom; paradoxically enough, it does so by the very fact that
it is a set of patterns for behavior. A person masters the routine habits
of dressing, eating, walking, getting to and from his place of work, using
language in speech and reading and writing, and makes them so habitual
that they require little conscious thought and effort. These habits free
his mind and energy for more creative thought and action and enjoyment
of life. Furthermore, by patterning the behavior of many individuals and
groups within a society, culture makes it possible to predict the behavior
of others, and thus enables the group to function more or less smoothly.
The control that culture exercises over the behavior of members of a
society eliminates much wasted effort and conflict.

Customs and norms. In the preceding chapter we referred to cultural
patterns of behavior as customs, the socially shared habits of a human
group, and as social norms, the ideal patterns of behavior, thought, and
feeling. These terms are essentially interchangeable, except that the
second is perhaps weighted more toward what *ought* to be than the first

is. They both refer to the conventional expectations that people mutually hold concerning the behavior of others.

Norms or customs may be classified in various ways. The most familiar scheme was developed by William Graham Sumner, who wrote the classic book, *Folkways*, more than 50 years ago. Sumner called all group customs *folkways*, and differentiated *mores* as those folkways that the society regarded as essential to its welfare. For convenience, however, the terms are often used as if they did not overlap. Because they are not mutually exclusive terms, and because modern culture contains a great many patterns of behavior that cannot definitely be put in either category, some sociologists prefer to think of customs in any one culture as forming a theoretical continuum from those rigid moral norms that are strongly sanctioned to the simple meanings that define possible behavior with no special praise or blame attached. We mention this attempt to refine the concepts to show the student that social science concepts are not immutable, cut-and-dried; they are tools to be worked with, to be refined and sharpened when the need arises. Here we shall, because of its familiarity to all social scientists and many laymen, present the widely used scheme of folkways, mores, laws, and institutions.

Folkways. Folkways are behavior patterns that define the proper, accepted way of doing things. They arose long ago, gradually and by chance, and as they were passed from one generation to another they developed the authority of tradition. (This much of our description also holds true of the mores.) Folkways govern most of our daily routine and ordinary contacts with other people.

Many folkways, like language, money, systems of weights and measures, driving on the right- or left-hand side of the road, and the like, are purely arbitrary conveniences. Others are rituals of behavior, like the method of celebrating a girl's coming of age, the number of meals per day (our "three squares" and a snack), or business hours (nine to five, or in Latin America eight to six with two hours in midday when stores and offices are closed up tight for a siesta). Folkways define "men's work" and "women's work." They set up ideals for gentlemanly and lady-like conduct. They provide patterns for greeting friends, from the casual "Hi!" we Americans so often use to the elaborate hat-doffing, hand-shaking, shoulder-patting routine, accompanied by inquiries after one's health and that of one's entire family, which is typical of encounters between middle-class Costa Ricans. The folkways govern our general style of housing, dress, recreation, child-rearing, courtship, and so on. Folkways compose the large underlying body of custom that is strongly rooted in tradition. They are by no means superficial or transitory.

Nonetheless, folkways change. The authors can remember when their mothers disapproved of lipstick, nail polish, bobbed hair, and women's smoking—so strongly, in fact, that they considered it not only improper, but verging upon the immoral to use them. Three decades later both mothers use lipstick and wear their hair short; one smokes an occasional cigarette and uses nail polish. Another folkway that is changing is the custom of rising for women on the bus or trolley. Today, probably employing the rationalization that women are competing with them in the workaday world and that even shopping housewives are probably less tired than they are (what with all their labor-saving conveniences!), men rarely offer their seats to women. In fact, people who rise for expectant mothers or for mothers with small children, or for elderly or ill-looking women, are most often matrons who can readily sympathize with others of their own sex. From a rational standpoint, strong young men and women, say of high-school and college age, should be the least in need of seats, but they seem to feel that their classmates would regard them as "sissies" if they made such a polite gesture.

Convention and *etiquette* are special kinds of folkways. People are aware that there is no deep meaning to them, but they are matters of convenience in social relations, smoothing the way and making people comfortable. Certain social groups expect their members to know when to wear what clothes and how to issue and reply to invitations. A person's standing in the social pyramid is often judged by the ease with which he observes the conventions and rules of etiquette.

Some behavior patterns are of such recent origin and so closely associated with new technological developments that they can hardly be called folkways. A convenient term for them is *technicways*. Technicways involve skills such as driving an auto and using modern appliances, or behavior such as watching movies or TV.

The sanctions that enforce folkways tend to be informal and non-deliberate but are nonetheless very effective. A person who does things in the right and proper way is rewarded by the approval, help, companionship, and friendliness of others. A child who politely shakes hands with guests is rewarded with smiles and words of praise. If he hangs back or is rude he is embarrassed by his mother's displeasure or the ridicule of his older sister. The adult who betrays ignorance of the proprieties may be punished by a raised eyebrow or a meaningful glance. People conform because they do not want to be regarded as rude, ignorant, uncouth, or just "queer." They want to "belong," to be "hep," to be "a big boy" or a "regular guy." They learn the technicways because modern life is full of delay, awkwardness, inconvenience, and even ridicule for people who cannot drive a car or tune a TV set.

Mores. Mores are customs that are considered vital to the welfare of the group. Mores are not simply proper, like folkways; they are obligatory. They are intimately tied up with the dominant values of the culture (see Chapter Five), and like values they are often so deeply im-

"Remember, Harriet, you must be tolerant—they have different mores down here."

bedded in the personalities of individuals, so taken for granted, that they are rarely articulated or consciously formulated. The mores define right and wrong, moral and immoral, without answering the question "Why?" They may be expressed in terms of "must-behavior" or "Thou shalt," or they may be negative—"Thou shalt not"—in which case they are called *taboos.*

In our culture, the mores include wearing a certain amount of clothing, having only one husband or wife at a time, and being loyal to our country. Bigamy, murder, theft, treason, and incest are among our taboos.

The mores can make anything right. Like folkways, mores vary from culture to culture. In some cultures it is moral to have several wives, to wear only a loincloth, or to be loyal to a leader whom others would regard as a tyrant. In some societies it is considered right to kill baby girls or helpless old people. Cannibalism has been considered moral in some cultures. In fact, cannibals are shocked at the conduct of modern warfare—to slaughter our enemies and then allow all those bodies to go to waste! Even incest, which is almost universally tabooed, has been moral in some societies under certain situations. The Ptolemies of Egypt were considered too royal to marry anyone but a brother or sister.

The folkways of other cultures are apt to strike us as interesting, amusing, exotic, colorful, and fantastic. The mores, if they differ sharply from our own, are likely to shock and horrify us; we cannot conceive of such behavior; it is wrong, sinful, immoral. Other peoples often feel the same way about our customs, though anthropologists have found that some presumably primitive peoples are much more tolerant of strange ways than we are.

The sanctions that enforce the mores are invested with greater emotional content than are those that enforce the folkways. Respect, approbation, public esteem, and praise are often the portion of those who obey the mores or personify them to the society. The Congressional Medal of Honor, the Order of Lenin, and the Victoria Cross reward patriotism and courage. A person is not likely to risk a reputation as an honest employee, a faithful wife, or an obedient son.

Violators of the mores experience feelings of guilt, sin, and shame. Their reputations suffer from gossip or from news stories in the mass media. They are ostracized by their peers, and stoned, pilloried, tried, imprisoned, whipped, killed, exiled, demoted, or excommunicated. The deserter is made an example to other soldiers. The rapist, too, though he may be psychologically unbalanced and not truly responsible for his act, is nonetheless held accountable for it. For unless individuals are held accountable for their behavior, the web of mutual expectations crumbles and with it the social order. Wrongdoing is punished not so much to teach the guilty person as to remind others that the norms must be obeyed.

Mores, like folkways, are subject to change, but somewhat more painfully and slowly than the folkways. Some customs pass from the mores into the folkways, but while they are changing it is hard to tell just which they are. Our changing attitude toward women's smoking is a case in point. Some groups in our society still consider the practice immoral;

in others it has become a folkway; but in general it is "permissive be-havior," open to individual choice. The use of contraceptives is another example. The attitude of the Catholic Church and the legal restrictions put on dissemination of information indicate that contraception is still considered a violation of the mores in a substantial portion of our society. Statistics, however, indicate that the use of contraceptives is passing into the realm of permissive behavior. Premarital chastity is still in the mores, still an ideal pattern, but research shows that the real pattern deviates considerably. Slavery was once considered moral; it is now clearly im-moral in our culture. But while the change in attitude was taking place, bitter conflict almost tore American society apart permanently.

The conflict over slavery is but one example of the fact that com-peting mores may exist in a society, particularly in a rapidly changing society or one in which many different sub-cultures exist. They may even present a problem in choice to an individual. For example, a descendant of a Confederate general may consider race mixture highly immoral. He may also consider obedience to the federal law a moral "must." When federal law says he must allow his children to attend school with Negroes, he is faced with a conflict of mores. Perhaps his solution of the impasse will depend on how he interprets his dilemma in terms of another source of moral norms—his religion.

Laws. The folkways and mores set the pattern for most behavior in a small and unified society. In more complex societies, where different groups within the society have different folkways and mores, a special organization is necessary to formulate laws that serve to coordinate the behavior of these groups sufficiently so the society can continue to func-tion. People usually follow folkways and mores without much conscious reflection. *Laws,* however, are deliberately formulated, clearly stated rules of behavior that are enforced by a special authority. Many laws enforce the mores. Monogamy, responsibility for the welfare of wife and children, and the taboos against murder, theft, and rape are all reinforced by law. But in a dynamic society, new situations constantly arise that are not covered by custom. The invention of the railroad, automobile, radio, airplane, and television have all necessitated legal regulation. Laws also meet crises in which traditional ways prove ineffectual. During the depression of the 1930's the old ways of doing business left many people hungry and ill-clothed, and the government had to enact laws to provide for them.

Occasionally laws are enacted that are really contrary to the mores, or if in a moral category, are not backed up by the mores. Their passage comes about through the influence of pressure groups. Drinking was not tabooed by the mores, and as a result many people violated prohibition. Traffic regulations are not a part of the mores; that is why so many people brag about getting away with violations. The most effective laws are firmly grounded in the mores.

Law may, however, be used as an instrument of social reform, especially where the real patterns do not coincide with ideal patterns. Americans like to speak about equality of opportunity. In actual practice we are guilty of discrimination in housing, education, employment, and other fields. Fair employment practices acts and federal Supreme Court decisions against state-upheld discriminatory practices have operated to bring real behavior more closely in line with the ideal patterns. Often legislation and judicial decisions prove so-called "practical" objections invalid, and thus bring about real social change.

The sanctions that enforce laws are specific and formal, and are carried out by designated personnel. Fines, damages, imprisonment, and even execution are the lot of people convicted of breaking the law.

Fashions and fads. Fashions and fads are highly transitory patterns of behavior. They too, are cultural patterns, however, for as sociologist Kingsley Davis says, "Curiously, the human animal manages to be a conformist even when he is seeking change." [1]

Fashion appears to be most prominent in a complex urban society where the class system is not rigid and a person is judged largely by externals. In our culture, for example, fashions are followed by the majority of women. The wealthy initiate style changes, but in an incredibly short time copies are seen in the windows of low-priced dress shops. Fads are fashions that alternate very quickly, are utterly superficial, and have an irrational and intense fascination, particularly for adolescents. High-school students are especially subject to swiftly changing fads in wearing apparel and dance steps. Crazes are much like fads. Examples are the Pyramid Club and the chain letter craze that still pop up occasionally and die down just as fast. The wildfire craze for hula hoops spread to many countries in 1958.

Sally, your college classmate, wears something to cover herself because the mores (buttressed by law) dictate it. For the sake of modesty she would not dream of coming to class unclothed. The fact that she wears a sweater and skirt instead of an East Indian sari or a Japanese kimono may be traced to the folkways of our culture. Hearkening to convention, she wears her sweater and skirt to class instead of her Saturday costume of "skinny pants" and pullover. Etiquette dictates that she change

Watusi Ritual Dance.
*The folkways of other
cultures are likely to
seem exotic, colorful,
and fantastic.*

to an evening dress and slippers and wear a corsage sent by her escort
when she attends a formal dance. The length of her skirt, the lines of her
sweater, and the colors she chooses are dictated by fashion. The bleached
streaks in her hair in 1958 represented a fad. She considered it fun, the
latest thing, a sign that she was "hep."

Institutions. Folkways, mores, and usually, but not necessarily, laws, are
organized into meaningful clusters around central needs. These clusters
of norms are called institutions. "An institution is a formal, recognized,
established, and stabilized way of pursuing some activity in society." [2]

The fundamental or pivotal institutions of a society are built around
man's imperative needs as a biological organism living in a social group.
Five such institutions are usually recognized by social scientists: marriage
and the family, the economic system, the religious and ethical system,
governmental organization, and education. A sixth, the expressional and
aesthetic system—recreation and the arts—is often added.

To illustrate the meaningful clustering of customs around a function,
let us consider the family. The functions of mating, reproduction, and
child-rearing are essential to the perpetuation of society, as are gratification of the individual's sexual drives and his need for security and
affection. Numerous folkways and mores and laws cluster around the
satisfaction of these needs. In our culture, dates, engagement rings, honey-

moons, bridal showers, and homes apart from the in-laws are among the folkways associated with marriage. Mores include pre-marital chastity, post-marital fidelity, monogamy, and rights and duties of husband and wife to one another and to their children. A legal framework has grown up to support the mores: licenses, legal ceremonies, laws against bigamy and non-support, laws providing for divorce under certain conditions, laws against intermarriage of close relatives, and, in certain states, of members of different racial groups, laws against marriage of children under a certain age without parental consent, and so forth.

The pivotal institutional systems are the chief agencies of external and objective social control and have recognized authority to punish deviation from the norms. They define the relationships among and within social groups and thus form the essential structure of the social order. They channelize human behavior. Through the institution of marriage the generalized, uncoordinated sex impulses are defined and guided into a pattern of socially acceptable ways of achieving satisfaction. The tension and imbalance of a hungry, thirsty, chilly human organism need not go unalleviated while a person individually seeks solutions by trial and error. The society has a technological and economic system whereby food, clothing, and shelter are wrested from the environment and distributed in organized ways.

Besides primary or pivotal systems, our definition of institutions also encompasses organized ways of pursuing secondary needs or desires. Television is an organized way of communicating moving pictures and speech across distance without wires. Big-league baseball is an organized way of satisfying people's acquired need for vicarious participation in sport. The press is an institutionalized way of gathering and disseminating news and opinion.

An institution may be *crescive,* may develop gradually and without deliberate planning over a long period of time in answer to a long-apparent need, or it may be *enacted,* deliberately formed in order to satisfy a need. Thus, government as we know it is a crescive institution. Social security as an organized formal way of guarding people against the hazards of old age is an enacted institution. Modern society has invented many institutions to satisfy the needs of a complex culture and urban living.

We can see why institutional social control is especially important to complex modern societies when we turn the noun "institution," into a verb, "institutionalize." A casual love affair, a dip in the old swimming hole, a mother showing her son how to tie his shoelaces, and a friend's newsy phone call are not institutionalized. But a marriage is institutionalized, and so are a swimming meet at the neighborhood "Y," a teacher showing a pupil how to multiply fractions, and the evening paper. To institutionalize an activity involves formalizing and stabilizing it and according it social recognition as an established way of doing something. If many segments of human behavior were not thus regulated, there would be very little order in modern society.

An institution is regarded as having a concept and a structure. The concept is the idea or need that the institution fulfills. The structure of an institution includes (1) its personnel; (2) the instruments or equipment it uses; and (3) the norms, techniques, and usages or rules it follows. Let us consider the concept and structure of medicine. Medicine is built around the need for healing the sick. It has a selected personnel; a person is either a doctor, nurse, hospital attendant, medical technologist, and so on, or he is not. It has its own special equipment—hospitals, uniforms, surgical instruments, medicines, symbols, and language. And above all it has its own customs or norms—the folkways, mores, and laws that pattern the behavior of its personnel. A doctor learns not only the skills, but also the ethics of his profession. A nurse learns the folkways that govern her relationship with doctors as well as her duties to her patients.

The personnel of an institution—in fact, any human group that is organized for the pursuit of a common interest—is an *association*. Any specific family is an association; the family in general is an institution. The government of Peoria, Illinois, is an association; government is an institution. The National Broadcasting Company is an association; radio is an institution.

The concept of institutions is an extremely fruitful one for studying culture, society, and personality. Therefore, we shall employ it quite often throughout the book, analyzing the institutions of the family, education, religion, government, and politics, and their relationship to one another. "The quickest way to envisage the total social order of a society is to understand its major institutions and the relations between these institutions." [3]

F I V E

Cultural Integration and Cultural Change

In discussing the nature of culture, we remarked briefly that each culture is more or less integrated into a meaningful whole. Integration we defined as mutual adjustment between cultural elements, absence of conflicts and inconsistencies, and unity of beliefs and practices. In this chapter we shall discuss the means or agents of cultural integration, its importance to a society, and its relation to

63

cultural change. Then we shall look at American culture from the perspective we shall have gained.

Agents •
of Cultural
Integration

Beliefs and values. The system of *knowledge and belief* within a culture is a unifying and integrating force to the extent that members of the society agree about what is real and what is true. The San Blas Cuna, for example, believe in such things as the culture-bringer Ibeorkun, *purbas,* and a universe of eight layers above and below the earth plane. To the extent that education in Panamanian schools and preaching by missionaries woo some Cuna away from these beliefs, the integration of the society suffers.

The system of *values* is also an important integrative force, for values are the underlying standards or principles by which social and individual goals are chosen and the criteria by which means and ends are judged. When members of a society use the same criteria to judge behavior and choose goals, the society is highly integrated. Obviously there is more agreement on values in a unified, homogeneous society than in a complex, urban society such as our own, where many groups hold different and conflicting values. But even in a multi-group society members must agree on some basic principles for governing thought and behavior.

The concept of values is somewhat elusive. We shall try to illuminate it by considering the relationship between values and norms and goals both for the society and for the individual.

Values are not the same as norms. Values are the principles by which the norms are justified and explained. The San Blas Cuna bathe frequently. This pattern is a norm; the value that guides their behavior is *cleanliness.* "Thou shalt not steal" is a norm; honesty is the value that underlies it. Lip service to the dominant values of a society is often considered more important than faithful adherence to norms, for society regards an attack on its value system as a greater threat than deviation from the ideal patterns of behavior. "Thus in our society it is easier to commit adultery than it is to advocate it." [1]

The value system. The core values of a culture are the dominant, ultimate, or basic social values that people are expected to accept without question. They are enduring and carry an emotional aura. People accept them as naturally as they accept food and drink. Many of the most important values are implicit in a culture, and are rarely if ever put into words, save perhaps by philosophers and other intellectuals.

If we rated values in terms of their importance or desirability, these ultimate values would be at the top of the scale. They determine, or at least justify and explain, the chief goals of the society. All other values and goals tend to be measured in terms of the dominant ones and to be oriented toward their fulfillment.

"Progress," for example, is a dominant value in American culture. People accept the idea without questioning it. If a goal or an action can be justified in terms of "progress," we accept it as good and right and worthy. Should a new dam be built if it entails flooding farms in a valley? Should men be thrown out of work temporarily by automation? "Progress" is the criterion that justifies these actions. Subsidiary values— the freedom of the farmers to keep their land, the right of men to employment—are sacrificed to the greater value—progress for the society as a whole.

Individuals, too, have scales of values that govern their decisions about means and ends. One person puts material gain above all else; another regards spiritual salvation as the ultimate value. Each orients his behavior accordingly. In any one situation, a choice between two important values may be demanded. Should a woman frankly tell a friend that her new dress is most unbecoming? Honesty is a value, but so is kindness, and kindness is likely to dominate in this case.

Clues to values. There are a number of clues to a society's scheme of values. One is choice. What do members of the society choose to do, to say, and to buy? In a monetary society a good yardstick is what people spend their money for. Judged solely by this yardstick, education would appear to be a relatively unimportant value in American culture, for Americans spend more on tobacco or liquor than they spend on schools. Here is a disparity between real and ideal culture patterns. Most Americans would place education far above hedonistic pleasure in their scale of values; but perhaps without being fully aware of it, they part more willingly with money for amusement and intoxicants than for school taxes and assessments. With the lion's share of the national budget earmarked for past wars and present armament programs, an outside observer might think that war is high in the American scale of values. Actually, we value peace. But we value freedom, too, so much so that we deliberately arm to protect it.

Besides choice or preference, we may measure people's values in part by what they say they are—that is, by what they express approval or disapproval of, what they consider worth while, and the reasons they give for their actions. This yardstick is also tricky to apply, for no person consistently practices what he preaches. But even when not expressed directly, people's values may be inferred from the subjects that arouse them to heated argument, condemnation, or enthusiasm.

The folklore, history, literature, and art of a culture are other valuable sources of information. The traits attributed to Abraham Lincoln, to Paul Bunyan, to the central figure of a best-selling novel, to the hero of a Western TV program, to the current hero of the baseball diamond, or to the crooner of the moment—these are traits highly valued in our culture.

The system of rewards and punishments throws more light on the value system. What infractions are most severely punished? An American mother is far more likely to spank her five-year-old son for stealing than for "sassing" her. Juries are likely to acquit a man who kills his wife's lover and to condemn one who kills his wife for her insurance. A political grafter does not suffer the same punishment as the accountant who embezzles from his employer. And who makes the most money and receives the most adulation? statesmen? poets? movie stars? scientists? writers? singers?

Functions of values. The value system serves two functions. (1) It laces together a culture, uniting its elements and institutions, making them appear consistent, and justifying and rationalizing them in the minds of its members. This function is so important that one sociologist defines a society or community as a group of persons "adhering to the same ultimate set of values and pursuing the same set of common ends." [2] (2) Values also provide individual members of the society with a purpose or meaning in life. "Instead of looking at their actions as attempts to satisfy their motives and then examining the worthwhileness of those motives, they think of their actions as attempts to reach goals which are ends in themselves. Those things which have the highest social value to any group become the life goals of its members and provide a reason for existence." [3]

Because they are grounded in emotion, values tend to endure. Nonetheless, values change through time. "Democracy," now perhaps the most precious value of the American people, was once a smear word in our country.

Different values can create misunderstanding between societies and between sub-cultural groups within a society. Much of our discussion of institutions will deal, explicitly or implicitly, with conflicts of values— between capital and labor, farmer and consumer, different sexes and generations, political ideologies and religious faiths, and within a personality. Another source of conflict arises from the fact that for some people the means of achieving cultural values may be blocked. We shall discuss this situation in connection with race relations, the class structure, and education.

Myth. Beliefs and values are woven into a body of *myth*. In the social scientists' language, the concept of myth does not imply falsity. "By myth we mean the value-impregnated beliefs and notions that men hold, that they live by or live for. Every society is held together by a myth-system, a complex of dominating thought-forms that determines and sustains all its activities." [4]

A myth system takes values and beliefs out of the realm of the abstract and sets them down into the sphere of reality. It explains how things came to be, justifies them, and holds out hope for a better future life, whether in this world or the hereafter. It prescribes a course of action by which people can attain the better life and thus justifies the self-control and sacrifices that they are called upon to make in the normal course of living together. It provides a faith that encourages and sustains men in working toward a goal. To the extent that the myth system is accepted by all or most members of a society, it holds that society together.

Some myths are more important than others. There are dominant myths within a society and less important ones that enhance minor values and beliefs in the myth-complex. Several great myths have in turn dominated the Western World: the Greek and Roman hierarchy of gods (which is what occurs to most of us when we hear the word "myth"); the Christian myth with its accompanying values and beliefs; the myth of the divine right of kings; the Democratic myth that came to the fore with the French and American revolutions; and the fascist myth and the Communist myth, now competing with the Democratic myth for dominance. These myths are identified with ultimate values and with the promise of a good life or a heavenly reward.

Lesser folk beliefs and values are made stronger and more real by their accompanying myths. The belief that intermarriage of Negroes and whites is wrong is supported by the recurrent myth of the black baby appearing to an unsuspecting husband and his supposedly white wife, who was perhaps adopted as a child. The story is usually couched in terms of "someone a friend of mine told me about." The myth of George Washington and the cherry tree brings the copybook maxim that honesty is the best policy—that is, the *value* of honesty—down to the child's level of understanding. By emotionally identifying themselves with the hero, children are helped to understand the meaning of honesty and remember the moral of the legend.

> Myth is the all-pervading atmosphere of society, the air it breathes. ...Wherever he goes, whatever he encounters, man spins about him his web of myth, as the caterpillar spins his cocoon. Every individual spins his own variation within the greater web of the whole group. The myth mediates between man and nature. Inside his myth he is at home in his world.[5]

Symbols, ritual, and ceremony. Values and beliefs are expressed in *symbols* and periodically reinforced by *ritual* and *ceremony.* The Japanese culture, for example, is integrated around the value of "honor," which is symbolized in the person of the emperor. The British regard their queen as a symbol of their highest values and dearest traditions. The Russians use the embalmed body of Lenin as a symbol of the Communist Revolution. The hammer and sickle, the Stars and Stripes, the Union Jack, the tricolor—all have a profound and emotion-packed meaning for the citizens of Russia, America, Britain, and France.

Ritual and ceremony are powerful means of sustaining the social order. A *ceremony* is a formal, dignified procedure that impresses observers and participants with the importance of an occasion. Its most distinctive element is usually *ritual*—a formal, rhythmic series of symbolic acts that are repeated on appropriate occasions. Ritual gives an occasion an air of solemnity, and evokes emotional, unreflective responses. The individual effortlessly associates the appropriate ideas, which come to seem right and inevitable.

> Ritual and ceremony impress without explaining, without reasoning. They convey a feeling of larger realities, of faiths, of unities, of social establishments, of the myths themselves, which can never be fully experienced or wholly comprehended by individuals. "The Church," "the State," "the Law," and "God" are distant abstractions, but the rites of the church, the coronation of the king, the inauguration of the president, the protocol of the court of law, the orderly procession at the grave or wedding, seem to bring near to men ...these invisible things.[6]

Ritual has its roots deep in the past and keeps traditional meanings alive. The ritual of the Passover dramatizes an important historic event and through its emotional impact contributes to the coherence of Jewish culture and creates a feeling of unity among Jews. The ritual of the mass, rich in symbolism, re-enacts the Last Supper and impresses its participants with its importance to their lives. Religious ritual in every society dramatizes, makes important, and defines the meaning of the major crises of life—birth, initiation or confirmation, marriage, and death. Each ritual explains the individual's relationship to nature and to society.

Many religious rituals long ago became interwoven with pagan seasonal rites, elements of which still survive. Christmas trees and candles are survivals of rites that used to be held during the winter solstice. Many ancient rites of spring, of rebirth and creation, survive in the Christian observance of Easter.

Religious ritual obviously has a great emotional impact and cohesive effect. Similarly, coronations are blends of the values and symbols of state and church. Our presidential inaugurations are relatively meager

Symbols and Ritual. *The brightly lighted Christmas tree is a survival of ancient pagan, religious, and seasonal practices hedged about with custom and tradition.*

in symbolism and ritual, and consequently have less emotional effect upon viewers than the British coronation ceremony, for example.

The processes of every institution are more or less ritually conducted. Parents learn that their children will go to bed more willingly if they prepare a little ritual for the youngsters to follow. Robes and rituals clothe courts and judges with dignity. A wise teacher finds that a certain amount of ritual smooths the educational process.

Ethos. Each society has its own characteristic quality, its own *ethos*, that springs from many contributing factors, particularly from the beliefs and values around which its culture is integrated. Comparable to what we would call a person's disposition or character, a society's ethos is rather elusive. It "deals with qualities that pervade the whole culture—like a flavor. [and]. . . . includes the direction in which a culture is oriented, the things it aims at, prizes and endorses, and more or less achieves." [7] The ethos of the Italian Renaissance was sensuous and passionate; that of the north-European Reformation was puritan and ascetic; Hindu civilization is mystical and other-worldly, Chinese civilization is temporal and matter-of-fact.[8] The ethos is easier to describe when one ruling principle such as religion—or even Communist totalitarianism—is the chief integrative force in a society than when a number of conflicting tendencies are at work, as in modern American society.

The ethos of a culture may be predominantly *sacred* or predominantly *secular*. A sacred culture is based on a systematic theology and is conservative and stable, reveres tradition, and provides dogmatic answers to all questions. Everything that happens has a religious motivation or explanation; nothing is simply a means to a practical end. Deviation from traditional behavior is severely punished. In a secular culture, on the other hand, ideas and things and people are evaluated in utilitarian terms. Change is readily accepted; in fact, it is sought, encouraged, guided, and called "progress." Instead of passively bowing to divine will, the secular society believes that "God helps those who help themselves."

For a picture of medieval society dominated by sacred values, a person has only to read a novel like Edith Simon's *The Golden Hand.* In the fourteenth and fifteenth centuries, *secularization,* the trend toward secular values, began. The Renaissance and the age of invention and discovery were characterized by a new interest in life on this earth and a belief in the scientific approach to human problems. Although this trend has continued, many customs and institutions are still sacred to us, and thus our culture is a mixture of sacred and secular elements.

Value • Integration is a matter of degree, a tend-
of ency. In a simple and unified society
Integration members generally agree on beliefs and
values. In a society that embraces many
different sub-cultures members prob-
ably agree on only a few beliefs and values, and differ over many of
them.

A highly integrated culture produces a sense of security and satisfaction among its members. There is, however, such a thing as an undesirable degree of integration; for when a highly integrated culture is
subjected to pressures of one kind or another, even in only one area, it is
likely to become disorganized. A culture in which the various elements
are less perfectly coordinated adapts more easily to circumstances that
bring about change. In a Utopia, a perfectly integrated society, as anthropologist John Gillin points out, there would be no new goals to establish,
nothing to strive for, to hope for, nothing to awaken ambitions or to cause
disappointments. Living would no longer be fun. A highly integrated
society, whether a sacred one like that of the Cuna or a secular authoritarian one like Nazi Germany, sacrifices freedom to control. But if there
is insufficient integration, there is conflict, confusion, and waste. Relative
lack of integration accompanies rapid cultural change.

A culture can successfully incorporate a number of inconsistencies
and conflicting elements as long as its members are in substantial agreement about ultimate values and overt behavior patterns. Agreement on
core values creates *esprit de corps;* agreement on behavior patterns makes
for smooth functioning of the society. Let us take two very simple
examples. If half the people of a society drive on the right side of the
road and the other half on the left, the society obviously suffers from
lack of integration in overt behavior patterns. If half the people believe
in free enterprise and the other half in state socialism, the lack of integration will be equally serious. There would be no way to accommodate
the various beliefs, values, and norms.

Cultural Change • Culture is dynamic; it changes through
time and it spreads through space. The
process of change does not conform to
the uniform growth of biological evolution, which occurs according to
fixed principles of mutation and selection. Cultural change occurs in
response to the wants and emotions of men living in groups. It displays
no even, "upward" trend, no inevitable progress from one cultural stage
to the next. Social scientists can gauge scientific and technological

progress by measuring such things as man's harnessing of energy; but they are very reluctant to judge changes in religion and morals, social organization, art, and the like, by any set standard of progress. Only in modern society—and especially in our own—is change as such deliberately sought and easily accepted in the name of progress, though most often only in such fields as science, technology, recreation, and fashion.

There are, however, certain generalizations we can make about the processes of cultural change, its causes or sources, its mechanisms, and the principles by which new elements are incorporated into an existing culture.

Mechanisms of cultural change. Cultural change may originate from within the society as a result of discovery or invention, or come from outside, via diffusion. A *discovery* is any addition to knowledge, such as finding a new continent or island or travel route or discovering that copper ore will melt, and it always implies the previous existence of the thing now known. An *invention* is a new application of existing knowledge, such as the combination of the steam engine and the river boat to make a steamboat. *Diffusion* is the process by which elements spread from one culture to another, and accounts for most changes within all but the most isolated cultures.

Many persons think of discovery and invention in terms of great men, geniuses gifted with such inborn intelligence that they added something completely new to a culture. *But every invention rests on existing knowledge.* There has been little if any change in the size and complexity of man's brain in the last ten thousand years, yet invention has proceeded at a constantly increasing rate. No man, however intelligent, can invent anything except on the basis of existing knowledge. Thomas Edison might have been a great man if he had lived 500 years earlier; but he would certainly not have invented the electric light or the phonograph, because the earlier steps that laid the groundwork for these inventions had not been taken. Leonardo da Vinci, for all his fascination with the idea of flight, could never have succeeded in inventing the airplane, for the gasoline engine was still far in the future. Isaac Newton gave credit to the predecessors who made it possible for him to formulate the law of gravity: "If I saw farther, 'twas because I stood on giant shoulders."

Parallel or simultaneous invention proves that invention does not await a predestined genius. Given the proper stage of cultural development, someone is likely to come up with an invention. Sociologist William Ogburn lists 148 inventions that occurred almost simultaneously without the inventors being in communication. Galileo and three others discovered sunspots; four men introduced the decimal point; two discovered oxygen; two the function of the pancreas; four the telegraph.[9] Thus the old saying that "Necessity is the mother of invention" would be closer to the truth if it were rephrased: "The existing culture is the mother of invention." The same holds true of discovery. If Columbus had never been born, someone else would have discovered America, for the time was ripe. The invention of the compass and the development of other improved navigational devices were enabling men to sail great distances, and the spur of economic rivalry between nations made imperative the discovery of new markets.

Out of the fact that invention depends on the existing "storehouse of knowledge" rises another highly significant truth: *the tendency of culture to accumulate at a geometrically increasing rate.* If there are ten thousand elements in a culture and they yield one invention, a culture with ten times that number of elements will yield not ten, but far more, for as the number of elements increases, the number of possible combinations increases at a greater rate. Stuart Chase drives home this point by telling of the farmer who agreed to the blacksmith's proposition that for each of the 32 nails needed to shoe his horse he would pay twice as much as for the previous nail. Since the price of the first was a penny, the farmer agreed. But the total came to $42,949,672.95! [10] Anthropologist Robert Lowie likened the progress of mankind "to that of a man one hundred years old, who dawdles through kindergarten for eighty-five years of his life, takes ten years to go through the primary grades, then rushes with lightning rapidity through grammar school, high school, and college." [11]

We have referred only to material and technological inventions, but a very significant number of inventions are so far removed from any material basis that they are called "social inventions." Often they are ways of adapting to changed conditions created by technological inventions, but not necessarily so. Such social inventions as minimum wages, maximum hours, and collective bargaining were adaptations to the factory system. Health insurance is a social invention; so are baby-sitting, social security, the cooperative store. Most laws are social inventions.

Invention is, of course, basic to cultural growth but *the great bulk of any rich and complex culture comes from diffusion.* The Tasmanians, when first visited by Europeans in the eighteenth century, had a Stone Age Culture. Cut off from the rest of mankind about twenty thousand years before, they had doubtless produced some minor inventions, but the content of other cultures was not available to them, so their own culture changed with glacial slowness.

Diffusion. *Through such cultural contacts as British sailors and American movies, Western culture is brought to Calcutta.*

Causes or sources of cultural change. The causes of cultural change are many and complex. They are especially difficult to analyze because one change triggers or eventually leads to another or others, and cause and effect factors may take a circular form in which the effect of one change is the cause of another.

Changes in environment, such as prolonged periods of drought, depletion of available food or mineral resources, and erosion of soil, may lead to changes in the subsistence economy, which, in turn, may lead to changes in other aspects of culture. Epidemics, changes in the birth and death rates, changes in the number of young and old people, all call for cultural adaptations. Historic "accidents" may initiate cultural changes. For example, the fact that Russia happened to orbit a space satellite before the United States did triggered many changes in such aspects of American culture as the administration of scientific research, the value placed on space flight, and educational curricula and methods.

Cultural contact is a potent source of cultural change, whether it occurs deliberately or more or less accidentally. Thus, most new cultural traits have been brought to the San Blas Cuna by their young men who have served as sailors in different parts of the world, and more recently by tourists, missionaries, and public schools. Propaganda and advertising, government coercion, and conquest also may bring about cultural change. Missionaries introduce new doctrines, new moral codes, and often other new customs in dress, hygiene, and schooling. Commerce diffuses movies, soft drinks, chewing gum, clothes, utensils, and gadgets of all kinds to all the corners of the earth. Dictatorships use strong punishments and threats of punishment to impose their reforms. The Turkish leader, Kemal Ataturk, westernized his Oriental country considerably by means of decrees backed by strong measures. History is also rich in examples of diffusion by conquest, though not in every case was the culture of the conquerors triumphant. The Romans, for example, took over much of the culture of the conquered Greeks.

As we pointed out in the preceding chapter, the individual is more than a mere sponge soaking up the culture about him. He may not be "adjusted" to the culture; every society has some deviants and some skeptics, and thus some innovators. Possibly the significance that the Plains Indians attached to seeing visions in a frenzy originated with some deviant personality who was able to impress upon the tribe the importance of his own ways. For cultural elements usually are introduced by individuals and thus enter the fringe of the culture as individual peculiarities. If adopted by others, an element becomes an alternative. It is tried out and compared with existing elements, though not necessarily with any deliberate thought. If it proves satisfactory, it becomes established as a specialty or universal and enters the core of the culture.

Change in one aspect of a culture almost invariably produces change in other aspects. Minor, emotionally neutral, and immediately practical cultural traits such as a minor food item or a passing fashion produce few if any accompanying changes. Other changes have revolutionary results. The change to agriculture from hunting and food-gathering led eventually to the development of civilization. The change from hand labor to the machine, powered by steam and electricity, made possible the Industrial Revolution that led to tremendous changes in all aspects of life. A third revolution in technology is now occurring, paced by the harnessing of the atom and solar energy and the elimination of much drudgery through electronic automation. Similarly, changes in one realm of knowledge have repercussions in another. Promulgation and acceptance of the theory of evolution necessitated a new and less literal interpretation of the Bible.

Adoption or rejection of new cultural traits and patterns. People are attached to their own culture through habit and emotional conditioning; they tend to prefer an element of their own culture to an innovation. Yet culture changes, and often changes rapidly. But new elements are not added indiscriminately. Culture is *selectively* accumulative. What factors determine whether a new trait will be accepted or rejected? Social scientists have formulated several general principles of cultural change.

(1) Some aspects of a culture are more hospitable to change than others. We Americans are comparatively eager to accept new "scientific" discoveries in medicine, labor-saving devices, and mass-produced material things; but we are far less interested in social inventions. In fact, we resist changing our beliefs and institutions to make them fit our technology.

In general, aspects of culture that carry heavy emotional overtones, such as religion, are especially resistant to change. The Guatemalan Indians have been under Catholic influence for four centuries, but still cling to shreds of the Mayan religion. In the parish of Chichicastenango, the priests have wisely adapted their methods of worship to Indian customs and silently tolerate the fact that after praying in church with candles, incense, and rose petals, their parishioners climb a nearby mountain and conduct what appears to be substantially the same ceremony before an ancient stone image. The San Blas Cuna have adopted mass-manufactured utensils and abandoned pottery-making except in the meaningful areas of religion and native medicine in which they still use handmade vessels. Emotional involvement may also be a significant factor in slowing down changes in technology, in economic systems, in education and modes of government, even in customs of dress, speech, and recreation.

(2) There is a "strain to consistency" in each culture. New traits are accepted most easily if they fill an obvious need and if they are compatible with other elements of the culture. The cultivation of maize spread rapidly from the New World to Africa and Europe because there was a need for such a grain. But rice-eaters like the Orientals and Central Americans show little interest in the starchy potato. Because a culture must appear to be consistent to its practitioners, must "make sense" to them, people are apt to reject elements that conflict with accepted values and adapt those that fit them. The San Blas eagerly adopted American soaps, talcums, and perfumes because these products jibe with their emphasis on cleanliness and love of fragrance. They also embraced Protestant moral teachings and in many respects Protestant conceptions of the supernatural because these beliefs were remarkably similar to their own.

New ideas are often ridiculed and even bitterly opposed when they are first introduced. Pasteur's germ theory and Harvey's hypothesis of blood circulation are examples. Another is Galileo's discovery that the earth revolved around the sun, which utterly contradicted the established conception of the earth as the center of the universe. Galileo was branded a heretic and forced to renounce his belief in his new discovery. One generation violently resists "drastic reforms" that may be commonplace to the next. Workmen's compensation is a case in point; national health insurance may prove to be another. The next two principles of cultural change help explain why many such "radical" ideas eventually are accepted.

(3) Resistance to change is greatest among the older members of a society. "To the young, unformed personalities all habits and ideas are equally new and all can be incorporated with ease," says Linton.[12] He contrasts a boy of 17 and a man of 70 learning to drive a car. Both may become adequate drivers, but the youth will feel much more at home behind the wheel. The present generation of children, growing up in an age of rockets and space flight, will accept air travel as an everyday affair. This "turnover" in the personnel of a society is a very potent factor in cultural change.

(4) Inventions and borrowed elements are more easily adopted during periods of crisis and social disorganization than during periods of comparative stability. During World War II the need for victory spurred a hothouse growth of technology. Nonmaterial changes also came thick and fast. Women entered previously masculine fields; they drove cabs, operated turret lathes and riveting machines, even joined the military forces. During the depression of the 1930's, in spite of press and other organized opposition, changes were made in our economic system that five years before would have seemed inconceivable.

(5) New cultural elements will be resisted by vested interests who see them as competitive. French wine interests raised a furor about the introduction of American soft drinks into their country, depicting the whole idea as a threat to the integrity of French culture. Shipping interests opposed the construction of the first railroad across the United States, and the railroads in turn later opposed construction of the Panama Canal.

(6) Form is more easily diffused than meaning or function. The San Blas Cuna buy sheets and pillowcases, but only a few use them on beds. Most of them sleep in hammocks and hoard the linens as a sign of their wealth and acceptance of American culture. The women eagerly scan American magazines for new ideas for their appliquéd blouses, but they use such schemes purely because the design and colors may appeal to them, not because they are aware of their meaning. Any cultural element can mean different things in different cultures. Black means mourning to us; white means mourning to the Chinese. The hula is a very formal and semi-sacred dance in Hawaii. Americans regard it as a gay

and rather wanton form of entertainment. The Navaho borrowed the colorful masked dances of the Pueblo Indians, but associated them with the healing of disease rather than with fertility, rain, and good crops, the original Pueblo interpretations.

Form also persists long after its original meaning has disappeared in any one culture. The buttons on the sleeves of a man's suit are supposed to be a vestige of the buttons that once were sewed on uniforms to discourage soldiers from wiping their noses with their sleeves! On the Midwestern prairies, pioneer farmers continued to build haylofts over their barns as they had done against New England hillsides, and then built artificial "hills" to get the hay in. As settlement moved westward to the mountains, people tried to build roads along section lines as they had done in the flatlands. Every year we turn millions of city children out for a long summer vacation "to hoe corn and 'bug' potatoes." Edward A. Ross, a pioneer social scientist, called this tendency of social practices to persist in form after the original justification has disappeared *ossification*. He attributed it to our mental laziness, to the fact that emotions are involved, to our failure to understand the dynamic character of society, and to self-interest.

(7) Lack of a written language or difference in spoken language may be a barrier to the adoption of a new element. Items that need no interpretation easily cross cultural bariers. Anthropologist John Gillin, in studying the village of San Luis Jilotepeque in Guatemala, where Indian and Ladino (or Spanish-speaking, westernized Guatemalan) cultures exist side by side with relatively little borrowing, found that the Ladinos have completely accepted tortillas, an Indian food, while the Indians have accepted the Ladinos' coffee. But Ladino traits that require literacy for their adoption are not found in the Indian culture.

(8) The attitude toward the lending culture affects willingness to adopt a cultural element. American women are well-disposed toward Paris fashions and perfumes, men toward London tailoring and leather goods. Although many Latin-Americans deplore what they believe is "American materialism and imperialism," they nonetheless admire American productive efficiency and strive to acquire gadgets, household goods, and cars made in our country. They also admire our athletic prowess and have adopted such sports as baseball and basketball. Similarly, in Guatemala the Ladinos have a higher status than the Indians, and Ladino women never adopt Indian dress. But Indian women occasionally wear Ladino dresses.

(9) Adoption of a trait may generally be considered desirable but is resisted because it would prove temporarily very disruptive and irri-

tating to some members of the society. For example, English spelling could certainly be simplified; there are valid arguments for a 13-month calendar; the United States has an awkward system of weights and measures in contrast to the convenient metric system used in Europe and Latin-America, as well as by scientists in our country. But adopting any of these obviously rational improvements would require years of difficult adjustment, and most of us are unwilling to go to so much trouble simply for the convenience of posterity.

(10) Some cultural traits cannot be adopted because of the technological stage of the society. Sewing machines may be found in remote jungle huts, but sewing machine factories are located only in industrial countries.

Incorporation of new elements. Some new traits and patterns are easily incorporated into a culture. The introduction of such practical items as coffee and tortillas, for example, requires little readjustment on the part of the borrower and has few if any repercussions. Other patterns disturb established habits and values. Employment in Panama and the Canal Zone and the sale of coconuts for cash have largely converted the Cuna to a money economy and caused a conflict between old values of hospitality and sharing and new ones of individualism and competition. The Cuna have, however, managed to achieve a degree of integration. Coined money has been fitted into the cooperative work pattern. Cash payments to the father-in-law or the village are accepted as substitutes for labor; money is now buried with the dead as a "cash payment" for the canoe, which until a generation ago was destroyed upon a man's death.

Another example of the way new elements are modified to fit pre-existing ones is the "creative synthesis" by which the Virgin Mary was identified with pagan regional goddesses as Christianity penetrated certain areas. Pagan religions often centered about one great goddess who was the mother and guardian of life. As Christianity began making inroads, the identity of the local deity was merged with the person of Mary, and the local goddess became the local Madonna.

What happens to displaced cultural elements? Some persist for a while as alternatives (as in long full skirts among old peasant women whose daughters wear modern dress), then as individual peculiarities, and finally drop out of the culture altogether. It is conceivable that the gold nose ring may take this path out of the San Blas Cuna culture. Some elements, like madrigal singing or classic cars, are deliberately and carefully kept alive by devotees. Others, like the bow and arrow, have lost their utilitarian function and now persist as toys, sport items, or in some other guise.

Often people accept a new element, particularly a technological element, as obviously advantageous. Then, when they begin to see its disruptive effects, they bewail the innovation—but rarely will give it up. Americans eagerly seized upon the automobile, then found it created new problems—accidents, parking space, highway financing, and changes in courtship patterns that disturbed many people.

Cultural Lag   •   Culture is continuous, yet constantly changing. It is rebuilt bit by bit as new elements are invented or borrowed and worked over to fit the rest of the culture and as old elements that have become obsolete or poorly adapted to existing conditions are dropped. A culture does not change evenly, with the various related

School in a Firehouse. *Is the inadequacy of postwar school facilities an example of cultural lag?*

elements adjusting quickly and easily to a change in any one of them. Some parts change much more rapidly than others, and when those that are interrelated are much slower to change, a period of maladjustment follows. This maladjustment is called a "cultural lag." The sociologist who introduced the concept, William F. Ogburn, writes: "A cultural lag occurs when one of two parts of culture which are correlated changes before or in greater degree than the other part does, thereby causing less adjustment between the two parts than existed previously." [13] For example, highways were adjusted to the burden of auto traffic in 1910, but since then have never caught up with the tremendous increase in traffic and the development of more powerful and wider cars. Often a cultural lag occurs when some scientific or technological advance poses new problems that can be solved only through a readjustment of values. A most dramatic instance of cultural lag is our society's encouragement of nuclear weapons production at the same time that many of us consider the idea of a really effective world organization to cope with armament and other related problems an outrage to the sacred principle of national sovereignty.

Other examples of cultural lag are inadequate housing, the shortage of teachers and schools, and unsatisfactory provisions for the expense of medical care. Reformers, planners, and government leaders constantly try to reduce cultural lags. When they fail and the lags become too critical, a revolutionary change may occur, such as the Protestant Reformation, the French Revolution, and present-day revolts against colonial rule.

American Culture • The United States is a huge country. Across its vast territory are spread 170-odd million people of many national and religious backgrounds, of different racial extractions, of different economic and social statuses. What holds this society together?

As we have seen, it is most important to a society that its culture be integrated in two areas: (1) overt behavior patterns that permit the everyday life of a society to flow along with the least possible friction—like rules of traffic that prevent hopeless snarls and delays on our roads and highways—and (2) in the core values or dominant cultural orientations upon which a majority of people can agree, and that make for coherence in family life, work relationships, and political actions. These values need not necessarily be perfectly consistent. But there must be sufficient agreement on them to give the people a sense of unity, of cooperation in a common cause that transcends pettier individual concerns.

Diversity of origin characterizes our people and our culture. Perhaps the most fundamental contribution to our culture was made by the British colonist, but many other cultural strains run strong in America. Though the Indian was nearly wiped out and the Negro long enslaved, each has made a strong imprint on our culture. Germans have re-settled here in great numbers, along with Irishmen, Scandinavians, Czechs and Poles and Serbs, Greeks and Italians, Austrians and Hungarians, Jews from many lands, Orientals, and most recently, Mexicans and Puerto Ricans.

They came because they saw America as a land of promise and opportunity. Promise has been the outstanding feature of the American myth throughout its history. America had made a fresh start, and its history was contemporaneous with the rise of industrialism, democracy, and capitalism. Pioneering, promise, and action are America's ethos.

Values, as we have said, are not always obvious or easy to analyze. And Americans, unlike loyal citizens of a totalitarian state, have no explicit ideology that they can rattle off on cue. But we do hold sacred a vague myth we call "The American Way of Life," though we are not always clear about all its details. Many acute foreign observers such as de Tocqueville, James Bryce, and D. W. Brogan, and many of our native social scientists, carefully thinking through the results of community studies and other research—the Lynds' "Middletown," James West's "Plainville," and so on—agree that certain dominant "value clusters" are held by the majority of Americans. If these values seem painfully obvious to you as we list them, that simply confirms their dominance; for values, as we have said, are "given" and unquestioned. Those who hold them consider them natural and unarguable.

(1) *Freedom, democracy,* and *equality* are core values in our culture and are closely interrelated. They are based on belief in the dignity and worth of the *individual* and imply that man is inherently good. If he is left free to pursue his own self-interest in *competition* with others, society will benefit. But freedom does not mean untrammeled personal liberty, for the individual is responsible for his actions. Everyone has an equal right to life, liberty, and the pursuit of happiness, and should have an equal opportunity to make the most of himself.

(2) The *"Puritan ethic"* is another cluster of values that emphasizes individualism. Unlike the Catholic, who has a hierarchy of priests and saints to intercede between him and God and assure him of forgiveness for sins, the Protestant faces God alone. His own efforts will determine whether he reaches the Kingdom of God in this world and the next. He can and must improve and discipline himself. He must work hard, save money, be thrifty. "Waste not, want not." If he works and saves, he will pile up material goods, and these are a sign of virtue and respecta-

Jet Pilot. *In the American value system, progress is closely identified with scientific and technological advances that extend man's mastery over time and space.*

bility. Thus did the Puritan ethic emphasize beliefs, values, and goals that encouraged the rapid growth of capitalism and that are now accepted by Americans of all faiths.

(3) *Progress* for the society and *success* for the individual are closely related. Our "golden age" lies not in a hoary past encrusted with sacred tradition but in the future. The future will be a time of freedom from want, of an abundance of material possessions for everyone. Progress is identified with advances in science and technology that can be used to increase the production of goods and extend man's mastery over time, space and nature. What is new—if it falls into this category—is good. Change is not merely accepted; it is sought. But this attitude, insofar as nonmaterial cultural elements are concerned, extends only to pleasure and entertainment, not to changes in the Constitution or in the theory of private enterprise, for these elements are sacred.

83

Success, like progress, is usually measured in terms of wealth and material possessions, which give a person power, prestige, and security. An individual *achieves* success through *self-reliance* and *initiative*. The hero is the person who comes up the hard way, through his own efforts. The myth of "log cabin to President" gives this value reality.

Mobility—to "get ahead" and "get around"—is also characteristic of Americans. We say, "You can't keep a good man down," and encourage youngsters to "Hitch your wagon to a star." The restless energy that pushed the frontier ever farther West expresses itself today in migration, travel, and efforts to climb the ladder of social status.

(4) Americans have, in Gillin's phrase, a *"mechanistic world view."* They see the physical and social world as made up of parts that fit together like a machine and work more or less satisfactorily. When the parts don't work, a person doesn't theorize, plan, or simply abandon the machine. He *acts*. He tinkers with the machine to make it work better. He must be *practical, efficient,* and *ingenious;* he must have "know-how."

The values of material progress and practical action combine to make the clever tinkerer one of our great culture heroes. Edison and Ford produced down-to-earth results measurable in material gains. Americans like precise measurement. They want a report card clearly marked in terms of competitive standing. They have faith in statistics. Quantity and size are valued for themselves. "The biggest" and "the most" are "the best." Paul Bunyan is a hero tailor-made to American values.

(5) Americans are *moralizers,* not shoulder-shruggers. They see things in terms of good and bad, right and wrong, and cannot resist passing judgment on almost everything. They tend to be less sensitive than Europeans to the grays of a complex situation. Things are either-or, black or white. They have a sense of mission. Our way is the best way, and it is our duty to enlighten and guide and help others to see and do things our way.

(6) *Humanitarianism, fair play,* and *cooperation* counterbalance the rugged competitive aspect of individualism. Americans have a sense of personal responsibility for the welfare of others. They feel they *should* give to the March of Dimes, send CARE packages, join the PTA, and ring doorbells for the Community Chest. The millionaire sweetens his money by establishing philanthropic and educational foundations.

(7) With the accent on the future and on individualism is linked an accent on *youth* and *romance,* which places the lovely young girl in her teens and early twenties at the center of attention. Monogamous marriage is unquestionably the right way; women are more chaste, more

moral, more spiritual, and more "cultured" than men. Love makes the world go around, and nothing is too good for the children. Along with this value cluster goes a growing preoccupation with sex, with techniques of love-making.

(8) Laymen and social scientists alike display concern over the growing acceptance of two values that compete with individualism: *security* and *conformity*. They observe that today's young men prefer a mediocre job in a big corporation to the risks and possible rewards of going into business for themselves. "The welfare state" is an epithet. The courageous pioneer, the brave Western marshal, the imaginative entrepreneur stand out in contrast to the faceless organization man in the gray flannel suit.

Many Americans now think in terms not of hierarchy but of equality, and measure themselves by their peers rather than by their betters. We glorify the common man rather than the expert or the intellectual. People are asked to adjust to each other and to things as they are. David Riesman sees the trend in America toward "other-directedness," toward being "hep" and responding from moment to moment to signals from one's peers as a break away from "inner" principles firmly built in by home, school, and church and used as guides throughout life.

(9) Another growing value is *hedonism* or devotion to pleasure. Although Americans have long valued material possessions as a reward for and a proof of hard work and success and therefore of virtue, they have felt guilty about actually enjoying leisure and comfort. This attitude apparently is changing. There is a new emphasis on frank enjoyment of leisure and sensual pleasure—of fun, food, and drink. And yet, say some, Americans do not really relax and enjoy life; they work hard even at having fun, pursue happiness earnestly and deliberately.

(10) Other values we frequently hear mentioned in connection with Americans are *order, cleanliness, punctuality, casualness, frankness, humor,* and *informality.*

Do these values seem self-evident to you? They might not to other people. The Chinese place family above the individual. The Japanese place "honor" and "face" above life and liberty. Europeans value the different, the unique, the outstanding—not the standardized and big and mass-produced. The English value formal ritual above casualness and informality. The Germans value order, cleanliness, efficiency, practicality, and hard work as much as we do. In fact, American soldiers quickly felt at home with their erstwhile enemies after World War II because they shared certain common values with the Germans. And yet it was obvious that important conflicts of values existed, or World War II would not have happened. In the next chapter we shall consider what happens when people think their values are the only valid ones, and we shall sum up the importance of our study of the culture concept.

Ethnocentrism

As the individual is socialized, he comes to feel that "the axis of the earth runs right through his home town." A person's belief that his own group and culture are superior to all others is called *ethnocentrism* (from the Greek *ethnos* or nation).

Ethnocentrism is a universal phenomenon; every group sets "us" off from "them." "We" are the center, and all others are scaled in

87

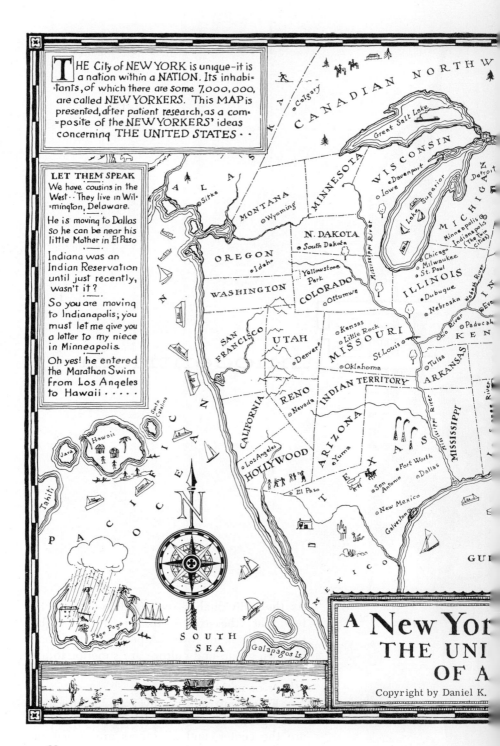

THE City of NEW YORK is unique—it is a nation within a NATION. Its inhabitants, of which there are some 7,000,000, are called NEW YORKERS. This MAP is presented, after patient research, as a composite of the NEW YORKERS' ideas concerning THE UNITED STATES · ·

LET THEM SPEAK

We have cousins in the West · · They live in Wilmington, Delaware.

He is moving to Dallas so he can be near his little Mother in El Paso

Indiana was an Indian Reservation until just recently, wasn't it?

So you are moving to Indianapolis; you must let me give you a letter to my niece in Minneapolis.

Oh yes! he entered the Marathon Swim from Los Angeles to Hawaii · · · · ·

A New Yor
THE UNI
OF A
Copyright by Daniel K.

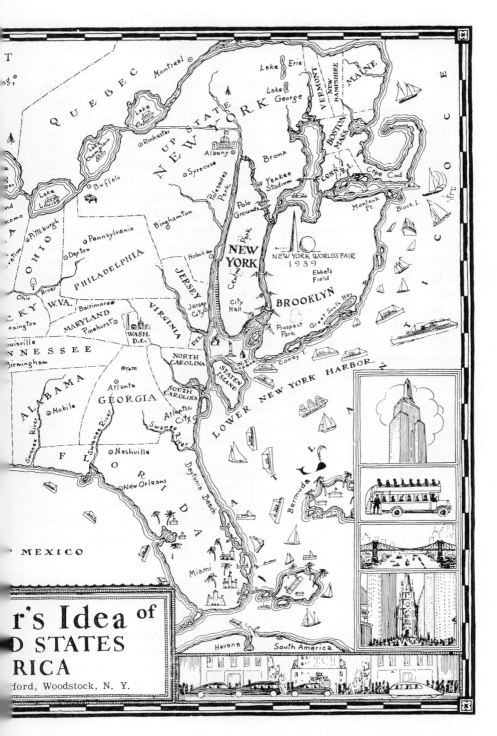

r's Idea of
D STATES
RICA
ford, Woodstock, N. Y.

reference to us; *our* ways are "human nature," our motivations inevitable. The Greeks thought that people who spoke no Greek "babbled"; hence our word "barbarian." Finnish immigrants in Minnesota and Michigan refer to people who do not speak Finnish as "toiskielinen" or "other-tongued." The Navahos call themselves "The People," and Eskimos refer to themselves as "Men." The San Blas Cuna believe that they are of the noblest origin and were the first created of all peoples. The Chinese used to call their country "The Middle Kingdom." Walking down a street in Peiping with a journalist one day, the senior author heard a child call to his mother. His companion translated, "There go two foreign devils!" Visiting a Japanese schoolroom, he was struck by a brilliantly colored map on the wall. Right in the middle, where the United States belonged (so he felt, for thus he had always seen it), was Japan. The United States was relegated to the fringes of the earth.

We Americans are prone to boast that ours is the richest country in the world, the one with the highest standard of living, the most democratic, the freest, and the most advanced technologically. Our cultural heritage includes a belief in "progress" that many other cultures lack. This assurance in turn reinforces the feeling that other groups are inferior and that we are doing them a favor if we change them to fit our pattern. Ethnocentrism does not by any means always include this attitude. Many peoples, although believing they are somehow "chosen," tolerantly ignore other cultures or brush them aside as "different" without any zeal to dominate or reform them.

Ethnocentrism is not the same as nationalism, though nationalism is the most prominent—and dangerous—form of ethnocentrism today. A person's belief in the superiority of his group may range from pride in his community or home town, his school or fraternity, to pride in his state, or to more insidious and socially disruptive forms such as racism, class solidarity and antagonism, religious bigotry, and zealous and belligerent patriotism.

Inevitability **of Ethnocentrism** •	This feeling that a person's own group is superior, this tendency to judge others by his own standards, is practically inevitable. Society *teaches* its

members to be ethnocentric, both through the informal processes of socialization and social control and through deliberate instruction by school, church, and government. The ways of the group seem natural, right and human; our moral standards, our values, are the only standards we have for judging behavior. We may be willing, as we become aware that there are other groups with other ways, to think in terms of their cultural values; but we are unable to. Our thinking stems from certain premises; members of other cultures think according to different premises. So with equal logic we and they arrive at different conclusions.

Few of us are aware of how little of our own culture we have created. Ralph Linton's classic description of a "100 per cent American" drives home the point that ignorance of a culture's many and varied sources fosters ethnocentrism.

There can be no question about the average American's Americanism or his desire to preserve this precious heritage at all costs. Nevertheless, some insidious foreign ideas have already wormed their way into his civilization without his realizing what was going on. Thus dawn finds the unsuspecting patriot garbed in pajamas, a garment of Indian origin; and lying in a bed built on a pattern which originated in either Persia or Asia Minor. He is muffled to the ears in un-American materials: cotton, first domesticated in India; linen, domesticated in the Near East; wool from an animal native to Asia Minor; or silk whose uses were first discovered by the Chinese. All these substances have been transformed into clothes by methods invented in Southwestern Asia. If the weather is cold enough, he may even be sleeping under an eider-down quilt invented in Scandinavia.

On awakening he glances at the clock, a medieval European invention, uses one potent Latin word in abbreviated form, rises in haste, and goes to the bathroom. Here, if he stops to think about it, he must feel himself in the presence of a great American institution; he will have heard stories of both the quality and frequency of foreign plumbing and will know that in no other country does the average man perform his ablutions in the midst of such splendor. But the insidious foreign influence pursues him even here. Glass was invented by the ancient Egyptians, the use of glazed tiles for floors and walls in the Near East, porcelain in China, and the art of enameling on metal by Mediterranean artisans of the Bronze Age. Even his bathtub and toilet are but slightly modified copies of Roman originals. The only purely American contribution to the ensemble is the steam radiator.

In this bathroom the American washes with soap invented by the ancient Gauls. Next, he cleans his teeth, a subversive European practice which did not invade America until the latter part of the eighteenth century. He then shaves, a masochistic rite first developed by the heathen priests of ancient Egypt and Sumer. The process is made less of a penance by the fact that his razor is of steel, an iron-carbon alloy discovered in either India or Turkestan. Lastly, he dries himself on a Turkish towel.

Returning to the bedroom, the unconscious victim of un-American practices removes his clothes from a chair, invented in the Near East, and proceeds to dress. He puts on close-fitting tailored garments whose form derives from the skin clothing of the ancient nomads of the Asiatic steppes and fastens them with buttons whose prototypes appeared in Europe at the close of the Stone Age. This costume is appropriate enough for outdoor exercise in a cold climate, but is quite unsuited to American summers, steam-heated houses, and Pullmans. Nevertheless, foreign ideas and habits hold the unfortunate man in thrall even when common sense tells him that the authentically American costume of gee string and moccasins would be far more comfortable. He puts on his feet stiff coverings made from hide prepared by a process invented in ancient Egypt and cut to a pattern which can be traced back to ancient Greece, and makes sure they are properly polished, also a Greek idea. Lastly he ties about his neck a strip of bright-colored cloth which is a vestigial survival of the shoulder shawls worn by seventeenth-century Croats. He gives himself a final appraisal in the mirror, an old Mediterranean invention, and goes downstairs to breakfast.

Here a whole new series of foreign things confronts him. His food and drink are placed before him in pottery vessels, the popular name of which—china—is sufficient evidence of their origin. His fork is a medieval Italian invention and his spoon a copy of a Roman original. He will usually begin the meal with coffee, an Abyssinian plant first discovered by the Arabs. The American is quite likely to need it to dispel the morning-after effects of over-indulgence in fermented drinks, invented in the Near East; or distilled ones, invented by the alchemists of Medieval Europe. Whereas the Arabs took their coffee straight, he will probably sweeten it with sugar, discovered in India, and dilute it with cream; both the domestication of cattle and the technique of milking having originated in Asia Minor.

If our patriot is old-fashioned enough to adhere to the so-called American breakfast, his coffee will be accompanied by an orange, domesticated in the Mediterranean region, a cantaloupe domesticated in Persia, or grapes, domesticated in Asia Minor. He will follow this with a bowl of cereal made from grain domesticated in the Near East and prepared by methods also invented there. From this he will go on to waffles, a Scandinavian invention, with plenty of butter, originally a Near-Eastern cosmetic. As a side dish he may have the egg of a bird domesticated in Southeastern Asia or strips of the flesh of an animal domesticated in the same region, which have been salted and smoked by a process invented in Northern Europe.

Breakfast over, he places upon his head a molded piece of felt, invented by the nomads of Eastern Asia, and, if it looks like rain, puts on outer shoes of rubber, discovered by the ancient Mexicans, and takes an umbrella, invented in India. He then sprints for his train—the train, not the sprinting, being an English invention. At the station he pauses for a moment to buy a newspaper, paying for it with coins invented in ancient Lydia. Once on board he settles back to inhale the fumes of a cigarette invented in Mexico, or a cigar invented in Brazil. Meanwhile, he reads the news of the day, imprinted in characters invented by the ancient Semites by a process invented in Germany upon a material invented in China. As he scans the latest editorial pointing out the dire results to our institutions of accepting foreign ideas, he will not fail to thank a Hebrew God in an Indo-European language that he is a one-hundred per cent (decimal system invented by the Greeks) American (from Americus Vespucci, Italian geographer).[1]

Advantages of Ethnocentrism • Ethnocentrism is not altogether objectionable. It has certain definite advantages for the "we group" and its individual members. It makes for social integration, reduces conflicts within the group (by deflecting many frustrations outward), and promotes cultural stability and uniformity. If what we do is right and natural and human, why change? In a nation at war ethnocentrism is obviously an asset, and is fostered by various means.

Besides holding the group together, ethnocentrism is psychologically satisfying to the individual. The lowly substitute's ego is enhanced if he is a member of a championship team, however little he may personally have to do with the team's success. The barefoot Costa Rican coffee worker, riddled with intestinal parasites and weighed down by poverty, is proud, because he has been taught that his country is the most advanced in Central America. A person participates vicariously in all sorts of wonderful things that other members of his group have or do.

Disadvantages of Ethnocentrism • But the harmful effects of ethnocentrism outweigh its advantages, for the following reasons. First, extreme ethnocentrism is accompanied by a sense of satisfaction with the status quo—with things as they are—and a resentment toward any healthy questioning of conditions or suggestions of ways to improve the cultural and social order.

Social changes, when they come, then prove much more disruptive and violent than a gradual process of intelligently guided change.

Second, our modern society is highly complex, with its parts interdependent, and no group within such a society can live in a vacuum. Extreme ethnocentrism in sub-cultural groups in our society incites conflict among them, or at best prevents them from working together as effectively as they might for the good of the whole society. Intolerance and misunderstanding among racial, religious, and nationality groups stem largely from each group's conviction of superiority.

Most important of all, ethnocentrism prevents nations from working together effectively to solve their mutual problems and settle their disagreements. A narrow nationalism is the chief stumbling block to really effective world organization. Ethnocentrism, when displayed by people from one culture in their dealings with people from another, breeds ill will. We have heard American tourists who apparently think that any of "these dumb Latin Americans who can't even speak English" will understand them if they just shout loud enough. Only an extreme conviction of the superiority of English over native cultures enabled the British to rationalize their imperialism in terms of "The White Man's Burden." Europeans and Americans in their contacts with underdeveloped areas have been especially prone to tread roughshod over the cultures of other peoples, bringing confusion and disorganization to many societies. As the anthropologist Melville Herskovits says, "Acceptance of European beliefs and values, coupled with the withholding of opportunities to achieve an equitable way of life under them—the most common form, over the world, of the contradictory situation that ensues on the imposition of Euroamerican controls—induces bewilderment, despair and cynicism." [2]

Cultural   •   Relativity   The best antidote to the poison of extreme ethnocentrism lies in making an honest attempt to grasp the culture concept in all its implications through reading anthropology and the other social sciences, through travel, and through exchange of students, teachers, and technicians. Thus we can counterbalance our natural ethnocentrism with an attitude of cultural relativity.

Cultural relativity is an attitude of respect for cultural differences. It involves the realization that each culture has its own values and should not be judged by those of another; that each body of custom has an inherent dignity and meaning; that a person's own culture is but one among many, which he happens to prefer because he grew up in it.

Cultural relativity does not imply that "all systems of moral values, all concepts of right and wrong, are founded on such shifting sands that there is no need for morality, for proper behavior, for ethical conduct." [3] (This is a crucial point, for upon it rests much of the uninformed criticism of social science.) We are suspicious of relativity, because we are taught morality and truth and beauty in terms of absolutes, of either-or, of black and white, of extremes with little shading between; and we tend to think that to accept the validity of other moral codes is to abandon our own. But to say that each culture develops its own moral codes, its own standards of truth and beauty, is not to deny morality, truth, and beauty. The set of standards by which each group guides its life is as valid *for them* as our own is for us. Morality, truth, and beauty are values in every culture, though they take different forms.

Nor does cultural relativity mean that an individual need not abide by the codes of his own culture, that he is "emancipated" from social control. The ways that are right for a South Sea Islander are not right for us, because they do not fit into our cultural pattern. We do not read

Overcoming Ethnocentrism. *Travel, which furthers an appreciation of other cultures, is a most effective antidote to the poison of extreme ethnocentrism.*

anthropology like a seed catalog, deciding to try this custom and that. The exotic plant would not fit into our garden. An intelligent under- standing of cultural differences does not prompt a person to kick over the traces and say, "Oh, boy! What haven't I been missing!" Instead, it im- presses him with the necessity of a certain degree of conformity to the code of the group, both for his own satisfaction and for the unity and survival of the group. Although cultural relativity means respect for other ways, it does not mean loss of respect for our own. A person may decide, after rational reflection, that his own ways are the best, or the best for his group, or the best for him to follow, since it is important to adjust to his own group. Even the most objective social scientist is hardly likely to abandon the dominant folkways and mores of his culture. A comfortable, orderly life hinges on a reasonable degree of living accord- ing to group expectations. As Clyde Kluckhohn says, anthropology does not destroy standards or "the useful tyranny of the normal." [4] It does teach us, as Ruth Benedict points out, to recognize that other cultures are as significant to their members as ours is to us. [5]

Nor does cultural relativity mean that all cultures are equally "good." This fallacy would be as dangerous as extreme ethnocentrism. It is a pre- carious thing, indeed, to judge cultures, but they can be measured against two criteria: (1) How well do they fulfill the basic functions of pro- tecting the individual and preserving the society? (2) How well do they satisfy the needs and wants they themselves create; that is, how well do they live up to their own values and goals? Other standards also may be used. We Americans use our own pride in bigness, speed, and material advancement as a yardstick by which we estimate other cultures. The Latin nations judge in terms of art, literature, music, and enjoyment of life. Even anthropologists use measuring devices such as freedom for individual variation, lack of conflict in interpersonal relations, the zest and vigor that the cultural orientation lends to existence, and the absence of indications of maladjustment, such as insanity, family disorganization, and the like. We *can* judge other cultures, but we must be conscious of the criteria we are using and admit that other criteria might produce other results.

Value of the   •   There are many advantages to be had
Culture Concept   from the comparative study of cultures.
A person cannot understand human be-
havior merely from looking at his own
culture. Small isolated societies with nonliterate cultures serve as "labora- tories of social forms." The study of various cultures points up the im- portance of cultural conditioning to human behavior.

An understanding of human behavior gives an individual a more objective attitude toward his own culture. Knowing the possible range of human behavior, a person can look at his own with somewhat more detachment, though he can never escape its emotional values entirely. He can evaluate his own institutions, using those of other cultures as a yardstick. If he still prefers his own, as he probably will because of early emotional conditioning, at least he does so with a more enlightened allegiance. Furthermore, this person grows more tolerant of socially harmless deviations from the pattern, less demanding of rigid conformity to every custom.

A grasp of the culture concept opens up a new perspective on history. As Stuart Chase says,

Formal history with its Caesars and Napoleons tends to be a record of the abnormal, the geniuses, sports, freaks, and misfits, the glandular cases of mankind. It stands the social pyramid on its apex. The culture concept puts it back on its base. The kings and warriors are dramatic, true enough, but the real story concerns the society which protected its children and organized its food supply down through the ages.[6]

Finally, the culture concept provides a new and more hopeful approach to social problems (quite aside from the important fact that an attitude of cultural relativity will in itself go far toward solving such problems as are based on prejudice). This does not mean that drastic reforms can be accomplished overnight, for culture itself is a brake on social change. In human affairs there is no such thing as a completely fresh start; no one can wipe clean the slate of tradition and past experience. In effecting any reform, the would-be reformer must be realistic and take into account the values and customs involved. "No reform can ever bear fruit unless it is grafted successfully to the living tree of culture." [7]

Nonetheless, an understanding of culture produces an objective approach to social problems that is essential to their effective solution. A person can study foreign or nonliterate cultures with greater detachment than his own because his emotions are not involved. Thereby he gains perspective by which to appraise his own culture more clearly. Ability to appraise our own institutions objectively makes orderly change possible.

The culture concept also encourages optimism regarding the eventual solution of social problems. If the people of a warlike nation were "born that way," little could be done to change them. But they are aggressive because their culture has shaped them that way, and there is hope that eventually they will change and that this change can be intelligently guided. If the rapist, the thief, or the murderer were fulfilling an inborn instinct, there would never be a decline in the incidence of crime. However, he is shaped largely by his life situation, including his culture; under different circumstances he might have been a good citizen.

Recognizing the strong influence of culture on the individual does not mean abandoning entirely the ideas of individual responsibility and free will. In fact, the realization that culture is man-made places the responsibility for man's destiny squarely on his own shoulders. Man does change his culture. Why then should he not be expected to apply the resources and knowledge now at his command in a constructive way?

SEVEN

Society

In discussing a subject as complex as modern society, the social scientist sometimes wishes he could "say everything first." The phenomena of culture, society, and personality are so interwoven that in discussing culture we already have had to mention such overlapping concepts as social groups, institutions, integration, and norms. Now and in later chapters we shall sharpen and expand these conceptual tools and acquire some new ones. In this chapter we are especially concerned with social structure, social interaction, and social change.

Sociology is the "science of society," and a society, as we have seen, is a group of people who share a common culture and a sense of common identity. In its most general sense society refers to human associations, the web of social relationships. The sociologist focuses on social organization, the behavior of people in groups, and studies the ways in which social relationships are organized into groups, classes, and institutions, and how this organization sometimes breaks down and social problems arise. He also is concerned with population trends, social change, and social psychology.

Animal Societies • Culture, we saw earlier, is peculiar to man. Society, however, is not. Many species of insects and animals live in societies. Their population aggregate is organized into a system of division of labor that persists in time, lives in a certain place, and shares common goals. Protection, nutrition, and reproduction are made easier by strength of numbers and specialization. The social organization of animals and insects is based on instinct; their responses are largely rigid and inherited. Division of labor among social ants, bees, wasps, and termites, for example, is based on definite physiological differences. Within each class there is no individuality. Bees are standardized, interchangeable units. The queen bee and the drones produce new generations; the workers build hives and gather nectar; the nurses feed the larvae; soldiers guard the colony against attack. Such societies do not change; some were perfected 65 million years ago. They need tolerate no deviants, no rebels or criminals. Every individual is born with the right responses. There is no need for socialization or for sanctions.

Most of the sub-human primates, too, are organized into families, herds, and clans. They are social animals in part because of the long infancy of the newborn, the fact that the adult sex impulse knows no special season, and because births are single. They can communicate by cries and gestures, and much of their behavior is learned. They display a sense of belonging to the group and manifest such emotions as love, hatred, grief, and happiness.

Insects and primates alike, however, lack the ability to speak, and therefore lack culture. Culture enables man to live in societies based not simply on interdependence but on shared beliefs and values and faith in a common destiny.

The Human Group   •   *Social interaction and social relations.*
A *social relation* exists when two or more people are in contact and mutually aware of one another. This contact may be direct or indirect, but it invariably involves communication on a symbolic level, whether by gesture or by language. And the behavior of each person modifies the behavior of the other or others. Each person responds to the others and shapes his actions according to their behavior. This mutual stimulus and response is called *social interaction.* The social relation consists of their reciprocal expectations. The relations between father and son, friend and friend, and employer and employee are meaningful only in terms of the mutual and reciprocal expectations on which their interaction is patterned.

Much social interaction is channeled by social norms, which define rights and duties according to established cultural definitions. A set of social relationships that is defined by the norms is a social system, and such a system always implies interdependence of the interacting persons. If there are no norms to govern social interaction in a given situation, social scientists call the interaction *collective behavior.* Collective behavior, which we shall discuss later, includes the behavior of mobs, crowds, and publics.

The nature of social groups. We all belong to groups—to our families, to bridge, drama, or astronomy clubs, to churches, to cities, to the United States of America. We also fit into "groupings" or categories—we are male or female, under or over 21, golfers, chess-players, or bowlers, Elvis Presley or hi-fi fans, college graduates or illiterates. We find ourselves, too, in aggregates—clusters of people waiting for a bus or watching a movie or walking along Main Street. But categories and simple aggregates, significant as they are to the social scientist, are not *social* groups.

A social group is an aggregate of two or more people who (1) may or may not be in contact with one another but who are aware of common membership in the group, (2) interact according to mutually accepted norms that define their expected behavior and set members off from non-members, (3) are organized around one or more common interests or activities, and (4) are united by a sense of emotional solidarity. Thus a family is a social group; Pat Boone fans are not, though some may be organized into groups called fan clubs. A college class and its instructor form a social group; the people shopping in a department store do not. There can conceivably be more groups in a society than there are individuals, for each individual may be a member of many groups. And the society itself is a group that includes all the other groups of an organized population that sense they belong together; [1] it links these groups together through the systems of rules called institutions. The society may be only one village of nonliterates, or, as in the case of the San Blas Cuna, a number of village communities belonging to one tribe. It may include many peasant communities centering in villages in a rural region, or it may be a nation-state with a population in the hundreds of millions. Its limits are marked by the sense of common identity and group loyalty of its members; very few people have any greater loyalty than their loyalty to the nation. The members of a society both interact more with one another than with members of other societies and hold more values in common. This interdependence and sharing of values help to hold the society together.

A society is not necessarily located within certain geographical bounds. A cluster of people living within a continuous small area, who share a common way of life, form a community, or local territorial group. [2] Community and society are one in most preliterate societies. Today, in modern society, people living within the bounds of a metropolitan area share a common life in terms of *symbiosis*, or mutual dependence, for such purposes as making a living or distributing goods. But within its bounds are many *ways* of life. "Social organization in modern society is veering away from community." [3]

Formation and integration of social groups. Social groups are formed for many reasons. One reason involves sheer survival. The family group originally was formed to protect infants and mothers, and bands were formed for the security afforded by numbers. People may not deliberately decide to form the group. It simply arises when people interact, when this interaction persists in time, and when the members become interdependent through division of labor. This functional interdependence of the group gives rise to the kind of "mechanical integration" that characterizes insect societies. When later the group begins to agree on values and beliefs, or decides to work to keep the group going, *consensus* is established.

Consensus is the socio-psychological basis of human society. It sets limits to conflicts of interest within a society because conflicting groups become convinced that in spite of their differences they must sacrifice some of their own self-interests so that the society will hold together. Another factor that increases the cohesion of the group is a sense of its goodness and rightness, a sense that it satisfies needs and is better than other groups, a sense of *esprit de corps* or morale.

When group integration is lacking, a state of *anomie* exists. Literally "normlessness," anomie refers to a sense of isolation, of being cast adrift from group ties. This feeling may be present in a person or a number of persons or may permeate a whole society.

Groups are, of course, often deliberately formed to promote the satisfaction of socially and culturally induced interests and values. Such groups are called *voluntary associations*. Unlike the rules that govern membership in a family, the rules of voluntary associations leave a person free to join or free to leave the group as he wishes. Estimates indicate that there are well over 100,000 such groups in our nation of "joiners"— PTA's, bowling leagues, Boy Scouts, bridge clubs, discussion groups, unions, study clubs, fraternities, alumni clubs.

Structure of groups: status and role. From the viewpoint of structure, a social group is a set of interrelated statuses and their accompanying roles, both of which are defined by the norms that have been accepted by the group. A *status* is a position in a society or a group. It has an identity of its own apart from any given individual who occupies it; it is an item of culture. Age, sex, kinship, and marriage define statuses in all societies; in most societies rank, occupation, class, and other considerations also define statuses. The statuses into which a person is born or which he automatically reaches with the passage of time are *ascribed* statuses. An *achieved* status is one an individual may reach by his own efforts or through some stroke of good fortune. A person doesn't strive to reach the status of a woman, a child, or a cousin as he does the status of club secretary, gang leader, president of the United States, minister of a church, or teacher.

The pattern of behavior that accompanies a status is a *role*. It is the dynamic aspect of status. A person *occupies* a position or status, but he *plays* the accompanying role. In the commonly used analogy of a stage play, the part the actor is assigned is his status; the script is his role. Another actor could step in and occupy the same status and play the same role, but individual interpretation would make the actual performance somewhat different.

Any one individual occupies a number of statuses and plays different roles at different periods of his life and in the different social groups to which he belongs. One man may within one day play the roles of father, son, husband, boss, underling, church member, poker crony, PTA president, customer, neighbor, host, guest, casual acquaintance, intimate friend, and voter, depending on which social relationship is in effect at any particular time. His behavior in any one role is largely patterned by cultural norms—the folkways, mores, and laws of his society that set forth the right and proper and legal ways of doing things. These patterns of group expectations, together with the sanctions that enforce them, are the basis of social organization and enable the society to function and to fulfill its main purposes—protection of the individual and perpetuation of the group itself.

Types of groups. There are many perspectives from which we could attempt to classify groups. We have already mentioned voluntary associations, which imply the existence of involuntary ones. We could classify groups by their duration: the enduring nation and the fleeting mob; by their purpose, which would entail many subsidiary categories such as the needs they satisfy; by their institutional affiliation, whether economic, familial, educational; by the traits of their members—youth groups, Negro groups, nationality groups; by their degree of organization, from the amorphous peer group to the government bureau. But perhaps the two most important classifications are by size of the group and type of social relationships.

Small and extended groups. Why is size an important consideration in social groups? Social scientists have in recent years focused on this question, and have concluded that small groups are extremely important in the functioning of a society because there are fewer social relationships in a small group and roles are more clearly defined and more personal than in larger groups and members are thus motivated to work harder. There are four possible relationships in a group of three, but the addition of a single member increases the number of possible relationships to eleven. If A, B, and C form a group, there are the relationships of all three, of A and B, of A and C, and of B and C. If D joins the group, we add to those four relationships seven more; that of all four; of A and D; of A, B, and D; of A, C, and D; of B and D; of B, C, and D; and of C and D. Interaction obviously becomes more complex as more members are added to a group. The army recognizes the importance of small groups by breaking down its organization into platoons and task forces. The small group is "the molecular unit of social structure." [4]

The extended group is also very important in all societies. A number of small "nuclear" families are joined by a system of norms into an extended family. The statuses of cousin, uncle, and the like, are much more meaningful in most small societies than in ours. Membership in a kinship group is the key to most of a person's social relationships in such societies. Among the Yirkala of Australia, for example, a man may usually marry only the daughter of his mother's brother, and he has a very special responsibility for contributing food and other gifts to this uncle. In modern society the extended family is less closely integrated with the rest of the social organization than in a folk society. Other extended groups such as the army, the large church, and the state are far more important.

The elements of extended groups are the small or nucleated groups that make it up, the system of communications that defines the relationship between the individual groups and the total extended group, and a system of control that makes these relationships permanent. In these extended groups statuses are formally defined; the army line of command, the state bureaucracy, the church hierarchy can all be clearly charted.

Primary and secondary relationships. Human groups are differentiated according to the type of contacts or social relations that predominate in the group. In the city when we go out to work or shop, the majority of our contacts are fleeting and impersonal. From the time we go out till we get home, we may rub elbows with hundreds of people, engage in minor transactions or brief conversation with dozens, without knowing their names, their family background, anything at all about them except what they look like and their function in relation to us. Most are merely obstacles to be avoided as we walk along, or fellow passengers to be ignored or classified and dismissed with a glance. Others are means to ends: the bus driver who lets us out at the proper stop, the salesgirl who helps us match a color, the bank teller who cashes a check, the traffic policeman who untangles the rush hour traffic jam.

At home, too, we come in contact with hundreds of people whom we know in only one aspect of their personalities—the newspaper reporter, the radio announcer, the TV master of ceremonies. They in turn are aware of us only as part of a mass of readers, listeners, or viewers who, if sufficiently pleased and entertained and convinced, will buy the sponsor's or advertiser's product or believe the message of the editorial writer or political speaker.

With our families, in the intimate circle of friends, and in a close-knit neighborhood, however, we know others as whole personalities. Any errand in a village is protracted by friendly conversation, for the villager knows everyone he meets and is interested in them. If a person is not a friend then he is a stranger and is treated with hostility or hospitality. In the city, the individual is anonymous and is greeted with indifference by those who do not know him.

We call this contrast the difference between primary and secondary

Primary Groups. *The cracker-barrel philosophers of the rural general store enjoy intimate face-to-face contacts.*

contacts. This distinction is so fundamental to social relationships that groups and even whole communities or societies may be characterized as "primary" or "secondary" (also called *Gemeinschaft* and *Gesellschaft*) depending on the proportion of warm, personal contacts to impersonal ones.

Primary groups are characterized by intimate, face-to-face association over a long period of time. The family, the play group or circle of close friends, and the neighborhood are the chief primary groups and are fundamental to every society. They are, as the pioneer sociologist, Charles Horton Cooley, said, "the nursery of human nature," for every individual starts life in them, and they transmit the culture to him and shape his personality. Primary group relationships are warm, personal ones, regarded as good in themselves; they involve the intimate sharing of common values. Primary contacts are "personal, spontaneous, sentimental and inclusive." [5]

Primary contacts are present in urban living, too, but the proportion of secondary contacts is overwhelming. Secondary contacts may be face-to-face, but they are impersonal, superficial, transitory, and segmental. We could not possibly know intimately all the persons with whom we come in contact in city living. The salesclerk, the bus driver, the grocer, the mailman, even the teacher and the priest, are essentially functionaries; we may not know where they live, who their "people" are, what they are "really like." Secondary relationships are means to ends. The relationship

106

with the other person or persons involved would be little if at all changed if another person performed his role.

As a member of a political party, a student body, an audience, or as a customer in a store, an individual acts not as a whole person, as he does in the primary group, but in the segmental or partial role. He is a voter, a student, a spectator, or a customer. When he leaves the group there will be no sense of loss or bereavement or loneliness. The group will simply be smaller by one, and anyone else can fill the gap and make up the loss to the party's registration rolls or the store's profits. Instead of an "intimate sharing of common values," the secondary group involves a rational pursuit of common interests, or at least interests that happen to coincide at a certain point.

The trend toward larger, more highly urbanized societies has inevitably meant an ever-increasing importance of secondary groups. Extended groups such as governments, churches, schools, and business corporations grow larger, more formal, and more elaborate. Associations spring up about various specific interests, and many of them also fill the need for communication with one's fellow men and for congenial interaction.

It is interesting to notice that primary relationships often tend to arise within secondary groups. In the army, for example, a soldier has "buddies"; in the factory men who work together become friends. In all large organizations cliques form and communication proceeds by grapevine as well as through formal channels. Informal spontaneous groupings arise; persons see one another as persons, not just as functionaries. For "however formalized and systematized and 'rationalized' an organization may become, the basic primary group process continues to operate, erecting its informal collectivities both within and without the large-scale associations." [6]

Communal and Associational Societies

Social scientists often develop "polar" concepts that are useful in analyzing complex social phenomena. Such concepts come in pairs and are regarded as occupying opposite ends of a straight line or continuum. They are "ideal" or abstract types that perhaps describe no concrete situation perfectly but which permit analysis of a particular phenomenon by considering the place that its various elements occupy on the continuum. One such continuum is represented by the polar concepts of "communal" and "associational" societies. The San Blas Cuna society is communal. Our own society or the society of any similarly urbanized and industrialized nation-state is associational.

The Communal Society. The communal or "folk" society is small, ranging from a few families to a few thousand people. It is isolated and has little or no social contact with other communities. It is self-sufficient and provides for all the needs of its members. There is little specialization or division of labor in the communal society except on the basis of sex. Every member of the society knows every other member; all share the same interests and experiences, the same biological and cultural heritage. Statuses are ascribed on the basis of sex, age, and family. Roles are clearly defined by the culture and their interrelationships are fixed; behavior patterns change little from one generation to another. Kinship ties of all kinds are formalized and each status is clearly distinguished and its accompanying role is prescribed. The extended family or kin group is the basis of social organization.

This rigidly unified social organization is dictated by an inflexible cultural pattern that changes very slowly. It is highly integrated, consistent, and static. It presents values and goals upon which there is an agreement so fundamental they need never be formulated in words or laws. Thus there is a strong feeling of group unity and loyalty among members.

The communal or folk society is a "sacred" society. The ways of life are folkways, and the folkways tend to become mores. Even food may be personalized, and the technological procedures of planting and harvesting and hunting assume the character of sacred rites. "Nothing is solely a means to an immediate practical end. All activities, even the means of production, are ends in themselves, activities expressive of the *sacred* values of the society."[7] Tradition is unchallenged by science. All institutions are crescive rather than enacted. No legislation is needed, for informal controls keep members in line. The culture affords a strong sense of rightness and security.

Behavior in the folk society is "traditional, spontaneous, and uncritical." Members spend little time reflecting on the whys of behavior or on alternative patterns. Relations are personal and primary rather than impersonal; people are not treated merely as things. Even nature is treated personally. Human qualities are attributed to trees, rocks, hills, the sun and moon. Behavior is meaningful in terms of a consistent whole. "Life, for the members of the folk society, is not one activity and then another and different one; it is one large activity out of which one part may not be separated without affecting the rest."[8] The cultural goals impart great meaning to action and make a person feel that what he is moved to do by the culture is well worth doing.

The associational society. At the other extreme of the continuum is the "associational society." Highly urbanized and industrialized, the associational society depends on other societies for raw materials and markets. It is never self-sufficient, nor is any one of its citizens. The extensive division of labor makes each citizen dependent on many others for most of his needs, and the various specialties are coordinated in a vastly complicated system of production and distribution.

The society is a mosaic of sub-cultures, for its people have diverse racial, cultural, and religious backgrounds. As a result there is a variety of values and tolerance of different patterns of behavior. The society is therefore "secular." Few objects are regarded as meaningful in themselves, few activities as any more than means to ends. Much behavior is rational and calculating. Religion is set apart from everyday affairs; sacredness is confined to religion and to a few values such as patriotism, the flag, the king, the constitution. Science challenges traditional knowledge.

Persons in such a society see many of their fellow citizens daily but recognize very few except in terms of the situation in which they appear at the moment. Many statuses are open to achievement. The culture changes swiftly and roles and their relationships are therefore in flux. People frequently find themselves in situations and relationships where their roles are not clearly defined by the culture and the old patterns do not fit. As the power of the folkways and mores crumbles, and many groups with conflicting customs and interests are interacting within a limited space, legislation is needed and new institutions must be enacted to define roles and statuses, reconcile interests, and channelize interaction. Formal sanctions are necessary to control behavior. The "we-group" feeling is far weaker than in the folk society.

Bureaucracy. A characteristic feature of social organization in the associational society is bureaucracy. We tend to associate the term with "red tape," "petty bureaucrats," rules and regulations, endless technical forms to fill out in triplicate, and with "going through channels." But essentially bureaucracy is designed to make the administration of large-scale organizations more efficient, not only in government but churches, schools, business corporations, the armed services, professional sports, and large voluntary associations. A bureaucracy is "the type of organization designed to accomplish large-scale administrative tasks by systematically coordinating the work of many individuals." [9]

The four basic characteristics of bureaucratic organization are: (1) specialization, with clear-cut division of duties and responsibilities, (2) coordination by a hierarchy of authority, (3) rules and regulations that fix "standard operating procedure," and (4) formal and impersonal—i.e., secondary relationships. Bureaucracy is typical of a large society based on a money economy. When special administrative problems arise, bureaucratic organizations are set up to handle them. The advantages of such organization are: (1) technical efficiency made possible by the precision of the organization, the specialization of employees, and the fact that the organization has continuity aside from any individuals who occupy particular statuses at a given moment; and (2) fairness. If people are only "cases," it is also true that prejudice is, ideally at least, not allowed to enter into the treatment of the "cases." Some "dysfunctions" also inhere in bureaucracy. Strict adherence to rules makes for inflexibility when conditions change or unusual cases come up; initiative may be stifled, and bureaucrats may not see the forest of goals or ends of the organization for the trees of its petty regulations. Also, as the amusing book, *Parkinsons' Law*, puts it, administrators, subordinates, and inspectors are more or less bound to multiply and memoranda to breed memoranda.

An acute student of modern bureaucracy, Peter Blau, says such dysfunctions are not necessarily inherent in bureaucracy, if we define bureaucracy as simply "organization that maximizes efficiency in administration," rather than as a system of rigid procedures. Bureaucracy he says is distinct from both democratic and autocratic forms of organization. "Neither the will of the majority nor the personal choice of a ruler or a ruling clique reigns supreme, but the rational judgment of experts." [10] Considerations of efficiency outweigh all others. Once the social goals are decided upon, whether autocratically or democratically, they are implemented through the most effective means—i.e., bureaucratic ones. We shall discuss this point more fully in connection with economic and political institutions.

Social • Society is rooted in social interaction,
Interaction the mutually conditioned behavior of persons and groups. "Both culture and society are the products of social interaction, which in itself is the fundamental category to which the countless ways of people of all times and places are reducible. . . . Social interaction is the . . . elemental social phenomenon from which all the specific varieties of social phenomena are compounded." [11]

The various forms of interaction are called the social processes. Cooperation, competition, conflict, accommodation, and assimilation are the chief social processes and are found in all societies in varying proportions.

Cooperation and Competition.
Competition is a value in American culture, accepted not only in sports but in other fields as well. Cooperation among oil-drillers is essential. Team play combines both cooperation and competition.

Cooperation. The basic process of interaction is cooperation, which pervades all forms of group life and is indispensable to it. *"Cooperation is the continuous and common endeavor of two or more persons to perform a task or to reach a goal that is commonly cherished."* [12] Cooperation is an element in all situations except those of overt personal conflict. It is a continuous and pervasive process, a unifying force, essential to the preservation of the group and the achievement of a measure of civilization.

Most interaction in the routine of daily life is cooperative simply because of the interdependence of persons that results from the division of labor. In a small face-to-face group, one is often aware of cooperating as he helps with the dishes, holds his mother's yarn while she rolls it, works on the school paper, or catches a pass in a football game. In the small nonliterate society of the San Blas Cuna, cooperation is one of the chief cultural values, consciously used to channel the interaction of members in farming, fishing, and house-building.

In a highly complex society such as ours, division of labor is carried to such extremes that cooperation is even more necessary than in the small society. Members of the society may not often be aware of cooperating as they go about their daily routine; but all the traffic of a city, the schedule of a university, the buying and selling of the stores, depend on cooperation. When you stop for a red light, when you appear in class at the same hour as your instructor and classmates, when you answer the telephone or doorbell, even when you reply to an acquaintance's greeting, you are cooperating. In order to get to your destination without being interrupted by a traffic policeman, you must allow traffic in cross streets to go across when the light is in their favor; you and the other drivers are cooperating so all can arrive at their destination without confusion or danger. The large city would be an impossibility without these arrangements.

Competition and conflict. Competition and conflict are social processes that are distinct in certain important respects but so alike in others that sometimes it is hard to tell where competition leaves off and conflict begins. *Competition is the striving of two or more persons for the same goal, which is limited so that all cannot share it.* The competing persons or groups may or may not be aware of one another. Their primary aim is to get the satisfaction for themselves, not to defeat or destroy their competitors. When they are aware of their competitors, as in a football game or a political campaign, the culture has laid down certain rules of fair play for the situation, and the losers are supposed to bow to the decision with good grace.

Like cooperation, competition is present in all cultures. In any society, people will compete for status according to the cultural values. The San Blas Cuna measure status by stored or hoarded wealth and by adherence to the moral norms; therefore the Cuna compete to hoard "white man's goods" and to abide by the mores. In a monastery where piety and austerity are the chief values, status may be won by the monks who most zealously deny themselves physical comforts and spend much time in devotions. Among both the Cuna and the monks, however, cooperation is the predominant value.

Competition is a conspicuous element in much interaction occurring in a society where many statuses can be achieved, whether in jobs, politics, business, school and college, sports, and even in the family ("Mommy, do you love me best?"). Our culture is distinguished for making competition a positive value, a "good thing." We are convinced that although cooperation gets things done, competition assures that they will be *well* done.

Conflict is "the deliberate attempt to oppose, resist, or coerce the will of another or others." [13] As in competitive situations, a goal may be desired that all cannot share, but instead of impersonally competing to attain it the persons or groups involved direct their efforts at defeating or annihilating the other parties pursuing the same goal. Although a person may or may not be aware of competitors, he is always aware of the other parties in conflict. A student who gets the only "A" in a small class denies that satisfaction to others who might have won it had he not excelled. He may have been aware of the other good students in the class, but he was not in conflict with them, for his efforts were aimed not at their defeat but at getting an "A" for himself. He used fair tactics, studying hard, passing his exams, writing a good term paper. Winning the hand of a popular girl denies others the privilege of marrying her, but conflict is not present unless two suitors quarrel over her. And the losers are supposed to congratulate the successful suitor and dance at the wedding.

Because the aims and purposes of different individuals and groups are inevitably incompatible, conflict is always present in society. A mother slaps her toddler's hands when he takes books and knickknacks off the shelves. Playmates fight over a toy or come to blows if one of them feels his ego has been damaged by being called a "sissy." Racial groups riot in the streets; laborers picket a plant; public figures accuse and counteraccuse through the newspapers; a revolutionary group overthrows a shah or president; one country attacks another and a war is on. Obviously the potentialities for conflict multiply with the number of groups in a society; their incompatible interests and values set the stage for conflict.

Although competition may go on for long periods of time, conflict by its very nature is intermittent. Latent conflict or tension may, however, exist for long periods before erupting into open conflict in the form of riots, strikes, revolutions, or wars. Tension between the native Panamanians and the Forty-niners who crossed the Isthmus and waited for ships to take them to the gold fields of California existed for years. Then a small spark set it off. A rough-and-ready American refused to pay for a slice of watermelon and a riot began that ended in death and injury to many persons.

Conflict may have positive results. The baby coming into conflict with his mother is developing his sense of self. The group in conflict with another group is strengthened in its "we" feeling. Conflicts within the group may dissolve or be temporarily checked by an outside threat. If a stranger attempts to interfere in a fight between two brothers, both may jump on the intruder. Families and nations alike prefer to reserve the right of criticism to their own kind and band together against criticism from outside. Conflict may also clear the air. When husbands and wives refrain from personal abuse and confine a quarrel to issues, they may eliminate points of tension. By harmlessly expressing envy and resentment, jokes and anecdotes lampooning a boss or a government or gossip about a public figure serve as safety valves to let off steam before emotions can explode into open conflict. During a period of social change, conflict serves to define the status of persons and groups; the labor-management conflict of the last few decades is a case in point.

Much conflict, however, is destructive and breeds more problems than it solves. A conflict of values in a person's mind may cause emotional and mental disturbances. The conflict between generations in a time of rapid change or between immigrant parents and their American-born children causes deep rifts in a family and much unhappiness among its members. Strikes and lockouts mean lost wages, production, and profits. War and the threat of war mean waste of life and property, grief, insecurity, and hate. For this reason men strive through such agencies as social workers, mediation boards, diplomatic parleys, and the United Nations to resolve conflicts before they become destructive.

Accommodation and assimilation. *Conflict is adjusted by the social process called accommodation.* Examples are the truce, the labor-management agreement, and the "racial etiquette" of the South. None of these measures really makes the interests and ends of the opposing groups compatible, but they are arrangements whereby the groups can go about their business without overt conflict. In one sense, accommodation is the basis of all formal social organization. Government, for example, is designed to harmonize the interests of different groups sufficiently so the society can function effectively. Because the potentialities for conflict, the incompatible values and goals, still exist, accommodation may be called "antagonistic cooperation."

Assimilation is the social process whereby individuals and groups come to share the same sentiments, values, and goals. It commonly refers to the absorption of immigrants into the culture of a large modern society such as the United States. It could with equal accuracy be used to describe the process of adjustment in a successful marriage or even the socialization of the growing child. The cultural assimilation of new members of a society may or may not be accompanied through the years by a

Assimilation. *Cultural assimilation of immigrants need not entail the loss of their rich and colorful traditions.*

process of biological *amalgamation* in which the physical differences of the incoming groups also disappear through intermarriage with members of the receiving group.

Cultural assimilation and biological amalgamation occur most frequently in multi-group societies such as ours. Cooperation, competition, conflict, and accommodation occur in every society, but they are found in varying proportions depending on the complexity of the society and the value placed on any one process. The San Blas Cuna stress cooperation; the Kwakiutl Indians of our Pacific Northwest built their culture around competition; the Comanches glorified the warrior and conflict. Counterparts in modern society might be found in Scandinavia, where cooperation is important, in the United States, where competition is believed to promote efficiency, and in Russia, where class conflict on a world-wide basis is the idea that justifies and motivates public policy.

Social Change   •   Change of all kinds is very much a part of our lives. Within the last two decades television has entered almost every living room in the United States and is fast spreading throughout the world. Plastics and synthetic fabrics, "wash-and-wear" clothes, stretch socks, automatic washers and dishwashers, food freezers, packaged mixes for pizzas and cakes have changed the housewife's lot. The authors cherish a newspaper clipping from the summer of 1940. On one side is an announcement of their engagement. On the other is a picture of a model wearing the first pair of nylon stockings!

These changes, like the man-made satellites circling the earth and the jet planes and guided missiles and nuclear reactors that have been developed during the same period, are primarily technological ones. But all cultural change is so interwoven that it is difficult indeed to untangle cause and effect. In concentrating on that aspect of cultural change that we call social change, we are concerned primarily with changes in social organization—in statuses and roles, social relationships, groups and institutions. Technological change may, of course, lead to social change. To dramatize this point Professor Ogburn once attributed the emancipation of women to the invention of the automobile self-starter, which enabled women to drive cars, freed them from their homes, and permitted them to invade the world of business. Of course, social change is never so simple and linear as that; in fact it is immensely complex. And cause and effect may be reversed; social change may lead to technological change. The dispersal of population to the suburbs may lead to adoption of an invention such as the monorail to bring suburbanites into the city fast and inexpensively without clogging expressways with cars.

Disturbances in one institution have inevitable repercussions in others because institutions within a society are interrelated in a "dynamic imperfect equilibrium subject to constant change." [14] A change in the economy, such as a period of prosperity or depression, or a shift from small businesses to huge corporations, affects government, education, the family, and even religion, as we shall see in subsequent chapters. And changes in the international power structure have had an immeasurable impact on many institutions. Young men in our society have been compelled to incorporate into their plans a new role—the role of peace-time soldier. The economy and the national administration are heavily skewed toward "cold war," foreign aid, and many other new developments. As we shall see in the next chapter, changes in population also are cause and effect of far-reaching changes in social institutions.

How social change occurs. Institutions often seem to change gradually, with no planning, as the result of the convergence of many individual actions and decisions that were not oriented toward change at all. This type of change is called *socio-cultural drift.* This gradual emergence of new forms may be seen by comparing courtship patterns as they exist today with the patterns your parents and grandparents followed.

> Similarly, changes in laws, in administrative patterns, in business practices, and in most other areas of our life take place in just such an unplanned and unheralded manner. As people learn more, experiment, work out problems concerning their daily life, and as they communicate their ideas and methods to one another, major social changes take place with none of the reformer's zeal or the revolutionist's violence. It is probable that such socio-cultural drift accounts for much of the social change that occurs in America today and perhaps this form of change is the most important, if not the most dramatic, form that exists.[15]

Social movements relate to behavior that is oriented toward planned changes in the social order, either reforms or revolutionary changes. Women's suffrage was once a dramatic social movement, as was the movement for the abolition of slavery. Revolutionaries may aim merely to get the "ins" out and the "outs" in, as is the case in many Latin-American changes of government; or they may aspire to change the whole social order, as in Russia.

In terms of the processes of social interaction, cooperation may play a definite role in social change, either in the research that leads to conquest of a disease and thus affects the population and many other aspects of the social order, or in a planned and institutionalized way of coping with a social problem, such as slum clearance. When a group of southern whites migrates to a northern city, the dominant group must accommodate to their presence and attempt to assimilate them. This interaction is reflected in changes in education, social work, housing, employment, and many other aspects of community organization.

Competition may contribute to social change by stimulating people and groups to try new and better ways of doing things, whether producing packaged foods for the housewife or political programs for the citizen. Conflict is, of course, the most dramatic agent of social change. Whether or not the militant group wins, it draws attention to problems, and its proposed solution may eventually be incorporated into the social structure, perhaps to alleviate the threat of revolution or of loss of power by the elite.

Collective • A major area of sociological interest is
Behavior the field of collective behavior. Unlike the study of social organization, collective behavior research focuses on interaction that is not guided by established cultural norms. A "collectivity" in the sociological sense is "the kind of group characterized by the spontaneous development of norms and organization which contradict or reinterpret the norms and organization of the society." [16] Crowds, audiences, and publics are collectivities. Collective behavior occurs frequently, but it is not normal or routine behavior. It may be spasmodic or brief, or it may be long lasting.

Collective behavior begins when group cohesion breaks down. We saw that the integration of social groups rests on interdependence of roles, consensus in regard to norms, and a flow of communication through which social control is exerted and understandings are kept in force. Failure of any one of these cohesive factors means social disorganization and unrest; when there is no cultural definition of the situation upon which to rely, collective behavior results.

The crowd. Crowd behavior takes many forms: a screaming audience of teen-agers gathered to watch their current idol; a lynch mob; a rioting crowd tearing down a Bastille or celebrating a war victory; a panic-stricken crowd fleeing from a disaster; a cluster of spectators watching the aftermath of a street accident. It originates in *milling*—restless, random movements that stimulate others to behave similarly, release energy, and communicate various possible meanings in an undefined situation. Milling may be primarily physical. Groups of people drift around, forming interacting knots, and break up and drift again. Or it may be verbal, as in the spread of rumor. Usually it is both. Milling is the basis of "social contagion," the development of a uniform mood and a uniform image. If the milling process is very slow, the crowd is "emergent," not yet formed into a collectivity. If on the other hand the milling process is unusually swift and a common mood and image are quickly formed, mob or panic behavior may result. The crowd may storm the jail to lynch an accused man, converge on the bank to withdraw money, or flee a city on the basis of a rumor, as in James Thurber's classic sketch, "The Day the Dam Broke."

All crowds have several features in common. Members are uncertain about how to behave and what to expect. A feeling of urgency grips them, a feeling that something must be done *now*. The interaction of the emergent crowd produces a common mood or imagery and a conception of some kind of appropriate action. There is pressure on individuals to conform to this developing image or mood. The crowd is permissive; persons feel free to express attitudes that are ordinarily repressed, and express them more emotionally. They may also evolve new ways of acting and new attitudes.

Types of crowds. The two main types of crowds are the *acting* crowd and the *expressive* crowd. An acting crowd is organized for a common purpose, whether to lynch a victim or to demonstrate against an unpopular governmental measure. An expressive crowd aims to create subjective and internal feelings and moods in its individual members, as in a revival meeting.

Crowds may also be considered in terms of their solidarity. They may cooperate in attaining an objective, or they may act in similar ways but for individual objectives. In the latter case the crowd weakens inhibitions; a looting mob includes individuals who would not steal under ordinary circumstances.

Crowds may be spontaneous, emerging in a new and unanticipated situation. They may be conventional, deliberately planned for a patriotic celebration or a religious service. Or they may be manipulated, as by a clever dictator or demagogue who creates the illusion of spontaneity. Once a crowd has emerged, it may be conventionalized; that is, when a

similar situation recurs, people remember their past experiences and behave as they did before. When a lynching mob forms, many of its members act from past experience. A religious sect may plan meetings on the basis of the spontaneous crowd behavior from which the sect emerged, hoping to repeat the expressive behavior and generate the same emotions in its members as formerly.

The audience and our mass society. The *audience* is a number of people who respond in similar ways to a common source of stimulation, but who do not have much communication with each other. They may be grouped together physically, as in a movie theater, or they may be as widely dispersed as the nationwide television audience or the readers of the *Saturday Evening Post*. In either case they are aware that they are members of a group, for they know that others read the same magazines and newspapers and see the same movies and TV programs, and often their attitudes and behavior are affected or influenced by this awareness. The directors of the mass media try to promote this feeling by having a studio audience present at broadcasts, by dubbing in laughter

Television, Press, and Radio. *Media of public opinion provide entertainment and spread ideas throughout every country of the globe.*

and applause, by printing letters from readers, and by numerous other devices. This feeling is reinforced when in talking with others a person finds they have shared the same experience.

In modern society the audience is so numerous and the stimulation that reaches its members is so nearly simultaneous that we speak of a *mass audience,* and even a *mass society.* Although the mass does not interact as do the public and the crowd, the mass media are constantly functioning to create a common body of images and understandings, which encourages in publics and crowds a constant readiness to interact.

Mass society, said a famed sociologist, Louis Wirth, is a phenomenon of the modern age, a product of division of labor, mass communication, and a more or less democratically achieved consensus.[17] The mass is an aggregate of numerous, dispersed, heterogeneous, anonymous individuals. It is unorganized, has no recognized leadership or defined program of action. It has no common customs or traditions, institutions or rules; therefore its members are open to suggestion and its behavior is capricious and unpredictable. Its members consist of individuals who at the time of reacting to the stimulus are not playing roles within a group. In modern society we are so fragmented by our numerous group memberships that no one group speaks for the whole person. Therefore "there remains for all of us a quite considerable range of ideas and ideals which are subject to manipulation from the outside and in reference to which there is no appreciable reciprocal interaction between ourselves and others similarly situated. It is this area of life which furnishes the opportunity for others to entrap us or to lead us toward goals with the formulation of which we have had little or nothing whatever to do." [18]

The mass media in our society depend for their very existence on a mass market and mass advertising. This situation tends to commercialize much that is printed and filmed and broadcast. Producers in search of a mass market are inclined to reduce the content of the media to the least common denominator. The passive recipients of these common stimuli tend to be uncritical, for they feel they are getting a lot of entertainment and information very cheaply. But as Mr. Wirth implied, these media could be used to manipulate collective behavior. "Mass communication is becoming, if indeed it is not already, the main framework of the web of social life. . . . If it is consensus that makes an aggregate of men into a society, and if consensus is increasingly at the mercy of the functioning of the mass communication agencies as it is in a democratic world, then the control over these instrumentalities becomes one of the chief sources of political, economic, and social power." [19]

The public and public opinion. The type of collectivity known as a *public* is especially important in modern democratic societies. A public is a vaguely defined number of people who for a time share a particular interest, such as concern about some controversial issue. A public is not a fixed or permanent group, but changes as the interests and attitudes of the individuals composing it change. A person may join and leave a public freely.

The public, through discussion and argument, strives to arrive at *public opinion*—a collective opinion or a collective decision on the issue around which the public has formed. Although it is not unanimous or even necessarily the will of the majority, public opinion is nonetheless a collective product.

Although the mass media are used to influence public opinion, a public is not an audience. Instead of responding individually to a common stimulus, the public interacts; its members discuss different points of view, weigh alternatives, and argue. A true public depends on freedom of association, of speech, and of the press. If these freedoms are missing, what might have been a public becomes an audience. The Soviet leaders have very cleverly arranged to give their citizens a feeling that they are members of publics by arranging numerous small local "discussion groups." The right solutions to the problems to be discussed are, however, specified in advance and strong pressure is exerted against any "incorrect" or deviationist thinking. And the communication and participation at the "grass roots" have little effect on what goes on at the top level. True public opinion affects policies; it is communicated to the decision-makers and affects their decisions.

Social movements. We can conceive of human behavior as forming a continuum from disparate individual behavior at the one extreme to organized group behavior regulated by traditions and rules at the other extreme. Collective behavior falls between these two extremes. At the end nearer disparate individual behavior we might place panic behavior. Near the other extreme, and often merging into it, are social movements, for compared with other forms of collective behavior, social movements are comparatively stable and organized and persistent in time.

A social movement is a collectivity acting with some continuity to promote a change or resist a change in the society or group of which it is a part. As a collectivity, a movement is a group with indefinite and shifting membership, with leadership whose position is determined more by the informal response of the members than by formal procedures for legitimizing authority.[20]

True social movements may be distinguished from quasi-movements of three kinds: mass movements, followings, and cults. Mass movements, such as mass migrations and gold rushes, involve large numbers of people who may cooperate in some respects, but who are seeking essentially individual objectives. Followings are made up of the "fans" of some hero, such as a baseball pitcher, a crooner, or a movie star. Cults have the continuity of social movements but their members are content to remain apart from society and feel somehow superior to non-members and do not seek to enroll or to change them. There are cults of art, religious cults, health cults, and many others.

Social movements seek to change the social order; countermovements seek to prevent such a change. We may distinguish social movements in which the leaders seek power for themselves from those reform movements in which permanent reorganization of the society is the objective. Classic examples in recent history are not hard to find. Hitler sought power; Gandhi sought a profound change in the social order. One manipulated crowds through clever techniques that gave people the illusion of spontaneity and the feeling of emotional participation in something exciting. Participation in expressive crowds erased many of their repressions and encouraged behavior that would have been repressed under established social norms. Repetition gave their behavior the sanction of a righteous cause. Gandhi's movement, on the other hand, appealed to ultimate values that were being violated by the British colonial system, and it was built slowly upon publics and small groups, villages and schools. Another recent illustration is the bus boycott in Montgomery, Alabama, in which Negroes responded to the informal leadership of a minister who, like Gandhi, preached passive resistance and nonviolence to dramatize neglected values.

Leaders, intelligentsia, and followers. As the preceding paragraph suggests, the type of leadership of a social movement is crucial to its success. Social movements arise out of a condition of unrest; people want a leader who promises to free them of the causes of their discontent. He is typically a "charismatic" leader whose power over his followers is based on the force of his personality. He is endowed in their minds with "charisma" or exceptional power that may verge upon the supernatural or superhuman or actually be regarded as such. The followers believe that his exceptional personal qualities symbolize their aspirations. The

Leaders and Followers. *In the minds of his followers, Adolf Hitler was endowed with superhuman or exceptional qualities that symbolized their aspirations and promised them relief from their discontent.*

quality of charisma is shared by saints and demagogues. In contrast to the charismatic leader stands the legitimate leader such as the traditional patriarch or legal president. Some legitimate leaders may also be charismatic, and most charismatic leaders have or acquire some legitimate standing. During a period of unrest a charismatic leader has more appeal than the legal or traditional leaders, who are identified with the institutions that are now regarded as dysfunctional.

The myth or ideology of a social movement that seeks change explains how things came to be as bad as they are, proposes a solution that justifies taking action against the status quo, and suggests tactics. These explanations, solutions, and suggestions are all given reality by symbols and emotion-laden terms. A countermovement in turn calls for loyalty to the old myths and symbols. The myth is put into words by the *intelligentsia.*

Out of the unrest produced by a critical situation in which old meanings are inadequate and people are seeking new ones comes the rank and file membership. When individuals believe that they have found a solution to their problems in one movement or another and find the ideological explanation meaningful they join the movement as *followers*.

Institutionalization. As a movement grows its leaders see in its sheer size a threat to their continued authority. Therefore they tend to regularize procedures to support their own power and policies. Thus traditions and norms are born. The followers, too, want responsible leaders whose actions they can predict, and they welcome a certain amount of stability. When a movement is not only stable but also has achieved recognition within the larger society as having a continuing function to perform, it becomes institutionalized, and thus its stability is further reinforced. The labor movement, once regarded by most people as a threat to society, now holds an established place in American society, seen by some as desirable and by others as unavoidable. Its leaders are legitimate and are held responsible for the movement by other members of the society. Sometimes the legitimate leaders are the same ones who were charismatic leaders during the early days of the struggle. In the same manner religious sects may become institutionalized as churches (see Chapter Fourteen).

Collective behavior and the social order. Collective behavior may promote social change. When the culture and social organization of a society fail to satisfy needs, unrest and discontent flare up, which are manifested in panic behavior, in expressive crowds, and in acting crowds that easily become violent. Power struggles may develop, as well as mass movements with a revivalist orientation—that is, engaged in emotional expression rather than reformist activity.

If, in the midst of their unrest and discontent, people begin to believe that things could somehow be made better—an idea that often comes through cultural contact—then collective behavior develops around the new ideas. Publics form, many and small and ephemeral at first, but diminishing in number and growing in size and becoming more permanent as the issues become fewer and more sharply defined. If these issues are urgent, they may give rise to acting crowds, some supporting and some attacking the status quo. If such crowds and publics are repressed by the society, feeling heightens and crowds become focused on goals more specific than the mere expression of emotion. Crowd behavior may unify a public and provide it with symbols and heroes; if it goes too far, however, it may lose the support of the public out of which it springs. A bloody strike, for example, may turn people against the labor movement, and a lynching may prove embarrassing to a white-supremacy collectivity.

By providing common symbols in terms of which people will interact, the mass media facilitate the formation of crowds, publics, and social movements. By giving their participants an exciting sense of escape from social control, crowds may weaken willing adherence to the social order. People are then receptive to new ideas and values, and may join movements headed by charismatic leaders. In the push-and-pull of publics and social movements and countermovements, new cultural directions and forms of social organization are being sought and worked out.

These new ideas may be absorbed into the social order in various ways. Where public opinion matters, the decision-makers take it into account. Social movements, as we have seen, may become institutionalized parts of the society. Or they may have their "teeth pulled" by reforms that incorporate their chief ideas, as the teeth of the Townsend movement, which advocated large monthly pensions for the aged, were pulled by the passage of social security legislation. They may also fade away as the reasons for their existence, the conditions that caused unrest and discontent, disappear. And, of course, the revolutionary movement may succeed in upsetting the social order, and then its leaders seek to legitimize their position and establish a new order.

Collective behavior may, on the other hand, actually contribute to social stability. A certain amount of collective behavior is institutionalized and fitted into the existing social order. Conventionalized publics, for example, discuss issues within the limits set by the culture. They channelize the expression of differences of opinion. Social movements not only merge into institutions; movements may emerge *within* institutions and pursue their aims in an orderly fashion, supporting the general social structure and culture. Recognizing the hold of the charismatic leader, society tries to endow authority with charisma, surrounding the person of the Pope, the king, the president, the dictator, with ritual, symbol, and myth.

Conventional expressive crowds in all stable societies reaffirm the values and dominant myths of the society with ritual and symbol and counteract the effect of dull routine. The church service, especially the revival meeting, is an example. This reaffirmation is particularly necessary when unusual demands are to be made of the people. War bond rallies and football "pep" rallies make sacrifice and do-or-die effort easier by asserting group ties and evoking emotional response.

Crowd behavior is a "safety valve" through which emotions that could be destructive are harmlessly dissipated. It also serves to test a person's commitments to the dominant values. In the process of challenging them a person may find he is really loyal to them after all.

Thus, in summary, collective behavior has a place both in change and in stability. In stability, it helps to maintain a certain fluidity which resists tendencies toward total inflexibility in the social structure. And it helps to maintain some of the vitality and vigor and religious devotion to values that characterize periods of change. While institutional behavior is associated with man's submission to essential routines, collective behavior is associated with his ideals. The institutionalization of collective behavior helps to weld these two aspects of life together.[21]

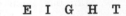

EIGHT

Population and
the Urban Trend

"Of all the people who have ever lived, 1 in
20 is alive today." "The birth rate of underdeveloped countries averages twice that of advanced countries." "At present rates the population of the world will double by 2000 A.D."
"Fifty-seven of every 100 Americans live in
162 metropolitan areas."

Facts such as these have profound implications for society. As the number of people

129

in the world changes, as their distribution in space and in age and sex categories changes, the social order also changes. The science of demography, or the statistical analysis of human populations, affords a firm basis for understanding these changes. In this chapter we shall consider population trends and urbanization and their effects on the social order.

The Population   •   A population "explosion" is in process
Explosion   throughout the world. There are now
                              about 2,750,000,000 people on the globe
                              —about twice as many as there were 70
years ago. There is every sign that in the next 40 years this figure will again be doubled. By 2000 A.D. there may be nearly 6 billion people in the world, by 2050 nearly 13 billion.[1]

Man has been on earth more than a million years, but not until about 1650 A.D. did the total world population reach half a billion. In the 300 years since then the world population has increased five-fold. This spectacular change has been called the Vital Revolution or the Demographic Transition, and can be traced to an astonishing rise in the *rate of growth* of population.

The rate of growth is determined by the balance between births and deaths. Obviously a population will not grow if the number of people born each year is sufficient only to replace those who die. The present rate of growth of the world's population, however, is 1.33 per cent per year. What does this mean?

Let us assume with demographer Karl Sax that the human race began with Adam and Eve in the traditionally fixed year of 4004 B.C. If, starting in 4004 B.C., the population had grown 1 per cent a year there would have been 4 billion people by 1900 B.C., and by the time of Christ there would have been "standing room only" on the face of the earth.[2]

But for many millennia the rate of growth was extremely slow. About 8,000 to 10,000 years ago men lived in small bands, hunting and gathering food. There were only about 5 million to 20 million people in the world then, and the growth rate was perhaps .02 or .03 per cent a year. After agriculture was developed, growth was faster; the population reached about 100 million a thousand years before Christ. At the beginning of the Christian era there were 200 to 260 million people on earth, and the rate of growth had risen to about .06 per cent. But by 1000 A.D., war, famine, and pestilence had checked the increase and left the population figure at around 300 million.

Then about 1650 began the Demographic Transition in the Western world; death rates dropped while birth rates remained high, and in three

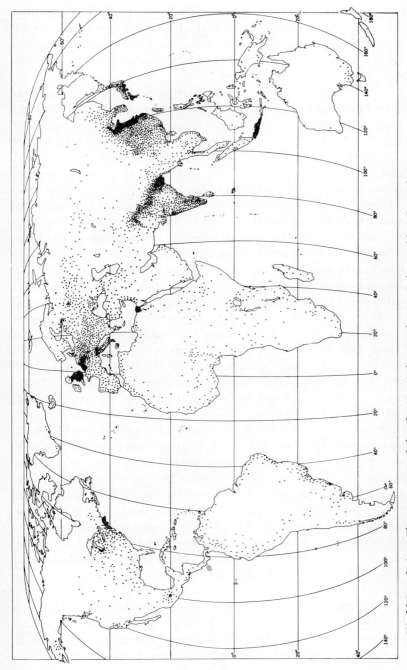

World Population. *The very unequal distribution of the population of the world is due only in part to climate. Manufacturing as well as agriculture has helped to create the congested spots. A map made in 10,000 B.C. would have shown a much different distribution.*

hundred years there were five times as many people in the world as there had been in the mid-seventeenth century. This Vital Revolution accompanied revolutions in agriculture and industrial production, advances in medicine and sanitation, and the settlement of the Americas.

Stages • in Population Growth

There are four possible combinations of mortality and fertility: a high birth rate and a high death rate, a low birth rate and a low death rate, a high birth rate and low death rate, or a low birth rate and high death rate. The fourth combination is obviously unusual and has occurred only in technologically primitive societies that have been ruthlessly exploited by other societies. Demographers have analyzed population trends throughout the world in terms of the first three combinations, and perceive a pattern of three successive stages, which describe what has occurred in the past and what may be seen occurring today in different regions of the world. These stages are, of course, not inevitable; they may be combined or skipped, but they serve as a convenient shorthand for describing what has happened and what is happening now, and to some extent are useful in predicting what may happen. In any one country this cycle is changed by such factors as wars, epidemics, and religious and ideological differences.

(1) *The period of high growth potential.* During this period birth and death rates are roughly equal and both are very high; the population is stationary or slowly growing. A high proportion of the population is young and life expectancy is low. This stage is called the period of high growth potential because if anything happens to bring down the death rate a "population explosion" will result. Modern sanitation and medicine have their greatest impact on mortality among infants and young children; therefore more survive to bear children themselves, and a dramatic rise in population occurs. Agrarian folk societies are in this phase of high growth potential. A native of India, for example, had in 1930 the same life expectancy as a Frenchman in 1789. India has seven times as many children under five as adults over 65, whereas in the United States the two categories are almost equal. If these children survive to child-bearing age, and fertility rates remain high, the rate of population growth will be very high.

(2) *The period of transitional growth.* During this stage the death rate falls while the birth rate remains high, and population increases at an accelerating rate. This is the period of the "population explosion." It occurs in countries that are beginning to feel the effects of industrializa-

tion but are not yet modernized. It occurred in Western Europe and North America beginning in the seventeenth century and is happening now in the underdeveloped regions of the world. Egypt, for example, has grown 26 per cent in the last decade; her registered birth rate (doubtless smaller than the actual rate) is 44 per 1,000 per year. Turkey, Syria, Mexico, Costa Rica, Ceylon, Paraguay, Malaya, and Colombia will double their populations in less than 25 years if the present rate of growth of approximately 3 per cent continues. Latin-America's population is growing four times faster and Asia's three times faster than the population of northwestern Europe.

Reduction in mortality is almost invariably a goal of human society, and the underdeveloped nations of the world are gladly accepting aid from the advanced countries in conquering endemic and epidemic diseases. The World Health Organization has helped cut the death rate in Ceylon, for example, from 20.3 to 11 in one decade. With the use of DDT the death rate from malaria in Ceylon fell 34 per cent in one year, 70 per cent in a decade. At the some time Ceylon's birth rate has remained at about 40.

For birth rates do not inevitably follow death rates downward. High fertility has long been highly valued by human society and encouraged by religion, government, and other institutions. High death rates long made it necessary for man to "be fruitful and multiply" in order to "replenish the earth." And as we have seen, values are slow to change.

(3) *The period of incipient population decline.* During this stage the birth rate falls and the fall in the death rate slows down. Population increases, but at a decreasing rate. The number of middle-aged and older persons in the population is higher, and the number in the child-bearing ages is correspondingly smaller in proportion. Therefore an actual decline in population may be coming. Whether the population will grow, remain stationary, or decline depends at this stage on fluctuations in the birth rate, for mortality obviously cannot continue to taper off indefinitely. France is the only Western country in which population has actually declined during this century, and recently the French government has begun offering family subsidies in an effort to encourage births. England and the Scandinavian countries are in this stage and the age pyramid of the United States indicates that we too are approaching it.

The postwar "baby boom" in the United States, Canada, Australia, and New Zealand has made the "incipient decline" label that demographers have given this period sound premature, "but it still appears likely that urban-industrial societies will ultimately achieve a new demographic balance in which both birth and death rates are low and approximately equal. Such a balance is immeasurably less wasteful both of human lives and of material resources than the high-fertility-high-mortality balance which has existed throughout most of human history." [3]

Social Effects **of Current Trends** **in Population**	•

The rate of population growth is highest in the poorer countries of the globe. This fact has tremendous economic, social, and political implications.

In the past, the rapid growth of population occurred in Western countries at the same time that they were expanding economically and raising their level of living. It is now occurring in agrarian peasant societies, not as an accompaniment to industrialization and economic advancement but by means of cultural diffusion of Western advances in medicine, sanitation, and agricultural production, many of which are exported in the form of foreign aid. Two-thirds to three-fourths of the world still lives in agrarian folk societies with sacred cultures and simple technologies. The crucial fact is that their economic systems are not keeping pace with their rapidly rising populations.

With population constant, it requires an investment of three to five per cent of national income to produce a one per cent increase in per capita income, whereas, with a population growing at three per cent per year, the rate of investment must be somewhere between 12 and 20 per cent—extremely hard to achieve under conditions of poverty and governmental inefficiency. [4]

In 1938, the average per capita income in 15 of the richest industrial countries was 10 times the per capita income of 20 non-industrial countries; by 1954 the gap had widened to 11. During that period the population of the industrial countries increased by 7.3 per cent, while in the non-industrial countries population increased by 10.7 per cent. According to French demographer Frederic Tabah, two-thirds of humanity consumes less than 5 per cent of the world's primary resources. Estimates indicate that 44 per cent of the Europeans are underfed, 80 per cent of the Latin Americans, 93 per cent of the Africans, and 98 per cent of the Asians. Americans, of course, are overfed. [5]

Population pressures, especially when combined with poverty, make for political instability. The high proportion of young people in a rapidly growing population means that each member of the labor force has many dependents. Young people growing up in an economy that is not expanding find jobs hard to come by, and are easy prey for panaceas such as communism and for demagogues of the Hitler, Mussolini, and Tojo variety who led their countries into aggressive warfare on the plea that their nations had no room for all their people.

The Distribution   •   People are distributed very unevenly
of Population   over the face of the globe. Most are
concentrated along the rim of the
North Atlantic Ocean and the Asiatic
border of the Pacific Ocean in three main areas: India-Ceylon-Burma, East China and Japan, and Europe. Over the rest of the surface of the earth, especially the dry cold north of Asia and America and the interior stretches of South America, Africa, and Australia, population density is extremely low.

Asia has over half the population of the world; Europe and Asia together have 78 per cent. In 5 per cent of the land area of the world are crowded 53 per cent of its people, with an average density of 394 per square mile. In some areas such as Java, the figure is about 800 per square mile.

Migration relieves some of the pressure on overpopulated areas. From 1825 to 1925, about 65 million people left Europe, mostly for the Americas. They were "pushed" by famine and oppression and political instability, and "pulled" by the promise of liberty and economic opportunity in the New World. But since 1925 migration to New World countries has almost been shut off by restrictive legislation that has struck hardest at the very countries that suffer most from population pressure.

Migration, however, still goes on. During the first postwar decade 50 million people migrated from their homelands in search of greater economic opportunity and political freedom. About 20 million of these were eastern and central Europeans. West Germany accepted 11 million immigrants, of whom 8 million were ethnic Germans who were expelled or were escaping from eastern and central European countries. Today one West German out of every five is a refugee or immigrant.

Twenty million more postwar migrants were Asians. The division of India into Moslem Pakistan and Hindu India was followed by a shift of about 17 million people between the two new countries. Other millions have fled Communist China, North Korea, and North Viet Nam.

Israel is, of course, almost entirely a nation of migrants, and in United Nations camps along her borders 800,000 Arab refugees are cared for. Since the 1956 revolution about 200,000 Hungarians have fled their homeland and sought refuge elsewhere. Puerto Ricans fleeing their crowded island have created a new immigrant colony in New York, attended by all the social problems that usually beset impoverished and culturally different groups.[6] Similarly, West Indians have migrated to Great Britain.

These migrations only temporarily alleviate population pressures. They indicate the turmoil of a world divided by religious and racial and political hatreds and suffering from poverty and persecution.[7]

Evaluations of Population Trends • Perhaps the most influential student of population the world has ever known was a gloomy English divine named Thomas Malthus. In his famous *Essay on Population*, published in 1798, Malthus said that population depends on the means of subsistence but will always tend to outrun the means of subsistence. Because of man's strong sexual drive, population when unchecked has a tendency to double every 25 years; it increases in geometrical ratio—1, 2, 4, 8, 16, and so on. Food supplies, however, because of the "niggardliness of nature," increase only in arithmetical progression, as 1, 2, 3, 4, 5, and so on. Two kinds of checks hinder the growth of population: positive checks such as vice, misery, poverty, famine, disease, and war; and preventive checks such as late marriage, celibacy, continence, and moral restraint. Although he did not have much faith in man's ability to practice such restraint, Malthus disapproved of birth control, which his followers, the "neo-Malthusians," advocate as the only ultimate solution.

The current population explosion and the fact that it is occurring in the poorest countries have led to a revival of Malthus' gloomy predictions. A few decades ago demographers were concerned about the declining birth rate in industrial countries; now their great concern is with the rapid rate of growth in the underdeveloped areas—the "Malthusian countries," as they are sometimes called, for they appear at the moment to be bearing out Malthus' predictions. Neo-Malthusians see "the stork gobbling up every advance in technology and food production." Books with titles such as *Our Plundered Planet* and *The Road to Survival* warn us that our resources are not sufficient to support a greatly expanded population for any length of time.

Others agree in essence with the philosophical Costa Rican peasant, who welcomes each new addition to his large brood with the observation that "each child brings his bread under his arm." The optimists say that man's ingenuity will enable him to feed many billions more. Agricultural knowledge now exists for raising world food production by half; and chemistry promises such marvels as food from algae, yeast, and the plankton of the sea. When the earth's coal and oil are gone, we can use nuclear and solar energy. Demographers also point out that industrialization and urbanization have always been accompanied by a decline in the birth rate. As living standards improve, people tend to limit the size of their families, whether the ideal values of their culture as expressed in religion and other institutions change concurrently or not. In such Catholic countries as Spain, Ireland, and France, for example, the birth rate is among the lowest in the world. And in the United States, size of family is more closely correlated with socio-economic status than with religious affiliation. The Catholic Church, though a staunch opponent of artificial means of contraception, also sees the current population explosion as a serious threat to the peace and prosperity of the world and has offered inducements for solutions that are compatible with Catholic doctrine.

The arguments that science is ingenious and resources are plentiful and that a drop in the birth rate will follow industrialization and urbanization come up against strong counterarguments. Ingrained social habits and attitudes may inhibit the application of scientific and technological knowledge to underdeveloped countries. And to wait for the now teeming agrarian societies to make the transition to modern industrial societies will be to permit the population to grow enormously meanwhile. Perhaps this very growth of population will be a handicap to modernization.

Almost all demographers, whether gloomy or optimistic, see population as having come largely under the control of man's ingenuity. He first applied this ingenuity to check mortality rates. In some countries he is now applying it to control birth rates. In the industrialized and urbanized countries preventive checks are practiced individually, mostly by the urban upper and middle classes and increasingly by others, and the resulting change is a socio-cultural drift. In other countries a government-sponsored movement is under way to induce people to practice preventive measures. Japan, with 617 people per square mile, has embarked on such a program, and from 1948 to 1955 her birth rate dropped 41 per cent, to a level slightly below that of the United States. Similar programs are under way in Puerto Rico and India. The government of Communist China, alarmed that her population, shown by the 1954 census to include 583 million people, is increasing by 14 million a year, has also urged such measures on her people.

Population   •   Against the perspective of world popu-
Trends   lation figures, let us look at some demo-
in the United States   graphic data for the United States. Her
population, totaling nearly 152 million
in 1950, increased about 18 million dur-
ing the following eight years. The annual rate of growth in the first five
of these years was 1.6 per cent a year.

The median age of the American population has climbed from 16.7
in 1820 to about 30 in 1950. These figures mean that half the population is
under and half over that age, and the rise indicates a tremendous gain
in length of life. Life expectancy is nearly 69 years, about three years
higher for females and three years lower for males. As the proportion of
aged people in the population increases, many new social adjustments
are required.

Under the age of 15 there are about 104 males for every 100 females,
but the sex ratio drops thereafter so that for all ages in 1956 there were
only 98.4 males per 100 females. Above the age of 65 the discrepancy
is greatest—only 85.7 males per 100 females.

The crude birth rate (live births per 1,000 population) dropped
from 30 in 1910 to a low of 18.7 in the depression year of 1935, and then
climbed steadily to about 25 in 1956. The death rate of 14.7 in 1910
dropped to an all-time low of 9.2 in 1954 and rose slightly in subsequent
years. Of every 1,000 babies born alive, about 26 die within the first
year. This low infant mortality rate is as low or even lower in Australia,
New Zealand, Switzerland, the United Kingdom, and Scandinavia. In
fact, Sweden registers an infant mortality rate of only 17.4. In contrast,
177 babies of every 1,000 born in Burma die before reaching their first
birthday, 148 in Egypt, 120 in Chile, 114 in India, 110 in Pakistan, 108
in the Philippines, and 104 in Costa Rica and Colombia.

The Urban Trend   •   Of even greater interest to the social
scientist than the number of people on
the earth is the kind of societies they
live in. The kind of society is, however, closely related to the numbers,
density, and spatial arrangement of the population. As we have already
mentioned, from two-thirds to three-fourths of the earth's people live in
agrarian peasant societies, which tend to exhibit traits associated with
the polar type folk or "communal" society. In the industrialized parts of
the world, as many as three or four people out of five live in cities, which
dominate societies of the "associational" type. There is a constant trend
from the rural or communal society to the urban or associational society,

a trend reflected not merely in the growth of cities but in the extension of urban influence to the countryside.

The growth of cities. The social scientist sets out with a working definition of a city as a "relatively large, dense, and permanent settlement of heterogeneous individuals." [8] Cities are not, of course, strictly modern phenomena. There have been cities ever since man learned to produce and transport enough food so that some men did not have to worry about wresting food from nature for themselves.

Prehistoric man, like some tribes today, lived by hunting and food gathering, or by tending herds of animals. He wandered in small bands, estimated to have numbered less than a hundred people. When man learned to plant seed and harvest and store food, he had taken the first step toward urban living, for he then had a dependable food supply and had to stay in one place to tend it. People then congregated in villages in fertile valleys, on mountain tablelands, and on the plains, going out each day to work the surrounding fields. The earliest of these agricultural villages date back to the New Stone Age. Even today many rural areas present this village-farmer pattern. Our American open-country neighborhoods, with widely scattered farms grouped around a local trading center, are largely a result of our unique frontier history.

Until man learned enough about farming to produce a surplus, there could be no true cities. The first cities arose where fertile land was well watered, the climate warm, and transportation easy—in the valleys of the Nile in Egypt, the Tigris and Euphrates in Mesopotamia, and the Indus in India. It is no coincidence that in these cities—Memphis, Thebes, Babylon, Nineveh—men worked out the beginnings of civilization: the alphabet, mathematics, and some rudiments of natural science; for the city and civilization grew up together and civilization functions through the structural framework of the city. Cities arose quite independently in our own hemisphere among the Mayas, Incas, and Aztecs.

Early cities served as forts, religious shrines, and monuments to the vainglory of rulers. They were economic parasites subsisting on the resources of the countryide. The change to a comparatively free economy and a mutually beneficial exchange of services between city and country appeared with the growth of Greek and Roman cities. Several Greek cities reached a population of 100,000 and were centers of a far-reaching maritime commerce.

Rome, proudest of all ancient cities, had a thoroughly urban system of community life. Its aqueducts and highways, its amphitheaters and public buildings, testify to skillful engineering and municipal administration. As the political center of a far-flung empire, Rome had over a million inhabitants in the first century B.C. With the decline of empire, Rome lost population and importance; during the Dark Ages it was a straggling town of some 20,000 people. The scattered, walled medieval towns were centers of the petty power of feudal lords and Church dignitaries, serving as trade centers only for the immediate vicinity.

The Crusades of the late Middle Ages stimulated a revival of trade, which was led by Venice and other coastal cities on the Mediterranean, the Baltic, and the northwest coast of Europe. Commercial cities grew up and broke away from the feudal form of government. The rise of

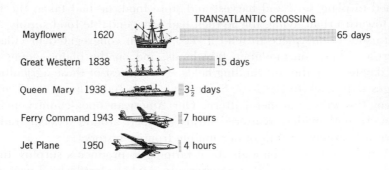

		TRANSATLANTIC CROSSING	
Mayflower	1620		65 days
Great Western	1838		15 days
Queen Mary	1938		$3\frac{1}{2}$ days
Ferry Command	1943		7 hours
Jet Plane	1950		4 hours

Our Shrinking World. *The four stages show how man's increasing rate of speed in crossing the Atlantic—from the 65 days of the Mayflower to the four hours of the modern jet airliner—has shrunk the relative distance across the ocean. Modern transportation plays a vital role in the shift from rural to urban living.*

unified nations and comparatively long periods of peace over wide territories made larger cities possible. The discovery of America and the opening of a water route to the Far East stimulated the growth of cities all along the coastal rim of Europe.

Then toward the end of the eighteenth century there began that spiraling series of developments that we call the Industrial Revolution. This involved more than a change in industrial technology; it was accompanied and fostered by new processes in agricultural production, distribution, and transportation.

Beginning with improved machinery for making textiles and with the harnessing of steam to run larger machines, the factory system developed first in England. Released by a revolution in agriculture, people huddled close to the factories and towns sprang up almost overnight. The application of steam to transportation made it possible for the growing cities to trade their manufactured goods for food, raw materials, and the finished products of other cities. People and ideas, too, traveled more swiftly and easily than before. The power press and machine manufacture of paper made it easy to print huge numbers of newspapers, books, and magazines.

New inventions came faster and faster during the nineteenth and twentieth centuries. Canning and refrigeration made possible the preservation of food during shipment and storage. Swift advances in sanitation and medicine made cities more livable. The telephone, telegraph, and radio speeded up communication. Gasoline engines turned the wheels of autos, uniting farm and city and allowing city-dwellers to live farther from work. Electric power also relieved the congestion of factory towns because, unlike steam, it could be transported cheaply over long distances. Economic systems became ever more complex with work divided up into hundreds of highly specialized jobs. City-dwellers became ever more interdependent, not only with their fellow townsmen, but also with producers and consumers in other areas.

The extent of urbanization. The word "urban" is variously defined in different countries. In the United States, the urban population is now taken to mean (1) residents of incorporated places of at least 2,500 people, (2) residents of densely settled but unincorporated suburban fringes clustering about large or medium-size cities, and (3) residents of other unincorporated places of 2,500 people or more. By this definition two Americans out of three are urban. In some countries, 1,500 people make a city; in others, 30,000. Therefore data on urbanization are not strictly comparable.

Looking at urbanization on a worldwide scale, in 1950 about 13 per cent of the world's people lived in cities of 100,000 or more; 21 per cent in cities of 20,000 or more. Four per cent lived in one of the world's 40 cities of over a million population.[9]

In the British Isles eight people out of ten live in cities, the ninth in a village, and the tenth on a farm. In Australia, the Netherlands, and Germany seven out of ten are city-dwellers. The percentage in the United States, Argentina, New Zealand, Spain, and Denmark varies from 66 per cent to 59 per cent or roughly 6 out of 10. Evenly divided between urban and rural are the people of France, Sweden, Canada, Venezuela, Cuba, Chile, Austria, and Czechoslovakia. Although recent census statistics for the Soviet Union are not available, it is estimated that about a third of the Russian population live under "urban government."[10]

Japan is the most highly urbanized country in Asia; in fact, Tokyo is a contender for the title of the largest city in the world. Although China and India have many large cities, and the urban trend continues, the bulk of their huge populations still live in agricultural villages and subsist by farming small patches of land. At least four out of five residents of India are rural. Africa's population is largely agricultural and pastoral.

Latin America, though preponderantly rural, shows a marked trend toward urbanization. Thus far, however, the trend has been less a product of industrialization than of depopulation of the countryside by the magnet of the capital city. In each Latin-American country, with the exception of Brazil, a single metropolis dominates—politically, culturally, and economically—and is rapidly growing.

Migration. Where urbanization is most rapid, cities grow much faster than the population in general, in spite of the fact that rural areas typically have far higher birth rates than cities. The explanation, of course, is migration.

The greatest migration in American history, when measured in numbers, at any rate, took place, not during the pioneer days that opened up the West, but during World War II. Between December, 1941, and March, 1945, over 27 million Americans, including 15 million civilians, migrated. Much of this movement was over long distances, and the predominant current was westward. As a result, many western states gained about 50 per cent in population between 1940 and 1950 and many metropolitan areas in Texas and California grew from 50 to almost 100 per cent in that decade.

Only about one American out of eight now lives on a farm. More people are classified as rural non-farm than as rural farm; they rent houses and yards but do no farming, or live in institutions, summer camps, motels and tourist camps, or villages under 2,500 population. The farm population has shrunk in actual numbers as well as percentages. In 1920, over 31 million persons lived on farms; in 1956, only slightly over 22 million did.

Why do people move to the city? The pull is strongest on young people in their productive years. They think of the city in terms of opportunity: better paying work, freedom from the restrictions of the small community, excitement, an easier life, and a higher standard of living. Those with special talents or ambitions must go to the large city to make a name for themselves in the fields of art, literature, or entertainment. While they are being "pulled" toward the city, they are also being "pushed" off the farm by labor-saving machinery.

The Suburban   •   *The metropolitan area.* Cities, then,
     Trend   have a long history. But super cities,
or metropolitan areas, are a new phe-
nomenon, largely a product of recent technological developments.

Just as the city was very much the product of the wheeled vehicle,
the sailboat, the steamboat, and the railroad, as well as of improved
agriculture and industrial development, the modern metropolitan area
is very much the product of the internal combustion engine and improved media of communication. In the Western Hemisphere a functional and spatial arrangement of people has adjusted to the automobile, the truck, the telephone, the airplane and the helicopter, the
shorter work-day and the shorter work-week to give us the metropolitan area.[11]

A "standard metropolitan area" consists of a central city, the entire
county containing the city, and any other counties having metropolitan
characteristics that are integrated with the central city.[12] Nearly a third
of the population of the United States lived in such areas in 1900,
although they were not then so defined by the census; in 1952, 57 per
cent of the population lived in such areas. And during that half century,
73 per cent of the country's population growth occurred in metropolitan
areas.[13] One American out of five lives in the metropolitan areas of our
five largest cities: New York, Los Angeles, Chicago, Philadelphia, and
Detroit.

Frederick Lewis Allen, long the editor of *Harper's* magazine, saw the
growth of the suburbs as having occurred in five stages. (1) Beginning
in the nineteenth century, in the "horse and buggy era" of commuting,
some people decided not to move back to town after their summer
holidays, but to commute by train and trolley. They lived along the
"North Shore" or the "Main Line."

(2) In the twenties, the "automobile revolution" occurred and made
commuting easier and faster. There were only 9 million cars in 1920; a
decade later there were three times that number. Real estate operators
opened "sub-divisions" all around the fringes of towns and cities. The
suburban life carried a great deal of prestige, and people moved to the
suburbs to build substantial houses and put down "roots."

(3) During 15 years of depression and war, the chinks between
towns and their suburbs were gradually filled in and new roads were
built, but the suburbs grew no faster than the population as a whole.

(4) Since World War II there have been two strikingly different

but overlapping kinds of change in the fringe areas of cities. One is the postwar boom in mass-produced, GI-mortgaged houses, which has produced enormous homogeneous suburbs laid out for the automobile age. Suburbs have always tended to be segregated according to income level; the new suburbs also tend to be segregated by age. A preponderance of young married couples and children live in these new mass-produced suburbs. In the decade between 1940 and 1950, nearly half the population increase of the country took place in outlying parts of metropolitan areas. Estimates of the number of suburbanites in the United States run as high as 54 million (when those near the outer edge of the central city are included); but according to the 1950 census, about one-third of the urban population, or one person in six in the United States, is a suburbanite.

(5) The other striking postwar development has been the discovery of the suburbs by business. The regional shopping center is something quite new and typical of the recent suburban trend; with its cluster of dozens of different stores, its enormous stretches of parking space, and its general air of modernity and convenience, it has almost outmoded the corner grocery and drug store. Businesses are also moving headquarters and plants to the suburbs, where they find lower tax rates, more parking space, and room for expansion.[14]

"Where once you had countryside interrupted by towns and cities, you now have an urban spread marked here and there by patches of open land." [15] Indeed, there is a tendency all over the United States for city and countryside to merge. Some towns that were once suburbs have long since been surrounded by the central city. Detroit has two such enclaves; Los Angeles has fourteen. Brooklyn was once a suburb of New York, Glendale of Los Angeles. From north of Boston down into the state of Virginia the eastern seaboard is almost solidly urbanized. The same thing occurs on the shore of Lake Michigan and along the Pacific Coast, especially in California. A French geographer, Jean Gottman, hypothesizes that industrialism in its modern form tends to distribute population with rough equality across the face of the land.

Types of suburbs. *Residential suburbs* are "bedroom" or "dormitory" towns from which most of the breadwinners commute to the central city to work, and come home to sleep. These suburbs may be planned, like many of the postwar suburban towns such as Levittown. They may have grown up around villages, which attracted more and more commuters. Or they may be fringe areas with a minimum of social organization. *Industrial suburbs* are less dependent on the central city; many of their residents work in the same suburb where they reside. Often they are satellite cities, having no political connection with the central city; they are, however, part of its social and economic sphere of influence as measured by department store charge accounts, newspaper circulation, and travel for recreational purposes.

Ecology · *Ecology,* as used in biology, refers to
of the City   the way plants and animals are distributed over a given area and to their
interdependence. *Human ecology* is concerned with the distribution of various functions, groups, and institutions within a given area and the processes involved in that distribution. Both refer to the adjustment of organisms to their habitat.

If we are to understand the physical and social structure of the city, we must avoid several pitfalls: the notion that the pattern of cities arises out of man's nature as man; the fallacy that economic competition alone determines the pattern; the idea that once we understand American city structure we understand human ecology all over the world. These mistakes stem from a tendency to overlook the importance of culture. It happens that in our culture the money motive is of great importance, but even here its effect on urban structure is modified by other factors. Because ecologists have not studied foreign cities as intensively as they have studied ours, we shall confine our remarks on ecology to the American city.

Ecological processes are the steps by which a city grows and changes. *Concentration* is the drawing of population into a given area; the degree of concentration, or *density,* is measured by the number of persons per square mile. *Dispersion,* or scattering of population—the opposite of concentration—is measured the same way. *Centralization* is the drawing together of institutions and activities, the assembling of people to work rather than to reside in a given area. Such areas, though highly centralized, may show a low density of population in census statistics, which are based on dwelling rather than working place. The downtown area is usually the area of greatest centralization, but sub-centers scattered through every metropolitan district display the same process. This clustering of activities in outlying sections is also evidence of *decentralization,* for it indicates the spread of activities and dwelling places farther and farther out from the center of the city. *Specialization* refers to the clustering of particular types of institutions and activities in "bright lights" districts, wholesale areas, financial districts, and professional or business office buildings, sometimes called "streets stood on end."

Rural and Urban Living. *Man's relationship to nature and his fellow man is quite different on the farm, in the small village, and in the city.*

Of special interest to the social scientist are the processes by which "birds of a feather flock together"—segregation, invasion, and succession. *Segregation* is sometimes used synonymously with specialization to refer to functions of different areas. More often we think of it as the drawing together of similar types of people. Whether they want to because of similar background or are compelled to by prejudice and poverty, individuals tend to gravitate to areas where they can compete most effectively and where others of similar race, culture, economic status, and point of view dwell. The "black belt," the ghetto (Jewish immigrant neighborhood), Little Italy, Chinatown, "Nob Hill," the "Main Line," and the "wrong side of the tracks"—known by different names in different cities—are all results of segregation.

The clusters of similar people, institutions, and interests resulting

147

from segregation and specialization are called *natural areas* because they are the spontaneous, unplanned results of social and economic forces. Each natural area is somewhat of a unit, with a relatively homogeneous population, local color, perhaps its own peculiar traditions, customs, conventions, standards of decency and propriety, and often a language of its own. Each large city has its hobohemia, its Bowery or Skid Road, its Greenwich Village or Latin Quarter, where flock the unconventional, erotic, or eccentric; its cultural and racial colonies; its ultra-smart residential area; and its dingy world of furnished rooms.

But these areas are not static. Areas change through the process of *invasion*, the penetration of a segregated area by an institutional function or population group different from the one already there. In a rapidly growing city, the commercial and industrial districts invade residential areas. One racial or cultural group invades an area occupied by another, or an economically inferior but otherwise similar group may invade an upper-class area, as in the rooming house districts that once were rows of dignified brick and brownstone residences. Invasion may be resisted, even to the extent of mob behavior. In other cases, invasion is successful and rapid, as in Harlem in the 1920's. When an invasion is successful and the new type of institution or population is established in the area, we say *succession* has taken place. One section of Chicago was successively inhabited by Czechs, Jews, Italians, and Negroes. The Black Belt is located in what was once the heart of the ghetto.

These ecological processes produce a pattern that is roughly similar in American cities. Various theories of urban development, none of which we need go into exhaustively, have been advanced. One much-discussed theory is that of *concentric zones*, advanced by Ernest W. Burgess.

Burgess observed that cities tend to grow outward in concentric rings from the central core, with each ring containing different types of subareas. Zone I is the *central business district*—in large cities the "loop," "downtown," or skyscraper district. Here department stores, business and professional offices, financial institutions, hotels, theaters, and restaurants are concentrated. Waves of workers and shoppers flood into the district from all parts of the city every morning and rush out noisily in the late afternoon, with a smaller wave converging on the bright lights district in the evening.

Zone II, encircling this district, is called the *zone in transition*. Often it was an upper-class residential area when the city was much smaller. Now the old mansions have been converted into cheap rooming houses and hotels, offices of the less prosperous business and professional men, pawn shops, eateries, secondhand stores. It is the area of the greatest concentration of vice, crime, delinquency, poverty, and mental breakdown. Often the owners of the property are merely holding on in hopes that the central business district will expand and send the value of their lots soaring. Meanwhile, they allow the zone to become a "blighted area."

Shading off from the rooming-house area is Zone III, an area of deteriorated housing where the poorer foreign immigrants cluster. Slightly better housing is found somewhat farther out, in Zone IV, the area of workingmen's homes. Zone V is a middle-class area of apartment buildings and houses with yards and gardens. In the suburbs live upper-middle class and upper-class people, often in business or the professions.

The concentric zone theory is most applicable to American cities that have grown up in the industrial era. Even so it is a highly simplified concept. In any one city the pattern is modified by the geographic setting, the historical background (whether it began as a trading center, a break-of-transportation center where rail and water routes met, or a specialized-function city such as a factory or mining town), its economic development, and occasionally by sentimental preference for a certain area, such as Beacon Hill in Boston.

Problems • Rapid social change inevitably pro-
of the duces disruptions in social organization.
Metropolitan Area Problems become critical as population
spills over the official limits of central
cities. The city loses its tax base as
upper- and middle-income families move to the suburbs, and yet is called upon to expand its services. Its central business area must compete with regional shopping centers. The blighted area of the zone in transition attracts one wave of migrants after another. Since the beginning of World War II, for example, many unskilled laborers from the South have moved to northern industrial cities and settled in such areas.

Compounding these problems is a cultural lag—the fact that political structure is antiquated, out of step with the realities of metropolitan living. One social scientist says that there is an average of 96 overlapping political units in each metropolitan area. The central city is also subject to county, state, and federal government; the suburbs, enclaves, satellite cities, and unincorporated fringe areas have many administrative units. Many problems such as sewage disposal, water supply, transportation, and industrial development would most efficiently be handled by regional planning. But suburban dwellers tend to resist cooperation or consolidation with the central city; they are apprehensive lest their lower taxes, restrictive zoning, and other perquisites be lost.

The rapidly growing suburbs, too, have problems. They have had to build schools in a hurry, and often as not they are overcrowded the day the doors open. They have had to cope with problems of health and sanitation, with transportation, with rapidly changing land values. From the viewpoint of the larger society, the city's encroachment on good farm land also creates problems.

Urban Planning and Renewal

Sociologists are working with city planners and administrators in the new and rapidly growing field of urban renewal and planning. The growth of American industrial cities was typically uncontrolled and unplanned; the result is an uncoordinated sprawl with the only patterning produced by the ecological processes that result in natural areas. The new movement, made more important by the postwar surge in population, has three aspects:

(1) *Redeveloping the old core area of the city.* Slum clearance projects get rid of blighted areas. Many cities, aided by federal subsidies that cover two-thirds of the cost, build huge low-rent projects to house the people displaced by slum clearance. Other construction on the cleared areas includes medical centers, higher-rent apartment buildings, and park areas. Even commercial districts, such as Pittsburgh's Golden Triangle, are transformed.

(2) *Conserving middle-aged but still livable neighborhoods.* Invasion and succession are occurring in many of these areas, and urban planners find their problem complicated by panic or apathy of the residents. Some "pilot projects," however, have met with considerable success.

(3) *Guiding the development of new areas.* Most new growth areas are planned and zoned with far more care than the old central cities ever were. Some whole cities, such as Levittown and the "garden cities" of England, are planned carefully on paper before the soil is turned for the first building.[16]

Rural Life in Modern Society

Only in a few isolated pockets of the United States do we still find the folk community, and under the far-reaching influence of the mass society even these are disappearing. Of our nearly 43 million families, only a little over 5 million still live on farms, and 10 million more live in rural areas or villages but do not farm.[17] In few respects do these 15 million families resemble the farmers and villagers of half a century ago. The automobile, radio, and television have helped dispel isolation. Commercialized machine agriculture has made many farmers specialists; the wheat farmer sells his wheat and buys "store bread" and prepared cereals for breakfast and studies reports on the national and international markets to determine when to sell. Agriculture has become a competitive enterprise oriented to a world market. It has its insecurities and casualties as does urban industry—its foreclosures, sharecroppers, and technological unemployment. The farm family joins more formal associations and participates in more secondary groups than a generation ago. The farmer's children see the same movies, hear the same radio programs, increasingly watch the same TV performers, wear the same kind of clothes, read the same comics, magazines, and schoolbooks, and even use the same slang as their city cousins use. His daughters go to the city to seek work; his sons serve in the armed forces. The farmer's wife yearns for and often gets an automatic washer, wall-to-wall carpeting, and a picture window displaying a fancy lamp, just as does the urban housewife. She drives farther to the shopping center. As churches and schools are consolidated, the small local church and school that served as focal points for the primary community are abandoned. Mass production, mass education, mass communication, and rapid transportation are erasing the most striking differences in levels of living and social participation between townsman and farmer.

We must not, however, minimize the importance of rural life in American society. Although only 11 per cent of employed adults are farmers as compared with 21 per cent in 1930, they have, in many ways, an influence out of proportion to their numbers. Our system of political representation makes country-dwellers powerful in Congress. The smallest farm state has as much influence in the United States Senate as New York, and within a state the urban-dweller typically has less voice in state government than the outstate citizen. In Michigan, for example, the Detroiter's ballot is worth only about half the vote of a fellow citizen in a sparsely populated country district. Farm pressure groups are also powerful; farmers, particularly during hard times, consider their interests to be directly opposed to those of city people.

Many city-dwellers grew up on farms and many others were brought up by farm-bred parents. As a result, many rural folkways and mores have been carried over into urban life, even though they may no longer be relevant in the new environment. Examples are the belief in the old maxims "early to bed and early to rise," or "woman's place is in the home," and the idea that everyone should own his own home. The things denounced as "frills and fads," on the other hand, are all urban. Rural values can contribute greatly to strengthening national morale in crises; on the other hand, rural prejudices often block social reforms.[18]

Significance • Louis Wirth once described urbanism
of the as a distinctive way of life. Much of
Urban Trend what he said fits the description of the
polar type associational society we discussed in the preceding chapter. For
urban life is characterized by great numbers of people in a comparatively small area, heterogeneity, mobility, secularism, a preponderance
of secondary contacts or *Gesellschaft,* formal and voluntary associations,
formal social controls, extreme specialization and interdependence of
persons and groups, rapidly changing culture and social organization,
and a comparatively slight sense of belonging and unity.

Great numbers of people. Cities are overcrowded, noisy, dirty, beset with
traffic and parking problems, and lack adequate play space for children
because *great numbers* of people often come together rapidly and with
very little planning. This does not mean that crowding, traffic problems,
noise, dirt, and lack of play space are inevitable aspects of city life. Not
even the nervous strain and hurry that produce the executive's ulcers
are caused by city life as such; perhaps they follow from competitive
emphases in some cultures. But it is not necessarily abnormal for men to
live in cities. Until recent decades, it is true, cities were fine breeding
grounds for epidemics, and the birth rate was far lower and the death
rate higher in cities than in the country. But modern sanitation and increased medical and dental care have changed the situation. The infant
mortality rate and the death rate from tuberculosis are now lower in
cities. Psychological tests show that city children are better "adjusted"
and more adaptable than country children. Differentials in the birth and
death rates are decreasing. The educational differential, however, is increasing, with urban systems usually far superior to rural systems.

Heterogeneity. The city is *heterogeneous,* populated by an extreme
variety of people. It could not exist without specialization and it in turn
fosters greater specialization. The jack-of-all-trades does not succeed in
the city; he must specialize in order to compete successfully. He may
spend the entire working day—usually a certain fixed number of hours—
typing letters, selling insurance or handkerchiefs or suits or furniture,
filing papers, reporting news. He may render any of a number of highly
specialized services: landscaping lawns, disposing of garbage, delivering

diapers, directing traffic, answering phones, repairing furnaces, reading meters. He may attach the left rear wheel to car after car as it comes down the assembly line of an automobile factory or inspect parts for flaws without much idea of how those parts fit into the final product. A lawyer may handle only certain kinds of cases; a teacher may teach only one highly specialized subject; a doctor may treat only skin diseases, or only eyes, or only pregnant women. These thousands of specialized jobs are meshed in a highly complex web of interdependent parts. The urbanite is never economically self-sufficient.

In this complex economic system of which the city is the center, different activities are rewarded with different amounts of the society's goods, and there is a wide range between poverty and wealth, which is accentuated by the possibilities that the city offers for persons to exploit others. Modern cities are often called "melting pots" because they have so many nations, physical types, and cultures represented in their population.

Along with this heterogeneity of occupation, economic status, and racial or national background goes a heterogeneity of beliefs and values. There is little on which all the members of the community would agree, few shared values and goals.

Heterogeneity offers distinct advantages. Specialization means efficiency in utilizing talents and interests, and thus more goods and services for the members of a society. It also means less self-sufficiency, greater dependence upon a complicated economy. On the whole, most people are willing to accept the material rewards of heterogeneity. Some are disturbed, however, because the self-sufficiency and independence of the rural folk community cannot be carried over "as is" to the urban society. They also are disturbed by the real problem that with a high degree of specialization people may lose contact with one another. A highly specialized education, for example, leaves great gaps in the understanding of many people. Educators are struggling to balance the courses a person needs to compete in a highly specialized society with those that will make him a good citizen of a democracy and a "rounded" personality capable of human understandings and enjoyment of a full life.

Differences in cultural, religious, national, and racial backgrounds can be used to enrich experience and add color to the culture of the group as a whole. People are "interesting" largely because they are different. Unfortunately, this heterogeneity is a source of difficult problems in modern society. The complex, multi-group society invariably must cope with conflicts based on prejudice, as we shall see in Chapter Ten, and with conflicts of interests and values.

Mobility. Mobility, or ease of movement, is of two types: physical—over the surface of the earth; and social—up and down the social ladder. Rural communities are far more stable than urban communities in both respects. Farm folk and villagers are more likely to stay put; they often develop a close attachment to the ancestral acres and have deep roots in their birthplace. The comparative homogeneity and lack of competitive emphasis in their way of life make them less conscious of social class, less ambitious to climb.

Physical mobility is present to a high degree in any urbanized country, but is most pronounced in ours. The city itself presents a picture of hurry and bustle as people stream through the streets afoot, on bicycles, by bus, streetcar, commuter train, by car and taxi. Urbanites move from city to city or from one section of a city to another with little regret for the place they leave. They expect to move—from the small apartment of the newlyweds to a house with a yard when they have children; farther out to the suburbs when they can afford it; back to a small apartment or away to a warmer climate when the children are grown. Only in the South and in New England do we find many city-dwellers who cling to their ancestral homes. In March, 1956, one American out of five lived in a different house from the one he occupied a year earlier.

Social mobility is closely related to ease of physical movement. The shifting nature of the city's population tends to reduce the importance of ascribed status and open more statuses to achievement. The individual is judged far less by his family background—whether or not it is something to be proud of—than by his own appearance and manner, his accomplishments in his occupation and in social and community life. Competition for status is a major preoccupation of urban life. Inequalities are tremendous in the city, but they are not determined by birth so much as by the use one makes of his abilities and opportunities. Even in the cities of India, rigid caste lines tend to break down. It was in the growing commercial cities of the late Middle Ages that serfs became free men.

Mobility offers certain advantages. In a physically mobile nation, heterogeneity is lessened as regional differences are diminished. A mobile labor force adds to productive efficiency. Mobility means more diffusion of cultural traits, more borrowing of ideas and inventions. The migrant has an objectivity that stay-at-homes lack.

On the other hand, the rapid shift from farms to cities creates problems of crowding and unplanned city growth. It is a strain on many persons who find it difficult to adjust to a new environment. Mobility breaks down neighborliness. Many city-dwellers do not even know the names of their next-door neighbors; they are "nigh-dwellers," not true neighbors.

Robert Cooley Angell, in studying the "moral integration" of cities—their group loyalty, morale, and civic spirit—found it to be least in cities where the population was most heterogeneous and most mobile.[19] The feeling of belonging is weaker in the city than it is in the rural community. City-dwellers tend to think of their city not as a group of people to which they belong but as a place where they happen to live, a statistical and geographical entity commanding little allegiance for itself. They lack a strong feeling of their role in the community, and feel only slightly dependent on it. They have one foot in the air ready to take off for greener pastures and leave with little sense of loss.

Secularization. Secularization has been accentuated by urban living. Where so many conflicting values are found, to live together at all people must develop a "live and let live" philosophy, a tolerance of differences, a relativistic perspective. Nothing surprises the urbane city-dweller. The danger here is that he may abandon his own values, perhaps taught him in primary groups in a rural community, and find nothing satisfying to take their place. The sacred values of a folk society are shared by all and are highly effective in fostering and preserving a sense of unity. A multi-group society that is unable to agree on sacred values must still hold together somehow. Is symbiosis, or mutual dependence, enough to impart a sense of unity?

Secondary contacts. In the preceding chapter we discussed the contrast between primary and secondary contacts and the relative preponderance of the latter in urban society. Here we shall consider the relationship of this fact to social control and freedom, voluntary associations, and anonymity.

New forms of *social control* arise of necessity in urban society. The control of the folk society or primary group over its members is informal but highly effective. In the rural community standards of conduct are passed on from generation to generation. The group is so unchanging, its members so much in agreement, and the problems met by succeeding generations so much alike, that these standards are seldom questioned. Withdrawal of affection or approval is a powerful sanction in the family or play group; gossip and ostracism are the punishments of the larger neighborhood. Everyone knows a person's work habits, his lapses from the mores, his "queer" ways. Each person has a reputation—his family's

Secondary Contacts. *The anonymous city crowd impersonally brushes elbows.*

156

and his own—to live up to. If he feels restricted, at least he has a sense of belonging, and takes the same interest in the conduct of others that they take in his.

In the heterogeneity, anonymity, and mobility of the city, an individual can escape such controls very easily. If a person has come from elsewhere, he may have left primary group ties and controls behind him and may find his conscience less strong than the new and heady sense of freedom. In the secondary group, too, the lack of sentimental and emotional ties allows a spirit of competition and exploitation to develop. Therefore, the urban society must rely upon formal and organized controls and sanctions. Laws and ordinances, policemen and courts and prisons, the clock, and the traffic signal regulate much of the individual's behavior. To the controlling agencies he is not a whole person, simply a legal and statistical entity.

Although his public behavior is strictly regulated, the city-dweller enjoys great freedom in his private behavior. The heterogeneous groups have different standards of behavior; seeing them all existing side by side, city-dwellers develop a feeling of social tolerance, a blasé, sophisticated, rational attitude toward the behavior of others. "What is it to me?" The primary group of family and close friends, even of neighbors in the numerous places where close social relations still exist in urban neighborhoods, take an interest in his conduct, of course, and exert control over his behavior. But when close bonds and controls grow too irksome he can escape for a while into the anonymity of the city, knowing eventually he can return to the circle of those who care. He has a double refuge.

But what of the person with no primary group ties? The young person from the farm or village, alone in the big city, finds it can be the loneliest place of all, for no one cares what he does. In the rooming-house districts, the anonymity of the city approaches the picture of a "dust heap of unrelated individuals," in the famous sociologist Durkheim's classic phrase. Many of the problems that find their way to police and social workers arise from this "freedom" from primary group ties, this anomie.

Even for the person with family and friends, primary group ties are less binding in the city than in the folk society or rural community. Interaction in the city is more and more between members of age and interest groups rather than between family and neighbors. In the densely populated, heterogeneous city there are hundreds of groups a person may join, hundreds of acquaintances who may become friends. This opportunity for *voluntary association* is another aspect of the freedom of the city. A person may prefer to spend his time with the degenerates of the vice district, the study group at the museum, the crowd at the corner bar, or the neighborhood bridge club. An American city-dweller can join stamp clubs, camera clubs, civic clubs, luncheon clubs, bowling leagues, volley-ball teams, Ladies Aids, Junior Leagues. He can attend plays, movies, concerts, horse races, poker games, night clubs, lectures, prayer meetings, revivals, language classes, dancing classes. The possibilities are almost endless, for every conceivable interest is organized and catered to. This multiplicity of choices permits far more *individuation* than is possible within the circumscribed limits of the rural community, more enrichment of personality in the sense of developing talents and interests.

There is, of course, another side to this freedom from close ties and controls and the voluntary association in other groups. A person is not simply *free* to join. He may *have* to join in order to promote his own interests, because the individual in the mass of the city is powerless un-

Elks Club Ceremony. *Civic clubs provide an urban substitute for the congenial neighborhood group.*

less he is part of a group. Furthermore, he may feel the need to join because primary group ties are either entirely lacking or are emotionally unsatisfying. He joins "to escape from freedom," for everyone needs some ties that approach the warm personal ones of the primary group. The hearty camaraderie of the luncheon club or convention, the fellowship of the store-front church, the "brotherhood" of the revolutionary cell, even a nodding acquaintance with a bartender help to fill the void left by the dissolution or weakening of primary group ties. "Group membership in a Rotary club may seem radically different from membership in the American rural neighborhood of a half-century ago, but the loss of the latter has been a substantial factor in the growth of the former." [20] So deep is a person's need for primary interaction that, as we have mentioned, even within the framework of a large and formal secondary organization such as a business office or a factory cliques invariably form. Politicians, employers, teachers, and other leaders of secondary groups try to bring primary group values into the secondary group relationship to strengthen morale. The media of mass communication are used to keep in touch with the other members of a person's society. Although there is disagreement on many basic cultural values, there is an area in which one American knows he is speaking the same lingo as others—the area of nationally publicized ball teams, movie stars, radio and TV comedians, and comic-strip characters.

The urbanized society, in transferring many functions from primary to secondary groups, has in general weakened primary group ties, but in one sense the primary group has gained. There is more spontaneous choice, more informality in family life and among friends. Courtship is a matter of individual choice; even parenthood is often voluntary. The group is held together by affection rather than by outside pressure and lack of alternatives.

For a full, rich life, an individual needs both primary and secondary group contacts and relationships.

The great community brings us opportunity, stability, economy, the constant stimulus of a richer, more varied culture. But living in the smaller community [i.e., the primary group] we find the nearer, more intimate satisfactions. The larger community [i.e., the secondary group] provides peace and protection, patriotism and sometimes war, automobiles and the radio. The smaller provides friends and friendship, gossip and face-to-face rivalry, local pride and abode. Both are essential to the full life process.[21]

Suburbanism as a   •   The tremendous growth of the suburbs
Way of Life   represents in part a forcing out of a
                              growing population; many young fami-
                              lies can find no suitable homes, espe-
cially modern ones, in the central cities. But this growth also results
from man's attempt to recapture values lost in city living. He seeks to
escape crowds, dirt, noise, smog, gas fumes, and barren streets, and find
sunshine, fresh air, quiet, privacy, and space. Especially does he want
these things for his children. He wants to feel independent, to own his
own home, to put down roots and do things with his hands. He may also
want congenial neighbors and a house that indicates his social status.
To what extent does he find what he seeks? Does he really escape from
the city?

Suburbs may seem like rural retreats at first, but often the spreading
metropolis engulfs them and the grove of trees framed by the picture
window gives way to a raw new housing development. Still, population
density is far lower than in the central city, and certainly there is far
more homogeneity. Suburban neighborhoods tend to attract people of
the same income level, for mass housing is produced within a narrow
price range in each neighborhood, and new developments are zoned for
certain types of houses. In some suburbs upper-middle-class business and
professional men predominate; in others, white-collar workers and skilled
laborers; in still others, industrial laborers. To this homogeneity of
occupation and income has been added homogeneity of age; many of
the postwar suburbs are solidly populated by married couples of about
the same age whose children are also contemporaries.

One social scientist is testing the hypothesis that this homogeneity
favors primary contacts, that there is far more informal neighboring in
the suburbs than in the city. She hypothesizes that not only does socio-
economic level play a role in this process, but also that the suburbs
tend to attract people who are predisposed to "neighboring." [22] Certainly
there is an informality to suburban life, and Allen, among others, has
commented on its gregariousness.

These are very gregarious communities, in which people wander
in and out of one another's houses without invitation, and organize
themselves into everything from car pools to PTA's and hobby clubs
of numerous sorts; and in which the churches are far more important
institutions than anyone who was brought up in the twenties or thirties
would have imagined they would be. Such gregarious communities
are paradises for the well-adjusted; by the same token, they are less

inviting to residents who prefer a modicum of seclusion and resist being expected to live up to—or down to—the Joneses.[23]

The suburbs, then, with their comparative homogeneity and neighborliness, may work toward conformity and against the individuation and freedom of the anonymous city. As for mobility, many of the young men who establish homes in the suburbs are most likely to be transferred shortly to another city, for physical mobility often goes with promotion in business, and even in the academic profession. Perhaps it is partly for this reason that people seek their own kind in suburbs; they can feel at home at once, for the few years they will be there before moving on.

Other disadvantages of suburban living often pointed out are the cost in time, money, and energy of commuting, the fact that women are left alone all day and fathers have little time for their children, and that the sense of belonging is weakened by working in one locality and living in another. However, the shorter work-day and work-week have given the suburbanite more time with his family and suburban families may do more together than city families. Suburban schools are said to be superior, because classes tend to be more homogeneous than in the central city, and community support of the schools is greater. A higher than average percentage of children finish high school and go on to college.

The Future of Urban Society • Like all great and sudden changes, urbanization has brought mankind so many new and challenging problems that many people view the city as a man-made monster that will devour society in the end. Man's urge to cluster in cities is blamed for all the woes of the modern era from war on down: crime, the decline of religion, the "breakdown" of the family as evidenced by falling birth rates and rising divorce and desertion rates, overcrowding, dirt, disease, noise, vice, materialism, and the drive to keep up with the Joneses. Like the Hebrew prophets calling down destruction on Tyre and Sidon and Babylon, like the English poets at the beginning of the Industrial Revolution vilifying cities as places "where wealth accumulates and men decay," some modern philosophers see in his rapidly growing cities the seed of man's destruction.

Even in a nation of city-dwellers like ours there is a tendency to regard urban living as artificial, abnormal, and inferior; our congested metropolises are condemned as "admirably fitted for the habitation of robots." Cherishing a nostalgic picture of an idealized rural life, many

Americans are inclined to consider it inherently charming and delight-ful and city life inherently nervewracking and riddled with insoluble problems.

As we have seen, the heterogeneity, mobility, and anonymity of urban life are not in themselves problems; in fact they offer many rewards. What does concern social scientists greatly is the loss of a sense of unity or be-longing in modern urbanized society. As George Homans, a student of the human group, points out, civilizations have fallen, but never beyond the level of the tribe or village, each of whose members can have firsthand knowledge of the others. Within the tribe, there are few problems of internal social organization; the members are able to cohere, to band together.

In Egypt, Mesopotamia, classical India and China, Greece, and Rome, the ruling class lost the capacity to lead, the formal organizations fell to pieces, faith was lost, and much of the technology was forgotten for lack of the large-scale cooperation needed to put it into effect. All these civilizations fell and the people sank back to a dark age "in which the mutual hostility of small groups is the condition of the internal cohesion of each one." Can we, asks Mr. Homans, keep our Western civilization, which grew out of medieval Christendom, from falling too?

Perhaps the solution would be to apply to the large group whatever it is that makes the small group cohere, to produce a feeling of belonging and eliminate emotional isolation. The myths that weave together values and beliefs do this to some extent; it is the aim of the totalitarian state to make loyalty to the state replace other loyalties. In our own country, we try to solve this problem by means of a complex of democratic in-ventions—representative government, universal suffrage, the secret ballot, the Bill of Rights—all of which are attempts to maintain the values of the small group on the national level.

"Civilization," concludes Homans, "means centralization. It means that men and women will be related to one another in increasingly large organizations, and that these organizations will be brought more and more under the influence of the central directing body of the society, the government. The real problem is not how to keep social groups (i.e., small primary groups) wholly independent and autonomous but how to organize their relation to central control in such a way that they main-tain their own life while contributing to the life of organized society." [24]

Many social scientists see in the trend toward decentralization that has just begun in our country the greatest promise for our civilization. Technology, with its advances in easily distributable power and rapid transportation and communication, has broken down the ancient dichotomy between city-dweller and countryman. The suburban trend may be seen not merely as a continuation but in many ways as a reversal of the urban trend. This does not mean that we can ever recapture the world of Grandma Moses and Currier and Ives.

Men do not go back to a rural existence. They do not find again the settled life, lived in the frame of bounded distances and concrete attachments. In the megalopolis of the near future the citizen has interests and needs which far outreach his immediate environment. His community is wider than he can see or can know in its entirety. His place of shelter, his shopping, his work, his recreation, his cultural pursuits, take place at scattered points, bound together only by the mysterious whole of his personality and the network of communications and transport which modern science provides. . . .

The new citizen may for a while draw comfort from pretending that he is the citizen of an older order. He creates his suburban existence in the pattern of a rural retreat. He dreams of moving still farther out where he can really take up farming. Yet in the end he must face the fact that he lives in a new environment, to a frightening degree without precedent, actually upon a frontier as hazardous to the soul, if not to the body, as the frontier to which generations of Americans moved in the past century. New strains and anxieties possess him, as he strives to make a meaningful life for himself in terms of education, of leisure, of civic responsibilities. The contrast between the simple, gregarious pleasures of the laborer and the tense uncertain enjoyments of the housewife of surburbia is a measure of the ground which is still to be explored before we can say that we are at home in the new world of our making.

Yet it is a world . . . that is in key with the best hopes of the future. We have all felt that the nineteenth century city was inadequate to contain and fulfill man's strivings. We have felt that it must wither away under some process of decentralization. That result is coming about in ways that could hardly have been predicted or foreseen; it still is subject to all the dangers of our folly and shortsightedness. Out of this new type of decentralized urban community we may create something as frustrating, as alien to the humane ideal, as the ant-heaps from which men are escaping. Yet at its best we have here a development which takes its character from the inwardness of our civilization—from the capacity to produce energy without being tied to a coal mine or waterfall, the incredible advances in transport and communication, the promised revolution in agricultural techniques.

We have on a smaller scale, moreover, a reproduction of the world community, where men's interests are broader than the geographical entities within which they live. As men find substitutes for the local attachments which sustained them in the village or town, they find, as well, substitutes for the narrow patriotism which has too often been at war with their better instincts.[25]

If, in this attempt to predict what decentralization may mean for modern society, we read "values" for "instincts," we too may see in the new trends the beginning of a new type of society, with a way of life neither rural nor urban but possessing the values of both.

NINE

Social

Stratification

All societies arrange their members in terms of superiority, inferiority, and equality. This vertical scale of evaluation, this placing of people in relatively stable and enduring strata, or layers, is called *stratification*. Those in the top stratum have more power, privilege, and prestige than those below, with each succeeding layer possessing less of these attributes than the one above.

An army is a perfect example of stratification. Two general strata are clearly marked off—officers and enlisted men. Within each of these there is a hierarchy that clearly marks off each position from those above and below in terms of obligations, privileges, power, and prestige. Each status is clearly designated by outward and visible signs—stars, eagles, chevrons, and the like—and the behavior of each person toward every other is governed by his relative status in the hierarchy and is guided by rituals and taboos. Inferiors must accord their superiors such symbolic acts of deference (to the rank, not the man) as saying "Sir," saluting, and standing at attention.

The army is not, however, a society, for it does not encompass all the life activities of a group of people of all ages and both sexes who share a common culture and a sense of identification. Societies, too, are stratified, some almost as clearly as an army, some into strata with no clear line of demarcation between them.

**Inevitability
of Social
Stratification**

•   An army must be stratified in order to get its job done. It needs a line of command from the few generals who plan strategy to the thousands of lowly privates who peel potatoes and attack machine-gun emplacements. A corporation must have a few persons on the board of directors to plan production, expansion, and employment policies; it must have many more persons to run its machines and type its letters. On the whole, both army and corporation distribute the greatest rewards of privilege and power and prestige to the few who do the thinking and planning, the coordinating and controlling of the whole organization, with proportionately smaller rewards all down the line.

Less clearly, perhaps, but just as inevitably, social stratification is a means of getting the society's various essential jobs done through distributing differential amounts of prestige and privilege. In a small non-literate society there may be little differentiation except on the bases of age and sex, with perhaps a little more prestige for medicine men, good hunters, and strong leaders. As soon as division of labor enters the picture, however, there is differential evaluation of functions and hence stratification. The larger a population grows, and the more complex its technology becomes, the more elaborate is its system of distributing prestige and privilege. There must be some correlation between the rewards held out for the different functions to be performed and the difficulty of finding people with the skill, talent, training, and willingness to fill those jobs. There is no necessary correlation, however, between the *importance* of a job and its rewards; if it is easily filled it need not be heavily rewarded.

These rewards are the incentives for doing the jobs that must be done in society. They may be economic, aesthetic, or symbolic rewards, material or psychological satisfactions. Since they must be unequally distributed, stratification results. "Social inequality is thus an unconsciously evolved device by which societies insure that the most important positions are conscientiously filled by the most qualified persons." [1]

In addition to getting the work of the world done, stratification controls the relations of human beings with one another. Within each stratum, *social distance,* the extent to which individuals or groups are excluded from participating in each other's life, is at a minimum; while between people of different strata there is comparatively little intimate participation, and consequently little sympathy and understanding (i.e., greater social distance). Certain expectations of behavior go with each social status; the desire to climb socially, or to avoid ostracism, may keep persons in line. The phrase "noblesse oblige" (noble rank requires honorable conduct), the concept of a "lady" and a "gentleman," and a person's desire to be esteemed by his equals are powerful influences on conduct.

The dream of a classless state seems doomed, then, by the very nature of society. Even Russia, which was supposed to turn the social pyramid upside down in establishing the "dictatorship of the proletariat," cannot, any more than any other society, escape the necessity of ranking people according to their functions. The criteria of rank have changed along with the values of the society, but they are essentially such as to form a hierarchy of economic and political power with differential rewards for different strata. True, the senior author found as a student traveling on the proverbial shoestring before World War II that classes had been abolished in Russia—but only in the vocabulary. Elsewhere in Europe he had traveled third class. In Russia he traveled in third "category."

Systems   •   Societies and communities exhibit
of Social   widely varying systems of stratification.
Stratification   The *number of strata* varies; in some
there are only two broad classes such as
royalty and commoners, rich and poor,
the elite and the masses. In others there is a series of four or five or more distinguishable classes. The *sharpness with which strata are marked off* also varies considerably. In some societies certain outward signs of status differentiate one status from another as clearly as do army uniforms. In others one class merges into another imperceptibly and it is

only after weighing several criteria that a person can place any individual in an approximate social status. The American class system is a gradient rather than a series of clearly marked strata.

The *criteria* used to place people in their social position also vary. In a very small nonliterate society, status may rest on personal achievement, as it does to a great extent among the Cuna. In larger societies it may be based on differences in birth, race, wealth, learning, occupation, "refinement," or authority, or on a combination of two or more of these factors. The *rigidity* of the structure also varies. In some societies a person can never change his social status; in others it is comparatively easy to do so.

Caste. The most clearly graded and rigid system of social stratification is the caste system, which consists of closed social groups ranked in a fixed order. A person is born into the caste of his parents and can rise no higher. Religion and custom explain and justify the system.

India is the outstanding example of a caste society. For three thousand years Hindu society has been organized into castes, each with a hereditary occupation. It is possible that the caste system originated when Aryan tribes from the north conquered the darker-skinned Dravidians, and the Aryan priests or Brahmans imposed a caste structure sanctioned and perpetuated by religious ritual.

Ancient tradition classified all Hindus into four chief castes. The Brahmans were the priests and teachers of the sacred lore. The Kshatryias or warrior caste were charged with protecting the social order. The Vaisyas were peasants, craftsmen, and merchants. These three castes shared the right to wear the sacred thread which symbolized spiritual rebirth and ritual purity. This right was denied to the lowest caste, the Sudras, who were manual laborers and menial servants who served the upper castes. Outcastes were all the tribes outside and below the Hindu spiritual community.

This simple classification probably never described the reality of Indian society. Through the centuries to these four traditional divisions were added several thousand different castes. About a fifth of the population were the exploited "untouchables" who lived in abject poverty. Stratification was most evident at the village level and varied from one village to another.

Not only do Hindus marry only within their caste, but they do not even eat with members of other castes, and the very shadow of an "unclean" or "untouchable" person is considered to pollute a member of a higher caste, who must purify himself with a long ritual bath. A person who violates caste taboos is ostracized or made an outcaste. It is impossible to rise in the caste system except in another incarnation, and a person's only hope of achieving reincarnation at a higher level is to fulfill the duties of his present status.

This system of inherited inequality functions to maintain the status quo. But it has never been entirely ironclad, and in the new industrial and commercial cities the rituals and taboos are becoming increasingly impossible to observe. New occupations are springing up, and the secondary relationships of the city as well as new ideas from Western democracy are blurring caste lines to some extent. In the crowded cities it is impossible for a person to take a ritual bath every time an "unclean" shadow falls on him. The new constitution has abolished untouchability and made its practice punishable; but any attempt to legislate social change, as we saw in Chapter Five, is completely successful only when grounded in the mores, and these still sanction endogamy, or marriage

Caste in India. *Tradition rules every aspect of life. Even in acts of mercy, a person of higher caste avoids pollution from contact with even the shadow of an untouchable.*

only within each caste.[2] Abolition of the caste system will take many generations.

Estates. Under the estate system, upon which the social organization of medieval Europe was based, a person's social position depends on his hereditary relationship to the land. As in the caste system, strata are clear and rigid. The customary rights and duties of each stratum are, however, buttressed primarily by law rather than religion, and a little mobility is possible.

After the Roman Empire crumbled and commercial towns declined, the economy of Europe was based on agriculture. The highest estate included the royal family and a landed military aristocracy that formed a hierarchy designated by various titles such as "duke," "baron," and "lord." On a par with the nobility were the clergy, who formed an intellectual elite. Because they were the only literate group, the clergy also served as administrators. The Church was a temporal as well as a spiritual power, with dominion over large areas of land. As in the nobility, a hierarchy existed within this estate. It was based on position in the Church and on land ownership. Because of the rule of celibacy, this estate was not hereditary. Sons of nobles entered the higher clerical orders, and the lower orders were often recruited from among the poor.

Below the nobles and clergy were the merchants and craftsmen, and at the bottom of the social scale, the mass of peasants. Various degrees of dependence and bondage distinguished freemen, villeins, serfs and slaves, but such distinctions became blurred by the fact that they were all bound by heredity to the land they tilled.

The close relationship of status to land tenure and its foundation in law tended to make the system of estates static. Nonetheless, some mobility was possible. A serf could be freed by his lord. He could enter the priesthood or the military service, and could obtain a title from the king by virtue of outstanding service. Occasionally a commoner rose in status through marriage to a noble.[3]

Class. A class system does not consist of organized or closed social groups whose status is defined by law or religion, nor are the various strata as clearly marked off or as rigid as in a caste or estate system. In modern society, and especially in American society, class is defined in different ways depending on whether we are considering a local community or a larger area such as a region or the nation as a whole.

On the scale of the society as a whole we may conceive of classes primarily as statistical groupings of people with similar occupations and incomes. It is almost exclusively at the local level that class differences give rise to *status groups*, "informal social groups whose members view each other as equals because they share common understandings, as expressed in similar attitudes and similar modes of behavior, and who treat or regard outsiders as social superiors or inferiors." [4] Members of status groups belong to the same clubs and share the same leisure-time activities, encourage their children to intermarry, and enjoy similar amounts of prestige in the community. Status groups correspond fairly closely to class structure as measured by wealth and occupation, because these factors make possible a certain "style of life" in each group. But only when a person's wealth is translated into this style of life is he accepted as a member; and other factors, such as the *source* of income and social attractiveness, also enter the picture.

Modern class systems first arose in medieval towns, quite apart from the feudal system. A class system based on wealth and occupation was headed by the bourgeoisie, or successful merchants and traders. The French Revolution sounded the death knell of the feudal system, and since then Western society has been stratified primarily according to pecuniary values. The class structure of many European societies, however, still displays vestiges of feudalism. The aristocracy of England, the concentration of most Italian and Spanish land into large estates, and the continued existence of a poor peasant class are holdovers from medieval times.

Russia was still an estate-stratified, agrarian peasant society at the time of the revolution in 1917. During the dramatic process of its rapid transformation into an industrial behemoth, its leaders did not create Marx's vision of a classless society. There exists in modern Russia, according to the Harvard research center studying the country, a police state hierarchy and a structure of five distinct classes: the intelligentsia, the white-collar workers and managers, skilled workers, rank and file workers, and peasants.

Mobility, or movement from one class to another, was high during the turmoil of the post revolutionary period, but has been curtailed by the authoritarian regime. Many categories of people, from school children to coal miners, have been put into uniforms, which serve as external signs of status. The spread in income is much more extensive than in Western Europe and the United States; high incomes are subject to a relatively small tax. Even educational opportunity, recently praised by many Americans as greater in Russia than in other countries, is limited for those at the bottom of the social pyramid.[5]

American Beliefs   •   The American political ideology is
Regarding Class   based on the idea expressed by the
                            Founding Fathers—"All men are cre-
                            ated equal." It denies the existence of
social classes, and none of our laws recognize such divisions. Our ideas
of democracy are based upon the equality of all men, as we saw in
Chapter Five.

Reality has forced us to modify this ideal. We interpret it to mean
that all men are entitled to equal opportunity to climb in the world.
Lincoln is our culture hero, for he was born in a humble log cabin and
rose to occupy the White House.

In thus admitting that all men are not born equal, Americans are
not really admitting that there are social *classes*, but simply that some
individuals have achieved higher status than others. And other individuals
can do the same, if they but subscribe to the beliefs expressed in the
Protestant ethic, the Horatio Alger novels of "rags to riches," and Ben
Franklin's proverbs. Hard work and thrift, honesty and perseverance will
bring success. Ambition is a good thing. Success is the shining goal, the
chief value. A person who succeeds thereby proves his merit. It follows
that those "at the top" deserve to be there; those at the bottom of the
ladder are just lazy. They would get somewhere if they believed that
"God helps those who help themselves," and that "A penny saved is a
penny earned."

Many of us Americans, then, take such pride in our traditional belief
in equality and democracy that we vehemently deny that we have any class
divisions. Identifying the notion with Karl Marx and the class struggle,
or with the hereditary inequality from which the early colonists escaped
by their migration to the New World, we regard class divisions as
practically "un-American."

Yet, as we have seen, no society is classless. We admit its reality
in our own society in our everyday speech. Do we not speak of being
ambitious, of getting ahead, of getting up in the world? Of "big shots"
and "high mucky-mucks"? Of "fine old families" whose ancestors came
over on that crowded ship, the *Mayflower?* Are there not a "country club
set" and a "street corner gang" in most cities? Are not some people "born
with silver spoons in their mouths," while others grow up "on the wrong
side of the tracks"?

Much of the stuff of our novels and dramas, too, comes from the
reality of class. Do we not recognize the obstacles to the happiness of the
night watchman's daughter, Kitty Foyle, and Wynnewood Strafford VI
from Philadelphia's Main Line? Do not the tabloids play up the Cin-

derella quality of a Rockefeller's marriage to the daughter of an immigrant? A dozen middle-class businessmen we know are epitomized in *Babbitt;* we catch a glimpse of the slums in *A Tree Grows in Brooklyn,* and sympathize with the impoverished and dispossessed migrants of *The Grapes of Wrath.*

Perhaps nowhere else than in the United States has it been easier for people to rise in the social scale. But even we cannot escape the fact that every individual starts life with an ascribed status—that of his family. If it is high, he has an initial advantage in the competition characteristic of a dynamic society. If it is low, he is handicapped in the struggle for status. A completely open-class society is a dream apparently impossible to realize.

Since everything points to some ranking of social status in our country, and we know that it must exist in ours as it does in others, any attempt to understand our society must necessarily include a consideration of our class system. Many American values are thrown into clear relief when considered in relation to our social pyramid. Instead of insisting that we have perfect equality (and therefore no class system) or denying that we have any equality (and therefore our class system means we have no democracy), we might try to appraise the ways in which reality can be brought closer to our ideal. Certainly, as individuals, we may find a better understanding of our own attitudes, ambitions, and problems, and a more realistic orientation toward possible goals than we could without some knowledge of our class structure and how it works.

The Criteria • What determines a man's position on the
of Social Class social pyramid? "Money," most Americans would answer promptly. And indeed, in our materialistic, highly competitive society, wealth is correlated to a considerable extent with social status. But this is not true of all societies. *The criteria of status are determined by the values of the culture.* In a society that puts a premium on warfare, the warrior who collects the most enemy scalps enjoys the highest status. Among the San Blas Cuna, being born with a caul ascribes to the newborn child the potential status of a *nele* or seer, which he may later achieve by study and training. In the Costa Rican town of Heredia, the chief division is between manual and non-manual workers. In a close-knit Old World Jewish community, education was a mark of high prestige. No objective criterion, then, is important in itself; it is made important by the *attitudes* of the people.

Housing and Class Status. *A middle-class street in a New England community and a working-class street in a mining town.*

We say a man is "worth" half a million dollars. This indicates the high value we place on wealth. The distribution of privilege and prestige among the population corresponds in a general way with the distribution of income. A pyramid of incomes would not, however, quite match the classic Egyptian pyramid with which we are accustomed to describe the class structure. It would be very broad at the base and taper off very thin and high. "If we made such an income pyramid out of a child's play blocks with each layer portraying $1,000 of income the peak would be far higher than the Eiffel Tower, but almost all of us would be within a yard of the ground." [6]

Wealth is, then, of great value as an index of social status. But even more important is the *source* of income. If a person's income comes from clipping coupons on inherited bonds, then he is almost certainly "top drawer." If from newly successful business ventures, he is probably just below the top. No matter how wealthy a man is, if he is identified with the "rackets" he is outside the pale, probably accepted only in the glittering tinsel world of "café society."

Closely related to source of income is *occupation*. Of every hundred working adults in the country, roughly 40 are in unskilled or semi-skilled labor, 19 in clerical and sales work and the like ("white-collar jobs"), 14 in skilled jobs, 8 are farmers and farm managers (ranging from the poor tenant farmer to the wealthy wheat rancher), 9 are "managers, proprietors, and officials," and 9 are professional and technical workers. [7]

Two other objective indexes of probable social status are the *kind of house* and the kind of *neighborhood* a person lives in. Social scientists have worked out a weighted table that gives different occupations, sources of income, houses, and neighborhoods different numerical values.

The test of social status at the local level is, "What is the highest status group in which I am accepted as a social equal, an intimate friend?" An incident in Sinclair Lewis' novel, *Babbitt*, illustrates the validity of this criterion. George Babbitt, a businessman, took advantage of a class reunion to invite the McKelveys, who belonged to a higher status group, to dinner. The McKelveys came, but left early. Instead of mentioning a return invitation Mr. McKelvey remarked that he and George really should lunch together sometime.

Another classmate, Ed Overbrook, an unsuccessful insurance salesman, invited the Babbitts to dinner. They reluctantly suffered through an evening with the lower-status Overbrooks, and left early. At the door George mentioned the possibility of lunching with Ed. The Babbitts decided it would not be fair to invite the Overbrooks to dinner; they would feel out of place.

The Class Pyramid	•	How many classes are there in the
in the		United States? The answer depends on
United States		many things: the criteria used to deter-

mine class structure; the area encom-
passed, whether a rural community, a
small town, a large city, or the entire nation; and the type of community
studied, whether old and stable or young and changing.

A broad approximation on a national scale, using wealth and occupation as indexes of status, defines three general strata in American society.
Skilled, semi-skilled, and unskilled laborers; urban workers; and farm
laborers and tenants form the "working class," comprising about 55 per
cent of the population. About 1 per cent of the population belongs to an
influential "upper class" of big businessmen and top corporation officials.
In between is a large, heterogeneous "middle class" made up of small
businessmen, independent farmers, intellectuals, professionals, and white-
collar employees.[8]

Finer distinctions are made in studying any one community, where
mutual evaluation of prestige qualifies the rough approximations arrived
at simply by using income and occupation as criteria. Let us consider
studies of three American communities.

Landaff, New Hampshire. The 72 families of this New England agricultural village scorn pretension of any kind. The distinguishing feature
of upper-class behavior is hard work, sobriety and thrift. Laziness, in-
temperance, and improvidence relegate a person to lower-class status.[9]
Most people belong to the upper class, which consists largely of dairy
farmers and their families with a history of generations of residence in
Landaff. Farm laborers, tenants, and lumber workers comprise the
lower class, for the fact that they are propertyless is taken as an indication that they lack upper-class virtues.

Elmtown. Five classes were delineated among the 10,000 people of
this Middle Western city. A very small upper class is differentiated somewhat into "old families" and recent arrivals who are prominent in the
business world. Protestants of pioneer American stock, they give financial
support to their churches and control the political affairs of Elmtown in
their own interest; at the same time they seldom attend church or hold
public office. Leisure-time activities are shared only among equals and
are governed by a rigid social ritual.

The upper-middle class includes 6 to 8 per cent of the population
of Elmtown, and is predominantly Protestant and "old American." Professionals, business officials, the "better" businessmen, and a few leading

farmers comprise this group. They are extremely active in civic affairs and social organizations such as the Chamber of Commerce, Rotary, and the D.A.R., and they dominate church affairs. They hold more college degrees in proportion to their numbers than any other class. Although they are not completely accepted by the upper class—in fact, they are dominated and manipulated by them—members of the upper-middle class identify themselves with the upper class and try to emulate their style of life.

The lower-middle class includes 35 to 40 per cent of the local population, mostly small businessmen, lesser professionals, clergymen, foremen, workers in the skilled trades, and owners of small farms. The majority are also Protestants of pioneer ancestry. They are more active, although less influential, in both political and church affairs than their superiors, and support lodges and women's auxiliaries. They place great stress on respectability.

The upper-lower class, about 40 per cent of the population, are almost exclusively manual workers and include more Catholics and people of recent foreign background than the lower-middle class. Few belong to civic organizations, many to lodges and salvationist-cult churches. They look upon themselves as poor but honest and hard-working. Their social life is restricted almost entirely to members of their own class.

Unskilled laborers comprise the lower-lower class, about 12 to 15 per cent of the population. Although three out of five families trace their residence in Elmtown to pre-Civil War days, this class contains a larger proportion of people of recent foreign origin than do the higher classes. They are excluded from participation in religious, fraternal, and civic organizations by their own choice and by the attitudes of their superiors, who regard them as dishonest, dirty, drunken, and shiftless.[10]

Yankee City. Anthropologist William Lloyd Warner and his associates have spent years studying class, particularly in Newburyport, Massachusetts, which they call "Yankee City." There they distinguish the following classes:

Upper-upper class—1 per cent of the people
Lower-upper class—1½ per cent
Upper-middle class—10 per cent
Lower-middle class—28 per cent
Upper-lower class—34 per cent
Lower-lower class—25 per cent

Volumes have been written describing and analyzing these classes, but we shall be brief at the risk of being sketchy.

Only "old families" with inherited wealth and several generations of upper-class position belong to the top 1 per cent. Not all communities have this "old aristocracy"; it is most often found in the stable old cities of New England and the South. The lower level of the upper class is wealthier, on the whole, than the "upper crust," but its money has not been sweetened by the passage of time. Its members are "new rich" who have made their money in finance and industry and business.

Business and professional men make up the bulk of the upper-middle class. They and their families are solid, highly respected citizens, active in civic affairs, and considered "the backbone of the community."

Below the sixth of the population who form the top three classes comes the level of "the common man"—that catchword of the twentieth century. The 62 per cent of the people who belong to the lower-middle class and the upper-lower class are far removed from the three classes above them. They might be called "the working class." Their chief values are thrift, hard work, honesty, and decency. The lower-middle class is composed largely of white-collar workers, clerks, small tradesmen, and skilled workers. They own small, neat homes but have little other property. The upper-lower class is made up of "poor but honest workers" who more often than not are unskilled or semiskilled. They are anxious to do the right thing, to be respectable, and to offer their children more opportunities than they have had. They are greatly concerned lest they slip into the lowest class.

The lower-lower class is looked down upon as a shiftless lot "from the wrong side of the tracks" or the slums. They are the families of unskilled laborers, who go from job to job and live on charity or relief between jobs.[11]

Metropolitan areas. Studies such as those made in the three communities we have just mentioned are impossible in large cities. The range of income, power, and prestige is greater in the huge modern city than in the smaller town, but the strata are less clearly marked off from one another. Only in a fairly small community can social status be conceived of in terms of the actual people in each class and their interaction; in the city status is more categorical and impersonal. "Precise and stable discriminations can be maintained in a detailed way only within the confines of a community small enough to be comprehended as a whole. . . . In the larger urban areas, the recognition of prestige differences becomes closely tied to the symbols of wealth and power, and only within the limited circles of more or less intimate association are more complex criteria employed and finer distinctions drawn." [12]

**Variations
in
Class Structure** • Class structures, then, show considerable variation from one locality to another. A rural community may ignore any other criteria of status but hard work and morality. Birth is more important where there is an "old aristocracy"; money is more important in newer communities.

The class levels of different communities are not strictly comparable; what is considered upper class in one might be middle class elsewhere. The "big frog" in the Elmtown pond might be considered a nobody by the leading citizens of Yankee City. One reason so many American tourists jump to the conclusion that there is no middle class in Latin America is that the level of living of the Latin-American middle class is far lower than that of the American middle class. But by the criteria of their own countries they are both middle class. The attempt to depict the American class structure in terms of a neat pyramid runs into another great obstacle —that of minority groups, of which the Negro is an outstanding example. Where does this tenth of our population fit? There are some elements of a caste structure in the position of the Negro. The taboos against any relationship that implies social equality or intimacy are still present in parts of the South, where the maintenance of separate schools, drinking fountains, and sections of busses and trains is only slowly giving way, and the law forbids intermarriage with whites. Skin color, in particular, makes the status hereditary to the extent that Negroes are identifiable by their color. Other aspects of the Negro's position do not fit the definition of caste, however. Although the mores and the law uphold his status as a "second-class citizen" in many states, religion and political ideology do not sanction it, as they do in a true caste system. In fact, the treatment of the Negro so violates our own democratic ideology, our insistence that "all men are created equal," that the race issue generates much tension and conflict and has been spoken of as "an American dilemma." In a caste system the lower castes are accommodated to their status; they believe in it because the values and beliefs of the society sanction it. In our country, where the values are directly in conflict with reality, many Negroes are not content; restless and ambitious, they are striving for higher status and resorting increasingly to political action to improve their lot.

In the century since emancipation, a class system has evolved among the Negroes themselves. Business and professional men are at the top.

There is a middle class of clerical and skilled workers which emphasizes respectability, industry, and morality as does the white middle class, and a lower class from which many Americans have derived their picture of all Negroes as shiftless and uneducated.

Significance   •   Class structure in terms of both status
of Class   groups and statistical abstractions is so-
                           ciologically important. Class status is
                           closely related to a person's chances for
"health and wealth, knowledge and experience, wisdom and happiness." It also determines and is mutually determined by a person's "style of life."

Life chances. Life expectancy is closely related to income. One study in Chicago found a difference of 7.6 years in the life expectancy of the highest-income and lowest-income white groups and of 18 years in the life expectancy of the highest-income whites and the lowest-income non-whites.[13] Health and medical care are consistently better in higher-income groups. Educational opportunity is also highly correlated with income, and it follows that those who can provide their children with a good education are also improving their chances to enter an occupation high in monetary and prestige rewards which will in turn enable them to provide these same opportunities for their own children. Justice and legal protection, it has been demonstrated, are also more readily available to those with money and prestige than to those who lack them.

Style of life: classes as sub-cultures. In our mobile society, classes are hard to define, and in some respects our class system is a continuous incline rather than a series of layers. Nonetheless there are other influences besides income and occupation and ancestry that tend to make social classes distinct. These influences produce differences in culture, or way of life, among people of different social status and thus produce social distance between people of different status.

To begin with, a child is born into a family and his initial status must be that of his parents. It is this fact that leads to the perpetuation of class distinctions. He learns his version of the culture—such things as table manners, vocabulary, hygiene, games, standards of right and wrong—from his parents, brothers and sisters, and later from his playmates. His playmates are very likely to have parents in approximately the same economic circumstances as his own, for neighborhood housing is usually of similar value. The American ideals he is taught in school may or may not agree with what he learns at home and on the playground. In the upper class there is great stress on being "well-bred"; among the middle class on being "respectable," as neat and well-dressed and well-behaved as one's classmates, and if possible getting better grades than they do; on being clean and hardworking and careful of what the neighbors will say in the upper-lower class; and on being "tough" in the lower-lower class.

When an individual takes a job or goes on to college he continues to associate with those of his own class, or a bit above it if he can manage it. When it comes to choosing a mate, he is very likely to marry one from his own general social level and settle in a neighborhood where others of his status live, usually moving to successively better ones if he is fortunate enough to earn more money as the years go by. He and his wife associate mostly with others in the same business office or the same profession, at any rate in the same socio-economic level. Thus they reinforce the tendency of people with the same income and occupation to act and think alike.

This limitation of intimate interaction and intermarriage to one's own general socio-economic level produces a tendency for classes to become sub-cultures. The style of life learned in childhood in any one class is so hard to unlearn that it tends to ascribe status in spite of any later rise or fall in income. "The subtle hints of status carried in manner, manners, dress, speech, and social attitudes can inform fairly accurately where any individual 'belongs' because of where he was born." [14] Thus it is that an impoverished aristocrat continues to be welcome in upper-class homes, while a "new rich upstart" commits social blunders and must "wait a generation" before being accepted, usually only after his children have acquired proper polish in the proper schools.

In a general way each social class in our society has the same attitudes, behavior patterns, and ideologies. Let us take a few examples.

Education, for one. How far an individual goes in school and how well he does are tremendously important to the middle class. *Which school* he attends is far more important to the upper class. Among the upper social strata, attending the proper preparatory and finishing schools and colleges is the thing. A Ph.D. from a state university is far less impressive than an Ivy League bachelor's degree. The Lunts once appeared in a play with a line pointedly illustrating this distinction. Discussing the granddaughter's new boy friend, they were happy to hear that he was studying at Harvard. Their satisfaction was short-lived, for someone observed, "But he's just a graduate student. Lord knows *where* he got his B.A.!"

In some respects, religion and politics also exhibit class characteristics. The elite tend to shun politics, or are content to stay behind the scenes, while members of the middle class occupy the prominent positions.

This is in contrast to England, where members of the upper class are active in government circles, and, in fact, feel it their duty to serve. Denominational affiliation tends to run along class lines to a large extent, from the Episcopalian elite to the store-front sects of the lower class. Family life also is different, as studies of child-training, sex behavior, and the birth rate have shown.

Most sports typically begin as upper-class pastimes and filter down the social scale. Tennis and golf are examples. At present, upper-class sports—polo, yachting, owning a string of race horses—are too expensive for the lower classes to take up. Summer resorts are also to some extent exclusive, though the days of palatial "cottages" and lavish balls appear to be over.

Formal organizations cut across class lines to some extent. The middle class are the great "joiners." In some activities, such as civic affairs and charities, they work with upper-class people. In informal organizations, cliques, and circles of intimate friends, however, class lines are rarely crossed. If a person is accepted as a member of a "clique" of higher-class people, he has passed the test and completed a step upward in the social scale.

Frequent interaction and intermarriage occurring among people of similar economic or occupational status, then, tend to turn status categories into sub-cultures, with the same style of life, shared interests, and similar attitudes, and to produce social distance between people of different classes. In some countries these tendencies have been at work so long that the different classes are worlds apart. In the United States this is not the case, for counteracting influences have retarded the separation of people into distinct sub-cultures. Mass production, communication, and education have operated to produce cultural homogeneity. When members of all classes read the same magazines and newspapers, see the same TV shows and movies, use the same schoolbooks in grade and high school, eat the same breakfast cereals, and take an interest in the same sports, they "speak the same language" to a great extent. Our heterogeneous racial, religious, and ethnic backgrounds, with important exceptions, cut across class lines. Both geographic and social mobility retard the formation of clear-cut, self-conscious classes, as does the great range of incomes, occupations, and family backgrounds in our comparatively large middle class.

The great cultural stress on informality and democratic manners has also discouraged the formation of clear-cut classes. Even the upper-upper class feels constrained to avoid acting superior in inter-class contacts. Aristocratic birth and manners handicap the politician; newspaper cartoonists made much of the contrast between Roosevelt and Hoover in the

1932 campaign, showing one as a Little Lord Fauntleroy tended by serv-ants, the other as a "barefoot boy with cheek of tan" going off to the fish-ing hole. One Minnesota housewife, who was a delegate to the 1952 Republican convention, could find no higher praise for her candidate, Dwight Eisenhower, than that he seemed so "ordinary, so common, just like one of us."

Social Mobility   •   In most democratic societies, there are no formal or legal barriers to social mobility. But no other society values mobility so highly as does our own. Our values stress opportunity, getting ahead, success, bettering one's self. We think continually of going up the social ladder, both in terms of income and occupation and in gaining entry to higher social groups, as a valid goal.

Because so much emphasis is placed upon outward signs of status in our culture, we Americans are often accused of having superficial, materialistic values. And indeed there is much to justify this judgment. But most Americans prefer to regard this system of values as having a very laudable aspect. They are proud of the fact that a person is not condemned to stay in the social class into which he was born, that acquir-ing these outward signs of status can help an individual rise in the social pyramid. And how does a person acquire the fine home, the shiny car, the "responsible position"? By his own efforts, on his own merits, is the Ameri-can answer. By hard work, sobriety, and thrift anyone can raise himself up by his bootstraps. Most of us accept the competitive struggle because we really believe that we can better our lot as individuals. There is great admiration for the man who makes it the hard way, little for the boss' son or son-in-law or nephew who, no matter what his abilities, is always suspected of having got his position by "pull."

There is ample historical explanation for this tenacious belief in mobility by individual effort. The immigrants to the New World, from Plymouth and Jamestown on, came partly to escape the restrictions of a hereditary class system. They came to a vast area rich in natural resources, where land could virtually be had for the taking, and many a strong, able, and resourceful man could make his fortune. Their children and their children's children saw Abraham Lincoln go from log cabin to White House, Andrew Carnegie from rags to riches. Technological progress opened up undreamed-of new jobs and business opportunities. Although the gap between rich and poor widened, there was always "room at the top" thanks to an expanding economy and the low birth rate of the upper class. Millions of immigrants "pushed" earlier arrivals upward in the social scale by taking the lowest-paid jobs.

The growth of cities both demanded and promoted mobility. In the competitive, specialized, impersonal city, what a man does and how he looks are more important than who his parents were. In the smaller community, classes more nearly approach the form of self-conscious social groups; in the city they are, with the possible exception of the upper-upper class, more nearly statistical aggregates. Particularly in the city a person strives to rise in terms of material rewards and of comparative success as measured against his job colleagues and intimate friends. John P. Marquand wove an entire novel around this contrast (and wove Warner's study into the plot!). Back home in a small Massachusetts town, Charles Gray, the hero of *Point of No Return,* was not considered quite good enough to marry the daughter of the town's leading citizen. In New York, his consciousness of family background receded. He was aware of striving to get up in the world chiefly in terms of competition with a colleague for a vice-presidency of the bank where both worked, and when he got the position he thought of his victory in terms of membership in an exclusive club, better private schools for the children, and social equality with the president of the bank.

Besides emphasizing the nature of urban mobility, this novel illustrates the fact that occupation and income are only *means* of achieving social status, not signs that a person has arrived. "Money must be translated into socially approved behavior and possessions, and they in turn must be translated into intimate participation with, and acceptance by, members of a superior class." [15] Physical mobility often facilitates such acceptance. By moving to another city, a man with new wealth or a promotion in a corporation sheds his old lower status; and if he acquires the style of life of the higher status group to which he aspires, he is likely to be more readily accepted than in a similar group in his former place of residence.

Means of mobility. Education is undoubtedly the chief prerequisite to occupational advancement today and thus to higher income and social status. Parents in the upper-lower and lower-middle class are particularly anxious to see their children through high school at least, and then through business school and college if possible, so they will escape the necessity of manual labor and "have it better than we did." Upper-lower class parents are usually content if their children acquire "good" white-collar jobs or become teachers or nurses. Middle-class parents often aim at graduate and professional degrees for their children.

Whatever the occupation, a person is expected to "succeed" in it and to display that success by means of "conspicuous consumption." An individual must look successful not only to convince others that he is successful, but also because "nothing succeeds like success."

Mobility through education and effort is usually step-by-step mobility within the middle class, often by means of promotions. The civil service employee, the single employee among thousands in a giant corporation, even the doctor or lawyer, rarely rise in spectacular fashion.

Not that the modern era is lacking in rags to riches stories. A barefoot girl in cotton dress and sunbonnet walked into Dallas' most fashionable store not long ago and spent thousands of dollars on a wardrobe; her father had just struck oil. Luck rather than industry would probably be Horatio Alger's theme if he were writing for modern youngsters, for the success stories that appeal to the rising generation are such stories as that of Lana Turner, who was "discovered" while sipping a soda at the drugstore, and of Bing Crosby, who modestly explains his success in his autobiography, *Call Me Lucky*. Luck can happen to *anybody!*

Girls in particular are conscious of the chance to capitalize on beauty and charm by making a "good marriage," for the wife commonly assumes her husband's status. Many girls choose "careers" as nurses or white-collar workers with one eye on their possibilities for contact with desirable men.

Consequences of mobility. The opportunity to rise socially is a distinct stimulus to effort. It keeps a society dynamic, its members optimistic and energetic. An open-class society relies upon competition to get its work done effectively. The prodding of American youth to "Hitch your wagon to a star," to go "Onward and Upward" has helped to make us a people noted for optimism, daring, energy, creativeness, and courage.

But the mobile society has many casualties. The stable folk society may be static and stifling, but it is secure. In our modern, highly urbanized society the social elevator goes down as well as up and generates a feeling of insecurity. Many are pushed beyond their capacities or into the wrong field. By preaching the doctrine of ambition to one and all, we encourage many who would be happier and more useful tinkering with engines and machinery to aspire to a career in law or medicine or politics. The son who cannot make the grade feels that he has failed his parents. The Milquetoast who plods along in a clerking job and putters with his hobbies is reproached by his family for failing to get ahead and to provide them with luxuries. There is no room in our culture for a "contented

"Will you *ever* learn that I will never be a success!"

failure." A person who has not managed to maintain at least the same social position into which he was born, or who has not risen as high as his brothers or classmates, is made to feel inferior. Thus mobility exacts a toll in discontent and frustration, in mental illness, in maladjusted and neurotic individuals.

The doctrine of ambition keeps us living for the future, often at the expense of future as well as present happiness. There is no stopping place on a ladder whose rungs are marked with dollar signs. Each step higher opens up a new vista—new things to buy, a flashier car, a better address, a more exclusive club—all just out of reach unless the aspirant makes it up the next rung. In chasing money and fame, many people lose lasting satisfactions. The hard-driving businessman piling up money to send his children to exclusive schools and to buy his wife a mink coat looks forward to enjoying life after he retires. By then he may be a physical wreck, may have lost contact with his family, and may find that he has never taken time to learn to live. "Success" is often an empty thing.

There is another danger in the starry-eyed preaching of the doctrine of ambition. When young people see that hard facts do not exactly fit the promises held out in "rags to riches" stories, they may turn to ideologies that seem to them more in keeping with reality. It should not be surprising that many young people who were taught "the American dream" in the optimistic 1920's and found that no amount of willingness and strength, intelligence and energy could get them higher than a WPA job or the CCC in the 1930's should have turned—even though temporarily— to communism. The harsh disillusionment they suffered made them easy marks for the ideology of a classless society. Their disillusionment with the Russian perversion of this ideal is another story.

186

Is mobility declining? "Our social structure is hardening." Thus many social scientists have expressed their belief that actual mobility has declined in our society faster than has our cultural faith in it. They point to the closing of our geographical frontiers, the sharp decline in immigration, the rise of the giant corporation, and the decrease in competition as causative factors.

It has become harder to make spectacular rises in the business world. Many fields, the main province of giant corporations, are denied to small new businesses. Similar situations are also found in farming, where subsidies are given on the basis of *previously* planted acreage; in the professions, where younger men are sometimes barred from lucrative practice by various means; and even in labor, where immigration restrictions and the closed shop sometimes make it hard for newcomers.

Other social scientists disagree that mobility has declined. They consider recent empirical studies of mobility as indications that ours is still the land of opportunity. Most such studies use occupation as an index of mobility, charting it in two ways: comparison of the occupation of fathers and sons, and changes in occupation of individual persons.

Summarizing several such studies, sociologist Arnold Green notes the following findings: (1) that from 1870 to 1950 the same proportion of lower-class Americans reached high positions in business; (2) that the depression of the 1930's was accompanied by a slight decline in mobility as fathers made room for their own sons in their businesses; (3) that big corporations afford the maximum opportunity for lower-class status men to rise; and that (4) a college degree is no longer a guarantee of success in the race, but it is increasingly a requirement for entering the race at all. He also notes (5) that the gap between manual and non-manual labor is less important than formerly.[16] Recent surveys show that this gap, long the chief barrier to mobility in either direction, is now crossed with comparative frequency; and this movement is more often upward than downward.

Studies of occupational mobility also indicate that although there is a great deal of mobility, and more of it is upward than downward, it is fairly limited in extent. "Over two-thirds of the sons work at occupations on the same level or one immediately adjacent to that of their fathers."[17] An unskilled worker's son seldom becomes a professional man.

In evaluating these studies, we must take into account several considerations. Our occupational structure has changed, thanks to technological progress and economic development. Fewer people are needed for manual labor than formerly, many more for skilled jobs and office and sales work. The fact that the higher classes have a lower birth rate than the lower classes leaves room for achievement and advancement.

We must also note that occupations not only change in nature in the course of time—the possessions, work, and income of today's farmer are very different from those of his grandfather, for example—but also that within any one occupation there is a wide range of skill, income, and prestige.

Levels of living in our whole society have advanced (with a few significant exceptions, such as people living on pensions, who suffer from inflation). Americans in each class are considerably better off in many respects than were people of comparable status in 1900. More people have the comforts and amenities of life, fewer go without necessities. The shorter work week has given wage-earners far more leisure time than their predecessors of 50 years ago would have dreamed of. Not only has the lower class risen absolutely, in terms of real wages, but in comparison with the middle class it has advanced considerably. In fact, the loss of teachers to industry and business, and often to factory work, indicates that salaries of white-collar and professional workers have not kept pace. Semiskilled and skilled workmen are far better off financially in many cases than teachers, nurses, and office employees. Furthermore, minimum wage laws and unemployment insurance have given them greater security than formerly. At the same time, the graduated income tax has brought the peak of the income pyramid considerably closer to the bottom. This leveling and equalizing process has made middle-class possessions available to many wage-earners. More and more, class differences are becoming differences in style of life rather than in wealth. A skilled worker may spend as much on a new car as a professor who drives an old model spends on a trip to Europe.

Class Attitudes · When asked to which class they belong,
in the most Americans—87 per cent according
United States to one poll—say "middle class." The
reasons lie mostly in our belief system.

Most Americans will deny that there are any real strata of any permanence and admit only that there are *individual* differences in prestige and privilege, and that a number of people happen at any given time to have more or less the same amount. Furthermore, it is thought snobbish to claim upper-class status; only 4 or 5 per cent do so. "Lower class" carries a connotation of insult, of immorality. People will admit that they are poor but despise the term "lower class." When the category of "working class" is added to the poll questions, only 40 per cent claim middle-class status, and most of the rest say they are "working class."

In Minneapolis, when people were asked, "To which social class do you belong?" many asked the interviewer what social class means. Even when they were prepared for this question by a series of questions about the various classes and their characteristics, 14 per cent insisted that they belonged to "no class," 20 per cent answered "don't know," and 5 per cent refused to answer.[18] Similar studies all point to a low degree of awareness of class status in the United States compared with Europe and Latin America. In small communities, however, as we have seen, there is greater awareness of class status than in large cities. And a person may be highly conscious of status in many ways without employing the concept of social class. Vernacular terms such as "getting up in the world" and the "country club set" betray an awareness of status differences.

Awareness of social status is keenest in regard to those just above or just below a person. The upper-upper class makes much of the distinction between their own kind and the "new rich." Although the new rich are eager to display their wealth, the "old families" are "ostentatiously shabby." They abhor the limelight and avoid being conspicuous. Quiet good manners are their hallmark. Members of the middle class who have climbed or tried to climb several steps upward are keenly aware of such distinctions in status as they themselves have experienced. Members of the lower class are prone to speak of almost all above them as "big shots" or "people who think they're somebody." If they have upper-lower class status, they are sharply conscious of those below and dread the danger of slipping into their class.

Each class tends to think important those things of which they have most, in comparison with other classes, and minimize the attributes of others by speaking of them condescendingly or scornfully. The lower class stresses toughness, being able to "take it," and attributes the position of those above to luck, pull, and inherited wealth. In the upwardly mobile middle class, the values that we think of as "typically American"—the stress on competition, respectability, industry, and education—are strongest. The lower-upper class stresses wealth as the criterion of status while striving at the same time to meet the standards of those above, in spite of loudly voiced scorn for "blue blood." Members of the upper-upper class emphasize lineage and tend to believe they deserve their higher status because they come from "better stock."

Class solidarity. In spite of their low degree of class awareness, people of various socio-economic levels demonstrate marked differences in opinions

and attitudes on a wide variety of social and political issues, as demonstrated by public opinion research. These cleavages of opinion, however,
do not lead to class consciousness because many dominant values are
widely accepted in American society—belief in opportunity for all, in

Social Class Perspectives in One Southern City. *The words in
caps under each class indicate how its members think of themselves. The words in upper and lower case indicate their opinion
of those in the classes above and below them.*

UPPER-UPPER CLASS

"OLD ARISTOCRACY"	UU
"Aristocracy," but not "old"	LU
"Nice, respectable people"	UM
"Good people, but 'nobody'"	LM
"Po' whites"	UL
	LL

LOWER-UPPER CLASS

"Old aristocracy"	
"ARISTOCRACY," BUT NOT "OLD"	
"Nice, respectable people"	
"Good people, but 'nobody'"	
"Po' whites"	

UPPER-MIDDLE CLASS

"Society"	"Old families"	UU
	"Society" but not "old families"	LU
"PEOPLE WHO SHOULD BE UPPER CLASS"		UM
"People who don't have much money"		LM
"No 'count lot"		UL
		LL

LOWER-MIDDLE CLASS

"Old aristocracy" (older)	"Broken-down aristocracy" (younger)	UU
"People who think they are somebody"		UM
"WE POOR FOLK"		LM
"People poorer than us"		UL
"No 'count lot"		LL

UPPER-LOWER CLASS

"Society" or the "folks with money"	UU / LU / UM
"People who are up because they have a little money"	LM
"POOR BUT HONEST FOLK"	UL
"Shiftless people"	LL

LOWER-LOWER CLASS

"Society" or the "folks with money"	
"Way-high-ups," but not "Society"	
"Snobs trying to push up"	
"PEOPLE JUST AS GOOD AS ANYBODY"	

individual achievement of success, and in democracy. The widespread achievement of material comforts and the democratization of behavior in all classes also work against class consciousness.

Those most aware of class status and most conscious of their class as having common interests, are those at the extreme ends of the social scale. The small upper class is notably homogeneous in shared political and economic attitudes and interests. They accused the late President Roosevelt of "betraying his class" in sponsoring social legislation during the 1930's. Class consciousness in the sense of solidarity made little headway among the working class until recent years. In general, the workers have shared the American belief, now typically middle class, that status is an individual matter. The growth of mass industries using machines that require little skill to operate, and of huge labor unions with programs of education and political action as well as their primary purpose of collective bargaining, have tended to make American workers somewhat more conscious of themselves as a group, and more concerned with security as a group than with individual advancement in social status. Although they champion social security and collective action, they are not the militant working class envisioned by Karl Marx when he predicted the "class struggle."

Lack of class conflict. Marx predicted that the "proletariat"—the propertyless wage earners—would unite and overthrow the "bourgeoisie" or property owners. His ideology has had great influence on recent history and on events still in the making. His predictions have failed to come true in the United States, however. In discussing the reasons why the "class struggle" in a revolutionary sense has not occurred in the United States we shall be summing up many of the things we have said about our class structure and how it works.

Far from being the two-fold system of bourgeoisie and proletariat described by Marx, our class structure may best be described as a continuous incline. Any division into a certain number of classes is necessarily arbitrary.

The growth of clearly defined and self-conscious social classes has been hampered by the ethnic, racial, and religious heterogeneity that characterizes all income brackets (although least pronounced in the upper bracket). At the same time mass production, mass education, and mass communication have fostered cultural homogeneity among all classes. Physical and social mobility also operate against crystallizing people into clear-cut groups.

The gap between top and bottom has been narrowed considerably in recent decades by such measures as the graduated income tax, social security, and minimum wage laws. The lower classes have enjoyed a rise in real income, meaning that they have more comforts and necessities than they had before.

The large middle class serves as a stabilizing influence in society. Its values—equality of opportunity, thrift, achievement, and industry—are the core values of American culture. Possible envy and resentment are counteracted to some degree by a belief in luck that is very strong in the lower class and by the observance of informal, democratic manners in all inter-class contacts. There is a cultural dislike of anyone who "puts on airs."

There is still considerable opportunity to rise in the social scale and considerable faith in the future. "If we don't get very far up in the world our children will"—if we give them a good education. Ambition has moved over only a trifle to make room for security as a dominant American value.

Intergroup Tensions in a Multi-Group Society

We have seen that in our heterogeneous, mobile society, distinctions between classes are not particularly clearcut nor productive of tensions. We cannot say the same of distinctions among other kinds of groups—those of different national background, religious belief, and racial type. American history is to a certain extent the story of such tensions and of efforts to alleviate them and to bring inter-

193

group relations into closer agreement with our cultural beliefs in freedom
and equality.

Nationality • The story of intergroup tensions in
Conflicts America began with the arrival of the
first European immigrants. Upon reach-
ing these shores, the newcomers almost
immediately collided with the only native Americans—the Indians. Bitter
campaigns of annihilation and conquest lasting through more than two
centuries reduced the Indians to a fraction of their original numbers, and
many now exist under conditions that, as Americans increasingly realize,
run sharply counter to our values of equality and justice.

These early colonists were largely people of Anglo-Saxon stock who
impressed their cultural traditions, especially their religious beliefs, on
our early history. During the first half of the nineteenth century, many
more Europeans came to America to escape religious and political persecution and the want that followed the breakdown of the peasant economy
in their homelands. Most of the newcomers were from western and northern Europe and closely resembled the earlier arrivals in appearance and
culture. The frontier was still open; there were opportunities for all
comers. The new settlers found a place in the growing society with comparative ease.

About 1880, immigrants began to come in greater and greater numbers from southern and eastern Europe. They were culturally different
from the earlier arrivals and often physically identifiable as different.
With the frontier closing up, they furnished the labor force for the mush-
rooming industrial cities, each new group of arrivals starting at the bottom
of the ladder. When times were hard and jobs few, they were the butt of
much discrimination and were called "Wop," "Hunky," and "Polack."

In the century after 1820, about 35 million immigrants came to this
country. In 1924 restrictions were clapped on, discriminating against the
"new" immigration from southern and eastern Europe and allowing liberal quotas for the old. No longer does the verse at the base of the Statue
of Liberty apply freely to all European countries:

> Give me your tired, your poor,
> Your huddled masses yearning to breathe free. . . .

The process of Americanization or assimilation typically began with
the newcomers quickly accommodating to the new environment in order
to live, for the immigrant was often almost penniless and had to have a
job at once. Those immigrants were fortunate who had friends to meet
them and help them find jobs and housing, usually in an island of their

native culture that eased the shock of adjusting to the new environment. Often the next step was naturalization, perhaps encouraged by political machines hungry for votes; naturalization required a minimum acquaintance with the English language and American history. The immigrants' children were usually taught the culture of the Old World at home and that of the New at school. Typically they were ashamed of one but not quite at home in the other. The story of the conflicts and maladjustments of this generation is a familiar one.

By the third generation, the assimilation process is typically complete, for these children learn only a smattering of their grandparents' language and traditions. In fact, many Americans have come to feel that the process can go too far, that our country should not be the "melting pot" of the tired cliché but should enrich its culture by incorporating what can be salvaged of the colorful and rich traditions of the immigrant generations. Each decade the number of foreign born whites is smaller; from 13 per cent of our population in 1900 it declined to 11 per cent in 1930 and to only 6.7 per cent in 1950. Roughly four out of five of the foreign born live in urban areas. Including both the immigrants and their children, the largest group of foreign stock is German, followed by Italians, Polish, Russians, Irish, Canadians, and English.

Religious • The increasing secularization of our
Differences society, together with our historic tradition of religious freedom, has encouraged tolerance among people of different faiths and reduced friction in their personal contacts in many areas of interaction. Most of the approximately 100 million church members in the United States belong to various Protestant denominations. The largest single church enrollment is that in the Roman Catholic Church—about 33 million members, while Jewish congregations include about 5½ million members. The 300,000 or more churches and synagogues dotting the country testify to the continuing strength of the Judaic-Christian traditions of our culture.[1]

There is undeniably religious misunderstanding and prejudice in America, for in a sense the very nature of religion means that each group considers itself possessed of the truth and the others in error. But there is little conflict except in a few areas where religious beliefs and public policy clash—such questions as religion in education, birth control, and the pacifism of a few sects. Often the churches themselves are active in interfaith activities designed to promote understanding and cooperation. The bitterest religious conflicts occur at the personal level, as in interfaith marriages (see Chapter Twelve), and in local politics.

Interracial   •   Most people do not wear their religious
Tensions   beliefs written on their faces, nor, in
                             mid-century America, betray their na-
                             tional origins by dress or speech. Re-
ligious and cultural differences are learned rather than hereditary, and
have "low visibility."

But other features are clearly different and are passed on from generation to generation in the germ plasm. For complex reasons, certain of
these hereditary traits—in our society, dark skin, woolly hair, slanted eyes,
a certain shape of nose—mark off their owners as targets for prejudice and
discrimination.

These differences are purely biological, and are unimportant to the
physical and mental capacities of human organisms. Why, then, do we
treat these "biological trivia" in a social science text? Because they are
culturally defined as important.

Differential treatment of biologically "visible" groups is "justified"
in the minds of the dominant group by "racist" doctrines. These doctrines
include the following beliefs: that there are pure races of men, clearly
marked off from one another; that these physically distinguishable groups
have different mental and emotional traits that can be rated on a scale of
superiority and inferiority; that the superior races are destined to lead and
dominate; that any individual of the superior race must be superior to
any individual of the inferior race; that biological crossing means degen-
eration or "mongrelization," and that therefore it is safest to forbid contact
between the races. So insidious is this doctrine that it hardly knows any
limits. It applies, in the mind of the prejudiced, even to groups with few
if any apparent biological differences. It applies to persons whose group
membership is betrayed by nothing more than a surname or known family
connection.

Obviously there are physical differences among the earth's people.
How do biologists and social scientists account for these differences?
What importance do they attach to them?

Physical   •   *What races are.* A *race* is a large group
Differences   of people distinguished from other
                        groups by inherited physical differences.
                        The term is often used to refer to people
who speak the same language, live within the same political boundaries,
or share a common culture. Sociologically, such definitions of race are
significant. But they are not based on biological reality.

What races are not. Take the "Aryan race." Originally the term was used to refer to those who first spoke the Aryan language. But no one knew exactly which people these were nor what they looked like. The man who first used the term later took it all back, saying, "To me an ethnologist who speaks of Aryan race, Aryan blood, Aryan eyes or hair, is as great a sinner as a linguist who speaks of a long-headed dictionary or a round-headed grammar." Not admitting this, the Nazis used the term "Aryan" to describe themselves as the master race as well as for several other purposes, all of them mistaken. Other examples of the confusion of race and language are references to the "Latin race" and the "Semitic race." Race and language are not the same.

"The French race," "the English race," "the Swedish race,"—such phrases indicate a belief that the people of any one country belong to a common race. Nothing could be further from the truth. No nation is made up of members of only one race. History shows that the French and English are mixed almost beyond belief, and the Swedes, who are often thought of as racially pure Nordics, actually differ so much among themselves that only a small minority have the combination of physical features usually thought of as Nordic. A study of 45,000 Army draftees found only one Swede in nine who was blond, tall, blue-eyed, and long-headed. Less than one in five had both blond hair and blue eyes. Race and nation are not the same.

"I can spot a Jew a mile away," a person in a discussion will occasionally insist. When pinned down he speaks of short people with dark eyes and hair and hooked noses. Then the fun begins. A tall red-haired man says he is Jewish. A pretty little pug-nosed, blue-eyed blonde announces she, too, is Jewish. A young man remarks that because of his name and the shape of his nose he is often mistaken for a Jew, but actually his father is a Protestant minister and he knows of no Jewish background in his family.

There is no Jewish race. Jews are a people. They share some common cultural traits. They think of themselves as Jews and are so regarded by others. They are characterized chiefly by their religion, but even in worship there are marked differences among Jews. A substantial percentage of the younger generation no longer hold with the faith of their elders. Yet most of these young people still think of themselves and are thought of as Jews. They still share a number of the items of their parents' culture.

In addition to the Jews with whom many of us have had contact, there are Negro Jews and Oriental Jews. Jews are found among all the major racial stocks. They tend to resemble the people of the country in which they live more than they conform to any supposed Jewish type. In the Caucasus they are round-headed; in Arabia they are long-headed. In Poland and Lithuania they are short; in London they are tall. There is no common Jewish physical type. Race and culture are not the same.

How races came to be. From an original home, probably somewhere in Asia, our earliest ancestors went slowly on foot or by primitive water craft wherever they could find food. They had some crudely shaped stone tools but knew nothing of agriculture or domestic animals other than dogs. Some of these expeditions took hundreds of thousands of years. Some of them succeeded only after many trials. Some were halted for centuries by jungles, massive mountain barriers, or wide expanses of water. Some groups found themselves unable to get back to where they had come from and were sealed off from the rest of mankind for tens of thousands of years; they were forced to breed only among themselves.

In some of these relatively isolated groups, man underwent slight physical changes. Through inbreeding, some of these changes spread to the entire group. One of the most obvious of these differences is skin color. Skin color is simply a matter of the amount of chemicals—carotene for yellow and melanin for brown—in the skin, along with the pinkish tinge from the blood vessels showing through the surface. Whites have some of these chemicals. Negroes have more. Only the pale, milky-skinned albinos, who are found among all races, have none. These chemicals enable the skin to filter out the actinic rays that are very good for man in moderate amounts but which are overabundant in areas of great light intensity. In regions where there is much sunlight, skin color tends to be dark; in more northern areas, on the other hand, most people are light-skinned and are thus able to take advantage of the weaker actinic rays in these areas.

Many times during the thousands of years when modern racial types were developing, isolated groups must have acquired somewhat distinct hereditary characteristics. In many cases, such groups must later have mingled with others and given rise to peoples of more varied and less uniform characteristics. No one knows, or probably ever will know, the history of inbreeding and outbreeding that has produced the modern racial types.

Racial divisions. "Races are not so much real things which man has discovered as they are pigeonholes which man has constructed." [2] And no system of classification is universally accepted, for no matter what system is used, many groups just do not fit into any neat pigeonhole.

Three main stocks are usually recognized: the Caucasoid or whites,

the Negroid, and the Mongoloid. Traits especially characteristic of Caucasoids are light skin, abundant body hair, hair type ranging from wavy
to straight, thin gray lips, and high thin noses. Mongoloids have yellowish-
tan skins, eyelid folds, dark eyes, straight black head hair, scanty body
hair, and predominantly broad heads. Negroids have dark skin and eyes,
dark and kinky hair, red and full lips, broad and low noses, and predominantly long heads.

Actually, populations with these distinct characteristics are clearly
present only in three areas of concentration—the Caucasoid in northern
Europe, the Mongoloid in east central Asia, and the Negroid in west central Africa. It is customary to extend these three main stocks to include
the great bulk of the world's population. Thus the peoples of the area
from the Mediterranean to India are usually spoken of as Caucasoids,
while the darker-skinned peoples of Africa south of the Sahara are usually
grouped as Negroids. The Indian aborigines of the New World as well
as most of the peoples of eastern and Southeast Asia, although few of
them show the eyelid fold in typical form, are usually called Mongoloid.

The Three Main Racial Stocks. *A is the area of strongest Cauca-
sian development, B of Mongoloid, C of Negroid. Most people
in the world have in-between-color skin.*

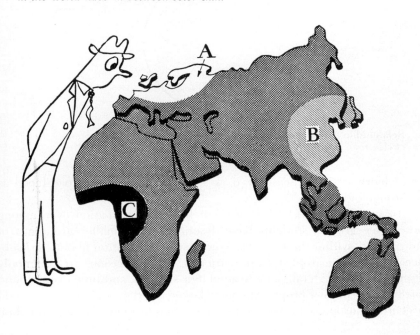

These larger groupings are basically conventional and no one really knows if all the peoples thus classed in a major racial division are actually more closely related to its typical members than to other main types. Some Caucasoids have darker skin than some Negroids. All stocks vary tremendously in skin color and range in height from very short to very tall. Certain groups resist all attempts at classification. Native Australians

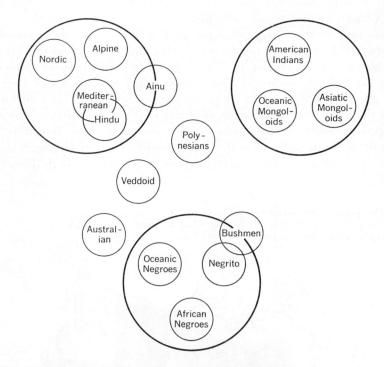

Relationship of Human Races. *Distances between the centers of circles represent the degree of relationship.*

are as hairy as the Caucasoids, dark as the Negroid, and broad-faced as the Mongoloid.

In spite of the lack of a clear-cut line of demarcation even among these three groups, students have described even smaller groupings of "pure types" within these stocks. Much has been written about the "subraces" of the Caucasoid stock in particular. Three divisions are commonly described: Nordics (tall, long-headed, fair-skinned, and blue-eyed) found chiefly in northern Europe; Alpines (darker, shorter, and broad-headed) in central Europe; and Mediterraneans (long-headed, darker, and thinner than Alpines) in southern Europe and elsewhere. No such pure groups can now be found. Possibly they once existed. Today, however, they are very much mixed.

There is no doubt that physical differences can be distinguished among large groups of people. Anthropologists have employed some 50 measurements and marked the minutest variations in tabulating population characteristics. How significant any of these variations are is another question, and one on which we have little undisputed evidence despite a great deal of study. Scientists laboring to classify people into groups and sub-groups according to physical differences have unintentionally given spurious authority to such fallacies as that of the "superior race," which has been used in recent decades to glorify the "Nordic" peoples in particular.

Our common heredity. In the eager search for race differences, it has been very easy to overlook the similarities found among all men, similarities that spell out an interesting story of human brotherhood. For beneath the skin you cannot tell one race from another; heart, lungs, skeleton, and muscles are all alike. All races are very similar in physical prowess. All four blood types—O, A, B, and AB—are found among all peoples, although there is some evidence that one blood type is more common in one group than in others. A white man with type B who needed blood to recover from an illness could not be given a successful transfusion from his brother with type A—although his brother is obviously of the same race. But he would be on the road to health after getting blood from a Negro or Mongol with type B. The donor's racial type would make no difference.

Still other items prove our common heredity. The intricate structure of the human foot with its delicate arrangement of muscles, joints, and bones could scarcely have happened twice in quite the same combination. Look at our teeth. All humans have the same number and arrangement of molars, canines, and front teeth. Take the human brain. An anatomist skilled in brain examination and using the finest equipment cannot distinguish the brains of one race from those of another. A scientist once published a 79-page article detailing his most interesting findings—that the frontal area of the Negro brain was less well developed than the white, and also that there were more convolutions in the white cortex. He was probably honest, but he knew while he was examining each brain from which race it came because it was already labeled for him. Then the doctor under whom he had done the work re-examined the brains just to make sure, but took the precaution of hiding the labels from himself so he would not be prejudiced in any way. Employing this scientific method, the doctor found exactly the same brain development in both the white and Negro groups.

Men of any race can mate with the women of any other race and the hybrid children prove vigorous and healthy. This biological test proves that we are all members of the same single species. The range of variation in the human species is decidedly less than that found in the black bear, and about half that found in a species of South American spider monkeys. When we turn to domestic animals we find the range several times wider than among man. Only one very obvious conclusion is possible: We are all closely related. "All the peoples of the earth are a single family and have a common origin." What Shylock said about Jews may be said of all mankind.

> Hath not a Jew eyes? hath not a Jew hands, organs, dimensions, senses, affections, passions? fed with the same food, hurt with the same weapons, subject to the same diseases, healed by the same means, warmed and cooled by the same winter and summer, as a Christian is? If you prick us do we not bleed? If you tickle us, do we not laugh? If you poison us, do we not die? . . .

Mental • As far back as we can trace what one
Differences group has been saying of another, we
find them looking down on the other as
mentally inferior.

"Do not obtain your slaves from Britain," Cicero warned Atticus in the first century before Christ, "because they are so stupid and so utterly incapable of being taught that they are not fit to form a part of the household of Athens."

"Races north of the Pyrenees are of cold temperament and never reach maturity," declared a Moorish intellectual in the eleventh century; "they are of great stature and of a white color. But they lack all sharpness of wit and penetration of intellect."

A century ago the Count de Gobineau wrote his famous *Essay on the Inequality of Human Races*. His work was eagerly read by those anxious to carry "the white man's burden" with a good conscience. Since then, a flood of material has appeared to prove the inferiority of some races and the superiority of others. Psychologists appeared with their new "intelligence tests" and added profound weight to these beliefs, carrying out as they did the "inferiority" of Negroes to whites to three decimal points. Many scholars added a tremendous degree of respectability to the assertion that Negroes were by their very nature inferior to whites. In 1939 a survey by *Fortune* magazine found most Americans believing Negroes intellectually inferior to whites at birth.

As testing improved, it was discovered that the old tests reflected the increased opportunity, incentive, command of English, and schooling that most whites had. The famous scholars pointed out that they had been in error and helped revise the estimates.

We now know that the ratings achieved in so-called "intelligence tests" may change. A child placed in a foster home with a superior family may raise his score markedly, for he has an opportunity to develop. Negroes in some northern states got higher ratings than whites in some southern states when as draftees they took the same army intelligence tests, for the Negroes had had better educational opportunities in those northern states.

Despite centuries of study, there is no real proof of any relationship between level of intelligence and race. If any such relationship existed, surely it would have been found by now, for many have been only too eager to prove it. On the contrary, as Franz Boas said, "If we were to select the most intelligent, imaginative, energetic, and emotionally stable third of mankind, all races would be represented."

Cultural • Psychologists attempting to test racial
Differences *intelligence* have thus concluded that no group is superior. Physical anthropologists with their calipers and other measuring tools have also been unable to find *physical* differences among peoples sufficient to rate one group as superior to another. But a point remains that deserves our attention—the so-called *cultural argument*. Whites must have greater intelligence, initiative, and perseverance than other races, goes the argument, for they have achieved greater wealth, education, leisure, and power than the other groups.[3]

There is no doubt that the whites are now "sitting on top of the world" with their unparalleled political might and their great share of the material things of life. But does this fact prove their biological and permanent superiority? Not in the least. It is a recently achieved and probably temporary superiority. Only a matter of a few centuries ago, when the European whites were living in a comparatively primitive fashion, Africans were working iron and the Chinese were living in a manner that astounded Marco Polo and other European adventurers.

Nor would everyone agree that the whites are to be envied even at the height of their dominance. Certainly they are far superior in their mastery of the machine and the amount of their material possessions. But many people place other values far above material ones; nor do they envy the whites their power, although they resent the misuse they have often made of it.

Even among the whites, many people recognize the importance of nonmaterial values and are turning to so-called "primitive" or "backward" groups in search of clues to such things as emotional security. White groups live in dread of a war that may destroy them and their possessions.

A third telling point against the belief that race and culture are closely related is that within each race there are wide differences in culture. The Incas, who developed art forms of great complexity and beauty, are grouped in the same race as the most primitive American Indians. Many think of the Negro as naturally carefree and happy, but many West Indian Negroes in Panama are chronic worriers and seldom smile. They also consider the Negro innately musical, yet Negro groups have been found among whom music was utterly lacking.

Finally, the argument that race and culture are related implies that a group remains always the same. This, too, is obviously a fallacy, for history has shown us that groups change, and often change tremendously. The reserved Englishman of today is not the Englishman of "merrie England;" the warlike Swede of several centuries ago has become today's pacifist. Habits, attitudes, beliefs, and behavior are not inborn and unchangeable.

Prejudices · and Stereotypes — Biologists and social scientists agree, then, that racial differences are simply the result of mutation and selection within the same species and that they have no inherent relation to the mental or emotional make-up of any individual nor the culture of any group. This is not to say that these differences are unimportant. They are extremely important *if and when they are thought to be important.* Where shades of skin pigmentation and other external traits are held to be unimportant, people who look different live in harmony within the same society. Where these traits are the basis of prejudice and discrimination, they produce intergroup tension and conflict, and have inevitable consequences for social unity and personality development.

Prejudice means, literally, "pre-judgment." It means that instead of withholding judgment on an individual until we know him, we believe we know what he is like simply because of some one distinguishing trait. We carry around in our minds a stereotype based on that one trait. The term "stereotype," taken from the word for metal molds used in printing, refers, in the social scientist's usage, to one group's or individual's preconceived image of what all members of another group are like regardless of their individual characteristics. The trigger-tempered redhead, the absent-minded professor, the thrifty Scot, the jolly fat man, the monocled Englishman—all these are stereotypes. A stereotype may be favorable; a Guatemalan movie fan upon meeting the junior author was sure she could sing like Doris Day—and that all American girls could! Usually, however, the word "stereotype" refers to unfavorable preconceptions that cloud the judgment of the prejudiced person.

The prejudiced American sees "slanted" eyes and thinks of sly, untrustworthy Orientals who will live on scraps so they can compete unfairly with Americans. He sees a dark skin and thinks the person inside it must be happy, childlike, subservient, ignorant, and shiftless. Or he sees a combination of a certain shape of nose with dark hair and eyes and thinks the person must be selfish and clannish. He would greatly resent it if he were told that anyone thought of him—a white, Christian American—as a materialistic, amoral, pleasure-mad creature with an insufferably superior attitude toward all others. But certainly many foreigners have that stereotype of Americans. Our "typical American" might defend himself, "Perhaps some Americans are like that; I'm not!" For stereotypes typically distort and exaggerate the unpleasant features of a few members of the group and apply them to all without exception.

Although the causes of group prejudice are many and complex—embracing ignorance of the meaning of differences in race, culture, and religion, a feeling that the out-group is a threat to economic or social status, and other elements—any one individual may be prejudiced simply as a result of the normal process of socialization. Prejudice is not inborn. Small children feel no revulsion against people of different appearance until they are taught to feel it, sometimes deliberately but more often in the thousand and one informal and unplanned ways in which attitudes are passed from older to younger children, from parents, teachers, and other culture carriers. A sign of disgust on the part of the parent, a casual remark to the effect that "That's just like a Jew (nigger or Wop, or what have you)" sinks into the child's consciousness. Nursery tales, scare stories, carelessly interpreted Bible stories, and comedy routines containing jokes that perpetuate stereotypes all instill prejudice slowly and surely.

Racial prejudice, then, is not an inborn revulsion against someone different; we do not find tall men aligned against short, fat against thin, redheads against brunettes. As Lt. Cable replied to Nellie Forbush in

South Pacific when she expressed the belief that Americans are born with
race prejudice:

> You've got to be taught to hate and fear,
> You've got to be taught from year to year;
> It's got to be drummed in your dear little ear,
> You've got to be *carefully taught.*
>
> You've got to be taught to be afraid
> Of people whose eyes are oddly made,
> And people whose skin is a different shade,
> You've got to be carefully taught.
>
> You've got to be taught before it's too late,
> Before you are six or seven or eight,
> To hate all the people your relatives hate,
> You've got to be carefully taught! [4]

Discrimination   •   Hand in hand with prejudice goes discrimination. When the prejudice is
shared by most members of a dominant
group, it is used to justify discrimination against the minority or subordinate group (who may actually be numerically in the majority).
Discrimination *may* involve political and legal barriers; it *invariably* involves social and economic barriers. The minority group is restricted to
certain menial occupations, if possible, and forced to live in segregated
areas, ride in separate sections of public vehicles, drink from separate
fountains, attend different schools and places of amusement, even be
buried in separate cemeteries. An American Indian killed in Korea was
denied burial in an Iowa town. Mob violence kept a Negro family from
moving into an apartment they had rented in Illinois. Certain residential
areas, hotels, and clubs are "restricted" to white Gentiles. South Africa
and the American South (and to a lesser extent some northern institutions) enforce a policy of *apartheid* or Jim Crow. White Europeans in
colonial areas deny the "natives" access to their residential areas; a foreign
district in prewar China bore the sign, "Dogs and Chinese not allowed."

Although the white people are a minority—about one-third of the
earth's population—the picture of white domination and Negro or Oriental
subordination has been world wide. In the era of colonialism and slavery,
there was a high degree of accommodation to this arrangement. The
dominant group shouldered the "white man's burden" of looking after

their "inferiors," while the subordinate group accepted their status with comparative resignation.

Today, however, accommodation has given way to unrest and rebellion. Colonial peoples revolt; South Africans live in a climate of ever tighter restrictions and ever greater fear; Americans wrestle with their consciences and consider the costs of prejudice and discrimination.

The Costs · of Prejudice These costs are heavy indeed. The burden to the minority group is obvious. The median income for the United States in 1955 was $3,926 for employed white males, but for non-white men it was $2,342. Although only 14 per cent of "families and unrelated individuals" had incomes below $1,000, when the non-white group was separated, about 28 per cent of them had such low incomes.[5]

The consequent difference in the non-whites' level of living, life expectancy, medical facilities, and infant and maternal mortality has been well documented. Members of the group suffering discrimination often develop an idea that they really are inferior, and their self-hatred is reflected in aggression, anxiety withdrawal, use of drink and drugs, high crime rates, and, when possible, acquisition of more elegant clothes and higher-priced cars than are owned by most members of the dominant group.

But the cost does not fall upon the minority alone. Although individual members of the dominant group may feel that perpetuation of the system ensures their superior jobs and incomes and general level of living, the high rents they can charge, and the low wages they need pay, the economic costs of discrimination can fall heavily upon them as well upon the whole society. The potential talent and productivity of the minority group are lost. They have less purchasing power, which means a loss to the entire economy. Discrimination and segregation entail great cost for public financing of separate facilities—schools, hospitals, transportation, and the like. They aggravate social problems. There is more disease among all groups, for bacteria show no prejudice and can easily pass from a malnourished person living in a segregated slum to the white person whose house he can enter only by the back door. Society also bears the cost of delinquency and vice that flourish in the frustration and want of the minority group. Much time and effort is spent enforcing segregation and deliberating over policies and problems. The costs of the pseudo-caste system of the South are reflected in the fact that there the median income for males in 1955 was $2,470 compared to $3,354 in the country as a whole.[6]

Prejudice and discrimination breed destructive conflict—race riots in Detroit and Chicago and Harlem, mob violence in Clinton and Little Rock, lynchings in Mississippi, rebellions in colonial areas. They not only give rise to overt group conflict, but also warp the individual personality, often exacting a toll in such destructive emotions as fear, guilt, hate, and anxiety. Although prejudice may serve as an outlet for a person's aggressions, it does him no service in the long run by directing his problems away from their real causes.

Another danger in race prejudice is that when it exists within a multigroup society any group can become its target. Discrimination usually means differential justice, unequal application of laws and standards of behavior. "When laws are misused or ignored, they become weakened, and illegality becomes part of the entire culture. Where a dangerous cultural practice exists, any person or group may become its victim." [7] Pearl Buck's description of how it felt to have light hair and blue eyes in China during a revolt against the dominant whites illustrates the point.[8]

Another grave cause for concern is that the American race problem diminishes our country's prestige not only with the non-white majority of peoples in the world, but also with many nations where race prejudice is less apparent and discrimination is negligible. In her position as leader of the free world, the United States is often told, in effect, to put her own house in order. Our treatment of people of Oriental background and of the one American in ten who is a Negro provides the Communists with highly effective, ready-made propaganda to use against us in the worldwide struggle for the minds of men.

Why Prejudice   •   Persists   If prejudice is not innate, and if it entails such heavy costs to society and personality, why does it persist? Some of the factors in its persistence we have already touched upon: the "natural" and informal way attitudes of prejudice, like other attitudes, are transmitted in the process of socialization, the lack of knowledge of the unscientific and irrational bases for prejudice, and the fact that most people do not realize its costs.

It persists also because advantages accrue, in the short run, to the dominant group. Material advantages are obvious in the case of colonial exploitation and in the high rents and low wages of a caste or pseudo-caste system. Often when there is a threat to the economic security of one group, they will turn upon a "visible" competing group and blame them for their plight. Factory laborers are notably prejudiced in hard times. The Panamanians have "racist" prejudice toward the West Indian immigrants—although Panama itself has a large group of native-born, Spanish-speaking Negroes—largely because the West Indians speak English and thus have an economic advantage with the Canal Zone Americans. The Panamanians, being in their own country, use their national power to enforce discrimination.[9]

Prejudice may persist because certain people may want it to persist. A dominant group may turn several subordinate groups upon one another, following the principle of "divide and conquer" and diverting attention from their own dominance. Rabble-rousers and demagogues know that prejudice can be exploited for their own ends; today the media of mass communication are at hand for such exploitation and magnify its dangers a thousandfold.

The presence of a minority group also gives members of the dominant group, no matter how low their status, a feeling of prestige. There is someone to look down upon. The poorest white sharecropper feels superior to the best educated of Negroes.

Almost always, in one way or another, the minority serves as a scapegoat. Just as Aaron called down upon a goat all the sins of Israel and sent it off into the wilderness (Leviticus 16:20-22) so a dominant group places the blame for anything that goes wrong on a minority group. In the days of the Roman Empire, whenever anything caused the populace to grow restless and critical of the rulers, it was "To the lions with the Christians!" Hitler whipped a latent sentiment of anti-Semitism to such a frenzy that many of his followers really believed that the Jews were responsible for all of Germany's problems. The presence of a scapegoat minority gives discontented people someone to blame, a target for their hostility, a socially acceptable release for aggression. They can take out their frustrations on this group without experiencing acute feelings of guilt.

In discussing the persistence of prejudice and discrimination, it is impossible to escape the formula of the vicious circle. As an Irish observer remarked, "The haughty American nation . . . makes the Negro clean its boots and then proves the . . . inferiority of the Negro by the fact that he is a bootblack."[10] The prejudiced majority forces the Negroes to live apart and do menial or unskilled work, keeps them from getting a good education and from living in comfort and decency, and then points to the fact that they are uneducated, work at menial jobs, and have a low level of living to "prove" that they are inferior.

Another reason for the persistence of prejudice has already been touched upon: its irrational nature. Instead of asking exactly what Negroes—to refer again to our chief minority group—want, and what they are entitled to under our democratic tradition, the prejudiced person jumps from consideration of such civil rights as equal justice, the vote, and a job to the conclusion that the next thing you know Negroes will "expect to marry your sister." Actually, as Gunnar Myrdal, the Swedish social scientist who, with a team of American colleagues, took a long look at this "American dilemma," points out, what the Negro wants and what the prejudiced white thinks he wants are very different. If the bars and discriminations that the whites impose are ranked in order of their importance to whites and to Negroes, the order is almost reversed. The whites are most worried about preserving the ban against intermarriage; the Negro's interest in intermarriage is "distant and doubtful," if it exists at all. Second on the list of white anxieties is social segregation in activities implying intimacy and equality; third is segregation in public facilities; fourth, political rights; fifth, equality before the law; and finally, the thing they are least worried about is economic opportunity. And it is jobs and bread the Negro wants most, closely followed by equality before the police and courts, the right to vote freely, and an end to segregation in public facilities.[11] Racists insist, nonetheless, that the Negro works toward eventual intermarriage, and only by keeping him "down" occupationally and educationally can this be prevented.

Reducing • All over the world more people are
Intergroup Tension becoming increasingly conscious of the
costs of prejudice and discrimination.
Evidences of this new attitude are many.
The American Indian denied burial in Sioux City was buried in Arlington National Cemetery with full military honors. Negroes and whites live peacefully side by side in many cities. South Africans like Alan Paton write masterful novels revealing the costs of *apartheid*. Colonial authority is relinquished, in whole or in part, to more and more native peoples, while those colonial administrators who remain often take native values into account.

More and more Americans, North and South, realize the great cost of prejudice and discrimination to society as a whole and to the individuals of both the dominant and subordinate groups. They have begun to attack the problem on many fronts. In general, these attacks attempt to break the vicious circle previously mentioned in which the attitudes of prejudice that bring about discrimination are reinforced by the low status resulting from that discrimination.

Intergroup Contacts.
Contacts on a basis of equal status in the pursuit of common objectives help to diminish prejudice.

This vicious circle can be attacked at either of two critical points—attitudes or conditions. The problem of attitude change is a complex one. One aspect of it is prevention of prejudice—a sort of immunization against its poison, which, like smallpox vaccine, is best administered early in childhood and regularly thereafter. Although prejudice is not innate, it is learned very early and very easily. Dr. Ilg, a well-known psychologist, advocates a program that begins with the child at age three, when he should play with children of other racial groups. The four- and five-year-old can be told in simple language about the world and its people, the six- to eight-year old guarded against absorbing stereotypes from the rhymes and clichés of the culture. ("Eenie, meenie, minie, mo, catch a nigger by the toe.") The nine-year-old's horizons can be broadened by such activities as taking him to different churches and temples. At age ten the "intellectual approach" can reinforce the emotional acceptance that earlier contacts, if carefully guided, have inculcated; he can be taught facts about race, minorities, discrimination, and scapegoating. Social scientists are giving serious study to training teachers in this area, for the teacher's role is crucial in any long-range program aimed at changing attitudes.[12]

None of these attempts will be effective unless the parents, too, demonstrate healthy attitudes. Nor can the pressing problem wait until a new and unprejudiced generation grows up. Adult attitudes are harder to change, but it can be done. The intellectual approach is only part of the job. Actual contact in concrete situations does more to teach people their essential similarity than all the scientific research and formal teaching in the world. The factory worker who stands next to a Negro day after

211

day soon sees him as an individual. The college student whose class is mixed is more likely to judge members of minority groups on the basis of individual traits and abilities than one whose school excludes minorities, no matter how many fine books both may read on race relations.

During World War II, 1,710 white American enlisted men in France were asked this question: "Some Army divisions have companies which include Negro platoons and white platoons. How would you feel about

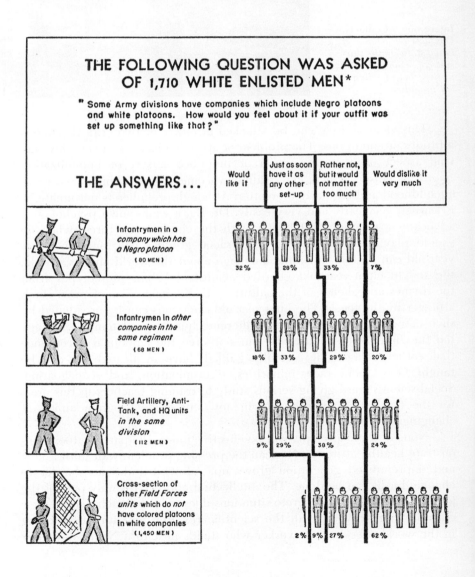

THE FOLLOWING QUESTION WAS ASKED
OF 1,710 WHITE ENLISTED MEN*

" Some Army divisions have companies which include Negro platoons and white platoons. How would you feel about it if your outfit was set up something like that ? "

THE ANSWERS...	Would like it	Just as soon have it as any other set-up	Rather not, but it would not matter too much	Would dislike it very much
Infantrymen in a *company which has a Negro platoon* (80 MEN)	32%	28%	33%	7%
Infantrymen in *other companies in the same regiment* (68 MEN)	18%	33%	29%	20%
Field Artillery, Anti-Tank, and HQ units *in the same division* (112 MEN)	9%	29%	38%	24%
Cross-section of other *Field Forces units* which do *not* have colored platoons in white companies (1,450 MEN)	2% 9%	27%		62%

it if your outfit was set up something like that?" The highly significant result was that those with the most contact expressed the least prejudice. Only 7 per cent of the infantrymen in a company that had a Negro platoon said that they would dislike it very much and 32 per cent said they would like it; 28 per cent said they would just as soon have it as any other set-up, and 33 per cent answered "Rather not, but it would not matter too much." Infantrymen in other companies in the same regiment were more prejudiced, soldiers in other units in the same division somewhat more so. Significantly, those with the least contact showed the most prejudice. A cross section of other field forces units that had no colored platoons in white companies showed 62 per cent saying they would dislike it, and only 2 per cent reporting that they would like it, while 9 per cent would "just as soon have it" and 27 per cent would "rather not." [13]

This brings us to the other chief angle of attack on the "vicious circle"—changed conditions. Fortunately these are easiest to achieve where most urgently desired—in housing and jobs. If asked what they think of fair employment practices, of having Negro sales clerks or bus drivers or teachers or nurses or neighbors, people often object vehemently, predicting dire results and destructive conflicts. But if the policy is put into effect firmly and without fanfare, the results are almost always surprisingly contrary to these predictions. Fair employment practices legislation and nonsegregated housing projects have been highly successful where they have been tried. According to a prominent psychologist, Gordon Allport, "Prejudice tends to diminish whenever members of different groups meet on terms of equal status in the pursuit of common objectives." [14] Legislation helps create a changed social climate and thus helps change attitudes. "A *fait accompli* that fits in with our democratic creed is accepted with little more than an initial flurry of protest." [15] When people realize, in other words, that a city's decision to employ Negro bus drivers, a baseball manager's hiring a Negro pitcher, a Supreme Court decision against segregated schools, is designed to bring reality closer to the American creed, most of them accept the action philosophically. And the resultant contacts on a basis of equality help to eradicate prejudice and encourage acceptance of individuals on their own merits.

A recent attempt to change conditions was made not by civil rights legislation but by a passive resistance movement among Negroes in Montgomery, Alabama. Boycotting the segregated buses, they "walked and prayed," dramatizing to the nation and the world that a tired Negro seamstress has as much right to a seat as any other citizen. The world-wide publicity given to such episodes, as well as to the more violent occurrences elsewhere, contributes to a realization that Americans are on trial in a world where they are judged not alone by the ideals they share but by the realities of their social order. Despite the greater news value of violence and conflict, the numerous instances of intergroup amity and cooperation are bringing those realities closer in line with our cultural values.

The Formation
of Personality

We now approach the subject of human behavior from a third angle—that of the individual human being, or person. In discussing culture and society we have necessarily said much about the person, for culture, society, and personality are so intimately connected that in discussing any one of them we must constantly refer to the other two. Culture, we saw, is possible only because of the potentiali-

215

ties of the human organism, and it serves as a ready-made set of be-havior patterns for individuals. Society we defined as a set of reciprocal relationships among individuals and groups. So, too, we cannot isolate the individual person from society and culture, for the newborn baby becomes human only through interaction with others in social groups, and this interaction is largely patterned by culture.

Like "culture" and "society" the word "personality" means different things to different people. We often hear one person say that another has "lots of personality"—that is, charm, vivacity, attractiveness. For the social scientist, however, every person—every socialized individual—has personality. *Personality* is the more or less organized ways of behavior, both overt and covert, which characterize a given individual.

The social scientist who concentrates on personality is called a social psychologist. He is concerned with such topics as socialization, motivation, and perception—with "why we behave like human beings."

<table>
<tr><td>**Theories**
of Personality
Development</td><td>•</td><td>It appears especially appropriate in this chapter to touch upon several conflicting theories of human behavior. The student will find much of what we said in our very first chapter on</td></tr>
</table>

"science and social science" illustrated here; he will also find the concepts introduced in connection with the discussion of culture and society useful in appraising these theories. They illustrate the development of rational thought as applied to an eternally interesting subject—himself—and help explain why he is the way he is.

Biological determinism. A school of psychology that was influential in the early decades of this century and with which we associate the name of William McDougall theorized that all human behavior was rooted in a certain number of instincts (see p. 37). McDougall posited 13 instincts; others said there were 2, or 250, or 1,500. Instinctivists paired each instinct with an emotion or "sentiment." We have said enough about instincts in previous chapters to dismiss this theory, which has been in disrepute since about 1924.

Attempts to explain behavior by inborn tendencies, however, recur continually. Theorists attempt to catalogue certain numbers of needs, drives, or urges and explain all human behavior on this basis. Aside from the obvious fact that man is an animal organism and must have organic satisfactions of various kinds, social scientists now conclude that "people need whatever they think they need." Even the long-accepted sociological classification of "the four wishes"—the wish for response, the wish for recognition, the wish for new experience, and the wish for security— is now regarded as useful in describing rather than explaining human behavior. As the famous psychologist Gordon Allport has said, "Not four wishes, nor 18 propensities, not any and all combinations of these, even with their extensions and variations, seem adequate to account for the endless variety of goals sought by an endless variety of mortals." [1]

A somewhat different variety of biological determinism seeks the explanation of variations in human behavior in glandular make-up or constitutional or anatomical differences. The theory of *somatotypes* put forth by William Sheldon has attracted much attention in recent years. Basing his research on four thousand photographs of male students, he classified three main types of physiques. The *endomorph* tends to softness and roundness; the digestive viscera are highly developed. The typical *mesomorph* is hard and rectangular, with a predominance of bone and muscle. The *ectomorph* is linear and fragile, thin and lightly muscled, with a large brain and nervous system in proportion to his size.

With each of these physical types goes a characteristic temperament. The endomorph is "viscerotonic"; he loves comfort and relaxation, takes pleasure in digestion, depends on social approval, sleeps deeply, reacts slowly, is even-tempered and needs people when he is troubled. The mesomorph is "somatotonic"; he is characterized by assertive posture, energy, need for exercise, direct manner, unrestrained voice, need of action when troubled, and physical courage. He looks older than his years. The ectomorph is "cerebrotonic"; he is characterized by restraint, inhibition, self-consciousness; he is afraid of people, prefers small, enclosed areas, and seeks solitude when he is troubled. He reacts overquickly, sleeps poorly, and is youthful in appearance.

This theory has stimulated a great deal of empirical research, but much of this research finds no such close correlation between personality and physical type as Sheldon indicated. Such study is of great importance to social psychology, however, for it is quite possible that many aspects of behavior, such as intensity of emotional reaction, are correlated with biological variables. Too heavy a dependence on any biological explanation of behavior, however, leads to neglect of social and cultural influences as determinants of behavior.

Psychoanalytic theory. The theory of human behavior advanced by Sigmund Freud has had a tremendous impact on social science, in spite of the fact that a substantial portion of it has been questioned or disproved. It also has had far-reaching effects upon the treatment of mental illness, upon child-rearing, and upon such attempts at public persuasion as advertising. Many Freudian concepts are now in common parlance. There are many schools of psychoanalytic thought, but all agree on three basic points: the significance of the unconscious elements of personality, the use of "depth therapy" in treating mental illness, and the primacy of childhood influences on personality.

The structure of personality. Freud saw personality as consisting of three component parts: the id, and ego, and the superego. The *id* is the raw, primitive, blind core of the unconscious, swayed by two overwhelming drives: sex or libido and aggression. It is an evil force at war with society. The *ego* is the rational, conscious portion of personality; it begins to develop in infancy as the child becomes aware of himself as separate from surrounding people and objects. It creates defense mechanisms against the demands of the id. The most important of these defense mechanisms is the repression of undesirable drives and impulses, forcing them back into the unconscious. These repressed desires make themselves felt in dreams and fantasies. The *superego* or conscience begins to develop in the stormy years between the ages of 2½ and 6 when the famous "Oedipus complex" emerges. The growing boy wishes to possess his mother completely and sees his father as a rival; he feels strong emotions of love and hate toward both parents. The girl feels the same conflict in reverse. This stress the child resolves through *identification* with the parent of the same sex. The moral judgments of the parents become his superego.

Stages of personality development. During the *oral* stage, the infant gets sexual pleasure from sucking. At first he is passive and receptive, later active and incorporative in seeking oral satisfaction. If his needs are not satisfied during the oral stage, insecurity, anxiety, and conflict develop. The differentiation of the id and the ego begins as the child establishes relations with his mother and with objects about him. During the *anal* stage, when he discovers the mystery of the defecatory process and finds his pleasure in soiling a diaper and otherwise thwarting his toilet-training, retention and elimination become the center of interest and the source of pleasure. Toilet-training is the "ego's first conscious struggle for mastery over an id impulse." His ego begins to develop during this conflict with his mother. During the Oepidal or *phallic* stage, already mentioned, he becomes aware of his genitals.

All personality structure, the Freudians believe, is based on what happens at these three stages. If the child is handled incorrectly or "arrested" at any one stage, he will bear the scars for life—unless therapy succeeds in ridding him of the anxiety, traumas, and perversions that may occur. The working out of the Oedipus complex and the development of a mature superego take years.

The *latency* period dates from about the beginning of school. The ego, mediating between the id and the superego and the id and reality, represses sexual tendencies. During the latency period the basic biological tendencies such as giving and taking, retaining and eliminating, continue to develop into more complex forms. The pleasure from oral reception now manifests itself as pleasure at receiving gifts, and pleasure from retention develops into a desire to collect things.

During puberty and adolescence, latent conflicts are reawakened by physical maturation and repression is again attempted. Expansion of interests and achievements indicates sublimation. The old Oedipal conflict is revived as the boy quarrels more with his father and the girl with her mother. As maturity is reached, both the sexual drives and social regulation of them are accepted. Adulthood is represented in the Freudian scheme as simply a working out of earlier genetic occurrences.

Mental behavior. Freud saw mental behavior as the result of the interplay of libidinal forces from within and environmental forces from without. This conflict gives rise to tension or anxiety, which the ego tries to dispel by activity. To the extent that the ego succeeds in mediating between the insatiable demands of the id, the stern voice of the superego, and outer reality, behavior is normal, sensible and satisfying. To the extent that the ego fails, behavior is neurotic or even psychotic.

The activity of the ego may take the form of defense mechanisms rather than rational thought. *Repression* is the ego's principal defense against unbearable impulses, particularly in infancy and early childhood when the ego is weak and cannot cope with these impulses. If he does not wholly resolve the Oedipal conflict, for example, and represses his ambivalence, a person may never experience a fully satisfying emotional attachment with a person of the opposite sex. The severely repressed adult spends much energy in blocking his impulses and therefore exhibits fatigue, anxiety, boredom, and a feeling of meaninglessness or futility.

Regression means sliding back from a more advanced level of satisfaction, which has proved impossible to achieve or disappointing or has aroused anxiety, to a more infantile form, such as overindulgence in eating or drinking. If a person never attempts a more advanced form of satisfaction and persists in clinging to an infantile form, the mechanism is called *fixation*.

Sublimation is a diversion of the libido from directly sexual aims to desexualized and socially acceptable ones, from crude satisfaction of the urge for sex or aggression to refined, subtle, and indirect satisfactions. Freud saw sublimation as the source both of human culture and of the individual's ability to participate in and contribute to culture.

In *projection* the ego reacts to something internal as though it were outside the person, perhaps attributing to someone else an unacknowledged feeling the individual himself harbors. Projective tests such as the Rorschach or ink blot test are based on the idea that the person's interpretation of a vague shape will reveal much about his unconscious self. We shall have more to say about projection a bit later.

Freudian interpretation of society. All our prescriptions for living, according to Freudians, are based on man's eternal effort to handle the problems of sex and aggression. The social roles people play are crystallizations of mechanisms people have collectively decided upon as acceptable for handling libidinal and aggressive drives.

The concept of *identification* is also used to explain the nature of society; as we identify with an admired person or one we wish to replace, so we identify with others on the basis of common choices, interests, and qualities. Identification is the cohesive force in the structure of groups. Crowd behavior is explained by the reign of the libido. Inhibitory behavior is relaxed in favor of guiltless expression of desires and repressed impulses; a member of a mob is released from the compulsions of the superego.

Psychoanalysis or psychotherapy. Psychoanalysis is aimed at freeing the person from "the tyranny of the unconscious." Because the impulses and experiences that create neurotic anxiety are buried so deep in the unconscious, psychoanalysis is a time-consuming process. The analyst tries to dredge up these trouble-makers from the unconscious and allow the ego to focus conscious attention on them and thus permit the person to rid himself of his anxieties. The analyst proceeds by the process of "free association," encouraging the subject to recall everything he can.

Criticism of Freudian theory. Social scientists, as well as many neo-Freudian psychologists, have pointed out that this scheme of personality development almost ignores the role of language; personality development includes intellectual as well as emotional factors in a close interrelationship. Freudians believe that learning is primarily concerned with harnessing the id. The theory is based on the "genetic fallacy" in which the last event in a chronological series is identified with the first.

The genetic approach of the Freudian analyst gives his explanations a narrative character. If it is asked why two persons whose childhood experiences appear to be substantially the same turn out very differently as adults, the analyst's answer will frequently consist of two biological narratives.[2]

Being based almost entirely on clinical cases—that is, on abnormal psychology—analytic theory does not lend itself to testing and checking by empirical research. Anthropologists find that in some societies there is no evidence of many of the stages and mechanisms that the Freudians hold to be universal. The development of the superego is too exclusively linked with identification with parents and with sexual development; broader cultural influences are ignored. Another criticism is that the theory allows little or no room for development during adulthood.

Freud and his followers, nonetheless, have presented a significant and challenging theory of human behavior that stresses the subtlety of human interaction and the existence of concealed factors in behavior. The neo-Freudians have broken away from strict biological interpretation based on the libido; they admit the role of developmental factors beyond the age of five, and the importance of language to human behavior.

Behaviorism. In sharp contrast to the psychoanalysts, behaviorists try to avoid dealing with any behavior that cannot be directly observed. Like the psychoanalysts, however, the behaviorists see man as an ego acting according to the pleasure-pain principle. Psychology they regard as a science of animal behavior. Human behavior, the behaviorists believe, is based on narrow physiological needs such as for food, water, and a mate, rather than on massive instinctive foundations. These needs provide the energy for all psychological processes. Aside from them, the human being is infinitely plastic. The learning process is one of stimulus and response; if these are correctly manipulated by rewards and punishments, the behaviorist believes that any desired results can be obtained. As the leader of the behaviorists, John B. Watson, said,

> Give me a dozen healthy infants, well-formed, and my own specific world to bring them up in and I'll guarantee to take any one at random and train him to become any type of specialist I might select—doctor, lawyer, artist, merchant-chief, and yes, even beggar-man and thief, regardless of his talents, penchants, tendencies, abilities, vocations, and race of his ancestors.[3]

Psychologists who subscribe to behaviorist theory tend to believe that human behavior can be understood by studying lower animals—"rats in mazes"—and then transferring the knowledge thus gained directly to human behavior. This theory obviously ignores the great chasm that exists between man and the lower animals because of man's mastery of language. In concentrating on the conditioned response, on overt behavior, and seeing all motivation as deriving from self-interest and society as a maze in which a person learns the rules of the game by receiving suitable rewards and punishments, behaviorism ignores the complexity of social situations and the subjective nature of much behavior.

Cultural determinism. Whereas the biological determinists see human behavior as deriving directly from the nature of the human organism, the cultural determinists see the individual as a mere reflection of his culture, which "somehow hovers above the members of society and pushes them around." A pioneer sociologist, Emile Durkheim, propounded just such a view. He called the cultural norms or images shared in the minds of members of a society "collective representations," which are prior to the individual and external to him, and have an existence above and beyond the lives of particular individuals. The collective representations exercise a constraining influence on the individual, coercing him and channeling his conduct into conformity. Culture Durkheim saw as a reality in and of itself and not just a name for the activities of disparate individuals.

This scheme, say its critics, does not explain either how the individual takes on culture nor how it is possible for cultures to change if individuals are merely passive recipients of a fixed prior reality. It ignores the great portion of human interaction for which there are no collective representations as well as the capacity of individuals to select, interpret, and decide on which patterns of behavior they will follow.

> Cultural patterns do not exercise a direct, mechanical, unmediated influence but an indirect and symbolically mediated one. Patterns are shaped and transformed as they are assimilated into the person's own individually defined view of himself and the world.[4]

The theory put forth by Karl Marx in *Das Kapital*, which has had such a tremendous influence in the modern world, is essentially one of cultural determinism. The group—especially the social class into which a person is born—is regarded as the basis of motivation, and the economic factor as the basic determinant of human life. This theory is discussed further in Chapter 27.

Symbolic interactionism. As we have implied in our comments on the theories already discussed—and there are others upon which we have not touched—neither inborn drives, nor culture, nor man's capacity to learn to respond in conditioned ways to external stimuli, is a sufficient or satisfactory explanation for human behavior. The social scientist sees the key to all that is distinctively *human* in man's behavior in *language*. The social psychological theory based on this fact is called *symbolic interactionism*. Unlike the theories we have already mentioned, this one does not separate the individual and society, but sees human behavior itself as inherently social.

George Herbert Mead, a famous psychologist, outlined a broad theory of human interaction and the development of personality upon which much current research is based. This theory involves ten key concepts which are closely interrelated.

Social interaction may be viewed as a *conversation of gestures*. This is not a simple stimulus and response situation but has a threefold character. It consists of (1) the gesture or stimulus, and (2) a response on the basis of (3) the indicated or anticipated completion of the stimulus. A dogfight is a conversation of gestures on the rudimentary level. For humans, the spoken word is the most satisfactory kind of gesture. When it stimulates both the speaker and the hearer, arousing in them both the same response or feeling, it is a *significant symbol*. The common set of significant symbols shared by members of a society is their *culture*. The *society* is a system of interpersonal relationships based on this culture. An individual who has internalized an organized set of significant symbols has acquired a *self*.

The self develops in the process of socialization. The infant has no conception of himself as an individual set apart from other individuals. Only as he interacts with his mother and others does he gradually become aware of his separate identity. The very frustrations that are part of every child's experience as he learns that his impulses must be satisfied only in certain ways and at certain times contribute to the development of a self. Roughly at the age of two the child begins to use the pronouns "I," "me," and "you," indicating that he is conscious of self and of other persons as individuals like himself.

Mead described the rise of the self in terms of "taking the role of the other." Only man can perceive *roles* and their relationships. As the child observes and responds to his mother and others in the household, they become objects to him, meaningful objects that bring him pleasure, frustration, security, and the like. In order to win from these people the responses he wants, the child must learn their attitudes. He gradually takes on their responses and attitudes toward him—that is, he "takes the role of the other." In so doing, he becomes an object to himself. Anyone who has watched a small child at play knows that he "tries on" various roles, switching from one to another with ease, addressing himself as storekeeper and answering himself as shopper, or playing mother and child. When several children play together, each adopts a role. As they grow older and participate in games with rules, where each person is expected to respond in a certain way to a given stimulus, the conception of the self in relation to others becomes more clearly defined. The child of eight or so playing baseball must carry in his mind a knowledge of the roles all others play in the game. In order to do what he should do, he must know what behavior to expect from them.

Like the ball game, society is an organized system of roles. As the process of socialization continues, knowledge of the roles and attitudes of others becomes more generalized. The child is aware not only that "Mother say it's not right to do this," but also that "It isn't right to do this." A larger, more inclusive "other" now controls his actions. He is aware of the moral voice of the community as a whole; he has internalized its mores and values; he has acquired what Mead calls a "generalized other," which in everyday language is often referred to as "character." At this point, the basic design of the self has been established. "As the individual incorporates into himself the system of mutually related attitudes in the community with reference to the common activities and goals

Socialization. Parents, teachers, and peers often provide varied types of socializing experiences that aid in building a satisfying self-conception.

of the group as a whole, he becomes a complete self, a social product in the fullest sense."[5]

Structure of the self. Like Freud, Mead conceived of the self as composed of three parts, and these parts correspond roughly to the id, ego, and superego. The *"I"* is the impulsive, non-reflective portion of human nature. The *"me"* is composed of the significant symbols internalized from the culture, its system of norms. It can anticipate the consequences of impulsive behavior; so it halts responses, deliberates, and selects the appropriate way to behave. The *generalized other* is a sort of ideal self, the conscience or superego in which the more abstract values and norms of the society are organized into the self. The *mind* is the conversation of the I and the me supervised by the generalized other.[6]

Mead's ten interrelated concepts—culture, society, the significant symbol, the self, the I, the me, the generalized other, roles, the conversation of gestures, and the mind—are the framework for modern social-psychological theorizing. Taken together they comprise a theory that is highly abstract. It describes the form of human interaction without detailing the content and is not subject to empirical verification. But it has proved very useful as a basis for sub-theories on more concrete matters such as the nature of perception, motivation, group interaction, leadership, collective behavior, roles, personality change, and personality disorganization, many of which have been empirically verified. It leaves room for explaining the wide variety of human behavior, as determinist theories do not. It concentrates on truly *human* behavior, i.e., language behavior.

| The | • | The self-conception develops as the |
| **Self-conception** | | result of a person's differentiation of |

The
Self-conception • The self-conception develops as the result of a person's differentiation of himself from others and his awareness of their attitudes toward him. The self as determined by the attitudes of others is called "the looking glass self," a term first used by a pioneer social scientist, Charles Horton Cooley.

As we see our face, figure, and dress in the glass, and are interested in them because they are ours, and pleased or otherwise with them according as they do or do not answer to what we should like them to be; so in the imagination we perceive in another's mind some thought of our appearance, manners, aims, deeds, character, friends, and so on, and are variously affected by it.

A self-idea of this sort seems to have three principal elements: imagining how we appear to another person; imagining how that other person judges our appearance; and some sort of self-feeling, such as pride or mortification.

> . . . we always imagine, and in imagining share, the judgments of the other mind. A man will boast to one person of an action—say a sharp transaction—which he would be ashamed to own to another.[7]

Not all "others," of course, are of equal importance to the self-conception. Each of us has some "significant others" whose judgments of us concern us far more than do the judgments of the rest of those with whom we come in contact. For a student trying to earn a good grade, his teacher is a "significant other." For most of us, our parents, spouses, and intimate friends, and the experts or colleagues within our fields of special interest—whether in work, sports, or hobbies—are our "significant others," the people we seek to please and impress.

Robert Burns wrote, "O would some Power the giftie gie us, To see oursel's as others see us." We are endowed in some measure with that gift, and therefore each of us has a self-conception. All his life the person who is not barred from social interaction by mental deficiency or mental illness is conscious of the attitudes of others. He never has an entirely accurate picture of them, but if his self-conception is too far removed from the evaluation that others have of him he is a misfit. The person who sees himself very differently from the way others see him is the bore who thinks he is the life of the party, the ineffectual male who exhibits unwarranted feelings of superiority, or the pretty girl who suffers from a conviction that she is unattractive.

One of the chief duties of parents is to help the child build a sound and satisfying self-conception. By giving him a feeling of belonging, by accepting him, the family gives him the self-confidence and security that he needs to adjust to other people and to meet new situations easily and with assurance.

Defending the self-conception. A person often encounters threats to his self-conception from changes, from criticism or pressure from other persons and groups, or from failures or other frustrations. He may meet these threats on a rational, conscious level, or he may resort to unconscious psychological mechanisms of adjustment to defend his self-conception.

Rational action rests upon intelligent choices. Need we try to please everybody, or should we decide which people's opinions really matter—which are our really "significant others"? Which values are highest in the scale? Which goals are most important and reasonably sure of attainment? How can they best be reached? By answering these questions clearly and decisively a person can avoid the consequences of action that is irrational, guided simply by tradition or inability to see alternatives, or dictated by such emotions as anger and hostility. He will be spared the need for relying too heavily upon unconscious and sometimes costly and dangerous methods of adjustment.

These unconscious mechanisms, like other habits, are socially acquired. Insofar as they reduce conflicts and tensions within the individual, they help the person adjust. If they fail to reduce tensions or if they lead to harmful self-deception, they become "neurotic" devices that signify maladjustment. We have already mentioned some of the most familiar mechanisms of self-defense that are associated with Freudian psychology—repression, projection, sublimation, regression, and fixation. Other common defense mechanisms include compensation, displaced aggression, fantasy, and rationalization.

Rationalization induces a person to give "good" reasons rather than real reasons for his actions. These reasons are emotionally satisfying and prevent self-condemnation and ward off criticism by others. The person who says "sour grapes" is rationalizing. When a student has made up his mind to study for an examination and an inviting opportunity to go out arises, he may rationalize that "I will feel fresher if I get my mind off the subject for a while." He may repress his awareness of the real reason for going out, thus avoiding guilt feelings. By preventing self-condemnation, rationalization may contribute to mental health. If carried too far, however, it becomes self-deception and fosters an inability to face reality.

Compensation is a device whereby a person makes up for his inadequacies by emphasizing assets, real or imagined (see cartoon, p. 228). The inadequacies may exist in his personality, in his environmental situation, or in his biological appearance or constitution. A man who failed in college may take satisfaction in piling up more money than the honor graduates. A physical weakling may compensate by studying hard, an unattractive girl by cultivating interests that will make her an interesting conversationalist. The poor family may take pride in the fact that they are hardworking, honest, and respectable. Compensation helps to relieve the tension induced by frustration; it also serves to conceal from others and from the person himself his own inadequacies or weaknesses. It is a constructive mechanism of adjustment insofar as it helps a person keep his self-esteem and/or stimulates him to achievement. If it is based on fancied assets, however, it is not constructive.

Fantasy, or day dreaming, is normal in childhood; the small child playing at different roles is indulging in fantasy. Adults also use fantasy to solve their frustrations in several ways. "Daydreaming" may or may not be productive. The boy daydreaming of accomplishments may be setting goals for himself; but an adult "Walter Mitty" is merely escaping from

"You're beautiful, sophisticated, lovely—What do you care if you got 'D' in history?"

reality. If overdone, indulging in fantasy is very wasteful and unproductive. Some mental illnesses are characterized by continual fantasy. A boy pretending he is Napoleon is usually playing at trying on a role; the man who insists he is Napoleon is put in a mental hospital. In some cases, fantasy may be highly productive. The imagination of a talented mind may produce inventions, books, music, or great works of art.

Projection explains much interpersonal and group misunderstanding and conflict. It means that a person attributes his own faults, his own un- acceptable urges, to others, as a means of reducing his own anxiety. It is the psychological device upon which scapegoating is based. It helps to explain unreasonable jealousy. It may with equal accuracy refer to the tendency of a naive and trusting person to believe everyone else is good and trusting, the belief of a materialistic person that everyone is out for all he can get, and a man's insistence on his son's becoming a doctor because he himself could not afford to attend medical school.

Displaced aggression or deflected hostility is often based on the pro- jection of unacceptable urges, and also helps to explain scapegoating. When hostility in regard to one person or group must be repressed, it is often taken out on another. The frustrations of the German middle class help to explain why they so eagerly seized upon a chance to vent their spleen on the Jews. The disgruntled employee who must repress his hostility at work "takes it out on the dog" at home.

Desire for self-enhancement. Besides defending his self-conception, the person is motivated to enhance it. This is especially true in our competi- tive society where a man is measured against others, even one child against another. The emphasis on ambition and success, on striving for goals and achieving them, makes the desire for self-enhancement strong.

> Therefore in our society the well-adjusted individual is one who not only conforms to the standards of the group but competes with others for a place in the sun ... [and] behaves not only as the com- munity wishes but in ways which will give him the greatest degree of self-expression.[8]

A person's desire for self-enhancement is related to the goals he chooses as he interacts with others, and he measures his success or failure only in those areas of achievement that he has come to consider worthy of his efforts. If he sets his sights too low, he derives little or no satisfaction from reaching his goal; if too high, he is bound to experience the frus- tration of failure. Rational behavior means that a person will evaluate his capacities and possible accomplishments before determining how high he will aspire.

The self-conception, then, can be understood in terms not only of what a person believes himself to be, but also in terms of what he would like to be and the ways in which he goes about achieving this ideal. Some of the mechanisms of self-defense we have already mentioned serve to conceal failures in self-enhancement.

Factors • Personality is the result of the interplay
in the Formation of three factors: biogenic factors, in-
of Personality herent in the human organism, psychogenic factors, and socio-cultural factors.
The dynamic interplay of these factors
means that each of us is in some respects like all other men, like some other men, and like no other man. This view of personality avoids the pitfalls of deterministic theories that stress one factor alone. It also avoids the sterile dualism of mind vs. body, if we are careful to remember that in analyzing these interdependent factors we are separating them only for purposes of rational thought.

Biogenic factors. The way the genes happen to combine into a nuclear cell at the moment of conception determines all the "hereditary" aspects of an individual. *Sex* is fixed at this moment by the presence of an X or Y chromosome in the sperm cell. The particular combination of genes also determines a person's probable *appearance*—his eye and hair color, stature, and other physical features (though prenatal and subsequent environmental factors affect his actual stature, weight, muscular development, and the like). Heredity also determines the limits of a person's *intelligence,* and probably has much to do with his *temperament* or prevailing mood. Closely related to growth, temperament, and behavior is the organism's glandular balance, which affects many bodily functions.

At birth the individual has certain *reflexes*—automatic and rigid responses—each of which is attached to a given stimulus. The heartbeat, breathing, salivation, and other reflexes are largely involuntary and can be modified only slightly. Although, as we have seen, the theory that human beings are born with certain instincts has been repudiated, the organism does have certain needs or *drives* that must be met (see Chapter Three). These inborn needs or urges are felt as states of tension or lack of balance; the organism seeks to satisfy the need, to dispel tension and restore equilibrium. And, as we have already mentioned, the specific pattern for satisfying these drives is not innate; it is cultural.

The primary defense reactions that prepare the organism to deal with dangers and hazards produce emergency responses that many psychologists believe are the basis of such emotions as fear, rage, disgust, shame, and grief. At any rate, emotions appear to be closely linked with the physiology of the organism, for under stress of emotion there are measurable and often striking changes in body functioning. The emotions, like the more distinctly primary or innate drives such as sex and hunger, are subject to considerable conditioning through experience. *Conditioning* means attaching a response to a stimulus that would not ordinarily call it forth. A baby is emotionally conditioned to love his mother. After being fed, rocked, cuddled, and cared for over a period of time, the infant will respond favorably at the sight of his mother or at the sound of her voice.

Some of the potential traits of the organism appear only with physical growth at a given level of development. Until the eye is capable of discerning letters, the child cannot learn to read. Until leg and back muscles are sufficiently developed, no amount of encouragement will persuade the infant to walk. Until the sphincter muscles have developed to the point where they can be controlled, toilet-training is futile. This development of the ability to respond to certain stimuli at certain stages of growth is called *maturation*. Although the rate of maturation varies from one individual to another, it always follows the same developmental sequence; that is, a child sits before he stands, walks before he runs. He is never ready for any stage of development until his organism is ready.

The biological heredity of the individual may predispose personality in certain directions, and set limits to possible development. The favorite topic of high-school debates a generation ago, "Which is more important, heredity or environment?" has been abandoned as fruitless by students of human behavior. Although it is possible to speak of *predominantly* hereditary factors and *predominantly* environmental ones, neither heredity nor environment can be regarded as the sole factor influencing development, nor even the chief factor. By the time any such aspect of the personality as intelligence or temperament can be measured, environment has affected it. In fact, *only* after environment has played upon the organism are these things apparent. Even physical appearance is conditioned by environment. Identical twins reared apart often differ in appearance as well as in intelligence and temperament.

Intelligence. Intelligence is the capacity of the organism to adjust to its environment. As a potential of mankind in general, intelligence is the basis of human culture. As an attribute of individuals, intelligence varies greatly among members of any society. This variation is a function of both heredity and environment. The quality of the brain and nervous system is the inborn potential. It cannot be measured at all accurately; it can only be guessed at from the way the brain functions as a result of an individual's experience. It is not yet clearly understood whether intelligence is a general ability or a number of specific abilities. But it is clearly a biological potential that emerges only as a result of social experience.

Innate intelligence sets limits to a person's capacity to learn. As a matter of fact, man rarely uses his intelligence to capacity. A meager culture, emotional blocks or anxieties, a narrow ideology, or simple illness or lack of time may prevent a person from utilizing all his intellectual potential.

Psychogenic factors. The family plays a crucial role in the development of personality. One of Freud's chief contributions to the study of personality was to stimulate an appreciation of this fact, even by those who disagree with his interpretation. Before the newborn infant has learned to respond to significant symbols, he responds to the care his mother provides. The nature of this care has dramatic consequences for personality. Studies of infants reared in foundling homes as compared to those cared for by their own mothers in prison show that the tender fondling of the infant is far more important to his development than hygienic surroundings and nutritionally perfect food. And middle-class mothers who stressed hygiene and schedules and letting the child "cry it out" had sicklier infants than warm, nurturing, lower-class mothers who were indifferent to strict rules of baby care.[9] As a result of such studies, a standard prescription for hospitalized infants is now "t.l.c.," tender loving care. Authorities now widely believe that the manner in which babies are fed, weaned, and toilet-trained lays the basis for deep and enduring personality traits, such as the capacity to love and respond to others. Although some research has carried this theory to the extreme of deriving almost all cultural values and behavior patterns from the manner in which the infant is disciplined, the subject is of such great importance to an understanding of personality that any empirical research along this line may prove enormously profitable.

Socio-cultural factors. As he develops mastery of the significant symbols of his culture, the child also incorporates its meanings and values, *internalizing* them into his personality and acquiring a self. The particular combination of cultural meanings and values to which he is exposed depends on the groups to which he belongs. The primary groups—of the family and playmates—exercise the earliest and most basic influences. Their class status, their racial, religious, or ethnic sub-cultures, determine which values and norms he will incorporate into his personality.

Non-cultural factors in group interaction also influence personality development. The number of children in the family, a person's position within it, the age of his parents, the nature of their personalities, and the particular atmosphere of the home, in whatever sub-culture, affect his conception of himself. As we have seen, it is in social interaction within the family and the play group that the person acquires his basic conception of self.

But this process of personality development does not come to an end at any specific chronological age. Throughout life a person's self-conception changes with changes in his body functions, in his age status, class position, and the groups to which he belongs or would like to belong.

Reference groups. A reference group is any group with which a person identifies himself, either as a member or an aspiring member. He evaluates himself according to the standards of the reference group and orients his behavior accordingly. The group to which he aspires may have more influence on his conduct than the one to which he belongs. In our mobile society, for example, many people orient their behavior not to their current status group but to the one just above, copying their style of life in the hope of attaining membership. The feeling of identification and loyalty toward groups is more important than actual group membership. Group identification provides the person with the "frame of reference" in which he views the world and chooses his goals.

Socialization   •   There is no more fascinating or vital subject than *socialization,* the process whereby the individual organism is transformed into a person, the human animal into the human being. Only through socialization can society perpetuate itself, culture exist, and the individual become a person. Socialization is the common meeting ground of biology, sociology, anthropology, and psychology, and the focus of interest of educators, religious leaders, and parents. In spite of its tremendous importance, no one yet understands the subject thoroughly.

In the process of socialization, the individual learns culturally approved habits, ideas, and attitudes. He is fitted into the social group by being taught the rights and duties of his position. His drives are guided into approved channels of expression; the cultural rules and restrictions are so internalized that they become part of his personality. Probably most people resist socialization to some degree because it interferes with the immediate satisfaction of impulses, but it is remarkable how narrow a gap there is between what most people want to do and what society would have them do. Those who cannot compromise with society without great resentment and frustration are said to be maladjusted.

Because socialization is so important, every society institutionalizes it. There are two main channels of socialization: those with authority over a person and those with equality. Parents, schools, and church have au-

"How are you, Mary Lou?"
"How are you, Mary Lou?"

"I'd like very much—"
"I'd like very much—"

"To have you come—"
"To have you come—"

"To my birthday party Saturday."
"To my birthday party Saturday."

thority over a child's conduct and are made responsible for his discipline. His peers teach him the child culture and during his interaction with them he learns how to adjust to them; this same process of adjustment to one's peers goes on throughout life.

Role. The concept of *roles* is crucial to an understanding of the socialization process and the rise of the self. We tend to conform to the beliefs and expectations of others all our lives. Our roles—the patterns of behavior in any one status or situation—are culturally defined. We are assigned the roles that go with ascribed statuses such as sex, age, race, class, occupation, and nationality.

We usually consider certain traits "masculine" and others "feminine," as if they necessarily go with the biological fact of sex. A comparative

234

study of personality in different cultures by Margaret Mead shows how little the biological fact of sex actually has to do with personality, and how much more important are the cultural definitions of sex differences. Comparing three New Guinea tribes, she found two that make no personality distinctions between men and women. Among the mountain-dwelling Arapesh, the cultural goals are growing yams and rearing children. Both men and women act in a fashion we would call "feminine." Both are cherishing, gentle, maternal, mild. Not far away live the fierce, cannibalistic Mundugumor. Both men and women of this tribe act in ways we would call predominantly "masculine." Both "are expected to be violent, competitive, aggressively sexed, jealous and ready to see and avenge insult, delighting in display, action, and fighting." [10] The things that give greatest satisfaction are fighting and the competitive acquisition of women. Every man is against every other, including his father and his brothers. Children are unwanted. The world is charged with hostility and conflict.

Instead of ignoring sexual differences in personality, the third tribe, the Tchambuli, define male and female roles in a way that is the reverse of ours. Women manage and dominate. Men gossip, wear curls, and go shopping, are emotionally dependent upon and less responsible than women. The people live chiefly for art, the event celebrated by a ceremony being less significant than the elaborate and lavish ceremony itself.

How does a child in our society acquire the cultural definitions of sexual roles and accept his status as a boy or girl? Studies have shown that sexual definition is a learning process. At first children employ such criteria as dress and hair styles; as they grow older and their vocabularies increase they mention hands, complexion, strength, and gait. By the time a boy is aware of primary rather than secondary or cultural sexual distinctions, the cultural definition of what it means to be a boy is basic to his self-conception.

Cases of mistaken sexual identity show how decisive are cultural definitions of sexual roles in the formation of personality. Lindesmith and Strauss relate the history of "Frankie," who had been reared as a boy because of uncertain genital structure. At the age of five Frankie was discovered to be a girl. Nurses and interns in the hospital found it difficult to treat Frankie as a girl because she considered girls' toys and activities to be "sissy," refused to wear a dress, and became extremely belligerent when anyone tried to treat her as a girl. [11] The socialization process had effectively organized her behavior along masculine lines quite independently of her feminine anatomy. Sexual deviations and varying attitudes toward sex also demonstrate how decisively this basic drive is defined, channeled, and patterned by symbolic interaction.

Role-playing. Each of us plays a number of roles, dropping one and assuming another temporarily. A woman talking with another in the living room may drop her role of friend briefly to play her role of mother or to answer the doorbell as a housewife. All these roles are part of her self-conception, and are thus unified. When a person adopts a new role, at first he feels he is play-acting. It takes a new bride some time to realize she is now "Mrs." To be incorporated into personality, a new role must become firmly linked with the self-conception.

Role-taking. Role-playing is to be distinguished from "role-taking." When we "take the role of the other," we imagine his attitudes and emotions; to the extent that we succeed in doing so, we achieve sympathy and understanding. Some practical work is being done in such fields as labor-management relations and family relations. A parent and child, for example, switch roles in a familiar situation and act them out, often achieving new insight into their problems.

The entire concept of role is a more fruitful one for the study of personality than the concept of *traits,* which are regarded as more or less fixed attributes of a person. The role concept resolves the dilemma posed by the fact that conflicting traits are attributed to the same person by defining his behavior in terms of different roles he plays in different situations. A woman may appear stingy in one situation and generous in another because in one she is playing the role of budget-conscious homemaker and in another that of hostess.

Human Behavior and Significant Symbols • We have repeatedly said that all that is peculiarly human about man's behavior is a consequence of his power to communicate, think, remember, and foresee by means of language. Let us consider this paramount fact as it determines his motives, the way he sees the world about him, and even the emotions he feels.

Motivation. Why do we behave like human beings? Why do we arrive at work on time, dress carefully and fashionably, eat dinner, make love, read books, go to the movies, scold our children, celebrate birthdays, smile, and weep?

Motives, or purposes, are our reasons for acting as we do in anticipation of certain consequences. People and groups may do the same thing for different reasons and different things for the same reasons.

Motives, we repeat, are not inborn, biologically given drives or instincts. Our gross organic needs ordinarily lead only to random or restless behavior. They "become motivational, as a rule, only after the organism has learned to *interpret* them in certain ways and to associate certain objects or modes of behavior with the satisfaction of the need." [12] These interpretations and associations are acquired through communication and are verbalized either partly or fully. Motives "are learned in social experience, vary from group to group, and are relative to a social context." [13]

On the other hand, it is not enough to say that motives are completely derived from the socio-cultural milieu, as the cultural determinist would have us believe. The social psychologist, in short, explains human motivation in terms of the relationship between basic needs and the social goals toward which they are channeled and directed by the human group and its culture. Furthermore, as we have seen, there are numerous motives that have no relation to innate organic drives—needs and goals that a person acquires in the human group. Man derives his patterns of goal-directed behavior from five specific aspects of the socio-cultural milieu: the system of status, the accompanying roles, the system of authority, the social norms, and the cultural values. These define his needs and orient his behavior toward the goals that will satisfy them.

It is the socially inculcated pattern for the satisfaction of any need that makes human behavior predictable. Behavior is meaningless except in terms of the goals toward which it is oriented. Hunger, thirst, and the sex drive have no predictable bearing on human conduct. A hungry man may do any one of a number of things. He may glance at the clock and ask his wife when dinner will be ready; he may resolve to stick to his 1,000-calorie diet and ignore the rumblings of his stomach; he may forego his rations so his children may eat; he may enter a hamburger shop or an exclusive restaurant. In any case his behavior is not a simple matter of stimulus (hunger) and response (eating). He has acquired cultural definitions of his hunger drive and cultural patterns for satisfying it.

Perception. The human organism is not a camera or a tape recorder that automatically responds to the sights and sounds within range of its senses. Human perception—"the way in which persons respond to the stimuli picked up by their sense organs" [14]—is influenced by needs, interests, and past experience, and is a complex process. Social psychologists are currently carrying on a great deal of empirical research and theorizing on the subject of perception. They agree on certain principles that govern the way a person perceives the external environment.

Perception is *selective*. Not all the possible stimuli in the environment are cues. They function as cues only when the organism responds or pays attention to them. At a party we must ignore many stimuli to concentrate on a conversation. Our "mental set" influences perception, as illustrated by experiments with students. A picture of a face is briefly presented to a class. Then a murder is discussed. When the face is again presented, the discussion of the face is colored by the foregoing discussion the class held about the murder.

Experiments with a tachistoscope, which flashes words or images on a screen very swiftly, show that those words or images that relate closely to a person's self-conception are the ones he most readily recognizes; he avoids recognizing those that might prove damaging to his self-conception. A minister, for example, readily recognizes words about religion; an atheist does not. Hungry men tend to see images of food; but significantly, conscientious objectors deprived of food and subjected to similar images do not, because their self-conception includes pride in self-sacrifice. Selectivity is determined by a person's social attitudes, which are defined as "a readiness to experience certain events in certain consistent and selective ways." [15]

Stimuli are *organized* by the perceiving person. He does not react with equal intensity to all cues. He organizes them. An illustrative experiment consists of sending two people out of a room. One comes in alone, and a person is described to him as "intelligent, industrious, impulsive, critical, stubborn, and envious." He is asked to give his impression of the person described. Then the second person enters, and the same list is read to him in reverse order. Because in each case the first words made more impression than the last, the two perceived the person described quite differently.

We also tend to *categorize* stimuli, classifying them in terms of the vocabulary at our command. This classification has two aspects: *generalization* and *differentiation*. We generalize a moving object in the sky as a plane; if we command enough images we further classify it by differentiating it as an F-94 Starfire rather than a T-33. "People see what they have words for."

Generalization is a means of economizing our limited span of attention and our memory. It means that we tend to see all succeeding stimuli in terms of the way we saw some previous stimulus. We cannot notice, much less remember, all the potential cues in a situation. "If we noticed every detail our senses equip us to notice, life would be a stream of unique, never-recurring events. We categorize because we want to know and need to know how to anticipate the future." [16]

Stereotyping is one form of generalization. A few cues are enough to elicit a response in terms of a preconceived image. We discussed this concept in connection with race prejudice. It means that on the basis of one cue—skin color—the perceiving person reacts to a Negro on the basis of the category into which American society has placed him. We also recode stimuli from within our own group, using categories of "social type" to generalize about persons: wolf, playboy, teen-ager, and the like.

Although there are dangers in such categorizing, constructive thought is impossible without a third form of generalization, that of "ideal types," which have been devised by specialists as aids in analysis and understanding. The concepts of "folk society" and "associational society" are ideal types, as are the terms "extrovert" and "introvert." No one specific society or person may exhibit all the characteristics of the ideal type, but such types serve as guides to accurate perception.

Differentiation means making finer distinctions than those afforded by type categories. The authors once took a Panamanian student of whom they were very fond to a social gathering in the Canal Zone. They had responded to her on the basis of special cues, such as her charm and intelligence. On the Panamanian side of the border, which is merely a street, they had not been conscious of her as a Negro. In the race-conscious Canal Zone, they noticed Americans reacting to her on the basis of one cue alone—skin color—and suddenly perceived her as several shades darker than she had looked among her classmates. Perception is affected by the social situation, whether in the direction of generalization or differentiation.

Accentuation is closely related to selectivity and organization. In perceiving a situation a person pays more attention to what fits in with his interests; to him this central element is the "figure," the rest of the stimulus field is background. Suppose that a group of three men is visiting a slum area—one an architect, one a doctor, and the other an artist. To the architect, the buildings will be the figure; to the doctor, the people's physical appearance; to the artist, color and form.

Emotion. We tend to think of emotions as basic human feelings—love, fear, anger, shame, guilt, pride, and the like—which are the same all over the world. But from the symbolic interactionist point of view, emotions, like perception and motivation, are "to an amazing extent regulated, prescribed, and even defined by groups." [17] The social situations that arouse shame or fear differ from one culture to another. In many folk societies people fear "the evil eye"; in our own we fear depression and war and traffic accidents. The expression of basically similar emotions is also culturally defined. We tend to show anger by loud talk and violent movement, whereas the Chinese express anger by staring with their eyes wide open.

The physiological aspects of emotional response to a stimulus are not learned, but the interpretation of stimuli that lead to emotional states and their expression is learned. Often a child goes through the outward forms of an emotion-arousing ceremony such as a funeral, but does not feel the emotion of grief himself until he has internalized the definition and significance of death.

We name, evaluate, and interpret our emotional reactions according to cultural definitions. Because we can think and talk about them, we can to a large extent control emotions and inhibit their expression. The intimate relation of emotional states to language is apparent in the fact that we can imagine a future occurrence, such as a death or parting or a wedding, or remember an insult or humiliation or death that occurred in the past, and feel the emotion aroused within us almost as if it were occurring in the present.

Memory. Past experiences are somehow preserved in the organism. Remembering, like perception and emotion, is a symbolic process, and the accuracy of remembering largely depends on the accuracy of verbalization. We cannot remember things that occurred before we learned to talk. Two-year-olds remember better than one-year-olds, according to experimental research, because they know more words.

Which experiences are most clearly remembered depends on a person's interest and attitudes. A young woman may remember the names of all the boys she ever dated but forget the names of her teachers. In one experiment, pro-Soviet and anti-Soviet subjects were tested for their memory of pro-Soviet and anti-Soviet reading material, and were found to remember most clearly the materials that they favored.

Memory, like perception and emotion, is patterned by the frame of reference provided by groups and culture. We perceive and remember events in terms of dates, calendars, clocks, and seasons; primitives remember them as connected with seasons or with other outstanding events such as a typhoon or a great feast.

We tend to preserve family memories in part because they are so closely allied with our self-conception, and also because families revive past events during their intimate interaction. A student remembers a particular class and professor far more clearly than the professor remembers particular students and classes, because to the student the situation was unique, to the professor it was recurrent.

Personality • An integrated personality is one lacking
Organization in contradictions, conflicts, and inconsistencies. Like cultural integration, personality integration is a matter of degree, never completely realized. A relatively high degree of integration exists if: (1) the person plays only roles that are clearly defined and compatible, (2) holds compatible attitudes, (3) pursues goals that are not mutually exclusive, and (4) is a member of groups with compatible cultures and values.

All these criteria of integration are easily measured up to in a stable, sacred society where one set of values is held in common by the homogeneous group and where roles and goals are clearly defined by tradition. In a changing, complex society, however, personality integration becomes a problem. Many groups with different values compete for the person's allegiance. Definitions of roles and goals break down. In such a society a person must make choices and achieve a satisfactory personality organization or suffer a great deal of tension, frustration and anxiety.

The roles of good father and church member, of good mother and good wife, are compatible. Harder to reconcile would be the roles of father and gambler, or—a more common dilemma in modern society— good mother and breadwinner.

The problem of compatibility of attitudes is more complex. Actually, a person can quite unconsciously and without serious cost to his personality hold two diametrically opposed beliefs, such as a belief that "Business is business" and anything goes, and that "Honesty is the best policy." These inconsistencies bother intellectuals or "thinkers" more than others; most people do not reflect upon their attitudes. But when incompatible attitudes toward the same value are strongly grounded emotionally—for example, love and hate of the same person—we speak of *ambivalence*. The growing child typically loves his mother deeply and dislikes her for frustrating his urges. Most people harbor some degree of ambivalence, such as love of the mother and mild resentment of her dominance, without much tension. But the adult who combines strong love and strong resentment of the same person has a serious personality difficulty.

The question of mutually exclusive goals is a typical problem of adolescence. Undecided about the future and confronted with a wealth of possibilities, the youth often wants to be "all things to all men." He wants to be approved of at home and approved of by the "gang." A boy may want to be a successful lawyer, an accomplished musician, and a rich playboy. Or a girl wants to marry and have children, pursue a career in art, *and* be a glamorous social butterfly. Either may be acutely conscious of what everyone may be thinking of him as he rides a bus or walks down a street. He has not learned that most people are only slightly aware of him and very little interested if at all. He has not narrowed down the number of significant others. A sign of maturity is the ability to choose goals that can reasonably be reached together, and forego the others without too much regret. Many a chronologically adult person still has not achieved such maturity.

The problems we have heretofore mentioned—of choosing compatible roles, goals, and attitudes—confront most people in an urban society. The fourth, that of incompatible cultures, is less often a question of making choices. In modern society, it is visited upon millions of people by circumstances. It is often a result of mobility. This mobility may be social; a man of lower-class status who achieves great success in business and moves to the upper-middle or lower-upper class is often ashamed of his background but not quite at home in his new situation.

More frequently migration produces "culture shock." Within our own country, migration from rural to urban or from southern to northern areas is a strain on the personality. A newcomer to the metropolis from a tightly knit rural community may come first to the area of cheap lodgings, where he feels anonymous and isolated. The city is indifferent to him. The freedom he longed for is his, but he has no sense of belonging, of security. The standards of proper behavior back home do not fit here, and there is no one to enforce them by caring what he does. He may develop no new standards and feel no restraints and drift into unconventional or delinquent behavior.

In *The Gold Coast and the Slum,* Harvey Zorbaugh depicts Chicago's "world of furnished rooms" as "a mobile, anonymous, individual world, a world of thwarted wishes, of unsatisfied longing, of constant restlessness, a world of atomized individuals, of spiritual nomads." [18] He tells of a girl from Emporia, Kansas, who went to Chicago dreaming of a career in music but found she had to live in miserable rooming houses and take any kind of work. After she was told she had no future in music, she felt she belonged to nothing and no one. She tried a church, but found it impersonal, went to a social agency and was treated as a rag doll. She felt "like an atom whirled about with three million other atoms." When a chance came to accept the companionship of a man, she took it. Obviously she had not been trained in the values and choices of a complex urban society. She had no moorings in a primary group. When the verdict that she had no real musical talent came, it was a great shock to her self-conception, and she had no one to build up her self-esteem and offer response and security.

A person identified with two cultural groups but not wholly at home in either is called a "marginal man." The most common example of the marginal man in our society has been the immigrant. A European peasant, transplanted after a difficult journey to the land of his dreams, has been socialized in one culture and now must learn to live in another. The strain is evident in the fact that the rate of suicide and murder is highest among immigrants. Their children, too, suffer from the same problem, for they are taught one language and one set of standards at home and are exposed to another in the school and the street. Delinquency and crime rates among immigrants' children are significantly higher than among children of native-born parents.

Marginality has also been imposed upon many "native" cultures by Western man, whether he went as conqueror, missionary, or trader. Whatever elements of his own culture he introduced, and no matter with what good intentions, they were frequently so incompatible with the native culture as to entail disorganization and demoralization. Minority groups within a culture also suffer from marginality. The "emancipated Jew" brought up in an orthodox home, feeling more identified with the Gentile culture but not accepted fully by Gentiles, and the mixed-blood mulatto or Eurasian not fully accepted by either racial group suffer the tensions of living in two incompatible cultures.

Being confronted with incompatible roles, values, and cultures is sometimes a stimulant to achievement. It gives a person a sense of objectivity lacking in the stable and secure personality that has never been offered a bewildering variety of choices. Some immigrants have achieved great success in business and the arts. Many Jews have profited from their experience in two or more cultures and have become eminent social scientists and anthropologists. Negroes have contributed richly to our art and literature in part because of their experiences with marginality. Many tales of urban success, too, began on the farm, for although the city threatens the newcomer with culture shock, it also offers great opportunities for those who can overcome the strain of adjustment.

Personality · Because personality is organized sym-
Disorganization bolically, in terms of roles and goals, and depends on group relationships, personality disorganization can be best understood in the same terms. From the symbolic interactionist point of view, personality disorders are not inevitably and without exception the result of childhood traumas.

We have already suggested the problems posed by conflicting roles that the same person tries to play, and by social change resulting in disagreement about how roles are to be played. Loss of an accustomed role, such as wife or mother or breadwinner, confronts the bereaved, divorced, and aging. Failure to play a role central to one's self-conception may result in personality disorganization. Loss of his job is a blow to the self-esteem of the breadwinner; failure to bear children may disturb a married woman. Failure to achieve goals, to reach a higher status group or become an actress, may contribute to disorganization.

Preventing a person from satisfying his basic needs may have the same effect on him as confinement has on prisoners. And the collapse of a person's entire social world leaves him disoriented and bewildered. War breaks up families and destroys towns, and the survivors truly become "displaced persons."

According to a very simple definition, the mentally healthy person is one who is "happy and responsible." He is happy because he has no serious mental or emotional conflicts; he has achieved a stable and satisfying self-conception. He is responsible in that he performs his social role as he is expected to, conforms to group values, and pursues acceptable goals—in short, he is adjusted to society. Being adjusted to society does not, however, rule out some dissatisfaction and constructive attempts to solve social problems.

A maladjusted or disorganized personality, to reverse our simple definition of mental health, is "unhappy and/or irresponsible." If unhappy, he lacks sufficient integration of his goals, roles, and values to function without much tension and conflict. He may carry on, outwardly conforming, but actually be full of mental conflicts and possibly of physiological symptoms induced by his emotional disturbance. On the other hand, he may be perfectly at ease within himself, but not be capable of social living because he does not perform his social roles well enough to fit into normal society. Or he may be both unhappy and unable to keep contact with reality.

Probably no one escapes mild and temporary disorganization as he faces crises, bereavements, failures, and new and strange situations. Somewhat more chronic and severe than these situational troubles are "personality problems" that impair happiness and adjustment. Most of us probably have one or more of these problems—shyness, tactlessness, feelings of inferiority, sexual maladjustment, irrational fears and worries, laziness, cynicism, dissatisfaction with our work, extreme ambition or lack of it, and any of a long list of other traits and attitudes.

Maladjustments that impair a person's happiness and usefulness more or less severely are *neuroses*. The term *neurosis* "refers to a self-conception which is so damaged, so beset by cross-purposes and contradictory goals, that any action, forward or backward, is painful. The neurotic personality is so loaded with guilt and anxiety that it cannot determine what its desires are." [19]

The late Karen Horney, a psychiatrist, sought to explain neurotic conflicts in cultural terms. The American emphasis on competition takes exaggerated form in the neurotic personality. A neurotic may constantly measure himself against all others, whether or not the situation calls for it. Not only does he want to be better or greater or more important than others, but also he wants to be the only one who attains the pinnacle. If he is discouraged in one area of competition, he tries another and another. He feels intensely hostile toward his competitors, real or imagined. The exaggeration of competition in our culture makes for a diffuse hostile tension among individuals, and an emotional isolation. The neurotic in our society, where love is regarded as the solution for all problems,

Personality Disorganization. *Skid Road is the haunt of many who have lost group ties and self-esteem.*

has a great need for affection but is incapable of really loving others.

A neurotic displays a certain rigidity of reaction. Although a normal person may be suspicious under certain circumstances, a neurotic may be suspicious under any and all circumstances. The same goes for fear, spitefulness, indecision, or any other attitude. All neurotics have anxieties. They may try to escape these by interpreting them as rational fears. The chronically worried and overprotective mother may point out the fact that children do get run over as a reason for keeping her seven-year-old confined to the yard. Or the neurotic may deny the existence of his anxiety, but certain "psychosomatic" symptoms appear that he may interpret as symptoms of organic illness. He may try to drown his anxiety in drink or work or drugs or sleep or excessive sexual activity. He may withdraw, avoid all situations that arouse anxiety. He may be subject to compulsions such as constant hand-washing, or to obsessions that occupy almost his whole attention, or to morbid fears or *phobias,* such as fear of enclosed places.

A person's friends and acquaintances may not be aware of his neurosis, for he may be capable of continuing to play his normal social roles. There is no clear-cut dividing line between normality and neurosis; the difference is one of degree, except that extremely neurotic individuals are no longer capable of playing their social roles satisfactorily.

Psychoses (commonly called insanity) are not merely more severe forms of neurosis. The neurotic has not lost touch with reality; he knows how he should function in society, but his effectiveness is diminished by inner tensions. The psychotic may know how to function, or he may not; at any rate he cannot. He is likely to require institutional care. If there is a physiological basis for the psychosis, it is called *organic;* that is the case in mental illnesses associated with alcoholism, drug addiction, syphilis, glandular changes, senility, and the like. Organic psychoses are responsible for almost half of the patients in mental hospitals. Psychoses in which there is no traceable organic change are called *functional;* there is some evidence that they, too, may be at least partly organic in nature. Three chief types of functional psychoses—schizophrenia, manic-depressive psychosis, and paranoia—are generally recognized, although the symptoms overlap.

Schizophrenia or split personality, also called dementia praecox, is characterized by a withdrawal from contact with others, preoccupation with the self, inability to concentrate, and dulling of emotional response. It comes on gradually and often strikes young adults. Alternating attitudes of deep depression and maniacal excitement characterize the manic-depressive psychosis, which often strikes in middle adult life. The paranoic harbors delusions and hallucinations, but he may appear to be highly intelligent and emotionally adjusted to reality and may not be recognized as psychotic. In fact, he may attain such a high position that his name will go down in history.

The appearance of psychotic symptoms is accompanied by a breakdown in communication; words are used eccentrically; their meanings are private. The psychotic individual may be said to be *desocialized;* he once was normal and now he is not, for he no longer interacts with others on the basis of common meanings and values.

Social structure and personality disorganization. Both the frequency and the type of personality disorganization vary from one culture to another and from one class, region, and nationality group to another. In India, for example, schizophrenia is infrequent, manic-depressive psychosis predominant. There is some evidence that psychotic disorders are more frequent in the blight areas near the center of cities than in surrounding zones. Rates for psychosis are higher in the lower classes, and neuroticism in the higher; but it should be kept in mind that doctors may be more likely to attach the psychotic label to a lower-class person.

Not only the type of disorder but the behavior and treatment of the patient varies with the culture, for some effects of the socialization process linger. Guilt is relatively absent in African social life, and hence in psychiatric disorders suffered by Africans. A lower-class psychotic frequently resorts to physical aggression and violent movement; a middle-class person with a similar disorder resorts more to conceptualization and meditation.

Personality deviation. Psychotics cannot conform to group norms because personality disorganization has desocialized them. Some human infants, perhaps 3 per cent, in contrast, cannot conform to group norms because they lack the capacity to learn.

Still another type of deviation from social norms exists—unwillingness to conform to the norms of the larger group. The "lone wolf" nonconformist is an eccentric. Some criminals, homosexuals, and drug addicts pattern their code of behavior after a deviant sub-group within the society. Members of such a sub-society are subject to its norms and sanctions. Other deviants, such as "white-collar" criminals, drug addicts in countries where they are not defined as criminals, and some homosexuals belong to no such sub-groups. They share some of the values of the larger society and are in conflict with others.

Freedom   •   *Dynamic nature of the self.* Although
of Personality   many people strongly believe that every
in Modern Society   man is master of his fate, others just as
strongly believe that the person is help-
less in the face of social and cultural
influences. By picturing the individual as a passive recipient of outside
influences, a person can blame his or another's faults and misfortunes on
something external, completely denying the older idea of free will. This
is a false interpretation of the findings of social science. If it were true,
no one would be responsible for his actions. But the socialized individual
is in large measure able to choose and decide, to set goals and strive to
reach them. The goal of socialization is to make him able to direct his
choices and his efforts for his own best interests and those of society.
"Personality is a unity, a purposeful, striving unity, at the core of which
lies the self-conception. . . . [Its chief motivation is] to attain and maintain a stable and flattering self-conception and to strive for certain goals,
within a range of inner limitations and outer circumstances." [20] This
interpretation of personality does not deny that in some situations persons
have less opportunity to succeed in making such choices and achieving
such goals than do those in more favorable circumstances, but it is more
constructive and optimistic than either the notion of a completely free
will or complete passivity.

The autonomous person in the "lonely crowd." David Riesman and his
associates, in a widely read book called *The Lonely Crowd,* subtitled *A
Study of the Changing American Character,* advance the thesis that different personality types are predominant during each phase of the population cycle (see Chapter Eight). The population curve is used as a
sort of shorthand for the sweeping changes involved in the transition
from agrarian folk society to urban industrial society.

Riesman believes that a society is characterized by a different mode
of conformity or character structure during each phase of the population
curve. The tradition-directed person is typical of the first phase; there is
a well-worn path marked out by the elders, and the sanctions impose
shame on the person who does not conform. The inner-directed person
is predominant in the second phase. His elders have built into him a set
of principles that will guide his conduct even under the changing conditions of the dynamic society, a sort of "gyroscope" set spinning at
home, in church and at school, which guides his behavior throughout
life. When he violates these implanted principles he is punished by guilt
feelings. Just beginning to appear on the scene, particularly in the urban

middle class, is the other-directed person, who is guided always by a desire to adjust to peer-group expectations, to catch in his "radarscope" the signals that are being sent out by others and to act according to them. The other-directed person does not want to be too "different," just marginally different. A process of "taste-exchanging" among members of the peer group trains them in consumption along approved lines. Instead of shame or guilt, an other-directed person feels a diffuse anxiety lest he fail to conform. He harbors an insatiable psychological need for approval. The parents make the child feel guilty not so much about his violation of inner standards as about his failure to be popular. Teachers emphasize cooperation and adjustment. The mass media reinforce the pressures of the school and the peer group. The goals of the other-directed person may at times shift; only the process of striving itself and of paying close attention to the signals from others remains unaltered throughout his life.

There is a "characterological struggle" within a society among the different types as one gains ascendancy over the others; this struggle also occurs on a worldwide scale. The inner-directed person, who possesses a relatively inflexible standard for judging success and morality and is buttressed by his steady internalized values and personal sense of discipline, may feel resentful when his formulas no longer work, when standards seem to shift with situations, and when the people who succeed are the flexible ones who to him appear unprincipled. His ambition for an individualistic career is outmoded by the antagonistic cooperation of his peers who wish only to be marginally different. The ambitious inner-directed person feels guilty when he fails; the other-directed person feels guilty when he succeeds too well!

The attitudes of the inner-directed toward work and play differ greatly from the attitudes of the other-directed. The first thinks of work in terms of the difficulty of the material, non-human objects with which he deals, of production in terms of impersonal technological and intellectual processes, of an "invisible hand" that seems to guide production through anonymous cooperation, of long-term ambition and long-term investment in expanding production. The other-directed man thinks of work in terms of people, of the "glad hand," of marginally differentiated products with "fair trade" prices.

Having described the other-directed as passive, cooperative, and tolerant, Riesman draws on Ruth Benedict's classic comparison of three modal personalities in *Patterns of Culture* and declares his conviction that Americans are more like the peaceable Pueblos than the suspicious Dobuans or the boastful, vengeful Kwakiutl Indians.

Riesman explores rather tentatively an alternative mode of personality organization—*autonomy.* The other-directed person usually seeks *adjustment;* if he fails, he may drift into anomie, become rootless or normless. But he may seek autonomy. An autonomous man is capable of conforming to the behavioral norms of his society (which the anomic cannot do) but is free to choose whether to conform or not. A person cannot find autonomy in a tradition-directed culture because he cannot conceive of people being other than they are. It is possible to be autonomous in an inner-directed culture, for there are many more roles and opportunities for exercising choice; there is more leisure and mobility, more literacy and education, and thus there are more social and personal models to copy and more time and incentive for imagining ourselves in other roles. In the society that is experiencing an incipient population decline Riesman sees even more hope for autonomy, an opportunity for a person to change his life style and character more or less deliberately. To become autonomous a person does not necessarily have to rise in the class structure; autonomy can be found within the middle class, of which he speaks almost exclusively.

Autonomy means that in a rich, complex culture such as ours, with the significant symbols of many ages and many nations from which to draw, it is possible to construct a set of values and a flexible mode of behavior that is more creative and satisfying than wan conformity to peer-group tastes and norms.

The key to autonomy is heightened self-awareness or self-consciousness. A person must recognize and respect his own feelings, potentialities, and limitations. In the sphere of play especially he can try to develop skill and competence in the art of living. We must, says Riesman, make more use of the free and large market for friendship, must enjoy both play that is private, reverie-filled, and fantasy-rich and play that is sociable, even ceremonial.

Riesman asks, in the light of the behavioral sciences as well as of his knowledge of history and of contemporary culture, the old question, "What is the good life?" and he means the good life for the *individual* human being. "We need to realize," he says, "that each life is an emergency, which only happens once, and the 'saving' of which, in character terms, justifies care and effort. Then perhaps we will not need to run to war or a fire because the daily grist of life itself is not felt as sufficiently challenging, or because external threats and demands can narcotize for us our anxiety about the quality and meaning of individual existence." [21]

Marriage and the Family

The family is the basic and universal institution. Upon it depends the survival of every society. Everywhere the family produces new raw recruits for society in the form of newborn infants and socializes them sufficiently so they can play adult roles in the other institutions of the society and in turn establish their own families.

The family is the most "primary" of

primary groups, for it receives the infant first and keeps him during the years most crucial for the formation of his personality. It is the group with the most intimate interaction and the most frequent and continuous face-to-face contacts. It is also the primary group that endures longest.

Need we define the family? Do we not have a mental picture of it as a rosy-cheeked father and mother with a rosy-cheeked son and daughter, gaily eating the latest breakfast cereal in a shining kitchen? This idea of the family as a man and woman and their children comes close to reality in most societies; but in order to apply universally, our definition must be more carefully fashioned. The family really has its origin in the fact that the human infant is born after nine long months of gestation, during which time the mother is hampered in her ability to provide for herself; and for a long period after birth the child requires constant care and supervision. Thus the family may in one sense be defined as "a woman with a child, and a man to look after them." This man is usually the child's father, but in some cultures he is the woman's brother. To include the essential elements of all families everywhere we define the family as "the institutionalized social group charged with the duty of population replacement." [1]

Every society recognizes marriage as the legitimate way to found a family, though its rites for signalizing this step may consist only of wrapping a blade of grass about the fingers of a man and a woman. Marriage is a "formal and durable sexual union of one or more men with one or more women within a set of designated rights and duties." [2]

In spite of its basis in the biological nature of man—the fact that sexual desire knows no season, the need of mother and child for help and protection, the long period of pregnancy and infancy—the family, like any other social institution, cannot be explained solely on biological grounds. These needs could conceivably be satisfied in other ways. Sociologist Robert Bierstedt sees bisexual reproduction as a necessary but not a sufficient condition for the existence of the family. "The sufficient conditions lie in society itself . . . the family performs a number of functions that no other group can perform so well." [3]

Basic Functions   •   *Reproduction* is, of course, a basic func-
of the Family   tion of the family in all times and places.
                                 In one way or another, society instills
                                 in its members the desire to have chil-
dren, reinforcing the powerful sex drive with injunctions to "Be fruitful and mutiply, and replenish the earth." Even in societies with great freedom of sexual expression, conception is surrounded by norms and sanctions that legitimize reproduction and bring stability and order into this

vital activity, insuring that the newborn will be given a chance to survive and that the species will continue.

Another primary function of the family in every culture is to provide for *socially approved expression* of a powerful organic drive—that of *sex*. Usually the outlet that is distinctly preferred is that between married couples. Among many peoples, including the Manus water-dwellers of New Guinea, the San Blas Cuna, and in our own ideal culture pattern, there is no other approved outlet. The mores decree that an individual be chaste and innocent until marriage, and after that he be faithful to the mate. Sexual taboos exist in every society and always with reference to the family organization.

The third basic and universal function of the family is *protection and care of children* through their long period of dependency. Although the actual physical care of the child might be more efficiently and economically handled by larger institutions, the family "combines an intimate, personal response with social care, and it is a combination that no other institution can successfully challenge." [4] We have already commented on the tremendous importance of the family in shaping personality (See Chapter Eleven).

The family also functions as the chief agent of *cultural transmission* during the early years of life, teaching the language, the folkways, mores, values, and beliefs of the culture as interpreted by the parents. In short, it socializes the child and prepares him, with varying degrees of success, for participation in the larger society.

Finally, the family *ascribes many statuses*. Our family names identify us to the larger society. "Our ethnic status, our nationality status, our religious status, our residential status, our class status—sometimes our political status and our educational status as well—are all conferred upon us by our families and, although most of these may later be changed, it is in terms of these statuses that we first gain social recognition." [5]

These five functions are performed by the family in all societies, and taking them all together it is doubtful that any other arrangement would serve these purposes quite as well as does the family.

Subsidiary Functions of the Family • In many societies, the family also serves other functions. In folk societies the entire social organization may be based on kinship. The family is the unit of economic production in folk societies and the chief unit of consumption in all societies. Traditionally the family has also protected and cared for its disabled, indigent, and aged members. Many recreational and religious activities are also primarily family functions. As we shall see later, these subsidiary functions of the family are the ones most affected by the worldwide trend toward an urban industrial society.

Forms • As we noticed earlier, the existence of
of the Family   the family is to be explained not in
terms of the biological imperatives it
satisfies but in terms of society and
culture. Because man is one species, the biological imperatives are the same the world over, but the institution of the family has many variations, especially in such matters as the number of spouses, the locus of authority, the rules of mate selection, and the kinship structure.

Number of spouses. The number of spouses, as we noted in our definition, may be "one or more." Man has, interestingly enough, hit upon all the possible combinations—one man with one woman, one man with more than one woman, one woman with more than one man, and two or more men with two or more women.

We are most familiar with *monogamy*, the marriage of one man and one woman. The natural balance between the number of males and females makes this the most common form of marriage even where other forms are permitted. *Polygamy*, or plural mating, includes *polygyny*, the marriage of one man with two or more women, *polyandry*, the marriage of one woman with two or more men, and group marriage. Least common is the last type, sometimes called *cenogamy*, in which two or more men are mated with two or more women. Where this arrangement exists, it is by no means promiscuous and unregulated. It is usually practiced only among "age mates." Among one group in New Guinea, all men born within a given period of time share duties and privileges, including the sharing of individual wives. Another group in Africa arranges similar reciprocity among all males circumcised at the same time.

Polyandry is rare; among the few places where it is practiced are the arid highlands of Tibet, where it takes several men to support a family. The husbands of one woman are usually brothers. Polygyny is found in many societies, but even where it is sanctioned monogamy is also practiced. Polygyny is not based simply on a desire for sexual variety; in most societies such a wish can be satisfied in other ways. The decision to take another wife may stem from one or all of the following motives that one anthropologist, Edward Ward, found among the Yoruba tribe of Africa—the desire for children, the desire to prove virility, a taboo against sexual relations for three years after the birth of a child, lucky inheritance of a wife, usually from a brother, the death of men in warfare, the economic usefulness of wives in bargaining and labor, and the fact that the number of wives indicates a man's wealth and prestige.[6]

Americans, using their own cultural values as a basis for judgment, are sure that when two or more women are married to the same man there must be a lot of friction. Actually such marriages appear to work quite well in societies where they are approved. The women are often sisters. Usually each woman has a separate hut for herself and her children, and the husband must spend time with her periodically. Women do not appear to be disturbed about the arrangement. Some even encourage their husbands to acquire more wives; after all, it means less work and more prestige for the wife. Also, among nonliterates, where women often far exceed the number of men because of hazards of hunting and warfare, almost all women are thus assured of a husband. It is true that the woman does not have the claim on her husband that she would in our society, but then she has not been brought up to expect it. Jealousy appears where a person senses a threat to his dominance or security in a personal relationship, but where plural marriages are permitted, emotional attachments between man and wife do not have the intensity characteristic of our society.[7]

Locus of authority. In a *patriarchal* family, the father's word is almost law to wife and children. The mother or grandmother controls a *matriarchal* family. In an *equalitarian* family, decisions are jointly made and control is shared between husband and wife, with children also having a voice in family affairs. This type of family is also called "democratic" in contrast to the "authoritarian" family where one of the parents holds the reins tightly. Some cultures actually have child-centered families or very nearly so. Margaret Mead relates in *Growing Up in New Guinea* that if a three-year-old Manus child refused to go home from a visit, the mother would resignedly stay and await his pleasure. She saw in this situation a parody of some American families.

Kinship structure. The family may be conceived of in two ways: as a *conjugal* unit or as a *consanguine* unit. Conjugal families consist of husbands and wives and their children. They may be extended families, in which three generations live within one household and interaction with related conjugal units is intimate and frequent. Or they may be restricted conjugal units, as in our society, where the typical household includes only two generations, other relatives often live far away, and the ties of "uncle," "cousin," and the like, evoke comparatively little loyalty. In a consanguine unit, "blood" or kinship is of greater importance than marriage ties.

Every society recognizes both units, but in some societies—and ours is an example—conjugal relationships are far more important, and in others, such as the San Blas Cuna, consanguine relationships take precedence. In some societies kinship is even more important than among the Cuna, and the entire social organization is based on an elaborate system of kinship relations. Where marital relations are subordinate to blood relations, the family provides more continuity and security for its members. It is not dissolved by death, desertion, or divorce of marital partners. Descent is traced either through the mother's line or the father's, but rarely through both. In the former case, the descent is called matrilineal, and the family consists of a woman, her children, her daughter's children, the children of her daughter's daughters, and so on. The consanguine family where descent is patrilineal includes the patriarch, his children, and the children of his male descendants. Resident in matrilineal consanguine families may be either patrilocal or matrilocal, but in patrilineal families the wife usually moves into the husband's household.

Although the consanguinal family offers stability and security, it discourages individualism. The relative freedom from family ties afforded by the restricted conjugal family is compatible with a culture that stresses individualism and progress.

Endogamy and exogamy. Every culture includes norms that prescribe whom a person may or may not marry. *Exogamy* means that a person must marry outside a certain group and universally includes prohibitions against incest. Incest prohibitions may be limited to near blood relatives or may include an entire clan or a kinship unit within the clan. *Endogamy* demands marriage within a certain group, which usually is determined by residence, nationality, class, race, religion, or other criteria.

Families of orientation and procreation. All but an insignificant number of us spend our early years in a family of *orientation,* into which we are born. Nearly all of us eventually form families of *procreation,* an act that has a more voluntary character. We belong, then, as children to the first, as parents to the second.

The American Family	•	Few aspects of American life have been the target of more criticism than the family. We find in traveling abroad that from movies and magazines for-

eigners have garnered many curious notions about our family folkways and mores. They are sure that unchaperoned dating is synonymous with sexual license, that marital fidelity is neither expected nor desired by American husbands, that most marriages end in divorce, and that our palatial homes are mere stopping places on a gay round of pleasure. These impressions are usually greatly altered when students and other visitors are invited to American homes, most often of middle-class families. They are amazed that the husband does not consider it beneath his dignity to help with the dishes or put the baby to bed, that married couples enjoy mutual friendship and joking relationships with other couples without jealousy, that many parents enjoy companionship with their children, and that a girl who accepts an invitation to go to a dance with a man is not compromising her reputation.

But of cries of woe from Americans themselves there is no end. On the one hand clinging and overprotective "Moms" are blamed for most of the problems of our society, while on the other, parental neglect is decried as the cause of juvenile delinquency. The fact that in recent years there has been one divorce decree granted for every four marriage licenses issued is viewed with great alarm as a sign that the American home is crumbling. Reports of scientific studies of sexual behavior, which need careful interpretation, are used to boost the circulation of magazines and stir up heated controversy over our sexual morals. Journalists, psychiatrists, judges, and ministers combine to give the impression that premarital chastity, parental wisdom, respect for parents on the part of children, marital fidelity, and family unity are at the vanishing point. Many of these critics give the impression that the only solution is to return to the old patriarchal rural family, the solid, stable household of turn-of-the-century America.

After looking long and hard at the American family, social scientists agree that its forms and functions have changed in many ways, and that the values and attitudes of Americans toward marriage and family life have changed along with them, though not always consistently. They see no rational basis, however, for the plea that all we need do is revive the old type of family. That is gone, along with the rural society of which it was a part. The changes that critics decry, social scientists see as part of the process of social change. True, this process is painful, but present disorganization does not bode the eventual end of all family life. Disorganization, they say, is a prelude to reorganization.

Many students of the family hold out the optimistic theory that a new kind of family, better suited to our modern way of life, is emerging from the ruins of the patriarchal rural family. Meanwhile, as new forms and functions emerge, there must necessarily be some confusion and disorientation, for disorder accompanies change in any institution. So many patterns of behavior exist that it is difficult to isolate any one mode of behavior upon which the majority of Americans might agree. In their valuable volumes on the family, social scientists are careful to point out that there is no such thing in our heterogeneous society as a "typical" American family, for there are variations between social classes, rural and urban areas, geographical sections, and between different racial, ethnic, and religious groups. Where some average or typical family is implied in their studies, however, it is usually the urban middle-class family.

Besides trying to trace the trends in family life, social scientists have made numerous studies that can be useful to the young person searching for a mate, the adult wishing to make his marriage more satisfying, the parent anxious to raise his children to be happy and useful members of society, and the adult approaching old age or coping with the problem of aging parents.

Changing Functions of the Modern Family

Economic function. The rural family in folk society is a production unit, largely self-sufficient. The home is a veritable factory. Bread and butter are made there (or whatever their cultural equivalents may be); clothes are fashioned there, perhaps from hand-woven cloth; soap and preserves and fuel and many tools are made and used right on the premises. Each member contributes to the work of house and farm at an early age. Even the toddler does his part; he can feed the chickens, gather eggs, and haul firewood on his sled. As he grows older he tends the herds and learns to help with the planting and harvest. When he is past his physical prime a person still pulls his own weight by doing small but necessary tasks. In rural America children were a financial asset, and a widow with a large brood was a matrimonial prize.

The small urban family is no longer a production unit except in the most limited sense. Usually one person—the breadwinner—is "independent," and the others are "dependents." The breadwinner goes out of the home daily to work for some secondary group—a business, a school, a protective agency—and returns with periodic cash wages that pay for most if not all of the family's needs. Many household jobs have been taken over by commercial agencies—laundries, bakeries, and so forth—or at least eased by modern appliances—electric sewing machines, washers, driers, vacuum cleaners, water heaters and automatic furnaces. The little chores that make children genuinely useful are few in the city home. There may be a lawn to mow, a baby to tend, trash to carry outdoors, the table to clear and set; but there is little really productive work in which the average child can take pride.

This transfer of economic functions to outside agencies or automatic "servants" has convinced many people that the average American housewife has almost nothing to do. This is certainly not the case, especially where there are children. In some ways her tasks are far harder than her mother's, for there is no unmarried sister or aunt or widowed mother in the typical home to ease the isolation and confinement that paradoxically enough is one of the urban housewife's chief problems. Nor do even the best of automatic servants run themselves. Although they ease the back-breaking work, they force housekeeping standards ever higher and, in fact, bring back into the home many of the functions that for a time were frequently delegated to outside agencies. The family is still the chief consumption unit, and on the wife falls the main burden of distributing the available cash to best advantage.

In the old rural society there was little place for the unmarried adult; in fact, he or she was economically at a disadvantage and usually dependent on married relatives. The single male in urban America is, in contrast, better off financially than the married man with a family. Many businesses seek to cater to his needs and wants. Nor does the American girl need a husband to support her. When a young couple marry after a period of economic independence, they find their standard of living drops unless the wife continues to work. Children are economic liabilities for whom parents must buy food and clothes, pay baby sitters and pediatricians, and provide space helmets, music lessons, and an education. And for all this, no economic return nor even any easing of the burden can be expected until the law permits the children to work or until their long education is complete and they can support, not their parents, but themselves.

Women make up more than a third of the nation's labor force. Of nearly 21 million women working at regular jobs today, almost 60 per cent are married. Twenty-seven married women out of 100 work outside the home.[8] It is obvious what a departure this is from the traditional ideas that men are the providers and that woman's place is in the home.

Other traditional functions. State and local governments have taken over many of the protective functions that used to be the province of the family. Fire departments, police departments, welfare agencies, and social security systems all give a measure of security that the small family cannot provide. The religious function has been left largely to Sunday school and church; grace at meals and evening prayers are not often part of the family ritual. Education, too, is regarded by most parents as the province of the schools. The home still plays a large part in inculcating attitudes toward religion and education, however, and can to a large extent either reinforce or nullify what is learned outside.

In urban society recreation and social participation are largely by age and sex groups. Husking bees, harvest festivals, and holiday "gatherings of the clan" have few if any counterparts in urban life. In the city, Junior goes to Cub Scouts, Big Sister to a dance, Mother to her bridge club, and Dad to the bowling alley.

The American family, then, has relinquished many of its traditional social and economic functions. What of the inescapable functions of bearing and rearing children and satisfying the sex drive and the psychological needs of its members?

Reproduction. In the past century and a half, the birth rate has shown a spectacular decline. The number of children per fertile married woman has dropped from 7.8 to 3.5 since 1790, while the size of the average family (defined by the census as a group of related persons living together in the same household) has dropped from 5.7 to 3.4. The graph on page 261 shows the sharp and steady decline from 1871 to the mid-thirties, and the trend since then.

This decline represents a revolutionary change in the reproductive function of the family. In traditional rural society, every additional child was welcomed as an asset. Only in recent decades has the impact of newly invented methods to prevent conception of children been registered in a sharply declining birth rate. The decline has been greatest among urban, upper-income, and non-Catholic groups.

Urbanization is significantly associated with acceptance of the idea that married couples may decide if they want children at all, or how many they want and at what intervals. Everywhere the urban birth rate is lower than the rural. We saw in Chapter Eight that the crude birth rate in many agrarian folk societies is as high as 44. In many urbanized countries, it is half that number. In the United States the crude birth rate is about 25.

One married woman out of six never bears a child; probably half of these are involuntarily childless. Although only one farm woman out of nine is childless, in urban areas one woman out of five is childless; and in general, the larger the city, the greater the percentage of childless women. In 1952, for every 1,000 urban women ever married and having passed their child-bearing period, 2,453 children had been born. Rural non-farm women had had 2,975 children per 1,000 women and rural farm women, 3,514.[9]

There is also a class differential in the birth rate. It tends to form a gradient from a high birth rate in the lower class to a low birth rate in the upper class. For every 1,000 women past their child-bearing period, those in the income group under $1,000 had borne 3,551 children, those in the income group $7,000 and over had borne only 2,095. Broken down by occupational groups, farm laborers and foremen had the largest families, farmers and farm managers next, with laborers third. Professional, technical, and kindred workers had the smallest families, with the families of sales workers only slightly larger.[10]

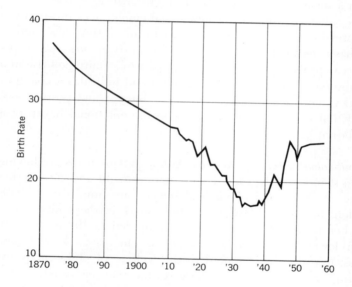

The number of births per 1,000 population, 1871-1958.

Children are a drag on the ambitions of the upwardly mobile middle class, an economic liability interfering with the high standard of living, an obstacle to individualistic pleasure-seeking. Nonetheless, most middle-class couples desire children for various reasons, such as the desire to appear respectable and stable, the desire to enhance the ego and have the affection of children, and the belief that children are necessary to a full life. The lower class has far less knowledge of medically approved contraceptives than the middle class, less ambition, less tense awareness of the responsibility of bringing children up by the latest methods, a more easygoing attitude toward having children, which may reflect the fact that they themselves often came from large families, and a tendency to emphasize living in the present rather than for the future.

Since World War II, fertility has risen in the United States, and the increase has been proportionately highest in urban areas and among the higher-income groups. In 1940 of women 15 to 44 who had ever married, 26.5 per cent were childless; the percentage had dropped to 18 by 1954. During those same years women up to age 35 showed a spectacular increase in number of children born; in the age category 20-24 alone, a 35 per cent increase was registered. "These younger women (those 35 years and younger in 1954) spent most of their child-bearing years in a social climate favorable to high fertility." [11]

The salient feature of this new social climate was prosperity. During the depression the birth rate dropped to an all-time low, and the fact that it has continued to rise long after the postwar spurt was expected to be over can probably be traced in large part to a continued rise in income. Some observers also think that the new trend indicates a change in non-material values, that many people faced by war and postwar insecurity decided that the only real security is in the emotional haven of a home and children.

Care and socialization of children. Although Americans are having fewer children than formerly, they devote more thought and care to those they do have. With the aid of medical science and improved nutrition and sanitation, for every 1,000 babies born alive in the United States only 26 die before their first birthday, as compared to 100 in 1915; this rate is even lower in some other countries. The psychological and social sciences, too, have contributed to the welfare of children by exploring the nature of their needs and the ways they can be socialized with best results for individual happiness and the good of society. They have by no means arrived at "all the answers." In fact, in some respects they have made socialization a heavier burden to conscientious parents haunted by the dicta that "A child's personality is fixed by the time he is five" and "There are no problem children, only problem parents." Swings in the fashion of child care leave some parents confused. The young mother may be told by her mother to "Let him cry it out," for that was the fashion a generation ago. But her grandmother believes in rocking and cuddling and feeding a child when he is hungry. Today the swing is back to Grandma, with the blessing of the scientists. Mothers consult their books by Dr. Spock, a pediatrician, and Dr. Gesell, a child psychologist, to find out how to handle problems of care and discipline. The latest admonition is that they are taking their job too seriously: "Relax; be spontaneous; follow your impulses." For the character of the total relationship between parent and child—one of rejection or acceptance, of affection or ambivalence—is in the long run more important than any detail of technique.

Other agencies contributing to the care and socialization of the child are nursery schools, kindergartens, and public health services. School lunch programs, boys' clubs, and city facilities for recreation and special training also take much of the burden from the home, minimizing the differences in "life chances" for children at various income levels.

Psychological functions of the family: response and security. The individual in urban society has lost so many of the relationships that afforded him intimate response in the extended family and rural neighborhood that he depends on the immediate family almost entirely for satisfying his wish for response. Happiness has become the criterion of success in marriage. Children are desired chiefly for ego satisfaction and affection.

Security, too, is found in the family. "Home," says Robert Frost, "is the place where, when you have to go there, they have to take you in."[12] The homeless are social misfits, highly vulnerable to mental and emotional disorders. In most families a person is sure of an affectionate welcome and knows that interest will be shown in what he is doing. Though feelings may be ambivalent and a person might not choose members of his own family as friends, still there is a tie that can be broken only with much distress and grief.

Many social scientists believe that the stability of the family will depend increasingly upon its ability to satisfy these psychological needs. "Mutual affection is becoming the essential basis of marriage and the family."[13]

Channelization of the sex drive. Although the sex urge is natural and powerful, it is susceptible to social control. Every society has standards of sexual behavior, and although no society is completely successful in keeping sexual behavior within the mores, in a stable society with primary group controls strongly operating, there is comparatively little deviation.

In a changing society, however, the real and the ideal culture patterns may be far apart. Certainly this is true of our complex society. We still subscribe to the mores of premarital chastity, marital fidelity, and modesty in public behavior. The only approved sexual outlet is between a man and his wife. Observation shows, and scientific studies prove, that many Americans either furtively violate these norms while giving them lip service, or openly flout them. About half the women interviewed by Kinsey and his associates had engaged in premarital intercourse (although of these, 53 per cent confined their intimacy to the man they later married). The average American male, according to the same team of researchers, is unfaithful at least once after marriage.

Class differences are reflected in sexual behavior, especially among males.

> Lower-class males, having acquired an intimate and realistic knowledge of the "facts of life" at an early age, often consider sex relations a "natural" part of life. In contrast to the better-educated members of the middle class, they place little value on virginity, have premarital intercourse frequently and do not consider extramarital affairs especially reprehensible. On the other hand, they look upon petting and other erotic techniques widely practiced at the middle-class and especially the college level as abnormal and perverse.[14]

Many forces operate to channel the sex drive into the socially approved outlet of marital relations. Among these are the idea of romantic love, which supposes that you find the one and only mate and live happily ever after; gossip and social ostracism for those known to deviate; pressure to marry; and the constant advice of church, school, and parents. But the counterpressures are strong. The heterogeneity of our society makes for disagreement on what is moral and immoral behavior. Its mobility and anonymity make it possible to escape the control of the primary group. The auto whisks young people miles away from the scrutiny of parents and neighbors; the motel asks few questions; birth control techniques are more efficient; fear of the loss of heaven and pain of hell seems to be diminishing. Mass media of communication and entertainment play up sex heavily in a way that would have shocked Americans of a generation or two ago.

The divergence between our ideal and real sexual behavior may be at least partly explained by our cultural tendency to think in terms of opposites, extremes, either—or. Heterosexual love is regarded as either spiritual or physical rather than as a blend of the two. If a person does not subscribe to Victorian prudishness, he must be an advocate of "free love." Morality is made to sound somehow grim, unattractive, puritanical; the sign of sophistication is supposed to be either frivolity or brutal frankness. From the hush-hush attitude of a few decades ago we have swung to great frankness even in mass-circulation magazines. This ambivalence almost invariably strikes observers from cultures where sex is accepted as part of the mature person's life, but is not so heavily emphasized, as an evidence of immaturity.

Ascription of status. As we have seen, the family ascribes many of our statuses. Its class status determines our "life chances" and its "style of life," the atmosphere in which we are reared. In modern urban society, and especially in a mobile, individualistic society such as ours, however, this function diminishes in importance, for how a person appears to others and what he does are frequently far more important in determining his status than is the status of his parents. The original nationality status of the parents and grandparents, too, becomes increasingly less important in our society.

Other statuses, however, are harder to shed, for biological, cultural, and emotional reasons; race and religion are the chief instances. Citizenship status is still ascribed at birth and can be changed only by formal legal procedures.

Romantic Love   •   The ideal of romantic love is as old as our literary heritage, perhaps older. We find it in Homer's epics and Sappho's lyrics, in the medieval tales of knights and ladies, in the sighs of Elizabethan poets. But only in a few countries, and almost exclusively in modern times, has romantic love been associated with marriage.

The cult of romantic love has flourished in the United States, where individualism and the belief in happiness as a life goal furnish fertile soil for its growth. From childhood on, Americans are taught its creed and its code. Our movies and magazines and popular songs all reflect and promote this cultural belief. We may distinguish several articles of this creed.

There is a perfect mate for each of us decreed by fate as "the right one," the "somebody who" we are destined somewhere, somehow, to meet. Some enchanted evening, we fall in love at first sight, on the basis of physical attraction. Therefore romantic love emphasizes external characteristics that can be appreciated at once: physical beauty, youth, glamour, vivacity. Most of us do not, even with the aid of fashions, cosmetics, elevator shoes, and padded shoulders, measure up to the ideal of "tall, dark and handsome men" or "glamour girls." How, then, do most of us manage to find mates? Because love is blind, and under its spell and magic we idealize the beloved.

Love overrides all considerations of differences in social status, family background, and the like. In fact, great differences and difficulties only make the affair more "romantic," adding interest to the period between "boy meets girl" and "boy gets girl." Love is all that matters; "love conquers all."

How do you know it's love? Because there is an ecstasy, a thrill, that lifts the relationship out of the realm of the ordinary. You can't eat, you can't sleep, you think about nothing but the lover. You are "crazy" about each other. The love affair is carried on in an unreal atmosphere of moonlight and roses, of glamour and excitement. What about sexual intimacies? The long-established romantic code does not sanction them; they must wait for marriage. Of late, however, popular songs, like other elements of mass entertainment and communication, play up sex more and more heavily.

The love affair leads to marriage and a rose-covered cottage filled with healthy, happy babies. But here, too, there is ambivalence. In our American culture you find two diametrically opposed ideas—often subscribed to by the same person. One is that youth is the time for love and romance, marriage and adulthood a drab anticlimax. "Have fun while you're young; these are the best years of your life. Time enough to settle down later," oldsters advise young people. On the other hand, the ideal marriage is one in which the romantic excitement of courtship is carried on, in which the two never take one another for granted, in which souvenirs and places and dates are surrounded with sentiment and ritually remembered. If love "degenerates" into anything as colorless as conjugal affection, then the marriage is considered a failure.

To question this intense cultural belief in romantic love almost amounts to heresy. But many social scientists have done so. One writer calls it "a sort of socially approved and temporary insanity . . . a pleasant form of mass delusion," and remarks that in many cultures cases of such violent emotional attachment are regarded as pitiable, disgraceful, and tragic.[15] They observe, however, that romantic love serves a useful purpose in our society. It is a "definition of the situation" and as such a means of social control. People behave according to its expectations because they have been taught to do so. It is a cultural modification of the sex drive, providing adolescents with a means of sublimation and redirection of this impulse.[16] But certain elements in the romantic complex place serious obstacles in the way of wise mate selection and successful marital adjustment.

There are perhaps hundreds of people with whom each of us might achieve a satisfactory marriage relationship, provided we ourselves are good marriage risks. The belief that there is only one, and sooner or later we are fated to meet him or her, minimizes the importance of adjustment. When problems arise in marriage, it is easy to decide that it was all a mistake, and this was not the right one after all; the marriage must therefore end so the person can go on looking for the right one.

The belief in love at first sight and the stress on external attributes emphasize physical attraction while minimizing traits of character and personality, cultural and social background—factors that social scientists have found to be more important to successful adjustment than is powerful initial attraction.

The belief that marriage is a failure unless it preserves all the ecstasy and thrill of courtship is an obstacle to adjustment, for adjusting to another person in an intimate relationship means forming interdependent habits of life, which inevitably creates the comfortable routine and "taking for granted" that the romanticists deplore.

All this does not mean that social scientists do not believe in love nor in the importance of sexual attraction. Physical attraction is the strong foundation of most marriages. But love requires time to develop, for it involves emotional identification, sympathy and understanding, tenderness and affection. There is, of course, such a thing as strong mutual attraction upon short acquaintance; our culture has prepared us to interpret it as "love at first sight." But only as a couple become really well acquainted and discover "mutual interests," enjoy one another's company, reach a certain measure of agreement on goals and values, and learn to accommodate to the personality traits of the other can they be said to have the kind of love necessary to successful marriage.

Stages • **in American** **Family Life**
Dating. In almost all societies the selection of a mate is the business of parents, matchmakers, or other designated adults. The young person may be betrothed even before he reaches puberty, and may not even see his mate until the wedding night. In many countries, even today, young people meet only under strict supervision, and choice of a mate is restricted to those considered acceptable by the family, who put considerations of economic and social status above the wishes of their children.

In our society, by long tradition, each person is supposed to be free to choose his own mate on the basis of love. Our belief in individualism and the pursuit of personal happiness tolerates no interference from others in the course of true love. The impersonality of city life and the loss of many primary group controls also made necessary some way in which young people could get to know one another. Dating has been the American answer for several decades.

Dating—making social engagements with a person of the opposite sex—begins at different ages in different sub-cultural groups; in general, it begins earlier in the city, often roughly coinciding with puberty. Dates are usually planned around specific recreational activities such as parties,

"Plymouth convertible, 1954, no radio!"

movies, picnics, and dances. The nature of these activities is closely correlated with class status. The study of "Elmtown's youth" revealed that lower-class youngsters go on jalopy rides and patronize taverns, middle-class students are in the majority at high-school dances, and children of the country club set prefer to congregate there. On the rare occasions when class lines are crossed in dating, the persons involved are on adjacent levels of prestige.[17]

Dating is a matter of extreme importance to young people, for much of their recreational life and their status with friends and schoolmates depend on the number and nature of their dates. One social scientist found much campus dating connected with status considerations. Girls won prestige by dating fraternity men with cars, money, ability to dance, smooth manners and clothes, and a good "line," while boys rated available dates according to popularity, smart clothes, ability to dance well, a smooth line, and sorority membership. Although doubtless somewhat exaggerated, this study does emphasize the prestige function of dating.[18]

Although dating has overtones of courtship and romance, the fact that it is often a preliminary to courtship and marriage is not especially important during adolescence. It is primarily a vehicle for having fun and getting acquainted. But it serves other important ends. Dating is a socializing process, one of the ways in which young people acquire understandings and social skills that later prove valuable in adult life. It affords an opportunity for becoming acquainted with various types of people and deciding which kinds are most congenial. It is a time for "window shopping ... with no commitment to buy the merchandise on display." [19]

A cultural pattern of increasing importance is "going steady." The frustrations of competitive dating are avoided and couples are assured of dates for all important school and college affairs. Some observers call it "training for monogamy," believing that it encourages a more sober outlook on marriage than does competitive dating. It provides emotional security during the turbulent period of adolescence. Boys and girls who "go steady" typically see one another in many different situations, including the family setting, that do not have the tinsel and glamour of a dance or a movie; they do homework together, and talk about many subjects instead of exchanging "lines." Critics of the trend believe it leads to early sexual experimentation and early marriage and deprives young people of the excitement that usually attended the older pattern of dating.

Courtship and engagement. It is used to be that if a boy walked a girl home from prayer meeting twice, people assumed that he was courting her. Today dating carries no necessary implication of courting. But it is expected that after a certain number of years of "having a good time," a person will "fall in love" and "take someone seriously."

The average young American rarely balks at public demonstrations of affection and often is convinced that he is "in love," that this is "the real thing." A person may be in love several times before he marries, but according to at least one study the heartache over a broken romance does not ordinarily last long.[20] Our romantic complex invests each such affair with thrills, doubts, excitement, and anxiety. It "defines the situation" in terms of questions: "Love or infatuation?" "Is he the one?" If it comes to marriage, then he is the one, and it is love. If the affair ends, then there are ego-salving explanations: It was infatuation; he was not the right one.

The confusion in American sex attitudes is perhaps felt most strongly during the period when a person is ripe for emotional involvement, with the thought of marriage always in the picture. It has been found that the sex drive in men is strongest at age 18, long before most are ready to marry. With sexual stimulation bombarding the couple from every side, with social controls weakened, and with the confusion of values we have already referred to, the real patterns of sex conduct deviate increasingly from the ideal cultural norms.

The decision to marry is formalized by an announcement of the couple's engagement. With society notified of the marriage plans, the two can spend more and more time together. If they are not determined to shun every issue on which they might disagree—which merely postpones quarrels till after marriage—they discuss such questions as where they will live, whether or not the wife will work outside the home, their attitudes toward parenthood, and how they should handle the money. None of these questions would have come up half a century ago, for roles then were clear-cut and choices few.

Social scientists have found that happy marriages are usually preceded by a fairly long engagement period, with about two or three years the ideal length. The couple then has time to test their compatibility. This is regarded as the function of engagement today. Broken engagements are not, as they previously were, considered broken contracts.

Mate selection. Although few Americans lose faith in most elements of the romantic complex entirely, as they continue to mature and to associate with different types of people most abandon the less defensible tenets of the creed. Only the perennial adolescent insists on the same "man of her dreams" at twenty that she vowed she must find at fourteen. She realizes that externals are comparatively unimportant, but she is likely to feel there is something wrong about weighing the character and background of prospective mates rather than relying on emotional attraction alone.

The field of choice. Convinced that sooner or later the right man will come along, one girl may criticize another girl frank and realistic enough to admit that she chooses her school, her job, and her leisure-time pursuits largely with an eye to the matrimonial prospects available. But it may be a mistake to limit oneself to chance contacts. Even in a large city—perhaps especially in a large city—a person's circle of friends is small. By taking advantage of the many voluntary associations designed to provide opportunities for young people to meet—Y.M.C.A.'s and Y.W.C.A.'s, hobby clubs, hiking clubs, church groups, and youth hostels—a person can enlarge his field of choice.

The sex ratio indicates that women will be more successful in finding a mate in the West, in small towns and rural areas, and in the South. The college woman's chances of marrying are somewhat lower than average, for the boys she dates on campus are likely to wait a few years to get established before marrying, and then to choose younger girls. Her independence may scare off prospects, or she may just not meet them in her job. When she does marry, however, studies show that she is more likely to be happy than the girl with less education.

Many of us, wondering what one person "sees" in another, fall back on the old cliché that "opposites attract." Like many clichés, this one is just not true (except for opposite sexes!). Social scientists find that like tends to marry like, in racial, religious, and ethnic background, in intelligence and temperament, and in general physical characteristics. Men tend to marry girls three years younger than themselves. The average age at which girls marry is 20 and for men, 23. Even in large cities many people marry someone whose home is near their own. This is less surprising when we consider that neighborhoods are usually composed of families of the same general background.

Predicting success in marriage. Among those who have studied happy and unhappy marriages are sociologists Ernest W. Burgess and Leonard S. Cottrell, working as a team, and psychologist Lewis M. Terman. They analyze some of the important factors in the adjustment of American middle-class couples. Their statistical findings are probably most useful in screening out the worst likely combinations and pointing out the best. Individual couples fill out the prediction schedules of Burgess and Cottrell not only when they are dubious about marriage, but also because they want to go into it with eyes wide open, and being aware of likely points of friction, can deal with them in an intelligent manner. The chief conclusions of these two studies are in substantial agreement.

(1) *People are conditioned from childhood on to be good or bad marriage risks.* Those whose parents were happily married and who had a happy childhood are more likely to succeed in marriage.

(2) *Similarity of background eases marital adjustment.* Although biologists have found no ill effects resulting from racial intermarriage, the social difficulties that arise from such marriages in our society are enormous. International marriages are also risky, because of differences in

language, cultural values, and customs and manner of living. Interfaith marriages were found to be successful by Burgess and Cottrell, but no one in their sample had been married longer than six years. It is when children come along that the parents feel both churches and both families pulling at them. Terman found this was a serious hurdle, and most social scientists agree. They point out that although a Catholic and a Protestant or a Gentile and a Jew might agree on basic theological doctrines, their values and philosophies may be irreconcilable in the intimate relationship of marriage, even when both partners have renounced their childhood faith. Only when husband and wife are exceptionally mature and tolerant and when circumstances are such that they neither feel much social disapproval nor much pressure from in-laws, do mixed marriages appear to stand much chance of success.

(3) *Certain personality traits are distinctly favorable to successful marriage.* Among these the chief one is happy temperament, the "habit of happiness." Other important traits are adaptability and the ability to identify with others in a spirit of sympathy and tolerance. A positive approach to problems is also an advantage in reaching adjustment. Those qualities that indicate emotional instability, immaturity, or neurotic tendencies are hazards to marital happiness.

(4) *The sociable, conventional person is a good marriage risk.* These qualities may be tested by such facts as attendance at Sunday school and church, number of years of education, membership in several organizations, and residence in a neighborhood of single-family houses, where stability is greater than in areas of multiple-family dwellings.

(5) *Similar interests and values are very important.* There should be substantial agreement on such things as the proper role for women, handling money, sexual behavior, having children, leisure-time pursuits, and religion. This is one reason why social scientists advocate fairly long engagements with plenty of opportunity to observe the other person in different situations, especially in the family setting.

(6) *A moderate income at marriage rather than a low or high one is associated with happiness, as is a regular work record and a degree of security.* But economic factors are given very low weight in predicting failure or success in marriage because others are regarded as more important.

(7) *Age at marriage is important, largely as one indication of emotional maturity* (though many girls of 18 are more mature emotionally than others of 25) *and because older couples have probably had more time to test their compatibility.* Marriages between very young couples do not turn out as well as marriages between older couples. The optimum age appears to be between 21 and 25 for women and for men, nearer 30.

(8) *Certain occupations also appear to be more likely to make for success in marriage than others.* Men who do not travel or do not come into contact with many other women under conditions where few social controls are operating—professors and farmers, for example—are likely to make better husbands than do traveling salesmen and actors.

(9) *But what about love?* The reader may conclude from what has gone before that he should go about with a list in hand checking off prospects against all these factors and finally settling on the person with the highest score. But a person can be careful without being cold and calculating. The authors know a young college couple who were very much in love and thinking of marriage but very conscious of the importance of determining compatibility before marriage as much as possible. They filled out Burgess's prediction schedules and mailed them in. After analyzing them, Professor Burgess replied that they were likely to have a happy marriage but there was one serious lack. In answering the question, "Why do you want to marry this person?" neither one had mentioned love! We shudder to think what might have happened to the affair if one of them had given love as a reason and the other had not. As it was they laughed off their omission as stemming from college courses in which they were gravely warned against being trapped by the romantic fallacy! [21]

Husband-wife relationships. Even when a couple marries with everything statistically in their favor, with a long period of testing their compatibility behind them, there are many adjustments to make. They must learn to live together in the day-by-day intimacy of marriage. This learning process begins on the honeymoon, eased by the rosy glow of romance and discovery. The fact that the two are away from family and friends and usually in a very pleasant environment eases the transition from the excitement of courtship to the routine of married life.

Chief areas of adjustment. Not all honeymoons, however, are idyllic. Newlyweds sometimes find to their dismay that even sexual adjustment takes time. In a study by Judson Landis of the time it took 409 couples married an average of 20 years to reach an adjustment in six major areas, only about 53 per cent of the couples said that they achieved a mutually satisfying sex relationship right from the start. In many cases, it took months or years to reach adjustment, and in one case out of eight such adjustment never was achieved. It took longer to adjust sexual relationships than to agree on money, social activities, in-law relationships, religious activities, and mutual friends.

This does not mean that almost half these couples were biologically mismated and should never have married. Biologically speaking, satisfactory sexual relations are possible between almost all couples. But the solid facts of life are the facts of the imagination, and each person approaches marriage with some convictions on what is right, proper, and necessary in sex, and some attitudes and emotions regarding it. The man may, consciously or otherwise, subscribe to the Victorian notion that women are passive and men dominant, and that his own gratification is all that matters. His wife may shrink from the relationship because she considers sex degrading and shameful, and just a necessary concession to the brutal nature of the male animal. Or she may find it unsatisfactory because he does not try to gratify her needs, which are just as real as his, although she may be slower to respond. Or dissatisfaction with the sex act may be the result of tensions in other areas, for it is impossible to separate the psychic aspect of sex from the physical. The only way to achieve a fully satisfactory sexual relationship in most marriages is to resolve conflicts in other areas first.

Conflict in other areas, on the other hand, sometimes causes a marriage to fail, even though the husband and wife have reached a satisfactory sexual adjustment.

The question of money takes almost as long as that of sex to adjust in most marriages. Two simply cannot live as cheaply as one. Often there is a sudden drop in the standard of living of both bride and groom. The question of whether or not the wife should work comes up in many urban marriages, and may never be solved to the satisfaction of both. Spending habits may differ; one may be parsimonious and the other extravagant. There may be disagreement about how the money should be spent. Given enough to live on, the amount is not so important as is the agreement on how to handle it. The wife may expect to take charge of the finances or the husband may claim the privilege. In many middle-class marriages where there is general agreement on finances, a joint checking account with the wife as bookkeeper is a mutually satisfactory arrangement. Other couples prefer the allowance or budget systems.

About two-thirds of the couples in Landis' study agreed about social activities and in-law relationships from the start, while another 10 per cent took less than a year to reach a satisfactory arrangement. About three-fourths had no disagreement about religious activities or mutual friends.

In general, the sooner adjustment was reached, the happier the marriage was in the long run. If the couple failed to reach agreement in three areas the marriage was almost certain to be a failure; even two areas of conflict endanger the happiness of the marriage.[22]

Role confusion as a source of discord. The wife does most of the adjusting in American marriages. Much of the confusion and disorganization of modern family life is closely tied up with changes in the status and role of women. No longer does a girl grow up expecting to be a homebody, a wife and mother. She always considers that probability, in fact usually wishes for it, but she also dreams of a "career"—rarely a mere "job"—as an airline stewardess, teacher, nurse, department store buyer, actress, and so forth. It is never quite clear to her just how she will manage marriage and a career, too. Many girls prepare to be nurses or teachers but expect to work only a year or two. This is often a waste of time, money, and training, for they may not work as well as they would have if they really had planned a long-term career, they may never work at all, or they may find after marriage that they cannot keep up their skills for lack of part-time employment. Americans are proud of the fact that few if any fields are closed to women; but controversy is now raging on whether schools and colleges are doing an adequate job of preparing women for their inescapable role in the home. As one college graduate put it, she learned in college how to be a successful man, but had to learn by herself how to be a successful woman.

A *Fortune* survey in 1946 found that 25 per cent of the women questioned wished they had been born men while only 3 per cent of the men were dissatisfied with their sex. The feminist emphasis on the rights of women as something to be wrested from men has contributed to a feeling that the sexes are competitive rather than complementary.

Sociologist Clifford Kirkpatrick has illuminated much of the confusion over the status of women by describing three possible roles in terms of privileges and obligations.

(1) The *wife-and-mother* role is the traditional role of the married woman. It implies as privileges security, the right to support, alimony in the case of divorce, respect as a wife and mother, a certain amount of domestic authority, loyalty of the hubsand to one who has borne him children, and a more or less sentimental gratitude from husband and children. Corresponding obligations include bearing and rearing children, making a home, rendering domestic service, loyal subordination of self to the economic interests of the husband, and acceptance of a limited range of interests and activity.

(2) The *companion* role is essentially a leisure-class phenomenon. The privileges pertaining to this role include sharing pleasures with

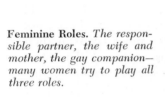

Feminine Roles. *The responsible partner, the wife and mother, the gay companion—many women try to play all three roles.*

the husband, receiving a more romantic emotional response, being the object of admiration, receiving funds adequate for dress and recreation, having leisure for social and educational activity, and the receiving of a certain amount of chivalrous atttention. On the other hand, it implies as obligations, the preservation of beauty under the penalty of marital insecurity, the rendering of ego and libido satisfaction to the husband, and the cultivation of social contacts advantageous to him, the maintenance of intellectual alertness, and the responsibility for exorcising the demon of boredom.

(3) Finally, there is the *partner* role, corresponding to a new definition of the cultural situation that is gradually emerging. This entails the privileges of economic independence, equal authority in regard to family finances, acceptance as an equal, exemption from one-sided personal or domestic service to the husband, equal voice in determining locale of residence, and equality in regard to social and moral liberty. The obligation side of the balance sheet would include renouncing alimony save in the case of dependent children, complete sharing of the legal responsibilities of the family, willingness to dispense with any appeal to chivalry, and equal responsibility to maintain the family status by success in a career.[23]

This multiplicity of roles contributes to personality conflict and marital discord in several ways. Women have difficulty in choosing which role they will play; they feel frustrated because in many ways these roles are mutually incompatible and yet they may be expected to play two or three. The young girl may have to shift roles. She may "play dumb" and act the clinging vine with men whereas actually she is a sturdy oak. Or she may be urged by her family to prepare for a career and in the same breath told to be feminine. Women may perform one role through duty or habit while yearning to play a different one. They may disagree with their husbands on which role is right for them. Finally, a woman may assume the obligations of more than one role without being given the corresponding privileges, or she may demand the privileges of a role she does not perform.[24]

The role of the homemaker. Biology decrees that most women must play primarily the wife and mother role, though they may at different times of their married life—or even at the same time—play the other roles as well. (See illustration "Feminine Roles" on p. 276.) Adequate performance of the wife and mother role is so essential to the happiness of the home and the welfare of society that it behooves us to ask why there is so much dissatisfaction with it and what can be done about it.

The role is by no means an easy one. Even with automatic servants, much housework is just plain drudgery. The woman "knows that she is the unhired help doing the hack work of the world." [25] The care of young children is an exacting, tiring, round-the-clock job. The young urban mother is also alone, more isolated in the city than was the farm wife in the extended family, where aunts and grandmothers were often part of the household, providing adult companionship as well as willing hands. The radio, TV set, and telephone are poor substitutes for primary contacts.

She has not been prepared for her role in terms of either skills or attitudes. Life in the typical middle-class small family affords little training in child care and housekeeping. Mothers often inadvertently instill in their daughters the idea that housework is menial and degrading. Either they give them the lowliest chores to do, such as dishwashing and dusting, or tell them to "run along and study," or "run along and have a good time." All through high school and college, the girl is guided toward earning a living outside the home.

Finally, the role is neither clearly defined nor, in American society, given much respect. The home-bound wife apologetically gives her occupation as "just a housewife." "Do you work?" "No, I am just a housewife." Father indulgently asks, when he comes home and flings himself into a chair after a hard day at the office, "Well, and what have you been doing all day?"

If the role of homemaker is defined as at least as essential as that of breadwinner, then it follows that it deserves as much preparation. Courses in home economics, child psychology, and marriage and family living, as well as women's magazines, stress not only the skills involved —important as these are to the home—but also the importance of an atmosphere of love and well-being.

Some progress—but very little—has been made in inventing agencies and techniques to ease the monotony and isolation of housework and child care. Cooperative nursery schools are increasingly popular. Some homemakers trade baby-sitting and even some household tasks. Some social scientists advocate the establishment of "community work centers" where mothers can meet to iron, wash, sew and mend together, while their small children play together. A common scene in campus housing projects after World War II was a young father in faded suntans hanging out the wash or taking baby out in the stroller to do the marketing. As the work day is shortened, more and more fathers help with the house and children. When the "partner" role is played by men at home, too, women have more time and energy for the role of companion.

Accommodation and release of tensions. When two personalities live together in the continuing intimacy of marriage, tensions and conflicts are almost bound to arise. Furthermore, many people use the marriage partner as a target for releasing frustrations that have nothing to do with family life. (See the cartoon below.) Resentments that a man cannot "take out" on the boss or his colleagues at work may emerge at home as snapping at his wife. She in turn may bewilder the children by turning on them with a sudden order or reprimand.

The family can, of course, serve as a "shock-absorber" by providing a place where a person feels understood and at home and need not be on his best behavior at all times. Many families have worked out effective

techniques for relieving frustration, such as postponing serious discussions until after the evening meal, working on a family "woodpile" or punching bag or absorbing hobby, asking permission to excuse oneself when he is becoming overwrought, agreeing on distress signals that gently warn husband or wife that one is "touchy," and going out together to "get away from it all."

When more serious tensions arise, help may be sought from a trained and objective marriage counselor. Some cities provide this service for families who cannot afford private counseling. Although prospects for a happy solution of problems are best when help is sought early, many marriages have been "saved" when neither partner could see any hope for reconciliation.

Parent-child relationships. When a child comes along, the marriage becomes a family. Every aspect of interaction is affected by the new roles of parents: the way they spend their time and money, their interests, their affection for each other, their time together, and especially their recreation. There is more noise, confusion, work, and expense. Growing children present numerous problems of health, discipline, and guidance, to say nothing of demands on time and money.

This responsibility appears to weigh very heavily on modern middle-class parents, as we pointed out earlier. Many tense and anxious parents feel that they have been cheated, that they are missing something, for they have always heard that having children is one of the most rewarding experiences in life. When they find it is also one of the most demanding, these individualistic, happiness-pursuing products of American culture find it difficult to retain their perspective. They may leave much of the task of socialization and care to others—in which case it may be done badly—or they may decide that "the children are all that matters."

In many folk societies, the family is a cooperative unit insofar as production and consumption, and even recreation, are concerned; and children are eased naturally into their adult roles as they work and play with their parents. In modern urban society, especially in the higher-income groups, the worlds of children, adolescents, and adults are to a large extent separate, with different cultural patterns.

Sociologist Arnold Green has analyzed the problem of the "middle-class male child" in the middle-income, well-educated urban family. The father is in the crucial years of his career when children come along. He feels ambivalent toward them because they cost time, money, and energy that could be spent on achieving success and hedonistic enjoyment. It is taken for granted that he must send them to college. Meanwhile, every magazine and book on child-rearing places a heavy psychological burden on the parents, and the father finds his wife cannot be as much of a partner and companion as he wishes. She feels a diffuse anxiety for the physical and psychological well-being of the children, and in her desire to do things "right," finds the job much harder than did her grandmother.

The child is constantly supervised. Great emphasis is placed on "love." He is made emotionally dependent on his parents, who demand good behavior as the price of love. They also prod him to compete with his peers, with whom they constantly and anxiously compare his behavior and achievements. Inside the home he has been trained to submission and dependence; now the love he has been taught to need demands that he succeed outside the home, and in order to succeed he must develop independence, firmness of purpose, and some aggressiveness. To these contradictory pressures Green attributes "much of the emotional insecurity and self-defeating striving in the modern world." [26]

A number of studies have shown that lower-class mothers are more permissive in the basic disciplines of feeding, weaning, and toilet-training than are middle-class mothers; but there is some likelihood that middle-class mothers, under the influence of the latest advice, are becoming more permissive. They still tend, however, to impose stricter discipline and to set higher standards of cleanliness, politeness, responsibility, and school achievement. Lower-class children stay up later, go to movies more often, play in the street without supervision, and are allowed greater freedom of emotional expression than middle-class children.[27]

During adolescence many chidren in our society are confused and rebellious, many parents bewildered and dismayed. In many societies children do not suffer a stormy and uncooperative adolescence. This is in part because values hold steady from one generation to another and because status is clearly defined, with tribal rites marking passage from one status to another. In our changing society, the confusion of values presents youth with many problems, and the fact that their role is not clearly defined in terms of privileges and obligations frustrates both them and their parents. There is no gradual easing into duties at the parent's side. Instead the teen-ager sees ahead years of dependence and schooling, and yet feels strong drives for ego satisfaction and sexual expression. He is told in one breath that he is old enough to do something, in the next that he is still a child. He is given considerable leeway, then is caught up short. The patterns are not clear. In urban society, parents are particularly vulnerable to the plea that "everybody does it." In some communities parents and teen-agers evolve "codes" concerning hours, places where they may go, and the like. Those parents are most successful who have established a habit of family agreement on important policies while leaving the youngster increasingly on his own as he shows he can handle more freedom.

The empty nest and old age. With the period of child-rearing shortened as families grow smaller, and with life expectancy lengthening, many parents find themselves in their forties or fifties with an "empty nest." This very often is a shock to the mother who has devoted years to home and children. Many of the difficulties of the menopause, doctors now believe, are associated with this loss of one role and the inability to replace it with another and equally satisfying one. Many in-law troubles also arise from the fact that parents are unwilling to relinquish the privilege of dominating their children and want to go on "living their lives for them." The mother who has used her spare time to cultivate other interests, whether talents, hobbies, civic and women's clubs, charities, or politics, is least disoriented when her children no longer need her. If she has not allowed her job or professional skills to get rusty, she may put them to use. At least one book on family life advocates that trained women be provided with part-time jobs during the child-rearing years so that they will be happier and benefit society by using their training.[28]

The husband-wife relationship also depends largely on the way it was developed or neglected during the years of child-rearing. If the two drifted apart in recreational and other interests, always speaking of the time they would have to do things together later on, they often find they no longer have the same interests.

An increasing proportion of our population (about 15 million) are over age 65. In many respects there is inadequate provision made for the aged in our society. The emphasis on youth, which is an outgrowth of our pioneering days when youth and strength were distinct assets in the difficult task of building a new country, has prevented us from adopting a sensible attitude toward aging. We fight every wrinkle and despair over each gray hair. Employers draw the line unreasonably low, often refusing to hire women over 40 and men over 45 for many kinds of jobs, and retiring them at age 60. Students of the subject of aging insist that one man of 70 may actually be age 50 in terms of physical condition and alertness, while a man of 50 may be a decade or two older in these same terms.

The feeling that a person is too old to be useful is a distinct blow to his self-esteem. Forced retirement is so often followed by steady physical decline and death that observers think the psychological stimulus of a job is one thing that keeps people alive. The person facing retirement is in the same situation as the mother facing the empty nest; he may prepare for it by cultivating other interests, perhaps developing a hobby or avocation into a part-time job, or working at some civic or community project.

Family Crises   •   All families face crises. But no critical period or occasion—be it desertion or death or loss of the job or the discovery of unfaithfulness—is exactly the same for one family as it is for another. An equation useful in understanding this variation is as follows: "A (the event) $\longrightarrow$ interacting with B (the family's crisis-meeting resources) $\longrightarrow$ interacting with C (the definition the family makes of the event) $\longrightarrow$ produces X (the crisis)." [29]

When Mr. Brown lost his job, his family held him blameless. The family had a conference and everyone pitched in to see what he could do. Mother found a part-time job clerking. The oldest girl took care of the smaller children. There was no nagging, and economies were practiced cheerfully. As a result father's self-confidence remained high, and although times were bad he found another good position in two months.

Mr. Smith had the same type of job as Mr. Brown. When he lost his job a big quarrel with Mrs. Smith took place in front of the children in which Mrs. Smith said she had married a failure. Smith's anxiety was further increased by this quarrel and the subsequent loss of face with his wife and children. He began to drink. The antagonism was reflected in a decrease in sexual relations with his wife. This family's definition of the loss of his job, added to its lack of crisis-meeting resources, intensified the tragedy of the original event and led to a major crisis in which the Smiths broke up and finally were divorced.

Divorce. Marriages end in death, divorce, or desertion. Each represents a severe crisis in the family, although in the case of divorce the crisis may have long since passed, the legal decree being merely formal recognition of it. In 1890 death and divorce together terminated 33 marriages out of every 1,000. Today the figure is closer to 30, so in a sense the family is more durable than it used to be. But today's lower figure can be traced mainly to the decrease in premature death. Actually, around four times as many marriages per thousand end in divorce today as in 1890.

In some ways divorce is a more serious problem than death. Society has organized to meet the emotional needs of the bereaved; but when divorce occurs, the emotional needs of those concerned are increased rather than met, and they are left to work out their own solutions. There are often ill will and bitterness; friends take sides; children may be fought over (in 1955, children under 18 were involved in half of all divorce cases); and there are still some people who think that any divorcee is an evil woman. Many people have religious scruples about divorce, regardless of the difficulties encountered in the marriage. Court procedures are such as to put the weight of guilt on one party. Finally, divorce is damaging to a person's self-esteem, for it is an admission of failure in an important area of living. Thus it is bound to leave emotional scars.

Our divorce rate has increased phenomenally since 1867, almost ten times as fast as the population. There are a number of ways of computing the divorce rate, none completely satisfactory. A crude measure often used is the ratio of divorces to marriages in a given year. If the fact that rarely does a divorce dissolve a marriage within the same year is kept in mind, this index can be useful. In 1870 there was only one divorce for every 32.1 marriages; in 1900 the rate was 1 to 12.7. Just before World War II the ratio was 1 to 6. In 1946 a sharp postwar rise in the divorce rate brought the ratio to one for every 3.8 marriages. In 1955 the rate was one for every 4 marriages. Why is this rate so high? Many think they know the answer: "Liquor," "gambling," "other women," "lack of religion." Others look at the legal reasons for granting divorces and conclude that cruelty, desertion, and adultery are the chief causes of divorce. The legal reasons and the real reasons, however, often bear little relation to each other, because the real causes of friction are so often not the grounds on which a judge can legally grant a divorce. Nor does the rise in the divorce rate necessarily mean fewer marriages are happier now than formerly, any more than additional hospitals are an index of a decline in health.

The high divorce rate is in part the result of historic trends that have changed the functions and values of the family. In the past, many things kept even unhappy marriages together: moral and religious convictions about the evil of divorce, the social control of the extended family and neighborhood, and economic interdependence that made it difficult for either husband or wife to get along without the help of the other. All these influences have all but disappeared in urban living. The family has lost many traditional functions; today affection is the chief bond that holds the family together. Our individualism and the emphasis on romantic love and happiness have led us to expect a high degree of personal happiness in marriage. In this connection, easy divorce laws may contribute to the high rate of divorce by presenting an easy way out for those who are disillusioned with romantic love and not mature enough to realize they must work toward building a successful marriage. "The point is sometimes made that in former times, when divorce was not socially acceptable, many people suffered through life in unhappy marriages because they had no escape. That is true. It is also true that many marriages now end in divorce that formerly would have been successful. If they had no easy way out, the partners in these marriages would recognize the necessity for working through problems." [30] The fact that most divorces now occur in the second or third year of marriage bears out this argument; the median duration of marriages broken by divorce is 6.6 years.

What can be done about it? A noted judge, Paul Alexander of Toledo, advocates new divorce laws—not more rigid, but more human, and certainly more uniform from state to state. Present laws are unrealistic. They carry the idea of blame; one party must be innocent, the other guilty. A large number of divorces actually do occur by mutual consent, but to admit this in court would invalidate the divorce. "Disagreeing disagreeably is all right, agreeably is illegal." [31] Positive measures would include establishing a family court much like modern juvenile courts, with special judges trained in family problems who would try to give advice or direct quarreling couples to marriage counselors. Instead of labeling a case "John Doe versus Mary Doe," Judge Alexander would call it "In the Interest of the John Doe Family."

But even the best of divorce laws treat the symptoms rather than the basic causes of divorce. "The big problem is not to keep people who want divorce from getting it but to keep more people from wanting it." [32]

Our society, say students of the family, needs a new philosophy of marriage. If affection is to continue to be the chief bond holding families together, then people must be trained to choose their mates more carefully, to expect no more from marriage than they are willing to put into it, and to replace the absurd tenets of love at first sight and of romantic ecstasy as the criterion of marital success with more realistic values. This would in no way rob courtship and marriage of their beauty; in fact it would add new meaning to both. But of course, all this is a large order in our culture, dominated as it is by the notion of individual happiness. Education for successful marriage begins in infancy. On the success of today's families depends the success of those established a generation hence.

**Future
of the Family**   •   The future is far from bleak. People still enter marriage with the idea that it will last. Americans believe in marriage as completely as they believe in anything. More Americans are marrying than ever before and are marrying younger than ever. College students want more children when they

marry than did college students before World War II. Social scientists are looking into the causes of happiness and unhappiness in marriage. Twenty years ago such research was not considered respectable. In the long run there is good reason to hope that marriages will be better adjusted than they are now.

We know that marriage and family living will continue to change, just as everything changes; but if the social scientist can make any long-range prediction he can predict that marriage and the family will continue to exist as long as man exists. "In the Götterdämmerung which over-wise science and over-foolish statesmanship are preparing for us, the last man will spend his last hours searching for his wife and child." [33]

THIRTEEN

Education

What picture does the word "education" evoke? The traditional symbol of the little red schoolhouse? The expensive urban high school with its mammoth gymnasium and football field? The ivy-covered halls of a college campus?

The word can just as appropriately call to mind a mother playing "pat-a-cake" with her baby, a Cuna *kantule* chanting tribal

287

legends at a puberty ceremony, a native of a South Pacific Island learning to use a G.I. hatchet, Spanish lads playing at bullfighting, a man reading the morning paper on the bus. For in its broadest sense education is synonymous with socialization, and includes any method whereby culture is passed on from one individual or group to another.

Recognizing that effective socialization is basic to the continuation of society, every society also practices education in a narrower sense: the deliberate transmission of selected knowledge, skills, and values to prepare individuals for effective membership in the society. In other words, society institutionalizes this function, organizing the process, designating personnel to carry it out, elaborating norms, and providing equipment.

As a tradition-perpetuating institution, education, like religion, tends to be conservative. It plays, however, a dynamic role as well, particularly in modern society. To prepare individuals for adulthood in a stable society means simply to teach them to be like their parents; their adult roles are chiefly ascribed and foreseeable. But in a society that is undergoing rapid social change, members must also be prepared insofar as possible to anticipate changes and be trained to guide those changes into whatever channels the society deems desirable and to expand the frontiers of knowledge. It is only in a changing society that education is a "problem," that people worry about "crises" and argue heatedly about solutions.

The social scientist's role in such a situation is to analyze the institution with the methods and techniques of anthropology, sociology, and social psychology. He begins with the premise that education, like other fundamental institutions, reflects the culture and the social order of which it is a part. The class system, cultural values, the power structure, the balance of freedom and control, the homogeneity or heterogeneity of race, religion, and nationality, the degree of urbanization and industrialization—all these factors exert a strong and inevitable impact on the school system of any community or society.

Just as inevitably, the school system is affected by social problems and social change. In spite of its essentially conservative nature education cannot escape the effects of changes in the form and function of the family and in the size, distribution and composition of the population; of technological changes and economic trends and crises; and of changes in political philosophy and political power. The school, however, often betrays a cultural lag in adapting to these changes; to cite just one example, the current "baby boom" overcrowds new schools as fast as they are built.

Furthermore, the educational system of a society—and each school in it—has a sub-culture and a social organization of its own. It has a system of statuses and roles, a body of values, skills, and traditions, its own rituals and ceremonies, and its own special language. Each school and each classroom within the school is an interacting social group, and social psychologists are especially interested in the relationship between the structure and atmosphere of the group and the behavior changes that result from its interaction.

Obviously, we cannot in a single chapter do justice to all these topics. We can only touch upon a few of the insights into education afforded us by social scientists.

Formal and Informal Education • In nonliterate societies education is largely the result of informal day-by-day interaction within the primary group. Father passes on to son and mother passes on to daughter the basic pattern of a man's or woman's work. Adolescence brings increasing responsibilities and privileges that culminate in a smooth transition to adulthood. In many societies few secrets are kept from children; they are allowed to learn by observing. Informal sanctions of ridicule or light punishment are usually sufficient to enforce "proper" behavior.

Even in such societies, however, not all is left to chance. Children (even as in modern society) are given toys that are small representations

A World-wide Phenomenon. *Every society institutionalizes the transmission of skills, knowledge, and values.*

of adult tools and possessions. They re-enact tribal rites in their play and imitate everyday adult activities. Their elders tell them tales and recite proverbs that incorporate and affirm the mores of the society. Children who are designated for special roles or vocations are trained early by an adult who is himself actively engaged in the role or vocation. The San Blas Cuna, for example, begin early to train a child born with a caul for his destined role of *nele*, for it takes years for a candidate to master the oral lore of the tribe.

In the rites and secret societies of nonliterate tribes an approach is made to formal education. The *kantule's* long recitations of tribal lore— the history, values, folkways, and mores of the group—are delivered on the special occasion of the puberty ceremony and their educational impact is heightened by the atmosphere of reverence and awe that surrounds the proceedings. The secret societies of some tribes are graded, like our schools, and each step a candidate masters means that he has gained more knowledge of the society's culture. Many tribes require young people to take a sort of "final exam" before they are admitted to adult status.

In rural folk society, as in nonliterate society, members "learn by doing," by actively participating in family and community life. In colonial and frontier America, for example, the family and the church were responsible for training the young in vocational skills, in proper behavior, and in the accepted value system. The little red schoolhouse was meant to impart only a little "book learning" and the 3 R's.

As a society becomes industrialized, heterogeneous, and urbanized, formal education becomes relatively far more important. There is more to learn as culture grows ever more complex. Modern technology, business, and the professions demand trained specialists. Many new statuses are available for members to achieve. Inevitably, a formal school system takes on the special job of educating the young.

Here, at the hands of experts, the too-big milieu was to be broken up into its elements, sifted for basic values, and organized into teachable bits. In short, the school was a device created by the community to do what it could no longer do well; namely, to educate children.[1]

Historical · A recent book on American schools is
Background entitled *A Fourth of a Nation*, for nearly one American in four is a teacher or student. Education is the largest industry in the United States in terms of people involved. This phenomenon —mass education—is a very recent one indeed and is typical of modern

Western society. It has its roots, however, deep in the past; a brief historical sketch will indicate the beginnings of traditions that still are valued by many educators.

The schools of ancient Egypt and Babylonia prepared a few men as priests, lawyers, civic officials, or scribes, who kept government and business records. Sparta, like Nazi Germany, trained men to be warriors and women to be the mothers of warriors. It was in Athens that the idea of education for citizenship first developed. Aristotle defined liberal education as education suitable for a free man—but only one Athenian in five was free. Athenian education stressed music, gymnastics, and citizenship; scholars concentrated on art, science, grammar, literature, and philosophy.

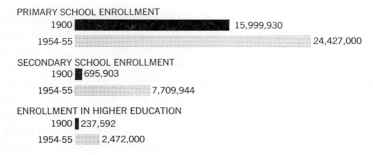

PRIMARY SCHOOL ENROLLMENT
1900   15,999,930
1954-55   24,427,000

SECONDARY SCHOOL ENROLLMENT
1900   695,903
1954-55   7,709,944

ENROLLMENT IN HIGHER EDUCATION
1900   237,592
1954-55   2,472,000

The Extension of Mass Education in America, 1900-1955.

The Roman schools (like those of the Aztecs) were divided along class lines. They were narrowly bookish for the patricians and utilitarian for the plebeians. No music or gymnastics were taught. During the Middle Ages the Greek language and learning were almost entirely forgotten in Europe. Schools were run largely by the clergy for the clergy and nobility and taught the Seven Liberal Arts—The Trivium: Latin grammar, rhetoric, and logic, and the Quadrivium: arithmetic, geometry, astronomy, and music. The "school" of chivalry exemplified by the noble Crusaders emphasized social graces, military skills, and moral virtues. For the less romantic work of the world young men were trained as apprentices under the system of craft guilds.

In the later Middle Ages the commercial revival and the rise of the business class stimulated cities and guilds to establish schools to teach reading and writing in the vernacular to prospective clerks and accountants. In the 1100's the first universities were established, and by 1500 there were about 80 throughout Europe. They trained lawyers, doctors, clergymen, and teachers, and they insisted on academic freedom—freedom to teach as they saw fit without interference from church or state. The universities fostered the age of scientific inquiry, which began about the fourteenth century; it was later that many of them became narrowly classical.

The Renaissance, which saw the revival of the Greek and Latin languages and literature, also witnessed the re-emergence of the Greek idea of a liberal education for free men. Such education was, however, still limited to the aristocracy, as it had been in Greece. Boys of "good family" attended schools modeled on the "Latin schools" of England; they studied classical languages and literature, Euclid's geometry, ethics, and politics, and participated in sports and games. Eventually the Latin schools developed into preparatory schools for the classically oriented colleges and universities.

Protestantism and the rise of nationalism gave impetus to popular education. Because the leaders of the Reformation insisted that everyone be able to read the Bible, parish schools for boys and girls were established to teach the 4 R's—reading, writing, arithmetic, and religion. This step represented the beginning of public education, for the pastor was in charge but the state helped support the schools, in Germany, Switzerland, Scotland, the Netherlands, and Scandinavia. In Catholic countries, schools for the poor were established by teaching orders. Finally, the whole series of social changes wrapped up in the terms "industrialization and urbanization" and the spread of ideas of democracy and popular suffrage made a formal system of public education inevitable.

The idea of popular education found fertile ground in the New World. Although the Puritan idea of elementary education made little headway in England, it flourished in Massachusetts, where the self-governing towns had established elementary schools soon after the colony was founded. In 1647 Massachusetts passed a law requiring towns of a certain size to establish both elementary and Latin schools, the latter to prepare young men for college. The academies of the 1700's were more practical secondary schools, which taught many subjects, including mathematics and its applications in bookkeeping, surveying, and navigation. The apprentice system still took care of training young people for the skilled trades.

The federal Constitution left the responsibility for education to the states. In early ordinances, however, the government set the pattern for tax-supported education by ordering that one section of each township in the western territories should be set aside for raising funds for education.

The steady trend toward government-supported compulsory education continued throughout the nineteenth century, stimulated by the
emphasis on personal reading of the Bible; the importance of an educated voting public to a democracy; faith in education as the means to
personal and social progress; the growth of industry with its need for
technicians and literate, skilled workers; and the stream of immigration,
which demanded a means of cultural assimilation. Landmarks in this
trend included the first public high school in Boston in 1821, the first
state normal school for teacher-training in Massachusetts in 1839, the
Massachusetts compulsory education law in 1852, and the decision of
Chief Justice Cooley of the Michigan Supreme Court in the Kalamazoo
case in 1874 that taxes could be used to support high schools as well as
grade schools. By 1918 all the states had laws providing for free, tax-
supported, compulsory, secular education.

Social Organization   •   The system of status—of prestige and
and Education   power—within a society determines
                                  who controls the schools and who shall
                                  be educated. The American system
stresses local control and social democracy, while the European system
stresses central control and a more rigid grading plan in keeping with
the more rigid class systems that exist there.

Control of the schools. Education in modern society is a public institution,
subject to public control. Because the schools transmit culture and
inculcate values, society dares not leave their performance unsupervised.
Whereas the doctor and the lawyer are entitled in our society to professional privacy, subject only to licensing and regulation, the teacher
is regarded as a public servant.

Teachers are often held to standards of conformity and propriety
not expected of other professions.... Willy-nilly the educator deals
with values; he has exceptional opportunity to examine the unex-
amined axioms of the culture and interpret its crucial but vulnerable
symbols. Since society is so largely equivalent to consensus, those who
deal with values and beliefs as part of their occupational role—
ministers, judges, writers, some artists, social scientists, teachers—
touch upon the sensitive fringes of the basis of social order. In part
for this reason, (they) are the object of special surveillance and concern.[2]

Although education is held to be the responsibility of the government and of the taxpaying public in all modern societies, the exact form of government responsibility and control varies with the general structure of each society. Centralized control, needless to say, is the pattern in totalitarian states such as Soviet Russia, where indoctrination of the young in the ideology of the regime is held to be a prime function of education. It is also the pattern in unitary states (see Chapter Twenty-six) that leave little or no power to geographical or administrative subdivisions such as provinces or counties. In France and in the Latin-American countries, for example, a national ministry administers all education, even the curricula and final examinations.

In the United States, however, there is a long tradition of decentralized control of education. Each state is an autonomous authority in educational matters. The states control roughly a third of public-school finance through aid grants based on attendance, and control the qualifications of teachers through their licensing systems. They also exercise some supervision over the curricula. They require, for example, that certain subjects, usually civics or American history, be taught, or define what may and may not be taught about religion in the public schools.

Local school boards—about 60,000 in number—appoint administrators, hire the teachers, build and equip schools, and manage the finances. They are usually elected by popular vote, less often appointed by a public official such as a mayor. School board members in urban districts tend to come from the upper-middle class, with smaller representations from the upper and working classes. Three out of four are business managers or proprietors, professional people, or wives of such men. In recent years labor has usually been represented, usually by union officials. Board members have higher than average incomes and usually more education than most other members of their communities.

Non-governmental influences and pressures on education. Part of the power structure of a community consists of non-governmental pressure groups of various kinds, which testify to their belief in the importance of education by trying to influence what is taught. Each pressure group is convinced that its version of the American way of life is the right one, and presents it in terms of faith in free enterprise, religion, and patriotism. The two main types of pressure groups are those primarily concerned with the distribution and control of wealth, and with war, nationalism, and international policy. Other groups are anti-alcohol (WCTU, for example), religious, professional, pro-minority and anti-minority.

The Chamber of Commerce, the National Association of Manufacturers, and public utilities, as well as individual business corporations, attempt to control what the schools teach about the economic system, to reinforce belief in capitalism and free enterprise, to influence the choice of texts, and to encourage the use of films, lecturers, and other "teaching aids" that present their point of view. In smaller towns business influence may bear less on belief than on the patronage or recognition given to various local firms by teachers and school organizations. Labor unions also offer their point of view.

The American Legion and the United Nations are polar groups, each attempting to influence the schools on international policy. Legion publications and pronouncements take a strong stand against teachers, texts, and schools that the organization believes are un-American or subversive. Materials presenting the United Nations in a favorable light have sometimes been deleted from texts and even from Girl Scout manuals at the insistence of some "super-nationalist" organizations.

Religious groups are vigilant about protecting their rights in regard to schools. Catholics have wherever possible organized schools of their own, and their right to share in tax money is never a dead issue. Jewish people have been content to support supplementary Hebrew schools, which teach their children values of the Jewish sub-culture in after-school and Sunday classes. The dominance of Protestantism in our national culture is evidenced by such organizations as the Hi-Y's in many high schools. Many pressures are brought upon public schools to teach religion or to teach about religions; for example, a law to require daily Bible-reading in schools is perennially introduced into the Michigan legislature. Recognizing both the historic importance of separation of church and state and the fact that even to ignore religion in public schools is to give it a value judgment, many people think that the ideal compromise is to teach the importance both of religious belief and religious tolerance without any sectarian bias—a difficult task indeed.

The federal government and education. In spite of local domination, the federal government plays a considerable and increasing role in education. There is no integrated federal program; it is scattered and uncoordinated. Separate arrangements are made for specific efforts with the states concerned and with individual colleges and universities.

Federal funds have gone to help areas where an influx of families connected with defense work or military bases has put a sudden strain on educational facilities. During the depression many high-school and college students were able to stay in school by taking jobs arranged by the National Youth Administration, and the GI Bill of Rights has enabled many veterans to attend schools and colleges since World War II. Federal agencies conduct training programs for their personnel and even operate colleges, universities, academies, and graduate schools, mostly for very specialized education in military and scientific fields. They also subsidize some vocational schools and agricultural experiment stations. The Department of State and the International Cooperation Administration provide for interchange of students and teachers with other countries.

The question of systematic federal aid to education is a thorny one. Inevitably it becomes tied up with such issues as segregation, the opposition of local units of government jealous of their power, the claims of sectarian schools anxious for a share, and the traditional American fear of centralized control of any kind. Proposals for federal aid have come up in Congress several times, and have always been defeated. Since the Sputniks were first launched by the Russians, however, the question has been re-examined. Many people have advocated a "crash" program in science and mathematics to be subsidized by national scholarships and similar measures. Others see a danger in concentrating on science; they fear that in competing exclusively on Russian terms, in technology, and neglecting the humanities and social sciences, we may sacrifice important values that we champion in the free world.

Effects of decentralization. Theoretically at least, local control of education makes for a feeling of pride and ownership in the community. In many places the school is the heart of community activities for people of all ages. Decentralization is seen as a guarantee that no dictator or demagogue will regiment and indoctrinate teachers and students. The absence of a central authority favors experimentation with various curricula and methods of teaching and permits the educational program to be adapted to the particular needs and desires of the community.

On the other hand, the lack of any national standards makes for unevenness in our school system as a whole. Since financial support also comes from state and local sources, and since the quality of teacher training and of facilities is closely related to the available funds, there is great disparity in the quality of education from one community and state to another. Because there is no national standard by which students can be compared and by which the level of achievement of schools can be measured, the high-school diploma, for example, can mean little more than that the student has attended school for twelve grades.

Social stratification and the schools. A superior education has traditionally been a badge of status. In the poorest nations of the Middle East,

Asia, and Latin America, the wealthy landholders and merchants have long provided a foreign education for their children and thus perpetuated the rigid class distinctions that prevail. Today, however, even illiterate peasants in thatched huts want education for their children and are increasingly able to send them to public schools. For as these nations become industralized, as agricultural techniques improve, as public health services expand, it becomes ever more necessary to train mechanics, technicians, nurses, doctors, and other specialists, and school systems are expanded accordingly. Wherever this happens, the school, in Margaret Mead's phrase, drives a wedge between the generations. With so many statuses open to achievement, and social change so rapid, it is impossible to predict in more than a very general way what a child will grow up to be and do. The peasant's son may turn out to be a clerk, the farmer's son becomes a lawyer. The immigrant's son becomes a fully acculturated American; the illiterate's son learns to read and write.[3]

All over the modern world, then, education is the most important avenue to social mobility. And nowhere is this truer than in the United States. Our system of education, as President Griswold of Yale phrases it, "casts the net wide and keeps the mesh tight," in contrast to the typical European plan of education. In most European countries sifting and selecting begin early. The controversial English system of giving difficult exams at "eleven-plus" to determine who shall be allowed to go on with academic training and who must be content with trade-school training is typical. The student's path from then on is studded with stiff competitive examinations that weed out failures at intervals. After their highly academic secondary training, students go directly into professional training; Europe has nothing equivalent to our more than 1,500 four-year liberal arts colleges. As a result, less than 20 per cent of the 16- and 17-year-olds in Europe and Great Britain are enrolled in school, as compared to more than 75 per cent in the United States. And while about one-tenth of the 18-to 20-year-olds in Great Britain, France and Germany are full-time students, one-fourth to one-third of Americans of those ages are in college.[4] Whether or not these statistics in themselves are grounds for pride we shall consider later.

Figures on occupational distribution demonstrate reasons why education is the great avenue of opportunity in the United States. For upper-middle-class occupations such as the professions and executive jobs in business, a college education is necessary, while a high-school diploma is regarded as essential for clerical work, skilled technical work, and many sales jobs. A study of occupational distribution shows that business, industry, and the professions have expanded at the expense of agriculture and unskilled or semi-skilled jobs. In 1820, seven out of ten gainfully employed persons were in agriculture; in 1920, the number had fallen to only one in four, and in 1950 to only one in eight. In contrast, although only 2.8 per cent of the gainfully employed were in public and professional service in 1820, and a century later the number was still only 5 per cent, by 1950, 13.7 per cent worked in those fields. Even more spectacular was the rise in the number employed in trade and transportation, the distributive occupations: from 1 person in 40 in 1820 to 1 in 4 in 1920 and 1 in 3 in 1950. The Bureau of Labor Statistics predicts that by 1975 professional and technical personnel must increase by 75 per cent (over 1957 levels) while the demand for skilled and unskilled labor will decline by 25 per cent.[5]

When we consider this shortage of trained people in conjunction with the differential birth rate, it is obvious that many lower-class people must be recruited to fill the occupational gaps. If the shortages are to be filled and recruitment is to be perfectly democratic, the intelligent, capable, and industrious will rise regardless of their family's class position. Ability alone, however, is no guarantee that a child will be motivated to study or be able or willing to continue in school. In numerous ways American schools discriminate against lower-class children.

The best-known study of this discrimination was made in "Elmtown," a corn-belt county seat of 6,000 people, by a team of social scientists from the Committee on Human Development of the University of Chicago. Over a period of several years they focused their attention on the 735 adolescents, age 13 to 19, in the town, testing the hypothesis that their behavior in and about school and their continuous acculturation were significantly related to the positions their families occupied in the class structure of Elmtown. The hypothesis was confirmed, and the team concluded that school-board policy, adolescent attitudes, participation in extra-curricular activities, membership in cliques, progress in school, and recognition by teachers were all consistently determined in large part by class background.[6]

This study and others have shown how class bias operates against mobility. Intelligence tests, being largely verbal, favor middle- and upper-class children. Teacher judgments are made almost entirely on the basis of middle-class values. Insofar as lower-class children are taught to accept these values, they learn the way of life of a higher class and mobility is promoted. There is, however, a lack of motivation in many cases, for the social distance between the lower-class child and his teacher may be so great that the child cannot see how anything he learns or is expected to learn in school is related to life outside of school, either in the present or the future. Unlike middle-class parents, lower-

class parents do not make the child anxious about success and respectability; they do not usually cooperate with the school and enforce the demands the teacher makes on his pupils. It is a rare teacher who has the
imagination or sympathetic understanding to work effectively with
lower-class children.[7]

Some factors in school teaching and administration can work either
for or against social mobility, depending largely on the people involved.
For example, homogeneous grouping by ability or achievement will
largely follow class lines if traditional IQ tests and middle-class standards of judgment are the sole criteria used in placing the children. But
a few lower-class children will enter superior groups in spite of this
bias, and more will be admitted if teachers make allowances. Lower-
class children in superior groups usually have stronger motivations and
a greater opportunity to learn the way of life of the middle class than
in heterogeneous classes.

A single-track high school in which all pupils study the same subjects will promote fluidity if it is not so academic as to encourage drop-
outs. A "multiple-track," European style school, early sorting children
into commercial, vocational and college-preparatory courses, is usually
highly correlated with class backgrounds and tends to solidify class
strata. Ideally, at least, the "comprehensive" high school, offering different curricula but mingling the students as much as possible and
offering a maximum freedom of choice, is the type least likely to perpetuate class distinctions.

An interesting experiment in combining mass education with the
European multiple-track system is going on in Soviet Russia. All youths
from 7 to 17 must attend ten-year schools with a rigorous curriculum and
a six-day session ten months out of the year. On the basis of long oral
examinations they may then be admitted to a university or institute of
higher learning. University students are paid according to their scholarship standing. Curricula are rigid; there are no electives. Though this
lack of freedom goes counter to American values, many Americans see in
the sure opportunity for all the talented, capable, and industrious a
lesson that we must quickly apply to our own society.[8]

**Cultural Values
and the Schools**   •   Schools have been called "museums of
virtue," for they are supposed to per-
petuate and transmit the most sacred
values of the culture, the ideal culture
patterns. And indeed they do. But just as there are values within a culture
that work at cross purposes, so do schools tend to violate some values at

the same time that they give them lip service. Both the core values of the culture and those that make their observance ambivalent are reflected in the school system.

Democracy. To illustrate this statement, let us examine one of the core values of our culture—democracy. Democracy is intimately related in our minds with other values such as freedom, equality, patriotism, and the pursuit of individual happiness. But though we laud the idea of democracy in our classrooms, we are not too sure just what it means, and often betray it in the same schools where we praise it.

For example, we take great pride in equality of opportunity, in our belief that everyone in the United States should have an equal chance for a good education. And as we saw, in contrast to many countries where the class system is less fluid, we have cast the net wide. However, differences in opportunity violate this ideal to such a degree that they have become problems for our educational policy-makers. A child in a small rural school does not enjoy the same facilities as a child in a modern urban or suburban school; a child in Mississippi does not enjoy the same per pupil expenditure on education ($123) as a child in New York ($362 as of January, 1954); Negro schools not yet "integrated" offer facilities that the Supreme Court has said belie the old "separate but equal" doctrine. Even within the same high school a senior with an IQ of 110 may be able to go on to college because his father is a successful businessman, while another with an IQ of 140 may have to seek work instead, because his father cannot stretch his wages to cover the cost of college tuition. Some 200,000 able students every year do not go on to college, at least 60,000 for financial reasons. When national scholarships for needy pupils have been suggested, however, the contradictory value of local control of schools and our somewhat dated belief in "every rugged individual for himself" have thus far proven more powerful than our belief in equality of opportunity.

Sometimes school administrators place so much emphasis on equality of opportunity that they actually subvert the essential meaning of the phrase. They refuse to divide children into groups on the basis of intelligence because they feel that such a step would be discriminatory toward slow learners. Actually, it would not. But the system of gearing the whole class to the pace of the slowest does discriminate against the bright pupils. Gifted children often become bored with school as a result and their talents are never fully developed.[9] Perhaps the terms "democracy" and "equality of opportunity" need to be re-defined in relation to education. Democracy, in popular and uncritical usage, means

"Everyone is equal." But this definition conflicts with educational reality, which shows that some students get 100, some get 75, and others flunk out. In many instances, this uncritical use of the word "democracy" has won out to the extent that our high schools are attacked by many critics as "conveyor belts" that grant a "guaranteed annual pass" and cheapen the diploma into a mere certificate of twelve years' attendance rather than an indication of the achievement of a set standard of scholarship.

Many educators argue that there is nothing democratic about keeping all ten-year-olds together when some have a mental age of seven and others a mental age of seventeen. Rather, they consider true democracy in education to mean equal opportunity for individuals to go as far as their abilities can carry them, unhampered by slower learners or by lack of funds, whether in the family or within the school districts, and maximum diffusion of knowledge, skill, and responsibility throughout society.

Faith in education. Our attitude toward education itself is ambivalent. We both respect it and suspect it. On the one hand, we think education is a good thing, a wonderful thing, the one and only answer to all the problems of our era. We hail it as the only hope, the universal panacea for race problems, war, and crime. We believe that education is a gilt-edged investment, for nothing is too good for our children, who represent the future in which we have such faith. Horace Mann, who worked long and effectively for the cause of public education in the early 1800's, was convinced that education is the sure road to prosperity, happiness, security, and salvation.

But the fact is that war, crime, and prejudice continue in spite of education. Though it is a fine investment, apparently it is not so highly valued as tobacco and alcohol, on which we spend far more each year. Our national per capita income in 1953-54 was $1,872. We spent only about 3 per cent, or $57.43 per capita, on schools.

Our faith in education is also belied by our anti-intellectualism. Many Americans tend to suspect people who are "too bookish." We distrust the scholar and label him "egghead"; the student who prefers learning to larks, A's to athletics, is a "grind" and a "square." There are no equivalent terms of opprobrium for the student who just "gets by" or for the campus good Joe who slides through courses on the strength of his fraternity brothers' notes and old exams. High-school students' attitudes toward scientists reflect the attitudes of their parents and the anti-intellectual images—the "mad scientist," the eccentric professor—that are conveyed by the mass media. Surveying a cross section of American high-school students, a Purdue professor found that 30 per cent believe that a person cannot be a scientist and hope to raise a normal family, 25 per cent think scientists are "odd," and 14 per cent think they are "evil." [10]

Material success and hedonism. Materialism and hedonism do not encourage scholarship. These values are reflected in the curricula, especially of our high schools, where new courses that are added are almost invariably courses in skills practical and impractical—in work that will "pay off" or play that will help us enjoy ourselves and "fit in" with others. The old saying, "If you're so smart why ain't you rich?" indicates our tendency to measure things by the dollar sign, which might be called, in softer terms, the pragmatic, practical, utilitarian bent of our culture.

We place less value on learning than we do on the diploma, which carries prestige value and is the key to material and social success. We even measure the liberal arts by this practical yardstick. We believe that to defend this type of training by the claim that it "pays off" is far more effective than to stress the intangible values of mental discipline, creativity, and aesthetic appreciation that it is supposed to instill. Not "the good life" but "a good living" is the goal. College graduates are reported to earn $100,000 more in a lifetime than nongraduates. A headline, "Bookishness Pays Off" is followed by a story to the effect that corporation executives find technical training gives new employees an advantage during their first five years, but that often it is the liberal arts graduates who forge ahead in the long run. The "solid disciplined thinking" that comes from studying history, literature, and philosophy "will ultimately succeed." [11] And "success" through individual competition is a dominant American value. American parents want their children to "get ahead."

Conformity. American schools also emphasize conformity, adjustment to the group, "other-directedness," in sociologist David Riesman's phrase. This conformity is measured almost exclusively in terms of middle-class values, which dominate our education as they dominate our culture. These values include general morality, especially in regard to sex and property, honesty, thrift, modesty, cleanliness, punctuality, industry, and ambition, most of which are taught to children under the rubric of "good citizenship."

Patriotism. Closely connected with good citizenship is another core value of our society—patriotism. There is no doubt that in each country the schools are a chief instrument of national solidarity. American schools stress American history and the lore of our great founders and presidents, the ritual of flag salutes and national anthems, the superiority of free enterprise, religious faith, loyalty in time of war, the feeling that our country is by far the best in every respect—all the national pride and ethnocentrism that we have studied in earlier chapters. When a school or a text leans too far in the direction of "internationalism" or "objectivity," supernationalists are sure to rise up against it. This opposition is especially effective where local control is strongest, in elementary and high schools. And, of course, it is precisely during these years that values are being deeply ingrained into the personality. Objective teaching in colleges and universities is often attacked by such groups as "red" and "subversive," and the tradition of academic freedom, of the university as a bastion of truth, is sometimes shaken.

Culture and Social   •   The school, both individually and as a
Organization   social institution, has a distinct sub-
of the Schools   culture and a typical social organiza-
                                    tion. In contrast with most other insti-
                                    tutions with which children and youth
come into contact, the school is characterized by a high degree of formalism and a singleness of purpose. Teaching and learning are the business of its personnel. They are formally organized by ages and grades; time is rigidly scheduled; lines of authority and subordination are clearly drawn. Traditionally there also are distinct lines drawn between the various school subjects. Grades are usually unequivocal competitive standings given by letter or number on report cards sent to parents or guardians. Rules and codes of conduct are explicit, as are the rewards and punishments used to enforce them.

The rituals of patriotism, of school yells and colors and songs, of athletic events, plays, programs, and graduation ceremonies are typical of American school culture. In European and Latin-American schools, the school uniform is a unifying symbol. To some extent schools—and certainly teachers and administrators—have a language of their own. Peer group culture is passed on in the schoolroom and the playground by the informal and diffuse groups that operate within any social structure. The code of solidarity that punishes the squealer or tattler and the teacher's pet is one element of this culture.

Each school follows or departs from these cultural norms in various ways. Substitute teachers have noticed that upon entering a new school for the day they quickly sense the atmosphere, whether it is one of strict authoritarian order, of cooperative industry, of anarchy, of uneasy competition, and so on. The formalism of the traditional school is avoided in schools by such experiments as "core" curricula that break down the rigid compartmentalization of subject matter, by attempts to rate the children with more regard for individual effort and talent ("Satisfactory," "Unsatisfactory"), or by replacing report cards entirely with parent conferences.

The culture of the school has a profound effect upon what children and adolescents learn and the ways in which they learn. There is a saying that children learn not what is taught, but what is "caught." Much of what is caught (attitudes toward learning, toward authority, values of right and wrong, and so on) comes not from the formal curriculum but from the pervading culture of the school.[12]

Kurt Lewin pioneered in studying interaction in the small group and the effect of various types of organization and leadership on group behavior and individual behavior changes. Two of his pupils, Lippitt and White, set up an experiment with four clubs, each consisting of five ten-year-old boys. Leadership alternated from *autocratic* (an authoritarian leader made policy, dictated activities step by step, and took no part in the group interaction except to bestow individual praise and blame) to *democratic* (policy stemmed from group discussion and decision, choosing between alternative goals, dividing tasks, with the leader as a source of suggestion and help) or to one of these situations from an atmosphere of *laissez faire* (freedom of action with no leader control, leader indifferent and not a participant, making few comments and no effort to enforce work rules). The contrast in group behavior was marked. Comparing work output, morale, and other factors, the researchers concluded that "democracy, while demanding skill and insight, is productive of high morale, a marked degree of teamwork, and creative talent."[13]

The success of the democratic method may be related to the behavior expected of children in our culture. One report seems to indicate that perhaps French children would have been less unhappy in an authoritarian group than American children. An exchange teacher who taught English in a French village school and French in an American school was struck by the contrast between the quiet subservience to authority of the French children and the exuberant self-expression of American children. He concluded that the American school prepares the child admirably "to meet the demands of social and political organizations in which persuasion, effective compromise, the individual vote, and the

collective will to abide by group decisions are the essential elements. . . .
In (France) it is the wisdom of a decision, rather than its acceptance by
a group, that is important . . . it is the adults who make the decisions. In
France, the family is sacred; in America this same reverence is held for
our democratic political institutions." [14]

Social organization of education. Like any other social institution, the
school in both the general and the specific sense is a complex web of social
interaction and an interwoven set of statuses and roles.

The school system in mass society tends to be bureaucratic. The
personnel of education are ranked in a hierarchy of authority and prestige, readily apparent in any one community or school, from the trustees
or school board, through the administration, down to the teachers and
pupils. The actual exercise of power does not always correspond to this
formal structure; a clique of teachers, for example, may control the
principal of their school.

We may use the school teacher to illuminate the concept of status
and role we introduced in Chapter Seven. The teacher's status is defined
in a certain way no matter who the specific person or persons are who
occupy the position at any given time. The teacher's role corresponds to
the set of behavior patterns that he and his fellow teachers are expected
to follow.

Status. The relative status of teachers varies from one society to another. In many societies teachers are highly respected and stand near the
top of the social scale. This was true in American society a century ago
and even more recently; it is still true in Europe. It is, as Americans
have recently become aware, especially true in Russia, where the
teacher at all levels occupies a position of great prestige. "With the
possible exception of top party leaders, no one is held in higher regard
than the university professor, especially in sciences and engineering." [15]
His salary is correspondingly high, starting at about $1,500 a month and
increasing as he writes texts and wins status in the National Academy
of Sciences. In American society today, however, the status of teachers
is far lower than our "ideal" culture pattern would indicate. In brief
interviews testing stereotype reactions to a list of 90 occupations, researchers North and Hatt found that a national sample of adults ranked
"public-school teacher" thirty-sixth.

About 90 per cent of elementary-school and 55 per cent of high-
school teachers in the United States are women. Young, unmarried women
fill most teaching positions; but wartime and the baby boom removed
the reluctance to employ married women, who now represent a sub-

stantial fraction of the total. Teachers used to come largely from the white-collar middle class; increasingly they are now recruited from farms and working-class families, especially for high-school teaching.[16] Two or three out of five teachers have moved at least one step upward in the social structure.[17]

Once established in the profession most teachers attain middle-class status—upper-middle in some communities, lower-middle in others. Although most upwardly mobile teachers have adopted middle-class values, attitudes, and ways of life, many come from backgrounds that may provide them with greater insight into the problems of working-class pupils than is possessed by teachers from middle-class homes.

The average teacher may enjoy middle-class status, but he doesn't enjoy a middle-class income. The average teacher's income is about on a par with the income of unskilled laborers. In October, 1957, the average salary for all elementary and secondary-school teachers in the United States was $4,330.[18] College professors, according to the report of a presidential committee, are the only group that has lost pay status since 1940. Although lawyers' incomes are up 29 per cent, doctors' 96 per cent, and industrial workers' 64 per cent, professors' incomes are down 5 per cent from 1940.

The American teacher's pay is in part a result of his ambivalent status. He is treated in part as a professional person with special know-how and in part as a public servant. He is often sunk in a morass of petty bureaucratic detail, of responsibilities for which professional training is unnecessary, such as hall patrol, lunchroom duties, numerous collections, slips to sign, and the like. Just as the shortage of nurses has forced hospitals to hire "aides" and "practical nurses" for routine duties that require little training, so a few schools have begun to employ "teacher's aides" to give the teacher more time to teach.

Roles. In a brilliant chapter on the social roles of the teacher, two educational sociologists, Robert Havighurst and Bernice Neugarten, describe a whole series of sub-roles, which are not separate or distinct but are helpful in analyzing the role performance of teachers.[19]

In the community, for example, the teacher plays several sub-roles. He is a participant in community affairs, especially religious and professional, but not as a leader or insider, rather as a worker at necessary but dull jobs. He is a "sociological stranger," in, but not of, the community. Even if he was born and raised there, his special training and his work of bringing the larger culture to the local community set him apart.

Other sub-roles in relation to the community include: surrogate of middle-class morality (a better model for children's behavior than their own parents); a person of "culture"; a pioneer in the world of ideas; a social reformer, working to improve the society, and at the same time a conservator of tradition or maintainer of the status quo; an expert in regard to children; and a public servant.

The teacher's role in the school setting also involves a set of sub-roles. In relation to other adults he is employee, subordinate, advisee, colleague, follower, and leader. In relation to his pupils, he is mainly a mediator of learning. The main role of the teacher is to teach—to induce socially valued change in his pupils. This is the role toward which his training was directed, and the role in which his behavior patterns are most clearly defined. A second classroom role, that of disciplinarian, is often a troublesome one, especially when the teacher's background is very different from his pupils. He is also a parent substitute, a judge (referee, detective, policeman), confidant, and again a surrogate of middle-class morality.

Within this framework and according to the situation and their own inclinations, teachers work out their own patterns of role behavior. Each teacher chooses to emphasize some roles and play down or ignore others, and to stress one aspect over others at different times. He can thus be creative in regard to the role; he creates his own behavior as a teacher, sometimes transcending conventional expectations, and thus he helps to define the roles further.

The Crisis in American Education • In considering education as an institution, we have at various points touched upon the present crisis in education, the long-simmering controversy over means and ends that came to a boil after the Sputniks demonstrated Russian advancement in science. Government leaders, parents, scientists, educators, all are examining the goals, the methods, and the values of our educational system.

Aims. First, what are the aims of education? We are not sure. Are the schools to concentrate on the child's intellectual development only? Should they also be responsible for his social, moral, religious, vocational, and physical and emotional development, as well as for his recreation?

The main reason for this uncertainty is, of course, the complexity and rapid change of modern society. A sociologist sees the fundamental aim of modern education as an attempt to teach children to realize "that they are the social order; that what they do or fail to do, and what goals they seek, make social order what it is." In this way, we may present to our children, and especially to adolescents, something more challenging and inspiring than the customary admonitions to be good, law-abiding citizens; to adjust to society, to conform to whatever exists. These teachings may have been adequate for a stable society, an intact culture, but they are worse than useless today.[20]

What shall we teach, then, to prepare our children for life in a rapidly changing society? The complexity of that society is reflected in the varied and controversial curricula the schools offer, especially the high schools and colleges. There are those who insist on a proper deference to tradition, to Old World culture, language, and literature. Others are equally insistent that science and mathematics get top priority.

American Satellite. *The advent of the space age and the race for scientific supremacy with the Russians have forced a re-examination of our traditional educational methods, goals, and values.*

Controversy over general and specific education became inevitable as occupations became more and more highly specialized. The Harvard Report on General Education in a Free Society sees the two as complementary: special education trains a person to be competent in some occupation, while general or liberal education prepares a person for life as a responsible human being and citizen. General education must represent "the common knowedge and common values on which a free society depends . . . Basic for all citizens are the abilities to think effectively, to communicate thought, to make relevant judgments, and to discriminate among values." [21]

Common values are crucial to the unity of a multi-group society. To promote social integration is regarded as one task of the schools; and an active program of "intergroup education" has been developed in recent years, especially in training teachers to meet the demands of heterogeneous schools. The teacher can build loyalty to the larger group and to the society by providing pleasant experiences for all to share, thus building loyalty to the group; providing various prestige pyramids that reward manual skills, citizenship, and athletic and artistic ability, as well as intellectual accomplishments; providing adult models of democratic attitudes; giving opportunity to members of minority and lower-class groups; teaching what is known about human behavior and the basic economic and social problems of our time; and condemning discrimination on moral grounds.[22]

To whom shall this education be "given"? The glib answer, "Everybody," is unrealistic. The question becomes especially pertinent at the college level: Who shall be accepted, and how can "poor but worthy" students best be helped? And how can we reconcile the idea that all should have a college education with the demand for higher standards? As the Gallup Poll showed in 1958, most parents believe all high-school graduates should be admitted to college. This Jacksonian idea is, of course, the basis of our widespread elementary and high-school educational system, but the problem of lowered standards goes along with it.

Who shall be responsible for education? The family? Studies have shown that children's attitudes correspond much more closely to those of their parents than to those of their teachers. By the time the school gets the child, the family has had five or six years to impart its own beliefs and attitudes to him.

Nonetheless, American parents have in large measure "passed the buck" to teachers, expecting them to teach manners and morals as well as math and music. According to a poll by Elmo Roper, 90 per cent of the parents expect the schools to teach their children the principles of fair play, the difference between right and wrong, and so on. The trend over the years has been to permit and expect the schools to take over more and more of the job of educating American children. The Costa Ricans, in contrast, consider it the parents' duty to *educate,* the school's to *instruct.* When they admiringly describe a person as "well educated," they refer to his character, his charm, his ability to get along with others. The educated person may also be "well instructed" in "book learning" and technical training, but it does not follow that a "well instructed" person is necessarily "well educated."

Methods. Perhaps the thorniest question of all is, How shall children and young people be taught? Teacher-training institutions are frequently accused of paying too much attention to method and technique and too little to subject matter, with the result that new teachers are far better versed in *how* to teach than in *what* they are to teach.

One aspect of this question is the great debate over "traditional" vs. "progressive" education. In a typical exchange, a traditionalist accuses the "educationists" of being anti-intellectual, of making the schools into "high-walled playgrounds." He cites the trend away from foreign languages, physics, and mathematics as one effect of the dominance of "educationists" and charges that far from being less important these subjects are more important today than ever. The defender of progressive education calls it "part and parcel of the general advance in modern thought," not only teaching the 3 R's and other school subjects but teaching them better than do rigidly academic schools. Three fundamental principles, he declares, guide modern education: that education is primarily character-building, not just instruction in subject matter; that it aims to develop each child to the full extent of his ability; and that only actual behaving—not merely knowing—really builds character. Replying to the charge of anti-intellectualism, he says that mind is more than mere intellect, that information alone is not enough, for attitudes and values carry thinking into action.[23]

Technological advances have introduced another element into the question of method. Adoption of and resistance to film strips, tape recorders, TV classes, movies, and other similar inventions provide us with a concrete example of the processes of cultural change in operation. Perhaps as a result of their traditional dependence on written and spoken words, teachers tend to have an anti-technical bias, a resistance to "gadgetry" and "hardware." "This attitude has inhibited creativity, imagination, and invention relative to how the educative processes can be made more *efficient, productive,* and *less costly* in terms of human energy expenditure." [24]

Vested interests also appear to be resisting the use of TV. In spite of the boom in enrollment and the shortage of teachers and classrooms, many teachers see in TV instruction a threat to their jobs. A number of their objections are, of course, legitimate criticisms that involve misuse of the medium, but experimentation is obviously necessary to find how best to use any new educational technique.

Most people seem to believe that mass media of communication generally do not need as much supervision and control as do the schools, because the movies, television, comic books and the like, are recreational rather than educational. Sociologists disagree. Willy-nilly, the mass media do a great deal of teaching. Herbert Blumer, in a sociological study of the effect of movies on the adolescent, states that they "define his role, elicit and direct his impulses, and provide substance for his emotions and ideas. Their modes of life are likely to carry an authority and sanction which make them formative of codes of living." [25]

More recent research has indicated that in the main, mass media do not have a direct effect on child conduct but rather are mediated by peer groups. That is, the more highly a child values his membership in the peer group, the less he will be affected by ideas and values that are contrary to those of the group; and he will judge and choose the material presented by the media in terms of their usefulness to his adjustment in the group.

The peer group, as we saw in Chapter Eleven, also is a major socializing agency, from which a person learns as long as he lives. It is the second group the child enters in point of time; it is not, of course, any one stable group but a succession of specific people and groups. Children and adolescents share a sub-culture of their own, with customs and rituals, even language, that are a mystery to adults.

The peer group also imparts adult mores and values, whether of the slums, of the American middle class, as reflected in the Scout movement, or of the totalitarian state, as seen in the Hitler Youth or the Young Communist League and the Pioneers of Communist Russia. The peer group gives children an opportunity to experiment with social relationships, trying out new roles and ways of behaving.

When we consider how uncertain they are about the aims of the schools themselves, it is not surprising that Americans concerned about education do not usually consider these other potent agencies of education part of the problem. This attitude is indicative of the segmented, disorganized, or unorganized nature of heterogeneous, secondary society. The formal institution, the school, is supposed somehow to counteract any undesirable influences of home, peer group, and mass media or fill in the gaps they leave in socializing the child. But most Americans do not feel that these agencies need any special guidance or control.

Freedom and control. If the schools are to be considered *the* educative agencies—and they are in our society so considered—then who is to see that they do their job? For example, who is to make the changes that must be made in our recruitment and training of scientists and engineers? Some have advocated a central planning agency. But it appears likely that our cherished principles of local control and voluntary action eventually will win out. Already many teachers are increasing the content of courses that may have been "watered-down." Administrators are voluntarily looking for ways to reduce cultural lag in schools and colleges and are tightening entrance and graduation requirements. Educators and laymen are examining curricula and teaching methods. Television is showing films of scientists at work and play to dispel the old stereotypes. Newspapers and magazines publicize all sides of the controversy. Parents urge their children to plug at homework a bit harder.

These diffuse and voluntary reactions to the educational crisis may not, however, be sufficient. Values do not change overnight. The "egghead" of October 3, 1957, did not become the national hero the day after Sputnik I was launched. Our policy-makers are considering ways of raising the pay and prestige of teachers and scientists, of providing opportunities for financially insecure students to attend college, of seeking out and training truly gifted children, of putting buildings to maximum use, and of fitting curricula to the needs of our times.

Can education be the vanguard of progress? Most Americans believe it can be, believe that a properly organized system of education will enable us to regain our lost prestige as the world's technological leader. More than two decades ago John Dewey declared,

It is not whether the schools shall or shall not influence the course of future social life, but in what direction they shall do so and how. . . .

There are three possible directions of choice. Educators may act so as to perpetuate the present confusion and possibly increase it. That will be the result of drift, and under present conditions to drift is in the end to make a choice. Or they may select the newer scientific, technological, and cultural forces that are producing change in the old order; may estimate the direction in which they are moving and their outcome if they are given freer play, and see what can be done to make the schools their ally. Or, educators may become intelligently conservative and strive to make the schools a force in maintaining the old order intact against the impact of new forces.[26]

About a quarter century after these words were written, most social scientists and educational philosophers—even his strongest critics—will agree with Dewey that the second course is the only one for Americans to choose.

Many Americans see the spearhead of progress, as well as a chief guarantee of freedom, in the university. Most college professors are permitted—even expected and encouraged—to teach as they see fit and to advance the frontiers of knowledge through research. Some research is purely individual and voluntary, stimulated by interaction with others in the same field at conventions and through books and professional journals. Some is subsidized directly by business corporations, philanthropic and educational foundations, and government agencies.

There is some danger that in measuring our school system against the European, and especially against the Russian, we may lose sight of the traditional value of academic freedom. This value is always on the defensive. It sometimes appears to be in sharp conflict with other traditional values—apparently, at least, to the newspaper reporter seeking headline material at a convention. Says Zechariah Chafee, Jr., a professor at Harvard University,

> The professor who indulges in heterodox views about economics, government, international affairs, and law . . . occupies the front page of newspapers beside bank robbers. . . .
>
> People are inclined to regard the multiplication table as characteristic of all education—something which is just so and not otherwise, which once learned stays with you through life. When a professor expresses to his class ideas about politics or economics with which the critics disagree, they think it just as bad as telling boys and girls that seven times nine is sixty-one. Of course there is a core of indubitable knowledge in education, but most of the teacher's task consists in imparting methods for understanding what is still unknown and dealing with it wisely. . . .
>
> Legislatures make it possible for scholars to think and teach. There

the political part in education should end. . . . If (universities) are deprived of freedom of thought and speech, there is no other place to which citizens can confidently turn for long views about public issues. . . . We need to make our fellow citizens realize that freedom is not safety, but opportunity.[27]

FOURTEEN

Religion as a Social Institution

Down through the ages, and to all manner of men, religion has given hope to those in despair, answers to those in trouble, solace to those who are bereaved. Little wonder, then, that religion is one of the cultural universals. And little wonder that men are often more defensive, more emotional, about their religion than about any other aspect of their lives. To millions of people, religious faith represents

315

contact with the ultimate, the unchanging, The Eternal. It answers the Psalmist's plea, "Lead me to the rock that is higher than I."

This fundamental importance of religion to mankind makes it one of the basic social institutions, and as such, it deserves careful study by social scientists. But because the aim of social science is to increase understanding, and not to support a particular point of view, the social science approach to religion must remain as free as possible from sectarian emphases. Hence, in this chapter we shall regard religion very broadly as that aspect of culture that deals with sacred things. As one well-known sociologist has phrased it, religion is concerned with "things set apart and forbidden," with the transcendental and the inviolable.

Such a conception of religion, in contrast to (but without judging) any sectarian claim to represent "the one true faith," encourages an analysis of religion's many forms. These forms include faiths as diverse as polytheism, or the belief in multiple gods, and monotheism, or the belief in one God; naturalistic humanism, or the agnostic disregard of spiritual beings; animism, or the belief that all objects have souls; and even magic, which is the belief that spiritual forces can be controlled through the medium of carefully conducted rituals. Religious diversity, as well as the relative strength of religious organizations, is also indicated by the figures included in the tables below and on page 317, which show the number of members claimed for the major religious bodies in the United States and in the world.

Basic religious orientations such as are listed in the tables are representative of all religion, as we have defined the word, because they are concerned with some aspect of the sacred. They and their institutional manifestations (churches, sects, denominations) are in most societies more or less intimately associated with cultural ideas and codes of right and wrong. Religious institutions often supervise and enforce these ideas and codes with such sanctions as the threat of supernatural punishment and the promise of supernatural reward. Even naturalistic human-

• **Membership of Religious Groups in the United States, 1956** [1]

Religious Group	Number of Members
Buddhist	63,000
Old Catholic and Polish National Catholic	351,068
Eastern Churches	2,598,055
Jewish Congregations	5,500,000
Roman Catholic	34,563,851
Protestant [2]	60,148,980
Total	103,224,954

ists go beyond the mundane level of ethics in ascribing a transcendental nature to many of their values. This tie-up of religion and morals is especially close in primitive societies, but it is easier to differentiate the purely moral or ethical from the sacred in complex cultures.

The complexity and importance of religion, as indicated in the foregoing comments and data, indirectly suggest that the social scientist can—indeed, *must*—approach religion from many angles. But no matter what approach he uses, his chief interest is in the consequences of religion's interaction with other aspects of society and culture. We now turn to some examples of these consequences, concentrating first on rep-

• **Estimated Membership of Major Religious Groups**
of the World, 1957 [3]

Religious Group	Estimated Membership [4]
Christian	835,564,542
Roman Catholic	496,512,000
Eastern Orthodox	129,192,755
Protestant	209,859,787
Jewish (all Jews)	11,936,871
Moslem	420,606,698
Zoroastrian	140,000
Shinto	30,000,000
Taoist	50,053,200
Confucian	300,290,500
Buddhist	150,310,000
Hindu	322,337,286
"Primitive"	121,150,000
Others or none	402,450,903
Total	2,644,840,000

resentative ways in which society and culture shape religion, and secondly on the religious impact on society and the individual. As we examine these topics, keep in mind that the group aspects of religious belief and organization, upon which social science concentrates attention, are only a part of what might be called "the whole truth" about religion.

Social Influences   •   *Socio-cultural influence in religious be-*
in Religion   *lief.* We learn specific religious beliefs,
                                            as well as religious faith in general, in
                                            the same way that we learn other attitudes and behavior. This elementary fact has profound implications. It suggests that the churches, ritual, dogma, and articles of faith which mean so much to many individuals and groups would be unknown or meaningless to them but for the chance combination of a multitude of

variables. Among these variables are the human group factors that are the particular concern of social science.

Why, John Doe might ask himself, am I a Presbyterian? If his case is typical, he can probably trace his religious belief to his family group, who introduced him to Presbyterian teachings early enough and for long enough so that now he sincerely believes in them. But if he is honest with himself, he will have to admit that he could just as easily have become a Methodist, a Catholic, a Baptist, or an adherent of Japanese Shinto if he had been reared in other cultural surroundings or times. Or what if his parents had been converted to some other faith before he was born? What if, when he was very young, his parents had suffered so much because of economic depression that they were attracted to a cooperative sect that preached communal ownership of property? What if some authoritarian government had dispersed all Presbyterian congregations as heretical? Would John Doe still be a Presbyterian? Probably not.

Specific religious beliefs, as well as denominational membership, are associated with socio-cultural surroundings. One particularly significant example is suggested by the statement, "Man creates his gods in his own image." Although this statement is one-sided and has been quoted so often that it has become a cliché, it is true to the extent that it means that members of all religious groups tend to attribute to their god or gods characteristics that are familiar, admired, or necessary in their own culture. This tendency, called *anthropomorphism*, explains why agricultural societies pay special homage to their fertility gods, why aggressive groups glorify their war gods, why hunting cultures venerate their animal gods, and why patriarchal societies revere their father-figure gods.

The influence of social change on concepts of God can be detected in the beliefs of the ancient Jews. When they were nomads following their herds, they believed in a vengeful tribal deity whose major function was to give them aid in battle. But when the Jews settled in an area where they were threatened on all sides by powerful enemies, they changed their conception of God to a figure of love to whom they thought all men should give their allegiance (a statement which is by no means a full explanation of Jewish monotheism).

So far as we can determine, men can never know, much less believe in, phenomena that are not related in some way to their own culture or personal experience. We can think and visualize only in terms of the symbols provided us by our culture. The truth of this fundamental principle will be explained in greater detail as we show how religion is affected by class stratification, economic institutions, government, science, and secular education.

A Basic Social Institution. *Religion is present in every culture and reacts intimately with other cultural patterns and institutions.*

Social stratification and economic factors. Many careful studies have shown that there is a close association between the socio-economic status of people and their religious beliefs and loyalties.[5] Stated in general terms, these studies indicate that most lower-class people tend to prefer religious emotionalism and promises of a happy spiritual future, whereas the majority of higher-class people prefer decorum in their religious services and an emphasis on adjustment to demands of the present. Although such preferences do not clearly prove the existence of any cause-and-effect sequence, they do indicate that the success or failure of particular religious beliefs and organizations is often related to nonreligious factors.

The culture complex known as "Negro religion" is one of the more obvious examples. Although the term "Negro religion" is a stereotyped designation that cannot be used correctly in a general sense, it is true that many lower-class American Negroes are adherents of religious sects that stress gaudy ceremonialism and ecstatic services. This tendency is usually ascribed to the fact that as members of a lower-class and disadvantaged minority group many Negroes find compensation in religious emotionalism and future-promise theology. In recent years lower-class Detroit Negroes, many of them migrants from the rural South, flocked to hear the sermons of "Prophet" Jones. Reverend Jones surrounded himself with uniformed and bedecked aides dubbed "Princes" and "Princesses," conducted his services in an ornate "throne room," and, so he said, refused to wear an earring on his right ear because God spoke personally to him through that orifice. After the prophet left Detroit, he was replaced by Bishop "Daddy" Grace, who has said, "If you sin against God, Grace can save you, but if you sin against Grace, God cannot save you."[6] The emergence of these colorful religious leaders illustrates the general principle that there is a negative relationship between the socio-economic status of various groups and the number of self-proclaimed prophets and messiahs who appear among them.[7]

The religious preferences of whites are also related to their socio-economic statuses. Various studies over the years have shown that lower-class American Protestant whites typically belong to demonstrative and fundamentalist sects, whereas upper-class people (Negro and white alike) are most likely to be members of reserved and tradition-laden Episcopalian or Congregationalist churches. In large Protestant and Catholic churches where the membership cuts across class lines, there are class-oriented clubs and other sub-organizations whose members can associate more or less exclusively with others who "speak their own language." When they are denied this privilege, as Hollingshead described in *Elmtown's Youth,* they often refuse to participate in any church activities at all.[8]

This class-caste orientation in religion is found in almost all societies. The ancient Polynesians believed that only nobles could hope to gain immortality. In Hawaii, before the island was Westernized, commoners and slaves were believed to possess much less of the spiritual power called *mana* than members of the ruling class. Among the ancient Chinese, members of the ruling bureaucracy were almost always Confucianist, while the masses were more likely to cling to Taoism, which promised that the faithful could obtain the magical help of spiritual beings in times of need. In modern Sicily, nominally Roman Catholic peasants, but not gentry, still pay homage to ancient nature gods.

There are three basic reasons for most such religious manifestations of social stratification: (1) the legally enforced group segregation found in some societies, (2) the fact that most people feel comfortable only when they are associating with other people who share similar values and tastes, and (3) the different psychological and physical needs of members of different status groupings.

The third factor helps to explain the popularity of the "peace of mind" type of religious emphasis in recent years. War prosperity and government-sponsored welfare programs have expanded the middle classes, whose basic religious need involves reassurance that middle-class striving for material gain is worth while, in contrast to the compensatory needs of the lower classes and the hope of the upper classes that their dominant position in society will be legitimized. Apparently the search for reassurance has, in part, persuaded more and more people to attend churches, to read books, and to listen to television programs that promise, in effect, "You can conquer the world if only you will follow ten simple rules of devotion." This form of religious emphasis will undoubtedly lose some of its popularity if hard times reduce many marginal middle-class members to a lower-class status.

Governmental factors. The impact on religion of social stratification and economic factors is matched or exceeded by the impact of government. Religious organizations and activities are sometimes curtailed and sometimes encouraged by different governments. The Roman Catholic Church, for example, is given special privileges in neofascist Spain, but it was all but outlawed in revolutionary Mexico. In Italy, Protestant churches must secure hard-to-get government permits before they can hold services, and in Norway the Jesuits were banned until 1956. Religious institutions very often have been amalgamated with the state. Shinto has been the state religion in Japan and Buddhistic Lamaism is presumably still the official religion of Tibet. The fortunes of religious organizations are, thus, often closely tied to the policies of the governments under which they exist.

Governmental institutions are also reflected in the internal structure of many churches. The emphasis on congregational control in so many American churches is in keeping with our cultural tradition of relatively decentralized government. In the United States, Lutherans have adopted a representative council type of church government that is quite different from the European Lutheran practice of organizing the church along *state* lines with controls running rigidly from top to bottom of an established hierarchy. According to one bishop, the American Lutheran denomination deliberately used the United States Constitution as a model for its church constitution. Only those Lutheran congregations that embrace many first- and second-generation immigrants still retain the authoritarian structure of large-scale European churches.

The Roman Catholic Church is, of course, the classic example of a church government that reflects secular arrangements. The popes "moved into the palace of the emperors" of the Roman Empire after a struggle for power among the various bishops.[9] There was nothing necessarily diabolical about this development, as some extremists would have us believe. When it occurred, it was in accordance with the cultural values of those involved and it facilitated the Church's proclaimed function of saving souls for the glory of God. The work of the Church was also aided by the establishment of a system of archbishops, parish priests, and other officials with authority and territorial supremacy that exactly matched the authority of the imperial bureaucracy. And the fortunes of the Church were controlled in large measure by the political situation within the Empire. In the East, where centralized political control was lacking, national Catholic churches such as the Armenian, Russian, and Greek Orthodox appeared very early and exist to this day. But in the West, where imperial control lasted long enough to establish firmly the idea of a supranational church, most Catholics remained faithful to Rome, which seemed natural in view of Rome's political supremacy. This supremacy was not seriously challenged until economic changes and the emergence of nationalism, along with religious grievances, led to the mass formation of dissident sects and national churches during the period of the Protestant Reformation.

Science and educational factors. During recent generations, science— its methods and its findings—has perhaps been the most important of all the secular aspects of life that have affected religion in the West. This is particularly true of urban areas where people are in constant touch with new ideas and discoveries. It is becoming increasingly true of rural and non-Western areas as mass media of communication and transportation, widespread secular education, and the constantly increasing interdependence of the people of the world minimize the effect of geographical distance and national differences.

The methods of science have affected religion because they have led many people to be skeptical about the dogmatic nature of the religious approach to knowledge. As one science advocate has expressed it, "It would be a shock to come across a university where it was the practice of the students to recite adherence to Newton's laws of motion, to Maxwell's equations, and to the electromagnetic theory of light."[10] Scientists everywhere have proclaimed that the way to "truth" lies in questioning every conclusion, conducting careful research, and keeping an open mind. Using this approach, they have shown that all known phenomena are subject to natural law, and they have given men the means of controlling many processes once thought to be "in the laps of the gods." Their spectacular success has inevitably led many people to doubt the reliability of the traditional religious use of intuition, sacred literature, and established dogma. The religious crisis thus implied has been made more acute by the fact that most teachers, who help to shape the beliefs of coming generations, are now graduates of higher educational systems that stress the tentativeness of generalizations and the relativity of truth.

The findings of science, as well as its methods, have undermined belief in a number of dogmas that once served as the foundation stones of religious conviction for all Christians. Rightly or wrongly, many people have discarded or modified their ideas that our world is the hub of the universe and that man is the center of God's concern, that morals are commandments from God, that man was created as a full-blown human being, and that every word in the Bible is to be taken literally. For better or for worse, such beliefs have been challenged by astronomical, biological, social, and Biblical research.

Astronomical studies have shown that far from being the center of the universe, our world is a mere speck orbiting around a minor star that is itself only a pinprick in one of millions of galaxies similar to our own Milky Way. Social science research has shown that though people may believe that morals derive from some ultimate source, in a practical sense moral ideas appear to be culturally determined and changing customs that a group accepts as best for its welfare. Biological studies have shown that man as a physical being is the end product of evolutionary processes in which the chance factors of mutation and selective survival have played the most important parts. This finding has been complemented by the social-psychological generalization that men are not born human but must learn from their fellows how to acquire their culture's version of human nature. In addition, chemists and other scientists have produced simple forms of life from non-living matter, and are on the verge of synthesizing higher organisms. Biblical research, finally, has demonstrated that the Bible we know is a product not purely of spiritual inspiration but of the historical views of men and women whose knowledge was limited, of a long drawn-out controversy and eventual compromise over which passages to include or exclude, and of imperfect translation.

Many devout people are, of course, not impressed with findings such as these. When they come upon scientific studies that have religious implications, they often accommodate by concluding that such discoveries simply demonstrate the final power of God. They also find comfort in the thought that perhaps God uses the dissemination of scientific knowledge as an acid test of faith. And, finally, they assert—and no one can prove otherwise—that science has not said and cannot justifiably say anything about belief in God as an ultimate creator.

Furthermore, there are many people who see no essential conflict between science and religion, for both are seeking *meanings*. Both reject the notion that life "is a tale told by an idiot, full of sound and fury, signifying nothing." One well-known writer sees the relationship between science and religion in these terms:

> Science represents the search for certainty, while recognizing that the ultimate and total certainties will always elude man, who did not create the cosmos but lives as one of its creatures within it.
>
> And religion, it seems to me, is a companion search for certainty, for the truth about man's relation to the Creative Power outside and within himself, and for the truth about creative relations with his fellow men.[11]

Many others, however, have not found it possible to rationalize their faith in the light of modern scientific knowledge. Their failure to do so has prompted clergymen on every hand to bemoan the loss of traditional religious beliefs despite the superficial figures that indicate a recent increase in church membership. Yes, people are going to church! But, as we have already mentioned, the most significant religious trend of our day is the widespread enthusiasm about "peace of mind" or "the cult of reassurance." [12] This religious emphasis pays little more than lip service to the old spiritual ideals, and places its major stress on how to be happy in the *material* world. And this emphasis is not confined to Protestants; the popularity of novenas among Catholics, peace-of-mind books among Jews, and sermons on such topics as "Your Hidden Resources Within" among humanist Unitarians suggest that its appeal is very broad indeed.

It is, perhaps, a measure of people's desperation that they have turned to the cult of reassurance. What else is left for many? Under the impact of modern science and secular education, so many of the old guideposts have been attacked and watered down that more and more people are confessing that they are confused and disheartened. They are no longer absolutely sure about what is right, what is true, what is good. This—to express a value judgment—is the real tragedy of modern man; he *wants* to believe, but he does not know *what* to believe. This is what science has done to Western religion and to men who once believed and were comforted by their belief. And this is what will probably happen in other areas as they become Westernized, secularized, and science-oriented.

How Religion Influences Man and Society   •   *Religion and sanctification.* Religion does not, as the preceding material might suggest, merely react to the social order and to other elements of culture. It is often a prime mover in itself. Perhaps its most basic function is "sanctification." Sanctification is the attempt on the part of religious associations in all cultures and at all times to uphold selected mores and values by relating them to the divine. The importance of this process—inculcating the belief that certain values or procedures are of transcendental importance and therefore inviolable—is that it constitutes the very cement of social cohesion. Religion, in short (or, at least, its sanctification function), is a prime essential for stable, long-term social organization.

No social order, especially during times of crisis, can long endure if the loyalty of its members is founded on nothing more than ordinary folkways or practical demands of the moment. The members *must* believe that something of the Eternal is involved in their organization if it is to have a permanence and stability that goes substantially beyond that of a club or fraternal association. The Eternal aspect of a stable social organization may include an institutionalized church complete with functionaries and sacred literature; or a set of political and economic theories such as Marxism, which is given unquestioned allegiance in a Communist state; or a vague sentiment such as "The American Way of Life." [13] The essential thing is that the people concerned must believe in the transcendental nature of their basic values or sentiments, however vague.

Religion in the broad sense, thus, is involved in man's freedom-control problems, which we have been analyzing throughout this book.

Religion and Sanctification. *In all societies and throughout all ages sacred objects such as this figure of the Egyptian God, Amon, symbolize to worshippers the transcendental and inviolable nature of their beliefs.*

When religion preaches adherence to a set of values, it tends to limit man's freedom to make rational choices. But such limitation and control is necessary if man is to be free of the anarchy and chaos that would arise if everyone was taught to make nothing but purely individualistic decisions.

Religious reactions to other institutions. In addition to its sanctification function, religion can have many other important consequences for the individual and for society. Some of the most significant of these consequences from the social science point of view are related to the degree of support given by various religious groupings to other social institutions. It is impossible to measure accurately the results of such support, or lack of support, but it is usually presumed to be vital, especially in a highly integrated society. In feudal Japan, for example, the Emperor derived much of his power from the Shinto belief that he was directly descended from the sun goddess, Amaterasu. When, between the eighth and seventeenth centuries, Shinto was all but absorbed by Buddhism, the emperor's loss of religious support contributed to a breakdown of centralized authority and a centuries-long period of civil war.

Although it is true that in most cases the effects of degrees of religious support or challenge of other institutions are not as clear as in the Japanese example we have just cited, it is possible to clarify the factors underlying such religious reactions. The basic principle involved is that *religious support or challenge of particular institutions depends on whether or not the adherents of given religions are accustomed to the institutions and believe they profit from them.* The following generalizations are related to this basic principle:

(1) It is the large, firmly-entrenched religious groupings that are indigenous or acculturated to a society that generally support the established institutions of the society.

(2) Criticism of particular social institutions frequently comes from religious groupings that (a) are small and relatively less well-established; or (b) are located in, or concerned with, societies to which they are not indigenous or acculturated; or (c) participate in a culture where antipathy toward certain institutions becomes part of the underlying ethos.

The foregoing principle and the two related generalizations do not mean that religious communicants and functionaries, even when they violate their religious ideals, are necessarily opportunistic or hypocritical. The principle and generalizations are simply expressions of the fact that *religion,* like all of culture, never does anything "by itself." It functions through *people,* and people are—among other things—products of conditioning. If people are conditioned to believe in a given stratification system, for example, and if they feel that it works for them, then *of course* they will make sure that their religion, as well as their other institutions, supports it. Similarly, if the members of a religious group find that certain institutional arrangements are not suited to them, they will generally challenge the institution, and—other things being equal— they will adhere to their religion only if it supports their actions or, at least, does not thwart them.

It is in the light of such explanatory factors that the social scientist, to be objective, must view the variety of religious reactions to different institutions. The contrasting judgments of fascism by southern European and North American Roman Catholics is a convenient example—and it is only an example; similar Protestant experiences could be cited. Fascism was not opposed by many southern European Catholics for the simple reason that it was compatible with the basic social values in terms of which they had been conditioned. Furthermore, once fascism became dominant in an area, most of those living in the area who wanted to share in the benefits of their society were forced to give at least lip service to the fascist philosophy. It is little wonder, then, that Roman Catholic officialdom signed agreements with fascist governments in such countries as Austria, Italy, Spain, and Portugal. But in the United States, most Catholic officials today are products of the same democratic ethos that influences non-Catholic Americans. Hence it is not surprising that the majority of American Catholic prelates are highly critical of totalitarian governments. It would not only be disadvantageous for them and their church to support totalitarianism in the United States; it would be foreign to them as citizens conditioned in terms of the democratic way of life.

The way in which different religious groups have reacted to Negro segregation and discrimination in the South provides another example. Until recently, various Protestant religious institutions controlled by white southerners gave explicit support to separation of the races. They supported segregation not only because their churches would lose members if they did not, but also because to those involved it seemed the natural thing to do since they had been taught from childhood that segregation was best for all concerned. But northern-controlled denominations gained no particular advantage from segregation and their members were conditioned in contrary terms. Hence it was relatively easy for them to criticize the southern caste system. They were joined in their criticism by many Roman Catholic Church officials in the South who were not southerners and therefore had not been conditioned to believe in segregation. Nowadays, southern as well as northern religious groups are challenging racial caste, at least partly in response to the fact that racial brotherhood—an ideal kept alive through the centuries by a variety of religious sects—has become a more widely accepted secular ideal to which all institutions must adjust if they hope to survive.

The support generally accorded established institutions by the large and prosperous religious groupings stems in part at least from the fact that as respectable organizations they attract influential people whose relatively high status depends on the maintenance of the social status quo. Society has been good to the influential or they would not occupy its upper brackets. Hence it is to be expected that they would bend every effort to prevent their churches as well as other institutions from criticizing existing societal arrangements. The disadvantaged, on the other hand, form or are attracted to dissenting churches, such as the early Quaker and Methodist, where they can express their frustrations by criticizing society (if the churches do not simply stress purely other-worldly goals). When such dissenting sects are successful in attracting large numbers of converts, their increased power tends to make social criticism seem less necessary. A religious grouping that undergoes this type of change in value orientation will then typically attain a measure of respectability that will in turn encourage higher-status people to become members. New generations of the dissatisfied will then find their needs unmet and will generally break off and form new sects. Thus, the degree of support given secular socio-economic institutions by religious organizations is part of the process that often produces new religious emphases.

Religion and insecurity. It is religion's contribution to mental peace that constitutes its most important function for the individual, according to some well-known psychological theories of religion. Those who adhere to such theories assert that one of the fundamental functions of religion is to help men find a common ground between the expectations that are set forth in the society's ideal culture patterns and the realities of their everyday experiences. The desire to find such a common ground appears to be universal, but is probably felt most keenly by those who are insecure, as suggested by the fact that interest in religion is greatest everywhere among those elements of society who live under some special disadvantage.

A pertinent illustration is the relatively intense religious interest of most American Negroes—and of lower-class groups generally, unless they are completely without hope or do not question their place in society. In Liston Pope's study of impoverished mill workers in an industrial county, he quotes one laborer's typical remark, "The prayer meetings are about the only entertainment we have."[14] The mill workers asserted that they wanted "a bucket of blood with every sermon," and their favorite hymns were those that promised release in the hereafter: "Beulah Land," "When the Roll is Called up Yonder," "Higher Ground," and "I Can Hear My Savior Calling."

The prevalence of messianic movements among Jews and among American Indians may also be explained to some extent by the hardships these groups have suffered. The American Indian Ghost Dance cult is a manifestation of and provides catharsis for Indian hates, fears, and insecurities.[15] The Ghost Dance, which proclaimed that Indian culture would once more be dominant in the Americas, appeared when the buffalo began to disappear; but Indian societies such as the Pueblo, which did not depend upon the buffalo, remained indifferent to the new cult. A similar situation explains the appeal of the Tigari cult on the Gold Coast of Africa.[16] Despite the great cost involved in maintaining its priesthood, Tigari has steadily gained popularity during the past 25 years because the introduction of Western culture has led to widespread personal and social disorganization among Gold-Coasters. They turn to Tigari as a prophylaxis against the *anyen* (evil magic) which, they believe, explains their inability to achieve the goals that are associated with the European way of life.

In complex societies religious "awakenings" are more widespread among relatively insecure sub-groupings than within larger dominant groups. As an example we can cite the study, conducted at the universities of Hawaii, Harvard, and Radcliffe, which disclosed that most students experienced types of religious conversion around the age of sixteen.[17] The explanation suggested by those in charge of the research was that adolescents in the American social structure stand uneasily on the borderline between childhood and adulthood. Insecure in status and uncertain about their proper role behavior, they very often turn at least temporarily to religion for an answer to their questions.

At the other extreme are the aged, who must adjust to the immediacy of death. Almost all qualified observers have noticed the preponderance of elderly people, especially women, on church membership rolls. Older people, too, are more devout and orthodox in their beliefs than younger people. Many of them seek the comfort that comes from religious sanctification of activities and beliefs that are associated with some form of permanent spiritual or material survival. The majority of church members are women, probably because of the subordinate position that women, relative to men, occupy in most societies. Correspondents abroad frequently mention how few men are seen in French Roman Catholic churches, and a comprehensive survey of nearly 67,000 Protestants in Indianapolis showed that only three out of ten church members there are male.[18]

Some latent consequences of the religious influence on society. It is, of course, the manifest purpose of most religious systems to facilitate favorable relationships with spiritual or supernatural forces. But religious beliefs and institutions often have latent, or unintended, consequences for human life. One homely example is the fish that certain American Indians placed in each corn mound to satisfy the spirits; the fish also served as an effective fertilizer which helped to enhance the food supply. The latter consequence would be regarded as a positive function from our material point of view. Religion can also have what are thought of as negative or dysfunctional consequences. The Dahomey of Africa, thus, endanger their food supply when they destroy crops during funeral ceremonies. Similarly, some psychiatrists have pointed out that certain types of religious beliefs contribute to fear and guilt feelings that may result in mental illness.

The latent functions of religion were investigated in a series of well-known studies by Max Weber, a German sociologist. In his most widely read work, Weber demonstrated a relationship between the development of Calvinistic (and Puritanical-Pietistic) Protestantism and capitalism.[19] Although he may have been wrong about the sequence of events he depicted, he was certainly correct in stating that the Calvinistic doctrines of stewardship and self-denial were the same values needed for the development of capitalism. He was also correct in his claim that the Calvinistic belief that a person should strive to master material forces (to demonstrate the glory of God) has been an important element in the growth of science, and that the individualistic stress in ascetic Protestantism indirectly helped to stimulate the formation of democratic governments. The irony of such latent consequences of religion is that the Calvinists certainly manifested no conscious wish to become rich and therefore worldly, to become scientific and therefore skeptical, or to become democratic and therefore tolerant of other faiths. But, according to Weber, these were the inevitable accompaniments of "the Protestant Ethic." The latent functions of other religions are similarly unavoidable and, as in Protestantism, are often more significant in the long run than the manifest functions.

In this brief consideration of religion as a social institution, we have not tried to inquire into the possible truth or falsity of the great variety of religious beliefs. Our aim, rather, has been to demonstrate some of the consequences of religio-social interaction. We have seen that specific religious beliefs, as well as membership in particular denominations, are learned reactions that depend on a number of human group variables such as social stratification, economic factors, government, science, and education. These and other components of the social order are, in turn, affected by the functions of religion. We saw that when the basic religious function of "sanctification" is fulfilled, the coherence of large-scale social organizations is facilitated. We also observed that religion has a significant part to play in its support of, or challenge to, established institutional arrangements, in helping to resolve fear and anxiety among the insecure, and in its latent effects. Religion is thus both cause and consequence of other social and cultural forces. Religion means, indeed, far more than this to those who feel their faith is "The true light, which lighteth every man that cometh into the world."

PART TWO

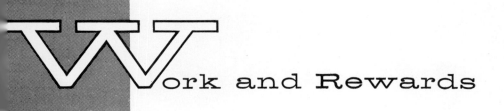

Work and Rewards

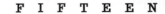

Economic Systems and Culture

An *economic system* is simply a means through which our wants are satisfied by the supply of goods and services. It is not something apart from the rest of the culture; nor can any individual—especially in our highly materialistic society—name many things he does during the day that are not in some way tied up with the economic system.[1]

We may not use the natural resources

335

around us as directly as does a South Sea Islander cultivating his yam patch or his wife weaving a grass skirt, but hour by hour we are doing things that reflect and affect our own American system of satisfying human needs and desires. Your breakfast of Frosty Grove Orange Juice, Peppo Wheat Flakes, and Stimulo Coffee; your decision to try that new striped toothpaste or to send a suit to the cleaners; your trip to the campus by streetcar or auto; your reading of ads en route; your certainty that the streetcars would run on schedule and the milkman would come in time for breakfast—these simple aspects of your daily routine are but a few examples of how you, as a consumer, are part of a vast and intricate system that caters to your needs and stimulates your wants along certain lines. Even in pursuit of "high learning" in the somewhat set-apart ivied walls of a college campus, you are oriented to our economy. You are probably preparing for a type of job that you have chosen largely because of its promise of money and security, perhaps rejecting one more suited to your tastes "because there's no future in it."

The economic system not only is very much a part of a person's daily life, but also is interwoven and "integrated" with all other aspects of a culture. It is difficult in many cases to say which is cause and which is effect in analyzing the relationship of an economic system to a society's system of government, its religion, family organization, schooling, and recreation. However, it is certain that all these reflect the influence of the economy and in turn affect it.

In India, among the Hindus, for example, people respond much more readily to religious beliefs than to material values. Hinduism teaches the sacredness of all life and forbids the slaying of cattle and the eating of beef by the natives. As a result, the groundwork for what might have become a prosperous native livestock industry was never laid. More subtle has been the influence of the Puritan ethic upon the rise of American capitalism. Puritan instruction consecrated the effort to become wealthy and preached the virtues of individual responsibility, thrift, and hard work with such devotion and intensity that these traits are still regarded by many Americans with much veneration and pride (see Chapters Five and Fourteen).

Where two patterns conflict, the society must make some attempt to integrate them or to eliminate the one more at variance with its traditions or its interests. These conflicts are numerous in a rapidly changing society such as our own. During the great depression of the 1930's many people were compelled to accept relief, a necessity that produced psychological conflicts in those who subscribed to our cultural value of individualism and our theory that "a man with any gumption can always make a living."

It was because of this conflict that public works projects and the food stamp plan were more compatible with our cultural values than the "dole." Changes in technology also may affect the other aspects of a culture profoundly. Industrialization, mechanization, and standardization have helped make our society urban and secular, and the rise of large corporations has been followed by government regulation of many aspects of business and legalization of trade unions, even though such changes long appeared to be inconsistent with our traditional cultural beliefs in individualism and free enterprise.

Why, then, do we study the economic aspect of culture separately? Because the economic system can be described as an institution—a complex of patterns clustering around one central function; because any scientific approach must *analyze*—examine component parts—while not losing sight of the whole.

In fact, why study economics at all? As we have already mentioned, each of us is affected by and affects our economic system. An understanding of that system can be of *personal value* to us and to our families in our everyday lives. Although a knowledge of economics won't necessarily enable us to make a fortune on the stock market, it can certainly help us to handle our own financial affairs.

In addition, a study of economics will help us *understand culture* in general, our own culture, and ourselves. Most adults spend most of their waking time working to satisfy their wants; no study of culture can afford to minimize this preoccupation. Certainly a culture like ours, dominated by an interest in material things and money-making, cannot be understood without paying special attention to its economic institutions. And since we reflect our culture, it follows that to understand ourselves we must understand this aspect, too, of our culture. It is a rare member of modern society who is not at least dimly aware that his fortunes are inextricably tied up with many things over which he appears to have little or no control.

Finally, a study of economic institutions will prepare us for *action as citizens*. An economic system is made by men—and can be changed by men. No given system is preordained, natural, inevitable. To vote intelligently, people need understanding and information about basic economic problems of the day.

As just one example of a question on which most Americans are confused, take foreign trade. We hear the slogan "Trade, not aid." That sounds fine. Then we are bombarded with arguments that this industry and that needs "protection" against competition from foreign meat, wheat, textiles, and the like, and wonder if we shouldn't retain some tariff walls. The argument that high tariff barriers turn our potential allies toward Russia swings us back in the other direction. It seems impossible to decide. Yet to this bewildering question and to many others there are good, clear answers to be found. With some knowledge of the basic principles of economics and some well-chosen reading, a person can be well informed about such knotty problems and use his vote and his influence to have them intelligently handled.

Wants • Human wants appear to be unlimited.
and Though people in every culture have
Resources the same basic wants such as food, shelter, clothing, security, sexual relationships, and companionship, these can be satisfied in a variety of ways. The natural environment and the culture determine what people will consider as suitable for the satisfaction of these basic wants. Tomatoes may flourish in the natural environment, but if people are taught that they are poisonous, as Americans were a century ago, they will not want them for food, regardless of their actual nutritional value. Certainly caviar, mink coats, and ultra-modern houses are elaborate and expensive means of satisfying the need for food, clothing, and shelter. Other factors, cultural ones, are extremely powerful here. The desire for prestige, for conspicuous consumption, for keeping up with the Joneses—desires stimulated by the advertiser—make the average American's wants apparently unlimited. Most people say that if they had one-fifth more income than at present they would be perfectly contented; but once they reach that goal, they set their sights higher.

In some cultures material wants do not loom so important as in ours. Nowhere, however, are man's wants freely provided for by a beneficent natural environment—not even in the South Sea Islands where breadfruit drops from the trees and the climate is ideal. Everywhere there is *scarcity* in relation to wants. Resources for satisfying wants are limited. Natural resources may be lacking or hard to extract. The population may consist primarily of children, or may be riddled with disease, or unwilling to work, or inefficient, or untrained, and thus unable to satisfy wants. As a result, there may be little productive capital in the form of machinery, factories, and savings. Even where resources are comparatively abundant, the population adequate and well-trained, and capital available, there is scarcity, for it appears that human wants always keep ahead of resources. Even in our highly productive American society there is scarcity, not merely in terms of the unsatisfied wants of those well supplied with the basic necessities, but even in terms of lack of adequate food, clothing, and shelter.

Everywhere, then, whether the standard of living is low or high, we find that resources are inadequate to satisfy wants. Therefore every society must *economize;* that is, it must develop social institutions to utilize the scarce resources for satisfying human wants. These institutions may take various forms. We call each society's system of organizing production and consumption an *economy. Economics* is the study of these organizations.

Are all human wants economic wants—recreational, religious and esthetic desires as well as biological needs? They are if they demand for their satisfaction the use of the scarce resources available—the time and energy of people, the use of capital, and the use of natural resources. Any goods or services that can be tagged with a price are economic commodities.

Decisions • Every society must make some basic
of Production decisions about its producing and consuming. First of all, *what shall be produced?* The society channels productive resources into the desired and needed types of goods. These may or may not be in proportion to the wants of individuals. At times the society must put group survival first and demand production of those things that will insure survival at the expense of those that satisfy individual wants not essential to group survival. In our society in peacetime the dollar votes of consumers guide production, on the whole. In wartime, however, our government restricts production of civilian goods to insure an adequate supply of war materials and to discourage inflationary spending by people with swollen incomes. In World War II our economy proved so flexible that through the full use of resources our level of living suffered little; on the whole we had both more guns and more butter, though some wants, such as cigarettes, nylons, and housing, were inadequately taken care of.

To get the goods and services it considers desirable, a society may encourage some types of production with subsidies, tax exemptions, medals, and other rewards, and discourage others by the imposition of quotas and high taxes. Some production may be tolerated because it does not seem wise or easy to interfere with it; some, such as coining money and making bootleg whiskey, may be forbidden.

The *method of production* must also be decided upon. Techniques vary. One man could take $1,000 worth of equipment to put 40 acres of fertile land into soy beans and through ignorance and error end up with a crop smaller than the number of seeds he had planted. By using other techniques the same man might produce a fair-sized crop, and through still other techniques a bumper crop. (We will assume weather conditions are the same in all instances.)

What method or technique, then, will be used? In our society we will generally use the technique that will bring us the greatest output in harmony with our mores and technology. If we find some better way, we are pretty sure to use it. Not all peoples feel the same way. Native peoples in the Pacific are said to have managed tolerably well with the American axes and shovels that they learned to use during World War II; but after they returned to their villages they, for the most part, again took up their own far less efficient but more customary tools and continued working much as they had before.

Among the mountain-dwelling Arapesh of New Guinea, each man plants several gardens, each one in cooperation with a different group of friends and relatives. They may be miles apart. He is host in one garden, guest in the others. Most of his time is subject to the plans of the "hosts" in the other gardens. This arrangement seems incredibly inefficient to us, for it is costly in terms of time and effort. There is no real physical need for cooperative gardening, but the Arapesh do not value individualism, efficiency, and competition. They consider warm human relationships, sociability, and cooperation more important.[2]

Still another problem involves the proportioning of *land, labor, capital,* and *enterprise*—the four basic resources or *factors of production* [3] available to man. To some extent, more of one and less of another can be used, depending on how efficient each factor is in relation to what it costs. For example, let's say a farmer can produce 100 tons of hay with *one-half* man-year and *75* acres, or *one* man-year and *50* acres, or *two* man-years and *30* acres. If the costs of capital and enterprise are the same in all cases, the most profitable of the three choices can be determined by figuring which combination of land and labor is least expensive.

In our country labor is expensive and employers substitute labor-saving machinery at every opportunity. In the Orient, however, labor is so inexpensive that big jobs, such as dam construction, are less costly when done chiefly by human labor rather than by machine. In any country a farmer may be land poor—have more than he can work efficiently. Enterprise, too, may be wasted. Henry Ford II, for example, could doubtless run a small foundry superbly well, but confining himself to such a small task would surely be a disservice to himself and his country.

From time to time and place to place, the proportions in which to combine land, labor, capital, and enterprise must be decided. One combination of the four factors of production will usually yield a greater return for each dollar spent than any other combination. Any enterpriser has a tremendous advantage over his competitors if he can come closer than they can to the most profitable combination. Those whose guesses or estimates are repeatedly poor will lose money and eventually be eliminated from production.

Decisions on what to produce and how to produce are not the only questions of production that have to be answered in every society. *Should a society produce for the present* (fish) *or for the future* (fishing boats)?" is another decision that has to be made continually. Obviously both present and future must be provided for, but where should the emphasis lie? In their five-year plans the Russians concentrated on turning out machine tools, the "tools of production," rather than consumer goods such as refrigerators, carpets, and autos.

Where should we produce? In Los Angeles or Detroit, or both, or elsewhere? Where labor is inexpensive, or where it is dear but efficient, or where natural resources lie near at hand? Why are some industries located in one area and others scattered everywhere? And why do those industries that concentrate pick precisely the locations they do? Although few businessmen would think of building boats in a desert, many other less obvious but very costly errors in choosing a location can be made. The history of Panama is studded with the tragedies of enterprisers who thought they had discovered El Dorado only to lose what capital they had invested. Obviously the location that seemed so promising was not the best place for them to invest their money.

Decisions • In the nursery story of the Little Red
of Consumption Hen, none of the other farm animals were interested in helping her plant or harvest the wheat, mill it into flour, or bake bread. However, all were eager to help *eat* the bread, but since they had had no share in its production, the Little Red Hen decided that only she and her chicks should consume it.

Like the hen, each society must answer the question: *Who gets the goods?* And there are many different answers ranging all the way from Captain John Smith's (and the Little Red Hen's) "No one eats who doesn't work" to "We'll take ours and the others be damned!" Deciding who gets what becomes especially pressing when there isn't enough to go around, where inequality is seen and resented, and where stress is placed on material things and great prestige is attached to getting them.

Society is deeply concerned with the division of goods. And quite rightly so! In Chicago, for example, people in certain upper-income areas live an average of ten years longer than people in certain poor areas. In Central America, near mid-century, farm laborers were toiling from dawn to dusk for as little as ten cents a day while some plantation owners lived like princes. Australia has a high level of living and almost as much land as the United States, but fewer than 8 million people. Northwest of Australia lies Java, only one-sixtieth the size of Australia, but with over five times as many people! Inequalities are glaring, both within and between countries.

Many people believe that extreme inequality is part of the natural order of things. They are sure that among all groups everywhere some have a lot and most have a little, and if everything were divided up equally, before long everybody would be right back where he started, "because that's human nature." Nonliterates, according to popular notion, are "savages" ruled only by "the law of the jungle." The strong members of the tribe are supposed to decide matters by sheer strength, to take what another has if they wish, to know no rule but "survival of the fittest." This notion is taken to prove that competition and inequality are universal.

Numerous studies of nonliterate groups show that nothing could be further from the truth.[4] Amassing wealth is a way to acquire prestige in some societies; to have more cattle or wives or shells or money than the next person is to be more respected and important. Among many other peoples, however, there is no lasting advantage to be gained from acquiring more than others have. Among the Dobuans, who live on a group of rocky islands near New Guinea, the couple with a rich harvest may be considered sorcerers; they remove their crops stealthily at night to avoid the suspicion of their neighbors. An unusually successful Arapesh gardener eats no better than his neighbors; he paints his yams and heaps them outside his door to be admired by all, and gives a feast at which the entire pile is given away for seed. In spite of the fact that possession brings no great prestige, nonliterates work hard and do not feel frustrated if they fail to amass a fortune.

The tradition is universal among nonliterate peoples that *none should want in the midst of plenty*. The hunter who returns with his catch over his shoulders sees that families of unlucky hunters also eat. He wouldn't think of doing otherwise.

With land ownership, *title rests on use*. If the owner isn't cultivating a particular field, others may do so. Few tribes will let a man avoid work by living on an income made by others who till his land for him.

Such customary rules are fairly consistent in guaranteeing that land benefits the group as a whole. They also operate effectively in regard to other property. If use of the particular property is essential to the welfare of the tribe, the owner usually becomes a sort of custodian. He may be recognized as owner of a canoe, for example, but if a fishing party is organized on which he does not go along, he has no right to prevent the group from using his canoe.

Most nonliterates do a good part of their work cooperatively. House-raising is often one big party in which the host provides the building materials, food, and liquor, and his friends and relatives put up his house with no charge for their labor. Much heavy field work is done in the same way. Often a group sings or chants to keep time with the rising and falling of their hoes as they move abreast down a field. In this way even the dullest and hardest sort of work is made lighter, and all share in its rewards.

Finally, nonliterates do not wake up one day to the realization that they are out of a job and in danger of starving. There is always work to be done.

Thus we can use nonliterate societies to clarify our ideas about "human nature." Obviously it is not inevitable that within a society there should be sharp competition for goods and services and great inequality in their distribution. Why is it that inequality is so widespread in modern society?

Certainly industrial technology offers far greater potentialities for production than the simple economies of nonliterate societies, and thus of greater material well-being for all. In the process of industrialization, however, many of the values of simpler societies were lost, and the struggle to regain them is only slowly bearing fruit. The Industrial Revolution turned the worker into a wage-earner utterly dependent on the job offered him by the producer and so far removed from the natural resources that if he lost his job all he could do was to try to find another. Cooperation and the sharing of wealth were usually replaced by competition and the desire of each member of society to "get his." As societies became larger, embracing more population and territory, their members tended to lose a sense of identification with those around them, except in certain periods of crisis such as war. Society has thus been faced with the problem of helping people identify with the larger unit in day-to-day living as well as during crises.

In American society a number of factors have kept the rich from identifying with the poor. A person could once acquire great prestige by piling up vast wealth almost regardless of how the money was accumulated and what he did with it after he got it. Our Puritan ethic identified virtue and success as almost one and the same thing, and the rich usually felt no compulsion to better the lot of the poor. Churches preached humility and patience and the rewards to come after death.

But important changes are occurring in modern American society. More and more Americans are convinced that to have a real political democracy we must have a fair and just economic system, and are even realizing that as leaders of the free world we cannot afford to ignore widespread poverty and disease anywhere. The "public be damned" attitude on the part of businessmen is no longer condoned, nor is the once widely held belief that millionaires make their money solely by their own efforts and contributions to society. To win public acclaim these days the tycoon must be known not only for his wealth and ability, but also for his civic interests and charities and for an enlightened approach toward his employees. In any society talent will tend to concentrate on the offices and positions that bring recognition, and thus through giving or withholding applause the public can do much to turn potential exploiters into desirable leaders.

Along with this shift in attitudes has come pressure for a more equitable distribution of wealth. As laborers have become literate and organized, they have done just what the upper classes so long feared—demanded a bigger share of the goods. And the churches have become much more interested in the rewards that people may win in this world. As most people have come to think of themselves as likely to remain in the employee class, they have brought many pressures to bear upon government for increased social services. These pressures have resulted in a great expansion of public services such as schools, parks, and care of the needy. These are paid for in part by a steeply progressive income tax that allows a man who makes over a million dollars a year to keep less than one dollar in ten. Compare that with 1900, when Andrew Carnegie took in 23 million tax-free dollars!

Like all social changes, this trend toward equalization of wealth has met bitter resistance from the groups who stood to lose most. Some employers claim that a steeply progressive income tax discourages enterprise and initiative. Business seems, however, to be doing very well in attracting men of these talents. Management has become what amounts to a trained profession, rewarded not merely by salary, but also by such devices as corporation expense accounts and by non-monetary rewards of prestige.

And finally, although this discussion may have led you to believe that if labor gets more, management is sure to get less, this is by no means the case. Time and time again we have found it possible for both to get more. The real hope for a greatly improved level of living lies in increased production. Fortunately, both management and labor are learning—although sometimes very slowly—that cooperation in raising output is both possible and profitable.

Exchange   •   It was early discovered that the jack-of-
of Goods   all-trades is the master of none. No doubt in many groups fat folk did much of the fishing, lean men did the hunting, and dreamers were the artists. Then, through exchange, all could get more and better things than if each did everything for himself.

Every group has at least an elementary division of labor. No society has ever been found where all the tasks that either men or women could do were shared by both.[5] But usually, specialization is extended much beyond the category of sex. One man may devote all his time to making pottery, another may be especially adept at woodcarving. But the potter and carver cannot eat and wear their products. Somehow the surplus built up through a division of labor must be exchanged. There are many culturally determined ways of distributing goods—by exchanging gifts, by pure trade, or by some system with elements of both. Whatever the method, sooner or later a person gets back from somewhere something in return.

Considerations of prestige are uppermost in those societies where goods are distributed by exchanging gifts. To many present-day Americans the idea of a man's taking yams he has grown to a friend's hut, where he is given more yams grown by his friend, seems as pointless as carrying coals to Newcastle. But important social values are involved—friendship, prestige, pride in one's providence, and generosity. The Kwakiutl tribe, which lived in the Pacific Northwest, practiced an even more fantastic form of gift-giving that emphasized competition. Individuals sought to shame their rivals by outdoing them in distributing property, and to avoid disgrace the recipient had to return each gift with 100 per cent interest!

Where exchanges are frankly in terms of trade, whether barter or cash purchase, everyday utilitarian values are usually stressed. Trade occurs only when people want things that others have and are willing to give up what others want. The price, or rate of exchange, fluctuates according to the possessor's notion of the relative worth of what is desired to what is given up. An individual may have to give a house to get something he wants at one time; at another time a knife may be enough.

Fish for Bills in Sumatra. *Money serves as a medium of exchange and a measure or standard of value.*

What one group regards as all important may mean little to another. No matter what the price, so long as exchange occurs both sides gain. Trade occurs only because each party feels he receives something worth more to him than what he gives up.

Neither division of labor nor exchange can be very efficient without *money*—pieces of convenient form, stamped by public authority, and issued as a *medium of exchange and measure of value*. These "tickets" come in large and small amounts and greatly increase the flexibility of an economic system. Using them as a *medium of exchange*, a person can sell for money, knowing that he can in turn buy what he wants for money. Money also serves as a standard or *measure of value*, for all exchange values can be expressed in terms of it. The reader probably has a fairly good idea of the prices of several hundred goods and services. Without money it would be almost impossible to estimate these values, and exchange would be slow and infrequent. In addition, money serves as a *store of value;* it is usable at any time, present or future. Parents may pay for their children's education with money that was saved long before. Finally, money also serves as a *standard of deferred payments*, which means that a person can judge by the present what he will owe or receive in the future. The national debt and the mortgage on your house are examples of deferred payments. In order to serve effectively as a store of value or standard of deferred payments, the value of money must remain stable over a comparatively long period of time.

It was once thought that nothing could serve as money unless it was desired as a commodity or good quite apart from its value as a medium

346

of exchange, but this is not true. As long as it is generally acceptable in exchange, anything at all may be used as money—coconuts, wampum, shells, salt, cigarettes, cattle, coins, or paper bills.

Who Makes   •   Although decisions of production and
the Decisions?   consumption and the means of exchange
                            between producer and consumer must
                            be made in all cultures, the methods by
which they are made are extremely diverse.

Custom is king in the sacred, homogeneous society. Most things economic are done the way they have always been done, and there are few decisions to make. What will be produced and when and where, and who is to get it, are matters that are governed quite satisfactorily, in the opinion of the group, by the ways of the past.

But we live in a secular, heterogeneous society. In present-day urban societies of this type there are two chief systems of control: the laissez faire or *free price system* and the *planned economy*. These are two different methods for parceling out goods when there are not enough for everyone.

It is important to know about the free price system because it has been part and parcel of the American ideology, and as a myth it is still important. Moreover, although we don't have a 100 per cent free price system, the economy we do have is a patched-up version of it.

For our society relies to a considerable extent on individuals making independent decisions guided mainly by prices and the desire for profit. This rather unusual economic system implies social goals, personal motivations, and legal institutions that are not universal. Despite the multitude of seemingly unconnected decisions, the system is not a chaotic one.

In brief, the key to the ideology of the free price system is that the social control of economic matters is left to the "natural results of unfettered individual decisions." Man is assumed to be a rational being moved by the desire to get the greatest possible satisfaction out of life. While acting in a purely selfish way, he will do the things that will also bring the greatest possible satisfaction to society. "If we let these rational beings alone, everything will be fine," is the basis of this philosophy. Obviously advocates of this system want a minimum of government. "Less government in business and more business in government," is the way they often express it.

The planned economy, on the other hand, is run by government. Thus those who believe in complete planning subscribe to another ideology, and are moved by different myths. But the economy of no big state is completely managed by government, although some come rather close to it.

In fact no economy is all free price or all planned; all economies are mixed to some extent. Our own American economy is certainly a mixed one. Over the decades we have been talking price economy but becoming more and more of a planned economy.

This entire section on "Work and Rewards" will analyze the American economy against a background of the free price ideology. Before doing so, however, we shall consider the essential differences between a laissez-faire economy, a planned or socialist economy, and a mixed economy.

Laissez Faire, the Mixed Economy, Socialism

We are sometimes told that an economy has the choice of producing under a plan or under no plan. Such a statement is misleading. Of course production must be planned. The question is whether production is to be carried on under the decentralized planning of thousands or millions of business managers, or under fully centralized planning with details set and administered by government, or under some kind of compromise between the two. We are considering here, of course, the various economic systems possible in modern industrial society.

In the preceding chapter we outlined the decisions that must be made in every economic system. The chief points of contrast between a planned and laissez-faire economy concern how, by whom, and according to what criteria these decisions are made.

Economic Decisions • In a laissez-faire, or private enterprise,
under economy there is a minimum of govern-
Laissez Faire ment intervention in the economy. Legend attributes the phrase *laissez faire*
to a seventeenth-century French mer-
chant named Legendre, who, when asked by the great minister, Colbert, what the state could do to assist the merchants, answered impatiently, *"Laissez nous faire!"*—"Leave us alone."

A laissez-faire economy is not planless. It is an economy in which planning is decentralized. In all modern economies—socialist, laissez faire and mixed—managers and employees alike try to obtain the highest incomes possible, non-financial considerations being equal; and every person spends his income in the way that brings him the greatest satisfaction. But only in a laissez-faire economy is the manager of each business free, within wide limits, to plan the operation of his own business as he likes. The more an economy is centralized, the more individual business managers are regulated and restricted by centrally determined rules.

The economy of the United States is by no means completely laissez faire; but it is more laissez faire than centrally planned. No one in Washington had to plan the production of the washing machines, electric irons, vacuum cleaners, tires, electric ranges, and radios that poured out of American factories at the end of World War II. Consumers had starved through the war for these goods. Producers were well aware that their goods would sell, even at high prices. Plants were promptly converted and equipped to produce these goods, and labor and raw materials flowed into their production. A year after Japan capitulated, production in each of these items was well above the prewar rate.

No central orders need be issued to managers instructing them to slack off production as the backlog of demand gradually is satisfied. Individual sellers find that sales fall off at current prices. They cut prices and sales still do not respond. They cut production, and some shift into other lines of production that now appear more attractive.

Sometimes such adjustments are painful. No one likes to find his money income falling, and not many of us like to shift from one line of work in which we are settled to another. But consumption is the purpose of production. The long-run interests of the consumer ought to rule.

The types and volume of goods and services produced should change (1) as consumer demand shifts, (2) as resources become more or less abundant, and (3) as techniques of production change.

At this point, a central question arises. Can such adjustments be made less painfully and more efficiently by individual business managers and employees as they decide what line of work they should go into on the basis of relative money incomes and relative attractiveness of work, or by a central (government) office?

Supply and demand. Let us generalize what we have just been talking about. In a laissez-faire economy, resources are allocated by the forces of supply and demand. In general, producers want to produce more of a commodity when the price rises. Perhaps dairymen will bring to market 5,500 pounds of butter a week when the price is 40 cents; they are encouraged to bring 8,000 pounds when the price is 50 cents and 11,000 pounds when the price is 60 cents.

Now for demand. In any good-sized area, we can be fairly sure that the higher the price of a commodity, the less of it consumers will want to buy. They will use it more sparingly and shift to substitutes. For example, 10,000 lbs of butter might be sold per week when the price is 40 cents a pound. But if the price goes up to 50 cents, only 8,000 pounds will be sold, and at 60 cents, only 7,000 pounds.

We can represent these conditions in a graph:

PRICE	SUPPLY	DEMAND
60¢	11,000	7,000
50	8,000	8,000
40	5,500	10,000

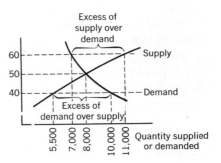

If these are the supply and demand conditions, the price of butter will hover around 50 cents a pound. At any higher price, say 60 cents, quantity supplied is greater than quantity demanded. Producers have been encouraged to put more butter up for sale than at 50 cents, and consumers have been discouraged from buying as much as they did before the price went up. The surplus butter accumulates in warehouses and stores. Producers and retailers eventually lower their price rather than keep on adding to the surplus.

At a lower price than 50 cents, say 40 cents, demand is greater than supply. The warehouses empty, and butter stocks sell out as soon as they are delivered to stores. So sellers raise the price because they can sell at a higher price all the supply they will receive.

Our general conclusion then—and this is a fundamental conclusion, applicable to many situations in economics—is that the price of any good or service seeks the level where *the quantity supplied equals the quantity demanded*. Price tends to fall whenever the quantity supplied exceeds the quantity demanded, and it tends to rise whenever the quantity demanded exceeds the quantity supplied.

The relationship between supply, demand, and price is the so-called *law of supply and demand*.

Our reasoning leads us straight to a first-approximation picture of how a laissez-faire economy adapts production to human wants. If people develop a special fondness for butter or if their incomes rise or if oleomargarine disappears from the market, then they will want to buy more butter. *At every price* the quantity that they want to buy is greater than it had been before (on the graph, the demand curve *shifts along its whole length* to the right). Consequently, the quantity supplied now equals the quantity demanded at a higher price than before. The price of butter rises, and producers are encouraged to supply more butter.

But if consumer demand for butter slacks off for any reason (the demand curve *shifts along its whole length* to the left), the price of butter falls, and producers are discouraged from supplying so much butter to the market.

The effect is the same if the supply curve shifts to the left or right.

If producers' costs rise for any reason, they will place less butter on the market. The price will rise, and consumers will buy less. The opposite occurs if producers' costs fall.

The invisible hand. We sometimes hear that a laissez-faire economy is one in which there is production for profit, not for use. This statement also is misleading. No one would argue that an economy should not produce for use; that is, should not produce to satisfy human wants to the full extent that scarce resources make possible. The question is, how is production best organized? A laissez-faire, or private enterprise, economy attempts to organize production by allowing each person freedom, within wide limits, to seek his own personal advantage.

Consider an idealized picture of a private enterprise economy in operation, neglecting for the present any faults and discrepancies. Each businessman, seeking to make more money, tries to produce as much of the goods and services in greatest demand as he can out of the smallest possible amount of the least valuable resources. His efforts are obviously in the public interest as well as his own.

The businessman is left free to charge as high prices as he pleases. But as he raises his prices, he faces the painful fact that his sales fall off. And if his sales do not fall off appreciably and his profits still remain high, other businessmen are encouraged to compete with him. The constant tendency is for profits to be pared by competition down to the minimum that just barely induces the businessman to stay in business.

Consumers (who are, of course, everybody in the economy—employees, businessmen, and owners of natural resources) are in effect voting, when they buy goods and services, for what should be produced. The man who buys a tube of Squibb toothpaste, or a loaf of wholewheat bread, or a Parker fountain pen, is voting economically for the production of that article. The voting is in a sense democratic: $1 equals, we might say, one vote. But the man who spends $10,000 in the course of a year has four times as many expenditure votes as the man who spends $2,500.

Now let's continue with our picture of the ideally functioning laissez-faire economy. In such an economy, inequality of consumption is justified by the need of our economy and of a poor world for increased production. The drive that makes men economize on scarce resources and produce more is, in the main, the very hope of obtaining a large income. Ideally we should have no more inequality than is justified by the need for incentives.

Adam Smith, in his *Wealth of Nations*,[1] published in 1776, presented this doctrine of economic liberty so memorably that his book has, more than any other, shaped the economic climate of the Western World in the past century and a half. Adam Smith was a rebel, with profoundly humane and ethical impulses. He was in rebellion against mercantilist doctrines that sanctioned restrictions on imports from abroad and against elaborate government economic regulations at home that gave monopolistic privileges to established businesses.

The government, he argued, should restrict its functions to defense against foreign aggression, the administration of justice, and the maintenance of certain public works and institutions, such as education, roads, bridges, canals, and harbors.

All systems either of preference or restraint being thus completely taken away, the obvious and simple system of natural liberty establishes itself of its own accord. Every man, as long as he does not violate the laws of justice, is left perfectly free to pursue his own interest in his own way, and to bring both his industry and capital into competition with those of any other man or order of men.[2]

Each individual, seeking his own self-interest,

necessarily labors to render the annual revenue of the society as great as he can. . . . He generally, indeed, neither intends to promote the public interest, nor knows how much he is promoting it. . . . By directing . . . industry in such a manner that its produce may be of the greatest value, he intends only his own gain, and he is in this, as in many other cases, led by an invisible hand to promote an end which was no part of his intention.[3]

If you feel that this logic relies too much on the selfish element in human activity, we can supplement Adam Smith's words with the gentle warning of another economist, Alfred Marshall: "Progress depends on the extent to which the *strongest*, and not merely the *highest*, forces in human nature can be utilized for the increase of social good."[4]

What prices do. At this point we should pause and sum up how prices work in a laissez-faire economy.

(1) *Prices allocate resources.* Prices encourage the use of labor, land, capital equipment, and management in the production of high-priced commodities and discourage their use in the production of low-priced commodities.

(2) *Prices determine incomes.* If the prices of your services and products are high, your income is high. If the prices of your services and products are low, your income is low.

(3) *Prices ration services and products.* All that is produced is, with rare exceptions, shared out among millions of people, all of whom want the goods and services and buy them. We have just seen how prices tend to move to the level where the quantity supplied equals the quantity demanded.

(4) *Prices encourage economic progress.* Progress is implied in the constant pressure on businessmen to use the least amount of lowest-priced resources in producing the greatest amount of products that can be sold at the highest prices.

And, remarkably enough, the price system performs all these functions without government officials having to administer it. In other words, *it works automatically.*

The world of Adam Smith. The world in which Adam Smith lived was mainly agricultural. The state-supported monopolies against which he inveighed were chiefly monopolies of merchants, not manufacturers. Factories were tiny; machinery was primitive. Human muscles were the main source of industrial power; a minor source was water power. Much of the manufacturing, especially the weaving of cloth, was carried on under the "putting-out" system—the worker received his raw materials from some merchant, worked on them in his own home, and returned the finished product to the merchant to receive payment by the piece.

There was a great deal of regimentation of social and economic affairs in the seventeenth and eighteenth centuries. Governments were hereditary dictatorships. In most countries—England, Holland, and the American colonies were the chief exceptions—people had no protection against arbitrary search of their homes by the police, no right to trial by jury, and no protection against arbitrary arrest and imprisonment.

Adam Smith's reasoning represents one phase of the protest against this kind of order. Since the chief oppressions resulted from government restrictions on the actions and thinking of men, the freedom that men sought was freedom from government restraints.

The basic doctrine of laissez faire was therefore highly attractive. With government restrictions removed, maximum production would result from the natural effort of everyone, employer and employee alike, to make money and to get on in the world. Competition would keep prices low.

But even in the world of the eighteenth century Adam Smith did not urge pure laissez faire. He was too humane and too observant of human nature. He realized that government had certain justified functions to perform and admitted other exceptions. He condemned not only government-established monopolies, but also those established through agreements among private businessmen. He castigated the "monopolizing spirit of merchants and manufacturers" who "complain much of the bad effects of high wages . . . and say nothing concerning the bad

effects of high profits." [5] He agreed that imports of certain goods might
justifiably be barred, and urged that bankers should not be permitted
to issue small-denomination paper money.[6] But these reservations were
minor deviations from the main theme.

Economic liberty in many ways reached its crest in the Western
World during the mid-nineteenth century. By then there remained few
survivals of medieval guild restrictions and of the swarms of town and
state regulations that had encouraged the growth of favored monopolies.
And only a few bits of regulatory legislation, like the British Factory Act
of 1833, sought to defend the poor and foreshadowed the future trend.
Economic progress seemed to justify the most extravagant claims of the
advocates of natural liberty. Laissez faire was triumphant.

<table>
<tr><td>Economic Decisions
in a
Mixed Economy</td><td>•</td><td>Since the mid-nineteenth century, the
gap between Adam Smith's vision of a
self-regulating economy with a mini-
mum of government intervention and
the reality of growing government par-</td></tr>
</table>

ticipation in the economy has widened. This development has been true
generally—in Europe, North America, and elsewhere among developed
economies. It has proceeded under governments that were antagonistic
to laissez-faire principles and under those that were devoted to them.

The attractively simple system of natural liberty has its own particular weaknesses. It clearly leaves many important public interests unprotected. It is based on the principle that private gain is public benefit:
The farmer grows his wheat, and thereby serves himself and the community alike.

But (1) there are many areas where the public is benefited by measures that carry with them little or no private gain, or where private
gain is served in ways that involve less than equal public gain. As examples of the former we can list public health measures, lighthouse
and harbor maintenance, and certain kinds of natural resource conservation, which, though justified from the social point of view, do
not repay private enterprise. Similiarly, the activities of some industries give rise to social costs for which they are not held financially
accountable—smoke nuisances, deterioration of real estate values around
factory sites, unemployment and poor relief, and the growth of social
discontent.

Furthermore, (2) laissez faire works to the advantage of the strong
against the weak. Those who are strong, mentally able, ambitious,
lucky, and least handicapped by scruples—these push ahead, and the

devil takes the hindmost. Economic power, once gained, tries to buttress itself and to advance further by the use of political power.

Adam Smith wrote during a period that was primarily agricultural. Since his time, the growth of cities has demanded more social services per person—water supply, sewage disposal, transportation, maintenance of law and order, hospital facilities, and the like—which for the most part have seemed best provided by government bodies. In addition, a growing sense of social responsibility makes us *unwilling* to tolerate social evils that were commonplace in 1600 and 1800; and increasing productivity makes it *possible* for us to maintain a higher minimum standard of consumption for those worst off.

Today the federal, state, and local governments enter upon the economic scene in five different ways. (1) They promote the interests of the public and of special groups through tariffs, subsidies to agriculture, labor legislation, and pure food and drug laws. (2) They regulate segments of the economy in the public interest: railroads, electric and gas utilities, the airwaves, and trade practices generally. (3) They carry on economic activities: production of gas and electricity, water supply and sewage disposal, production of munitions. (4) They conserve and develop natural and human resources: irrigation, flood control, soil conservation, public health and education activities. (5) Last, they maintain a legal framework of obligations and rights within which the economy and society function, and they provide protection through the police and the armed forces.

During World War II, the United States government specified in detail, by type and quantity, about one-half the total production of the economy, and controlled almost everything else that was produced. Following the war, the proportion of output produced at the direct or indirect order of government dropped to about one-seventh, but this proportion is still much above the prewar level.

It is easy to exaggerate the economic role of government. Despite the activities we have listed, most of us have little direct contact with Washington, our state capital, or our city or county governments. Most government economic measures affect us only indirectly by modifying the environment within which we work. Within wide limits, we do pretty much as we please.

The type of economy we have just been discussing—an economy that allows private enterprise a fairly wide scope yet provides also a large area of government enterprise and public economic policies—is a *mixed economy,* or *mixed-capitalist economy.* The United States economy today is a mixed economy.

Government Planning. *The Tennessee Valley Authority's effective organization of a large river valley gives evidence of man's capacity to control his environment.*

The reasonable argument for this undoctrinaire kind of organization is that the government should do whatever the people, in Lincoln's words, "need to have done, but cannot do *at all,* or cannot *so well do,* for themselves." [7]

Economic Decisions • In addition to the laissez-faire and
under Socialism mixed economies, there is a third type, the socialist or centrally directed economy. We do not discuss here how existing socialist or communist economies function. These are in, or claim to be in, transitional stages of development. They are likely to be, 10 or 50 years hence, organized somewhat differently, and perhaps much differently, from the way they are set up now. We are here concerned only with the basic operations of a centrally directed economy, which can be called briefly, *socialism.*

The nerve center of a socialist economy is some sort of central planning board that tries to direct production and distribution in the best interest of consumers. Does this mean that the members of the central

358

planning board try to decide what every person in the country wants every day, and try to get it to him, so far as resources permit? No. The job would be too big. There are millions of individuals in most countries, each with scores of changing wants. The planners would be stumped before they could start.

In some way the board must rid itself of the responsibility for making millions of these detailed decisions a day. It must decentralize decisions. Here is how it can do it.

Under laissez faire, we remember, the distribution of income is closely connected with production. The person whose services or goods are sold at the highest net price receives the highest income. Under socialism, however, distribution can be separate from production. The society distributes claims or tickets to the available output in accord with whatever compromise between equalitarian and incentive principles seems to it best. We might as well call these claims or tickets *dollars*. The socialist storekeepers deliver goods in exchange for these dollars.

In a socialist economy, as in any other, human wants are unlimited, whereas the work and other resources used in production are limited. The storekeepers are ordered by the board to limit total demand by setting appropriate *prices*. That is, the price of every commodity should be set at that level where the total demand of members of the society for the commodity (which reflects both the wants of the members and the quantity of dollars of income that has been issued to them) just equals current production. If the price were higher, people would not buy and supplies would pile up on shelves and in warehouses. If the price were lower, people would rush to buy, supplies would be quickly exhausted, and some members of the economy would have no chance to obtain the commodity at all.

The next and crucial question facing the board is, How much of the scarce resources of the economy will be allotted to the production of each commodity?

As products are "sold" in the socialist stores, the managers of industrial plants receive the proceeds, transmitted to them by the storekeepers. These proceeds, or dollars of revenue, are the claims of the industrial managers on the resources of the economy. With these dollars the managers are entitled to buy, at "prices" set by the central planning board, the kinds and quantities of labor and other resources that the proceeds will just cover—no less and no more. The industrial managers are, of course, instructed to use these resources as economically as possible. (The central planning board, in turn, sets such "prices" on the resources that the demand of all the industrial managers taken together just exhausts the available supply of the resources.)

Suppose, when such a system is operating smoothly, that consumer demand for shoes suddenly rises. Then the storekeepers must raise their price in order to comply with the rule that sales will just equal production. But this means that the "proceeds" of shoe factories increase; that is, they make bookkeeping profits, so that *the managers of the factories are entitled to demand more resources.* With more resources at their disposal, they can raise output. As more shoes flow onto the counters of the stores, the storekeepers will lower the price of the commodity somewhat, toward its original level.

If, instead, an improvement in technique is developed so that industrial managers can produce more from given resources, the increased volume of goods flowing into the stores causes the storekeepers to lower the price of the product somewhat. As their proceeds from sales rise, the industrial managers are enabled to demand more resources.

This skeleton outline of socialism sounds much like the working of price and output changes under competitive laissez faire, which we have already surveyed. And so it is. The economic logic of socialism and the economic logic of laissez-faire are identical. The aim in each case is that additional units of a resource will go into the production of a commodity so long as the community values the commodity more than the resource used in its production. In each system industries should expand production when additional products become worth more than the cost of the resources that go into the products; that is, when real or bookkeeping profits are obtainable. Industries should curtail production when the production costs of the last units of output are higher than the value consumers place on them; that is, when losses are incurred.

Even after this explanation of socialism and laissez faire, we are in no position to pass on their comparative merits. We have already mentioned the shortcomings of laissez faire. As to socialism, probably no actual system would work as smoothly as the one we have just described. The system might not be run with the idea of "economic welfare" in mind, but rather for the expansion of the power and prestige of the leaders or ruling group or for the expansion of the power of the state.

Nor can efficient performance be taken for granted. Incentives to work and produce might be missing. Bureaucratic red tape and inertia might slow progress to a stop and encourage demoralization. Corruption might become commonplace.

On the other hand, there is reason to be optimistic about nationali-

A Mixed Economy. *The American economy grants substantial freedom to private enterprise, embodies the cooperative principle, and provides for government regulation of certain utility industries vested with a public interest.*

zation if the public wants it, if administrative techniques are well developed, and if management problems (including problems of changing methods of production and changing kinds of products) are not too great.

In every kind of economic system, then, decisions must be made in some way with respect to allocation of resources, degree of employment of resources, and distribution of product. Resources can be organized to fulfill human wants (1) under a laissez-faire type of economy, in which there is a minimum of state controls; (2) under a mixed economy, in which the state intervenes frequently in economic life; and (3) under a centrally administered (socialist) system, in which the state directs the course of production.

In a laissez-faire system resources are allocated by the forces of supply and demand. The price of a product tends to rise whenever the quantity supplied is less than the quantity demanded at the existing price. A price rise, other things being equal, stimulates supply and discourages demand. The price of a product tends to fall whenever quantity supplied is greater than quantity demanded. A price fall, other things being equal, contracts supply and increases demand.

In an (ideal) socialist system, prices are used in a surprisingly similar fashion. Industrial managers and storekeepers are instructed to set prices at the level where consumers will just buy up current production.

No present-day economy, as we have seen, is either pure laissez faire or pure socialist. There are all varieties and extents of government intervention in the private economy.

Business Organization and the American Economy

In the preceding chapter we pointed out that in a laissez-faire economy the production and distribution of goods and services is determined largely by the pull of individual choices in the market place. This system is different from a centrally directed economy, where production and distribution are determined by government authority.

American economic life is founded upon

laissez-faire principles. The traditional American respect for freedom of individual action and opposition to centralized control make it only logical that this nation should believe in the freedom of each person to buy and produce what he chooses.

But, as we have already noticed, conditions in the late eighteenth century, when Adam Smith set forth the laissez-faire theory, were far different from what they have become in the mid-twentieth. The independent artisan of Smith's day has been replaced by the giant industrial corporation, his few neighborhood customers by a market of national or international scope, his journeyman or apprentice helper by thousands of workers, his simple tools by power-driven machinery. These changes have altered the nature and requirements of our economic system and have modified the validity of the laissez-faire theory in American economic life. This chapter will consider these modifications in greater detail and describe the ways in which our society has adjusted to the new situation.

The Industrial Revolution • An essential element of the laissez-faire theory is that business shall be perfectly competitive. Perfect competition means that there must be enough sellers bidding for the customer's patronage to give him a wide choice among them and enable him to turn to the one who offers the goods or services he wants at the lowest price. Only in this way can the money that each individual has to spend bring him the greatest possible return. Under no circumstances must one business unit become large or powerful enough to develop exclusive control, or *monopoly*, over the production of any good or service and thus get more of the customer's money than it would under competitive conditions.

All this was more than theory in 1776 when Adam Smith wrote his *Wealth of Nations*, and it was a particularly apt description of actual conditions in frontier America. The independent artisan made and sold his products to people who lived within a few miles of his doorstep. If the quality of his workmanship declined or if he failed to use his own labor and the labor of his hired man, his simple tools, and his raw materials in the most efficient combination, thus forcing his price to rise, it was a comparatively simple matter for a rival to set up shop and lure his business away. Competition between the two, or even the prospect of such competition, assured the consumer of the lowest possible price.

Smith's book was hardly off the press, however, when a Britisher named James Watt set in motion a chain of events that would profoundly alter the entire structure of economic life. To his contemporaries, what

Watt accomplished in 1777 was hardly startling. The principle that steam contained power to turn wheels and move levers had long been known. But when Watt applied that principle to a practical engine that pumped water from a flooded Cornish mine, the Industrial Revolution was born.

The years sped by and the wheels turned faster. To the power of steam was added the power from the black liquid that could be made to gush from the earth and the power created by falling water. This power applied to manufacturing during the nineteenth and twentieth centuries completely changed the economic world that Smith had known. It now became possible for one business unit to turn out a supply of goods undreamed of in Smith's day. The number of shoes that one cobbler could make in a week by hand, for example, was multiplied more than a thousand-fold by the use of power-driven machinery that could cut the leather, stitch the soles, and drive the nails. The same held true for virtually any article—books or bicycles, chairs or chandeliers.

In the last 180 years, therefore, the most efficient combination of the factors of production has involved not the skill of the individual artisan in using his simple tools to change the raw material into a finished product, but rather the application to the raw material of complex, power-driven machinery. Capital rather than labor is now the key. The independent artisan, unable to compete, has gradually disappeared from the scene, making his way to the factory where the output of goods centers around the machine.

But the new type of capital has done more than just destroy the independent artisan. The new machines are expensive to build and maintain. It has not been economically possible, therefore, for small business units to employ them. The maintenance or *overhead* costs are prohibitive unless the machines are used almost continuously. Thus, as the machines have developed, they have been concentrated in a few large plants, each producing a large share of the total market requirement.[1]

Of course, if the market of each business unit had remained confined to its immediate neighborhood, such concentration could never have taken place. But the same power that was applied to manufacturing has also been applied to transportation, and in the course of years ribbons of steel, later of concrete, and finally of invisible air have bound all sections of the nation and large parts of the world together. Over these ribbons, goods can be transported from one source quickly and cheaply. The contemporary development of means of preserving perishable items in transit has also increased the area that can be served by one producer.

Thus the application of power to transportation and manufacturing has permitted a great reduction in the number of business units. A smaller number of firms is able to turn out a greater number of products

Industry in Asia. *Cultural diffusion, as indicated by the label on the machine, brings industrialism to tradition-bound agrarian societies.*

and distribute them over a wider area than was possible before. The consequent ability of the large business unit to take advantage of the full use of power machinery has placed its smaller competitor at a serious disadvantage. And this disadvantage is intensified by the ability of the larger unit to utilize its size in still other ways.

Because its output is so great, the large unit may, for example, have each individual worker specialize in only one phase of the total operation. Time and motion studies have shown that constant repetition of the same task, rather than doing several different jobs, puts less strain on the worker's attention, reduces fatigue, and enables him to work faster. Specialized personnel may also be hired for managerial functions, purchasing, and selling.

In addition to specializing personnel, the large firm may, with the aid of its machines, standardize its output. Making all products from the same mold reduces the cost of design. Making the parts interchangeable lessens the cost of breakage or spoilage.

The large firm may also reduce costs by purchasing raw materials in bulk and developing a large-scale distribution system. Greater output may make it feasible to employ a research staff to find ways of increasing quality and reducing production costs. And the larger unit, because it controls an appreciable percentage of the market, may be better able than its smaller counterpart to adjust its output to shifts in demand, thus avoiding either being caught without enough goods on hand to supply a rising market or with an over-large inventory when demand has dropped.

And then, of course, the larger business may use advertising and public relations campaigns to build consumer good will, thus increasing sales at the expense of smaller competitors who cannot afford this outlay. There are, for example, many brands of watches, all of which run with reasonable accuracy. But how many of us would buy a make other than one of those that tell us the time every half hour on the radio?

All these advantages of large-scale operation, combined with the development of power machinery, have reduced the number of individual units doing business in our economy. And although we have been discussing the advantages in terms of manufacturing alone, they are equally applicable to *all* processes involved in getting a piece of raw material to the consumer, not only in the *form* that he wants it, but also at the *location* he wants it and at the *time* he wants it.

Types of Business • To utilize fully the advantages of
Organization   greater size, American business units
                      had to undergo a drastic change in their
                      basic organization. The small business
unit of pre-Industrial Revolution days, the type whose dominance was largely assumed by the laissez-faire economy theorists, was the *single proprietorship,* owned and to a large extent operated by one individual. Although the owner or proprietor sometimes hired others to work for him, he alone provided the tools, and he assumed the entire risk of success or failure. The size of each business unit, therefore, and its amount of capital, was limited by the amount of money that its proprietor could raise for investment purposes, either from his own funds or from funds he might borrow from others. Since most proprietors also acted as their own managers, the size of each unit was further limited by the ability of one man.

With the development of expensive power machinery it became acutely necessary to obtain more funds than the single proprietor himself could raise. One answer to the problem was the *partnership,* in which two or more individuals pooled their resources and assumed joint responsibility for the business. The partnership did mark an improvement over the single proprietorship in that more money could be obtained for capital equipment and managerial functions could be shared among the various partners, each assuming responsibility for the job he could do best. But two factors prevented the partnership from growing large enough to take full advantage of the economies of large-scale operation.

First, its future was uncertain because it was legally dissolved with the death or withdrawal of any one partner. Thus, should more than a handful of individuals participate, the business would be subject to constant reorganization. But even more serious than the threat of dissolution or reorganization was the fact that each partner was legally responsible to the extent of his entire personal resources for actions taken by any other partner in the name of the business. This situation meant that if one partner were to make a foolish contract on which money was lost, and there was not enough in the firm's treasury to cover the loss, each of the other partners might be sued to the full extent of his personal wealth, whether such wealth were invested in the business or not. If business activity were not to be hampered, therefore, by constantly referring all decisions to all partners, this *unlimited liability* factor required unlimited confidence on the part of all concerned. And since no man is likely to risk his home, automobile, and personal savings account on the actions of others, the partnership was also unable to expand sufficiently to meet the financial demands of large-scale operation.

There was, however, one form of business organization that was ideally suited to almost unlimited expansion. This was the *corporation* or, as it was sometimes called in its early days, the *joint stock company*. Because the corporation has today become the typical form of large-scale business enterprise, it will be worth while to examine its structure in some detail.

Unlike a partnership, which is simply a collection of individuals joined to do business, a corporation is an independent legal "person" whose life stems from a state government *charter*. Because of this independent existence, the corporation does not end with the death or withdrawal of one of its owners. There may be an unlimited number of these owners, and they may come and go at will without affecting the life of the business.

The owners of the corporation hold what are called shares of *stock*. Each owner risks only the amount of money that he invests in his stock, and he is in no danger of losing his other assets if the corporation should fail. The stockholders elect a board of directors to supervise the operation of the corporation, each stockholder having as many votes as he owns shares. The board of directors in turn hires trained executives to carry on day-to-day business. Profits earned by the corporation are distributed by the directors to the stockholders in the form of *dividends* at so many dollars per share.

Because a corporation can issue as many shares of stock as it requires to get the funds for needed capital equipment, it can meet the requirements of large-scale operation more easily than can the partnership or single proprietorship. But it is not limited merely to attracting people who might wish to become partial owners through the purchase of shares. There are actually three types of *securities* the corporation may issue: *bonds, preferred stock,* and *common stock*. The bond is not a certificate of ownership but is an evidence of indebtedness. The bondholders are, therefore, not owners of the corporation but creditors to it. As a reward for lending their money they receive, not dividends, but *interest*. Interest is not a share of the profits but a cost of doing business to be deducted before setting aside any profits. Should the corporation default on the payment of interest and other business obligations for an extended period and thus go *bankrupt*, the bondholders are the first to receive their investment back from the resulting sale of corporation property. The bond, then, is the safest type of security to purchase. But, because of its safety, it offers the lowest return. It is an ideal type of investment for people who wish to receive a modest income without great risk.

Preferred stock offers a somewhat higher reward for those who are willing to assume a greater risk. The preferred stockholders are owners of the corporation, although they generally are not allowed to participate in electing the board of directors. They have first claim on profits after the business costs, including interest on bonds, are paid. Frequently their claim must also be met for preceding years in which no profits were made. But, because of these safety features, the preferred stockholders are limited to a specified maximum dividend and do not receive the full benefit of large profits.

Those owners of the corporation who assume the greatest risk are the holders of *common stock*. Common stockholders receive no dividends at all until bondholders and preferred stockholders have been satisfied. But for assuming this risk they receive both the right to elect the board of directors and also the prospect of unlimited dividends should profits so warrant. For people who are willing to take the greatest chance with their money for the greatest possibility of reward, common stock is, therefore, the favorite investment.

Rise of the Giant Corporation • Because it can attract large amounts of money for the purchase of capital equipment and can also hire trained executive personnel, the corporation has provided the vehicle for enlarging the business unit. It has, indeed, become almost the only type of organization for large firms and also for most moderate sized firms whose owners wish to avail themselves of the *limited liability* feature. Business units organized as corporations are responsible for *over 80 per cent* of the total production of goods, workers employed, and wages paid in this country.[2]

Under the corporate form, American business units have expanded to the size most suited to the requirements of large-scale operation. This expansion has generally been in one or more of three directions: *horizontal, vertical,* and *lateral. Horizontal expansion* involves enlarging plant capacity in order to produce more items or establishing control by one corporation over a number of formerly independent companies engaged in the same business. For example, one large corporation might supply a world-wide market for its products from one plant in the United States, or a large railroad might consolidate the activities of many smaller independent lines.

Vertical expansion involves the establishment of unified control, not over an extension of the same activity but over related activities leading to the creation of a finished product. Thus the large American steel companies operate mines to extract iron ore from the earth, blast furnaces to reduce the ore to molten iron, mills to temper and finish the iron into steel ingots, and railroads to transport the metal in its various stages from process to process.

Lateral expansion involves bringing different and often unrelated activities under the same management to secure economies in financing, purchasing, distributing, advertising, management, and research functions. Thus the General Motors Company manufactures not only automotive products but also refrigerators, washing machines, and household appliances.

An overwhelming amount of America's business is now concentrated in the hands of the largest corporations. Of the 640,073 corporations in the United States in 1953, only 7,207 (slightly over 1 per cent) were large enough to have assets of $10,000,000 or more. Yet this tiny group earned over 52 per cent of the total gross receipts of all corporations.[3] Shortly before the outbreak of World War II, the United States government's Temporary National Economic Committee undertook what is still the most comprehensive study of the increasing concentration of business activity in the hands of large corporations. The study revealed that in the field of manufacturing alone, three companies produced 61 per cent of all the nation's steel, three companies made 80 per cent of the cigarettes, and three companies put out 86 per cent of the automobiles.[4]

But we need not rely on figures alone to understand the extent of concentration. Take a short walk and count the number of autos parked at the curb or passing on the street. How many of them have come from the assembly lines of Ford, General Motors, or Chrysler? What has happened to the cars of yesteryear when the industry was younger and the advantages of large-scale operation not so apparent? Where are the Graham-Paige? Oakland? Reo? and Stutz-Bearcat? Who but Jack Benny still drives a Maxwell?

Large-scale operation has not taken over every phase of the economy, however. Concentration is, of course, greatest in fields such as mining, transportation, and the manufacture of products for which demand is heavy and variety is not required. For a product with a small demand, such as snuff, there is no point in increasing plant size. Where style dictates an infinite variety, as in women's evening dresses, maximum

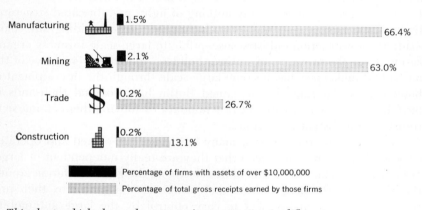

Manufacturing   1.5%   66.4%

Mining   2.1%   63.0%

Trade   0.2%   26.7%

Construction   0.2%   13.1%

■ Percentage of firms with assets of over $10,000,000
▨ Percentage of total gross receipts earned by those firms

This chart, which shows the extent of concentration in different fields, compares the percentage of firms in manufacturing, mining, trade, and construction with assets of over $10,000,000 and their percentage of total gross receipts.

standardization would only pile up many items that could not be sold. Where transportation costs are prohibitive, as in the construction of houses, it would be impractical to concentrate manufacturing at one location. And if the consumer's convenience requires a large number of small shops near at hand, as in retail trade, concentrating solely on department stores at central locations would be to ignore a large potential business.

The extent of concentration in different fields is shown in the graph on this page, which compares the percentage of firms with assets of over $10,000,000 and their percentage of total gross receipts for the fields of manufacturing and mining on the one hand and trade and construction on the other. The figures show that in manufacturing and mining a greater percentage of the firms are large, and these large firms do a greater percentage of the business.[5]

We might also notice that in contrast to its findings of extreme concentration in the steel, cigarette, and automobile industries, the Temporary National Economic Committee revealed that the four largest manufacturers of women's clothing produced only 2 per cent of the total output.[6]

But our table shows that some concentration exists even in fields where decentralization seems logical. Improved rapid transit may bring the suburban housewife easily to the department store in the city, or the store may go to her by establishing branches in outlying areas. The use of mass-production techniques in the building of homes, as seen in the Levittown developments, to say nothing of light, prefabricated structures built in the factory and transported cheaply to the building site, have made the construction industry susceptible to large-scale business organization. Even the provision of summer holidays, long the prerogative of the individual innkeeper, has become large-scale through the development of hotel chains. An Englishman named Butlin has provided thousands of his fellow countrymen with cut-rate holidays by moving them en masse to resorts as far distant as Bermuda.

Furthermore, the fact that many businesses are owned and operated on a small scale may not mean that they are really independent of larger organizations. The local automobile salesroom, the gasoline station around the block, and the drugstore on the corner may be owned by their proprietors, but they are subject to easy control by the large automobile, petroleum, or drug manufacturers whose power to withhold their products can spell economic ruin to the small businessman.

There is some disagreement among social scientists whether the expansion of business units will continue, and if so, how far. Clearly, large-scale operation can be extended beyond the point where it is profitable. Making work too specialized or routine may damage the morale of the employees and render them less efficient; the managerial ability of the executive staff may be overtaxed by the mounting problems of organization attendant upon the progressive increase in the size of the firm; and it may not be worth the cost to expand into the production of all parts and equipment needed to make the finished product. Thus not one of the "Big Three" automobile companies makes its own paint and finishes and only one makes its own steel. These products can be more economically purchased from independent producers who manufacture them on a larger scale than is required by any one of the auto firms.

But evidence seems to indicate that businesses generally have been growing larger and, if the present trend continues, may be expected to increase. According to the Federal Trade Commission, the number of consolidations reported in 1954 was three times the number reported in 1949 and just slightly below the number reported for each of the years 1946 and 1947, when concentration of economic activity reached a postwar peak.[7]

Thus the Industrial Revolution has clearly altered the pattern of American economic life by making it more practical to produce goods through a relatively small number of large business units rather than through a large number of small ones, and an overwhelming share of enterprise has been concentrated in the hands of the large units. This concentration has become particularly strong in the United States where no tariff walls cut off part of the potential market, as has so often happened in Europe.

The concentration of business activity has brought many blessings to the consumer by placing goods and services which under any other system would be considered luxuries available only to the wealthy within reach of the most modest pocketbook. And new products, designed to make life easier and happier, emerge from the research laboratories of the large corporations. A small businessman may conceive an idea that would be useful to society and make him a nice profit, but he rarely has funds for the experimentation necessary to perfect it. Large units, on the other hand, can set some of their income aside to investigate new ideas, and the fruits of their study range all the way from power steering and color television to Nylon stockings and Dacron suits.

Although he came upon the scene relatively late in the history of the Industrial Revolution, no one more truly symbolized its universal impact than did Henry Ford. Before his time the automobile, or "pleasure wagon" as it was sometimes called, was a toy for the rich. It chugged along the cobblestone streets of the town and dirt roads of the countryside, attracting some awe and much derision. To this seemingly useless luxury, Ford applied the techniques of mass production: the moving assembly line, standardized and interchangeable parts, an output of tremendous quantity that cut the cost of each unit to the bone.

"You may have any color car you want," he said, "so long as it's black." And the critics laughed. But the black Model T's flooded the inadequate roads of the land, and the roads were made adequate to handle them. City-dwellers, no longer forced to live within a short distance of their work, moved farther out into the country, and stores, movies, and city services went with them. People traveled over the length and breadth of the land in their own automobiles, and the hotel, the motel, and the tourist industry went with them. Trucks rumbled swiftly over distances of hundreds or thousands of miles, and the varied products of America were made more cheaply available to all.

Yes, the critics laughed. But Ford kept selling those black cars until someone figured out how to vary the color without disrupting the steady progress of the assembly line. And a visit to River Rouge or the plants of any of the other great auto manufacturers provides the perfect picture of industrial America. Down the long main line move the steel frames of the car bodies. From subsidiary lines the parts join them and are fitted together with the barest twist of the human wrist. Each part arrives at the proper time at the proper place and in the proper color. And, after less than an hour, the steel frame has become an automobile, ready for delivery at a price the consumer is willing to pay.

Monopoly Price   •   But what of Adam Smith in Henry Ford's America? With business concentrated in large units, what of the picture of perfect competition with the price of goods determined by the free play of the market place? This early picture, substantially true in the eighteenth and nineteenth centuries, has been profoundly altered in the twentieth. Let us see what has arisen in its place.

There are, we have noticed, limits to the advantages of concentration. Yet the growth of corporations has not always halted at the point where it becomes more economical for them to let further production be handled by someone else. *The reason for their continued expansion has been an attempt to overcome the hazards of a market price by creating a monopoly in order to exercise exclusive control over the production of an economic good or service.*

According to the laissez-faire theory, business units in competition with others each produce to the limit of their capacity and place their products on the market, where the price is determined by the relationship of the total supply to the total amount demanded by consumers. Those business units that cannot operate profitably at the price determined in the market are forced from the field. But if one business unit can develop a monopoly, it need not worry about the effect on price of goods placed on the market by competitors. It can, in fact, set the price to suit itself by determining at what point the greatest profit will lie. Thus, if the monopoly is in cigarettes, a firm can calculate that 8 million packs per week can be sold at a price of 20¢ each, 6 million at 25¢, and 5 million at 30¢. The higher the price, of course, the fewer sold. But the fewer produced and sold, the lower the total cost of labor, equipment, and material. The monopolist can, therefore, adjust both production and price to the point where he is receiving the greatest possible return.

We should also notice that monopoly may exist in purchasing as well as in producing and selling goods. If there are a number of small tobacco farmers but only one manufacturer of cigarettes, the manufacturer can set the price that he will pay the farmers for the raw material as well as the price that he will charge the consumer for the finished product. And the same is true, of course, for labor. If there is only one employer in the field, the worker cannot dicker over wages but must take or leave what is offered him.

Here then, in the ability to manipulate both production and price, lies a goal for the expansion of business units over and above the advantages accruing from the economies of large-scale operation. It is not even necessary that one business unit achieve 100 per cent control. The same results can be obtained under a situation of *monopolistic competition* where an overwhelming amount of production is concentrated not in one but in a handful of large corporations.

Competition among a few giants—or oligopolies—is far different from competition among a number of small producers because it is based primarily upon product innovation, quality, and sales effort rather than price. Each firm tries to increase the range of choice it can offer to consumers by varying its products and services, improving the quality of its respective brands, and then, through advertising, attempting to convince the consumer of their superiority and general desirability.

If demand is inelastic, oligopoly may stagnate product or process development and minimize competition. But in many industries today the demands of labor for higher wages and fringe benefits and of stockholders for dividends, along with the growth of investment trusts staffed by experts who select their investments from the companies that are performing best, compel big businesses to engage in dynamic competition even in the absence of a large number of firms in the industry. The few dominant companies, however, vie for the patronage of the customer by introducing a variety of brands, models, and price lines; only rarely does one firm make a significant effort to undersell its competitors. Take cigarette manufacturers, for example. We are told that one brand outsells all others, that another tastes better, and that still another is the choice of famous people. When we enter the corner drugstore, however, we discover that all brands almost always cost the same. And notice that the advertisements never tell us that one brand is less expensive than the others.

Now it is obviously not coincidence that makes oligopolists charge the same price for their products. It is, rather, enlightened self-interest, since price-cutting might only lower profits for all.

One study a few years back indicated that this indeed was the reasoning of the cigarette manufacturers when it reported that during the preceding 17 years, two leading cigarette companies had charged identical wholesale prices and that two other companies had joined in the practice for the preceding 12 years. Sometimes one, sometimes another of the companies would assume the *price leadership* by initiating the change, but the others would invariably and quickly follow suit.[8]

TYPES OF MARKET SITUATIONS

PERFECT COMPETITION

Many buyers and sellers, with an undifferentiated product or with substitutable ones. No individual's supply or demand, if removed from the market, is sufficient, by itself, to affect price.

PERFECT MONOPOLY

Many buyers and one seller, with no competing substitutes, creates perfect selling monopoly. Obviously such a seller can fix the price which suits him best and vary supply accordingly.

MONOPOLISTIC COMPETITION

A few sellers, who may actively compete for sales, yet may cooperate more easily than a larger number of sellers, to influence price and control supply.

MARKET LEADERSHIP

Another example of monopolistic competition. Here again there are few sellers, but one seller is large enough so that the others follow his leadership.

It is, of course, a moot point whether or not there was actual collusion in establishing the price. The economic advantages were plain enough to all.

This kind of price-fixing is impossible where production is divided among many small business units, because some of them would be ever ready to reap the advantages of a cut. But when the field is restricted to a few large corporations, it is a simple matter for them to realize the advantages of cooperating in matters of price and even production quotas in order to gain the same advantages that would be exercised by a single firm with a monopoly. An important agent of such cooperation is often the *trade association* to which all the competitors belong and which gathers supply and market information. Cooperation through the association also helps members develop strategy against the occasional small or new producer who refuses to hold the price line or adhere to a production quota. Although price warfare against such dissidents springs up periodically in situations of monopolistic competition, the already established large corporations almost inevitably win out. Being few in number and having enough financial reserves to operate temporarily at a loss, they can in concert undersell the price-cutter until he is driven from the field or bid up the price of his raw materials, labor, and equipment until it becomes impossible for him to operate at the lower price.

Since monopolistic competition carries with it the ability to establish a monopoly price, the tendency of corporations is to seek to expand at least to a size necessary to fix such a price. This expansion has occurred in many essential areas of American business, changing the nature of competition therein from a concentration upon price to a concentration upon innovation and upon quality. And the theory of the laissez-faire economy is, therefore, no longer completely valid in those areas.

The Corporation • The significance of the large corporation
as a Social in American society extends far beyond
Institution its economic position. In their drive for
size corporations have become social
institutions of prime importance whose
structure and functions must be understood if we are to comprehend fully the American way of life.

Up to this point we have discussed the corporation as a form of business organization that differed from the single proprietorship and the partnership only in its ability to expand to greater size. Such a description suffices for the early corporation whose stockholders never rose above a few hundred, where a relatively few individuals held a majority of the shares of stock, and where all owners took personal interest in the operation of the business even if they did not participate actively in it. The description is not sufficient, however, for the gigantic modern corporation whose need for additional finances has extended the number of its stockholders to the hundreds of thousands and even, on occasion, above the million mark.

The average stockholder in a modern giant corporation holds such a small percentage of the shares that he cannot conceivably, alone or in combination, have a significant voice in deciding policy. But over and above his lack of ability to control is his lack of desire to control. The average shareholder buys his stock not to acquire a voice in the business, but because he considers it a good investment, likely to return high dividends. Or the purchaser may not look upon the stock as an investment at all, but rather as a speculation. In this case he buys stock only because he thinks that others will soon desire it and offer him a higher price than he paid. Buying and selling shares in large corporations has become, therefore, an activity in its own right. Huge *stock exchanges* have been established in principal cities throughout the country where the shares of many corporations may be quickly bought and sold. And on the scene has appeared the *broker,* whose specialty is to advise investors and speculators about the possibilities for a rise or a decline in the value of stocks and then to handle their transactions in return for a fee.

With the bulk of a corporation's shares thus scattered among many people who are interested only in guessing what the results of business policy will be rather than in influencing that policy, the overwhelming majority of common stock is hardly ever voted in the election of the board of directors. It is possible, therefore, for those with only a relatively small financial investment to elect the board and thus control policy. Often as little as 5 per cent of the total stock will be sufficient.

Thus we see that despite the fact that giant corporations are widely owned, they are narrowly controlled, the control lying with those who own a significant portion of the common stock. Such a significant portion may be held by a small group of individuals, perhaps a single family, or by an *investment banking house,* which handles the issuance of a corporation's securities and perhaps keeps for its fee a modest but controlling percentage of the common stock.

Narrow control of major corporations facilitates cooperation within the field of monopolistic competition. It is easier for a few firms controlled by a small group of individuals to reach broad understandings on price and production quotas than it is to try to forge an agreement between stockholders from many different corporations. It is also simpler to agree not to compete at all, not even by improving products or by advertising, but instead to set up a *pool* wherein each corporation is given exclusive rights in a particular area of the country, or even a *cartel,* where exclusiveness is assigned on an international level.

In addition to such understandings, the relative ease of obtaining corporation control has led to further consolidation of erstwhile competitors in order to approach a more complete monopolistic position. A favorite means of such consolidation in the nineteenth century was the *trust,* pioneered by John D. Rockefeller and Standard Oil. Under the trust arrangement, controlling stockholders of competing corporations surrendered their shares to a board of trustees and received in exchange trust certificates that paid dividends but carried no voting power. The trustees would then vote the shares of the former competitors in electing boards of directors that would pursue a unified policy. Trusts as such have long been outlawed, but their name has attached itself in popular parlance to all devices for reducing competition and establishing centralized control in a particular industry.

A device similar to the trust in final effect was the *interlocking directorate,* an arrangement by which the controlling stockholders of different corporations would elect boards of directors with overlapping membership. Also outlawed, at least in regard to competing corporations, the interlocking directorate still exists among corporations not in direct competition, where it undoubtedly helps create a community of interest that facilitates cooperation in matters of mutual concern, particularly political.

Of more direct modern concern as an instrument for consolidation is the *merger,* which is usually accomplished by procuring stock or purchasing assets. Generally, either the acquired companies are dissolved and their stock and assets are taken over by the firm whose existence continues or a newly organized corporation absorbs all merging firms. In any event, a single corporation emerges from the multiple units. Studebaker-Packard and American Motors are examples of recent mergers.

Another integration device is the *holding company,* a separate corporation that is organized to control other firms by holding (owning) at least a controlling proportion of their stock. Although some holding companies engage in the production of goods and services, perhaps even in competition with the corporations whose stock they hold, others are concerned merely with buying and voting shares. United States Steel, General Motors, and American Telephone and Telegraph are examples of holding companies.

The tendency of those in control of large corporations to cooperate and consolidate is increased by a similar tendency among those entrusted with active business management. One of the great advantages of the corporate form of business organization is that it permits the hiring of expert managers. The modern corporation is so vast and requires so much executive leadership that there has arisen what might almost be described as a new social class, the corporation executive, whose role we must not ignore.

The young man who chooses a career within a large corporation has a far different life ahead of him from the one who strikes out on his own. The corporation offers him much in the way of security, opportunity to rise to positions of great responsibility, and higher salaries than might be made in independent business. But it demands in return not so much initiative and daring, qualities that might be cultivated if he were on his own, as loyalty to the organization, learning the ropes, and playing the game. Once instilled, these qualities are re-enforced by the fact that the corporate executive almost of necessity lives practically his entire business and social life in contact with others who have similar values. Not only does the corporation absorb his working hours, but by moving him frequently from one area of the country to another, it often prevents him from sinking roots in any single community and absorbing characteristics not involved in his way of life.

This type of training leaves its mark on the executive when he reaches a position of major responsibility. For men who have learned to play the game and maintain social contacts with and respect for their opposite numbers in other corporations, the "cut-throat" competition of a laissez-faire economy holds no thrills. The corporation manager thus is conditioned by experience to supplement the financial interest of the controlling group by eliminating and playing down competition, a conditioning that the manager or owner of a smaller business unit would rarely have undergone. Indeed in many corporations the top management is almost identical with the controlling owners. If no significant bloc of stock is held by a group of individuals or an institution, the corporation officers can frequently dominate the election of the board of directors by voting the few shares they themselves own and soliciting *proxies,* or authorizations to vote, from other stockholders.

The stress on work within large-scale organizations has an effect beyond the purely economic. For one thing it is a great leveling device. The widening of American educational opportunities has made engineers, accountants, and lawyers of rich and poor, farmer and city-dweller. And it is these men who are hired as executive personnel. The corporation places them in the same mold of experience, and they all come out very much alike. Many of the differences in our society are thus smoothed over and upward social mobility is increased. Opportunities to advance to positions of power and prestige are extended to more people than ever before.

For the American community in a broader sense, it is also significant that an increasing proportion of its leaders, men who wield economic power and its attendant social prestige, are men who are trained to live within organizations, to cooperate rather than to compete. As they set the pattern that the rest of us imitate, the free-wheeling individualist, the eccentric and non-conformist, whose imagination has often pioneered new developments in literature, art, and science, is losing his former high prestige. Even in the field of scholarly and scientific research, the modern stress is on large-scale projects undertaken by teams of experts rather than on the work of individuals. This stress has, of course, been aided not only by the example of the large corporation, but also by the fact that corporation grants frequently subsidize research teams, and large-scale projects appeal to the men who dispense the money.

Success in many phases of life has become the result, therefore, not of individuality and daring, but of adjusting to the rules of the game. America is bound to gain much from an emphasis on cooperation and teamwork over the days when the erratic and the unconventional were relied on to pave the way to progress. But it will lose something, too, no doubt, something in flavor and glamour. It was, after all, much easier to get excited about the "Lone Eagle" who first flew the Atlantic than about the "committee" that finally scaled Mt. Everest.

Corporations • We have now seen that American eco-
and Government nomic life is far different from what
Policy we like to picture it. Not only has free
price competition been replaced by the
giant corporation and the cooperatively
determined price in many areas, but the spirit of organization with its attendant stress on teamwork and large-scale activity has also pervaded elements of our society beyond the economic.

The actualities of life thus do not square with laissez-faire theory, and we are confronted with the alternatives of readjusting the facts to fit the theory or developing a new theory to fit the facts. To alter the facts would mean restoring price competition by destroying those large-scale business organizations that can, either alone or through cooperation, establish monopoly. To alter the theory would mean abandoning the no longer valid notion of a freely determined market price and recognizing that our economy is now based primarily on giant corporations engaged in monopolistic competition. Once that recognition has occurred, society must, of course, take steps to insure that such corporations do not use their power irresponsibly.

Either the breakup of large-scale business organizations or their regulation requires action by government, and it is to this area that we now turn. We must remember, however, that in any field, democratic government moves primarily in response to the demands of different groups in society, and that in the field of business concentration the action that has been taken is the result of pressure by interested parties—in this case, small business, the controlling, managing, and investing groups of large corporations, consumers, and labor organizations.

Early attempts to make fact and theory correspond centered about restricting the size of business units in order to insure price competition. The growth of corporations has been resisted by smaller businesses that have quite naturally feared the greater competitive advantages of larger units. Small businessmen have been joined frequently by consumers who have feared the imposition of monopoly prices and by workers who have sought to resist arbitrarily set wages. These opponents of corporate growth have entered the political arena in an attempt to induce government to restrict expansion; they have taken their case to the people in the name of the traditional American ideal of free competition and called for the government to intervene.

Their arguments were quite effective during the early and middle years of the nineteenth century; and the states, in issuing corporation charters, set up rigid controls on the activities in which the new business units might engage and the size to which they might grow. Almost invariably, for example, they prohibited one corporation from owning the stock of another. But as the years went by, the different states began to compete for the fees that were paid for the right of incorporation as well as for the prosperity and employment that followed whenever corporations located within their borders. Corporations, too, began to play a significant role in state politics, throwing their support to governors and legislators who promised to undo restrictive regulation. Both of these factors combined to make charters progressively more liberal, and by the end of the century several states, particularly Delaware and New Jersey, had eliminated practically all restrictions on corporate size and activity.

The opponents of the large corporations then turned their attention to the federal level, and it is there that the major battle against business concentration has been waged. In 1890 Congress adopted the Sherman Act, which was designed to restore the principles of a laissez-faire economy by outlawing "every contract, combination in the form of trust or otherwise, or conspiracy in restraint of trade or commerce among the several states," and by prohibiting persons from monopolizing or attempting to monopolize any part of such trade. In 1914 the Clayton Act prohibited some of the specific practices that large corporations used against smaller competitors when their use was intended to "substantially lessen competition." Prohibited were *discriminatory pricing,* by which certain retailers who had an opportunity to deal with a competitor were given cheaper rates than retailers who did not have such an opportunity, and *tying contracts,* whereby a retailer might be forced to purchase all his goods from the corporation in order to obtain some one item. The act also outlawed holding companies, interlocking directorates, and mergers, when designed to "substantially lessen competition." Finally, in 1914, Congress also created the Federal Trade Commission, authorizing it to investigate complaints of "unfair methods of competition" and to order offenders to "cease and desist."

The Sherman and Clayton acts and the act creating the F.T.C. have been the basis of the federal government's efforts to restrict the growth of monopoly power. But the government has tried to foster competition in other ways as well. The Reconstruction Finance Corporation, for example, which from 1932 to 1953 had the power to make loans to new business, has made funds available to newcomers in such fields as automobile manufacturing, shipbuilding, and housing. Government contracts for military and other supplies are frequently issued in such a way as to favor smaller business units, and the Atomic Energy Commission is forbidden to license any firm to use fissionable material if granting the license might maintain or foster monopoly.

Despite these and related activities, however, governmental efforts to halt the growth of monopoly have not been particularly successful. A major reason for its lack of success has been the counterpressure set up by the large corporations who have also entered the political arena in the name of free competition. It has been their contention that American tradition calls not for the intervention of government to maintain price competition but for the absence of government interference with expansion. In their political efforts the large corporations have had the distinct advantage of being able to coordinate their plans. The campaign has been directed by small controlling groups in each corporation that have cooperated in forging a common policy through such devices as the interlocking directorate and trade association. In later chapters we shall examine political devices, including pressure-group tactics, the spending of money on election campaigns, and the influence on public attitudes of the various communication agencies that are themselves big business. We shall simply say here that when a relatively few persons can turn vast wealth to this type of activity, the potentialities for their success are great. This is particularly true when the opposition is composed of a great many smaller organizations, each of which must be consulted and convinced before concerted action can be taken.

The success of the political efforts of the larger units can be seen primarily in the manner in which the acts seeking to restrict monopoly have been enforced. In its interpretation of the Sherman Act, the Supreme Court of the United States has adopted what is known as the *rule of reason.* Under this philosophy, no combination in restraint of trade is illegal unless it offends the Court's sense of reasonableness. However, the Court has never put itself on record with a comprehensive definition of reasonableness, although the current policy seems to be that *potential power* to exclude competitors is the prime consideration in determining whether a monopoly exists. The phrase in the Clayton Act that restrains only those practices designed to "substantially lessen competition" has the same effect as the rule of reason that governs the application of the Sherman Act. Here, too, there is room for wide latitude of interpretation. And the Federal Trade Commission, you will remember, is authorized to ban only those practices that it considers "unfair."

What all this means in effect is that the attempt to restore the principles of laissez faire to the economy has been placed in the hands of government attorneys who bring cases and of judges and commissioners who hear them. These men are, after all, products of our culture. When our society is particularly aroused by some well-publicized monopolistic practice, the F.T.C. and the courts will hold very strict ideas of what is unfair or unreasonable. On the other hand, in periods such as the decade immediately following World War I, when Americans had great faith that the giant corporation would pave the way to universal prosperity, the corporation's argument that the free economy was best maintained by leaving it alone carried great weight. The recent tendency has been to apply anti-trust laws with somewhat greater rigor to industries where sellers are relatively few in number and large in size.

Many more suits have been initiated by the government in the past 15 years than in the previous half century. However, the legal remedies applied by the courts have frequently been ineffective. For one thing, the fine (although it was recently raised from $5000 to $50,000) is not large enough to deter a company from a practice that is yielding it millions. Secondly, the suits can have only a negative effect by having certain acts declared illegal. They can restrain a company from entering some line of business or force it to get out of an enterprise by disposing of its holdings. But there is no assured way a decree in an anti-trust proceeding can affirmatively foster competition. Moreover, the government is often satisfied with something less than complete liquidation of properties.

In addition to trying to neutralize the enforcement of laws designed to restrict their activity, large corporations have, despite their attacks on government interference, pressured Congress into passing legislation to counteract the effects of the Sherman, Clayton, and Federal Trade Commission acts. Thus the Webb-Pomerene Act of 1918 exempted from the earlier laws associations among businesses engaged in export trade as long as such associations interfered only with foreign rather than domestic competitors. The National Industrial Recovery Act of 1933, declared unconstitutional after only a brief life, permitted within each industry the development of codes of practice designed to lessen competition. And the Miller-Tydings Act of 1937 permitted the producers of goods bearing a brand name or *trademark* to set the retail price within each state provided the state government consented and one retailer within the state agreed. The Supreme Court held resale-price-maintenance legislation invalid in 1951, but Congress re-enacted it in new form in 1952.

The giant corporations have been helped in their campaign against restrictive legislation by the obvious economic benefits of large-scale operation. Failing, therefore, to readjust fact to theory, American society has proceeded to recognize the role of the large corporation in our economy and to regulate its activities in the interest of the groups with which it deals.

Here, too, action has usually been attempted first on the state level. But as some corporations have extended beyond the borders of their legal homes, it has become increasingly impractical to regulate them from the state capitals. In the matter of regulation, therefore, as in the matter of size, the struggle for and against restrictive legislation has been concentrated more and more in Washington.

The divorce of control and management from ownership has been recognized in the Securities Exchange Act, which is designed to force the disclosure to prospective shareholders of the actual financial conditions of the corporation and to prevent certain financial manipulations by which corporate earnings can be withheld from distribution as dividends and instead manipulated in order to increase the power and profits of the controlling and managing groups. Many states had already enacted so-called *blue-sky laws,* which make it a crime to offer for sale securities that represent nonexistent gold mines, oil wells, or other properties—in short, securities that stand for little more than the bright blue sky.

In order to protect the worker in his dealings with the large corporation, laws have been enacted establishing minimum standards of wages and working conditions and guaranteeing the right to form unions. These laws will be considered in greater detail in the next chapter.

The consumer has been protected through increased power given to the Federal Trade Commission and the *Food and Drug Administration* to insure him not only products of reasonable quality, but also honest presentation of the facts in advertising. These matters, too, will be covered in detail in a later chapter.

The major issue in all cases has been, of course, just how much regulation and what type. That question has been answered in the long run by the respective strength of the different interest groups in the community. Just as the small investor, the labor union, and the consumer have demanded more stringent control of the large corporation, so the managing and controlling groups have demanded less. The end result has been a compromise ranging from almost total governmental regulation in some industries to almost total absence of regulation in others.

Generally speaking, the most extensive regulation is exercised in those industries that are clearly recognized to be monopolies. There are certain industries where competition would be extremely wasteful: communications, for example. To have two competing telephone companies would necessitate two sets of wires and cables and require most people to have two phones in order to keep in touch with all their acquaintances. The same thing is true of gas and electric companies, streetcar and bus service, and in some cases railroads, trucking, and airlines. Inasmuch as most of these activities are *public utilities,* of extreme importance to the daily life of the community, government usually forbids competition altogether and instead grants monopolies or franchises to particular corporations. In return for its *franchise,* the corporation must agree to render service to all who require it at a rate that the government deems to be fair. And since it can exist only by its franchise, such a corporation is also in a weak position to resist other demands that may be imposed on it at the request of investor and labor groups.

However, a monopoly established through consolidation and cooperation may be as complete as one granted by franchise, though perhaps not so obvious, inasmuch as some competition at least appears to exist. The government has therefore levied some stipulations in regard to financial, rate, and labor policies on other industries as well. Although corporations have opposed regulation in the name of traditional freedom from governmental restraint, those which depend in some measure on governmental actions have been less successful in resisting regulation than those that are completely independent of government. For example the shipping industry depends to a large extent on government contracts. Radio and television stations can broadcast only so long as government prevents chaos by parceling out wave lengths and channels. And in many fields, governmentally imposed tariffs grant protection from foreign competition.

Outside of the public utility field, therefore, and even to a certain extent within it, the battle over how much and what kind of regulation is a running fight among competing interest groups, with state and federal authorities bending first one way and then another in response to the pressures of the moment.

The final step in regulation is, of course, government ownership and operation of an industry. Like lesser forms of regulation, government ownership usually has been imposed on public utilities that represented a choice between authorizing a public monopoly or an obviously private one. Thus in the United States, as in the United Kingdom, we frequently find the local water, gas, electric, or transportation company publicly owned. But in these industries, as in businesses not obviously of a public utility nature, the issue is not settled on the basis of abstract political philosophy, but on the competition of interest groups. If the consumers of electricity in a particular community, for example, are convinced that they can get cheaper rates from a publicly owned company than from a privately owned one, and their political strength is greater than the private company's, the city probably will take over the utility. *Government will enter any business where the political pressure favoring the step is greater than the pressure opposing it.*

Business　•　In the battle among interest groups
Regulation and　　over government regulation and owner-
Political Reality　　ship the great political strength of the
　　　　　　　　　　　large corporations is thrown to the sup-
　　　　　　　　　　　port of the controlling and managing
groups who want as little regulation as possible. Although labor unions, as we shall see later, have grown to the point where they can pose as effective counterweights to the large corporations, most other groups seeking regulation, including small investors and consumers, have not organized into groups of anywhere near comparable power. And we should remember also that the fight is not a clear-cut one with controllers and managers invariably lined up on one side, and labor, con-

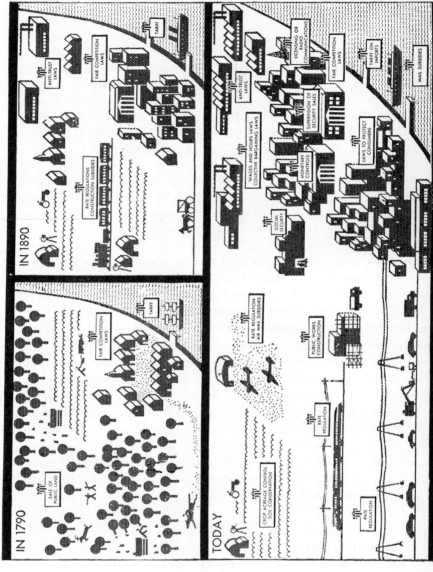

A MORE COMPLEX

LIFE MEANS MORE

"GOVERNMENT

IN BUSINESS"

sumers, and small investors on the other. Each of the latter groups is concerned primarily with its own problems, and may oppose regulation relating to the others. Thus the small investors frequently feel a community of interest with managers and controllers on the question of governmental regulation of labor conditions, or with labor unions on issues of consumer protection.

Finally, we must bear in mind that the battle is carried on within the context of laissez-faire economic theory. The average American, who after all must be convinced before government can act, has been reared on this theory and is reluctant to forsake it. He distrusts big government, and he is coming more and more to respect the large corporation that plays such an important role in society. To this corporation he has transferred much of the same friendly feeling that his ancestor felt for the independent artisan and small businessman.

This attitude does not mean that the average American is unaware that economic conditions have changed since the Industrial Revolution. He is, we have seen, ready to accept a certain amount of government regulation, particularly where monopoly is obvious, to assure himself that economic power will be exercised responsibly. He is also aware of the necessity for a virtually completely planned economy in time of war with direct price control, rationing, and allocation of materials and manpower in order to assure adequate supplies for the armed forces and a fair distribution of civilian goods.

But over the long pull, the tendency of the man in the street to think in terms of laissez-faire theory places those who advocate more governmental control in the economic field at a disadvantage. Steps in the direction of greater regulation are taken slowly, reluctantly, and only after their necessity has been clearly demonstrated. And they are, in most cases, less complete than in nations where laissez faire has not held sway quite as strongly. In the United Kingdom, for example, government owns and operates such industries, not obvious monopolies, as coal production and radio broadcasting. This type of control, accepted by the British, runs so counter to American tradition that it cannot be expected here in the foreseeable future. Far more in accord with our history and philosophy have been our attempts to destroy business concentration; and, failing that, our efforts to live with it so long as it conducts itself in a fashion considered reasonable.

To summarize: Although the laissez-faire economy remains the theoretical basis of the American economic system, it has been profoundly modified both by private monopoly and government regulation. What has emerged is a *mixed economy*: it has areas in which the pull of individual choices still prevails, areas in which goods and services are allocated exclusively by government, and intermediate areas where private monopolies make the decisions under varying degrees of governmental supervision. It is a complex economic system for a complex and mighty nation. It adheres to no abstract theory but is rather the result of years of experience and the interaction of countless political pressures.

The Laborer

One of America's most eminent historians, when writing of the ten happenings "that most profoundly shaped and shook history" during the first half of the present century, placed the "upsurge of labor" third on his list.[1] Some of our citizens view labor's increase in power during the twentieth century as an ominous trend; others view it as a hopeful one. But whether a person approves or disapproves, the hard fact that the organized labor movement has come to play a dynamic role in contemporary American and world society cannot be denied. No adequate understanding of modern economic systems and political systems or of the cultures of which they are a part is possible without constant reference to the subject of labor.

Before   •   The laissez-faire theory assumed that
the   individual workers would be able to
Factory System   bargain effectively with their employers
                             over wages, hours, and other conditions
                             of work. It further assumed that almost
automatic economic processes would assure to workers their fair share of the fruits of production. For the most part, these laissez-faire assumptions concerning the position of labor, as we have seen to be the case for other laissez-faire generalizations, operated more in the realm of theory than of reality. They never corresponded exactly to the economic facts of life.

Yet it is true that prior to the Industrial Revolution, which dramatically began to remake human society in the late eighteenth century, workers individually could bargain with their employers much more effectively than at a later period. Before the factory system prevailed in Western society, most manufacturing and business operations were carried on by small concerns. As a consequence, relationships between employers and employees were frequently highly personalized and intimate. The owner of the small shop was aware of his employees as individual personalities. He called them by their first names and took a paternal interest in their personal lives. At the very least, he knew of the weddings, births, and deaths in their families.

Moreover, before the establishment of the factory system, workers were usually not completely dependent on their jobs for earning a living. During hard times many of them fell back upon farming, hunting, and fishing as a means of support. Competition between employers was keen and genuine, and thus the likelihood that they would establish agreements to keep wages low or otherwise conspire to keep their employees at a disadvantage was not very great.

Workers generally produced a complete product rather than merely one part of it. The craftsman who produced a whole shoe probably derived a kind of satisfaction from his work that is unknown to the worker in a modern shoe factory who perhaps spends his whole working day attaching only heels to shoes. Formerly the all-important factor in the manufacturing process was individual skill, and it gave to the worker who possessed it a sense of pride and independence.

It is, of course, easy to idealize this vanished relationship of employer to employee and worker to product. Nostalgia for "the good old days" should be tempered with the realization that modern factory life, with all its demand for readjustment, has given factory workers a dramatically higher level of living than the independent artisan formerly enjoyed.

The Emergence • Modern industrial society and the vari-
of Modern ous patterns of living and working that
Industrialism we associate with it certainly did not appear on the scene like a flash of lightning. It emerged rather as a process that took place over a period of years. In the United States, this process was almost constantly stimulated by the general scarcity of labor that was an ever recurring theme in early American history. The Civil War with its huge demand for war supplies also stimulated the industrialization of American society. In the years that followed the war, Americans proved themselves to be more eager than any other people on the face of the earth to accept and devise new ways of manufacturing in almost every field. Such behavior cannot be understood apart from the fact that America was a young nation largely lacking in the strong sense of tradition that almost invariably impedes the acceptance of the new. During the 50 years that followed the Civil War, modern industrialism emerged in the United States with a flourish. American life was radically transformed. It was a period of great triumph for the industrial way of life and for the industrialists who had helped to bring it into being. The era was climaxed during the first decade of the twentieth century by the introduction of the assembly line that heralded the subsequent marvels of mass production.

The Worker • The onward march of industrialization
and the New profoundly altered the situation of the
Industrial Order wage-earner in the United States. Many manufacturing and business establishments grew so large that employees became useful to their employers as groups rather than as individuals. The widespread development of the corporate form of business organization further depersonalized relationships between employers and employees. The characteristic situation that now prevails in our important industries is one in which very remote and impersonal stockholders own factories about whose workings they usually know little. Their basic function, apart from providing capital, is hiring managers to direct production, and

even this is accomplished through procedures that the average stockholder only vaguely understands (see Chapter 17). Thus it is that nowadays we more frequently speak of "labor and management" disputes than of "labor and capital" disputes. The separation of the owner and manager function constitutes one of the most significant themes in the industrial history of the twentieth century.

Probably this modern industrial setting is conducive to patterns of mutual exploitation. All the parties concerned are psychologically able to evade moral responsibility with relative ease. Not infrequently managers respond to charges that workers under them are being mistreated by saying, in effect: "I only work here myself. I don't make all the policies of this company. My main job is to earn money for the stockholders." When similar complaints are registered with stockholders they often say something like this: "To tell you the truth I don't know much about the business. What do we pay managers for, if not to work out things like that?" In different but comparable ways, workers in modern industrial situations have also been prone to behave irresponsibly. It is not so much a case of passing the buck, as it is with the stockholders and the managers, but rather an "I don't care" sort of attitude. The modern factory is often so large and impersonal that workers would appear to say to themselves more often than is generally realized: "What difference does it make if I loaf on the job or waste materials? I'm not hurting anybody, and besides the company's so big and wealthy it surely isn't going to collapse because of what I do or don't do."

The emergence of modern industrialism had an especially important impact upon the situation of the skilled worker. Many highly trained artisans found that the jobs that they had once performed were rapidly being taken over by efficient and untiring, if inartistic, machines. An abundance of skill or training is not necessary to watch over machines. Henry Ford once judged that 43 per cent of the jobs in his plants could be learned in a day and that only 15 per cent of the jobs required as much as a month's training. Many of the dislocations that were involved in the mechanization of industry were, of course, temporary. Moreover, even though severe individual hardship was frequently involved, industrialization did, in the long run, promote general social well-being.

The advantages that were derived from the new modes of production, however, were distributed in a strikingly uneven way. The owners of industry frequently received fabulous returns from their investments, but the workingmen whose toil and sweat lay behind the value of these investments received no corresponding gains in wages or in other conditions of work or living. Wages generally tended to lag behind prices.

Many important industries came under the dominance of monopolies and semi-monopolies. Thus workers frequently had to buy goods that were monopoly priced, but they had to continue to sell their services under competitive conditions. The general result was that industrial workers did not receive sufficient wages to allow them to live in health and decency, even according to the standards of the time. To make matters worse, urbanization, which was part and parcel of industrialization, made it virtually impossible for workers to supplement their incomes in the traditional ways. Hunting, fishing, and farming were hardly possible on a meaningful scale in the urban setting.

The mechanization of industry eventually meant shorter working hours, but the dawn to dusk hours of the farm were initially carried over into the factory. Such long hours were doubtless difficult for agricultural workers to bear, but they involved much greater hardships for industrial workers who were constantly trying to keep pace with machines in noisy, poorly lighted, and poorly ventilated buildings that were totally lacking in anything resembling adequate eating or sanitation facilities. These conditions were conducive to a high industrial accident and disease rate. Yet during the early years of industrialism, safety devices and regulations were virtually unheard of, and injured workers received little or no compensation. One of the sorriest aspects of the situation was that women and children were frequently subjected to the same conditions.

The beginning period of modern industrialism has not infrequently been characterized as one of the most depressing eras in the long history of man's cruelty to man. Since the beginning of this new era, thoughtful observers have wondered whether the machine was slave or master of man. Perhaps the most distressing feature of modern industrialism was that it was accompanied by periods of depression and unemployment on a vaster scale than ever before known in recorded history (see Chapter 21). When large numbers of men starved and went without the necessities of life in earlier times it was usually because of crop shortages or other natural disasters. Modern depressions have been more tragic and less necessary in that they have been characterized by starvation in the midst of plenty. Men have gone hungry while they were almost literally knee deep in grain.

The machine age worked havoc with the older economic principles and institutions. The finely spun theories of the laissez-faire economists crumbled before it. Of course, among the various groups in society who were adversely affected by depressions, it was the workers—the group that did not fare well even during normal times—who invariably suffered the most hardships. The lot of the industrial workers was difficult not only in the sense that they faced privation, but also because of the general sense of insecurity inherent in their situation. Men engaged in agriculture, at least those who have been self-employed, have usually known where their next meal was coming from. Industrial workers in the event of depressions or even more temporary situations such as lay-offs, shut downs, or strikes, have not even had this assurance.

**Labor Organizes   •   Enough has been said to indicate that
in Self-defense   the organized labor movement devel-
                         oped as a self-defense reaction to the
                         ravages of modern industrialism. Every**
modern industrial society has an organized labor movement of one variety or another. The origins of the labor movement have been traced back to the beginning of the factory system. The lone worker was a helpless creature in the face of modern industrial conditions typified by the impersonality of the giant factory. As an individual he could not, by any stretch of the imagination, eliminate low wages, long hours, unsafe and unsanitary working conditions, or chronic insecurity, nor effect almost any other improvement in his lot. It was inevitable that he should join together with his fellow workers in order to attempt to make a better life for himself and his family. The consolidation of industry led to the consolidation of labor.

The labor movement is world wide. The basic stress of this chapter is upon the American labor movement, but some of the patterns that we shall point to will have application for labor unions throughout the world. Whether you look upon labor unions as a blessing or a curse, it is well to remember that they constitute an essential part of the social fabric of modern society. That more than 135 million of the world's people now belong to trade unions is strong testimony to this fact.[2]

Prior to the Civil War, there were only short, sporadic developments in the organized labor movement in the United States. It was not until after the close of the war that a nationally significant labor movement developed. The building of a trade union movement in the United States was no easy task. The early organizers of American labor were confronted by serious obstacles that required long years to overcome.

Early union leaders were attempting to organize persons of widely different backgrounds and traditions. American workers spoke different languages, practiced different religions, and had different national and racial backgrounds. To unify such a heterogeneous group was no easy undertaking.

Another obstacle to labor unity was that most American workers, as we saw in Chapter Nine, have been lacking in what is frequently referred to as *class consciousness*. That is, they have been to an unusual degree unaware of themselves as belonging to a distinct and separate group in society. The facts and myths concerning the great opportunities to climb the ladder of success in America have tended to make the average worker look upon his status as something very temporary, and traditionally he has been prone to think of himself as a member of the middle class. Tomorrow or the next day he expected to be a boss himself or at least to have gone up a rung or two on the social and economic ladder. Men imbued with this kind of psychology, who did not identify closely with their fellow workers, were not inclined to be interested in helping to organize or even in joining labor unions.

American federalism also made the task of improving the lot of the workers slow and difficult. In an era when it was not thought proper for the federal government to intervene in the nation's economic and social affairs, labor organizers would occasionally succeed in winning legislative concessions in particular states that would perhaps outlaw child labor or make employers assume responsibility for industrial accidents. But frequently the industries would merely move to other states where there were no laws or the laws were not so stringent. Thus the struggle to benefit workers via legislative channels had to be approached nationally.

Probably the most important obstacle that had to be overcome by those workers who wished to organize was a climate of public opinion that was generally unfriendly to the trade union movement. The dominant power in late nineteenth-century American society was wielded by businessmen; especially important in the scheme of things were the so-called "captains of industry." Business ways of thinking and doing were assumed to be correct by most Americans, and the supremacy of business was hardly challenged until the opening of the twentieth century. The suspicion and hostility with which the business community viewed the idea of workers organizing themselves into trade unions came to be shared by large numbers of Americans. It also was reflected in the attitudes and actions of the national and state governments. If and when government intervened in labor disputes during the nineteenth and early twentieth centuries, it almost invariably sided with capital as against labor. Two keen students of the American past have suggested that there came into being at this time "a double standard of social morality," one for capital and another for labor.

Combination of capital was regarded as in accordance with natural laws; combination of labor as a conspiracy. Monopoly was good business, and business men denounced or evaded the Sherman Act, but the closed shop was un-American. It was the duty of government to aid business and to protect business interests, but government aid to labor was socialistic. That business should go into politics was common sense, but that labor should go into politics was contrary to the American tradition. Property had a natural right to a fair return on its value, but the return which labor might enjoy was to be regulated strictly by the law of supply and demand. Appeals to protect or enhance property interests were reasonable, but appeals to protect or enhance labor interests were demagogic. Brokers who organized business combines were respectable public servants, but labor organizers were agitators. The use of Pinkerton detectives to protect business property was preserving law and order, but the use of force to protect the job was violence. To curtail production in the face of an oversupply of consumers' goods was sound business practice, but to strike for shorter hours in the face of an oversupply of labor was unsound.[3]

**The American   •   Despite the obstacles that had to be
Federation   overcome, a powerful organized labor
of Labor   movement did develop in America.**
Among the several nationally significant labor organizations that came into being in the second half of the nineteenth century, the American Federation of Labor was destined by all odds to be the most important. It was founded in 1881, but it was reorganized and given the name A.F. of L. in 1886. It almost completely dominated the American labor movement during the half century that extended from the time of its birth to the mid 1930's. Through 1920 the organization knew a rather steady increase in numbers and in general power and influence. By that year its membership included 4 of the 5 million workers who were then unionized.[4] With the exception of some of the railroad brotherhoods, who maintained close relationships with it, virtually all the major unions in the United States were affiliated with the A.F. of L.

Throughout its early history, the A.F. of L. was primarily concerned with the organization of the skilled worker. Most of its unions, though by no means all of them, were of the craft variety. A *craft union*, sometimes called a horizontal union, is organized on the basis of the skill that a particular group of workers possesses or in terms of the type of task that they perform. The building industry is a good example of a highly unionized and important industry that is organized along craft lines. The various persons who work in the building industry do not all belong to one union but rather hold membership in separate unions on the basis of the trade that they follow. Thus there is a bricklayers' union, a plumbers' union, a painters' union, and so on. And the membership of these unions is open only to persons working at these trades.

The *industrial union* or the vertical union is the other basic form of union organization. It organizes all the people working in a given industry into one union. For example, the United Automobile Workers is an industrial union. Its membership is open to all automobile workers regardless of the specific task that they perform or whether they are skilled or unskilled. It includes in its ranks foundrymen, machinists, painters, body polishers, upholsterers, janitors, and all other workers who are involved in the manufacture of automobiles.

The A.F. of L., as its name suggested, was organized along federal lines. Each member union had its own constitution but theoretically subscribed to the general policies laid down by the parent body. But the Federation was never a highly disciplined organization, and the affiliated unions, especially the larger and more powerful ones, did not hesitate to overlook its rulings when they so desired.

Many of the trade union organizations that had preceded the A.F. of L., as well as some that were its contemporaries, advocated a complete alteration of the economic, social, and political status quo. They often envisioned, among other things, a new social order wherein industry would be cooperatively or state owned. The Federation's leadership, however, did not look to the founding of a new society. Its orientation was essentially conservative. It favored cooperation with the established economic system, but, of course, it encouraged workers to struggle for as large as possible a share of the fruits of production. The general social outlook of the A.F. of L. was well summed up by one of its founders. "We have no ultimate ends. We are going from day to day. We are fighting only for immediate objects." [5] The spirit of gradualism dominated A.F. of L. thought and action.

This attitude was well reflected in the Federation's traditional position on politics. It shunned the idea of identifying itself with any particular political party or group. Its leaders advocated trade unionism pure and simple. They apparently feared that extensive involvement in politics would lead to disharmony among the member unions and ultimately divert organized labor's energies from its main goal—securing for workers higher wages, shorter hours, and other improvements in working conditions. Its advice to workers at election time was nonpartisan: "Reward your friends and punish your enemies." The A.F. of L.'s official position was that it preferred to achieve its ends through its own means without government intervention. The Federation was never quite as removed from political life as it officially claimed to be, but it did have a real and justified fear of governmental action in labor disputes, intensified by long years of government strike-breaking activities.

The   •   The policies we have just outlined
Decline of   seemingly served the A.F. of L. well
Organized Labor   until the 1920's. This decade, which has
                            been described as the "era of normalcy,"
                            was one of stagnation and decline for
organized labor. It was an era during which there was a well-organized and well-financed employer offensive against the trade union movement. An attempt was made to convince workers as well as the American people at large that unions were unnecessary and even un-American. Employer groups were frankly intent upon destroying unionism. They were seeking to establish the *open shop,* that is, the non-union shop, the country over. They attempted to lure workers away from bona fide trade unions by organizing company-dominated employee organizations of one kind or another. With this apparent innovation, employee associations, recreation clubs, insurance plans, and even stock purchasing plans were founded. The open-shop movement combined with company paternalism was heralded, at least in employers' circles, as the American Plan.

There is room for considerable argument concerning the whys and wherefores of organized labor's decline during these years, but there is no doubt that between 1920 and 1930 American unions lost more than a million and a half members.

Labor and the   •   In the opening years of the 1930's, the
New Deal   state of the labor movement went from
                            bad to worse. Prosperity appeared to
                            have drugged it, and the Great Depres-
sion appeared to be dealing it a death blow. Neither extreme in economic climate seemed to favor its survival. By 1933 the A.F. of L. had sustained, by comparison with 1920 figures, an almost 50 per cent loss in membership. The morale of organized labor was indeed low.

Organized labor, however, was soon to experience a revitalization that was fundamentally related to new forms of governmental action. A new era in relationships between government and labor was to be inaugurated. The federal government, which was once regarded in labor circles more as a foe than a friend, was now to become labor's great benefactor and protector. Even before the New Deal was officially launched in 1933, a new deal for labor had begun. The onset of the new era was marked by the passage of the Norris-LaGuardia Anti-Injunction Act, which was signed by President Hoover in 1932. This Act restricted the use of the labor *injunction,* which is in essence a court order that can restrain unions or other groups or individuals in society from engaging in specified activities. The injunction was hated by organized labor as the instrument by which many strikes had been broken. The Act also asserted the principle that workers should have the right to join organizations of their own choice. It also outlawed, in effect, the so-called "yellow dog" contracts. These were agreements that workers often had to sign as a condition of employment stating that they did not belong to a union and that they would not attempt to organize one while they were on the job.

A basic goal of the New Deal's economic recovery program was to increase the purchasing power of the mass of the American people. It deliberately set out to promote the development of a strong labor movement in an attempt to stimulate the economy. The theory was that the unionization of workers would tend to force wages up.

The first piece of New Deal legislation that importantly affected labor was Section 7a of the National Industrial Recovery Act of 1933. The historic significance of this part of the act was that for the first time *collective bargaining* was given legal sanction by the federal government of the United States. Section 7a stated that employees should have the right to organize and bargain collectively through representatives of their own choosing. It also forbade employer interference in the unionization process and prohibited employers from attempting to use coercion to prevent their workers from joining unions.

In 1935 the National Industrial Recovery Act was declared unconstitutional by the United States Supreme Court. But in the same year the National Labor Relations Act, better known as the Wagner Act, became law. This statute, which has with reason been referred to as labor's magna carta, not only included all the provisions of Section 7a, but also in greater detail protected workers from possible anti-union activities on the part of employers. Moreover, it created the National Labor Relations Board with powers to investigate unfair employer labor practices and to conduct elections in order to determine what unions should represent the various groups of workers as rightful collective bargaining agents.

Among the various pieces of New Deal legislation, probably none had more significance for wage-earners than the Social Security Act of 1935. Its provisions embody a complex pattern of federal-state cooperation that is designed to relieve the insecurity that industrial wage-earners have traditionally experienced. It set up a federal-state system of unemployment compensation and a federal system of old-age insurance. Its provisions also included arrangements for aid to the physically handicapped and to dependent children and the improvement of the public health. Though many European nations had adopted similar social security programs at a much earlier date, such legislation was unprecedented in American history. It signified a new form of governmental concern with the general welfare in the United States.

The Birth · The encouragement that the New Deal
of the C.I.O. gave to organized labor set the stage
for the revitalization of the American
labor movement. Unionization became
so powerful a trend that from 1933 to 1935 workers in many parts of the nation spontaneously organized themselves and sent telegrams to the A.F. of L. requesting admission. The most rapid trade union growth in American history got underway.

Organized labor's new vitality was to revive an old issue, an issue loaded with dynamite, which had haunted the house of labor for long years. Throughout the history of the A.F. of L., there had been groups within it who maintained that the craft union form of organization was not appropriate to the new industrial era. The gist of their argument was that it was pointless to put so much emphasis upon craft unionism when by far the greatest number of persons employed in the mass-production industries were unskilled or semi-skilled rather than skilled workers. They argued that the great task before the A.F. of L. was to organize the unorganized and that this could be accomplished only via industrial unionism. Every attempt, they observed, by the A.F. of L. to organize the workers in the important mass-production industries had failed. They charged that these failures arose from the fact that the craft union approach had involved, in the attempts to organize the automobile and steel industries, for example, dividing workers into dozens of different and competing unions. The duty of the A.F. of L., maintained the advocates of industrial unionism, was to unite workers and not to divide them along unrealistic craft lines.

Craft unionism versus industrial unionism was heatedly, sometimes violently, debated at the 1935 convention of the A.F. of L. Most aspects of the controversy were fundamentally related to a struggle for power that was raging within the Federation, but there was, nevertheless, genuine disagreement between the disputants concerning organizational principles. Just after the close of this stormy convention a group of important Federation leaders formed the Committee for Industrial Organization. The avowed purpose of the C.I.O.—as it was soon to be known to the American people—was to promote the industrial organization of the mass-production workers of the country under the auspices of the A.F. of L.

The new organization that was brought into being by the leadership of the United Mine Workers, the International Ladies' Garment Workers, the Amalgamated Clothing Workers, and of several other important unions was equipped with all the things necessary to the achievement of its purpose. It possessed a workable idea, an able and experienced leadership, large financial resources, and a challenging task. With "Let's organize the unorganized" as its battle cry, it succeeded where the A.F. of L. had failed. In three years it had unionized large segments of the steel, automobile, and rubber industries. During these first years, the C.I.O. remained within the A.F. of L. but functioned much as an independent organization. By the autumn of 1938, after three years of controversy between the C.I.O. leaders and those labor leaders who had remained more loyal to the A.F. of L., the C.I.O. formally emerged as an independent federation of labor organizations. The C.I.O., which had become well known to the American people, changed its name but not its initials. The Committee for Industrial Organization now became the Congress of Industrial Organizations.

The significance of the C.I.O. extended far beyond the industries that it organized. The C.I.O.'s successful organizing campaigns impressed the whole world of labor, including the staunch craft union leaders. The result was that as the years went by many of the craft unions altered their structures so as to include larger numbers of semi-skilled and un-skilled workers within their ranks. Thus it was ironical that as the C.I.O. and the A.F. of L moved farther apart, their organizational practices became more alike.

These two giant federations of labor unions were similar in many ways. The general structure of the C.I.O. was clearly modeled after the A.F. of L., and it maintained a similar pattern of relationships with its member unions. But the C.I.O. exercised a somewhat greater degree of control over the behavior of the unions that were affiliated with it. And the C.I.O. had a less conservative orientation than the A.F. of L. That is, it was more disposed to challenge the economic, political, and social status quo in America. The C.I.O. became deeply involved in American political life on both national and local levels. The developments that led to its birth rose out of governmental action, and quite naturally the C.I.O. maintained a keen interest in politics.

A.F.L.-C.I.O • The A.F. of L. and the C.I.O. went their separate ways for 17 years. During this period the leaders of both organizations publicly maintained that they favored a unified house of labor but that the leadership of the other group was blocking it. Bitter jurisdictional disputes between A.F. of L. and C.I.O. unions, which were trying to organize the same industries, were not uncommon. November, 1953, saw the death of William Green, long time President of the A.F. of L., and the death of Philip Murray, President of the C.I.O. George Meany assumed the presidency of the A.F. of L. and Walter Reuther took over the reins of the C.I.O. Soon afterward, unity discussions were begun between the two organizations. In December of 1955 the A.F.L.-C.I.O. held its founding convention.

The A.F.L.-C.I.O. clearly has the right to speak for organized labor. It is a federation of 150 independent unions with a collective membership of some 16.5 million persons. Only about 2 million of the unionized workers in the United States are not affiliated with it.

The A.F.L.-C.I.O. has a federal structure along the lines of the two organizations that brought it into being. However, it appears to be more inclined than were either the A.F. of L. or the C.I.O. to exercise authority over its affiliates. The rather vigorous way it has been dealing with corrupt unions within its ranks is a case in point.

The American labor movement has long had a lively interest in international relations and in the plight of workers in other lands. The A.F.L.-C.I.O., in keeping with this tradition, established an International Affairs Department and is an active and influential member of the International Confederation of Free Trade Unions. The I.C.F.T.U., a non-communist association of labor organizations, was founded in 1949. It has 125 affiliates in 90 countries and a membership of some 55 million. Its chief rival, the Communist dominated World Federation of Trade Unions has about 80 million members.[6] But many of the W.F.T.U. affiliates are not genuine labor unions in the Western sense. They are, in effect, disciplined arms of the Communist states in which they are located.

The Culture • Understanding the role of the laboring
of the Factory   group in contemporary society requires more than a discussion of its formal organization into trade unions. The behavior of men in group situations is determined as well by processes that are not so formal or tangible as the labor union and the various patterns

of behavior that we associate with it. Social science is just as much concerned with informal means of social control as with formal means of social control.

The large modern factory can be accurately viewed as a society that possesses a culture, much as does the larger society of which it is a part. Factory cultures, for example, exhibit folkways and mores that regulate the behavior of industrial workers. That workers can and do use informal social control devices to curtail or increase output has been well established by industrial psychologists and sociologists.[7] In most factory situations the new worker soon learns that his fellow employees are likely to resent him if he produces too much or too little. Both the "eager beaver" and the slacker are sure to bump up against group resentment.

It has also been established that a worker's basic attitude toward his job, whether he works with zest or indifference, may be determined by the quality of his social relationships with his fellows. Patterns, either of cooperation or of hostility, as between one employee and another or between employer and employee, may be so thoroughly internalized by the members of a factory society that they may dominate the whole picture of industrial relationships. All who have had much work experience know that some places of employment are characterized by a feeling of togetherness or a strong we-feeling, while in others it is each man for himself.

The culture of the factory also embraces a system of social stratification. Members of a factory society, just as members of every other human society of which we have knowledge, enjoy differential social status. Positions of social superiority and inferiority exist that are determined by whether a person belongs to the management group, the foreman's group, or the ordinary workers' group. There are also differences in the social status and prestige that are accorded to the white-collar or the office worker, as distinct from the person who actually works among the machines and gets his hands dirty. These differences, however, do not loom as significantly as they once did, for the trend would now seem to be that plant workers, being the better organized of the two groups, generally receive higher wages than office workers. Hands that hold money appear somewhat less dirty. Industrial unionism has tended to have an uplifting effect upon the social position of the unskilled worker, yet it remains true that the skilled worker continues to enjoy a higher status in the industrial hierarchy than the unskilled worker.

The factory has been well described as a society of unequals.

Union Activities. *To many members, unions mean political action and family vacations and friendships, in addition to strikes and bargaining sessions with management.*

Every person except one within the structure has a boss; and every boss in turn, has his boss, until finally at the top of the heap we find that rare and practically sacred individual, the president, the owner, the big-shot-who-has-no-boss. . . . The whole structure forms a neat pyramid, with the Big Boss at the top and each rank of lesser bosses increasing in numbers as they decrease in importance. . . .[8]

Collective   •   During the last two decades, remark-
Bargaining   able changes have taken place in the pattern of labor relations in the United States. The picture that was so recently one of anarchy and jungle law has changed to one wherein a large degree of order prevails. This is not to suggest that the struggle between labor and management has ceased. Nor can it be safely assumed that an era of genuine cooperation between labor and management is about to begin. More accurately, it would appear that both sides have learned the rules of the game. Conflict between labor and management continues but it continues within the framework of rather well-established collective bargaining procedures. In effect, collective bargaining has become an institutionalized process whereby wages, hours, and other conditions of work are determined.

It is important to realize that collective bargaining does not function only when representatives of management and labor sit down in order to negotiate contracts. The notion of collective bargaining includes the procedures that have grown up in the sphere of industrial relations for the adjustment of disputes between labor and management that occur on a day-to-day basis. In fact, labor-management agreements now almost invariably outline what are usually called *grievance procedures*. They are written into contracts in order to give the worker some recourse if he feels that management is not living up to its bargain. Moreover, even the best of agreements fail to anticipate many conflict situations that arise and that require adjustment. The general practice is for workers to choose a steward or a shop chairman to represent them in grievance matters. Such persons are frequently granted special immunities from layoffs to encourage them not to be unduly submissive to management. In this connection we should point out that a fundamental fact that helps to explain the growth of unionization in the mass-production industries is that workers were seeking relief from situations in which foremen or other bosses abused the power that they possessed. At present, probably the most important day-to-day activity of unions is the administration of contracts, which in large measure involves helping settle grievances.

Most industrial disputes are successfully adjusted by negotiation between representatives of labor and management without the intervention of outsiders. In the vast majority of union-management contracts, however, provision is made for the referral of unadjusted union disputes to *arbitration.* This process varies from agreement to agreement, but it usually entails the selection of an impartial person as an arbitrator who becomes chairman of a committee composed of an equal number of representatives of both labor and management. The essential feature of arbitration is that both parties to the dispute agree in advance to accept the decision of the arbitrator as final and binding. But, of course, each side is given the opportunity to present its complete case to the arbitrator before he arrives at his decision.

Mediation is similar to arbitration as a process for settling labor disputes. Mediators, like arbitrators, are outside persons. The basic difference is that mediators only have the power to assist in the settlement of controversies. They do not possess the arbitrator's power actually to lay down the terms of settlement. The keystone of mediation is that it is a voluntary way of adjusting labor disputes. Arbitration, even though it comes about through mutual consent, is clearly less voluntary.

Labor and management are both opposed to *compulsory arbitration.* This type of arbitration is not the result of voluntary agreement. Rather, it is a situation wherein a third party, namely government, intervenes and hands down decisions in labor disputes without being invited to do so by the parties concerned.

Collective bargaining in its various forms is still far from being a perfected process. Yet it has considerably reduced the unexpected elements in labor-management relations. Each party, now that there are some rules to go by, is better able to predict the behavior of the other. Consequently, strain and bitterness are no longer so prevalent in labor relations as they once were. For example, strikes of major proportions have occurred in the post-World War II period, but they have been notably lacking in violence. And the greatest likelihood is that labor relations will continue in this non-violent pattern now that collective bargaining processes have become institutionalized.

Cooperation   •   During the last several decades, the
and Conflict   study of labor-management relations
                        has emerged as one of the important
                        areas of social science research in the
United States. This trend clearly reflects the fact that our whole society now exhibits a deep interest in industrial relations. Labor-management

disputes receive headline attention in our newspapers and in our radio and television newscasts. Labor "problems" are discussed on street corners, in buses, in barber shops, at social gatherings, and almost everywhere Americans come together. But it is unfortunate that many of these discussions shed more heat than light. Most Americans have taken sides, and it is not uncommon for arguments concerning labor-management relations to resemble disputes between fans of different baseball clubs.

The central theme of these discussions is "How can labor and management work together?" It is somewhat of a paradox that the American belief system, which emphasizes the sanctity of competition in economic life, at the same time assumes that cooperation between labor and management is both necessary and possible.

The relative lack of class consciousness among American workers, which we have already discussed, has probably increased the possibilities for labor-management cooperation in the United States. Workers who do not quite look upon themselves as workers are not likely to be the most enthusiastic trade unionists. The fact that only half of the American workers who are eligible for trade union membership in terms of the nature of their employment belong to unions tends to substantiate this generalization. In fact, a person is justified in concluding that a sizable number of workers, but, of course, not all non-union workers, are anti-union in their outlook. It is doubtless true that some American workers identify themselves more closely with their employers than with their fellow workers.

In our heterogeneous society, the most intense forms of conflict occur between workers of different racial, national, religious, and regional backgrounds. Antagonisms between Negro and white workers, between foreign-born and native workers, between Catholic and Protestant workers, between northern and southern workers are widespread in the United States. There is another form of conflict between workers; namely, rivalry between different union organizations. Thus we have the spectacle of bitter *jurisdictional* disputes between unions that attempt to organize the same group of workers. For example, over a long period of years the Brewery Workers' and the Teamsters' unions were literally at each other's throats over which union should organize the truck drivers who hauled beer. The Brewery Workers claimed jurisdiction over them by virtue of the fact that they were working in the beer industry, and the Teamsters based their claim on the fact that they were truck drivers. We should also keep in mind that workers are divided among themselves by the patterns of social stratification that exist within the factory.

In short, despite the fact that organized labor is a powerful factor in contemporary American life, and growing stronger as the years go by, the solidarity of all labor, the grand goal to which unionists have long aspired, is a long way from achievement. Moreover, despite the existence of the National Association of Manufacturers, the United States Chamber of Commerce, and other employer associations, it would be hardly accurate to suggest that management is a highly united group in the United States. The consequence of this absence of a very high degree of unity among either labor or management has produced *group conflict* rather than *class conflict* in the field of labor relations in the United States. A situation in which all workers have been pitted against all employers or all management has never developed. Rather it has been individual groups of workers as against individual employers or groups of employers.

The degree to which labor and management can cooperate fundamentally depends on the goals that both sides have in mind. Precisely what these goals are is extremely difficult to determine. Indeed, there seems to be a question whether the members of the two groups are certain in their own minds about their goals. Nevertheless, social scientists have attempted to make generalizations concerning these goals, and it is

THE FOUR GOALS OF LABOR . . .

1. SECURITY   2. A CHANCE TO ADVANCE

3. MORE HUMAN TREATMENT   4. MORE DIGNITY ON THE JOB

THE FOUR GOALS OF MANAGEMENT . . .

YOUR JOB IN XYZ CO.

SALES
PROFITS

1. THE ECONOMIC WELFARE OF THE COMPANY   2. GOOD RELATIONS WITH LOYAL EMPLOYEES

DEP'T. A

ACHIEVEMENT

BUDGET

RULES

BINDING AGREEMENT

3. FREEDOM TO MANAGE   4. BUSINESSLIKE, RESPONSIBLE RELATIONS

well to be familiar with some of their conclusions. One of America's most prominent public opinion analysts, after carrying on a ten-year study of workers' attitudes, concluded that the basic goals of workers could be summarized in four points:

(1) *Security.* He defined this goal as "the right to work continuously at reasonably good wages."

(2) *A Chance to Advance.* Described as "just the good old American chance to get on in the world, to go from one job to the next higher job."

(3) *Being Treated Like a Human Being.* He said this was rather intangible and hard to define, but manifested itself in an insistence that management recognize that "workers, too, have daily lives, personal problems, temptations, ambitions, loves, and hates."

(4) *A Desire for Simple, Genuine Human Dignity.* Defined to mean that "most workers want to feel that they are personally performing creditably in a job which contributes something to the aggregate of human security, advancement or happiness." [9]

Another important social scientist and labor relations expert, after interviewing 60 leaders of management, summarized management's goals under four headings:

(1) *The Economic Welfare of the Company.* The first objective of industrial relations, like that of every function of management, is the economic welfare of the particular company.

(2) *Good Relations With Its Own Employees.* Industrial relations are primarily and basically a matter of relations between management and employees, its own employees.

(3) *Freedom to Manage.* Industrial relations arrangements must leave unimpaired management's prerogatives and freedom essential to the meeting of management's responsibilities.

(4) *Businesslike, Responsible Relations.* All parties to industrial relations should be businesslike and responsible.[10]

Not only have social scientists endeavored to outline the respective goals of management and labor, but an interesting attempt to mark out certain stages in union-management relations has also been made. These stages may be summarized in the following way:

(1) *Opposition.* This stage characterized the situation through the late 1930's in the United States, until the major industries such as steel

and automobiles were organized. There was great mutual hostility between organized labor and management during this period. Management was determined to block unionization at almost any cost, and labor was equally determined to unionize. Both sides were inclined to use extreme methods to accomplish their ends. The emphasis here was almost completely upon the distribution of the fruits of production. Each side struggled to increase the size of its share of the pie.

(2) *Toleration.* This stage came into being after the unionization of the mass-production industries. Management and labor lost no great love upon each other, but each was resigned to the existence of the other. Each side continued to emphasize, almost exclusively, the matter of how large its share of the pie was to be.

(3) *Cooperation.* This is the stage that is now theoretically in the process of emerging. But, of course, there are still many areas in American industrial life where the first and second stages prevail. Where the third stage prevails, management and labor have come to view each other somewhat more objectively. The attitude of toleration has become more an attitude of acceptance. Both labor and management are supposed to be on the point of forgetting old antagonisms. Both parties have adjusted their behavior to the fact that the union is now a permanent factor in the industrial process. Labor relations have, so to speak, matured. Unions behave less aggressively since they no longer have to carry on a struggle merely to exist. Likewise, employers are less aggressive in that they have been forced to abandon dreams of union-busting. Finally, according to this theory of stages, labor and management are now beginning to emphasize not only how much of the pie they should receive, but also to concern themselves with increasing the total size of the pie to be shared, and are orienting their behavior toward that end.[11]

Certain cautions are in order at this point. Both the goals of labor and management and the stages in the development of their relationship that we have just listed should be viewed with a critical eye. Labor relations are complex and changing and such attempts to define goals and stages as those just mentioned inevitably simplify and thus to a degree distort. Both series of generalizations would appear to be founded on the assumption that genuine and thoroughgoing cooperation between labor and management is possible—an assumption that some students of labor relations are not ready to accept.

Those who view labor-management relations in a less optimistic light argue that labor and management are two opposing groups that have quite different interests. They say that what helps one frequently hinders the other. They agree that increasing productivity would be advantageous to both parties, but they are quick to add that there is only one pie and if management gets a larger piece it follows that labor gets a smaller one and vice versa. Their general conclusion is that cooperation between labor and management is possible only on the most superficial level.

Moreover, it should be pointed out that cooperation between labor and management can conceivably take the form of cooperation against the rest of American society. Or it can manifest itself as cooperation between union leaders and management at the expense of workers. Indeed, some conflict between labor and management is probably to be desired. Each group now, for example, performs the socially valuable function of carefully observing the behavior of the other group and making the public aware of its shortcomings.

A realistic and democratic goal for our society in the sphere of labor relations would be to minimize industrial conflict rather than to eliminate it. Most of us have at one time or another been personally inconvenienced and perhaps angered by strikes. Some persons react to strikes by demands for vigorous action. They talk of abolishing all strikes. They frequently make the unwarranted assumption that strikes are almost always the fault of organized labor rather than management. They overlook the fact that strikes are rarely called for minor reasons and they almost invariably involve more severe and more direct hardships for the workers concerned than for either management or the rest of society. When all is said and done, it is usually the workers who have to tighten their belts.

Moreover, those who talk of doing away with strikes fail to consider that such an end could be achieved, given modern industrial conditions, only if society were completely dominated by either business, labor, or government. Few Americans would prefer total dominance by any of these three powers to the occasional strikes that we now know. After all, conflict as well as cooperation is probably basic to the functioning of a free society.

Let it be clear that we are not maintaining that every instance of conflict between labor and management is desirable. Though it is probably true that the social costs of strikes and other labor disputes have been exaggerated, especially by the enemies of organized labor, nevertheless, they are real and should not be too easily dismissed. Not only do workers and owners lose out when labor disputes stop the wheels of production, but the whole of society loses the product that might have been produced. In some cases, moreover, lost production can never be regained. Also, it is obvious that in a highly complex and interdependent economy such as our own strikes in key industries can paralyze the whole of society.

Labor Comes   •   By the time of America's entry into
of Age   World War II, most of the mass-production workers in the United States
had been successfully unionized. The
great goal was won. Organized labor had come of age. One eminent American economist even goes so far as to argue that "A laboristic society is succeeding a capitalistic one." [12] Such a conclusion has not yet been well supported by evidence. Most social scientists are inclined to argue that the power of labor is still surpassed by the power of business

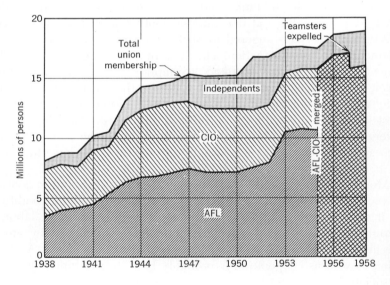

Membership of labor unions, 1938-1958.

and government. But no student of American life would deny that organized labor constitutes one of the most important power centers in the United States. It exerts a tremendous influence upon our collective destinies. The evidence of organized labor's newly acquired status in America is abundant.

The membership increases that organized labor has known in recent years are in themselves striking. From 1933 to 1958 union membership increased more than six-fold, from less than 3 million to almost 19 million. Or, to put it differently, by the middle of the century one out of three non-farm employees belonged to a union. Moreover, organized labor indirectly affects the wages, hours, and other conditions of work of an additional 25 to 30 million workers.

Another important indication of organized labor's new position in American life is that its representatives have an unprecedented access to and influence over government in the United States. Apart from the large staff of paid lobbyists that unions have stationed at Washington and at numerous state capitals, it is a commonplace nowadays for labor leaders to request and receive audiences with high government officials. In fact, they are frequently invited to confer with government officers. Similarly, the representatives of labor meet with representatives of business on a footing of greater equality than ever before in American history. Also, as union treasuries become larger, organized labor is increasingly gaining access to the mass means of communication, which were once almost completely monopolized by business. Unions now sponsor a number of radio and television programs at both national and local levels. They publish a variety of newspapers, magazines, and pamphlets. They are also now financially able to purchase considerable amounts of paid advertising space in non-union papers. Thus labor unions are now in a position to present their point of view to the public with a reasonable degree of effectiveness.

An important aspect of labor's coming of age is that more and more of its leaders are looked upon as respectable civic leaders rather than as bogey men to be feared. There was a time, and it was not very long ago, when labor leaders were looked upon by large numbers of Americans in terms of a much less than flattering stereotype. They were thought to be rabble rousers, who had dirt on their clothes and under their fingernails, shaved infrequently, had bloodshot eyes, and spoke the poorest sort of English. Fortunately, these and similiar distorted notions concerning labor leaders are not as prevalent today as they once were in America.

What is the typical labor leader actually like? There is no simple answer. A basic but inadequate generalization is that the leaders of the large and powerful labor unions are becoming increasingly like the executives of the large and powerful corporations. The following profile of one of America's important labor leaders is a telling description of what one union leader is like, and it also sheds much light upon the characteristics that the newer generation of labor leaders are developing.

> . . . what has happened . . . in general is that to a considerable extent, he has slipped into the character mold of the American managerial type: the personality of neutral efficiency. [His] private personality has increasingly been absorbed by, or become a function of, his social role. As he has consolidated his power in the [union] he has unwittingly, perhaps unavoidably, taken on a number of characteristics and outlooks of the managerial caste which functions in large areas of American industrial life. The way he dresses, the way he talks, the large, almost frightening emphasis on *efficiency* in his recent statements would all seem to support this hypothesis.[13]

It is hardly surprising that labor leaders are now frequently dubbed "The New Men of Power."[14] Trade union leaders not only have an important influence upon the lives of their followers, but also have an important influence upon the whole of our economy. And their influence increases in proportion to the steady growth that the labor movement is at present experiencing. Leaders of the larger unions speak, at least formally, in behalf of very large groups of men and women. Many individual unions have several hundred thousand members; several approach or surpass the million mark.

Labor • The emergence of the organized labor
and Society movement as one of the great power centers in American life has not been without its problems. In the light of recent congressional committee revelations even staunch friends of organized labor have to admit that all is not well in the labor movement or, at least, in many segments of it. There is disquieting evidence to the effect that some labor leaders have been unable or unwilling to make necessary distinctions between their personal funds and those belonging to union treasuries. Many union leaders enjoy a suspiciously long tenure of office. There are numerous instances in which unions have denied their members the most elementary civil liberties. Some union leaders, moreover, have violated their basic obligation to promote the best interests of workers by accepting loans and sometimes outright bribes from management. Repayment for such favors has been made at the expense of workers in the form of "sweetheart" or soft contracts, which are highly

favorable to the interests of management. Instances of union corruption are frequently related to comparable moral laxity on the part of management.

Any attempt to explain these shortcomings of unionism, as manifested in the behavior of some of its present leaders, must take into consideration the large-scale nature of the contemporary American labor movement. The problems inherent in the workings of the mammoth union are not unlike those that afflict mammoth business organizations and mammoth government.

It appears to be difficult to maintain democracy and honesty in giant organizations. We are still sorely lacking in effective techniques for making executives behave responsibly toward those who have granted them their authority. But it is not simply a case of lack of techniques. At the heart of the problem we find an apathetic citizenry. It would be idle to expect persons who pay but scant attention to politics and elections in society at large to behave as effective citizens within unions. Sheep who are willingly led to the slaughter must bear some responsibility for their fate.

One staunch friend of unions has shrewdly suggested "that the tragedy of the labor movement has been its corruption by the mores of the world it once challenged." [15] Yet it seems that organized labor is becoming more sensitive to its internal weaknesses and problems. The A.F.L.-C.I.O. appears to be making a determined attempt to implement its new codes of ethical and democratic practices, as the expulsion at its second convention of three of its affiliates, including the enormous and powerful Teamsters, indicates.

Despite these impressive housecleaning activities we can safely predict that the organized labor movement will know, in the future, greater federal control, especially concerning its financial affairs. The positive intervention of government in industrial relations is now taken as a matter of course by most Americans. During recent decades, society has intervened to regulate the behavior of both management and labor. The National Labor Relations Act of 1935, which encouraged labor to organize and which forbade employers to interfere in the process, was modified by the National Labor-Management Relations Act of 1947, more widely known as the Taft-Hartley Act. This legislation was founded on the assumption that organized labor had too much power and that employers and the general community had to be protected from union abuse of it. This assumption is still prevalent in the United States.

Few pieces of legislation in recent years have been the subject of so much public controversy as the Taft-Hartley Act. The act loomed as a major issue in the presidential campaigns of both 1948 and 1952. Probably its most significant provision resulted in the outlawing of the *closed shop*. That is, it banned labor-management agreements that made it necessary for workers to join unions before they could be hired. Furthermore, it rigidly restricted the *union shop,* wherein individuals have to join the union immediately upon receiving employment or at some specified period thereafter. Its other provisions included granting wider powers to the federal government in situations where strikes affect vital services or industries, outlawing strikes by federal government employees, prohibiting unions from making financial contributions to political campaigns in national elections, and requiring union officials to sign noncommunist affidavits.

The basic significance of the Taft-Hartley Act lies in the fact that it indicated that the pendulum had once again swung in the field of relationships between government and organized labor. If government once deliberately facilitated the growth of the trade union movement, at this juncture in our history it seems determined to regulate some aspects of union behavior. A person might quarrel with specific pieces of legislation, but society clearly has the right and sometimes the duty to undertake such regulation. Labor unions are no longer merely private associations in any realistic sense. They are clearly semi-public organizations that wield enormous power over the community, and this exercise of power must at times be controlled.

Yet such control should be applied cautiously and judiciously. The aim should be to regulate, not to cripple or destroy. A strong and free labor movement is a prerequisite to social and economic democracy in modern industrial nations. The degree to which a society is totalitarian or democratic can often be measured by the health of its labor movement. The darkness that is totalitarianism is quick to engulf the free trade union movement. In the setting of the democratic society, free labor movements flourish.

Labor • Despite the prospect of increased regu-
and the Future lation, labor unions in all probability will play an increasingly important role in the lives of their members, in the industrial community itself, and in American society as a whole.

American labor unions are in the process of becoming much more than "bread and butter" organizations. They are no longer merely content to fight for higher wages and shorter hours. Now, in increasing numbers, they are expanding their functions to the point of offering educational, recreational, and health services to their members. They are well aware of the fact that the men they represent are more than economic animals.

Now that the older goal of collective bargaining in large segments of American industrial life is an accomplished fact, organized labor has set its sights toward a new goal. The grand end that it would appear to have in mind is the achievement of middle-class status for American workers. Significant headway toward that status is represented by the various social security benefits now available to millions of American workers. Employer-financed health and pension plans have become almost standard in our major industries. Moreover, several major unions have won a modified guaranteed annual wage in the form of employer-financed supplements to state unemployment insurance. Union leaders justify such a demand on the ground that workers are entitled to have what members of management have enjoyed for long years; namely, the sense of security and the status that the prospect of regular paychecks brings.

It would appear that technological changes even more than union leaders will determine the shape of organized labor's future demands. Automation—a new word in the American language, meaning the tending of machines by machines—is destined to revolutionize industrial relations in the United States, as the development of mass production did in an earlier era. A significant difference is that mass production was introduced when American workers were without powerful unions and thus their interests were frequently subordinated to the needs of an advancing technology. Organized labor realizes that automation is here to stay, but it insists that workers be given adequate protection against unemployment and other possible employee hazards in an automated industrial environment. Hence some unions are strongly committed to guaranteed employment ideas and to severance pay plans based on the number of years of service rendered by the worker. Spokesmen for organized labor are increasingly demanding that workers receive a fair share of the increased production made possible by new technical developments. As automation increases productivity with the use of relatively less labor it is inevitable that organized labor will campaign more vigorously for the four-day week and similar plans designed to maintain wages and reduce hours.

Organized labor's reach has always exceeded its grasp, and if the four-day week does become a reality it will not mean the end of labor's quest to improve the lot of American workers. In future years the labor movement will doubtless develop new goals and confront American industry with new demands.

The Consumer

A century and a half ago, Adam Smith wrote that consumption was the sole end of production. The laissez-faire economy is based on the theory that each individual buyer or "economic man," equipped with a supply of wherewithal, will buy what he needs on the open market with a canny concern for his own welfare, after he has deliberately decided what his most important wants are. He

421

knows the comparative values of the different products and services available. In pursuing his own selfish interests, he will buy from the producer who gives him the best quality for his purposes at the least cost, and thus he will encourage competition and the smooth functioning of the system.

But this ideal picture is a far cry from the actual position of the consumer. How many people buy as coolly and rationally as the "economic man"? How many know all about the comparative worth of different goods and services? How many have paused to examine their personal scale of values as reflected in the ways they spend their money? And to get down to real fundamentals, how many have the wherewithal to satisfy their most important needs?

Inequality   •   Let us consider the last question first. Income levels vary greatly from country to country, especially from the modern industrialized countries to those in "underdeveloped areas." The United States, with approximately 6 per cent of the world's population, shares 40 per cent of the world's income. Western Europe, with around 25 per cent of the population, shares another 40 per cent. The people of Africa, Asia, and parts of Latin-America—almost 70 per cent of the world total—are left with about 20 per cent of its income.

These underdeveloped areas include nearly half of the world's 2,750,000,000 people and half the earth's surface. Their tiny income obviously forces them to live at levels "which deny them a reasonable freedom from preventable disease, a diet adequate to physical well-being, a dwelling that meets basic human needs, the education necessary for improvement and conditions of work that are technically efficient, economically rewarding, and socially satisfactory." [1]

Agriculture—often a very primitive agriculture based on methods centuries old—is the chief support of these people. Increasing population, war, and political disturbances have made their food sources even more scant than before. The poorer a family is, the larger the portion of its income that goes for food. In many countries nine-tenths of the family's income is spent on food, and sometimes this amount is not enough to keep them from starving. The average diet is 20 per cent below minimum health standards. In contrast, Americans long spent a quarter of their incomes for food, and now since food prices have risen out of proportion to other prices, they spend slightly over 30 per cent. Obviously this leaves a greater margin for comforts and luxuries. Citizens of modern industrial countries have more doctors and hospitals at their command and enjoy a greater life expectancy, in some cases more than double that in the poorer countries. They have more teachers, less illiteracy, more leisure and recreation, more telephones, radios, autos, and miles of railroad in proportion to the population.

The vast majority of the world's people have appallingly poor shelter. Most homes consist of one dim, unheated, glassless, and unscreened room crawling with insects. In some countries only a fraction of the inhabitants

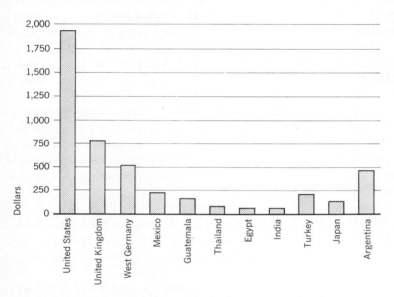

A comparison of per capita income in some industrialized and some underdeveloped countries of the world.

have shoes. Most people can be marked out by their dress as lower class. In only a few countries, and ours is one, is the level of living so high that the lower classes dress in the same street fashions as the middle and upper classes. "But where are your poor?" visitors to the United States ask.

These comparisons with other countries are likely to make Americans feel a bit smug and complacent; in fact, you may be wondering right now why we should bother about a chapter on consumer problems if we are as well off as we seem to be.

We may look at worldwide poverty from two points of view. First, we may ask whether the poor are satisfied because their culture does not teach them to want more, but rather stresses resignation, the beauty of poverty, and the rewards of the hereafter? By this criterion, many people, especially in Asia, are content with their lot. But as the world shrinks and they see other ways of life, they are likely to feel stirrings of discontent, as many already have under the prodding of Communist propagandists. Therefore we need to measure their level of living in terms of our own standards of health and decency. Inadequate nutrition, housing, and sanitation are reflected in ill health, shortened lives, and lowered efficiency. The strongest allies of communism are poverty, hunger, and disease. As a leader of the free world, the United States cannot afford to be complacent about poverty and inequality among its potential allies.

Our government has recognized this fact and stated a policy for dealing with it in the much-discussed "Point IV" of the Act for International Development:

> The peoples of the United States and other countries have a common interest in the freedom and in the economic and social progress of all peoples. Such progress can further the secure growth of democratic ways of life, the expansion of mutually beneficial commerce, the development of international understanding and good will, and the maintenance of world peace.

Based on this policy is a program for helping these peoples to raise their own level of living by improving their agriculture and industry. Our government has sent technicians to guide them in programs aimed at "grass roots" improvements.

Even in our own relatively prosperous country there is still great inequality of incomes. Over a period of years one family out of five has received as much income as the other four families put together. Although there has been some tendency toward equalization of income since World War II, partly as a result of a progressive tax program, full employment, and an increased number of wage-earners among lower income groups, the top fifth still receives about 45 per cent of the total income, with the top 5 per cent getting one-fifth of the total income. About a quarter of American families have less than $2,000 a year to live on. The 1950 census revealed that half our 40 million families earned from $2,000 to $5,000, 8 million earned over $5,000, and 10½ million less than $2,000.[2]

The last decade has witnessed a great expansion of the middle-income group. In terms of purchasing power average after-tax family incomes rose 20 per cent between 1947 and 1957, and the proportion of families with incomes between $4,000 and $8,000 rose from 37 to 43 per cent. One fifth of American families had incomes over $8,000.[3]

With the number in the middle-income group rapidly approaching half the population, it appears that our actual *level of living* is getting closer to the American "standard of living." A person can get a fairly accurate picture of this ideal culture pattern by leafing through a slick-paper women's magazine. It includes adequate amounts of the basic necessities, an ample quantity of semi-luxuries, and "cultural" advantages.

If our average family income is over $5,000, and nearly half our population is in a comfortable middle-income bracket, where is the problem? It lies in two areas: in the fact that two-fifths of the population get only one-sixth of the income, and in the fact that the wants created by our culture far outrun the means of most members of our society.

In discussing culture, we defined a "good" culture as one that satisfies

Average family income, 1935-1954.

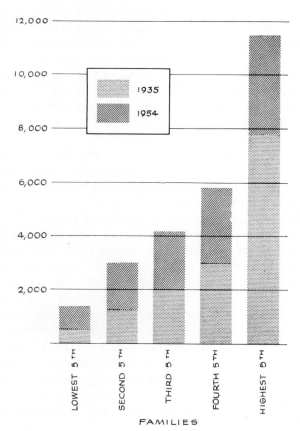

not only the basic biological and social necessities, but also the wants and desires created within the culture itself. In a society such as ours, where the "good life" is identified with material abundance, and "getting ahead" with financial success, where the rich are conspicuously rich, where wants are created and fostered by producers and distributors, the majority of people cannot satisfy the wants created by their culture. That is why economists consider inequality the Achilles' heel of our economy. When 80 per cent of the people hold only 7 per cent of the savings, and operate pretty much on a hand-to-mouth basis, says Roger Babson, the manufacturers and labor leaders who depend on the mass market must reduce their costs to fit the mass pocketbook, or their days are numbered.[4]

We cannot, then, afford poverty and extreme inequality either in Podunk or in Pakistan. It is not compatible with democracy within a country nor with our mission as leader of the free world.

Problems · of the American Consumer In addition to inequality of income and savings, there is another major respect in which the theoretical picture of the economic man does not fit reality. The great majority of consumers find it difficult to evaluate the differences between various goods and services. Nor do they determine their wants with any such degree of rationality as the "ideal" economic man would employ.

Mass production. In part this situation is the price consumers pay for the marvelous benefits of industrialization and specialization. Mass production has put on the market a *bewildering variety of goods* that are sold in numerous stores. Shopping takes a heavy toll of time and energy even when the buyer does not pause to compare prices and values from store to store. Most present-day Americans, of course, enjoy all the wonderful things on the market, even when a plate glass window intervenes, and would not care to return to the "good old days" of 50 years ago when supplies were simpler and fewer and were almost all concentrated in a "general store." But it was much easier to pick and choose when the variety of goods was limited, when the primary group pressures of a closely-knit neighborhood controlled merchants who were also neighbors, and when about the only times farm and small-town families were exposed to high-pressure sales talk were the annual visits of the itinerant peddler and the covered-wagon purveyor of "Indian medicine."

Ever greater specialization has made the typical consumer a producer

Consumer Choice. *The jammed shelves of an American super-market demand intelligent choices on the part of customers whose wants usually exceed their means.*

of only one good or service. He spends the money he earns to buy everything else he needs. He has, therefore, *no background of producer experience* from which to judge butter or cloth or apples or furniture. Some of us can remember the wonderful hearty bread our mothers and grandmothers made, and spurn the grocery's "glorified mattress stuffing" with its radiant whiteness, exaggerated softness, and artificially preserved freshness. But more and more people take grocery bread for granted because it is available in such abundance and they have no standard for comparing it with other types.

New types of goods, which even the all-around farmer-producer would find it impossible to judge, are constantly appearing on the market. The weaver of wool cannot judge the new synthetic fabrics; the metal-worker or cabinet-maker is as much in the dark as anyone else about what makes one TV set better than another; the housewife who has always been proud of her sparkling laundry but wants to eliminate some of the labor involved finds it difficult to choose from among the various automatic washers on the market and may select a brand simply on the basis of her favorite comedian's recommendation.

Since the beginning of World War II, however, there has been a significant trend reversing this over-specialization. More and more, the

427

housewife and homeowner, finding it difficult to pay plumbers, painters, carpenters, seamstresses, and odd-jobs men (a vanishing species) their current high wage scales, are learning to handle tools themselves, and with the advent of books and materials to help them, are largely dispensing with such services. Resin-based paints, ready-pasted wallpaper, drapery-making gadgets, simplified patterns for clothing, and books for the handyman all indicate this trend. Someone in most modern households knows how to replace a leaky washer in a faucet, repair an electric outlet, slipcover a chair, or refinish a chest of drawers. Surprisingly many people can install kitchen cupboards and appliances, make lamps and furniture, and turn out beautifully tailored clothes. This trend has been eased and encouraged by modern appliances and suburban living, where "do-it-yourself" is part of the culture.

Mass production, in bringing abundance, has practically eliminated the made-to-order market except in shops that cater to the wealthy. Under the old system a customer went to the tailor or dressmaker, cooper or smith, cobbler or cabinet-maker, and ordered just what he wanted. Now *goods are first produced in huge quantities, then buyers are sought.* This procedure entails *advertising* and other kinds of *sales pressures.* Mass production means a high overhead, for it is achieved by means of expensive factories and machinery; only on the sales the producer makes beyond the break-even point does he realize a profit. With most large producers of retail goods this means reaching a national or even an international market through advertising. And, as we shall discuss later, the advertiser tends to rely on the irrational in man rather than the rational to bring him sales.

Cultural values. Advertising would not be as successful as it is in "promoting new wants" were it not compatible with American values. *Our cultural values do not encourage rational choice.* Americans tend to think more of increasing their earning power than they do of getting the maximum satisfaction out of a limited income. Frugal homemaking is not highly regarded as an art. The good life is identified with an abundance of this world's goods, progress with more of the same. "Keeping up with the Joneses" is a powerful motive for spending money where it shows—on cars, clothes, and home furnishings. This desire for "conspicuous consumption" leads to an emphasis on style rather than durability. The urbanization of society, with emphasis on secondary relationships, has fostered this attitude, for in fleeting contacts people are judged by appearances, and to be successful in some fields a person must above all *look* successful.

It is true that in no society are wants limited to the simple satisfaction of elemental needs; every culture *creates* desires. But in our culture wants multiply so fast (thanks to "scientific promotion" and our own material values) that our earning capacity cannot keep pace with our *yearning* capacity.

Lack of reliable standards. Uniform standards of quality are almost entirely lacking in most lines of goods and services. Goods are inadequately or even misleadingly labeled. Such terms as "extra fancy" and "select" sound like top grades; actually they are not in many cases. A person buys a can of ripe olives marked "Select" and finds them to be tiny things; to get respectable-sized ones he would have to buy the "Jumbo" size; the largest are labeled "Colossal."

This situation is not the result of lack of knowledge of how to grade goods. Some private grocery companies use definite grade labels. Large businesses have purchasing departments and demand that the goods they buy meet certain requirements. This ultimately benefits the consumer, of course, but the buyer has no definite yardstick of quality with which to compare brands. Manufacturers insist that the brand name is a guarantee of quality, and to some extent this is true; but sales pressures so becloud the issue that the average consumer finds out which brands are best only by costly and slow trial-and-error, if at all.

The United States Bureau of Standards sets up scientifically determined standards for all government purchases. These are not, however, available to consumers. If they were, says a high official of a large mail-order house, the average person's level of living could be raised as much as 25 per cent with no increase in production.

There is a lack of any reliable correlation between price and quality, particularly in drugs and cosmetics, less so in food, clothing, and furniture. Laboratory tests of 130 brands of toilet soap sold during the depression of the 1930's found the most expensive brand, which sold for 35¢ a cake, deficient according to one federal specification and very much like a soap that sold for 5¢ a cake. In 1953 the same laboratory tested 102 brands of soap ranging from 5¢ to over $2 a cake and reported, "They'll all get you clean." Most soaps do a fairly good job of cleaning but little if anything else, no matter what the ads say about guaranteeing that a girl will be a lovely bride, or be accepted at the bridge club, or be protected around the clock. If they smell good, agree with a person's skin, and cost little, they are usually good buys.[5]

Producers have one eye not on this sale but the next; they make things just good enough, but not so durable that they will not need replacement within a short length of time.[6] Most things could be made to last much longer than they do. Many people who brought home or bought from surplus stores such things as woolen Army blankets and clothes, shoes, and towels find that they wear amazingly well. Neither the manufacturers nor the consumers apparently want things to "wear forever." Manufacturers would rather push style changes, and consumers are anxious to keep up with the current fashions. Thus we see changes not only in clothing fashions, jewelry, and cosmetic colors, but also in the shape and color of bathtubs, in the type of lamps and tables and rugs that mark a person as sophisticated, in modern cars and appliances.

Lack of awareness and organization. We are all consumers, but *few of us are aware of a "consumer problem."* In spite of the fact that they are frequently weary from shopping, are dissatisfied with the goods they have bought, feel let down after acquiring something they have wanted because the neighbors have it, or are vaguely dissatisfied with the struggle to earn more and more, most Americans fail to recognize such a problem. Most of them are firmly confident that "you get what you pay for"— a misleading slogan if there ever was one. Most of them do not think of themselves as consumers; they are much more conscious of their role as producers, and much more anxious to improve their earning capacity in that role than to improve the buying power of their dollars. Often their dual roles conflict. When a question of taxes or higher wages comes up, they are much more concerned with its immediate effect upon their income than with its ultimate effect upon the buying power of their dollars. That is why consumers are not a pressure group like laborers, farmers, or manufacturers, and why their interests are so often neglected.

Because of his lack of organization and information, the *consumer is discriminated against in much legislation.* Sales taxes, which weigh heaviest on the poor, are a prime example; there has even been some talk of a federal sales tax. Excise taxes on luxuries are legitimate sources of revenue—except when baby oil is defined as a "cosmetic"! As we saw in Chapter Seventeen, there is far less real price competition in American business today than most consumers imagine. Trade associations and price leadership policies operate to fix prices. Although federal anti-trust laws are designed to prevent price-fixing, other federal laws actually operate to keep a floor under prices. Some industries have developed into monopolies through ownership of patents, and federal and state "fair trade laws" have forced most retailers to charge the price fixed by the manufacturer. Tariffs and agricultural quotas and subsidies are other government measures that favor producers and thus raise prices to consumers.

Consumer credit. The consumer is tempted, because of sales pressures and the irrational nature of his wants, to mortgage his future income at a high rate of interest in order to have goods *now.* The path is made easy for him by *installment loans* that are available not merely on large and durable items such as cars, appliances, and furniture, but also on "total purchases of $25 or more." This practice is not compatible with the rational nature of the "economic man," for it usually results in a cost of about $12 to $20 more per hundred than the buyer would face if he paid cash for his purchases. Not only that, but cash purchasers often are granted discounts.

Perhaps installment buying is an advantage for people who cannot seem to save ahead for large purchases. This is the only way they can acquire large and durable items and buy better ones than they otherwise would. But buying an eight-cylinder car on a four-cylinder income is especially irrational when carrying charges are added.

Many buyers are convinced that the carrying charge is negligible. They are unaware that interest should always be calculated on the *unpaid balance.* If a person buys a $100 item at 6 per cent carrying charge, he may really believe he is paying only 6 per cent. But if he pays in twelve equal payments, at the end of six months he has paid half his debt and is still paying interest on the full amount for the next six months. Thus his interest is really closer to 12 per cent. Most things bought on credit come even higher. And should the buyer fail to keep up his payments the seller can repossess the goods, even if only one or two months' payment is still owing.

In spite of their convenience and their usefulness in establishing a person's credit rating, charge accounts also add hidden costs to everything the consumer buys. He must pay enough for his purchases to cover the clerical costs involved in charge accounts, and must also in many cases pay a percentage of any balance that remains unpaid from one month to the next.

Closely related to installment buying is borrowing money; in fact, installment purchases may be lumped with cash loans as "installment credit." The Bureau of Labor Statistics reports that the average city family in 91 cities of various sizes had about $4,300 income after taxes in 1950 but spent $4,700. Some of this extra $400 came from savings and gifts or inheritance, but much of it represented debt.

There are many reasons for borrowing money, from emergencies to careless management of income. Some people have the "debt habit," taking on new debts as fast as they pay off the old. "Credit cannot take the place of income. It can only alter the time when income is spent." [7]

One reason why many people acquire the debt habit is that they have never stopped to analyze how expensive it is. Credit unions and banks charge about 12 per cent a year on the unpaid balance; licensed small loan companies charge about 30 per cent (but it may be as high as 42 per cent), and "loan sharks" or illegal lenders trap the unwary borrower into an interest rate of 240 per cent on the average, and sometimes as high as 1,200 per cent! [8] The rational consumer would pay himself the money regularly (instead of a store or loan company), putting it in the bank each month and then buying what he needs with cash.

This is a very difficult procedure for many people to follow, however; and of course there are such things as emergency appendectomies, sudden moves to another city, and other unforeseen turns of events that can sometimes be met only by borrowing money. In such cases it is best to patronize a credit union, if a person is eligible for membership in one, or the small loan department of a bank, or to borrow on one's life insurance. In some cases, a small loan company is the only recourse, for it makes loans on little or no security, and makes smaller loans than some agencies with lower rates are willing to bother with. Whatever the source of a loan, the borrower should borrow only from a licensed lender and understand very clearly just how much cash he must pay in return, what security he is putting up and on what terms, and read carefully whatever he signs.

Advertising and the Consumer • The $10 billion business of American advertising, often much maligned by foreigners and occasionally resented by Americans themselves, is very much a part of the American scene. It performs certain very appreciable services for the American consumer.

Local advertising is especially useful to the consumer. He scans the daily paper for news of sales and seasonal merchandise, for classified ads, and for listings of current attractions at the theater and movies. Advertising foots the bill for much of our entertainment and news in the press and on radio and television. Some of us would groan if we had to pay a direct tax for the privilege of using a radio, as the English do. Much of our information about new products and the different varieties of commonly used items comes from advertising. National advertising often amounts to a guarantee of quality and gives the buyer confidence in the product. By stimulating steady demand it tends to reduce waste in production and distribution. Through promoting increased sales, ads may make lower prices possible, although price-cutting on competitive brands is not customary. Advertising draws money into circulation and keeps us working for the many things that are held enticingly before us (though some may question the ultimate value of this incentive!). As the advertisers themselves say, it "scientifically promotes new wants," and thus keeps the economy expanding.

Often the consumer is not conscious of the fact that he "wants" something until he sees it advertised, but then he is sure it will fill a definite need or satisfy a desire. Whether or not this is a worth-while function is an arguable question. "Making a man unhappy and then making him happy again is no great social service." [9] On the other hand, it is this very function of advertising that is seen as a lubricant to the economy, a stimulant to work and production, and thus one contributor to our great material abundance.

Motivation research. Advertising agencies recently have begun to employ sociologists, psychiatrists, and psychologists to advise them on how to exploit unconscious motivations and appeal to persons of different social classes and personality types. The best-selling book by Vance Packard, *The Hidden Persuaders,* describes this new field of "motivation research." The title of the book is based on the fact that these efforts take place below our level of awareness, and that therefore many of us are being manipulated much more than we realize through clever use of the mass media and of packaging techniques.

This new approach, according to Packard, is based on three premises. First, people cannot be trusted to behave rationally. Many do not know what they want, even when they say they do; and they cannot be trusted to tell the truth even if they do know. Therefore, their hidden motivations must be studied and exploited. Second, people are too easily satisfied with what they already have. Therefore, the "merchants of discontent" must create "psychological obsolescence," which involves changing the colors of cars and appliances, for example, to make them more appealing to consumers. Third, the growing similarity of products makes it necessary for the advertiser to base his appeal on some subtle but irrational differentiation that will build loyalty to his brand.

"Hidden desires." Packard mentions eight psychological "hooks" that the "motivation researchers" use. The desire for security, for example, is exploited in ads for home freezers; the desire for reassurance of a person's worth in ads for attractive luggage; the desire for a sense of power in automobile ads; the desire for a sense of roots in ads for wine "like Grandma used to make." The success of Liberace, he explains, can be traced to older women's desire for a love object. Steamshovel ads that depicted a huge machine that dwarfed the operator lacked pulling power; when "motivation researchers" tackled the problem, they decided the desire for ego-gratification would be better fulfilled by taking

a picture over the operator's shoulder, and sales climbed. Successful life insurance ads exploit the desire for immortality by picturing the departed father as the hero, who is still caring for his family even after his death. Cake mixes that directed the housewife simply "to add water" were thwarting her desire to be creative; mixes that call for fresh eggs and milk satisfy that urge.

Statements that chewing gum relieves frustration and pictures of huge bowls of ice cream are familiar examples of other advertisements that have been inspired by "depth" psychology. These ideas are based on the Freudian idea of an infantile longing for oral satisfaction. Ads for cigars appeal to the desire for masculinity and are more successful when no approving females are depicted. Ads for lingerie appeal to narcissism by showing a woman admiring her new slip before a mirror, and to hidden desires to appear naked in public by showing a girl dreaming she is in a public place fully clad except that above her waist she wears only a brassiere. Whether or not these "hooks" are based on sound psychological theory—and they could be interpreted in terms of cultural values rather than Freudian motivations—the advertisers say they work.

Impulse buying in the supermarket. Most purchases, major and minor, are made impulsively. Women who shop for food in supermarkets rarely take lists with them. Studies using hidden cameras have revealed that supermarket shoppers go about their business in a hypnoidal trance. As they finish their shopping, their eye-blink rate goes up, and at the check-out counter they abruptly snap out of the trance and often discover they do not have enough in their pocketbooks to pay for the gay packages in their baskets.

Exploiting this knowledge, supermarkets are carefully laid out so that the most expensive items are at eye level. Goods are constantly rearranged so that in hunting for staples the shopper will be attracted to many other items she had not planned to buy. And packages are cleverly designed to appeal to her hidden motivations. Certain colors and combinations of colors have been found to boost sales. In one test women were asked to try three detergents in boxes of different colors. They reported that the one in the yellow box was "too strong," the one in the blue box did not get clothes clean, and the one in the blue box with splashes of yellow was excellent. Actually, all the boxes contained the same product!

Brand images. Since most products are so much alike, advertisers strive to create an image of their brand and thus create an illogical loyalty to it. About 65 per cent of smokers are absolutely loyal to one brand of cigarette, but in blindfold tests they cannot identify it. They are "smoking an image." One brand of cigarettes, with its shiny red tip, was long designed to appeal exclusively to women. Then it was changed to a "cigarette for men that women like" (note the dual meaning!) and every ad shows it held in a rugged, tattooed male hand.

The automobile owner, too, "drives an image." Automobiles are "heavily laden with social meanings." A team of social scientists studying 352 car owners in the Chicago area correlated various personality traits with each leading make of car, and with different models and colors. The report indicated that people buy the car they think suits their personality and social status.

Social status and consumption. Warner's study of the six classes of Yankee City, and their motives, desires, and styles of life (see Chapter 9), excited great interest on Madison Avenue, New York's "ad alley." Warner's conclusion that 65 per cent of the population is in the lower-middle and upper-lower class turned the advertisers' attention to "Mrs. Middle Majority." The values and status symbols of our mobile society are considered in advertising: the importance of *bigness* (large stoves, large cars); the importance of the price tag (some items sell better when the price is raised, and the prestige of an exclusive car rubs off on lower-priced cars in the same line); and the effectiveness of testimonials by debutantes and social leaders (snob appeal).

Social scientist David Riesman, in his famous study of personality in modern society, comments at length on our increasing preoccupation with acts of consumption, in contrast to acts of production. The mass media serve as "tutors in consumption style," even with the Howdy Doody set. The child learns early that there must be a reason for consuming anything, and he couches his reasons in terms of advertising slogans and discusses them with his peers.

In the peer group, at all ages, taste-exchanging occurs, and a person who wants to conform and to belong must be "hep." The other-directed person does not splurge too much for fear of other's envy; he does not make an abrupt jump from Ford to Lincoln as he climbs in status. On the other hand, his envy of others keeps him from consuming too little. As we saw in Chapter Nine, he tends to conform to the style of life of the status group to which he belongs and, when possible, to acquire the status symbols of the group to which he aspires.

Morality of the hidden persuaders. Packard questions the morality of playing upon human frailties in order to sell goods. "When you are manipulating," he asks, "where do you stop? Who is to fix the point at which manipulative attempts become socially undesirable?" [10] To encourage waste, impulsive buying, and irrationality, to exploit hidden yearnings and desires, to capitalize on ignorance, to urge people to pile

up more and more material goods—do these violate our moral code? Are
we to allow the use of such devices as "sub-liminal perception," in which
messages are flashed on a screen too swiftly for us to be consciously
aware of them, but slowly enough to register subconsciously? And how
are we to guard against the use of "motivation research" to sell us not
only products but programs and politicians?

The popularity of *The Hidden Persuaders* indicates that, extreme as
some of its assertions may be, the public is uneasy about such questions,
and that many a consumer would like to bring his buying habits more
in line with the ideal of the rational man. He is aware that his
dollar still votes, but that in some cases the contest for votes is comparable to a dictator's plebiscite, where there is only room for "Yes" on
the ballot, and that in other cases it is comparable to a state or city election in which he is confronted on the ballot with a long list of names
among which he does not know how to choose. How can the voting power
of the consumer's dollar be increased?

Measures **to Aid** **the Consumer**	The classic phrase, *caveat emptor* ("Let the buyer beware"), has obviously been outmoded by mass production and or- ganized sales pressures. More and more consumers are waking up to the weak-

ness of their position and are seeking to strengthen it. Their organized
efforts have taken three general directions: pressure on the government
for protective legislation, improvement of buying habits through education
and information on scientific testing, and consumer cooperatives. Business
has responded with some degree of standardization and improved labeling.
As individuals, too, consumers find that they can improve their buying
habits in several ways.

(1) *Protective legislation.* Federal, state and municipal agencies give
the consumer considerable protection, but not as much as they give the
farmer, laborer, and businessman. There is no cabinet department to
represent the consumer; the Department of Health, Education and Welfare may be persuaded to act strongly in the consumer interest only if it is
subjected to sufficient pressure.

The two chief federal agencies operating in the consumer interest are
the Food and Drug Administration and the Federal Trade Commission.
The FDA administers the Pure Food and Drug Act of 1906, which was
amended and broadened in 1938 to include cosmetics and curative
devices, packing conditions of food, and drug labeling. It has greatly reduced the amount of spurious, adulterated, and injurious merchandise

on the market, mostly by providing for factory inspection. In 1952 the FDA prevented more than 18 million pounds of contaminated food from reaching the market. In 1953, however, the right of mandatory factory inspection was revoked, and how much harmful goods reached the market is anybody's guess. In most cases the producer can be charged only with the fault found with the seized shipment; he pays a light fine and may go on selling the same quality of goods, risking another negligible fine. Publicity could be very valuable in curbing such disregard of the spirit of the law; but news of cases is often not released until long afterward, and even then newspapers play it down for fear of offending their all-powerful advertisers. If consumers applied sufficient organized pressure, such agencies would work more effectively. Often they are handicapped by lack of sufficient appropriations to provide inspectors.

The other major agency working to protect consumers, the Federal Trade Commission, was originally established to protect businessmen from unfair methods of competition, but its powers have been broadened to punish unfair and deceptive acts that hurt the consumer. It can restrain producers from false advertising, enforce labeling of the different ingredients of wool and rayon products, enforce the truth of any labels guaranteeing against shrinkage (though the use of such labels is not mandatory), and promote "fair trade" practices (though this last is really a guarantee against competition and thus not a pro-consumer measure).

Several agencies of the Department of Agriculture work in the interest of consumers. The Production and Marketing Administration operates the school lunch program and provides a standardization and inspection service for processed foods. Some manufacturers take advantage of this service and can also use the label "US Grade A, B or C." The Department of Agriculture inspects meat entering interstate commerce and offers a valuable and inexpensive grading service, which has not been mandatory since the death of OPA. Since grading costs meat-packers only about a fiftieth of a cent per pound, consumers should demand graded meat. The department's Bureau of Human Nutrition and Home Economics provides bulletins and other informational and educational services to both rural and urban consumers. Its Extension Service is responsible for the valuable work of county agricultural agents, home demonstration agents, and 4-H clubs.

Though the Constitution gives Congress power over weights and measures, the situation is a patchwork of different state laws with varying standards of what makes a bushel and varying degrees of enforcement.

The consumer is given short weight and measures more often than he suspects, especially where there are not enough inspectors to keep tab on retailers and wholesalers. In one large city we were continually given short weight by the neighborhood branch of a local chain, and found it impossible to interest the local Bureau of Weights and Measures, even after we had made the several phone calls necessary to locate their office!

State and city governments work with the federal agencies, especially the Food and Drug Administration, and, in addition, provide licensing and inspection for such services as restaurants and dairy farms and control liquor sales, gambling, and utility rates. Some states have gone much further than others in establishing standards and providing consumers with information on such foods as milk, eggs, and butter, and other local goods. North Dakota has perhaps the best such laws in the country and backs them up with sufficient money for enforcement.

On a worldwide scale, the Economic and Social Council of the United Nations is working through its World Health Organization and its Food and Agriculture Organization to raise living standards and improve health and sanitation.

(2) *Education and information to improve buying habits.* As people learn to choose merchandise wisely, either by finding how to judge quality themselves or by relying on impartial and scientific tests, they can bring pressure to bear on industry to increase the supply of goods of dependable quality at reasonable prices. Our schools are doing something, though not nearly enough, to train students in choosing wisely. Some women's clubs, both local and national, have consumer education programs, as do some cooperatives and professional organizations.

Perhaps the most valuable service now being performed in supplying consumers with reliable information about specific products, as well as in educating them to standards, is that of Consumers' Research and Consumers Union. These are nonprofit testing organizations founded in 1929 and 1936. They depend on subscriptions, and did not become really popular until after World War II. They publish monthly magazines and annual buying guides for their subscribers.

Many mass-circulation papers and magazines refuse ads from these testing organizations, perhaps because they puncture many of the extravagant claims in the ads that keep these publications going. Educators and other professional people who know the social and economic need for such services have steadily supported them and regard them as a significant social invention.

The staff of such an organization decides what to test by questioning subscribers and making surveys. Shoppers who do not reveal their jobs buy items off the shelf in ordinary retail stores, never accepting manufacturer's "samples." These are then scientifically tested in the laboratory; in some cases "actual use" tests are also necessary, for many items cannot be tested by laboratory methods alone. They are scaled as "Best Buys" (the most for the money); "Acceptable" or "Recommended" (usually in order of quality without regard to price, or in order of increasing price); and "Not Acceptable" or "Not Recommended." The tests used are described. Each brand is further described in terms of any significantly good or undesirable qualities, and reasons for the "Best Buys" and "Not Acceptable" ratings are explained in detail.

These services are headed by scientists of unquestioned integrity, and are scrupulously free of connections with any manufacturer, distributor, or other commercial interest. They do not allow use of their findings in advertising.

In spite of a few drawbacks (many items are not tested, and "Best Buys" are not always available all over the country), these organizations perform a valuable service in consumer education and information. Besides testing specific brands, they explain what to look for so the subscribers themselves can check and judge. A sure indication of their value is the fact that they are imitated by many commercial interests that boast "consumer services," "seals of approval," and "scientific laboratory tests," although usually with less impartiality and less scrupulous regard for scientific techniques.

(3) *Consumer cooperatives.* A democratic "middle way" has become a significant part of the economy in a few countries. This is the cooperative movement. "Co-ops" are retail stores owned and managed by the customers, who supply the capital and share the earnings in amounts proportional to their purchases. In other words, they engage in non-profit-making self-management of economic enterprises, eliminating the middleman and the advertiser. Each member has only one vote regardless of the number of shares he owns. Return on shares is small, for most of the surplus is divided on the basis of purchases at the end of the year. Cash sales, grade labeling, and lack of sales pressures are typical of consumer cooperatives. Though cooperatives usually begin with a retail store, they may expand into other lines according to need —credit unions, gas stations and garages, creameries, meat-curing plants, telephone companies. They organize into wholesale units and even set up some manufacturing plants of their own. In theory there is no limit to the application of the cooperative principle.

Cooperatives do only a tiny fraction of the retail business in our country. Co-ops are found mostly among the Scandinavian and Finnish colonies in Minnesota, Michigan, and Wisconsin. In Finland, they do one-fourth of the retail business; in Denmark and England (where the idea originated in 1844) they do 15 per cent; in Sweden 10 per cent. One reason for the limited acceptance of the idea by Americans is our emphasis on greater earning capacity rather than on "petty" saving. In addition, some Americans are inclined to suspect that cooperatives are somewhat leftist. There is no basis for this in fact except that occasionally cooperatives do get entangled with other movements. In spite of its relative smallness in our country, the cooperative movement is significant. It gives people a feeling that they have something to say about managing their own purchases. It promotes consumer education and information, serves as a check on private industry, and encourages international cooperation.

(4) *Business-connected agencies.* Although a clear and uniform system of standards and labels upon which the consumer can rely is still lacking, some progress has been made by various commercial agencies. To mention a few examples, the American Institute of Laundering has promoted the use of labels indicating the washability of clothing; the United States Testing Company allows use of its findings by its commercial clients; underwriter's laboratories guarantee the safety of gas and electrical appliances; and some large chain stores have their own system of grade labeling—A & P uses "Ann Page" for Grade A, "Sultana" for Grade B, and "Iona" for Grade C. Better business bureaus in the larger cities warn citizens against fraudulent activities.

(5) *Individual improvement in buying habits.* Aside from joining testing organizations, consumer cooperatives and study groups, and a local chapter of the National Association of Consumers, which tries to centralize the various uncoordinated parts of the consumer movement, the individual can improve his own satisfaction as a purchaser in several ways.

The fundamental step is to examine his own system of values, to ask himself what he really wants out of life. Is he placing material success above all else and sacrificing to its attainment such other values as enjoyment of family life, travel, art and literature, hobbies, sports, music? Is he so weary from chasing after the almighty dollar that he has no energy left for anything else? Does he find himself at a loss for a way to fill his leisure time; does he "kill time"? Does he feel the urge to keep up with—or somewhat ahead of—the Joneses? A cartoon in a popular magazine well expressed the futility of this national sport. Two women were chatting over the backyard fence. Said one to the other with an expression of astonishment, "And all the while *we've* been trying to keep up with *you!*"

That ideal picture of the "economic man" that we drew at the start of the chapter is not a goal for all consumers to aim at. A perfectly cool and rational purchaser would get little fun out of life! People need variety, emotional release, an occasional sense of "a fling." But too many fritter money away so they have none left for the things they really want. A widely traveled professor said her friends envied her memories of the Taj Mahal, the Louvre, and the colorful Indians of Guatemala, and marveled at how she was able to manage so much travel. "I just don't buy a pretty handbag or scarf whenever one catches my fancy," she explained.

Time and energy are to be weighed, too, when considering the expenditure of money. Perhaps Consumers Union reports that the best buy in shirts is at one store, the best in shoes at another; but the stores are far apart and a person's time is limited. He must make compromises. The housewife who chases from supermarket to supermarket buying only the specials may pride herself on saving pennies, but she is probably wasting time and energy, or confessing that she has little in the way of more interesting activity on which to expend them. "A perfectly rational 'economic man'—one who decides every purchase rationally— would have to be not only very wise and judicious but endowed with the vigor of ten ordinary men to stand the nervous strain of choosing his purchases." [11]

A sensible, not too rigid budget on which the family democratically agrees is a standard recipe for happy management of family finances. Families and individuals can also try to avoid wasteful installment buying, carefully investigate sources of necessary loans, cultivate more pride in management of money and use of goods, recognize that top quality is not invariably necessary, nor price necessarily indicative of quality, and adopt an attitude of healthy skepticism toward advertising claims and the blandishments of salespeople.

The individual conscious of the importance of his role as a consumer should also realize that he has a duty as a citizen to ask for and support legislation that fights monopoly, improves price competition, and forbids the sale of inferior or dangerous goods. He can best do this by joining consumer organizations that can bring pressure to bear upon government and industry.

**Justification for
a Consumer Movement**   •   There are those who tend to be suspicious of any attempt on the part of consumers to organize and bring to bear such pressures. They are comparable to those who damned the labor movement in its embryonic stages. The Consumers Union board of directors stated the case for a consumer movement within the free price system admirably when answering charges

that they did not believe in private enterprise and were undermining faith in American business:

"So deeply is the philosophy of Consumers Union based on the free market, the competition of products, and the free choice of the consumer who wants to buy the best for his money—all mechanisms which are essential to the free enterprise system—that it is utterly obvious . . . where we fit into the scheme." After mentioning that business and government set up purchasing departments and testing laboratories, the directors went on to say:

> It appears to us unarguable that consumers [also] have the right and the need to provide themselves with such an information service to help themselves in dealing with the free market. Today more than ever, with all the rich variety of products made available by our industrial system, it takes more information than any one person can amass for himself to choose wisely. . . .
>
> An organization like CU is hardly conceivable in other than a free enterprise society . . . [It] is a characteristic expression of the American tendency to seek solutions to problems wherever possible through voluntary action. It is our aim to strengthen our economy, and hence our democracy, by giving consumers impartial and accurate product information which will lead to wiser choices. . . . We are opposed to the authoritarian guidance of production and consumption.[12]

The acid test of any economic system is, "Does it satisfy the wants of the consumer?" Economic processes are not ends in themselves; they are means by which the ends of human living may be served. Our version of the free price system, coupled with an abundance of natural resources and other advantages, has produced the highest average level of living in the world. As long as most Americans aspire to a standard achieved by relatively few, however, the system cannot be said to satisfy completely the needs and desires created in our culture. A more equitable distribution of income, a system of uniform standards, encouragement of true price competition, and an adjustment of value systems would relieve many of the stresses and pressures that endanger the continuation of the system itself.

The Farmer

In 1940 the United States Department of Agriculture issued a yearbook entitled *Farmers In A Changing World*. The editors of that volume set out to describe a great transformation that was re-shaping American agriculture. With remarkable foresight they stressed "change" as the dominant characteristic of rural life. Looking backward, it is evident that the transformation of American agriculture

443

which they described has continued at breakneck speed—that a bloodless revolution is re-molding rural America, that this impetus for change is still at full flood. The nature of this change, the problems created by it, and the search for democratic solutions to these problems are the subjects of this chapter.

The Technological   •   As a nation of city dwellers we are apt
      Revolution   to think of rural America as a placid island, untouched by modern trends. But any close examination will destroy this pretty picture at once. It is true that for centuries rural life flowed along like a quiet stream, as generation after generation followed the same farm practices. But in the past three generations the pattern of farm life has been altered more than in the previous 50 generations. As late as 1850 most farm work was done by human muscle. It was sometimes said that a farmer's chief qualification was a "strong back and a weak mind." The first great agricultural revolution harnessed the power of horses to machines—mowers, reapers, rakes, steel plows, and hayloaders. Shortly after this "horse-powered" revolution had run its course, another began.

The farm tractor. This new change centered around the gasoline-powered farm tractor. Unlike the horse, a tractor never grows weary. It is speedier than a horse and can haul and provide power for a host of new, efficient machines.

An example drawn from the harvesting of oats provides an excellent contrast between the old and the new. Standard harvesting practice as late as 1930 consisted of the following steps: (1) the oats were cut and bound into sheaves by a horse-drawn reaper; (2) the sheaves were manually placed in small "shocks" for drying; (3) the dry sheaves were later hauled by a horse-drawn wagon to a barn or stack and unloaded; (4) finally, the sheaves were threshed and the grain was stored in bins.

Notice that most of the effort was supplied by horses. Yet the procedure also required hard, heavy, human effort. The slow harvesting process likewise demanded extended periods of fair weather.

Modern harvesting offers an interesting contrast. A tractor-drawn or self-propelled combine reaps and threshes the oats in one operation. The oats are carried to storage bins by a motor truck, which uses power-driven augers for loading and unloading the grain. At no point are the oats touched by human hands. The pitchfork as a symbol of farm life has given way to the mechanic's wrench.

In a similar way other crops have felt the tractor's impact. Planting, cultivating, and harvesting have changed so radically that a farmer of 1900 would feel like Rip Van Winkle among the new machines. This change is dramatized by the tractor-horse census. In 1920 in America there was approximately one tractor for every hundred horses. Today they are nearly equal in numbers. In 30 years the horse-mule population has been reduced by four-fifths. The value of farm machinery has increased five times in the same period. Combine-harvesters in use doubled between 1945-1950, as did milking machines, hay-balers, and corn-pickers. Between 1930 and 1955, the number of corn-pickers increased by 1,300 per cent. Looking ahead, one agricultural economist predicts that for every 100 machines in use in 1955, there will be 270 by 1975. The horse, it would seem, is destined to follow the buffalo toward extinction.

Electric power. Another source of farm power has not yet been fully utilized. Electricity was available to less than 4 per cent of our farmers in 1925; by 1955 the percentage had risen to 92 per cent. There is still a great potential for expanded use of electricity in farm operations. Recently a power official remarked, "Our original power lines led to the farm house, and only as an afterthought to the barn. That was a mistake. The center of electric power consumption is in the barn."

Improved breeding. Agricultural scientists have kept pace with the designers of new machinery. Dramatic improvements have taken place in animal breeding. Artificial insemination has made it possible for one outstanding sire to produce thousands of offspring. Carefully controlled breeding programs have produced "new" animals such as the double-breasted turkey, the eleven-week broiler chicken, the "all-bacon" hog, and the high-producing milk cow. Plant scientists have created high-yielding and disease-resistant grains. Hybrid corn, for instance, has been accepted by nearly 9 out of 10 farmers in the last 20 years. Chemists have likewise contributed to the revolution. The use of commercial fertilizer has increased from 6 to 22 million tons since 1935; the use of chemical sprays for pest control increased 12 times in the same period.

Machines Force Adjustment • The past 30 years have been a period of great adjustment for farmers. Many of the new machines are efficient only if they are used on large acreages. Farm productivity per man hour has increased. But farm population has declined, as has farm tenancy; and farm capitalization has mounted. We can best trace these trends and their implications by examining some "before and after" statistics.

Farm population. The upward spiral of our national population is not reflected in rural population figures. In 1930 the United States had a population of 106 million, of whom 30 per cent lived on farms; by 1958, with a population of 175 million, less than 12 per cent lived on farms. Not only has the percentage fallen, but there are 11,000,000 fewer people living on farms today than were living on farms 30 years ago. From April, 1956, to April, 1957, nearly 2 million people left their rural homes. By 1975, if present trends continue, farm population will be less than 15 million, or only 7 per cent of the total population.

Increased productivity. Declining farm population has not affected American living standards. Thanks largely to the new machines and to scientific research, total farm output has actually increased. As contrasted with 1930, for instance, 37 per cent fewer workers produced 54 per cent more farm products in 1954. Farm productivity for a generation has increased more rapidly than industrial production—more than 4 per cent each year.

• **Farm Productivity in Terms of Man Hours, 1930-1955**

Product (100 bushels)	1930	1955
Corn	127 man hours	34 man hours
Oats	41	18
Wheat	70	26
Potatoes	63	27

A projection of current trends by one economist indicates that the average farm worker in 1975 will produce around 2¼ times as much as he did in 1955.

The trend toward bigness. For generations the family homestead, isolated from its neighbors, has been an American symbol of independence. In recent years these older farms have been consolidated into larger units. In most rural communities a number of abandoned farm houses stand as monuments to this change. In 1910 the average farm consisted of 138 acres; by 1955 the average was 242 acres. Meanwhile, the total number of farms declined from 6.4 million in 1920 to 4.7 million in 1955. These trends will probably continue. One cautious forecast anticipates that we will have 1 million fewer farms in 1980 than we had in 1954.

Although the over-all movement toward fewer and bigger farms is clear, the result in terms of farm families is in dispute. Does the disappearance of a million farms since 1930 mean that the older "family farm" is vanishing? Can a parallel be drawn between the farm situation and the earlier rise of giant industrial corporations and the destruction of small, family-owned businesses? Pessimists foresee the gradual elimination of an older rural way of life and the substitution of business agriculture (agribusiness), characterized by hired managers, cost accounting, and salaried employees. They point to the transformation of the chicken broiler business, in which the independent farmer has been displaced by hatcheries and feed companies who supply chickens, feed, and capital to a farmer-employee under contract. They also cite such developments in corporation farming as the United States Wheat Corporation of Harding, Montana, which harvests 95,000 acres of wheat annually; the King Ranch of Texas, which covers 920,000 acres and owns 85,000 head of cattle; or Adams Brothers and Company of Iowa, which harvests 6,500 acres of corn. Further, a critical examination of the existing 4.7 million farms reveals that only 2 million should be rated as "commercial" (those that produce over $2,500 in sales per year). These farms account for 90 per cent of all farm sales. The other 10 per cent of sales is a trickle derived from the remaining 2.7 million farms. In fact, 2 per cent of American farmers account for over 25 per cent of all sales. From these statistics it is easy to conclude that ownership and production are highly concentrated and that the pronounced trend is toward still greater concentration.

Other observers challenge this interpretation. They will agree that mechanization has displaced many farm families, but they do not believe that we are moving toward corporation farming. Even today most farms are of the "family" type, operated by a self-contained family group. Although the average acreage of farms has grown, this is only a realistic response of farm families to technological change.

Capitalization and tenancy. Because of the widespread use of machinery, the farmer's capital investment has also increased. The average farm worker now requires $14,000 of capital investment; in prosperous farm communities an average of $60,000 per man is not unusual. Expressed in another way, it would probably be cheaper for a father to establish his son as a surgeon than as a debt-free, prosperous farmer.

One noticeable effect of the new mechanization has been a reversal in the trend toward farm tenancy. From 1880 to 1930 the proportion of farms occupied by tenants steadily increased until over 40 per cent fell into this category. Today the percentage has dropped to 26 per cent and is still falling. Tenants are being "tractored out" or displaced by such machines as cotton-pickers.

Overproduction. The most conspicuous aspect of the new agriculture is the embarrassing flood of abundance that it has produced. The farmer could undoubtedly make the painful adjustments demanded by the new technology if it were not for this end result. His plight is in part the fruit of his own hard work and productivity. Other businessmen have generally been able to convert higher productivity into profits, but not farmers. For example, farm production in 1955 was higher than in any year except 1948. Yet falling farm prices cut total farm income to the lowest point in ten years. Higher production in agriculture normally brings glutted markets and unwanted surpluses. Periods of shortage are high profit years; abundance generally spells a deficit.

| The Farm Price Structure: Boom and Bust | • | The history of the past 40 years illustrates the "boom-bust" pattern of farm prices. During World War I farmers planted 20 million additional acres of wheat and raised cattle and hog pro- |

duction by one-fifth in answer to the government's call for increased agricultural output. At the end of the war this additional demand vanished almost overnight. From June to December in 1920 the price of wheat fell from $2.56 to $1.46 per bushel. A year later it touched 93 cents. The depression in American agriculture actually began in 1921. During the 1920's the average farmer's net income hovered between $600-$1,000. By 1931 wheat was selling for 36 cents a bushel.

The World War I pattern was repeated during World War II. During the Second World War nearly every farm product was in short supply— bread, butter, eggs, meat, and cotton. As a result the index of farm prices doubled between 1939 and 1945. These high prices stimulated farm output, but the return of peace quickly converted scarcity into surplus. Although demand fell, greater efficiency brought still higher production. Between 1949 and 1955 net farm income dropped by some 30 per cent in the face of rising industrial profits and higher wages. Net farm income reached nearly $17 billion in 1947. By 1955, despite inflation, it had fallen to about $11 billion. Meanwhile, farmers were faced with rising prices for farm machinery, gasoline, clothing, and the thousand-and-one other things farmers must buy. For example, a tractor that sold for $1,500 in 1955, sold for $1,605 in 1956.

If surpluses bring low prices, it would seem logical for farmers to grow less, thus forcing prices up. Why don't farmers cut production? A number of factors stand in their way. Over 5 million farmers make individual decisions about what to produce—they take no coordinated action. Also, farm expenses remain fixed. Each farmer needs a base income, and if he limits production or stops work, part of this income is cut off. Wheat farmers in North Dakota have little choice. They must grow wheat or quit. Dairy farmers or ranchers spend years building up their herds, and cannot afford suddenly to let them go. However, cows produce milk and sheep produce lambs and wool without regard for milk, meat, and fiber prices. The owner of a family farm cannot cut costs by laying off some of his help, because members of the family do all the work. In fact, low prices may even cause an increase in production as individual farmers attempt to meet their fixed costs in a falling market.

The fight for the consumer's dollar. Agricultural price patterns are determined in part by the farm share of the consumer's dollar. That share fluctuates widely. In 1939 the farmer got only 39 cents. During World War II he was receiving 54 cents. By 1954 he was getting only 43 cents, and the trend was still downward. Meanwhile, consumer prices were climbing upward, month by month.

Thus falling farm prices are not always reflected at the check-out counter of the supermarket. Various explanations of this fact are offered. Farmers are inclined to think that "middlemen"—processors, distributors, and retailers—are waxing wealthy at their expense. Although farm prices for pork were cut in half during 1955, for example, meat-packers generally earned record profits. Packinghouse workers also received a sizeable pay boost. Farmers are puzzled when they see consumer prices for bread and milk go up and at-the-farm prices for the same products fall.

The consumer has been blamed by other critics for the price spread. Purchasers constantly demand better packaging, processing, and service, and more liberal credit terms, which force suppliers and retailers to raise their prices and thus widen the gap between farmer-consumer prices.

A national or world market? Many issues would be clarified if the scope of the farm market were defined. Should the American farmer fix his production sights on a world market? Should he compete with all the world's farmers? Or should he try to trim production to our national demand? Is the downward trend of farm exports temporary or permanent? Can American farmers meet world market prices? Should any American export program be subsidized by the government?

Throughout most of American history the farmer has depended on a foreign market to absorb his surplus products. Before World War I we owed foreigners some $200 million yearly as a debtor nation. This annual payment was largely met through exports—nearly half of which were farm products. After World War I this tide was reversed. Foreigners now owed us $500 million a year. Nevertheless, United States tariffs were raised to keep out foreign goods. Retaliatory action by other nations cut the value of our farm exports by half in a single year. American farmers have never recovered the markets they lost during the 1920's, except on a temporary basis. The farmers of Argentina, Brazil, Canada, Egypt, and India have used their expanding production to take over markets that formerly were dominated by the United States.

The early Roosevelt New Deal was faced with a mountain of farm surpluses at home and a closed door abroad. Farm policy of the 1930's was built on the belief that our foreign market was gone, and an attempt was made to cut production to fit our domestic market. World War II reversed this policy. Food and fiber again found foreign markets, and a sudden decline in demand at the close of the war was prevented by such programs as UNRRA and the Marshall Plan. Now we have come full circle. Foreign demand is declining; farm surpluses are mounting; domestic farm prices are falling off. Will the program of the 1930's become our permanent agricultural policy, or will we try to win back foreign markets for our agricultural products?

The Farm Problem: Some Proposed Solutions • Solutions to the farm problem depend on our definition of national interest. Are we chiefly interested in low food prices? Is it important that we preserve the family-sized farm? Do we want foreign markets for our agricultural surpluses? Should government be responsible for a sick agriculture? Can farmers solve their own problems? Our answers to these questions will determine national agricultural policy.

The farmer helps himself. Throughout our history farmers have been regarded as rugged individualists—each one operating his own farm and making his own decisions about planting and production. In recent decades, however, a measure of farm unity has been achieved through several national and regional organizations. Nationally the Farm Grange has 800,000 members; the American Farm Bureau has 400,000; the National Farmers Union counts 100,000 farm families as members. These organizations speak for farmers in state legislative halls and in Congress. They also operate insurance, marketing, and purchasing programs.

Below the national level are several state and regional associations. Such bodies as the Eastern States Cooperative Association are purchasing agencies. Other associations have been organized to market fruit, vegetables, livestock and grain. The Livestock Producers Association, for example, sells livestock for farmers in most major markets.

Purchasing and marketing associations are established to insure the farmer a larger share of the consumer's dollar and to reduce the cost of his supplies. Success in either direction increases his net income. In the United States there are now 10,000 cooperative groups with more than 7 million members (obviously some farmers belong to several groups). In 1953 these co-ops did over $9 billion worth of business. Roughly one-quarter of all farm products move to market through cooperatives, and the limits of expansion have not yet been reached. It would seem that cooperatives offer one promising way to shave distribution costs.

Increased farm efficiency. Many farm experts feel that we have been too sentimental about farms and farming. Most small farms are inefficient and outdated in this modern age. A congressional committee in 1950 declared that rural poverty was a result of "too many people, using outdated methods, trying to make a living exclusively from agriculture." Some 31 per cent of our farmers produce less than 3 per cent of the total farm products; 60 per cent produce only one-tenth of the total. On the other hand, the most productive 14 per cent of our farms sell over half of all products; 40 per cent of the nation's farmers account for 90 per cent of all sales.

Following this reasoning, low average farm income ($3,917 per farm in 1950) is caused by the depressed half of the farm population. If these people (the inefficient workers) were shifted from agriculture to more profitable occupations, the average farm income would rise to $6,000 or more. Superior crops and animals, better machinery, and more efficient farm methods would lower costs and raise profits for the remaining farmers. The number of commercial farms would decline; their average size would increase. Meanwhile, the displaced farm families would be more profitably employed in industry. Consumers likewise would benefit from lower costs and more efficient operation.

If the farm problem is defined solely in economic terms, fewer, more efficient farms is an obvious answer. But in solving the problem of rural poverty we must guard against the creation of other complicated issues. The transition from rural to urban living is difficult in any society (see Chapter 8). When that shift is made rapidly on a wholesale basis, the migrants often become rootless, irresponsible citizens in their new environment. The recent migration to Chicago, Detroit and Cincinnati from impoverished mountain areas of the South, for example, has given city officials several headaches. The newcomers bring with them primitive notions of sanitation, relaxed standards of sexual behavior, a tradition of violence, and conflicting values regarding living standards, personal privacy, interracial relations, absenteeism from work, and the repayment of debts incurred through easy credit. The migrants, in turn, often feel at odds with urban society and dream of eventually returning to their native soil. Since they normally enter urban society as unskilled workers, many uprooted rural folk drift into impoverished, overcrowded sections of the city and intensify the spread of slums. When depression strikes, they are among the first to swell the ranks of the unemployed.

It should also be noted parenthetically that land concentration has historically produced unrest in countries as diverse as ancient Rome and modern Hungary, China, Argentina, and Mexico. The United States has been somewhat unusual in her century-old concept of isolated, family-sized homesteads, originally created for the most part by something approaching a "give-away" governmental program (the Homestead Act). This original goal should not be lightly tossed aside in the name of efficiency or high productivity.

Government farm programs. Since 1930 American farmers have turned to government for the solution of their problems. During this period several well-defined programs have emerged, most of them dependent on the concept of "parity."

Parity. Supporters of parity believe that a relationship should exist between prices farmers pay and prices they receive. The years from 1909 to 1914 have been chosen as the period that best reflects an ideal relationship between the two price levels. This ideal relationship is called *parity.* Farm costs and farm prices are measured each year and compared with these base years.

In simple terms parity may be explained in this way. Assume that a bushel of wheat sold for $1.00 in the base period and a hoe also sold for $1.00. If a hoe sold for $2.00 in 1958, wheat must sell for $2.00 to buy the same hoe. If wheat sells for only $1.50 it is selling for 75 per cent of parity.

The idea of parity is deeply embedded in all farm programs. Major debate centers around a secondary point—should government attempt to maintain farm prices at a fixed percentage of parity, or should a sliding scale be used? Few people advocate 100 per cent of parity. Most debate centers around the 75-90 per cent range.

Government purchasing programs. To maintain farm prices the government has been forced into the farm marketing picture. At harvest time farmers may get a government loan at a percentage of parity instead of selling their crops outright. The crops are then placed in storage, which tends to keep prices up by preventing a glut on the market. If the market price goes above the loan rate, farmers may pay the loan and sell their crop. If the market price stays low, the farmer may surrender his stored crop in full repayment of the loan. This system has diverted huge farm surpluses into government warehouses and grain elevators. In mid-1956 the government held nearly $9 billion worth of wheat, corn, dried milk, cheese, and vegetable oils. In all cases this mountainous surplus has been accumulated in the years since World War II. Some Americans argue that these supplies represent a stock pile—an "ever-normal granary" that is a cushion against crop failure. Others declare that the program is a gigantic fiasco, that government purchases have encouraged farmers to produce unwanted goods for government stockpiles. Critics point out that storage alone cost the government about $1 million a day in 1958.

How can unmanageable surpluses be avoided? Would a reduction of parity payments cut production? In other words, are high supports to blame? There is no positive answer to this question. Logically, lower prices should drive producers from the market. However, our experience in the 1920's indicates that falling prices may actually increase production. If a Kansas wheat farmer gets less per bushel for his crop, he may decide to raise more wheat to meet his expenses. Most farmers do not have a free choice.

Acreage restrictions. To prevent overproduction the government has also resorted to acreage restrictions. Individual farmers are assigned a maximum allotment for surplus crops, and those who exceed this figure are fined heavily. This approach has been unsuccessful largely because rising farm productivity has made it possible to produce more on fewer acres.

The soil bank. The Eisenhower administration contributed the idea of the soil bank to farm policy. Under this program farmers convert cultivated acres into grass or forest land. In exchange they receive a payment based on the potential return of their acreage as cropland. In 1957 this program cost over $1 billion.

Supporters of the soil bank have declared that it is the only effective way to reduce surpluses. By taking the land completely out of production (neither grazing nor harvesting is permitted) crop diversion is prevented. If sufficient land is placed in the program, all farm surpluses should disappear. The "bank" concept assumes that our rising population will eventually need these surplus acres.

Opponents of the soil bank have criticized the plan for being too expensive and as pampering farmers with taxpayers' dollars. In 1957, for instance, over $5 million was paid to 67 growers, the top sum being $278,000 to Garvey Farms of Colby, Kansas, for withdrawing over 22,000 acres from wheat production. These payments illustrate a dilemma: should we limit payments and regard the government funds as a sort of welfare program? Or is our primary concern with acreage reduction, irrespective of land ownership?

World   •   No discussion of the problems created
Agricultural   by surplus American food and fiber
Problems   would be complete without examining our relationship to world production and consumption patterns. A few countries other than ourselves struggle with problems of overproduction and low prices. Brazil has experimented with production controls and price fixing for coffee; the government of Argentina has had to face the problem of meat surpluses; the Canadian government, the problem of wheat surpluses. In global terms, however, such phrases as "overproduction" and "surplus" refer only to effective demand (demand backed by purchasing power). Actually, the world problem is hunger, rather than overproduction. The situation in a few favored countries should not obscure this fundamental fact. Viewed from a world perspective, then, the need is for increased production and better distribution. Half of the world goes to bed hungry each night; two-thirds of the world's population is undernourished; famine is still a recurring phenomenon. In these underdeveloped lands people with primitive equipment eke out a bare subsistence livelihood from an unyielding soil. Determined efforts since World War II to change their centuries-old mode of existence have been centered in the United Nations Technical Assistance Program, the American Point IV Program, and the British Colombo Plan.

The United Nations has worked on problems of food supply through the Food and Agriculture Organization, to which 63 nations belong. Its efforts have been concentrated in three areas: (1) reducing losses in the production and storage of food through campaigns to control locusts and hoof-and-mouth disease, (2) increasing yields by acquainting farmers with improved seeds and fertilizers and a host of other techniques, and (3) developing new farming areas through drainage and irrigation programs and the construction of dams. In 1955 the United Nations spent $7.5 million on technical assistance. Field work was supervised by 438 experts who worked on such projects as the control of locusts in the

Helping People Help Themselves. *A Point IV irrigation project in Jordan begins to show results.*

Arabian peninsula, the development of hybrid corn in Europe and hybrid rice for the Far East, the control of various plant and animal diseases, and the better utilization of water resources in Pakistan, Iran, and Tanganyika.

Somewhat older but similar to the U.N. activity is the United States program of technical assistance. On a more limited scale the Colombo Plan is designed to aid the technologically backward countries of the British Empire.

In our zeal to raise living standards it is easy to forget that economic welfare is but one phase of human existence, that the culture of any society is an integrated whole. The introduction of Western technology without its accompanying political and social structure may create impossible tensions within an underdeveloped country. When viewed in true perspective, then, the problem of development is one of social change in the broadest sense of the word.

The transition to our present society in the Western world was achieved in leisurely fashion over several generations. Even at that pace the change was painful. The new technology makes it probable, however, that underdeveloped countries will be thrust into the modern age in a decade or two. Those who aid in the economic development of backward nations must share responsibility for other problems of that transition period. Among these problems are those of land tenure, literacy, political structure, religious values (e. g. the sacred cow of India), the far-reaching impact of the scientific method, organization of business, and family ties. Certainly Americans would feel that our aid to underdeveloped nations

455

would be a colossal failure if rising living standards were accompanied by a denial of democratic values.

From a world point of view, then, the farm problem is a strange blend of overproduction and hunger, surpluses and famine. In a few countries the issue involves overabundance; yet many countries are still unable to provide an adequate diet for their people. Taking the long-range historical view, the problem of abundance is indeed very new. Throughout man's recorded existence, famine and starvation have been the rule rather than plenty. Only in the past century have we achieved a "break-through" on this difficult economic front. An optimist might conclude that where some nations have pioneered, others can follow. If this is true, American farm surpluses are a foretaste of abundance for all mankind.

Prosperity without Inflation

When 50 distinguished leaders in public affairs were asked recently to identify the most pressing United States domestic problem of the next twenty years, a majority agreed on inflation. When the man on the street is asked the same question, he is apt to say "depression" or "unemployment." Perhaps both the experts and the man on the street are right. In the past century capitalism has been characterized by a series of "booms" and "busts" that seriously disrupt normal economic life. The nature of these fluctuations, or business cycles, their effect on political, social, and economic life, and programs that are designed to reduce their violence are the subject matter of this chapter.

Such issues are of concern to every citizen. Job opportunities, wage scales, pension programs, the cost of living and a host of other items are directly related to the central issue of national economic health. Social unrest, revolution, hunger, and the destruction of democratic government are possible dangers if we do not develop effective controls for our economic system.

Communist critics from Marx to Khrushchev have long claimed that the business cycle is a cancer that will eventually destroy capitalism—that the capitalist economy carries within itself the seeds of its own destruction. The stakes, then, are very high. If capitalism can demonstrate an ability to provide full employment and maintain high production, a relatively stable price structure, and high living standards, it will have furnished the best possible answer to the claims of Soviet propagandists. If it cannot, the very existence of the free world will be jeopardized.

Federal Reserve Board Index of Industrial Production, 1929 to 1957.

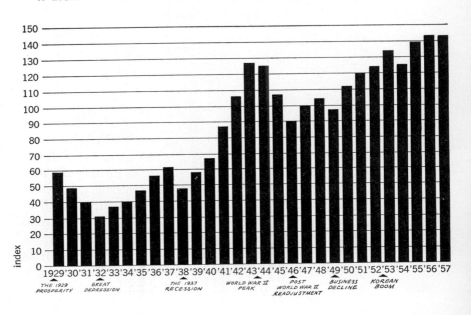

The Business · The modern business cycle appears to
Cycle be distinctly different from earlier periods of depression and prosperity. Perhaps the major difference stems from
the fact that most societies until modern times were erected on a broad
agricultural base. It is true, of course, that natural disasters such as hail,
storms, wind, drought, and floods can wipe out growing crops and cause
distress, hunger, and even starvation. But instances of prolonged depression in ancient times are rare. Long-term unemployment in agriculture is
unusual. Perishable food products must be grown each year, and workers
are generally attached to the land in a fashion that gives them work during hard times.

The frenzied economic activity that we associate with booms is also
a phenomenon of modern times. Only in a society geared to wages, profits,
and the interest payments of a money economy can the economic pendulum swing in such a broad arc from depression to prosperity and back
again.

Phases of the business cycle. Business cycles do not fit any simple pattern.
No two are exactly alike. Nor do they recur according to any time sched-

A Model of a Business Cycle.

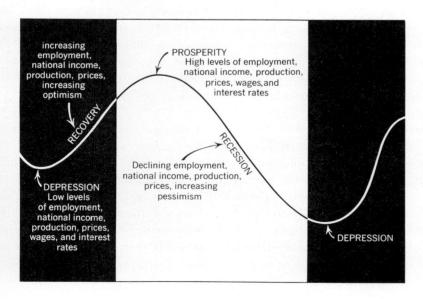

increasing
employment,
national income,
production, prices,
increasing
optimism

RECOVERY

PROSPERITY
High levels of employment,
national income, production,
prices, wages, and
interest rates

RECESSION

Declining employment,
national income, production,
prices, increasing
pessimism

DEPRESSION
Low levels
of employment,
national income,
production, prices,
wages, and interest
rates

DEPRESSION

ule that makes forecasting an exact science. Nevertheless, certain general characteristics are typical of all cycles. The four phases of the cycle are called: (1) prosperity, (2) recession, (3) depression, and (4) revival.

A period of economic *prosperity* is a period of peak industrial activity. Wages are high and unemployment is low. Prices, too, are rising, along with business profits. Credit is "easy" and expanding, while interest rates are rising because there is an active demand for money.

During the *recession* phase of the cycle industrial activity declines, unemployment mounts, wages tend to stabilize or fall, and most workers face the loss of overtime and a shorter workweek. Retail and wholesale prices meet consumer resistance and are "soft"—*i.e.*, often forced down by shrewd bargaining; profits are falling and business failures mount. The demand for money declines, and interest rates tend to fall. Nevertheless, credit is "tight" or hard to obtain because the business outlook is so uncertain.

All the recession tendencies are intensified during the *depression* phase of the cycle. Inventories of finished goods pile up and production is cut back. Unemployment increases; people who are still working watch their wages and salaries fall. Prices on consumer goods are low. More and more businesses fail. The demand for money dries to a trickle, interest rates reach new lows, and credit is very tight. Both borrower and lender are very wary about business prospects.

The period of *revival* reverses the recession phase. Inventories finally are exhausted and manufacturers resume production. Idle workers are hired and wages begin to move upward. Overtime and the full workweek are re-established. Shortages of goods force up retail and wholesale prices, profits pick up, and new businesses begin opening their doors. Money again is in demand, interest rates rise, and credit is easier. As these tendencies intensify, we re-enter the next phase of the cycle—prosperity.

Frequency. In spite of the neat pattern we have just described, business cycles do not follow a regular course like the movement of tides. Periods of prosperity may be long, interrupted only by slight dips in the economy. Or periods of depression may extend over years. Some economists have tried to find an "average" cycle on which to base predictions and remedies. Complete cycles appear to vary from thirty months to ten years, with the average being around four years. But such averages are not very useful to the economist. The average temperature in your community may be 61 degrees, but this figure is small comfort to you on a February morning when the thermometer stands at 10 degrees below zero. We can best understand the actual nature of business cycles by examining how they have fluctuated in a number of modern nations.

Business cycles: the British experience. As a victorious nation in World War I, Great Britain found herself in the midst of a roaring boom by 1919. Over 4,000,000 men were absorbed into industry from the armed forces. Wartime controls were abolished, and prices soared before the pent-up demand built up during the lean war years. But by 1920 the bubble burst, and over 2,000,000 unemployed were walking the streets by March, 1921. Throughout the 1920's unemployment remained high, and labor unrest erupted in the form of violent strikes. Relief payments, or the dole, became an established part of the British government's budget. The socialistic panaceas offered by the British Labor Party grew to be articles of faith in hundreds of drab mill towns whose inhabitants believed that capitalism spelled poverty. Finally, in the 1930's, the private British depression was merged with the world economic crisis. Full employment did not return to Great Britain until World War II.

Inflation: German and Chinese experience. Inflation may be of two kinds: (1) the type that accompanies a high level of prosperity and business activity, and (2) the type that stems from unwise government monetary policies. The second of these types brought on the notorious inflationary spiral in Germany in 1923. In that year French troops occupied part of Germany. The German government encouraged a gigantic sit-down strike of workers, which it financed by inflating its currency. The German mark had been valued at five to the dollar in 1914. By January, 1923, the ratio had risen to 20,000 to the dollar, and by April to 100,000 to the dollar. By August the mark was standing at 5,000,000 to the dollar—an almost meaningless relationship.

The German employee never knew how much his pay would buy. His wife went out to make her household purchases with a whole basketful of notes which might fall further in value while she stood waiting in the shopping line. A tourist with a few francs or dollars lived like a prince. A postage stamp or glass of beer cost millions. Paper investments, bank balances, savings, mortgages, annuities vanished.[1]

This mad period was finally ended by international financial aid that stabilized the German currency. Nevertheless, the damage wrought during these years left a serious blight on German society. For all practical purposes the German middle class was destroyed, along with its savings accounts, life insurance annuities, and other marks of thrift. In its frustration this group joined in the search for an economic scapegoat, which it found in the Jews, and an economic savior, which it thought it found in the person of Adolph Hitler. Although no other nation has suffered from inflation as much as Germany, where it has struck its results follow a similar pattern, varying in intensity with the degree of inflation.

An inflationary spasm almost as bad as the one that swept over Germany in the twenties convulsed China from 1947 to 1948, the last years of Nationalist rule of the Chinese mainland. By that date the official rate of exchange was 12,000 Chinese dollars to the American dollar. Unofficially, however, the exchange ratio was 93,000 to 1. As Nationalist troops suffered their final reverses, the rate of exchange reached even more fantastic proportions.

The business cycle: United States experience. The rapidity of economic change in the United States can best be shown by quoting from two presidential inaugural addresses. On March 4, 1929, President Herbert Hoover told the American people:

> In the larger view we have reached a higher degree of comfort and security than has ever existed before in the history of the world. Through liberation from widespread poverty we have reached a higher degree of individual freedom than ever before. . . . Ours is a land rich with resources, stimulating in its glorious beauty, filled with millions of happy homes, blessed with comfort and opportunity. . . . I have no fears for the future of our country. It is bright with hope.

Four years later to the day, President Franklin D. Roosevelt declared:

> Values have sunk to fantastic levels; our factories are without orders; taxes have risen; our ability to pay has fallen; government of all kinds is faced with a serious curtailment of income; the means of exchange are frozen; the withered leaves of our industrial enterprise lie on every side; farmers find no market for their produce; and the savings of many years in thousands of families are gone. More important, a host of unemployed face the grim problem of existence, and an equally great number toil with little return.

The impact of the great depression of the 1930's can be captured in part from the following figures. National income fell from 85 to 40 billion dollars between 1927 and 1933; earnings of the 550 largest industrial corporations dropped by nearly 70 per cent. Industrial production was cut in half. Unemployment ranged between 13 and 15 million. Construction fell to one-fifth of the 1929 volume. Receivers took over one-third of the national railway system. It has been estimated that between 1930 and 1939 we *failed to produce* goods valued at $389 billion because of unemployment.

The disaster that gripped America between 1929 and 1933 fastened itself on all capitalistic countries. In that brief period world commodity prices fell by one-third and raw material prices by one-half. Many nations saw their national incomes dwindle by two-fifths. The price of Canadian wheat reached its lowest level in four centuries. Everywhere huge stocks of unsold goods accumulated.

The scope of the debacle can be captured only partially by statistics. Red ink, falling graphs, and tumbling index numbers spelled out personal tragedy for millions of families. The world figure for unemployment probably reached 30 million. Shattered hopes, bitterness, and a demand for change were epidemic in such an environment. In the United States it ushered in a New Deal. It brought Hitler to power in Germany and launched the military leaders of Japan on their plan of Far Eastern conquest. British socialism as a major political force was also a product of the depression.

Inflation is as much a part of American history as depression. During the 1920's the United States gloried in an almost uninterrupted boom. Although one historian later tagged the boom the "Golden Glow," at the time it seemed very real. Many of us are familiar with the story. Speculation was rampant in real estate, especially in Florida building lots. On Wall Street the great bull market of 1928-1929 tripled the price of Westinghouse, Montgomery Ward, and General Electric stock, while the price of Radio Corporation of America shares increased five times. Millions of wage-earners took advantage of easy credit terms to buy on the installment plan, thus mortgaging their future earnings. We achieved almost full employment, and wage rates rose.

Since 1945 we have again been experiencing a strong inflationary surge. Personal income, which in 1947 stood at $189 billion, reached $303 billion in 1955. Installment credit in the same period tripled. Average weekly earnings in manufacturing were less than $24 in 1939; by 1955 they were $75. The scope of our industrial expansion is indicated by steel production, which was 53 million net tons in 1939 and leaped to 117 million net tons in 1955.

These statistical samples give some indication of the scope of the boom. But a large slice of the apparent gains was "phony," because the purchasing power of the dollar was steadily falling. Between 1939 and 1955 consumer prices nearly doubled. The 100 cent dollar of 1945 was worth less than 70 cents ten years later. Although the average worker increased his weekly earnings by nearly $16 between 1950 and 1955, in terms of purchasing power he gained only $9. Like the renowned frog in the riddle, he jumped forward two feet and slipped back one.

The tremendous spread between the top and bottom of the business cycle can be illustrated by charting the record of one sensitive business indicator, the American housing industry, for the 30 years from 1925 to 1955.

- **Housing Units Started, 1925-1955**

Year	Number
1925	937,000
1933	93,000
1940	602,000
1950	1,396,000
1955	1,328,000

Notice that building operations fell by nine-tenths between 1925 and 1933; that they increased by over six times between 1933 and 1940; that they doubled between 1940 and 1950.

Turning to the relationship between creditors and debtors, the confusion created by shifts in purchasing power is apparent. People who purchased a United States Savings Bond for $18.75 in 1945 received $25 when the bond reached maturity in 1955. Yet in terms of purchasing power they could actually buy less with the $25 they received than with the $18.75 they had originally invested.

Inflation affects all kinds of fixed investments in the same way. Contributors to social security and private pension plans find on retirement that inflation has made serious inroads on their income. One life insurance company years ago ran an advertisement captioned, "How I Retired On $100 A Month." The advertisement still appears, but over the course of years the sum has climbed steadily—$150, $200, $250, $300. In inflationary periods lenders suffer, while borrowers gain. A man who has borrowed $5,000 to build a house may find ten years later that his income has tripled and his house is worth $15,000. Payments on his house will now take only a small fraction of his income, while his housing investment has participated in the general inflation. In depression times, of course, the reverse is true.

The Causes   •   Both depression and inflation create
of   tensions and serious dislocations in eco-
Business Cycles   nomic life. What factors bring on a
depression? What causes an inflation?
Is there one cause? If there are many
causes, can they be modified? Are inflations or depressions man-made
or are they part of an inevitable cycle? To enjoy the benefits of prosperity
and full employment, must we suffer the evils of inflation? These questions are of vital concern to every citizen.

External causes. One set of factors that contributes to the business cycle
can be labeled external. Falling into this classification are those events
outside the economic system that have an impact on it. Alternating
periods of depression and prosperity are reported in the history of ancient
Egypt. The Old Testament tells of the Hebrew slave, Joseph, who skillfully managed the Pharaoh's estates by storing the abundance of prosperous crop years in anticipation of the "seven lean years" of unfavorable
growing conditions. Good weather can still produce abundance and low
prices; bad weather can produce scarcity and inflation. These cycles exist
today in such preindustrial societies as China and India.

War has always been a threat to economic stability. During wartime,
prices are apt to rise as goods and services become scarce. Postwar
periods are frequently depression years. Factors such as the weather and
warfare are not peculiar to the capitalistic system, however. Rather than
being part of the economic system, they are external factors that react
upon it.

Internal causes. Internal factors are those causes that operate within the
system itself to determine the course of the business cycle. Several elaborate theories have been developed to explain modern economic behavior.
Taken singly or in combination, they are the basis of attempts to curb
excesses of the cycle.

Self-generation. Some economists believe that each phase of the business cycle is directly responsible for the following phase. For instance,
the boom phase eventually produces recession; recession produces depression. If this chain reaction theory is correct, business cycles have a life
of their own, quite apart from economic systems and man-made controls.

Money velocity. Many economists believe that a direct relationship
exists between prosperity, the volume of money, and the rapidity with
which it is spent. During the boom phase of the business cycle money is

abundant and people spend it rapidly and freely. During depression, money is scarce and people curtail their spending. Few people actually accept the volume-velocity theory of money in the simplified form in which we have described it here, but many economic experiments of the past 30 years have been based on various modifications of the theory. Following this theory, the excesses of prosperity can be curbed by a "tight" money policy of high interest rates, loans only to first-class risks, and short periods for re-payment that will slow down borrowing and spending. Recessions can be halted by an "easy" money policy of liberal credit and low interest rates.

Psychological attitudes. Another theory about business cycles centers on people, rather than money. Followers of this theory believe that speculation stems from optimism and confidence about the future. Consumers feel secure and are willing to borrow and spend. Businessmen are in an expansive mood that manifests itself in new factories and full employment. Whenever this confidence and optimism are shaken, the economy takes a dip.

The optimism of prosperous years is matched by the pessimism of depression years. Consumers live from hand to mouth. Manufacturers regard the future skeptically, while creditors are reluctant to make loans.

Underconsumption-overinvestment. The underconsumption theory of business cycles places great stress on the role of the consumer. Depressions are caused, according to this theory, by an unwise distribution of national income. Too little purchasing power is left in the hands of consumers. Too much income is received by investors who expand plant capacity beyond the needs of consumers. Adherents of this theory argue that underconsumption caused the crash of 1929 since wage rates did not keep pace with the economy's expanded capacity to produce during the 1920's.

Overconsumption-underinvestment. This theory, which is the exact opposite of the one we have just discussed, is offered to explain our inflationary boom of the 1940's and 1950's. Consumers in this period, so the theory runs, caused the inflation because their purchasing power outran the economy's productive capacity. For example, citizens with the means to purchase 1,500,000 new homes a year bid for the 1,000,000 homes available, thus forcing prices up. This pattern was repeated over and over again in consumer markets, spreading a general inflation over the land.

There is probably some merit in each of these theories. Excess purchasing power is certainly an inflationary force. A shortage of purchasing power will leave goods on merchants' shelves and spark a deflationary trend. The delicate line between too much and too little purchasing power and too much and too little investment is difficult to fix.

The Communist analysis. We have already mentioned that the eventual collapse of capitalist society is a central theme of Communist theory.

Briefly, Marx and Lenin believed that capitalism had basic faults and contradictions that could not be eliminated. As capitalism evolved, they foretold, depressions would become more pronounced and prolonged. The wealthy owners of the means of production would grow richer; the poor, poorer. Since workers never received enough wages to buy the articles they produced, crisis would follow crisis in the capitalistic world until the workers united to destroy the system by revolution.

To avoid this crisis, Lenin predicted that capitalist nations would try to find new markets in underdeveloped areas. Capitalism, therefore, in its search for markets produced imperialism. Imperialism in turn led to war as the various capitalistic countries battled among themselves to capture markets.

This apocalyptic vision of the future—unemployment, colonialism, exploitation, and warfare—forms the central core of the Communist critique of capitalism. At first reading it may appear convincing and closely allied to other theories of the business cycle we have already outlined. We should, however, recognize one significant difference. Communists are convinced that reform of capitalism is a futile task, because the flaws they point out are inherent in the system. Any attempt to patch up or reform capitalism will only delay rather than prevent its inevitable end. So deeply embedded in Communist philosophy is this belief that Stalin, shortly before he died, publicly rebuked a leading Soviet economist who predicted that the United States would not suffer a depression during the post World War II period. When the former leader of the American Communist party, Earl Browder, declared that American capitalism was different from the system the Soviets described, he, too, was rebuked by Stalin. The ups and downs of the American business cycle, therefore, have world-wide implications. If we can control it, we will invalidate a central thesis in the Communist argument. In addition, we will prevent the domestic insecurity and suffering that accompany inflation and depression and maintain our position of economic world leadership. How effectively we are able to tame the fluctuations of the business cycle is a subject of major concern to the entire free world. In view of their importance, we shall now turn to various proposals that have been advanced for stabilizing the economy.

Stabilizing • What methods are available for insuring
the Economy economic stability? What can the government or private groups do when inflation threatens or when a depression
looks? Obviously our goal is to guarantee an orderly economic expansion that will provide a rising standard of living for our constantly increasing population. Although the following discussion applies to the United
States, similar stabilizers are available to other advanced capitalistic
countries.

The American economy. Modern statistics are of great help in getting a
panoramic view of the American economy. The most significant data are
set forth in the adjoining table. At the outset, however, several terms
require definition. Gross national product refers to the market value of
all goods and services produced. Aggregate effective demand, which is
always equivalent to gross national product, is the term used to describe
the three major factors in demand: (1) personal consumption expenditures, (2) investment (gross private domestic investment and net foreign
investment), (3) government purchase of goods and services. The factors
listed in the table determine the state of business activity. A decline in
aggregate demand causes unemployment, falling prices, and surpluses of
goods. When demand is rising, we tend toward full employment, rising
prices, and shortages of goods. It follows, then, that economic stability
can be achieved if we can prevent violent fluctuations in aggregate
demand.

• **Gross National Product and Aggregate Demand, 1954 and 1957**

	Billions of Dollars	
	1954	*1957*
Consumers (personal consumption expenditures)	236	280.4
Producers (gross private domestic investment and net foreign investment)	47	67.6
Government purchases (national, state, local)	77	86.8
Gross National Product	360	434.8

Glancing back at the table, we see that the largest source of demand
is consumer spending. This spending tends to be geared closely to personal income, although it may outrun income if credit terms are liberal,
or fall behind if a substantial amount of income is tied up in installment
consumer payments. Between 1945-1955 consumer expenditures ranged
between 91 to 98 per cent of disposable income (income minus tax payments).

The second factor in aggregate demand—investment—is closely related to savings. There are various kinds of savings—private hoarding, bank deposits, corporation surpluses, and insurance reserves. Either directly or indirectly, most savings are invested. At no point, however, are savings and investment apt to be in exact balance. In boom times investment tends to outrun savings; during hard times savings tend to outstrip investments.

Government spending is the third side of the national product triangle. Since the government obtains its funds from taxpayers, a close relationship generally exists between tax revenues and government spending. Government spending will exceed government tax income when money is borrowed; spending will fall behind income when tax money is used to reduce debts.

It is within the framework of aggregate effective demand—(1) consumer expenditures, (2) producer expenditures, and (3) government expenditures—that proposals for controlling the business cycle are developed. These proposals are closely linked to the various theories concerning the business cycle that we discussed earlier. Nevertheless, since government policies can be more easily regulated than consumer or producer expenditures, most proposals for control involve government action which affects consumer-producer expenditures only indirectly. The responsibility of government for economic stability is recognized by the United States Congress in the Employment Act of 1946, which declared in part: "The Congress declares that it is the continuing policy and responsibility of the Federal Government . . . to promote maximum employment, production, and purchasing power."

Monetary regulation. Monetary regulation involves government control of interest rates and the money supply through the Federal Reserve system. The system is semi-public in nature; the commercial banks belonging to the system hold over 80 per cent of all checking accounts. Control of the system is concentrated in 12 regional Federal Reserve banks, which in turn are controlled by a Board of Governors. These reserve banks are "bankers' banks" for they deal only with member banks, rather than the public. Since they control the reserve deposits of member banks, there are several devices they can employ to control the monetary supply.

Reserve requirements. All member banks are required to maintain a variable percentage of their total deposits on reserve with their regional Federal Reserve Bank. By raising or lowering this requirement, the system can curtail or expand the amount of money the member banks can use for loans.

Open-market operations. The same end is served by the rather complicated device called "open-market operations." Since most member banks use government bonds for their reserve requirements with the regional bank, the total pattern of reserves can be altered by bond sales or purchases of the regional bank. When the bank sells government securities, reserves of the member bank are reduced and money becomes tight. When the regional bank buys securities, money becomes easy.

Rediscount rate. Member banks can borrow money from the regional banks by offering as security the bonds and promissory notes which they hold. By charging a low rate on such loans, the bank encourages credit expansion. The regional banks can discourage borrowing by member banks by charging a high rediscount rate. When fewer funds are available, member banks are less inclined to loan money to their customers.

Selective controls. The Federal Reserve Board of Governors has sometimes used more direct measures to regulate consumer credit. To prevent stock-market speculation the Governors have the power to fix margin (down payment) requirements on stock purchases. To prevent a runaway housing boom they were empowered to define the terms of real estate loans. To restrict consumer credit the Board also has the power to fix down payments and periods of repayment for durable consumer goods such as refrigerators, automobiles, and washing machines. By relaxing such restrictions, of course, the Board may attempt to stimulate a laggard economy.

The system in action. Perhaps our somewhat theoretical description will become more realistic if we examine the actual policies the Federal Reserve system followed from 1955 to 1957. During these years the Board of Governors, under Chairman William M. Martin, operated on the assumption that inflation was the main threat to the United States economy. To curb this threat they took the following action. In April, 1955, the rediscount rate was 1½ per cent, a point around which it had hovered for several years. In a series of seven steps taken from that date until August, 1957, the Board raised the rate to 3½ per cent, the highest it had been in 23 years. By August, 1957, prime commercial debtors (*i.e.,* the best risks) were paying 4½ per cent on loans and others were paying 6 per cent. Apparently these tactics were successful. Nearly all business indicators turned downward in the last three months of 1957. Satisfied that the inflationary threat had been squelched for the moment, the Board cut the rate to 2¾ per cent in January, 1958, to stimulate borrowing and investment.

Evaluation. Most economists believe that the Federal Reserve Board can successfully curb inflation if it acts quickly and decisively. High reserve requirements, high rediscount rates, and high down payments, plus selling government bonds on the open market, can make credit so tight that investment and consumer demand will be effectively stifled. But some authorities doubt that the system is as effective in preventing depressions. Most authorities agree that the timing of any action is very important. A gentle nudge in one direction or the other at the right moment by the Reserve system may be worth more than a sledge hammer blow six months later.

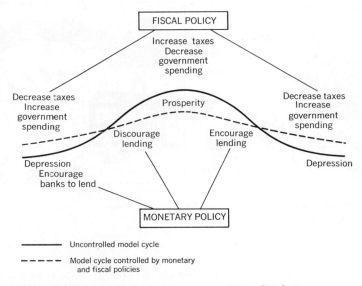

FISCAL POLICY

Increase taxes
Decrease
government
spending

Decrease taxes
Increase
government
spending

Prosperity

Decrease taxes
Increase
government
spending

Discourage
lending

Encourage
lending

Depression
Encourage
banks to lend

Depression

MONETARY POLICY

—————— Uncontrolled model cycle

— — — — Model cycle controlled by monetary
and fiscal policies

Controlling the Business Cycle by Monetary and Fiscal Policies.

Fiscal policy. Fiscal policy is probably a far more potent weapon to use against economic fluctuations than monetary policy. Whereas monetary policy is in the hands of the Federal Reserve Board of Governors, fiscal policy is determined by our elected political leaders—the Congress and the President. The two major divisions of fiscal policy are (1) taxes, and (2) government spending.

Taxation. Now that taxes and government spending represent more than one-fifth of the gross national product, any major change in the tax structure reverberates throughout the entire economic system. A program of high taxation, for example, can apparently curb inflationary pressures. When inflation threatened during World War II, for instance, excess purchasing power was drained off through high taxes and vigorous war bond

Stabilizers That Help Bolster the American Economy: *exports, contracts that maintain wages, farm price supports, and public works.*

drives. There are, to be sure, many kinds of taxes. If we accept the theory that inflation is a threat because of underinvestment in new plants and a resulting shortage of goods, heavy taxes should probably be levied on consumers. Investment might then be encouraged by reduced taxes on dividends and corporation earnings.

During periods of depression consumption can probably be spurred by lowering taxes on personal income. Businessmen argue that investment should also be stimulated by tax reduction.

Spending programs. Most Americans of an earlier age believed that government budgets should show a balance each year between income and expenditures. In their search for economic stability most modern economists are apt to minimize this earlier goal. Governments enjoy great flexibility in dealing with the ebb and flow of economic life, since their expenditures are not necessarily linked to current income. During depression years, for instance, it may be desirable to cut taxes and increase spending so that sizeable deficits put government deeply in the "red." In

472

prosperous times government may cut its spending below income, soak up inflationary dollars through taxation, and show a comfortable balance which it can apply to debts.

Keynesian theory. Current economic theory regarding taxation and spending owes much to the ideas first advanced by the English economist, John Maynard Keynes. Keynes' theory minimizes the impact of direct government payments to the unemployed during depressions, however necessary this may be to prevent human suffering. Much more important, according to Keynes, is government investment as a substitute for private investment. Government investment is far more valuable than relief payments because of the "multiplier principle." Government construction of a dam will mean money payments to manufacturers of cement, steel, and construction machinery, as well as to people who actually work to build the dam. Thus employment will be stimulated in these industries, payrolls will expand, and the workers in turn will spend more money in gas stations, barber shops, and grocery stores. These stores in turn will expand or replace their inventories. In other words, one dollar put in the investment hopper by the government may produce many dollars in consumer demand. The device was called "pump priming" during the New Deal period. Pump priming links private investment and government investment, with government investment being the "compensating" factor. If private investment declines in a depression, government spending will be increased. During boom times, when private spending is high, government spending will be greatly reduced to check any inflationary spiral.

One of the most difficult questions facing any government that adopts the Keynesian philosophy involves the nature of its spending program. Obviously, the free enterprise-private investment idea may be seriously undermined if the government builds and operates a shoe factory, even though the unemployed may need shoes. And many people are very critical of "make-work" projects such as leaf-raking, even though some economists would argue that pyramid building may stimulate the economy just as much as post office construction. Many government officials believe that a file of useful projects should be built up in good times, so that government may take swift action when a depression threatens. Items often suggested for such a list are government buildings, schools, highways, public housing, dams, and irrigation projects.

Critics of government spending believe that the cure may be worse than the disease. Government programs launched during hard times can seldom be cut back in good times when they are no longer needed. Tax-cutting is a very popular anti-depression measure among politicians, but once a reduction is voted it is extremely difficult to reverse direction and raise taxes should the need arise.

Built-in stabilizers. In addition to the devices we have already listed, the government has available what are called "built-in stabilizers." These stabilizers automatically adjust to changed economic conditions. One example is unemployment insurance. During prosperity a sizeable reserve of funds is built up, thus reducing inflationary pressures. During deflationary periods consumer purchasing power is maintained by making payments from the fund to the unemployed. Much the same process operates in respect to old-age pensions. People beyond retirement age may continue to work during prosperous times and pay into the system. If the economy slumps they may be discharged or quit and then be eligible for payments from the fund. Payments to farmers under the various agricultural programs are also apt to rise and fall with economic conditions, as are tax rates. During periods of prosperity, corporation and individual income taxes take a sizeable slice of potential consumer and investment spending that otherwise would have an inflationary effect. During depressions reduced incomes are taxed at a lower rate, thus expanding investment and purchasing power.

Evaluation. How effective are all these various policies and devices we have been discussing? Have we actually solved the riddle of the business cycle? Are depressions of the 1929 variety now impossible? Have we mastered the threat of inflation? There are no decisive answers to these questions. Some students of the problem believe that we have not yet mastered the business cycle. They declare that New Deal pump priming did not solve the depression of the 1930's—that full employment came only with the gigantic orgy of government spending during World War II. As for inflation, these same people point to our record since 1940—a period when consumer prices have nearly doubled. If control of the economy is possible, say these critics, it may well be politically impossible. During boom times a democratic government cannot afford to be a spoilsport by applying the economic brakes; in a depression such devices as the rediscount rate and highway construction are weak weapons to use against the giant grip of deflation.

Other critics believe that the various devices we now have can control only an older kind of business cycle. Traditionally, in a free market economy, falling demand brings falling production, falling prices, and falling wages. These trends are apt to respond quickly to positive government action. But in the "new economy" the prices of labor and manufactured goods are "administered" and do not react automatically to supply and demand. Wages are now determined without any immediate relation to the current demand or supply of labor. Instead, wages are fixed by union leaders who bargain from a semi-monopolistic position. Manufacturers' prices are determined in much the same fashion. An industry may be operating at only 50 per cent of capacity and may still not cut its prices. Union leaders may negotiate for higher wages in the face of widespread unemployment. Recent years have unveiled such puzzling phenomena as declining factory production and falling employment, side by side with rising wages and higher retail prices. Perhaps it is possible in modern America to combine inflation and depression in the same package, leaving government with conflicting roles to play. In any event, the great power exercised by industrial and union leaders in determining economic trends must be recognized. Price movements in modern society probably are determined by spokesmen for government, business, and labor, each having some voice in the outcome. The effectiveness of our current controls in this situation is still to be proven.

The World Price   •   Our analysis of price fluctuations would
Structure   not be complete without some discussion of the economic problems that confront the free world. Thus far we have directed most of our attention to the situation in the United States. But we are not an isolated island, and world economic conditions affect us just as surely as our economic condition affects the rest of the countries of the free world. Since 1945 especially our concern with the economic welfare of the free world has been growing. In part, this is a selfish interest. Foreign trade is directly related to our domestic economy. Approximately half of the American wheat, cotton, and rice crop is exported, while one-third of our tobacco crop is shipped abroad. Today 4.5 million United States workers (7 per cent of the total) are employed in the manufacture of goods that are exported. The list of our imports includes many items essential to our well-being. At the present moment 10 per cent of all raw materials we use comes from abroad. It is estimated that by 1975 a third of our iron ore, half of our copper, and three-fourths of our lead will be imported.

For most of the world the United States is an economic success story. Our per capita income and standard of living are a goal toward which all nations strive. Because of our economic strength, other nations look to us for leadership and fear even a mild recession in the United States. Our imports represent one-sixth of the world total, and we are the best customer of countries with such diverse economies as Brazil, Canada, Venezuela, and the Philippines. In 1956 we imported $12.5 billion worth of goods and exported $19 billion worth. The various nations of the world are now economically interdependent. If foreign sales drop, the American economy feels the pinch; if our foreign market is vigorous, our economy benefits.

Trade restrictions. The chief barriers to international trade are lack of purchasing power and artificial blockades such as tariffs and quotas. During our early industrial history we sought to protect the growth of our infant industries by enclosing them behind high tariff walls. During the decade from 1920 to 1930 many nations of the world embarked on a program of economic nationalism that led them to close their ports to foreign imports while they attempted to export their surplus goods. Under such a program world trade shrank to a small fraction of its earlier volume. United States exports dropped from $8.2 billion in 1920 to $3.8 billion in 1930; imports dropped from $5.3 billion to $3.1 billion. Beginning in 1934 with the first Reciprocal Trade Act, we have tried to lower trade barriers by negotiating agreements with other nations. This movement was strengthened in 1947 with the establishment of G.A.T.T. (General Agreement on Tariffs and Trade) by nations that represented three-fourths of world trade. This organization is committed to the reduction of tariffs and other trade barriers through general agreements between nations.

European programs. Probably the most significant attempts to abolish trade restrictions are the series of agreements that have been made between European nations since the end of World War II. In 1953 the European Coal and Steel Community was created, which eliminated all tariffs on coal and steel between the charter members—France, West Germany, the Netherlands, Belgium, Italy, and Luxemburg. In 1959 the same six nations inaugurated the European Economic Community with the express aim of forming a common European market in which persons and goods might move freely. Striking out in another direction, these same nations in 1957 created the European Community of Atomic Energy (Euratom) to exploit atomic energy for peaceful uses. The implication of these developments, if they were to spread, requires no comment.

The people of the United States remain split on the question of protective tariffs, despite the trends we have been outlining. Critics of the protective tariff believe that we must take the lead in cutting trade barriers. Most of our early infant industries are now industrial giants that do not need protection. With this great productive capacity we are constantly plagued by a trade imbalance, since we sell more to foreigners than we buy. In 1956, as we have seen, we exported goods valued at nearly $7 billion more than we imported. Since 1945 we have partially plugged this yearly gap by loans to other nations. The British slogan of "Trade not Aid" is aimed at replacing loans with a free exchange of goods.

American protectionists base much of their case on a whole series of special cases. Foreign residual oil should not be imported because we have idle coal miners; English generators should not be used on American dams because our domestic electric companies have unused capacity. Our watch-makers should have a tariff so that they will be available for skilled defense work in an emergency.

World investment policy. Any hope for major progress in the so-called underdeveloped countries depends on their ability to attract foreign investments and technical aid. The actual job of development must be borne by outside sources, because the underdeveloped lands lack the capital and trained technicians to carry out any improvement programs. Contemporary technical assistance programs are described in chapters Nineteen and Twenty-eight, but a brief description of investment policies would be appropriate at this point.

Private investment. Some underdeveloped nations have been successful in attracting private investors or corporations to develop their economies. United States corporations are pumping Venezuela's oil and mining her iron ore. In Iraq oil operations are divided between the British Petroleum Company, Royal Dutch Shell, Compagnie Française des Petroles, Standard Oil of New Jersey, Socony-Mobil Oil, and the Gulbenkian Estate. This type of operation has definite limitations. Not all underdeveloped nations have valuable natural resources and danger always exists that a nation may be stripped of her natural resources without any permanent improvements being made in the living standards of her people. And private investors are often skeptical of the political stability of the underdeveloped areas and are reluctant to make loans.

United States investment. In the absence of private investment, governments frequently take direct action. In 1947 the United States announced the Marshall Plan, a program under which loans would be made to European nations for five years. Later, under the Mutual Security program, financial aid was extended to other countries. In all, the United States has spent over $50 billion in foreign aid since World War II. Much of this money has gone into armaments, but a considerable amount has been aimed at strengthening the economies of the non-Communist nations of the world. In 1957, for instance, a total of nearly $4 billion in grants was made. Of this sum, 35 per cent was non-military.

The United States has made other loans through the Export-Import Bank, which was created in 1934. As its name suggests, this bank was originally organized to promote foreign trade. Today its loans are largely made to help the economic development of other nations. Total loans may be made to the amount of $5 billion.

United Nations agencies. At the international level there are several United Nations agencies that are concerned with economic questions. To lend stability to international trade the International Monetary Fund maintains a $9 billion pool to prevent violent fluctuations in national currencies. The International Labor Organization is concerned with such questions as world unemployment. The Food and Agriculture Organization attempts to raise living standards. The International Bank for Reconstruction and Development probably is the agency most directly concerned with questions of capital formation and investment. By 1957 this bank had made loans amounting to over $3 billion in 45 countries. Typical of the projects which it sponsors are $19 million for electric power development in Ceylon and $13 million for flood control in Iraq. These sums, we should notice, are loans rather than grants.

Outside the capitalistic system, the Communist world views our attempts to improve our economic health and that of our allies with the cynical certainty that capitalism is doomed. If any serious economic crisis were to overtake international capitalism, many more countries would probably be drawn into the Soviet orbit. American power and prestige on the world scene depend on her economic well-being and strength. This fact, however, should be good grounds for optimism, rather than pessimism. On the basis of her past achievements it would seem possible for the United States to achieve the good economic life, "prosperity without inflation," given a willingness to experiment and to profit from experience.

PART THREE

The Governing
of Man

Government

and Freedom

The story of government parallels the story of
man. In the simplest society, man's experience
with government was largely confined to the
family. Within the family circle, under the
leadership of the elders, government was carried on, rules were made and enforced, some
degree of social stability was assured. "Big
government" is an outgrowth of a more complicated social setting. As societies became

more heterogeneous, man had to grapple with new and increasingly complex social problems stemming from the rise of new types of property relationships and the growth of economic inequalities, problems of war and defense, the emergence of different social classes, and the growth of the power and prestige of a leader and the emergence of the principle of inheritance of office and privilege. These factors, influenced by local, regional, and national variations and by other integrative social forces, led to the gradual evolution of government as we know it today.

**Inevitability   •   Government is an aspect of culture. It is
of   an integral part of the fabric of society,
Social Control   and the best way to study it is to try to
                        understand its place and significance in
                        the whole setting of human activity.**

The culture of a society determines the society's patterns of organization and regulation. The very existence of society demands that people in countless situations subordinate their individual wishes, desires, and inclinations to the requirements of the group. This process by which the individual is required to conform to group expectations is the essence of social control. Philosophers through the ages have dreamed of societies wherein absolute freedom and liberty would prevail. Yet the authors of such undeniably beautiful dreams have failed to understand the elementary facts of social life. Group membership always involves the abridgement of individual freedom and liberty. Freedom and liberty even in the most democratic societies can never be complete. Society, by definition, means ordered relations among people. Yet the total absence of social control would not necessarily entail an increase of individual freedom. Individual liberty does not thrive in an atmosphere of chaos. The total absence of any restriction upon individual liberty would, in all probability, lead to the destruction of human freedom. Even democratic societies demand that individual liberty be restricted, at least to the point where individuals are not allowed to exercise their freedom at the expense of the freedom of others. In other words, a person's freedom to swing his fist ends where his neighbor's nose begins. Compromise is a major aspect of social life. The democratic society attempts to strike some reasonable balance between liberty and order, but it cannot dispense completely with social control.

Government   •   The origins of government are shrouded
and   in mystery. We cannot say precisely
Social Control   how or when government began, but
we do know that it is a very ancient as-
pect of human existence. Most social
scientists agree that the "breeding ground" of government was the family,
that social regulation originated within the family and eventually manifested itself as the organized state.[1]

Government, as we have already mentioned, is a man-made or cultural pattern of organization and regulation. It is one of the ways in which
society enforces rules and thus controls the behavior of its members. For
purposes of this analysis, we shall divide social control into *moral control*
and *political control*.[2]

Moral control exists when each person accepts as right and just the
rules that regulate his own conduct. He abides by the rules because he
wants to, and it would never occur to him to do otherwise. Moral control,
to a large degree, springs from within the individual himself. It is not
formally imposed from the outside. It begins in infancy when we learn
group ideas of right and wrong. These ideas become a part of our very
being; no outside policing is necessary to see that they are observed. They
become self-enforced. On the other hand, *political control* involves enforcement from the outside. The person responding to political control is
not necessarily convinced of the justice or the wisdom of the rule he is following but is simply conforming out of fear of punishment or hope of
reward.

Moral and political control are not mutually exclusive. They are,
rather, fundamentally interrelated and mutually reenforcing. "Political
control," argues one searching student of social life, "involves not only
authority, but *ultimate* authority, backed at some point by the use of
force."[3]

But this does not mean that *political control* is the most fundamental
or most effective variety of social control. Political control in a very real
sense grows out of moral control. If government is to be effective most of
the members of the society in which it operates must be disposed, on the
basis of habit, to recognize its authority almost automatically. No government that has to coerce, force, or threaten most of its members most of
the time can long survive. Such a society would obviously have to have
more law enforcement officers than citizens, and even the modern "police-
state" does not go that far. Governmental officers "do not merely push
others about as mere pawns. Social control is not like the sort of control
exercised over the cue ball by the billiard player or the handling of dolls

by children. Much of the mechanism of control is within the controlled individual himself." [4]

Government rests upon learning. It rests upon automatic and predictable responses to the symbols of government, which are provided by the culture. For example, we respond automatically to the traffic light, the uniform of the policeman, the office of the presidency. Most citizens obey traffic lights even if there is no patrolman standing on the corner. We accept direction from the men in blue in situations in which we would not accept the guidance of ordinary citizens. A few policemen generally are able to control the behavior of huge crowds, not because they actually possess superior force but because we have learned willingly to accept police directives. Similarly, most of us accord high governmental officers special deference. We usually treat presidents with the utmost courtesy even if we disagree with them politically or dislike them personally. In other words, we respond respectfully to the office of the presidency even if we do not always agree with or like the person in office.

Responses of the type we have just described are more fundamentally a matter of moral control than political control. They arise from internal cultural learning rather than simply from the threat of force.

If internal or moral control is so effective, why does a society need political control as well? The answer is that moral control becomes more certain when it is re-enforced by political control. Even the simplest of societies usually require something beyond moral restraint to insure conformity to group rules and customs. As one eminent social scientist has put it, "rules . . . have little value unless everyone keeps them, and force is needed to fill the gap between most people usually and all people always obeying." [5]

One society may place less emphasis on external force as a mechanism of social control than another. Simple societies with a slow rate of social change obviously can maintain order by relying mainly on moral control. A complex society like the United States, however, must rely heavily on political control. In a simple, slow-moving social setting, people are limited to similar group memberships and identifications, and, consequently, they share similar values and attitudes. Moreover, these values are long enduring and tend to be passed down from generation to generation relatively unchanged. On the other hand, in our multi-group society, people are exposed to many different group situations and are confronted with many alternative values and ways of life. And group values change quickly in response to the fast tempo of social change.

Members of a simple society, because of common values and group experiences, have a rather clear notion of what is expected from them in the various situations in which they find themselves. In a more complex society people must adjust to the expectations of many different groups. In American society, for example, standards we learn in the home, in school, in church and in the business community might well be at variance with one another. In church the person may be told to trust his fellow man in all matters, but in the world of business he may learn to be very wary about trusting anybody. Thus, the individual in our type of society frequently has no clear idea of the type of behavior expected of him in different situations. Moreover, he associates with other people who also lack clear behavioral guideposts. The seeds of social conflict and disorganization are embedded in this type of situation, where individuals, in fact, only vaguely understand the nature of their rights, duties, and obligations. Hence the complex society requires the force inherent in political control to hold it together.

**Government:
A Social
Institution** • Comprehending the significance of moral and political control is essential to an understanding of the nature of government, but it is not enough. Government is a very complex phenomenon that has to be viewed in the very broad and intricate setting in which it actually functions. We live within a vast network of social control systems, called *social institutions*.[6] Social institutions are found in every society. They are everywhere among the oldest and most durable organized aspects of culture. They do not change easily. Government is a major social institution. It is a very complex and powerful group habit, an established procedure through which society accomplishes some of its major purposes.

It is impossible to measure precisely how important one institution is compared to others, for the institutional structure of society, as we have already pointed out, is very much interlaced. Yet, in one respect, it is accurate to say that the institution of government is unique among institutions because the successful functioning of other institutions depends on the coercive authority that is vested in government. That is, the regulatory aspects of society's other institutions are implemented by the force of government. For example, persons who violate the fundamental rules and regulations of family, educational, and economic institutions in the United States are likely to be brought face to face with the power of government. Persons who engage in adultery, who refuse to support dependent offspring, who decline to send their children to school, who destroy the property of others are subject to possible punishment by the agents of government. Thus government lends support to the other institutions of society.[7]

Government • and State

In the course of this discussion, we have mentioned several times that the force of government rests upon informal or moral control and upon political or formal control. If we keep these thoughts in mind, we are well on the road to distinguishing between two basic concepts—namely, *government* and *state*.

The governmental process is present in every society. In simple societies government is carried out informally by the family or perhaps by the community as a whole. It is not necessarily formally organized or entrusted to a particular body of officials. A victim's family may take revenge for his murder and not be condemned for it. The violator of the treasured values and customs may be stoned to death by his fellows without a formal pronouncement of judgment by a court.

As societies grow in size and complexity, the activities of government are assigned to particular individuals. Traditionally developed and casually enforced habits become formally stated laws whose violation will be followed by reasonably sure punishment. When government develops to the point where political control is given over to special members of society and supplemented by formal rules or laws, the state has emerged.

The state is the formal, more or less tangible version of the social control process. It is not deliberately created at some point in a society's history, but rather emerges gradually in response to social needs. "It is a process that begins before there is any light of history and it is one that is still far from being fulfilled." [8] Yet it is obvious that all modern, complex communities have carried the development of government to the point where a state is discernible—in the eyes of some people, too much so.

It would be a mistake to conclude that government and the state are completely separate entities. It is only for purposes of analysis that we make an attempt to distinguish between them here. They are both highly related aspects of the web-like institutional setting of society. But it is probably helpful to assume, at least for purposes of this discussion, that the institution of government in complex societies becomes an aspect of the institution of the state. If we break down the concept of the state into its basic parts, we are confronted by three elements: territory, population, and government. With reference to this type of division, we may think of government as the state's functioning arm. It is the mechanism by which the state formulates and enforces laws.

State and Nation • Like the other great institutions of society, the state consists of individuals who are organized to carry out a particular purpose—the imposition of organized political control. But the state differs from all other institutions in two ways that are essential to the carrying out of its purpose. First, membership in the state is compulsory for all who are physically present within specified territorial limits. All other institutions are somewhat more voluntary in nature. A person need not be a member of a particular family group, or indeed of any family group at all, after he attains maturity. Nor need he maintain any particular economic, educational, religious, or other affiliations or relationships. But the physical act of standing on a given piece of ground at a given moment makes a person and all others within that demarcated territory members of the same state. And, since the entire land surface of the earth is divided into states, it is difficult for a person to leave one state without entering into the jurisdiction of another.

The second sense in which the state differs from all other aspects of social organization is in the complete nature of its political control. Political control does exist in other situations, of course. An employer can fire a non-cooperative employee; a church can excommunicate a member who disregards its articles of faith; a club, union or even a family group can expel a member who persistently violates expected patterns of behavior. But the state, and the state alone, can go beyond expulsion to punishment. It alone may seize such an amount of an individual's property as it deems necessary, may deprive him of his liberty by confining him in prison, or, in the last resort, may take his life.

Both of the attributes we have just mentioned are necessary if the state is to exercise organized political control. If an individual could resign from the state within whose geographical limits he lived and thus relieve himself of all obligation to obey its laws, he could defeat the very purpose for which the state was formed. And, since the state is confronted with the duty of enforcing behavior patterns on all persons within the limits of its boundaries, its government must have authority to use whatever sanctions are necessary to achieve this purpose.

We have now traced the rise of government and the state as a means of organizing political control. We must emphasize again, however, that no state could long remain in existence, no government could function effectively, if it were forced to rely on political control alone. As we said earlier, government formulates and enforces those standards of behavior that are generally acceptable to the members of society. Should government ever make the mistake of misinterpreting the basic standards of society and attempt to formulate laws in conflict with them, the laws would undoubtedly be ineffective.

Perhaps the clearest illustration of such a failure was the ill-starred attempt of the United States government, between 1920 and 1933, to prohibit the manufacture and sale of intoxicating beverages. Substantial segments of the American people countenanced drinking. Those who violated the law and those who abetted the violation by consuming illegal alcohol apparently did so without any sense of guilt and without much fear of the informal censure of their fellow citizens. Even the application of government power to fine and imprison proved insufficient to enforce the law. Eventually, the government recognized its failure and abandoned what had been termed the "noble experiment."

Although the government must take cognizance of the standards of society in formulating and enforcing laws, in most instances the standards of society demand obedience to the law. Prohibition was an exceptional case, and in the normal course of events the community expects each individual to conform to all the rules set down by the government, whether he agrees with a particular rule or not. This expectation is internalized as are other forms of moral control, thus giving to governmental actions an added force they would not possess if they depended solely on formal political means.

A sense of obedience to the law will be strongest among people who comprise a nation. The term "nation" identifies a group of people who have a sense of unity so strong that, despite inevitable areas of difference and conflict, they tend to accept one another as belonging together and regard others as foreigners or outsiders. Many things contribute to this sense of unity. The major elements are a common language, common literature, common history of triumphs and defeats, and the crucial sense of a common future. The governmental process functions much more effectively when the people of a state possess a feeling of nationality.

| **Democratic** | • | Democracy is a major myth of the |
| **Government** | | American nation. Yet there is no scientific way to prove that it is superior to |

other types of governmental arrangements. Governments everywhere rest upon beliefs about right and wrong that cannot be objectively evaluated. Different cultures give birth to different myths. In countless ways we are taught to prefer democracy. The key molders of opinion in our society, including the home, the school, the church, and the mass means of communication, continually impress upon us the virtues of democracy. Virtually everyone reared in American society

An American Political Symbol. *American children grow up associating our political values with such symbols as the Statue of Liberty.*

has internalized, in varying degrees, a faith in democracy. This is not to suggest that our democratic ideal is perfectly realized in American life. Indeed, there is always a disparity between a society's ideals and its practices.

Democracy means many things. It has political, economic, and social implications. It is hard to describe because it is a way of life with many dimensions, because it is a process that is never finished. For Americans, democracy has come to mean individual freedom, majority rule, equality, justice, and a great many other things. Democracy has become a yardstick that we increasingly use to measure the basic institutional structure of our society. We do not merely expect our government to be democratic; we also expect democracy to prevail in our social relations and in our economic, family, and educational institutions. Moreover, democratic government is difficult, if not impossible, unless democracy is practiced in these other areas of our social living.

Despite its many-sidedness and its broad implications for the whole of American society, democracy embodies two outstanding principles: individual freedom and majority rule. A fellowship of free men is the goal of the good society. The sacredness of the individual personality is unquestionably the prime democratic value. The democratic society, at its best, not only allows but encourages individuality of expression and development.

Democracy emphasizes the principle of majority rule almost as strongly as it does the principle of individual freedom. The Declaration

489

of Independence announced that government should rest upon the "consent of the governed" and later American constitutional developments firmly implemented the idea of majority rule. What is the justification for majority rule? It would be pleasant if we could say, with certainty, that the history of man reveals that the majority is always right or even usually right. But, unfortunately, the historical record provides us with no conclusive evidence to support such a contention. Nevertheless, it is probably true that democracy rests upon the recurrent suspicion that more than half of the people are right more than half of the time. And whether right or wrong, many people believe they have the *right* to decide most matters for themselves.

Majority rule contains no magic but it may be justified on practical and compelling grounds. Political decision-making on the basis of majority will leads to stable government. The explanation is simple. People are disposed to abide by decisions that they have had a share in making. Rule by the many means that governmental stability is virtually maintained by the sheer weight of numbers. It means that the necessity for governmental coercion is minimized. The unusually high degree of domestic peace and tranquility that the British and American societies have enjoyed for long years can be traced largely to majority-rule government, to the fact that the right to vote has been extended over the years to an ever-increasing proportion of the governed.

Democracy involves a compromise between majority rule and minority rights. At times, as we shall argue later, the minority requires protection from a tyrannous majority. Majority rule, to be consistent with democracy, also means that channels for becoming a majority remain open to the minority. In a democratic society delicate adjustments must be made between the rights of the individual, the rights of minority groups, and the rights of the majority. The matter of achieving a balance between liberty and order is a ticklish one for every society, but it is especially delicate for the society that is committed to protecting individual freedom. The degree and kind of liberty that the citizens of the various states of the world enjoy are clearly at the heart of the issues that divide the "free world" from the "totalitarian world."

Natural Rights   •   Why should men be free? History has given us many different answers to this question. Among these, the theory of natural rights holds special significance for Americans and other Western peoples. The ideology of Western democracy, including its politics, its literature, its arts, and its educational practices, has been profoundly influenced by the natural rights doctrine. Giving philosophic justification to the American Revolution, Thomas Jefferson argued in the Declaration of Independence (1776) that men are "endowed by their creator with certain unalienable rights." Similarly those leaders of the French Revolution who drew up the famous Declaration of the Rights of Man (1789) announced: "The aim of all political association is the conservation of the natural and imprescriptable rights of men." More recently, the framers of the Universal Declaration of Human Rights (1948), which was adopted by the General Assembly of the United Nations, wrote: "All human beings are born free and equal in dignity and rights." Thus these three great documents of human liberty were all predicated upon the philosophy of natural rights.

The origins of the natural rights philosophy can be traced back to ancient and medieval times, but the most significant expression of the theory occurred in the seventeenth and eighteenth centuries. The natural rights doctrine has been embraced by thinkers of many different outlooks. Probably its two most prominent exponents were the English social philosopher, John Locke (1632-1704), and the French social philosopher, Jean Jacques Rousseau (1712-1778).

Some natural rights theorists have believed that natural rights are God-given; others believed that they are granted by Nature, which was not quite equivalent with God, but which was controlled and designed by God. In general, the natural rights philosophers believed that human relations are governed by natural laws just as surely as is the physical universe.

The crux of the natural rights doctrine is that men are not granted such rights as life, liberty, and property by the political or social community but rather that these rights are an integral part of man's situation as a human being and existed prior to the creation of organized society. "A man's natural rights," explains one keen student of political thought, "are as essential parts of him as are his sense organs. They are not derived from and are not modifiable by laws of the state, and they are valid for all normal men, however men may differ in other respects. States may properly differ from one another only as to the ways in which they protect rights, not as to the rights which they ought to protect." [9]

One contemporary theologian argues that the philosophy of natural rights provides us with an indispensable standard for judging the acts of governments. The implication that a man has only those rights that the government sees fit to grant him, he argues, denies the existence of rights. A person's rights do not depend on his power to enforce them. Either right is what the citizens of a political community want it to be or else there is an objective standard by which the will of the state can be evaluated—either a totalitarian philosophy or the philosophy of natural rights.[10]

That men do actually possess natural rights has never been established by scientific procedures, and there is little likelihood that it ever will be. The fact is, however, that men have believed and still believe in the theory, and this faith clearly was an important factor in the development of modern democracy, with its central emphasis upon liberty for the individual.

Liberty and the Social Good   •   We do not have to believe that men are born with natural rights in order to justify democracy or to favor the free exercise of basic civil liberties.[11] A person may believe that civil liberties are granted men by the cultural or social environment rather than by God or Nature and still be an ardent champion of freedom.

John Stuart Mill, a nineteenth-century British philosopher, in his *On Liberty*, one of the most important defenses of freedom ever written, rejected the idea of abstract natural rights and rested his defense of civil liberties on the ground that the free expression of opinion promotes the social good.[12] He stated part of his compelling and tightly reasoned position as follows:

> If all mankind minus one were of one opinion, and only one person were of the contrary opinion, mankind would be no more justified in silencing that one person than he, if he had the power, would be justified in silencing mankind. Were an opinion a personal possession of no value except to the owner; if to be obstructed in the enjoyment of it were simply a private injury, it would make some difference whether the injury was inflicted only on a few persons or on many. But the peculiar evil of silencing the expression of an opinion is that it is robbing the human race; posterity as well as the existing generation; those who dissent from the opinion, still more than those who hold it. If the opinion is right, they are deprived of the opportunity of exchanging error for truth; if wrong, they lose, what is almost as great a benefit, the clearer perception and livelier impression of truth, produced by its collision with error.[13]

Mill would have agreed wholeheartedly with Justice Oliver Wendell Holmes, who reasoned that "when men have realized that time has upset many fighting faiths, they may come to believe . . . that the ultimate good desired is better reached by free trade in ideas—that the best test of truth is the power of thought to get itself accepted in the competition of the market." [14]

As both Mill and Holmes saw it, society profits from the existence of individual freedom. They both believed that civil liberty is a prerequisite to the intelligent direction of society. The atmosphere of freedom leads to the free exchange of ideas that makes possible the separation of truth from falsehood. It provides the setting for social experimentation and invention, for the enactment of wise public policy. "We do not protect freedom," argues Henry Steele Commager, an eminent student of the American past, "in order to indulge in error. We protect freedom in order to discover truth. We do not maintain freedom in order to permit eccentricity to flourish; we maintain freedom in order that society may profit from criticism, even eccentric criticism. We do not encourage dissent for sentimental reasons, we encourage dissent because we cannot live without it." [15]

Freedom and Personality • Freedom, of course, is not only desirable from the point of view of the needs of society, but seems to be preferable to most people. Perhaps the best case for liberty can be illustrated by a "story of a liberated slave who met his master on the street. The master asked, 'Are you as well off as before you were free?' The Negro admitted that his clothes were frayed, his house leaked, and his meals were nothing like the food on the old plantation. 'Well, wouldn't you rather be a slave again?' 'No, massa. There's a sort of looseness about this here freedom that I likes.'" [16] In short, an atmosphere of freedom seems to be conducive to the richer development of the human personality.

Government and Freedom • The fear of state power is an old and major theme in American political thought. The idea of limited government is perhaps the most fundamental characteristic of the American Constitution. Democratic government is not possible unless the power and authority of the state is subject to limitations and restrictions.

Yet in a century when "statism" is rampant we tend too often to assume that government is the only source of danger to liberty. In reality government is a neutral instrument that may protect freedom or deny it. "We must rely on the state," suggests one legal scholar, "to restrain powerful private individuals from unduly restricting the liberty of the weaker ones. One who is locked up by a kidnapper is deprived of liberty as completely as if he were imprisoned by the state. One who shuts up his shop to avoid the threatened violence of gangsters has lost his freedom to conduct his business quite as much as if he had to obey a law forbidding him to conduct it. When the state through its administration of criminal law, destroys the liberty of kidnappers and gangsters to engage in their activities, it is enhancing, not curtailing, liberty in general." [17]

It is not only through the exercise of police powers that government may enhance freedom. The fathers of the Constitution, taking for granted the British heritage of civil rights, did not deem it necessary to include a formal statement of these rights in the Constitution. Soon after the document had been completed, however, it became evident that they had misjudged popular feeling on the matter.

In order to secure ratification of the new Constitution the ten amendments generally known as the Bill of Rights were added in 1791. This precedent was followed in drafting the various state constitutions. Today, all state constitutions have their own bills of rights, which reassert the principles laid down in the first ten amendments to the Constitution of the United States.

Two Kinds   •   Under the Constitution Americans enjoy
of Rights   *substantive* and *procedural* rights. Substantive rights are positive. For example, the Bill of Rights of our Constitution guarantees freedom of religion, freedom of speech, freedom of the press, the right of assembly and petition. These rights are substantive because they allow the individual to engage in certain kinds of activities, to express himself in particular ways. Procedural rights, on the other hand, are safeguards against the arbitrary action of government, especially against arbitrary judicial proceedings. The Fifth Amendment prohibits the federal government from depriving persons "of life, liberty, or property, without due process of law. . . ." The Fourteenth Amendment, in practically identical language, places the same prohibition upon the states. The precise meaning of the due process clauses has been debated through the years by constitutional lawyers and historians. Happily, procedural rights are guaranteed more specifically in parts of the Fourth through the Eighth

Amendments, which were designed to safeguard the rights of persons accused of crimes. The Fourth provides for security from "unreasonable searches and seizures." The Fifth says that an individual may not be tried twice for the same offense, "nor . . . be compelled in any criminal case to be a witness against himself." The Sixth guarantees the individual a "speedy and public" trial and the "Assistance of Counsel for his defense." The Seventh establishes trial by jury in civil cases. The Eighth proscribes "excessive" bails and fines as well as "cruel and unusual punishments."

Documentary · Rights and Other Governments The United States, of course, is not the only government that gives documentary guarantees of liberty to its citizens. Virtually all constitutions drafted in recent times contain formal lists of rights that belong to the people at least in theory, if not always in practice.

Great Britain. Great Britain is the only major world power that functions without a written constitution and a formal statement of rights. The British have an unwritten constitution that largely embodies powerful and carefully observed tradition. However, the British constitution also includes such landmarks in the history of liberty as the Petition of Right (1627), the Habeas Corpus Act (1679), and the Bill of Rights (1688). These more specific parts of the British constitution in the main guarantee procedural rights. Technically speaking, moreover, parliament, which has supreme authority in Britain, has the power to rescind them. The more fundamental substantive rights have no specific constitutional backing today in Britain. Nevertheless, no people in the world today exercise more completely the great substantive rights of freedom of speech, freedom of press, freedom of religion, and freedom of assembly than do the British.

France. The preamble to the constitution of the Fourth French Republic (1946) "reaffirmed" the principles of the Declaration of the Rights of Man (1789). This famous declaration contains most of the procedural and substantive rights contained in the American Bill of Rights and, furthermore, strongly emphasizes the principle of social equality, which is not stressed in our Constitution. Yet the authors of the constitution of the Fourth Republic apparently did not believe the Declaration of 1789 said all that needed to be said in our time about human rights. In the 1946 constitution they supplemented the Declaration by proclaiming, among other things, equal rights for women, the right to employment, the right to engage in trade union activity, the right of children to free and secular education, and the right of the community to own public service industries and monopolies. Social and economic rights of this kind increasingly find their way into the constitutions of the era in which we live.

Russia. The Union of Soviet Socialist Republics provides no exception to the generalization that the constitutions of modern governments almost invariably contain written guarantees of civil rights. Chapter X of the Soviet Union's constitution, which was adopted in 1936 and amended in 1947, is entitled, "Fundamental Rights and Duties of Citizens." This section contains articles that formally grant to Soviet citizens "the right to work," "the right to rest and leisure," "the right to maintenance in old age and sickness," "and the right to education." The Soviet constitution also proclaims equality for citizens in all areas of Russian life, without regard to sex, race, or nationality. More surprising than the listing of these rights is Article 125 of the constitution that reads in part:

> In conformity with the interests of the working people, and in order to strengthen the socialist system, the Citizens of the U.S.S.R. are guaranteed by law:
>> (a) Freedom of speech;
>> (b) Freedom of the press;
>> (c) Freedom of assembly, including the holding of mass meetings;
>> (d) Freedom of street processions and demonstrations.

Despite these constitutional guarantees, freedom, in the Western sense, does not exist in the Soviet Union. The Soviet constitution proclaims freedom but the rulers of the Soviet Union are not inclined to allow the Russian people to exercise it. Insofar as "liberties" exist in the Soviet totalitarian state they "are reserved for adherents and denied to opponents of the regime. Freedom, in the Soviet constitutional lexicon, is the duty to ratify the policies of the ruling group and not the right to criticize them." [18] In some instances Russian citizens are allowed, and sometimes even encouraged, to protest the inefficiencies of minor government agencies and officials, but no dissent from Communist Party policy is tolerated. The tight party dictatorship of the Soviet Union renders the facade of Russian constitutionalism quite meaningless. When the principles of the constitution conflict with the interests of the party, as defined by its leadership, the constitution is invariably set aside.[19]

**The Essence
of Freedom** • The Russians, who have much in the
way of documentary rights, enjoy little
in the way of liberty; the British, who
have little in the way of documentary
rights, are among the freest people on earth. The explanation of this
seeming paradox tells us much about the nature of freedom and government. The point is that democratic government is not fundamentally a
matter of constitutions, or statutes, or documents of any kind. Bills of
rights do not implement themselves.

The freedom enjoyed by Russian citizens on paper is a far cry from
the exercise of freedom. In essence, freedom is a way of life. Its presence
or absence is in the last analysis determined by the cultural environment
—the socially inherited traditions of a people. Freedom develops slowly
and is not easily achieved. The roots of both American and English
democracy are embedded in the history of British political and social life.
British traditions have sanctioned and have been conducive to the development of civil liberty. Russian political and social traditions have
been largely authoritarian. Certainly, it would be a distortion of the truth
to suggest that the Russian people enjoyed much in the way of liberty
under the czars. The best that can be said for the old regime in Russia is
that it was an inefficient tyranny. Hence under the very efficient tyranny
of the Communists individual freedom is probably more limited than it
was in Czarist Russia. But whether one takes into consideration the new
regime or the old, Russian civilization has never stressed individual freedom as an important value.

**Majority Rule
or Majority
Tyranny** • The American Bill of Rights is essentially a bulwark against governmental
infringements upon individual freedom.
The First Amendment, you will remember, says that Congress may not pass
laws denying freedom of speech, freedom of press, and freedom of
assembly. Such restraints upon the power of government are of critical
importance, but government is not the only source of danger to human
liberty. Majority rule is fundamental to the idea of democracy, but
majority rule may become majority tyranny.

John Stuart Mill correctly maintained that one of the worst forms
of tyranny was imposed by society itself through informal means distinct
from political authority. He suggested that "social tyranny" might more
completely penetrate the various aspects of the life of a community
than would governmental tyranny. Protection against the tyranny of the

magistrate, he insisted, was not enough. Protection against the tyranny of the prevailing opinion and feeling, against the tendency of society to impose by other means than civil penalties its own ideas and practices as rules of conduct on those who dissented from them was equally necessary. Mill felt that there was a limit to the extent that collective opinion could interfere with individual independence. And to find that limit, and to maintain it against encroachment, he believed, was as indispensable to a "good condition of human affairs" as protection against political despotism. More than a century ago a Frenchman, Alexis de Tocqueville, published what is perhaps the most important book ever written about the United States by a foreign visitor. Tocqueville called his book *Democracy in America,* and in it he argued that public opinion could become a tyrant and that majority rule tends to lead to majority tyranny. It is incumbent upon the American nation to prove him wrong.

**Crisis in Civil   •   These are critical and perplexing times
Liberties   for honest believers in civil liberty and
                    democracy. Modern totalitarianism as
                    exemplified by Communism and fascism
has made it tremendously difficult to outline both a democratic and logical social policy with respect to human freedom. Thomas Jefferson, in his inaugural address in 1801, remarked: "If there be any among us who would wish to dissolve this union or to change its Republican form, let them stand undisturbed as monuments to the safety with which error of opinion may be tolerated where reason is left free to combat it." But, unfortunately, this civil liberties formula was easier to apply in Jefferson's day than in ours. In Jefferson's time free institutions were not threatened by secret, highly organized, tightly disciplined groups that were dedicated to the destruction of the democratic process itself.

Earlier we maintained that a society ruled by a majority needs the leavening of minority dissent. For its own sake the majority needs to be scrutinized by the minority. This is how the democratic society, in part, averts costly mistakes.

But our view that the democratic society is obligated to encourage dissent is not without its complications. It forces us to come to grips with one of the most crucial and difficult questions that supporters of democracy have to face. Is it incumbent upon those who believe that freedom is a practical necessity to justify the granting of freedom to those who do not believe in freedom, and to those who are perhaps bent upon its destruction?

The society that permits freedom of expression only to those who express the prevailing beliefs makes a sham of the democratic process. Even totalitarian governments allow freedom of expression to those who espouse the approved version of religion, politics, economics, or what have you. In the words of Justice Oliver Wendell Holmes, ". . . if there is any principle of the Constitution that more imperatively calls for attachment than any other it is the principle of free thought—not free thought for those who agree with us but freedom for the thought that we hate." [20] To be more explicit, a meaningful test of whether or not we practice freedom is whether or not we allow radical opinion that is significantly different from beliefs subscribed to by the majority to be expressed freely and openly. In our time this means freedom of speech—with certain limitations we shall discuss later—for the atheist, Communist, fascist, and socialist. It is a sobering thought to remember that many times in history

"I don't know what I'd do without you, mister."

beliefs that were looked upon as radical in one generation have become respectable in the next. The definition that suggests that a conservative is a person who worships dead radicals contains more than a little truth.

The curbing of freedom of speech, even if the restrictions are only imposed upon those who do not believe in freedom, is always fraught with danger for the democratic society. "Abuse of the freedom of speech ought to be repressed but to whom may we commit the power of doing it?" asked Benjamin Franklin. The point is that few men, if any, are so wise and so moral as to be permitted to decide who shall and who shall not exercise freedom of expression.

For the sake of argument, let us assume that we are not worried about protecting the liberties of the opponents of democracy, say Communists and fascists. We might argue that advocates of dictatorship forfeit their civil liberties because they believe in a system of government that denies individual freedom. Those who subscribe to this type of reasoning overlook the fact that the denial of liberty to one group may lead to the abridgement of freedom for other groups, and possibly for the community at large. Dangerous and contagious precedents may be established.

Inherent in the view that we may safely curtail the civil liberties of the opponents of democracy is the disheartening fact that it is not always easy to distinguish between the supporters and enemies of democracy. For example, socialism and Communism, although closely related in terms of origins, are very different in practice. The socialists, for example, who belong to the American Socialist Party and to the British Labor Party, have a democratic orientation; the Communists, who are advocates of the dictatorial regime of Soviet Russia, are in the totalitarian tradition. Democratic socialists are, in fact, staunch and long standing foes of communism. Yet, many Americans are unacquainted with this basic distinction between socialism and Communism and tend to equate the two movements.

A humorous anecdote is told about a policeman who was involved in breaking up a Communist rally. A person who was being dragged off to jail protested that he was an anti-Communist. But the policeman replied that he did not care what kind of Communist he was and continued to carry out what he thought to be his duty. This is not a true story, but the incident probably could have happened in your town or mine.

A very compelling and practical argument for granting civil liberties to those who do not believe in democracy is that people who are allowed to speak out about their feelings and antagonisms are probably less likely to act them out. In other words, we could argue that democracy is safer when its adversaries are allowed to release their feelings through the safety valve of free speech.

"Heresy, Yes; Conspiracy, No!" It is one thing to maintain, as we have, that civil liberty, including freedom of speech and assembly, should be granted to those who hold unpopular convictions, even to those who reject democracy and its basic principles. But it is quite a different matter to suggest that those who don't believe in freedom should be permitted to engage in activities that jeopardize the very existence of a free society. Apart from any considerations of what is right and wrong, every society attempts to protect and perpetuate itself. Political communities do not consciously encourage or tolerate situations that lead to their own destruction. Ethically speaking, moreover, a majority may not have the right to silence minority opinion, but it emphatically does have the right to protect itself from being overthrown by a minority. The minority, of course, has the right to attempt to become the majority, providing that in the process of making the attempt it lives by the rules of the democratic game. An individual's freedom must end where it interferes with the freedom of another individual. Likewise, an individual's freedom or a group's freedom must be curtailed when it becomes destructive of the welfare of the larger society.[21]

Oliver Wendell Holmes, in a famous Supreme Court decision, once argued that free speech could not be tolerated to the point where an individual would have the right to cause a panic by crying "Fire!" in a theater where there was no evidence of fire. He argued in effect that inherent in such behavior was a "clear and present danger" to the larger group, and that when free speech clearly threatened the security of the community it had to be curbed.[22] The clear and present danger doctrine had a profound influence upon Supreme Court decisions in the area of civil liberties, especially in the decade between 1940 and 1950. This doctrine has proved itself useful; but there is no magic in it, nor in any other formula that attempts to say when the democratic community may properly restrict liberty.

Yet the matter of deciding when and where the abridgement of freedom is justified is further clarified if the difference between heresy or dissent and conspiracy is made clear. The heretic or the dissenter is a person who embraces an outlook that is fundamentally different from the one held by his fellow citizens. The heretic openly espouses his beliefs and may attempt to persuade others to accept them. The conspirator, as distinct from the heretic or the dissenter, does not abide by the rules of the democratic process and is perfectly willing to undermine that process in order to accomplish his ends. Sidney Hook, an outstanding American social philosopher, puts it this way: "In general, whoever subverts the

CIVIL LIBERTIES
CIVIL RIGHTS

As America goes, so goes the world.

rules of a democratic organization and seeks to win by chicanery what cannot be fairly won in the process of free discussion is a conspirator." [23]

Evidence, which we do not have the time to review here, makes it abundantly clear that organized fascism and Communism constitute conspiracies on the basis of the criteria we have just outlined.[24] The nature of the Communist party has been well explained by one close student of world Communism. "Within the party and for its supporters, there is but one great commandment, laid down by Lenin himself: Thou shalt believe what the Party tells you and do whatsoever is necessary in the judgment of the Party to advance its interests. Every change of line, every lie or deceit or act of violence thus commanded, is right and holy." [25]

Conspiracies against the democratic process itself must be controlled. But if democracy itself is to survive, domestic Communism and fascism must be combatted along lines that are consistent with democratic procedures. In our attempt to crush conspiracy we must carefully avoid crushing heresy and dissent, which are necessary to the development and continuance of an experimental and dynamic society. Democratic societies have to guard against the suicidal procedure of adopting totalitarian practices in order to cope with totalitarian conspiracies. Burning down barns is hardly the best way to get rid of rats.

The American mind and civil liberty. How do the American people think and feel about some of the questions we have raised in this chapter? What is the nature of their beliefs concerning civil liberty? Recent social science research sheds some light on these questions. Under the leadership of Samuel A. Stouffer, a prominent social scientist, several of America's leading opinion research organizations recently attempted to assess American attitudes with reference to communism, conformity, and civil liberty.[26] "More than 6,000 men and women in all parts of the country and in all walks of life confided their thoughts in an interview that was as impartial as fallible ingenuity was able to devise." [27]

This attempt to look into the American mind revealed a great deal that was interesting and significant concerning American thinking and civil liberty. "Very few Americans," according to this study, "are worried or even deeply concerned about civil liberty" or the "internal Communist threat." [28] However, many of our citizens do appear to be interested in acquiring information about these matters. It would not be well if our citizens were panicky about civil liberties and Communism. But the present state of affairs leaves much to be desired! Mistakenly or otherwise, Americans, according to this study, assume that their personal involvement in problems of civil liberty is slight; therefore it is difficult to conduct sober and effective public discussion about these crucial issues.

One of the central questions that *Communism, Conformity, and Civil Liberty* addressed itself to is the degree to which various groups in America are willing to tolerate the expression of non-conformist opinion. Here are a few of the questions that were put to some of our fellow citizens:

> "If a person wanted to make a speech in your community favoring government ownership of all the railroads and big industries, should he be allowed to speak, or not?"
> "If a person wanted to make a speech in your community against churches and religion should he be allowed to speak, or not?"
> "Suppose an admitted Communist wants to make a speech in your community, should he be allowed to speak, or not?" [29]

What does the evidence gathered by this competent group of researchers reveal about the degree to which various segments of American society are willing to tolerate the expression of non-conformist opinion? Here are some of the more important conclusions that were arrived at:

(1) Community leaders, including public officials, party officers, industrial leaders, labor leaders, and heads of patriotic groups are more willing to extend civil rights to non-conformists than are rank and file citizens.

(2) The data showed that the older generation was less tolerant of non-conformists than the younger generation; also, that within each group the less educated were less tolerant than the better educated.

(3) City people tend to be more tolerant of non-conformity than do rural people.

(4) To a small degree, women tend to be less tolerant of non-conformity than do men.

(5) Church attenders are more likely to be intolerant of Socialists, atheists, Communists or suspected Communists than non-churchgoers.[30]

In general, the findings reported in *Communism, Conformity, and Civil Liberty* do not bear out the contention that Americans are on the verge of throwing overboard their long and great tradition of civil liberty. Neither does this report suggest, however, that the present atmosphere in the United States is conducive to the expression of dissenting or non-conformist opinion. For example, this study reveals that only 58 per cent of the American people would accord freedom of speech to a person advocating socialism, and even a smaller number of our citizens, only 37 per cent, would grant freedom of speech to an atheist.

Yet *Communism, Conformity, and Civil Liberty* arrives at many hopeful conclusions. Certainly, the fact that community leaders and the better educated members of society are significantly more inclined than rank and file citizens to allow the expression of non-conformist opinion should be encouraging to those who believe in civil liberty. In a nation that is becoming more and more urbanized it is also encouraging to know that city people are more tolerant of non-conformity than are rural people. And, finally, it is very heartening to know that the younger elements of our population, in whose hands lies our future, are more inclined to tolerate non-conformity than their elders.

Security • It is not the purpose of this chapter
and Freedom to make specific recommendations about
what our national policy should be with
respect to civil liberty. That policy will
necessarily, and quite properly, vary with the state of the times. There is no formula that will work forever and forever. Practically speaking, the policy will and should depend on the assessment we make of two

Security and Freedom. *No government can insure absolute security nor permit absolute freedom. The quest for absolute security would entail the abridgment of many basic freedoms. Unlimited freedom would imperil domestic peace and deny the principle of equal rights and justice to all citizens.*

important variables: the strength of particular conspiratorial groups and the strength of American democratic institutions at any given time in our history. Obviously, there is more justification for curtailing civil liberty during periods when our own institutions are weak and the conspiratorial groups within our midst appear to be strong than there is for restricting liberty during times when America is strong and when conspiratorial groups are weak.

Even a democratic society is clearly justified in restricting liberty if such action is necessary to avert its own destruction. Yet it has to realize that absolute security is just as elusive for nations as it is for men. There is no certain way of anticipating or guarding against all the various threats to our national security that may arise at some future time. The

505

quest for absolute security is as illusory as the quest for absolute freedom, for it would lead to the creation of the kind of society in which the activities of all citizens would be subject to police surveillance. But even a policeman on every street corner would be no guarantee of absolute security in a huge and complex society. People would be giving up their freedom in vain.

Despite the real difficulties involved in maintaining both freedom and security, the situation is not one that calls for despair. The American nation has thus far remained both free and secure, and its citizens are not likely to sacrifice either of these values if they become aware of danger to one or both.

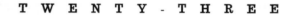

TWENTY - THREE

The Political
System and
Political
Behavior

One of the major areas of study within the
field of social science is political behavior, but
there has never been any widely accepted definition of just what part of human activity is
"political." Politics is certainly more than just
government. We speak of "office politics," and
"school politics," and the term "politicking" is
used rather widely in many spheres of activity. One of the best terse descriptions of

507

politics—although not a definition—is that it determines "Who gets What, When, and How." In this chapter we cannot discuss all the ramifications of political behavior in all cultures, nor can we develop a theory which will relate political behavior to economics, social and economic class, and the formation of national policies. But we shall explore the political system of the United States as it relates to government and also discuss some of the things social scientists have discovered about the way people act within the system.

The United States system of government is generally described as a democracy, and, as we saw in the previous chapter, a major element of our cultural faith in democracy is belief in majority rule. If someone asked you why the United States was a democracy, most of you would probably say because the government is controlled by the people. This answer is partly true. Let us examine the American political system to determine just how true it is.

Elections • The major technique of popular control in the United States is the *election,* the selection of a person or persons to fill an office by vote. If you think about this definition for a while, you will realize that there is nothing inherently democratic about elections. It all depends on who is voting for what. The right to vote in an election is called the suffrage. And all the people who possess this right are collectively called the electorate. Obviously the extent of the suffrage plays an important part in determining the democratic character of an election. We sometimes vote in elections where the pertinent question is not "Who shall fill a particular office?" but something of a factual nature such as "Shall the sale of alcoholic beverages be permitted on Sunday?" This kind of an election is called a referendum.

Under our system of government voting rights are established by the individual states. The national government forbids states to deny voting rights because of race or sex, but all other qualifications are up to individual state governments to determine. All states deprive some people of the right to vote. Children cannot vote. Citizens of one state cannot vote in another state. In some states non-taxpayers cannot vote; criminals cannot vote; and illiterates cannot vote. "People" control our government, but not "all the people."

The right to vote was at one time more sharply limited than it is today. In the earliest days of our history the suffrage was practically restricted to land-owning white males. Women were generally barred from voting before 1920. Negroes received the right to vote, on paper, in 1870 but are still effectively barred in some states. In many states property qualifications are still enforced in some elections, usually on referenda that involve state or city borrowing for specific purposes.

In view of the distribution of the suffrage we would have to amend our original explanation to say, "The United States is a democracy because it vests control of the government in the people who have the right to vote, and these voters constitute a large proportion of the population." But even this description is only partly true.

In most elections the voter cannot actually choose the person he would most like to see filling the office. If he could, he probably would vote for himself or for his closest friends. We usually must choose from a number of specified candidates. Although there are sometimes several people on the ballot, only on extremely rare occasions does anyone other than a nominee of one of the two major parties have a chance to win. To vote for anyone else is practically equivalent to not voting—except as a form of protest. This pre-selection of candidates is accomplished through political parties and primary elections. In a country the size of ours no one can get elected to office through his own efforts alone. The task of persuading enough people to come out and vote for him takes more time and money than any one person is likely to have at his disposal. The political parties are associations whose task is to organize popular support for a particular candidate or list of candidates.

In the late nineteenth century, when many people became disturbed at the power that the leaders of political parties had acquired through controlling the choice of candidates, a system of primary elections was instituted. *In a primary election people vote to decide who the final candidate of a particular political party will be.* Supporters of

"You mean some can and don't do it?"

the idea felt that the primary would make political parties more democratic by curtailing the power of the leaders to choose the candidates. As
a matter of fact, so few people vote in most primary elections that a well-
organized political party can still choose its candidates with every assurance that no outsider will beat them in the primary.

In some states primary elections are *closed*—that is, only people who
are willing to register as members of a particular party are permitted to
vote in the primaries of that party. Other states have an *open* primary—
anyone can vote in any party simply by asking for the ballot of the party
at the time of election. In California, the cross-file primary is used so that
a candidate can try for the nomination of both parties at the same time.
Obviously, the more nearly closed the primary is, the easier it is for the
leaders of the party to determine who will run for office. In many communities parties are not permitted to endorse people to fill local political
office. Under this "non-partisan" system the primary becomes a run-off
election to reduce the number of candidates to a manageable figure. Even
in a non-partisan election some sort of organization is necessary for waging
a *successful* campaign. The organization cannot, however, be one of the
major political parties.

Another characteristic of the political process in the United States is
the lack of interest in political matters on the part of most citizens. Turn-
outs vary from state to state and from election to election. A hard fought
presidential campaign may bring out as many as 75 per cent of the
eligible voters, but many elections for local offices attract less than 20 per
cent of those eligible to vote.

We can now revise our statement of what it means when we say the
United States has a "government of the people." It means that many important governmental offices are filled by providing those individuals who
have the right to vote and care to use it the opportunity to choose between
the candidates offered by our major political parties.

Political Parties   •   In most countries political parties offer
and   the public a choice of political pro-
Political Issues   grams as well as a choice of candidates,
particularly in Western European na-
tions and other countries that have an
active and relatively stable political system. In Britain, for example, the
Labor Party is pledged to strengthen government control and ownership
of basic industries, while the Conservative Party is opposed to such an
extension. In one-party countries political competition takes other forms.
In many parts of the world those organizations that are called political

parties are little more than personal armies organized to procure the complete control of the state for one man.

It may well be that the degree of tolerance of political opposition that exists in England, Western Europe, and the United States is not an exportable commodity. At any rate, the generalizations that we make here concerning political systems and political behavior hold only for those countries where elections mean something.

Our political parties are neither personal armies nor program-minded organizations. Our voters are seldom offered a clear-cut choice between policies. Furthermore, the parties do not control the political decisions of their members once they are in office. If you knew only that a man was a Republican, it would be impossible to predict where he would stand on federal aid to education. Some Republicans favor it, but many do not. A similar division exists on many issues within the Democratic Party. As a result foreign observers often comment that they can see no difference between our two major parties.

If we study the national platforms and campaign promises of the Republicans and Democrats we might begin to suspect that these observers are correct. The documents are very much alike in most presidential campaigns. In our country the voter rarely influences the future policy of his government simply by casting his ballot.

Elections do determine national policy, but not directly. The major issues in most *American* elections involve not what will be done in the future, but what has been done in the past. The Democrats ran against Herbert Hoover in 1952 and the Republicans ran against Harry Truman. The fact that neither was a candidate made no difference. This practice means that voters control governmental decisions only indirectly. Major governmental decisions are usually made with their political effects firmly in mind. What the politicians think of, however, is not their past promises. Rather they consider how any decision will affect future elections. This is not the ideal culture pattern of popular control that we may have learned about in high-school civics, but it does seem to work.

The Electoral   •   When we discuss politics in the United
College   States we are likely to turn our attention to the presidency, our most important office and the one that has had the most profound effect upon the behavior of our parties, our politicians, and our citizens generally. The president of the United States is chosen by the electoral college. This technique was developed by the framers of our Constitution to reduce the possibility of political parties being formed

in the United States. The original idea was to have the voters of each
state elect a number of leading citizens—the number depended on the
population of the state—and to have these men choose the president. The
plan didn't work out that way. What actually happened was that by the
time of the second presidential elections political parties were running
slates of electors pledged in advance to support the candidate of the party.
As a result, the whole purpose of the electoral college, to remove the
presidency from popular control, was undercut.

As it now operates the electoral college *does* have a profound effect
on our process of choosing a president, but not the effect that was originally intended. Each state is given a number of electoral votes equal to
its total representation in Congress. There are, therefore, 533 electoral
votes. To become president a man must win at least 267 of these. Under
our present system each state gives *all* its electoral votes to the candidate
whose slate of electors wins within the state, regardless of his margin of
victory. Depending on the distribution of his support, a man can become
president even though he has received a minority of the popular vote.
This eventuality is not common, or even likely, but it has happened.

The electoral college increases the proportionate importance of the
large states in determining who the president will be. New York, California, Pennsylvania, Ohio, Illinois, Texas, Michigan—these states control
such large blocks of electoral votes that their delegations to the national
conventions have great power in nominating the candidate. It is true that
any governor of New York is a presidential possibility.

Although this technique of choosing a president is not statistically
fair, there are two reasons why it is unlikely to be changed in the foreseeable future. First, the only people who could change the system have a
vested interest in preserving it. No politician from a large state is likely to
look with favor upon a change that would reduce his or his state's power.
Furthermore, our present method tends to balance our total political
system. The large states and particularly the large cities within these
states are severely discriminated against in the distribution of congressional seats. (See Chapter Twenty-four.) Politicians from rural areas already control Congress, no matter which party is in power. Politicians
from urban areas control the choice of a presidential candidate. This is
not the system that was foreseen by our founding fathers, but it does
work. Certainly it would not be improved if we changed only half of it.

Our electoral college is a good example of the two facets of our
political process which any serious political scientist must consider—the
political system and political behavior. Any serious observer of our political life must look at the structure of governments and elections. This is

the framework within which people act. The important thing is that this framework affects the way people behave by rewarding some actions more than others. It is also important to realize that people can change the system.

The Electoral · There are no national political party
System organizations in the United States.
and Third Parties What seem to be national parties are only loose associations of state organizations. The presidency is the only national elective office and a new political party is created every four years in order to choose a candidate and try to elect him. It is true that the parties always have the same names, but they are never really the same groups that tried four years earlier. Each national convention is a fresh attempt to build a successful compromise between state organizations. Sometimes the compromise is unsuccessful—four southern states refused to support Harry Truman in 1948.

On the state level, political parties endure. Here elections are more frequent and the returns are steadier, if not so large. No matter how long either of the major parties is out of office—and both have had long spells of lean years—it is always possible for them to re-create themselves out of their state organizations in order to campaign for the presidency.

The electoral system in the United States preserves the major parties in spite of long-term reverses they may suffer on the national level, but it makes the formation of a successful third party extremely difficult. We use what is called a single-member district system in choosing our political officers. Under this system the winner in a given district gets all the seats from that district—usually one. One party may win a majority in one district, another party a majority in another. This gives a major party something to fall back on. You might come in second nationally but as long as you come in first somewhere you are still in politics. A third party gets nothing unless it comes in first in some region or other. This explains why national third-party movements regularly fail in the United States while regional ones, like the Dixiecrats, sometimes succeed.

The best performance by a third party in a presidential election was carried off by the LaFollette Progressives in 1924. They took almost 17 per cent of the national vote, but carried only Wisconsin. Teddy Roosevelt did better in 1912, but most historians consider his Bull Moose movement of that year merely as a split within the Republican Party, not a genuine third party.

It is possible to create an electoral system that encourages the growth of many political parties. If a country adopts a system of proportional representation so that each political party gets seats in the legislature corresponding to its percentage of the total vote, then the groundwork is laid for a multi-party system.

Under the most common form of proportional representation each party submits a list of candidates to fill its assigned seats in the legislature. The parties are awarded a number of seats corresponding to their proportion of the total vote. In a 100-seat legislature a party winning 1 per cent of the total vote would get one seat, a party winning 20 per cent, 20 seats, and so on. To be certain of election a man must be at or near the head of the list of his own party.

On the other hand the party leader can control his organization by removing any dissidents from the list altogether. Party discipline is strong, but the personally ambitious man might frequently feel he is better off as top man in a small party than as a follower in a large one, particularly if he is obliged to compromise his own political principles more often than he likes.

France's post-war Fourth Republic had a multi-party system. No one of the numerous parties was large enough to control the legislature. Government was carried on by shifting, changing coalitions of parties mobilized to form a majority. When a coalition broke up, the government fell, and it was necessary to form a new majority coalition.

Our winner-take-all system means that it is more profitable for an ambitious politician to remain within one or the other of the major parties than it is to form a party of his own. Our lack of party discipline makes it possible for him to do so even if he disagrees with the policies of men within his party. He can win elections as a maverick within his party, but he can only lose them as an independent or third-party man.

Interest Groups and Political Issues • Even though political parties in the United States do not ordinarily present the voters with a coherent statement of political issues, it is apparent to anyone who thinks about politics for a while that political issues none the less exist and play an important part in United States politics. Since we cannot explain the importance of political issues in terms of political parties, we must go farther afield.

Most politically important issues arise as a result of proposed governmental programs. That is, they center around the question of what the government is doing or should be doing, or is not doing or should not be doing. Political parties are not generally concerned with such questions except as they affect elections. The organizations that *are* concerned with such problems are called interest or pressure groups.

There are literally thousands of organized associations in our society that devote part or all their activities to attempting to influence governmental programs on the national, state, and local levels. A neighborhood improvement association, the P.T.A., the American Medical Association, the United Automobile Workers, the National Association of Manufacturers—all these organizations spend a great deal of time, effort, and/or money in trying to change governmental programs or in opposing changes proposed by other groups. The groups may be more or less allied with one or the other of our major political parties. The UAW, for example, is closely associated with the Democratic Party, and the NAM with the Republican Party—that is to say, with particular factions within each group. But the political parties are primarily interested in compromising the demands of such groups in order to create support for a particular candidate, while the groups are primarily interested in government programs that are formulated as a result of the election. Of course, these areas of interest overlap. No political party completely ignores issues, and pressure groups cannot afford to ignore the party affiliation of candidates; but their main interests do seem to differ.

Political parties in the United States try to control governmental offices, particularly through elections, while pressure groups attempt to control political programs through elections and other techniques. The task of the professional politician is to get people elected. In order to achieve this task he needs resources—particularly manpower, publicity, and money. The interest groups control large amounts of such resources.[1] The UAW can provide precinct workers and some funds for publicity. The AMA can use its widely dispersed and influential membership to publicize the case against government health insurance. The NAM can provide funds. The politician must balance the conflicting demands of these groups in order to finance and man a winning campaign. If he succeeds, he is granted positions of prestige and authority in the society. If he fails he has to wait two to four years for another chance.

Some parts of our social system are more politically organized than others. Business organizations have a long history of successful political activity. Veterans' groups, particularly the American Legion, have achieved a great deal of political influence. Labor unions have risen to positions of political importance in the highly industrialized sections of the country, and the farmers' organizations, particularly the American Farm Bureau Federation, have been outstandingly successful in getting governments on all levels to pass laws favoring their members. On the other hand, con-

Once the candidate has entered the race he must please everyone . .

A sore throat and temperature of 102 cannot keep him from the hustings . . .

He must be against the Taft-Hartley Law and a champion of labor . . .

A few ill-chosen words on the golf course can kill the church vote . . .

and at the same time finance his campaign with management's contributions . . .

and a moment of absent-mindedness will cost him the support of the vets . . .

The candidate runs for office

He can lose the election by being
seen in a non-union barber shop.

Is it all worth it? Only the returns on election day can tell.

sumers have been relatively less successful politically, and have shown little tendency to band together to improve their political position. Negroes and minority ethnic groups have formed organizations to speak for them in the political arena, but their unfavorable social and economic position has slowed their progress in this direction.

Any political interest group is likely to be more powerful in some areas of political activity than it is in others. Although many organizations, such as the American Farm Bureau Federation, take a political position on a wide range of issues, they generally concentrate most of their activity on those matters that directly affect their members. Thus, the unions speak out most vigorously on labor legislation, the veterans on military pensions, and the farmers on subsidies for agriculture. This concentration of attention on one or two areas is also paralleled by a concentration of success as far as changing government programs is concerned. Politicians are more likely to listen to the American Legion when it thunders against a reduction in veteran's medical benefits than when it complains about United States foreign policy.

Political interest groups are just as active between elections as they are during campaigns. In trying to influence government programs they bring pressure to bear on both the legislative and administrative branches of government. In the legislature they present arguments to committees and try to line up individual members to support their position on important bills. On the executive side, their activities are much the same, but are often coupled with attempts to influence administrative decisions that concern individual cases of interest to the group concerned.

The operations of government are so complex that many people will turn to some organized group that will support and guide them in their efforts to get something from the government. The interest group may maintain a staff that is familiar with the ins and outs of government pro-

517

cedure in order to expedite such matters and thus cement relations with its members.

We now see that the political system in the United States is exceedingly complex. The political parties, which command so much of our attention, are actually little more than loosely organized groups that focus almost all their attention on choosing candidates and winning elections. The political interest groups are primarily concerned with changing those governmental policies that harm their clientele and preserving those programs that give them an advantage. The professional politician must turn to these groups for support in order to win elections. His job is to weave successful compromises between interest groups and candidates. If he succeeds, his prestige and power increase; if he fails, his influence may suffer a temporary, or even permanent, setback.

The Voter's Role • Social scientists have collected a great deal of information on the manner in which individual citizens participate in the political process. Although we know very little about why people vote as they do, the area of voting behavior has been studied more thoroughly than many of the other aspects of political activity. The most important thing that we have uncovered about political behavior in the United States is that it is relatively insignificant as far as most of our citizens are concerned. Most people care little about politics and know less.

Most of the early mistakes made in the investigation of voting behavior stemmed from an unwarranted assumption made by political scientists. They assumed that people were interested in politics. But no matter how you approach the problem—by studying voting rates, voter interest in political news, or voter information—you cannot escape the conclusion that most people just don't care about politics.

Of the few people who do show an interest in politics, most have already made up their minds. That is to say, the more interested a person is in political matters, the more likely he is to be firmly committed to one or another of the two major parties. The well-informed voter is likely to be a party-line voter. The independent is likely to be poorly informed and not to vote at all.

A study of firmly committed voters displays some interesting characteristics. We find that people from the small towns of the East and Middle West are quite likely to be Republican, while people from our larger cities are more likely to favor the Democrats. High social and economic status is frequently associated with Republican political preferences, low status with Democratic tendencies. Protestants are more likely to be Republicans, Catholics and Jews to be Democrats.

It makes little sense to talk about political attitudes except in the context of the entire personality. For most individuals political preferences are a fairly weak part of the self-image. People will change their political beliefs more easily under social pressure than they will their religious beliefs, primary group affiliations, and so forth. We tend to alter our political preferences to agree with the expressed political sentiments of our associates. The more important an associate is for our personal self-esteem, the more likely we are to accept his political ideas.

Social scientists who have studied the political preferences of a number of citizens through several campaigns and elections have found that most of the group belonged to organizations and primary groups that reinforced their political attitudes.[2] That is, every primary and reference group that was important to the individual asserted the same political values. Let us construct a hypothetical case on the basis of these findings. Stash Wosniak is a steelworker, and unions are strongly pro-Democratic; a Catholic, and Catholics tend to be Democrats; from Pittsburgh, and big-city residents are more likely to be Democrats; of relatively low social and economic status, and most such people are Democrats; and from a family of rabid Democrats. Add these together and Stash Wosniak is almost inevitably a Democrat.

Some of the people studied found themselves in social situations that conflicted with their political preferences. Our Stash Wosniak might become a supervisor, call himself Stan Wosniak, and move to the suburbs. He is now cross-pressured. His religious and family associations still push him toward the Democrats, but his neighborhood friends and work associates are Republican. What does he do? He keeps his mouth shut and quietly goes his own way, gradually becomes less interested in politics, and makes up his mind how he will vote late in the campaign, or maybe doesn't vote at all. Political participation has become uncomfortable for him and no longer important enough to warrant such discomfort. Perhaps in five or six years the change will be complete and S. Peter Wosniak, now executive supervisor in charge of the paper-clip division, will be a rabid Republican.

We know that politics is a relatively unimportant part of our hypothetical citizen's daily life. We are fairly sure that he builds his political attitudes out of his communications with his friends and acquaintances. A person who is socially mobile either through choice or accident may find that his political interests are too expensive to be retained. If some shattering event occurs, a war or a depression, it may jar large sections of

Familiar American Political Scene. *The excitement of the national convention is important in mobilizing party voters.*

the population into new patterns of political response. This happened in 1932 and possibly again in 1952. Generally, however, the pattern seems to be one of stable political attitudes in stable social situations and a weakening or change in political attitudes if the individual moves into or finds himself in a different socio-economic environment.

The Campaign • If we accept this theory of the political process in the United States—and it seems the most reasonable yet put forth —where do our political campaigns fit in? Large sums of money and immeasurably large amounts of energy are spent every four years and slightly lesser sums every two years in order to run our national political campaigns. We now see that the interested voter is likely to be already committed and the uncommitted voter is likely to be uninterested. Then what is all the shouting about? We might guess that campaigns are conducted to convert Democrats to Republicanism, and vice versa, but we know from research into the effects of propaganda that people screen their reading and listening through their existing stereotypes and are not likely to be so converted. A far more reasonable explanation is that the primary function of the campaign is *mobilization*. The Democratic candi-

520

dates are not trying to convince Republicans to vote for them. Their real goal is to get lazy Democrats excited enough to go to the polls. The Republicans must follow the same technique. In a way our political candidates spend large amounts of money and energy to talk to themselves. More precisely, they talk to members of their own political party in hopes that they will overcome the vast inertia that is characteristic of the American body politic. Mobilization is important, but it is not the function we might expect a campaign to fulfill at first glance.

Food for Thought   •   We have described the American political process as we think it exists. Like many real culture patterns, the way popular control of government actually works in our society does not correspond exactly to the ideal pattern that is part of our democratic myth. This is not necessarily a disturbing or alarming fact. The real pattern does seem to work and most people seem to be fairly satisfied with it. Some students of democratic political theory have suggested that the relative lack of interest of the American people in political matters is in fact a good thing. These men would argue that people do not get excited about politics because there is a wide area of agreement among all Americans on the duties and powers of government. A heavy voter turnout might be a symptom of basic disagreement in the society.

In Germany in the early 1930's voting rates approached 100 per cent of the eligible voters as the Nazis, Social Democrats, and Communists presented three completely inconsistent programs for the future of the country. People were literally voting for their lives. In the United States no one expects to find the Republicans or Democrats shooting or imprisoning their political rivals if they win. Nor is either party likely to change our form of government to such an extent that it will be completely unacceptable to the opposition. Voting rates may be low in our country because most people realize this fact.

You have often been told that our system of government depends on everyone being a good citizen; that we should all see to it that we are well informed on governmental affairs so that we may choose our elected representatives wisely. But our system of government would break down if it *really* depended on everyone being an active and aware political participant, for most of our citizens are not so inclined.

Apathy is the norm in American politics, yet the system requires people who are interested in politics if it is to function effectively. A small minority of our adult population—perhaps no more than 2 or 3 per cent—

Politics and the Citizen. *Standing room only at a New England town meeting reflects the ideal pattern of democracy in action.*

522

actually makes the political decisions that affect all our lives. Our whole political system depends on the activities of this handful of people who are willing to do more than merely talk about politics.

We do not yet know why some people are interested in politics, though most of us are not. This problem is, in fact, one of the most challenging areas of research in the field of political behavior. The answer might be found in a study of the social-psychological processes of politically active individuals, but such a study is still in the future. All we can say now is that some people perceive government and politics as a vital area of their daily life. It is easy enough to prove that governmental decisions on all levels affect the day-to-day behavior of all of us. Our probability of getting a job, the amount of money we will be able to spend, where we will be able to live and how much it will cost us to buy a house, all these things and more are profoundly affected by governmental programs. The fact is, however, that only a very few people perceive participation in government as a means of achieving these things, and even fewer are willing to devote some of their leisure to political activity. The rewards of such work are largely intangible, but a few years of effort can often bring positions of high political responsibility to some willing and dedicated people. The general level of apathy on political matters means that those who are interested in politics can become important

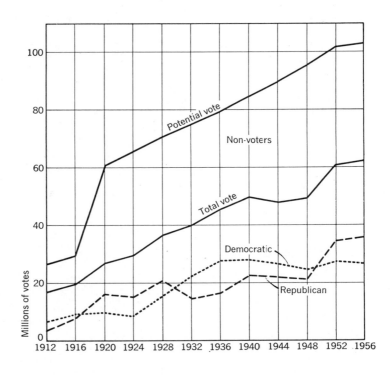

The Popular
Vote Since
1912.

participants in the political process with relatively little effort. Most of you will not be tempted to engage in political activity even though the odds are good that you could be a leader in public affairs at the lower level of government in a very short time. To those of you who are interested, good luck! Our whole political process depends on your efforts.

TWENTY - FOUR

The President
and Congress

Almost every issue of *Time* magazine carries a
lead article summarizing a few of the activities
of the President during the preceding week:
"Last week the President, also: Accepted a
226 piece silver set (valued at $7,000) from
Sir Peter Roberts ... in appreciation of ...
courage and leadership in World War II.
Sent Press Secretary Hagerty ... to look over
the Newport vacation site. ... Swore in Iowa's

525

lantern-jawed Republican ex-Governor Leo A. Hoegh, 49, as new Federal Civil Defense Administrator. . . . Cabled 'best wishes' to Spain's Dictator Francisco Franco on the 21st anniversary of the start of his revolt. . . . Told 764 visiting foreign exchange students from 30 nations —who chanted 'We like Ike'—that they had been in the United States long enough to decide 'whether most of us wear tails or horns. . . .' Named retired Navy Rear Admiral George Dufek, 54, veteran South Sea explorer (Operation Deepfreeze) to replace the late Rear Admiral Richard E. Byrd. . . ." [1]

The President   •   Such is a partial summary of the varied and complex schedule of the American president during a relatively uneventful week. In times of crisis, however, the tempo of activities increases and the burden of responsibilities seemingly becomes impossible to bear. In the early months of 1943, for example, Franklin D. Roosevelt hardly knew a single idle moment. In January, Roosevelt embarked on a 23 day, 13,823 mile trip, which carried him to Casablanca for a conference with Winston Churchill. En route he visited the Republic of Liberia and stopped on his return journey to greet President Vargas in Brazil. Three months later he was off again, this time on a 16 day, 7,600 mile tour of army and navy bases in the South, ending up in Monterrey, Mexico, as the guest of President Camacho. In between trips, Roosevelt submitted a $109 billion budget, endorsed pay-as-you-go taxation, ended a Pennsylvania coal strike, dedicated the Jefferson Memorial, planned a United Nations' food conference, proposed the independent election of the Puerto Rican governor, and found time to welcome President Beneš of Czechoslovakia.

One conclusion is inescapable—domestic events and foreign affairs have made the presidency the nerve center of the nation. When the president speaks, the country listens. Since he represents all the people, the president is expected to have a program of action and to throw the whole weight of his prestige and power behind his proposals. More than any other individual, he is held responsible for the affairs of the country. His office is the one place in our complex government on which the white light of publicity can be focused. As a small sign on the desk of Harry S. Truman appropriately read: "The buck stops here." The president's responsibilities have outrun our national boundaries. Because of our military and industrial might, the president has become a symbol of international influence. That skillful statesman, Prime Minister Winston Churchill, recognized this fact at the Bermuda Conference in 1953 when he offered Dwight D. Eisenhower the seat of honor between himself and the French Premier. Churchill recognized where the seat of power lay.

Growth of the presidency. Unlike the office of prime minister in Great Britain, which emerged in response to political need over a long period of time, the American presidency was brought into being by the ratification of the Constitution. It is a "made" executive. Yet the office has developed, has changed, and has fluctuated a great deal since 1789. There is no mention in the Constitution, for example, of the president's cabinet, the president's role as party leader, or the presidential press conference. Oddly, perhaps, the chief executive has not always been the focal point of leadership in American government. Congress has at times eclipsed the president and exercised fundamental power. Toward the end of the nineteenth century, House Speaker Samuel J. Randall could remark with some correctness that his office was ". . . the highest office within the reach of an American citizen. . . ." [2]

It was Theodore Roosevelt who reversed the trend toward congressional leadership and recaptured the imagination of the people by showing the ease with which the president could place himself squarely in the public eye and take political advantage of the situation. He talked "tough" to the Kaiser and tougher to the trusts. He sponsored conservation, played honest broker to Russia and Japan, settled capital-labor disputes, and acquired Panama Canal treaty rights from Panama. When the President announced that he planned to do what no other president had ever done —submerge in a submarine—Mr. Dooley, the humorous philosopher, prayed that "Teddy" would reconsider but finally concluded, "Well, you really shouldn't do it—unless you take Fairbanks [the vice-president] with you."

Theodore Roosevelt showed the potentialities inherent in the president's role as leader of the people and took the first steps toward structuring the role of the president as chief legislator. He also introduced the threat of veto. Roosevelt would acknowledge in advance his opposition to a measure while Congress was still considering it.

The ebb and flow of presidential power continued, however. William Howard Taft was more impressed with the restrictions and limitations imposed on the office than he was by the power he could exercise. His successor, Woodrow Wilson, strikingly illustrated that the president could articulate the needs, expectations, and aspirations of the people and play a significant role in national and international events. Wilson introduced the press conference, revived the practice, dormant for over a hundred years, of going before Congress in person and reading his messages, and formulated the pattern of the president as an initiator of action. Franklin D. Roosevelt broke the no-third-term tradition, served longer than any other president, and, among other things, devised the "fireside chat" as a means of appealing to the country over the radio to support his policies and program. The presidency under both Truman and Eisenhower has been constantly in the public eye. Incidentally, both men have vitalized the office of the vice-president and attempted to rescue it from its traditional low estate, a status which caused Jefferson to describe it as "a splendid misery."

Presidential roles. The American president must currently play many roles. In a splendid analysis of the office, Professor Clinton Rossiter notes ten different functions of the Executive—Chief of State, Chief Executive, Chief Diplomat, Commander-in-Chief, Chief Legislator, Chief of Party, Voice of the People, Protector of Peace, Manager of Prosperity and Leader of the World's Free Nations.[3] Even as Rossiter was writing, another important presidential role was emerging—the executive's power and responsibility as leader in science. Henceforth, every president will be required to take the lead in encouraging scientific research, attracting and promoting top scientists to key positions, creating an atmosphere both friendly and stimulating to the best scientific minds, and organizing scientific and industrial skills and directing them into national channels.

The president as a politician. Unconsciously, at least, most Americans recoil at the thought of associating the president with the role of a politician. We sympathize with George Washington's concept that the presidency should be above politics. This approach is, of course, unrealistic and one which the First President himself could not maintain. Washington could not prevent the rise of two political parties within his own cabinet and from time to time was called upon to make political decisions and to resort to political action. Few presidents have been great without possessing skill in the political process.

Actually, a presidential candidate is knee-deep in politics long before he is nominated. To win the nomination and the election, the candidate must be a master politician or have good political advisors. He should realize that prior to the nomination the office must seek the man. He must not appear overly eager. He must know, for example, that he should not wear a topcoat when he campaigns in California nor make the mistake of crossing a picket line on his way to a hotel or restaurant. In Texas he must praise Texas grapefruit and while in Kansas he should pay some attention to Kansas wheat. At some point he must go West and don the cowboy's Stetson, or straighten his Indian headdress and accept an honorary chieftaincy in the Blackfoot Tribe.

As chief executive the victorious candidate discovers that policy-making overshadows all his other functions. The president represents the interests of all the people; he is forced to take the lead in formulating a program of action. No program is ever self-executing. Hence, the president must constantly use the political leverage of his office to influence, to persuade, and to educate. He must be acutely aware of his remarks, and the wording and timing of everything he says. Bad news is postponed whenever possible until after an election and is usually couched in a "chins up" speech. Good news is frequently released at a strategic time and may often be accompanied by unpleasant realities and sobering problems. An effective executive must also create issues so vital and urgent that Congress will be compelled to dispose of them. The whole tendency of the separation of powers, the local orientation of Congress, and the loose system of political parties discourages prompt action. In strictness, it is only the president's skill as a politician, the interplay of politics, and the vigilance of the people that permits a program to be enacted.

The president's activities as a politician facilitate his role of party leader. It is the president who chooses the national chairman of his party, distributes patronage, frequently with a price tag on it, confers with party leaders in Congress, greets ward-heelers and party hacks, rallies the faithful at political powwows and fund-raising dinners, and endorses party hopefuls. The executive might wish to avoid some of his duties as party leader, but if he desires to be a successful executive he cannot. Power and party are woven together.

The president as head of state. Great Britain divides ceremonial and executive duties between the crown and the prime minister. Many cities distribute duties between the mayor and the city manager. But in the United States government there is only the executive who must both "reign and rule." It is the president who throws out the first ball to launch the baseball season, rolls the first Easter egg, pushes the button that sends waves of water into a new federal dam, lights the national Christmas tree, welcomes foreign monarchs and visiting statesmen, greets "Miss America" and Eagle Scouts, and addresses the American Legion assembled in national convention.

He also is besieged with minor administrative duties. Truman had to sign his name to legal papers on the average of 600 times a day. Herbert Hoover had to countersign every will made out by our American Indians and to affix his signature to the promotion of every officer in the armed forces. Frequently there were 1,000 documents on his desk awaiting his signature. President Eisenhower could sympathize with Hoover. While he was still recovering from a coronary attack, two promotional lists for foreign service officers were rushed to his sick bed. In addition to the expanding major functions, Eisenhower discovered that he had to approve the dates of tour of the Marine band, the rules for halibut fishing, and bond elections in Hawaiian counties.

The pressure of ceaseless ceremonial and trivial administrative duties makes it difficult for the executive to discharge his most essential obligations—to ponder, to reflect, and to lead. Professor Rossiter asks the question, "How much intelligent leadership can a dray horse give?" Woodrow Wilson, who knew the ordeal of the executive office as few men have known it, pleaded that only prudent athletes should run for the presidency. There are few rest stops and the demands upon the executive call for "hour by hour" leadership. The president lives in a goldfish bowl; he has little private life. This situation, according to Herbert Hoover, explains why he was so fond of fishing. It was one chance for him to be alone. Certainly many modern presidents would agree with Hoover—Coolidge fishing in his white gloves, Franklin D. Roosevelt on the high seas in his jaunty canvas hat, and Eisenhower pursuing the wily trout, describing himself as "a persistent if not a skillful fisherman."

President Eisenhower's coronary attack focused public attention on the multitude of "extras" imposed upon the executive and provoked numerous suggestions for reducing the burdens of the office. A proposal with obvious merit suggests shifting some of the ceremonial duties from the president to the vice-president. One student of the presidency, however, cautions against eliminating too many of the president's ceremonial functions. The president derives real political power from his status as ceremonial head of the nation, and in his role of chief of state he needs all the power he can muster.[4] In the last analysis it is the president who must make the tough decisions and see that they are executed. He must adjust military expenditures to the international situation, balance domestic spending against anticipated revenues, reconcile foreign aid to the nation's economy, and coordinate science and security.

The president as a legislator. The producing and rural interests gravitate to Congress for protection while the consumers, inhabitants of the cities, and families on low and fixed incomes look to the president for support. Unquestionably, the presidency is the one place in the American governmental system where the people in the cities get their proper share —no more, no less—of national power. Both political parties are conscious of this fact and every presidential candidate is aware that he must carry a significant number of the 12 or 15 largest cities in the nation in order to be elected. The urban areas are interested in a progressive program of social action. Hence, the president must take his stand on a dynamic platform and, once elected, must take the lead in seeing that that platform is enacted into law. As a national leader, the president is favored by almost complete access to public opinion. Everything he does is good press copy, from the golf he plays to the most solemn pronouncement he makes. By virtue of his status, the president has a built-in national audience before which he can present issues and problems.

The president also has constitutional prerogatives that help him shape legislative policy. Perhaps the most apparent power is the veto. Most presidents use the veto power sparingly, but when it is exercised it is frequently the decisive factor since only about one presidential veto in seven is overridden. On the positive side, the president has an opportunity to state his program in his inaugural address and in each state of the union message. He is also called upon for budget statements, special messages, and required reports.

As a follow-up to a state of the union message, the president may utilize many varied tactics to stir Congress into adopting his program. He may send prominent party leaders out to explain his program. He may tempt recalcitrant congressmen with patronage and federal appointments, particularly in the judiciary. The advent of electronic communication has provided the president with a powerful medium for taking his case to all the people. Franklin D. Roosevelt found the radio "fireside chat" to be impressive and effective, and Eisenhower has had considerable success with television.

The presidential press conference, the unofficial American equivalent of the questioning period in the House of Commons, was begun by Woodrow Wilson in 1913. Wilson disinherited his brain child after a hot hectic 30 minute free-for-all on the eve of the 1916 election. The president abruptly terminated the conference and the reporters never came back. Harding reinstituted the custom, but he lacked skill in handling the questions and soon required that all questions be written and submitted in advance. Coolidge and Hoover had little better success, but Roosevelt turned the press conference into an institution of creative leadership. Eisenhower once termed the conference a "wonderful institution."

The press conference can be used not only to promote legislation, but also to prevent it. Shortly after the Soviets launched their first space satellite, there was considerable agitation for the President to call a special session of Congress to push through a "crash" program in missile and rocket research. At his usual press conference following the Soviet announcement, the President calmed the fears of the country and quieted, to some extent, the demands for a special session.

To summarize, the potentialities of the president in influencing and promoting legislation are very great. During his first year in office, President Eisenhower recommended 44 specific proposals to Congress and 32 of them were enacted into law. In 1956, Eisenhower proposed 225 measures and despite the fact that the opposition party controlled both houses of Congress, 103 were approved.

The president as number-one diplomat. Writing in 1836, the prophetic Alexis de Tocqueville foresaw that if the "Union were perpetually threatened or if our government had daily contact with foreign nations," the Executive Department would assume greater importance. In recent years this is precisely what has happened. Emergencies, domestic and foreign, expand the role of the presidency, and in the last quarter century America has had her full measure of crises. President Eisenhower once remarked that he could not recall a day in 15 months when he had not faced a crisis. When the crisis occurs in foreign affairs, immediate action is required. Only the president can act with speed. Intelligent action presupposes background knowledge. Here again the president is the only one equipped with information, "the cables" that are necessary for decision-making. Much of this information has to be secret since general distribution might jeopardize security. Furthermore, you cannot negotiate in a glass house. As Harold Laski, a British scholar of the American system, noted, diplomacy, like romance, flourishes best in private, even though the marriage must be made public. The president is best equipped for all the exigencies and therefore must take the lead in foreign negotiations.

With the approval of the Senate, the executive may negotiate treaties and appoint ambassadors and ministers. The president has the power to recognize or to refuse to recognize foreign governments. He, and he alone, can speak for the United States in foreign affairs, and it is only through the executive that foreign governments can address the American people. By means of executive agreements, the president can negotiate arrangements with foreign countries that have the force of treaties but do not require Senate approval. The destroyers-for-bases accord with Great Britain in 1940 is an example of an executive agreement. Some congressmen have been highly critical of the vague and broad scope of these agreements. Senator Gillette of Iowa once asked the State Department to explain the difference between a treaty and an executive agreement. The Department wrote back saying that if the president asks the Senate to approve the document, it is a treaty. If the president decides the Senate does not need to approve the compact, then it is an executive agreement. Thereupon Senator Gillette remarked that this explanation was like differentiating between a male and female pigeon by throwing corn on the ground. "If he picks it up and eats it, he's a male. But if she picks it up and eats it, she's a female." However, much of the criticism directed against executive agreements has been partisan and emotional. Without the authority to make commitments and agreements, modern presidents would find themselves deprived of the immediacy and speed necessary in modern diplomacy. Over half of our commitments with foreign countries have been negotiated through executive agreements, and they have served our country well.

The president takes the lead and sets the tone in foreign policy. Occasionally, a pronouncement like Washington's Farewell Address or the Monroe Doctrine may become a traditional policy. On the burning issues of complicated foreign problems, there are bound to be many voices and many viewpoints, but it is equally obvious that there can be only one official voice—that of the executive. The Supreme Court reinforced this idea in the Curtiss-Wright case in 1936 when it upheld "the exclusive power of the President as sole organ of the Federal Government in the field of international relations. . . ." All these factors point up the significance of President Truman's statement, "I make foreign policy." [5] In the reality of politics, however, this is only partly true. There are solid brakes on the president's power. Congress, with its authority to appropriate and its readiness to investigate, can modify and also check presidential authority. Truman, for example, could elect to send troops to Europe under the North Atlantic Treaty Organization, but a congressional committee required Secretary of State Marshall to disclose, against administration wishes, the number of troops that were being sent. Finally, the president must contend with public opinion. A hostile public can thwart any presidential foreign policy.

The president as chief administrator. It is in the area of administration that the chief executive is less of an executive than in any other role he is called upon to play. Basically, the difficulty arises from the fact that the president's responsibilities are greater than his power. He is head of a vast, sprawling, administrative empire of some 2 million individuals; yet he cannot adequately direct, supervise, nor control this huge officialdom. The president's plight seems to be that he cannot always work well with the bureaucracy and he cannot work at all without them. In a loquacious moment, Calvin Coolidge once said that the federal government could close down for three months and the entire country would never know the difference. Today the president, Congress, and the Supreme Court could go on vacation for a limited time and the country would still be unaware of the change, as long as the bureaus and agencies stayed on the job. In many ways the agencies are the wheels that keep the government and the nation moving.

Nevertheless, bureaucracy has a bad reputation in many quarters. The general public uses the word to ticket inefficiency of any kind, and the politician exploits it as a watchword in campaigning. The operation of the federal administration is probably the most misunderstood phase of American government. To mention just four misconceptions: (1) *We could carry on the government very efficiently without administrators and bureaucrats.* On the contrary, bureaucracy is the everyday business of winning victory in war and achieving social gains in peace. Bureaucracy is an inevitable part of bigness. It exists in big business, big labor, and even in large universities. (2) *The growth of federal administration is largely the result of the efforts of a few ambitious Washington officials to increase their power.* Not at all. The expansion of government personnel has occurred because private rules of the road and the air and the business world are no longer adequate to meet complex conditions, and the growth of urban industrialism has caused the government to assume new duties and positive functions. (3) *Bureaucracy is inherently inefficient.* Not necessarily. The German bureaucracy under Bismarck in the nineteenth century, for example, was very efficient. (4) *Most government employees are concentrated in Washington, D. C.* Actually, the vast majority are scattered throughout the country. Approximately one-tenth of all federal employees live and work in Texas and Illinois.

The expansion of federal programs has often taken place during emergencies when an immediate program seemed to be the only way out. As a result, boards, agencies, commissions, government corporations, committees, and regulating agencies were thrown together in rag-bag fashion. There has been some streamlining of authority and consolidating of functions in recent years but the phrase "the headless fourth branch of the government" still applies to the federal administration.

Almost without exception, new agencies are placed under the Executive Department. For the most part, however, the president has little supervision over these agencies, and Congress has less. Congress may project itself between the executive and his administrative heads and thus blur the line of responsibility. Department chiefs are sometimes torn between a congressional committee, particularly if it is an appropriations committee, and the executive. As head of the Mutual Security Agency, Harlan Cleveland spent six months out of twelve preparing and presenting to Congress a program that he supposedly was administering.[6] The role of Congress, however, is important. Congress does render the country a service in spot-checking. Many cases of mismanagement are brought to light by congressional committees.

The redemption of the system lies in the fact that almost everyone in the administration empire works for the president. When the lines are drawn on issues, loyalties go to the "Chief." "The buck always passes up." [7] Career persons are the backbone of bureaucratic administration. The president cannot personally know all the facts; he must take the word of the department head, who in turn depends on the information and advice given to him by his assistants, the career personnel who stay on while directors come and go. A recent survey of secretaries and assistant secretaries of the Defense Department disclosed that the average tenure was 15 months, hardly long enough to learn the job.

There are at least 100 federal agencies or boards that make and interpret regulations, administer laws and, in general, dovetail legislative, judicial, and executive functions. The decisions of administrative boards affect the individual increasingly, and often more directly and obviously than actions of Congress, the president or the Supreme Court. Regulatory agencies affect his gas and electric bills, train and bus fares, television programs, stock market purchases, and the newspaper and magazine advertisements he reads.

Criticism of the federal bureaucracy is constant and spirited. Senator Byrd of Virginia once charged, "This bureaucracy is not elected by the people and is not responsible to the people. It does not answer for its acts at the polls, yet it wastes the people's money, flouts the will of the people's elected representatives, and down to the last crossroad, village and farm is extending its power over people's lives." It is also charged that there exists a close, even "cozy" relationship between some agencies and the businesses they are supposed to regulate. In other words, it is alleged that some agencies become captives of their clients—i.e., the CAB is dominated by the big airlines and the ICC is influenced by the railroads.

In defense of the agencies as they now operate, we may note that there are limits and restraints on their decision-making powers. Administrators share our democratic values and are highly sensitive to complaints from the man in the street. The citizen can always take his case to his congressman, who is generally ready to make an inquiry into any arbitrary administrative ruling. Finally, the regular courts are open to cases involving a violation of due process or to a damage suit against public officials. A writ of injunction may be sought to prevent an official from carrying out policy until a hearing is held, while a writ of mandamus will compel a public official to discharge his rightful duties.

Undoubtedly there is intercommunication between certain agencies and private groups. In relationships between the Veterans Administration and the veterans, the Department of Agriculture and the farmers, a sympathetic point of view is understandable and perhaps desirable. Both agencies would lose a great deal of their effectiveness if they did not recognize the difficulties of their clients and attempt to resolve their problems. The influencing of regulatory agencies by private groups is another matter, particularly if the national interest is overshadowed by private interests.

There is no simple solution to the problems posed by big government. Although the agencies cannot be abolished nor cut down to puppet size, reorganization of the executive branch to eliminate the overlapping of functions and to coordinate activities is essential. Congress has a responsibility for drawing up more specific laws. Frequently, administrators must "substitute their vision for the vision of the legislators." [8] The Tennessee Valley Authority was created in 1933 to develop the water resources in that region, but this agency has been shaped and styled into its present role largely through administrative decisions. Congress also has an obligation to revise and modernize existing statutes; only recently was the Secretary of the Interior relieved of the duty of selling surplus male reindeer and using the proceeds to purchase female reindeer! Finally, as a nation we must train and attract more competent officials to government service.

Limitations on presidential power. The foregoing pages have pointed up the growth of the office of the presidency, the importance of the executive as the initiator of action, and the virtually unlimited power of the president during wars and national emergencies. Important as the president's power may be, it is usually effective only over the short run. The president is effective as long as he commands public opinion, but public opinion is a perishable commodity. There is always the opposition press as well as the opposition party. And no president can completely control the voting disposition of many of the members of his own party in Congress. Franklin D. Roosevelt discovered this fact even during the first 100 days of the New Deal, and Truman experienced the same fate during his so-called "honeymoon" immediately following the death of Roosevelt. The president attempts to set the tone of events, but Congress may not be tuned in on the same station. Truman's plea to keep price controls after World War II fell on deaf ears in the 80th Congress. Any administration's attempt to keep the troops mobilized after World War II would have been frustrated by hostile public opinion.

There are also institutional checks on executive power. The president shares appointment and treaty-making power with the Senate, his power to dismiss the heads of regulatory agencies is limited, and presidential vetoes can be overridden by a two-thirds vote in each House of Congress. The authority of the Supreme Court to pass on the constitutionality of a law or presidential policy is always a gun behind the door. During the conflict in Korea, Truman seized the strike-bound steel mills under his powers as chief executive and commander-in-chief of the armed forces. In a test case resulting from the seizure, however, the Supreme Court held the action to be an undue assumption of power.

Two factors limit the effectiveness of the presidency as a political institution. One of these limitations results from the gap between the Executive Department and Congress, which divides power and responsibility. Today, recurring crises demand greater coordination between the two branches of our government. So ways must be found, for example, to channel the vast and urgent information which the president has on foreign affairs to the members of Congress who must ultimately vote appropriations to back up the president's program. If Congress is not adequately informed, stalemate will result.

Secondly, the president does not have the political machinery necessary to assist him in sharing the heavy responsibilities of his office. His cabinet is frequently selected to satisfy minority and sectional interests rather than to provide a unified team to head up the administration. The president does not usually regard his cabinet as his planning board. Truman's remark, "Roosevelt never discussed anything important in a cabinet meeting," has validity. Harold Ickes reported that Roosevelt's highly controversial Court reorganization plan was never reviewed in a cabinet meeting before it was introduced into Congress. Frances Perkins also notes that the practice worked in reverse, and cabinet members did not discuss their "pet" projects in open meeting but sought out the President privately to present their ideas.[9]

Strengthening the presidency. Virtually all authorities agree that the president's staff should be strengthened to relieve him of needless detail and to provide him with more time and more information to make the crucial decisions that are his and his alone. Sixty per cent of the public and a large segment of the students of government are in favor of giving the president authority to veto specific items in appropriations bills.[10] As matters stand, unimportant and often expensive riders are tacked on to large appropriations bills. The president is forced either to approve or to veto the entire measure. More debatable is the recommendation urging repeal of the constitutional amendment limiting the tenure of the president to two terms. Advocates of repeal point out that the amendment weakens the power and prestige of a president during his second term, reduces him to "lame duck" status, and deprives the country of the opportunity to return a tested leader to office in troubled times. Those who approve the two-term limitation argue that it prevents the perpetuation of power.

The presidency and the future. Opinions on the office of the presidency are divided. Some believe that there is a curious alchemy in the White House that causes the occupant of the office to grow in stature and rise to the emergency of the hour. Others feel that our success so far has simply been the result of good fortune. All will agree, however, with the perceptive comment of Harold J. Laski: "... the essence of the Presidency is the fact that it is an American institution, that it functions in an American environment, that it has been shaped by the forces of American history, that it must be judged by American criteria of its response to American needs." [11]

The Congress • *Representative government in America.* Even before landing at Plymouth in 1620, the Pilgrim leaders drew up a compact for self-government, and 12 years after the first settlement in Virginia, the first representative assembly met at Jamestown in 1619. From these simple beginnings, representative government grew until by the time of the American Revolution it was considered to be one of the basic rights of the people.

Independence from England produced only a few changes in governmental procedure. In the area of state government the power of the legislature increased and the powers of the governor as an elective executive declined. On the national scene under the Articles of Confederation, Congress exercised both legislative and executive power—a situation that proved very unsatisfactory. When the Constitution was drawn up, the Executive and Legislative departments were given separate but equal power.

Fortunately the new Republic was guided by several strong presidents who maintained the integrity of executive power that had been envisioned by the Founding Fathers. Following Jefferson, however, there occurred a long period of congressional supremacy during which time only Jackson, Lincoln, and perhaps Cleveland and Polk could be classified as vigorous presidents. In 1884, when Woodrow Wilson wrote a study of American government, he revealingly entitled the book *Congressional Government*. At one point in his commentary, Wilson noted, "Whereas Congress at first overshadowed neither President nor federal judiciary, it now on occasion rules both with easy mastery and a high hand." [13]

As President, Woodrow Wilson reasserted the position of the executive, and 20 years later the vigorous policies of Franklin D. Roosevelt caused critics to refer to his administration as presidential government. Harry Truman carried on the pattern of his two Democratic predecessors. The trend of President Eisenhower's administration, however, seems to be toward a system of balanced power, even to the point of inviting congressional revision of his program. The $71 billion presidential budget of 1957 was followed by Secretary of the Treasury Humphrey's announcement that excessive spending would cause a "hair-curling" depression. Humphrey's statement was an open invitation for congressmen to sharpen up their meat cleavers and go to work on the President's program. Perhaps the pendulum of power is swinging again in the direction of Congress. In any event, throughout most of American history, Congress and not the president has been the dominant element in American government.

Stereotype vs. reality. Congressmen are free to say what they please on the floors of Congress, but they have little protection against what is said about them in the public press, mass media, and the entertainment industry. Much of what is said does not enhance their public image. The Senator Phogbounds and Claghorns of the comic strips and radio are more common stereotypes than are the profiles of courage—Daniel Webster, John Calhoun, Robert Taft, Robert LaFollette.

Unlike the presidency and the Supreme Court, Congress is held in very little regard by the average citizen. Somehow this governmental institution has become a perfect target for jokes and biting derision. Mark Twain once jocularly remarked, "Suppose you are an idiot, and suppose you are a member of Congress—but I repeat myself!" Will Rogers used to say that when he ran out of jokes during his early days in vaudeville, he would simply buy a late afternoon paper and find out what Congress had done that day. Even sober critics such as Woodrow Wilson have added to the stream of anti-Congress material. Wilson wrote, "Congress is a despot who has unlimited time—who has unlimited vanity—who has, or believes he has, unlimited comprehension, whose pleasure is action, whose life is work." [12] We still hear the United States Senate referred to as the "Millionaires Club" and the lower House ridiculed as "The House of Misrepresentatives," or "The House of Reprehensibles."

In contrast to the widely held view of congressional inefficiency and ineptitude is the incontrovertible fact that Congress is the most powerful deliberative body in the world today. By action or inaction, Congress can irrevocably alter the fate of many nations. Parliamentary governments everywhere have a stake in the sturdiness and forceful vitality of Congress.

Most of the problems of Congress are the direct result of the tremendous growth of activities and functions that have been forced upon the federal government over the years. Congress reflects this expansion. In a single session, for example, 14,000 bills and resolutions may be introduced into the hoppers of both houses, and comment on these measures and other matters will fill 15,000 pages of the *Congressional Record.* The old days when a congressman's main concerns were sending out free seed, securing an Annapolis appointment for a boy back home, and getting back to the hometown law practice are gone. A Congress which spends approximately $700,000 per minute is bound to be a complex operation.

Perhaps some of the criticism of Congress can be explained by the seeming contradiction that its proceedings are open and unprotected and at the same time veiled from the public. When Congress debates, its forum is the nation. Disagreement is a matter of public record. There is no "front," no protective coloration, to conceal controversy or altercation. At the same time, the real work is done behind the scenes and, consequently, the matters reported to the public are usually only those that are public—a thoughtless comment or an absurd speech on the floor. This situation, of course, is a pitfall to the casual visitor who comes to Washington to watch Congress at work. Peering from the galleries, he sees a speaker droning on and on before a half-filled, inattentive chamber— members chatting with each other in low whispers, or smoking a furtive cigarette near the last back exit. If the visitor picks up his opera glasses, he may even spot a legislator busily working on a crossword puzzle or reading the editorials in the morning edition. The uninitiated usually react with dismay. "How can national statesmen behave with so little dignity?" The answer is that the visitor has seen congressmen at the wrong time and in the wrong place. Evaluating Congress on the basis of the average floor session is unfair; for a congressman does his serious work on the night and morning shifts—going to meetings, reading at home, and attending committee sessions.

Rarely is consensus achieved in open debate on the floor. The process of creating consent occurs in the deliberation of small groups over a cup of coffee or in informal conversation. For the most part, speech-making is aimed at influencing opinion, registering personal convictions, and going on record for the benefit of the folks back home. In a curious way, the United States Senate recognizes the facts of legislative life by refusing to install a loudspeaker system. The acoustics are so poor in the Upper Chamber that Senator Jacob K. Javits of New York recently complained facetiously that he wished he could hear what was going on. "I believe some great speeches are made here," Javits said. "I should like to hear them." The House, of course, has microphones, but the Senate, largely because of tradition, refuses to install them.

The role and structure of Congress. Congress suffers from a lack of agreement on what it is supposed to do. If it does too much, it is criticized for being too independent. If it does not do enough, or is usually cooperative in its relations with the executive, it is criticized for being a "rubber-stamp" organization. Probably Congress makes its greatest contribution as a *national forum*, where divergent and conflicting opinions can be aired and an opportunity is provided for working out compromise and consensus. It is precisely in its role of acting as a broker of opposing opinions and convictions, of not necessarily being of one mind, of not always settling everything "right," that Congress renders its greatest service to a democratic society. Striving for consensus is a function that many people do not understand, and lacking understanding become critics of Congress. Congress also is a *court of public accountability;* it is the one agency that can turn the rays of "pitiless publicity" on issues of national policy. Better than any other existing institution, Congress can raise questions regarding ballistic missiles, space satellites, defense spending, or foreign-aid expenditures.

The Constitutional framework of Congress has been altered in only two respects. The Twentieth Amendment, commonly known as the Lame-Duck Amendment, changed the date on which Congress convenes each year from the first Monday in December to January 3, "unless they [Congress] shall by law appoint a different day." Prior to 1933, a Congress elected in November did not convene until 13 months later. In the meantime the old Congress, including a number of congressmen who had been defeated in the November election, met for a final session beginning on the first Monday in December.

The second constitutional change affecting Congress provided for the direct election of United States senators. Up until the passage of the Seventeenth Amendment, senators were chosen by the various state legislatures. When the present method was instituted in 1913, a few prophets of doom predicted that popular election would down-grade the stature of United States senators. Democracy, however, lived up to the challenge. The caliber of membership today compares favorably with that of the Senate during any period of its history. Recently the Senate looked into the past and voted five outstanding senators into its newly created Hall of Fame. Two of the five selected—the late Robert Taft of Ohio and Robert LaFollette of Wisconsin—were the products of popular election. The fact that two-fifths of the group had been popularly elected was somewhat remarkable, since a condition for selection excluded from consideration any senator or ex-senator now living.

Obviously, there has been an increase in the size of both Houses since the time of the Founding Fathers. According to the Constitution, the number of representatives in the House was not to exceed one for every 30,000 persons. This provision might have been restrictive at one time, but if the same ratio were used today, the membership in the Lower House would be over 5,000 instead of the present 435. The latter figure was courageously set by Congress in 1929 after more than a century of expansion to keep pace with the census returns. Although the number can be changed by Congress at any time, it is doubtful that there will be further increases. (The admission of Alaska meant a temporary increase to 436, but Congress provided for a reapportionment after the 1960 census and a return to the 1929 figure.)

The framers of the Constitution in all probability intended that the House of Representatives should be the more powerful of the two chambers. The Lower House was designed to be the American equivalent of the House of Commons in England, representative of "The People" and guardian of the public purse strings. Ironically, the "undemocratic" Senate has come to be the dominant body. Usually, the Upper House represents more adequately the national interest and generally asserts a "superiority not in any serious doubt in this century." [14] The Senate is undemocratic in the sense that Nevada, with fewer people than crowd into Yankee Stadium during a typical World Series, has as many senators as the State of New York, which has 100 times as many people.

The more influential position of the Senate in our legislative system can be explained on a number of grounds. Because of its staggered membership, one-third of which is elected every two years, the Senate is a continuing institution. In a sense it never dies. It is also a smaller body, highly cohesive and very conscious of its traditions. In many ways, the Senate acts like an exclusive club, jealous of any attempt, real or imagined, on the part of the House or the president to infringe upon its prerogatives. The story is told that George Washington once went before the Senate to "advise them on the terms of a treaty . . . with the Southern Indians." The Senate proceeded to rewrite the treaty in his presence. Washington was crestfallen and later vowed that he would "be damned if he ever went *there* again." [15]

Largely because of its cohesiveness and marked *esprit de corps,* the Senate conducts its business with too few rules, particularly insofar as a relevancy rule for debate is concerned. The filibuster has been terminated by the closure rule only four times since 1917 and on no occasion since 1927. Filibustering Senators have read *Pilgrims Progress,* quoted Shakespeare, resorted to the *Congressional Record,* and submitted recipes for southern fried chicken on various occasions.

On the other hand, the House of Representatives is hampered by too many procedural rules. The greatest factor, however, that has caused the House to lose prestige is the locality requirement. By custom, this requirement dictates that a representative must live in his district; the realities of politics require that he respond to the demands of local pressure groups even when the objectives of these groups conflict with the national good. Beyond this handicap, the locality requirement causes people living in a congressional district in which there is little political talent to miss the opportunity of choosing a more able representative, and the entire country thus has fewer legislators who might think nationally rather than locally and regionally.

Finally, the Senate has two constitutional powers that are not matched by the House: the sanctioning of treaties and the approval of all important Executive appointments. The House of Representatives, it is true, has the constitutional authority to initiate all revenue bills and the prerogative, based upon custom, to originate appropriations measures. Once introduced, however, both revenue and appropriations bills may be amended by the Senate, even to the point of deleting everything but the titles of the bills.

The function and powers of Congress. When we visualize the separation of powers in our national government, we are inclined to think of Congress as being solely concerned with legislation and having no power that might rightfully be called executive or judicial. A more accurate analysis would picture our national government as a system of separation of personnel rather than of powers, since executive, legislative, and judicial powers are shared to some extent by all three departments. The Senate's sanctioning power on appointments is an executive power, and control of the purse, obviously, gives Congress great influence in the formulation of executive policy. Hostile congressional opinion is enough to frustrate a proposed invitation to the head of a foreign state to visit the United States, and a congressional measure on immigration may have widespread repercussions in the executive's conduct of foreign affairs. On the judicial front, Congress has the power to impeach all civil officers and to try impeachment cases. In addition, Congress may determine the appellate jurisdiction of the Supreme Court and can create new or abolish existing inferior federal courts. The main focus of congressional power, however, remains centered on the legislative function.

Making laws. In every session of Congress, between 10,000 and 15,000 bills and resolutions are introduced. On the first day of the 1955 session, 1,738 bills were placed in the "hopper" of the House of Representatives. Needless to say, most bills are dead even before they are introduced, and only about 12 per cent ever become public law. Even fewer of the measures that are introduced originate in the mind of the congressman who places his name upon them. Generally speaking, bills are promoted and sometimes actually drawn up by federal departments and agencies, congressional committees, lobbyists, interest groups, and individual constituents. It is also a growing practice for a major legislative measure to be sponsored by the executive and sent to Congress with a presidential message. Such bills are simultaneously introduced into both the Senate and the House and are accorded prestige and priority on Capitol Hill.

After a bill is introduced, it is referred to an appropriate committee. This process is usually automatic, but if a controversial measure permits consideration by more than one committee, the discretionary assignment by the presiding officer may be the ruling factor in the bill's survival. The chairman of a committee screens the measures which are sent to his committee and decides which are to be pushed during the session. He also schedules hearings and committee sessions on the bills. Frequently, the committee chairman refers a bill to a subcommittee for detailed examination. The subcommittee later reports its findings to the full committee.

When the hearings on a bill are terminated, the committee may do any one of four things: (1) report the bill out without change, (2) table or "pigeonhole" the bill, (3) substitute a completely new version of the original bill, and (4) amend or revise the original bill. If the bill is reported out, it is placed on the calendar for consideration. In the House of Representatives, placing a bill on the calendar is a rather complicated process, and it would take the skill of a Philadelphia lawyer to explain the intricacies of all of them. There are, however, three major calendars— one for appropriations bills, another for non-fiscal public bills, and a third for bills of a private nature. Actually, the key to the advancement of a measure at this point rests with the House Rules Committee, which serves as a legislative "housekeeper" and decides which of the bills reported out of committee shall be placed on the calendar and brought

HOW
A BILL·····

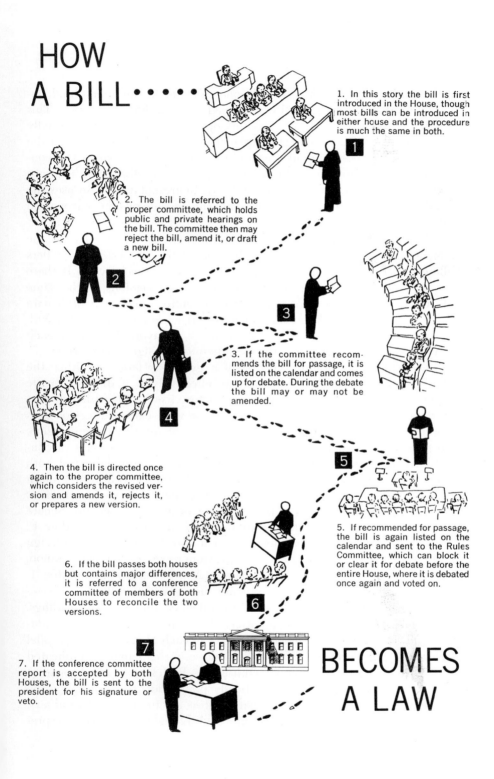

1. In this story the bill is first introduced in the House, though most bills can be introduced in either house and the procedure is much the same in both.

1

2. The bill is referred to the proper committee, which holds public and private hearings on the bill. The committee then may reject the bill, amend it, or draft a new bill.

2

3

3. If the committee recommends the bill for passage, it is listed on the calendar and comes up for debate. During the debate the bill may or may not be amended.

4

4. Then the bill is directed once again to the proper committee, which considers the revised version and amends it, rejects it, or prepares a new version.

5

5. If recommended for passage, the bill is again listed on the calendar and sent to the Rules Committee, which can block it or clear it for debate before the entire House, where it is debated once again and voted on.

6. If the bill passes both houses but contains major differences, it is referred to a conference committee of members of both Houses to reconcile the two versions.

6

7

7. If the conference committee report is accepted by both Houses, the bill is sent to the president for his signature or veto.

BECOMES
A LAW

up before the House. There is only one calendar in the Senate and important measures are generally advanced by unanimous consent. This practice is workable since the Senators opposing a measure will usually consent to its consideration. The explanation lies in the informality of the Senate, the absence of a rules committee which might control the consideration of certain bills, and recognized freedom of debate on a measure after it has reached the floor. The House of Representatives also uses the unanimous consent procedure to expedite the passage of noncontroversial bills and "preferred" status bills.

After a measure has been debated and perhaps amended from the floor, a vote is taken. Voting may be done either by voice, by tellers (filing between two tellers in the House), or by a record vote. If there are any differences in the Senate and the House versions of the same bill, the measure goes to a conference committee made up of Senate and House members. When this committee reaches agreement on a bill, the measure is re-submitted to both Houses. A favorable vote in each chamber sends the measure to the executive for his signature or veto.

The committee system. Obviously a group as large as either the House or the Senate could not operate effectively if it did not divide responsibility and, in some manner, restructure itself into smaller groups for detailed consideration of business. At a very early date, Congress adopted the committee system as a method of solving this basic problem, and today the committee system is one of the strongest features of congressional procedure. The committee system gives the members of both Houses direct contact with the making of public policy. It also provides a training school in which legislators may become recognized authorities in selected fields of public affairs. After years of service on the Senate Foreign Relations Committee, Tom Connally of Texas and Walter F. George of Georgia came to know as much about United States foreign policy as the Secretary of State. Certainly, Congressman Clarence Cannon, after decades of experience on the House Appropriations Committee, is as well informed on fiscal policy as is anyone in Washington.

Congressional committees can be catalogued under three headings. (1) There are the standing committees, 19 in the House of Representatives and 15 in the Senate. The committees in each House loosely parallel each other. The Foreign Relations Committee in the Senate is duplicated by the House Foreign Affairs Committee. As Professor D. W. Brogan of England humorously and parenthetically points out, the reason for the different committee names is not that senators are too old to have affairs, since the average age of senators is only slightly higher than that of representatives.[16] The reason is simply tradition. (2) Joint committees made up of members of both Houses study such complex problems as atomic energy, economic stability, and other pertinent and continuing problems. (3) Finally, there are special committees established for specific periods of time to consider special problems. Numerous investigating committees are special committees. Sometimes, however, perpetuity takes an investigating committee out of the class of a temporary committee. The House Un-American Activities Committee was created as a special committee in 1937 to investigate the Nazi menace and then concentrated on the Communist conspiracy. At the time of its inception, it was thought that the committee could clear up its investigation of "un-American activities" in seven months. Today, the committee is still going strong and is now a standing committee.

Without the committee system, orderly procedures in Congress would give way to wind and confusion. There are, nonetheless, several serious shortcomings in committee procedure. The House Rules Committee has great influence over every controversial bill that is introduced into the Lower Chamber. This committee decides which of the bills reported out of the other committees shall be brought up and the order in which these bills will be considered. The powerful Rules Committee may even force changes in a bill before permitting the measure to come up before the membership of the House. The committee may completely bury a bill. Of course, there are methods of overriding the action of the Rules Committee but such procedures are rarely used.

The power of a committee chairman to promote or to impede legislation is also disturbing, especially since the chairmanship of all committees is a prize that is awarded on the basis of seniority. By virtue of longer service, representatives of "safe" districts and senators from one-party states exercise stronger influence. Frequently, the system projects conservatives, perhaps even individuals with an antiquated social philosophy, into positions of leadership. When Dwight D. Eisenhower, for example, was elected in 1952 with the help of many independents and cross-voting Democrats, he found a number of his policies frustrated in Congress by conservative Republican committee chairmen. Particularly active in this respect was Republican Congressman Daniel A. Reed, who as Chairman of the House Ways and Means Committee fought vigorously against the administration's proposal for a retention of the excess profits tax. Reed had first gone to Congress in 1918, and in the sense of time, at least, was not an Eisenhower Republican.

Currently, not one of the important chairmanships in the Senate is held by a senator from north of the Mason-Dixon Line. The Deep South has eight of these chairmanships and the border states have two. Such a system emphasizes minority interests as opposed to majority, since none of the "one-party" states are urban, industrial states and, consequently, senators from these areas are inclined to represent rural interests as opposed to the needs of people in the cities. And, as we have already mentioned, the important Senate and House committee chairmen have great power and influence. They can set up work schedules for committee meetings, select sub-committees and frame their jurisdiction, determine, to a large degree, what legislation shall be considered by Congress, and help to mold the policies that are finally adopted. Legislation is made in committees. In the Senate the committee makes 99 out of 100 of the final decisions on any particular piece of legislation. The Senate's refusal to accept a report of a major committee, such as the Finance Committee, occurs less frequently than does the overturn of party government in Britain.[17]

Congress as a political process. A perceptive understanding of how our bills are made, or how they fail to become enacted, cannot be gained by reading the House and Senate rules or even by becoming familiar with the procedural steps involved in legislation. Political wisdom requires insight into the behind-the-scenes maneuvers that produce compromise and accommodation. No one, for example, could tell the full story behind the passage of a controversial measure without assessing the personal and political factors of influence that created the necessary consent.

In *Citadel,* Washington reporter William S. White stresses the loyalty and sense of community among the members of the Senate. White also notes the unsolicited but matchless influence of the elite who belong to the inner circle and the lack of influence of those who fall from grace. Senator Hubert Humphrey, by way of illustration, espoused the civil rights plank at the 1948 Democratic Convention in uncompromising terms. As a consequence, he alienated the elders in the Senate from the South and damaged his usefulness as a legislator. Recognizing the situation, Senator Humphrey became more tolerant and amenable and finally worked himself back into the good graces of the hierarchy. Ultimately, he was accepted as a Senate type. In the process of learning the legislative ropes Senator Humphrey dropped his earlier swashbuckling tactics. Yet in the long run it was the new and more skillful Humphrey who accomplished what liberals and conservatives had been attempting to achieve for a long time—the establishment, over initial administrative opposition, of a blue-ribbon commission to study the government's loyalty-security program.[18]

Through all phases of the legislative process there is constant political maneuvering to influence public opinion, and to appeal to large voting blocs. Committee hearings are ostensibly scheduled to bring out as much information as possible on pending legislation. Nevertheless, political manipulation is constantly carried on in an attempt to recruit support for a measure or to backstop the opposition.

An excellent illustration of the political nature of the committee hearing can be seen in the testimony on the North Atlantic Treaty when that document came before the Senate Foreign Relations Committee in 1949. The treaty had bipartisan support and the chairman of the committee, Senator Tom Connally of Texas, was personally committed to its passage. Senator Connally knew, however, that the treaty would need the broadest base of popular approval to hurdle the two-thirds vote requirement necessary for the ratification of treaties. Perhaps this is why the first two witnesses scheduled to speak against the treaty were Henry Wallace, presidential candidate on the Progressive Party ticket in 1948, and Eugene Dennis, General Secretary of the Communist Party. Mr. Wallace had been overwhelmingly repudiated in his bid for the presidency in the preceding November election, and as the result of his advocacy of negotiation with the Soviet Union, in the face of continued Russian aggression, he had been steadily losing prestige and influence. In fact, by 1949 Wallace had become a symbol of the misled liberal. The Foreign Relations Committee questioned Mr. Wallace for four hours. Almost everything he said against the treaty generated support for the document, and, needless to say, the pro-treaty members of the committee were ready to make the most of his remarks.

When Wallace testified, for example, that big business and British imperial interests were supporting the treaty, Senator Alexander Wiley was quick to inquire, "Would you include the C. I. O. in the Big Business group?" On another occasion Mr. Wallace stated that the Czechoslovakian incident was a "spontaneous" Communist coup. At this point Chairman Connally slyly inquired, "Wasn't Mr. Vishinsky there?" Wallace replied, "He was supposed to have been down there (Czechoslovakia) taking the cure." "Yeah," Senator Connally asserted, "he took the cure—but he gave it to the Czechs." [19]

In response to another question, Mr. Wallace remarked that Russia was afraid of the North Atlantic Pact and that this fear might turn her into a "wild and desperate cornered animal." Further, she would do "everything she can to avoid war." "That's fine," crowed Senator Connally. "Then we shall have peace." [20]

Subtle methods of political in-fighting and effective behind-the-scenes maneuvering can be seen in sharp relief in the legislative history of the 1957 Civil Rights Act. The House of Representatives passed a strong civil rights measure and sent the bill on to the Senate. In the Upper Chamber such a measure would ordinarily have been assigned to the Judiciary Committee. Senator Eastland of Mississippi, an avowed enemy of the bill, was chairman of this committee and supporters of the bill felt that referral to his committee would delay or perhaps completely emasculate the measure. Ultimately, by a Senate vote, the bill was placed on the calendar without going to the Judiciary Committee.

At this point, the southern bloc in the Senate threatened filibuster and wisely selected able and respected Senator Richard Russell of Georgia to mastermind their attack on the measure. During the ensuing debate on the bill, senators from both sides of the Mason-Dixon Line made statements and introduced amendments designed to reassure the voters back home. Senator Fulbright of Arkansas compared the bill with the totalitarian measures of the Kremlin or Nazi Germany. Senator Potter of Michigan served notice that he would introduce a bill exempting Negroes from the draft in those states where they are denied the ballot. Senator Russell of Georgia countered with a proposal suggesting an investigation of the civil liberties of a group of gypsies who had recently been treated in arbitrary fashion by law enforcement officers in Michigan.

In their strategy on the floor, southern senators avoided a showdown on the central issue—civil liberty—and concentrated their fire on two clauses: Section 3, which would permit the federal government to intervene to enforce school integration; and Section 4, which would have prohibited jury trial in contempt cases growing out of federal injunctions against interference with voting rights. Southern senators made it appear that the bill would limit the right of trial by jury in all cases rather than in the limited area of cases arising out of the denial of voting rights.

As a result of the efforts of the southern bloc, Section 3 (federal intervention in the schools) was overwhelmingly defeated on the floor of the Senate. In its place, an amendment was introduced to provide enforcement power only to protect voting rights. It was apparent that the vote would be extremely close on the jury trial provision. Majority Leader Lyndon B. Johnson of Texas was bent upon accomplishing two things: preventing a civil war in the Democratic Party and passing some type of civil rights law. He did not wish to rupture the party or to permit the measure to carry over as a burning issue into the following election-year session of Congress. Skillfully overcoming a five-vote margin that Minority Leader William F. Knowland had built up, Johnson collected "one of the oddest coalitions of strange political bedfellows ever gathered together in Washington" to defeat jury trial prohibition.[21] The coalition consisted of western liberal Democrats, southern Democrats, and a few independent Republicans. Johnson used the United Mine Workers, 12 railroad brotherhoods, fearful of the extended scope of the court injunction, and the American Civil Liberties Union to persuade doubtful senators.

With the two controversial sections deleted, southern leaders were willing to vote on the bill. At the last moment, however, Senator Thurmond of South Carolina revived the old image of moonlight and magnolias and raised the Bonnie Blue Flag of the Confederacy with a record-breaking filibuster. None the less the bill passed the Senate by a 60-15 vote. Since the Senate version was different from the measure passed by the House, the bill was sent to a conference committee. This committee strengthened the Senate's bill by providing that the judge in a civil rights case could dispense with a jury trial where the fine was not over $300 or the jail sentence not more than 45 days. The right of trial by jury was limited to cases arising out of denial of voting rights and was not applicable to all criminal contempt cases under federal law. The conference committee's recommendations were passed by both Houses and signed by the President to give the country its first civil rights legislation in approximately 90 years.

Congressional investigations. In recent years the most debatable issue involving the use of congressional power relates to the scope and method of congressional investigation. The legality of the power to investigate under certain conditions is unquestioned. Inquiry is inherently involved in the process of legislation. In *McGrain* v. *Daugherty* (1927) the Supreme Court stated, "We are of the opinion that the power of inquiry— with process to enforce it—is an essential and appropriate auxiliary to the legislative function." Without the power to investigate, Congress would find it difficult to secure the necessary information to promote policy or to pass legislation.

It is also indisputable that some congressional investigations have served both Congress and the country well. The Senate inquiry into the dismissal of General Douglas MacArthur was dispassionate and intelligent and did much to quiet the nerves of the country.[22] Harry S. Truman's

Senate Committee on Investigating Defense Spending saved the country $4 billion, won him a national reputation, and eventually projected him into the presidency. Recently, the work of the Senate Subcommittee on Constitutional Government provided an excellent example of how a committee can respect procedural rights and still accomplish the purpose for which it was established. This committee, under the leadership of Senator Thomas Hennings, Jr., of Missouri, was at all times judicious and restrained, yet it documented in full fashion the effect of hysteria on loyalty-security matters and its subsequent effect on individual freedom.

On the other hand, an uninhibited race for headlines has been an all too common characteristic of some recent congressional committees. Many times leaks from the committee have convicted an individual in the public mind before the person had advance warning or before he had an opportunity to appear before the committee to clear himself. Far too commonly, committees have been set up to investigate some despised or feared enemy, and the committee working on the most dangerous forces of evil becomes the prize to which congressmen aspire. In recent years, committees investigating labor racketeers, Communists and communist sympathizers, and underworld characters have fallen into this category. Admittedly, undesirable groups should be investigated, but it is doubtful that such investigations should be the function of Congress. Probably the greatest liability of certain congressional investigations is the tendency to present an unbalanced, if not a distorted, picture of the problem. Senator Gerald Nye's investigation of the munitions industry, "the merchants of death," during the 1930's created a one-sided picture of the causes of the United States entry into World War I and helped to promote the cause of isolationism. The climate of opinion that was fostered by this committee helped prevent the free world from preparing to meet the threat of Hitler's growing might. A single senator's pronouncements are taken with a sizeable grain of salt, but the findings and conclusions of a congressional investigating committee are often accepted as established fact.

There are, of course, limits to the power to investigate. In the case of *Watkins* v. *United States* (1957), the Supreme Court noted, "investigations . . . conducted solely for the personal aggrandizement of the investigators or to 'punish' those investigated are indefensible . . ." Because of general criticism, there have been numerous voices raised in Congress for the adoption of a fair code to govern committee investigations. Partly in response to the plea for a set of "ground rules," committee hearings of late have been more restrained and committee members appear to be more conscious of the importance of observing the procedures of due process.

Congress and the agencies. Congress has the perennial problem of checking on the vast administrative bureaucracy. Department heads, as well as some 2 million federal workers, are part of the Executive branch and, as such, are primarily obligated to the president. Nevertheless, as an arm of the Executive, a department head has the obligation both to consult and to inform the Legislature. He must also see that congressional intent as expressed through statutes is realized. Occasionally, Congress will discover an administrative agency exercising policy-making power that actually nullifies congressional intent. The Bureau of the Budget, for example, has been reported to be fixing the ceiling for defense, foreign-aid, and veterans services regardless of the final appropriation figures set by Congress.

Congress has difficulty in doing anything more than spot-checking even the independent regulatory agencies such as the Civil Aeronautics Board, Interstate Commerce Commission, and Securities and Exchange Commission. These agencies naturally need a great deal of flexibility to deal with the complicated problems which arise in our industrial democracy and, admittedly, cannot be run by any legislative book. On the other hand, some authorities charge that these agencies have a tendency to become autonomous empires or tend to become dominated by the private groups which they were set up to regulate. The president through his power of appointment can conceivably influence the philosophy and point of view of these agencies, and the Budget Bureau, an arm of the Executive, may assume a policy-making role through "suggestions" to an agency on what programs to cut or where to curtail spending. In any event, although the regulatory agencies may have started out as "creatures of Congress and responsible to Congress," in actuality they are practically self-operating.

Pressures on Congress. Any thoughtful analysis of Congress will reveal that power as well as purposeful activity in our national legislature is seldom conspicuous. Particularly is this true of pressure groups and their reason for existence—lobbying. Both lobbying activity and the lobbyist long ago outmoded early stereotypes to the extent that even periodic congressional investigations cannot keep up with them. The concept of the lobbyist as a cigar-chewing, derby-hat character, soliciting legislators with champagne, slinky women, and a bundle of greenbacks is as old fashioned as a buggy whip. The modern lobbyist does not like to be called a lobbyist. He prefers to be known as a "legislative agent" or a "legislative engineer." In a very real sense he is a professional public relations man. His activities are complex, multi-focused, and constantly changing. He ignores no method of projecting influence; he explores every technological device, every medium, in an attempt to mold the minds of men. In addition to conventional procedures of direct lobbying, the modern lobbyist uses indirect persuasion techniques, the "hidden persuaders." Staged hearings and demonstrations, letter and wire campaigns, institutional advertising, charged books and pamphlets, prepared editorials, canned news stories, and stereotyped letters-to-the-editor are used to create and to exploit emotionalized public opinion.[23]

In 1950 a House committee on lobbying activities reported that lobbying had grown into a billion dollar business and that lobbying activities were changing too rapidly to permit reliance upon a single method of control. The committee was particularly concerned with the effect of indirect lobbying or lobbying at the "grass roots" on our time-honored assumption that in a free society interest groups would balance each other. The application of the cancel-out theory to present-day events, the committee contended, is like "the elephant shouting 'Everybody for himself' as he stomps up and down among the chickens." [24]

Any attempt to prohibit lobbying would run counter to the ancient democratic rights of petition and would interfere with the activities of conscientious citizens. A prominent state legislator tells the story, with obvious enjoyment, of numerous visits by constituents while the state legislature is in session. Invariably, a citizen will ask the legislator to point out a lobbyist; the constituent wants to see what a lobbyist looks like. More often than not, this same citizen, before he takes his leave, will ask the legislator to vote for or against a particular bill that is currently up before the general assembly! Lobbyists also provide the congressman with much information. The trouble is that pressure politics creates a situation where the wheel that squeaks the most gets the most grease. Many of these pressure groups exercise an influence out of proportion to their numbers, and none are responsible to the people.

Unfortunately, attempts to control lobbying activity have not been encouraging. The most promising suggestions include streamlining the legislative and administrative process and strengthening the party system by increasing party discipline. When all has been said and done, however, the words of Professor Stephen K. Bailey seem to express the greatest wisdom. "No registration law, no listing of connections and salaries in the

Congressional Record, no system of party responsibility, by itself, can scratch the surface of the problem of controlling pressure politics. In the long run, a civilized morality is the sole key to the survival of democracy." [25]

Toward a more effective Congress. We remarked earlier that picking Congress apart has been a national pastime for Americans virtually from the beginning of the Republic. But along with the jibes and criticisms have come many sober plans and proposals for improving the legislative procedure and machinery.

Strengthening the party system. Since there is such a dispersal of control in Congress, with individuals, committees and sub-committees competing for power, and because of the inherent deadlock, sometimes icy, between the Executive and the Legislature, certain observers argue that the way to a more effective Congress lies in strengthening the party system. According to its advocates, this proposal would give Congress a focus for leadership and responsibility. It would tend to emphasize the interests of the people as a whole and provide a better channel for carrying out the will of the majority. After an election, the party would feel a definite commitment to translate campaign promises into effective legislation. At all times, parties would strive to create policy and to educate the public to the meaning of this policy.

Defenders of the present system point out that the loose party structure permits an infinite variety of opinions and at the same time provides for unity in national affairs. Substituting a tighter party system would introduce one aspect of the parliamentary system without providing for the fundamental clause—the ability to call a national election on issues in order to secure a mandate from the people. Moreover, many of the issues today are decisive questions that are stacked with irrevocable alternatives. Sharp and uncompromising stands upon these issues could be virtually fatal. The Labor Party in Britain has gone on record pledged, if returned to power, to restore nationalization in the steel and long-distance trucking industries. These industries were nationalized by the Labor Party in the period shortly after World War II. When the Conservative Party came to power, it proceeded to sell the industries to private investors. Assuming that such a seesaw political situation could continue, how long would the private citizen be willing to reinvest his money? [26]

Conservative bias of Congress. The essential tone of Congress is conservative. The geographical basis of representation in the Senate permits the eight largest states with one-half of the population to be matched in

"There must be some better way we can run this."

voting power by the eight smallest states with only 3 per cent of the population. Unbalance is also present in the House of Representatives, because congressional districts are drawn up by state legislatures that are almost invariably dominated by rural and conservative forces. Hence by skillful architecture, through a process known as gerrymandering, districts are created in which a rural-oriented congressional candidate has a distinct advantage. Professor Binkley, an authority on Congress, points out that 50 per cent of the membership of Congress is drawn from districts without a city of more than 50,000 population. In Texas, the Eighth Congressional District includes the city of Houston and has a population of 806,701. These 800,000 people elect one member of Congress while four other Texas districts, each electing a congressman, have populations of under 250,-000. One authority suggests that the advantage of this type of districting amounts to the control of 60 votes in each session of Congress—the difference between liberal, progressive action and congressional stalemate.

Congress represents rural conservative interests, but people in the cities look to the president for their leadership. This is why the president is elected on a program of social progress by the city vote. However, when the president places his program before Congress, the controversial social and economic issues usually run into trouble. If Congress takes any action at all, it will usually come up with considerably less than a dynamic program. There are some issues, however, which Congress, because of its sensitivity to local pressures, will invariably champion. The rivers and harbors appropriation contains a good deal of congressional "pork" and will generally pass with few dissenting votes. Other measures that are taking on the characteristics of sacred congressional cows because of the

556

backing of powerful minority interests are the oil tax depletion allowance
and the agricultural subsidy program.

Correcting the ills of Congress. Even the strongest devotee of the
present operation of our congressional system would agree that certain
procedural changes are warranted. There has been only one major over-
hauling of congressional machinery since 1789—the LaFollette-Monroney
Reorganization Act of 1946. The House could save time—up to a month
a year—by installing electric voting equipment, and both chambers could
save time by turning over picayune private bills to other agencies and
dropping the role of City Council to Washington, D. C. Congress spends
too much of its time on trivial legislation. In one session congressmen
rushed from a bill to protect the fish in Alaskan waters to a measure regulating left-hand turns in Washington, D. C. In 1950, in the middle of the
military operations in Korea, the House District Committee spent hours
trying to decide just how much a billy goat smells. A resident of the city
kept billy goats, much to the chagrin of his neighbors who demanded
legislation barring the keeping of goats within the city limits. The House
District Committee first had to pass on the proposed bill and spent hours
on this "bad-smelling" legislation.

Other important reform suggestions include joint Executive-Legisla-
tive committees to discuss broad questions of public policy and to formulate legislation. Congressmen and their committees need larger research
staffs, and the seniority system could well be revised to provide for the
rotation of committee chairmanships on a seniority basis. At present Congress has a very loose purse. On long-range appropriations, Congress
virtually loses over-all control when the funds are appropriated. A more
businesslike approach to long-range appropriations is necessary. A vision-
ary idea, yet one of considerable merit, is the proposal to extend the length
of the term of House members from two to four years. This provision
would make Congress less defenseless against local pressures, add stature
to the office of congressman, and offer a greater opportunity for statesmanship.

Evaluation of Congress. Violent criticism of Congress and radical suggestions for improving our legislative procedure are not as common today as
they formerly were. We see more clearly that the big issue is not whether
we substitute the British system of parliamentary responsibility for the
congressional system but rather that we recognize the threat of the totalitarian state to our free society. In an age when parliamentary institutions
all over the world are under attack we value more highly the vital work

which Congress performs. It is an agency of consensus, compromise, and even stalemate, a place where consent can be achieved through the conflict of interest groups. A more cohesive system might be successful in a more homogeneous society, but there is no guarantee that merging the Executive and the Legislature would get the job done in our heterogeneous society.

TWENTY - FIVE

The Constitution
and Its Judges

The mere existence of a written constitution does not guarantee a republican form of government nor a stable society. If it did, the Soviet Union would have the most democratic government in the world today, and insurrection would disappear as a national activity in a number of newly created republics. Underpinning a free society must be the force of fundamental law or constitutionalism, which

559

implies a belief in recognized procedures of law-making, protection against arbitrary government, and the open acknowledgment that the state is responsible to the citizens. A constitutional system is run according to basic laws and ordered justice. In essence, the spirit of constitutionalism demands safeguards for individual rights and shields for human dignity.

Late in the eighteenth century, Thomas Paine wrote that constitutions are "to liberty what grammar is to language" and ". . . a government is only the creature of a constitution." [1] Paine believed in written constitutions; so implicitly, in fact, that he assumed that since England did not have a written constitution, she had no constitutional restraints. Constitutions, of course, may be written on paper or embodied in a nation's traditions. The modern British constitution, for example, consists of unwritten custom as well as the great state documents such as the Magna Charta, Bill of Rights, Act of Settlement, and the great political and electoral reform laws of the nineteenth and twentieth centuries. It is not written into a single document as is ours. The broad, comprehensive view of a constitution was well described by the American political scientist Edward M. Sait: "A constitution may be defined as the sum of laws and practices which regulate the fundamental concerns of government." [2]

| Constitutional | • | *Beginnings of constitutionalism.* The |

Constitutional Development in America • *Beginnings of constitutionalism.* The Mayflower Compact of 1620 was drawn up before the Pilgrims landed in America, but it was not a constitution nor a compact in the strict sense. It was simply a written understanding. The Cambridge Agreement of 1629, however, virtually made a constitution of the Massachusetts charter. A few years later the Fundamental Orders of Connecticut (1639) and the Charter of Rhode Island (1644) approached the ideal of citizen participation in the making of a constitution. These landmarks are the beginnings of American constitutionalism. So important did this force become in early America that the failure of superimposed governmental systems such as "The Duke's Laws" in New York (1664) can be explained in part by the fact that they lacked a constitutional basis.

While the American Revolution was precipitated by events that occurred during the years of crisis, 1773-1775, the conflict had its roots in the previous century. The growing independence of colonial assemblies had created the elements of a federal empire. Failure to grant some form of "dominion status" to the colonies spurred the outbreak of hostilities.

Following the Declaration of Independence, the people demonstrated outstanding ability in self-government even though the machinery of government was defective. Both the Continental Congresses and the Articles of Confederation were imperfect instruments. At that time the people were suspicious of a strong central government. As colonists they had fought one war against the usurpation of power, and as Americans they did not wish to fight another one for the same reason.

The fatal weakness of the "Articles" was the frustrating gap between the scope of authority and the power of enforcement. In addition there were also specific difficulties growing out of the absence of a national court system and an executive and the lack of national authority and jurisdiction over the individual.

In short, the government under the "Articles" was a confederation and not a federal body. It is instructive to note the differences between these two political institutions. A confederation has no citizens; individuals are citizens of each sovereign state. A confederation executes policy—i.e., the enforcement of resolutions—through the tolerance of its members. A federal union has authority over individuals. A confederation is predicated upon the good faith of the sovereign states.

The constitutional convention. When the delegates assembled in Convention Hall in Philadelphia in 1787, prospects for a stronger union were brighter than they had been in the waning days of the Revolution when the Articles were adopted. Although the delegates generally agreed on the need for a more perfect union, they disagreed over the manner in which the union should be achieved. Fortunately, they were an extraordinarily able group of men who knew the value of consensus. As a result the final document, which was ratified in 1788 and went into effect in 1789, contained a bundle of compromises, a situation that augured well for the future of the new nation.

The great dispute in the convention involved representation. The question was finally settled by setting up a two-house legislature. Each state was granted equal representation in the Upper Chamber, while membership in the Lower House was based upon population. The issue whether Congress should be given authority over commerce precipitated another sharp controversy. Congress was finally given this power but was denied the right to lay duties on exports. Although the issue of counting slaves in the congressional apportionment and in the assessment of direct taxes evoked a spectacular debate, it was not a crucial topic in the convention. Ultimately the issue was settled by counting the slave "three-fifths of a man." The delegates skillfully "dodged" several controversial questions such as the status of state debts, the role and scope of the national judiciary, and the manner in which the national debt was to be paid. In postponing decisions on divisive issues, the framers of the Constitution contributed immeasurably to the success of the document.

Characteristics · *The Constitution as an article of demo-*
of the American *cratic faith.* The British statesman Wil-
Constitution liam E. Gladstone once described the American Constitution as "the most wonderful work ever struck off at a given time by the brain and purpose of man." Gladstone's high opinion, however, was not shared by many delegates. Alexander Hamilton argued persuasively for the document, but his role was more like that of a lawyer defending a client than of one who was thoroughly convinced. Patrick Henry refused to attend the Constitutional Convention and was openly hostile to ratification. A popular article of the times states that the Constitution pleased no one but the people. Actually, at first the people were probably the least pleased. Certainly public opinion was sharply divided. Supporters of the Constitution made strenuous efforts to secure ratification of the document. Their opponents argued that it was too conservative, permitted a dangerous concentration of national power at the expense of states' rights, and did not guarantee individual liberty against the encroachment of federal power.

The basic problem whether the Constitution was ultraconservative has been resoundingly answered in the negative by history. For the time, the Constitution was a radical proposal. Democracy, as we know it, had not yet become a household word or a national philosophy. The Constitution provided a liberal and flexible framework within which democratic institutions were to develop and flourish. The Constitution, for example, did not limit suffrage and specifically guaranteed certain rights by proscribing bills of attainder (legislative convictions) and ex post facto laws (retroactive criminal laws). There was also provision for the writ of habeas corpus (right to a court hearing on the charges of detention). In addition, the promise of a Bill of Rights as a condition of ratification actually made the first ten amendments an integral part of the original Constitution.

The Constitution as a baseline. Volumes have been written on the Constitution, and it is venturesome, to say the least, to try to summarize them. A few fundamental characteristics, however, do stand out like towering mountain peaks.

(1) The Constitution is built on the premise that man is essentially a rational and a responsible being and that the people are capable of solving the problems of human society. The Constitution recognizes this proposition by making the people the ultimate source of all governmental power and authority.

(2) The Constitution provides for limited government. Neither the states nor the federal government are granted unrestricted power. Both are limited by expressed restraints in the Constitution. Both are limited by the fact that ours is a government of laws, rather than of men. Both are limited by an area of private rights that cannot be invaded, denied or legislated out of existence.

(3) The Constitution creates a separation, division, and distribution of power on the basis of function, place, and sequence of time. Within the federal government, there is a separation of power among the Executive, Legislative, and Judicial departments. The separation of power concept is modified by the check and balance system in which the overlapping of power among the three departments permits each to check and balance the other two. There is also a geographic division of power between the states and the federal government. Finally, there is a political distribution of power over a period of time that results from staggered elections and appointments and fixed terms of office.

(4) The Constitution provides for evolutionary change and growth when broad agreement exists on the need for change. Change can be brought about through the amendment process, by custom and usage, or by judicial interpretation.

The Constitution as a symbol. Many attacks were leveled against the Constitution during the struggle over ratification, but within a few years the document became an object of admiration and esteem. Both of the two emerging political parties, the Federalists and the Republicans, showered praise upon the document. Whigs, Democrats, Republicans, the people at large, all venerated and respected it. On the eve of the Civil War both the North and the South used the Constitution as a reference to support their respective positions. Today the Constitution is sacrosanct. It is above party loyalties and has become a "living symbol of national unity." [3]

The Constitution as an instrument of growth. Woodrow Wilson referred to the Constitution as "a vehicle of the nation's growth." Because of its flexibility, we have been able to adapt an eighteenth-century document to the needs of our intricate, industrial society with relatively few formal amendments—only 12 if the Bill of Rights is considered an integral part of the Constitution. To a large degree, the process of adaptation has come about through the concept of implied power, which was given lucid and forceful assertion in *McCulloch* v. *Maryland* (1819).

Because the implications of *McCulloch* v. *Maryland* are so important, a few comments on the case are in order. In 1816 the federal government chartered the Second Bank of the United States and granted the institution the power to issue currency. Although there had been disagreement, no open clash or overt issue had developed over the First Bank of the United States. By 1816, however, growing sectional and group opposition precipitated a controversy. Opponents claimed that the National Bank was a privileged corporation and a number of states passed laws to restrict its operations within their borders. Maryland, for example, imposed a heavy tax on any bank, not chartered by the state of Maryland, which issued currency. McCulloch, a cashier in the Baltimore branch of the National Bank, refused to pay the tax. The litigation that followed brought the issue before the Supreme Court. In upholding the authority of Congress to establish a national bank John Marshall wrote one of his greatest opinions. A much celebrated quotation from the Chief Justice's opinion captures the spirit and flavor of the decision: "Let the end be legitimate, let it be within the scope of the Constitution, and all means which are appropriate, which are plainly adapted to that end, which are not prohibited but consist with the letter and spirit of the Constitution are constitutional."

Congress followed Marshall's counsel on the loose construction of the Constitution so diligently through the years that few people in 1820 could have foreseen the ultimate exercise of the commerce and taxing powers. Under the grant of power "to regulate commerce among the several states" Congress has, from time to time, barred convict-made goods, white slaves, and slot machines from interstate commerce. Similarly, by imposing high levies, Congress has eliminated the manufacture of white sulphur matches, reduced the competitive advantage of colored oleomargarine, and made unprofitable the traffic in sawed-off shotguns.[4]

The process of growth through law and custom. The first Congress was almost a second constitutional convention because it had to flesh out the skeleton framework of government with specific procedures. In one of its first acts, Congress established administrative departments. The heads of these departments became advisors to the president—his cabinet—although the Constitution makes no provision for such a body. Congress also set up a federal court system and established rules for its own procedure. The committee system, the transformation of the Senate from an advisory body to the president to an independent legislative body, and the functions of the Speaker of the House began to take shape at this time. As a matter of fact, almost all our governmental institutions, save the party system and the role of the Supreme Court, had their beginnings during the years from 1789 to 1792.[5]

In addition to the supplemental acts of the first Congress, custom and precedent have changed the Constitution far beyond the limits of its original 6,000 words. Usage has constricted as well as expanded the meaning of the document. Certain provisions of the Constitution just do not function today. The president, for example, is not really elected by the electoral college and he has never exercised his power to adjourn both houses of Congress. On the other hand, the party system, unmentioned in the Constitution, has profoundly altered the fundamental character of our government. The Constitution states that representatives must live in the states that they represent, but custom has decreed that they must also reside in the district that they represent. The Constitution states that in the event of the death of the president the vice-president shall *act* as president. Yet practice and custom have decreed that the vice-president shall *become* president upon the death of the chief executive.

**The Constitution
and the
Judiciary**
•
Article III. The clauses in the Constitution that relate to the legislative and executive branches of the federal government are far more adequate and extensive than are the corresponding instructions on the judiciary. *Article III*, the judiciary section, charges Congress with the mandatory power to establish a Supreme Court and the discretionary power to create such inferior federal courts as might be necessary. To encourage the independence of the judiciary, the Constitution provides that the judges shall hold office during good behavior, that they shall be paid at stated times, and that their salaries shall not be cut while they are in office. There are also direct and indirect controls imposed upon the courts. The president, with the advice and consent of the Senate, appoints the judges of the Supreme Court and of the inferior federal courts. As civil officers, judges can be removed by the impeachment process. The Supreme Court is given very limited original jurisdiction (cases involving ambassadors and foreign ministers and those in which a state is a party), and the appellate jurisdiction of the high court is subject to any exceptions and regulations that Congress may impose. Parenthetically, however, we should mention that Congress has rarely used this power. Finally, the Supreme Court is given no authority to en-

force compliance with its decisions since it possesses "neither the sword of the executive nor the purse of the legislature."

The constitutional courts.[6] The first Congress followed the discretionary lead of the judiciary article in the Constitution and set up a system of federal district courts. As the territory and population of the new nation grew, the number of district courts expanded. Roughly 246 judges sit in these courts. They are the real laborers in the legal vineyard of the federal government. Although understaffed, most federal district courts give reasonably prompt action to the 100,000 cases that come before them each year. Since 1940 the number of filings has increased 60 per cent, the backlog of cases has risen 125 per cent, but the number of judges has increased by only 25 per cent.

Ordinarily one federal judge sits in each case in a district court. Since the district court is the court of the first instance, both grand juries (juries which decide whether an indictment shall be returned) and petit juries (trial court juries) may be employed. Most of the cases coming before the district court involve suits between citizens of different states where the amount involved is $10,000 or over; violations of federal laws, such as revenue and postal laws; bankruptcy cases; and cases directed toward redressing the denial of civil rights.

Although a few important cases may go directly from the district court to the Supreme Court of the United States, the majority of appellate cases find review in the United States courts of appeals. Congress first established circuit courts in 1789. When these courts were abolished in 1911, their appellate jurisdiction was assigned to the circuit courts of appeals. These courts are now designated the United States courts of appeals. Currently there are 11 courts of appeals with 65 judges. Each court of appeals employs from three to nine judges. At least two of these judges must preside at the hearing of any case, and frequently three judges sit. In strictness, the courts have no original jurisdiction. The courts of appeals simply review cases from the district courts and consider contested decisions of administrative agencies such as the Interstate Commerce Commission and the Federal Trade Commission.

Since the courts of appeals are staffed with competent judges, most of their decisions are allowed to stand as final. Less than 3 per cent of all cases decided by the courts of appeals are reviewed by the Supreme Court. If the Supreme Court decides to consider a case from the courts of appeals, it usually grants a writ of certiorari upon the petition of a litigant. At least 80 per cent of all petitions, however, are denied review. In this way the Supreme Court can control the work load and devote its time to important cases of constitutional law and statutory construction. The Court may dispose of 1,500 cases in a single year, although only one-fifteenth of these cases will require a written opinion. The vast majority of cases will terminate in a denial of a writ of certiorari.

The Supreme Court. In many ways, the Supreme Court is America's most singular contribution to the whole subject of law, jurisprudence, and government. Despite intermittent criticism down through the years, the Supreme Court still ranks high in the confidence and respect of the vast majority of the American people. Yet the Court has not always been as highly regarded as it is today. When the Court first assembled in 1790, it did not have a bench on which the judges could sit and for many years was without a building of its own. George Washington experienced difficulty in getting outstanding men to accept appointments to the Court, and those who did accept frequently resigned to take state judgeships and other offices, which carried greater prestige at that time. The first Chief Justice, John Jay, withdrew from the Court firmly convinced that there was no great future in the job.

John Marshall, fourth Chief Justice, changed all this. When Marshall left the Court, after 34 years, the imprint of his keen intelligence and strong personality was plainly engraved upon both the Court and the country. He labored for a strong national government and a broad construction of the Constitution; and in 1835, when he hung up his judicial robes for the last time, both of these concepts were realities. In a series of striking and influential decisions, John Marshall and his Court clearly outlined the scope of the federal system, strengthened the authority of the federal government, and immeasurably raised the prestige of the Supreme Court itself. A number of these decisions, such as *Marbury* v. *Madison* (1803), *McCulloch* v. *Maryland* (1819), and *Gibbons* v. *Ogden* (1824) still rank among the most important decisions ever written. *Marbury* v. *Madison* is, of course, the most famous case since it expressed in written terms the preëminent power of the Court—the authority to invalidate acts of Congress and of the president on grounds of unconstitutionality.

Functions **of the** **Supreme Court**	*Judicial review.* The precise origin of the authority for judicial review is a moot question. Did the delegates at the Constitutional Convention intend that the Court should exercise the power of

judicial review, or was this authority usurped by the Marshall Court? There is no irrefutable answer to this question, although the weight of scholarship in constitutional history supports the cause of legitimacy. At least, the men who drew up the Constitution clearly intended that the Court should have the power to invalidate state laws. Some of the delegates thought the Court should have the full power of judicial review and said so. Alexander Hamilton, for example, regarded the Constitution as fundamental law and felt that the Court should interpret the meaning of the Constitution as well as the meaning of any particular legislative act that impinged upon it. Regardless of the intent of the Constitution-makers, the document does not spell out the function of judicial review in specific words. Consequently, the decision in *Marbury* v. *Madison* did much to map out the future role of the Court.

The facts of the case are simple. President John Adams, the first and last Federalist President, appointed a number of fellow Federalists to judicial positions during the last days of his administration. A few of these commissions remained undelivered when John Marshall, Adams' Secretary of State, left office. James Madison, who succeeded Marshall as Secretary of State, was instructed by incoming President Thomas Jefferson to refrain from delivering the certifications of appointments to certain justices of the peace in the District of Columbia. One of the undelivered commissions was consigned to William Marbury. Marbury brought suit under Section 13 of the Judiciary Act of 1789, which contained a clause empowering the Supreme Court under its original jurisdiction to issue a writ of mandamus directing federal officials to perform their rightful duties. Marbury contended that as Secretary of State, James Madison should be ordered to deliver the signed commission.

The Court acknowledged Marbury's right to the commission, but to the amazement of almost everyone it did not grant the writ that would have given Marbury the office. Instead, the Court went on to hold Section 13 of the Judiciary Act of 1789 to be unconstitutional. The reasoning was as unpretentious as it was debatable. According to John Marshall's opinion, the Constitution gave the Supreme Court original jurisdiction in only two classes of cases: those involving ambassadors and foreign ministers and those in which a state was a party. In granting the Supreme Court original jurisdiction to issue a writ of mandamus, Congress was adding to the Constitution in an unconstitutional manner. Since the justices had taken oaths to uphold the Constitution, Marshall contended that they had no other recourse than to declare Section 13 of the Judiciary Act of 1789 void.

In spite of this precedent, the Court's power to invalidate an act of Congress, established in *Marbury* v. *Madison,* was not exercised again until the Dred Scott decision in 1857. Then, in the years following the Civil War, the voiding of federal statutes became more frequent and the present concept of judicial review evolved. It must not be assumed, however, that the Supreme Court has ever invalidated federal laws on a mass-production basis. Since 1803 only about 75 acts of Congress and approximately 250 state laws have been annulled.

In the twentieth century, the wisdom of an active and aggressive Supreme Court was not seriously questioned until the days of the New Deal. Within a period of 16 months during the mid-thirties, the Supreme Court invalidated eight congressional laws. Many people felt that the Court was invalidating needed legislation because the new statutes did not conform to the antiquated social and economic ideas of some of the justices. In 1937 President Franklin D. Roosevelt called upon Congress to sanction a reorganization of the federal judicial system. The basic feature of the President's plan provided for the appointment of additional justices to the Supreme Court for each incumbent who, upon reaching the retirement age of seventy, did not choose to retire. Under this plan the Supreme Court could be expanded to a maximum of 15 justices. Critics labeled the plan "court-packing" and it was never enacted. However, since 1937 the Supreme Court, with one possible exception, has not overturned a congressional measure of any magnitude or consequence. This development has led the cynical to suggest that a "switch in time saved nine." Actually, the Court has changed its policy from activism to restraint in overruling congressional judgments. The 1954 decision on school segregation and a 1956 decision striking down an Illinois law regulating the money order business indicate that the Court has not surrendered its power to pass on state legislation.[7]

Misconceptions about the Court. Frequently in the midst of an argument a person will exclaim, "I'll sue you right up to the Supreme Court of the United States." The inference is, of course, that it is the birthright of a citizen to take a suit to the Supreme Court under any conditions. On the contrary, the Supreme Court screens all appellate cases very carefully and elects to review relatively few. This discretionary approach applies to nearly all cases that originate in both state and federal courts. Many people also believe that all unconstitutional laws are immediately spotted by the Court and declared null and void. This is a misconception. The Supreme Court will review only contested cases that involve an actual controversy. The Missouri Compromise stood as the law of the land for 37 years until it was finally set aside in the Dred Scott decision. A third fal-

The Judicial Process. *Here the Supreme Court of Canada is shown in the traditional robes that, along with ritual and ceremony, lend the courts of a nation impressive dignity and aid their essential function of social control.*

lacy concerns the belief that if one part of a statute is declared unconstitutional, the entire measure is invalidated. Only the specific clause or part of the law that is unconstitutional is voided. The remaining provisions may still apply, unless the clauses are interdependent. The idea that the Supreme Court may be consulted in advance of the enactment of legislation to pass upon its alleged constitutionality is another popular misconception. Although several state supreme courts have authority to render advisory opinions, the federal Supreme Court will not. Finally, many people believe that as long as an issue is important and relates to the Constitution, it may be brought before the Supreme Court. This, too, is not necessarily so. The Constitution requires that the United States shall guarantee each state a republican form of government, but the Supreme Court has consistently refused to rule on cases in which it is asked to arbitrate this question. The Court refrains from hearing a case if it involves a "political" or non-legal question or if the Court feels a matter rightfully is within the jurisdiction of the president or Congress. It is highly probable that if a question involving the disability of the president were brought before the Court, the judiciary would rule that it was a political question and as such was not within the province of the Court to decide.

The Supreme Court at work. The Supreme Court begins its yearly session in October and sits until late in the spring of the following year. Two weeks of each month are devoted to the hearing of cases. On these days the Court sits at noon and listens to arguments until two o'clock. At this point there is a 30 minute recess for lunch. Following lunch, the Court resumes hearing cases and sits until 4:30. After the day in court is over, correspondence and reading keep the justices in their offices until 6:30 or 7 o'clock in the evening.

In addition to this pattern of activity, a closed-door conference is held at the end of each week in which the justices discuss, analyze, and dispose of cases they have previously heard. The Chief Justice schedules cases to be considered and presides over closed-door meetings. He also initiates discussion by giving his opinion on a particular case. Each associate justice, in order of seniority, then gives his opinion. Ultimately a vote is taken. The justice with the least seniority votes first and the other justices follow in the reverse order of appointment. The Chief Justice votes last. Six justices constitute a quorum and a majority vote is necessary for a decision. The decisions of the Court are announced to the public on Monday of each week.

Much of the Court's influence and effectiveness lies in the opinions it hands down. When the Court has reached a decision on a case, the Chief Justice assigns the responsibility for writing the opinion of the Court either to himself or to another justice who voted with the majority, if, of course, the Chief Justice voted with the majority. If the Chief Justice abstained from voting or voted with the minority, then the senior majority justice assigns the writing of the Court's opinion. A written opinion explains the background of a case and the legal reasoning used by the Court or an individual justice in reaching a decision. If the Court is divided in its judgment, a dissenting opinion may be submitted. There may be concurring opinions and concurring dissenting opinions. Such opportunities provide the individual justice with an occasion to argue the case on a different basis from the one chosen by his colleagues.

The role of the Court. From what we have said so far, you might assume that the Supreme Court does nothing but sit in judgment on the work of

Congress. Although the review of federal laws is often dramatic, it is not the only function of the Court, nor is it even the most important. The Supreme Court serves as a "watch-dog" for the federal system in reviewing state laws that impinge upon the federal Constitution. In fact, the function of the Court in passing upon state laws of doubtful constitutionality helps to preserve the integrity of the federal union and goes far toward maintaining the supremacy of the national government. As Justice Oliver Wendell Holmes remarked, "I do not think that the United States would come to an end if we (the Court) lost our power to declare an Act of Congress void. I do think the Union would be imperiled if we could not make that declaration as to the laws of the several states." [8] In addition to the foregoing functions, the Supreme Court also supervises the federal court system.

There are, however, conflicting views regarding the policy of the Court in passing on matters relating to public affairs. One school of thought contends that the Court should exercise judicial review to balance interests and maintain equilibrium in our changing society. Advocates of this position feel that the Court should take the lead in formulating policy. Since, they argue, there are checks on the power of the Court, in the long run the will of the people will prevail. In other words, the Court is an instrument of power in our political system and should be recognized as such.

A second point of view insists that the Supreme Court should exercise only limited supervision over legislative action and observe great restraint in voiding state and federal statutes. This group holds that the Court does not have a monopoly on wisdom and as long as a popularly elected legislature does not clearly exceed constitutional limits, its judgment should stand. The Court should set aside legislative acts only when the justices are firmly convinced that the legislature has overstepped its accredited power.

There is also a middle ground between the active and self-denying concepts of the proper role of the Court. Those who hold this position believe that the Court should have greater power in the areas of civil liberty and personal freedom than in regard to economic matters. These individuals believe that the Court should take the initiative in expanding the margins of individual freedom but should not interfere when Congress or a state legislature extends or restricts the limits of legislation on economic questions.

Judges or legislators? Throughout the nineteenth century it was generally felt that the Supreme Court searched out the law in the law. That is, the

Court used the plain meaning of words in interpreting the law, considered the strict precedent of judicial decisions, examined the intentions of the legislators, and was at all times precise and legal. For over a century, the concept of judicial review postulated a mechanical, automatic, and completely logical process. Although by 1936 this view was seriously questioned in many quarters, a Supreme Court opinion in that year gave the legalistic approach to judicial review definitive expression: ". . . the judicial branch of the government has only one duty—to lay the Article of the Constitution which is invoked beside the statute which is challenged and decide whether the latter squares with the former." [9]

Roscoe Pound, former dean of the Harvard Law School, has colorfully styled this thinking as the "slot-machine theory." The litigant steps up, inserts a coin, releases the lever, and out pops the decision. A corollary to the "slot-machine theory" is the "isolation booth concept" of the jurist. This concept implies that a justice should not have any personal views on public affairs, but if he somehow has acquired any such ideas he should keep them to himself. When Justice William O. Douglas makes a speech or writes a book on domestic issues, eyebrows are lifted and voices are raised against the idea of a justice commenting publicly on issues. In 1957 retired Supreme Court Justice Stanley F. Reed resigned from the Civil Rights Commission to which he had been appointed because he felt the work that he might do as a commissioner might lower "respect for the impartiality of the Federal judiciary." [10]

In recent years, jurists and scholars alike have attacked the legal, objective, and mechanical concept of judicial review. In writing about the Supreme Court, Professor Max Lerner noted, "judicial decisions are not babies brought by constitutional storks." Decisions are the offspring of the men on the Court, and numerous judges have acknowledged paternity. In reply to the question, "Do judges make laws?" Jeremiah Smith, former Judge of the New Hampshire Supreme Court retorted, " 'Course they do. Made some myself." [11] Laws may be so loosely drawn that the court cannot define legislative intent; yet judges are required to make decisions. Even when the words of a statute are clear, there are always conflicting precedents that may be called upon to document a judgment. Certain constitutional principles such as "equal protection of the laws" and "due process of law" defy simple interpretation and application. The Supreme Court has consistently refused to define "due process." It merely decides whether in a specific instance the precept has been violated. In a facetious and indelicate mood, a Supreme Court justice revealed how he determined whether a law ran counter to the principle. "If a law is so bad that it makes me want to puke," said the justice, "I consider it to be a violation of the due process."

Judging the judges. If the judges in interpreting the law become in a sense law-makers and policy-makers, are there any limits to judicial power? Certainly, there are terminal points in the exercise of judicial authority. The judges, for example, are influenced by the same forces of public opinion that influence all of us. They cannot be unconcerned and unmoved by the commentaries in the important magazines and major newspapers on their actions. Judges are sensitive to the comments in the leading law reviews. If a dissenting judge failed consistently to justify his opinions in terms of what is reasonable and what is just and good for the nation, would not such a judge run the risk of being labeled incompetent, unsound, or just a plain fool?

In 1898 Supreme Court Justice David J. Brewer said, "It is a mistake to suppose that the Supreme Court is either honored or helped by being spoken of as being beyond criticism . . . its judgments [should be] subjected to the freest criticism. . . ." Effective channels of opposition are open to the critics of judicial power. Every instrument of public influence is called into service when the Supreme Court attempts to turn the clock too far ahead or too far behind. In a loose sort of way, Mr. Dooley was right when he remarked that the Supreme Court follows the election returns. The Court is always cognizant of the people and does not treat popular will with disdain. Over a half-century ago, Lord Bryce said, "The Supreme Court feels the touch of public opinion . . . judges are only men. To yield a little may be prudent. . . ." [12] Since the Court is an agency of power, it is a political agency, and all interest groups will attempt to influence it. In the long run, dominant groups will influence policy determination. As long as this process is carried out through accredited procedure, there is nothing reprehensible about it. In fact, such is the indirect way in which policy may be formulated in a democratic society.

Judges as jurists. There is a growing segment of scholarly and legal opinion that argues, ". . . judges not only can legislate, but also ought consciously to do so." [13] Equally respectable, however, is the opposing thesis that policy-making is incompatible with the role of the jurist. Most Americans want the Court to be as objective and as neutral as possible. They would raise serious objections to the proposition that the Supreme

Court should promote social equality, or that the Court should play the part of the reformer or the readjuster. The basic dilemma of relying upon the Court to protect us against the whims and recklessness of popular assemblies is that it denies the democratic assumption that people are capable of self-government. We are lulled into a situation in which we elect a Huey Long or a Joseph McCarthy and then pray to the Supreme Court to save us. We are frequently not saved and we are always kept in a state of political tutelage. The Court did not prevent the terror of the Ku Klux Klan in the 1920's nor the rampages of McCarthyism in the early 1950's. Perhaps what is needed is not less democracy but the extension of popular responsibility. To achieve this end, the Court might best confine itself to rather slender limits in exercising its function of judicial review.

The Supreme Court Today • The Supreme Court is currently being attacked by those who believe the 1954 school desegregation decision was unwarranted and by those who feel that the Court has put individual freedom above national security. The irrationality of some of the charges against the Court can be seen in a recent speech by Federal District Judge George Bell Timmerman, Sr., whose son is Governor of South Carolina. Judge Timmerman referred to the Supreme Court as "a hierarchy of despotic judges that is bent on destroying the finest system of government ever designed." He also went on to say, "The court has been construing the Constitution so as to make it a protective shield for the criminally disposed and disloyal elements in our populations." [14]

As the result of charges such as these, several bills have been introduced in Congress to restrict the power and jurisdiction of the Court. The most publicized anti-Court measure was the bill sponsored by former Senator William E. Jenner of Indiana which would have removed from the Court's authority cases involving congressional committees and would have deprived the Court of jurisdiction in federal loyalty-security programs and over state action in the subversive activities area. Local ordinances on alleged subversion among teachers would also be exempt from Supreme Court review.

It seems safe to say that the Supreme Court will survive all of the present-day attacks and justify, as it has in the past, Justice Felix Frankfurter's contention that if a Supreme Court did not exist we would have to create one. However, we should recognize that the future of the Supreme Court is irrevocably linked with the destiny of our governmental system and that, "judicial functions . . . can be discharged only in that kind of a society which is willing to submit its conflicts to adjudication and to subordinate power to reason." [15]

State and Local Government

If you are convicted of first-degree murder in Illinois, you will probably be executed. In Michigan, you would get life imprisonment. In Michigan, most things you buy cost you 3 per cent extra because of a state sales tax. Oregon has no sales tax but does levy a tax on personal incomes. Eighteen-year-olds can vote in Kentucky and Georgia, and can drink in New York. Michigan sets the minimum legal age for both these activities at 21, but you can marry at age 18. Why do the laws that govern our behavior vary so widely from state to state? The answer is *federalism,* and until you understand the workings of a federal system the American form of government will remain a mystery to you.

Federalism   •   Federalism is a compromise between two forms of government: (1) a *confederation,* of which the United Nations is an example, and (2) the *unitary state,* represented by England. Both a federal system and a confederation are technically associations of independent governments, and this degree of independence which the American states possess explains why laws differ so greatly from state to state. In a confederation, the central government has sharply limited powers and controls only the member states. As individuals, for example, we cannot be held accountable for violating the rulings of the United Nations; these laws are binding only on the United States government. A federal government, on the other hand, controls the actions of its individual citizens as well as the actions of the states which compose it. Each of us is therefore a citizen of two governments at once and is subject to two sets of laws, those of the state in which we live and those of the United States. In a unitary government, the individual is subject to only one set of laws, which are uniform throughout the country. The following illustration will help to make this distinction clearer.

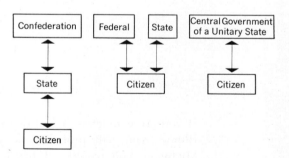

In order to place the study of state and local government in its proper perspective, we must realize that the government of the United States was formed as a result of the actions of separate state governments. The states are, in this sense, older than the federal system itself. The Constitution of our country, adopted in 1789, established our national government as one separate from and superior to the states, but it took a Civil War to assert the superiority of the federal government once and for all, and even today the exact relation between the states and our national government remains doubtful on many matters. The United States government is the most powerful federal system in the world today, but it is still in the process of evolution.

The expanding powers of the national government throughout our history have led some writers to suggest that the independence of the states is "nothing more than a legal formula, a myth." Even if this view is correct, and there are many who would dispute it, students of social science recognize the importance of myths in everyday life.

Although the activities of the federal government may corner most of the front-page newspaper headlines, in our daily lives we are more likely to depend on the activities of state and local governments. It is our state and local governments that supply our water, protect our homes and persons from injury, regulate our traffic, and haul away our garbage. Furthermore, the federal government often uses state and local units of government for the administration of programs established by the national government. For example, the recently proposed federal highway program may be paid for out of federal funds, but the roads will be built by state and local governments.

The programs, responsibilities, and budgets of the national government have expanded enormously in recent years, primarily as a response to economic depression, war, and international tensions. Although the states themselves have embraced many new programs and functions which simply did not exist in earlier generations, there are still periodic protests against the federal government "usurping the powers of the states." This "states' rights" movement is generally no more than a symbol of righteousness for those groups which oppose government action in certain areas and feel that the states would be less vigorous in social and economic regulation than the federal government. The famous tidelands oil dispute is a classic example of this sort of activity. Oil companies supported the states in their fight with the federal government over control of offshore oil because they felt they could make more profitable leasing arrangements with the state administrations of Texas, California, and Louisiana than with the federal government. Any specific governmental program will be opposed by some groups in this heterogeneous country of ours, and it sounds better to oppose certain programs on the high-sounding principle of "states' rights" than because it will lower profits or reduce the political influence of some special interests.

Many of the problems of state and national government under our federal system arise from the limitations that are placed on the national government by the Tenth Amendment to the Constitution. This amendment reserves for the states all powers of government that are not specifically granted to our national government. Supreme Court interpretations have through the years expanded the powers of the federal government despite this clause, but the police power remains largely with the states and is their most important privilege. The police power is the right of a government to control the private use of personal liberty and property in matters that are connected with the public interest. Almost all laws that control the actions of individuals or groups—for instance, the laws against murder, theft, and driving a car without a license —are examples of the police power of the states.

The major difficulty with this arrangement, as logical as it may seem at first glance, is the possibility of inconsistencies between the purposes of the national government and those of individual states. Our national

"In two words, yes and no."

HERBLOCK
© 1962 THE WASHINGTON POST

government represents the dominant political values of the entire population of the United States. These values may or may not be consistent with those dominant in any one state of the union. When they are not in agreement, the legal formulas which assert the independence of state governments within their proper sphere are severely strained, and usually are rewritten. Since the Fourteenth Amendment to the Constitution was adopted, just after the Civil War, it has been clearly decided that the federal government may protect its citizens from state actions which are inconsistent with the dominant national political values of the day. It has also been fairly clear that the states possess no similar power to interpose themselves between *their* citizens and the federal government.

Various branches of the federal government have in fact blocked state actions which were inconsistent with the dominant political values of the nation. In the 1880's many middle western states came under the control of powerful farmers' organizations and attempted to control railroad freight rates within the states. The national government reflected another set of political values and many of these early attempts at controlling the power of business organizations were set aside by the Supreme Court as a violation of the Fourteenth Amendment.

The most pertinent recent example of this sort of activity is the desegregation dispute between the southern states and the national government. In this case the dominant value position of the southern states seems to be at odds with both the national government and the world at large. The broader concerns of international relations, in other words, tend to force the federal government into intervening in what was at one time a purely regional problem.

For those who value tidiness in theory and operation over all other considerations, the federal government demonstrates severe shortcomings. The borders between federal and state powers in the United States are vague and state powers in the United States are unclear and ever-changing. When we consider the problems that would arise in attempting to administer one set of laws over a nation as heterogeneous as the United States and the conflicts of local interests in which the national government would be obliged to intervene, it is doubtful whether any other system operates any better than our own in actual practice. In spite of its clumsiness, the federal system has the advantage of permitting more direct popular control over local and state governmental units than any form of centralized government. Imagine the difficulties that would arise if all complaints about the performance of local government ended on the floor of the United States Congress. Exactly that sort of thing can happen in England, where the House of Commons is the only independent legislative body. In the United States, our state legislatures thus serve to insulate the national government to some degree from purely local concerns. The question is a truly academic one, however, for it is highly unlikely that it would be politically possible to drop the federal system after so many years of relatively successful operation.

State   •   Just as the machinery and powers of
Constitutions   the national government are defined by
the federal Constitution, so each state
has a form of government that is deter-
mined by its own constitution. As far as the Constitution is concerned, the exact form of government within the states is a matter for each state to decide for itself, the only restriction being that it shall be a "repub-lican form of government." In fact, however, all states have modeled the machinery of their government after the national system. Separation of powers is basic to all state governments, the two house legislature to all but one, and judicial review is standard.

State constitutions do differ from one another—no two are exactly the same. We can, however, generalize about them and compare them to the federal Constitution. As you know, the wording of the federal Constitution has remained relatively unchanged since its adoption. Since 1787 there have been only 22 amendments, and two of these, establish-ing and abolishing prohibition, cancel each other out. The Constitution has needed few revisions because it is written in very general terms and the United States Supreme Court can change its meaning through inter-pretation (see Chapter Twenty-five). State constitutions are generally much more precise and detailed, and, as a consequence, the state supreme courts are not able to revise the meanings as easily. The constitutions of our several states must therefore be rather frequently amended and often completely rewritten.

There is also a strong tendency among state governments to insert into their constitutions matters which could be handled through the nor-mal procedures of law-making. The Florida constitution establishes an independent commission to regulate freshwater fishing and hunting in the state. The California constitution establishes the amount of pensions to be paid to the aged. These matters, and many like them, could be handled much more efficiently by statute.

This unnecessary attention to detail seems to stem from a distrust in the judgment of the legislative bodies of the various states. In the middle of the nineteenth century corruption was widespread—the legis-lature of the state of Illinois, for example, gave the entire lake front of the City of Chicago to the Illinois Central Railroad—and one way to prevent a legislature from doing the wrong thing is to prevent it from doing anything at all. This solution to the problem has left most of our states with governmental systems that are drastically out of step with the twentieth-century tasks of government.

Another characteristic of state constitutions is the relative weakness of the Executive branch of government. In most states all important executive offices are elective. The governor, thoretically the most powerful state official, is often left with all the responsibility for seeing that the state is efficiently run, but with no power to enforce his decisions. Another problem, as we mentioned earlier, stems from the fact that the large centers of urban population are systematically underrepresented in our state legislatures. This often creates a situation in which a governor, whose political support comes from the urban areas, must try to cooperate with or accommodate to a legislature dominated by rural interests. You need only think back to the material on the urban vs. rural way of life in the early part of the book to see that conflict is highly likely in such circumstances.

State and Local   •   Unlike our national government, which
Finance   controls the money supply of the United
                                   States and is therefore able to engage in
                                   deficit financing with relative impunity,
state and local governments generally face financial problems similar to those of private industry. In the long run the states must pay for what they get in dollars whose value they do not control.

There are two possible ways of financing the activities of state and local government. The first is the pay-as-you-go plan where governmental units spend only what they collect in taxes during a given year. This technique, however, cannot be used for activities which involve massive capital expenditures. Highways, for example, cost up to a million dollars a mile, so our state governments and local units generally borrow money to finance these improvements.

The bond issue is a method of distributing heavy expenditures over a long period of years. Under our economic system, a person, corporation, or government must pay interest in order to borrow funds, however, and the long-term bonds favored by state and local governments usually force a high proportion of tax money into interest payments rather than into the projects themselves. Interest on 50 million dollars of 3 per cent 20-year bonds is $30 million. This means that only $50 million of expenditures are possible, even though a total of $80 million leaves the taxpayers' pockets. It is often possible to refund bond issues; that is, to borrow more money in order to pay back borrowed money. When governments resort to this technique, the cost of capital improvements often goes far beyond any realistic appraisal of their value. Fortunately the federal government does not tax the interest on state and municipal bonds, and state and local government units are therefore able to borrow at lower rates than private business. That is, the fact that income on these bonds is tax free tempts people to invest in them.

State and local governments also raise money through taxes. Local governments depend almost completely on the property tax, which is levied at a certain rate for every thousand dollars of the value of the property, as determined by a public official known as an assessor. The property tax is the oldest form of taxation in the United States. It is easy to collect, because it is impossible to hide real estate; but it is an expensive tax to collect, and it has harmful side effects. The side effects of taxes are very important, for a tax not only raises money, but also tends to force people into certain patterns of behavior in order to avoid heavy taxation. The property tax tempts people to move away from high-tax areas and, if they remain, it makes them reluctant to improve their property because any improvement will increase their assessment and total taxes.

The states at one time used the property tax very extensively, but they have tended to abandon this area to local government in recent years and to switch to other sources of revenue. The only tax common to all states is some form of levy on business. About 32 states also have adopted a form of the general sales tax, and a somewhat smaller number use a state income tax, which differs from the federal tax in that it is usually a flat rate at all levels instead of a progressive tax. The general sales tax is probably the cheapest and easiest tax to collect, but it falls most heavily on the poorest citizens who spend more of their income on those items on which the tax falls than do wealthy people. In addition to these categories, all states use some form of excises. Excises are taxes that are collected on the sale of specific commodities, particularly commodities with which some sort of moral disapproval is connected, such as liquor and tobacco. Obviously the intended side effect here is to reduce consumption of such items.

As the costs of state and local government increase both because of inflation and the expanding responsibilities of these governments, sources of taxation are becoming scarce and there is active competition between the different levels of government for new revenues and an increasing tendency to seek financial support from the federal government.

State Politics   •   The states are the real stamping grounds of the professional politician, who may or may not be a holder of political office himself. The professional politician uses control of the offices of government to act as a broker of political decisions. He balances the demands of interest groups, often trading governmental decisions for economic and political support. Since political parties in the United States are not noted for taking clear stands on political issues, most of the demands for, and opposition to, proposed government programs come from such organized interest groups as business organizations, labor unions, and church groups. The task of the politician is to translate these often conflicting demands into governmental programs.

The politician may be rewarded with financial contributions to party coffers and possibly to his own pocket, but considering the amount of effort required to win them, the direct monetary rewards of politics are not high. The successful politician, however, gains prestige and wins an entree into groups in the community which might otherwise exclude him. This situation probably explains why groups that are discriminated against socially and economically tend to participate in political activities. Politics is one area where upward mobility is still relatively easy.

The state governments provide the greatest number of political offices and therefore attract the attention of most of the professional politicians and exhibit the highest degree of political party organization. In most states there is at least one fairly well-organized political party which structures and channels the competition for political offices within the state. Many states have two such organizations; the national government has none.

Although competition for state political offices is keen, it is limited by the salaries that are offered. Few state elective offices pay salaries high enough to be attractive on that basis alone to competent men. Even fewer pay enough to cover the costs of a political career. State elective offices, therefore, tend to attract those individuals who can treat them as part-time occupations—farmers and lawyers, for example, or those who are rich enough to consider public service an honor or a hobby.

Most of our prominent national politicians have worked their way up through state political offices or through state political activity. In our federal system the states or sections of states are the units of election for all national offices, and it is not ordinarily possible to achieve national office without the wholehearted support of some state political organization. Politicians must win offices in order to be successful. A loser in politics is no better rewarded in American society than any other sort of

loser. He may be complimented and even admired, but he does not shape
governmental decisions. Party organizations in the United States have
one dominant purpose—to win elections. In the days of the "patronage
system," before civil service systems became widespread, the task was
somewhat simpler than it is today. A party leader could reward his supporters with government jobs. This basis for organizing political parties
seems to be disappearing throughout the country. The old-time political
boss who depended on patronage to create a legion of precinct workers
is fast disappearing. Today's successful political leader is one who can
stimulate and channel the activities of volunteer political workers during
election campaigns. Merit systems, organized welfare programs, and prosperity have made the cost of buying support too high.

Forms of Local   •   Local governments are created by the
Government   states. For many years local political
                          leaders in all the states have tried to
                          get some form of "home rule" whereby
they can be given the power to manage their own affairs without state
supervision—or as some would call it, interference. In spite of this movement, local governments are still generally subservient to the state, even
where such home-rule provisions exist. Michigan, for example, is a "home-
rule" state, but this means little more than that Michigan cities can re-
organize their own forms of government without getting permission from
the state legislature. When the city of East Lansing protested the State
Highway Department ruling banning parking on U. S. 16, which is also
the main street of the city, it lost. With few exceptions cities will always
lose such fights, for the state makes the rules under which the fights take
place.

Since cities are created by state government, they have no more
power than the state government chooses to give them. City governments
can be organized in several ways, and probably no two cities in the country have exactly the same charter. The document that establishes the city
and defines what powers it possesses is the charter.

There are four prevalent plans of city government in the United
States: the weak mayor-council plan, the strong mayor-council plan, the
commission plan, and the city manager plan. Common to both mayor-
council systems is a generally elected mayor, who is chief political and
administrative officer of the city. The councils may be either chosen from
the city at large or elected to represent certain districts, or wards. The
two plans differ, however, in the amount of administrative power that
the mayor possesses. A strong mayor will ordinarily have some control

over the budget process and complete direction of all administrative departments. In a weak-mayor city, budgeting may be strictly a council function, and some of the departments may be controlled by independent commissions or by the council directly. The adjectives "strong" and "weak" refer to the plans themselves and not to the personality characteristics of the mayors. Chicago, for example, is a weak-mayor city. But if the mayor and the head of the political machine are one and the same man, the mayor can often use his political power to augment his rather weak administrative position. Similarly, a strong-mayor system is no guarantee that the mayor may not be bullied by the city council.

The commission plan was first adopted by Galveston, Texas, in 1900 after a hurricane and fire had left the city's administration in chaos. It was very popular with smaller cities for almost two decades but now seems to be dying out. Under the commission plan the head of each city department is elected separately and these men act as a group to form the city council. The plan can work, but there are some obvious administrative problems as far as cooperation between the city departments is concerned. One commissioner, for example, may be more interested in protecting and expanding his own administrative sphere than in the city's business as a whole; and when this situation is coupled with the possibility of feuds among the commissioners, the problems which can arise are obvious. If the water and fire commissioners are political enemies, trouble can pop up at the hydrant level.

The newest city government plan is the city manager system. Under this plan, the city council employs a professionally trained city manager who takes responsibility for all the city's administrative departments. The council is supposed to restrict itself to legislative work and, if dissatisfactions occur, to replace the city manager. This plan has been very successful in small and medium-sized cities, but it deprives the community of the political leadership that the mayor-council system provides.

The strongest argument in favor of the city manager plan is that it takes city government out of politics. In our larger cities this is not necessarily desirable. The professional city manager may be more capable of administering the day-to-day work of government than an elected mayor. But the fact that he is an employee of the city council with no direct political support places him at a disadvantage when he is called upon to reconcile conflicting demands. In the heterogeneous society that is characteristic of our larger cities the resolution of conflicts between various groups is likely to be the major task of the head of city government. No amount of professional training can help a city manager in such situations.

Special Local   •   In most of our states special local gov-
Governments   ernments exist to provide one service
                           for a particular area independently of
                           the other governments that function
there. The most common special government is the school district, but
there are also drainage districts, park districts, water districts, and sewer
districts in many parts of the country. These organizations can usually
levy taxes to provide whatever service they are designed to render.

Rural Government   •   The most common system of rural gov-
                             ernment is the county-township system.
                             Under this system the state is divided
into counties and the counties into a number of townships, usually 16.
Each township elects one commissioner, and the 16 commissioners form
the board of county commissioners, which conducts the administration
of county affairs.

In addition to the commissioners there are also semi-independent
officials who are elected on a county-wide basis—the sheriff, clerk, and
county treasurer being most important. When some section of the county
is incorporated as a city, the city is granted a certain number of commissioners and the size of the county board increases. When an entire
county becomes urbanized, the county may assume new duties and continue as an important unit of government, as in Cook County, Illinois.
Sometimes, as in St. Louis County, Missouri, the county is abandoned as
a unit of government altogether. Sometimes it goes on and on collecting
taxes but provides services for an ever-narrowing area. The county is
not an appropriate form of government for urban areas. It lacks executive direction and represents a form of cultural lag when it persists in a
metropolitan community.

Intergovernmental   •   Possibly the greatest problem that the
Cooperation   federal form of government faces is the
                              fact that social problems overlap politi-
                              cal boundaries as our society becomes
more and more complex. On the local level, metropolitan area development is hampered by a lack of cooperation among cities and suburbs on
such area-wide problems as sewage disposal, drainage, police protection,
fire prevention, and water supply. If each local government attempts to
set up separate agencies to meet these problems, or if some economy-
minded localities simply close their eyes and hope the problems will
disappear, it will be difficult and expensive to coordinate their activities

and reach eventual solutions. More than half our total population now lives in metropolitan areas, and the figure is increasing. Complications set in when metropolitan regions become overcrowded.

Our eastern seaboard is practically one large city stretching from north of Boston to south of Baltimore. Aside from the fact that this heavily industrialized and populated area makes a very attractive target in time of war, the problems of water supply, transportation, waste removal, and recreation created by this enormous concentration of population cross municipal and state boundaries. There have been some successful instances of interstate cooperation, such as the New York Port Authority, which is chartered by the states of New York and New Jersey to develop harbor and transportation facilities in this region. But there are more instances of problems remaining unsolved because participating units of government cannot reach agreement. In Louisville, Kentucky, fire engines stopped at city boundaries because of squabbling over the assessed costs of such service. The states of California, Arizona, and Nevada are in a continual conflict over the waters of the Colorado River. Michigan, Ohio, New York, Wisconsin, and Canada are attempting to block the city of Chicago from using Lake Michigan water to flush out the Chicago River. West Virginia and Oklahoma both have turnpikes which go nowhere because other states have no linking roads. Voluntary cooperation between cities and states is still rare, except when the national government stimulates such cooperation by making federal grants contingent upon it. For example, *The New York Times,* May 15, 1956, reports that California receives an army of perhaps 2,000 homeless children per month who are shunted westward from state to state till they hit the Pacific Coast. When they get to California, that state rounds them up and ships them back to their cities of origin by train, where perhaps they start the journey all over again. Each state rejects their applications for welfare funds because they have not established residence.

Industrial development, national resources programs, highway programs, and various forms of social legislation all involve the solution of problems which overlap state boundaries; and these matters, among others, tend to produce demands for intervention by the federal government. There are two basic techniques whereby the federal government intervenes. The first is the establishment of a federal agency to handle the problem directly, as in the Tennessee Valley Authority, which was established to develop the resources of an entire region. The second is the adoption of a federal grant-in-aid program. Under this system the federal government provides funds for state and local governments subject to certain conditions which tend to induce interstate cooperation.

Old-age assistance, highway and hospital construction, and public housing are examples of areas in which federal tax funds are used to encourage the states to cooperate in a nation-wide program.

Let us summarize briefly the most important points for you to remember about state and local government. The states are separate governments, independent from, but inferior to, the national government. Each of us is a citizen of both a state and the national government at the same time. This is called a federal system. In theory, the powers of the states and the national government do not overlap; in actual practice they do.

The machinery of government for each individual state is determined by its constitution. State constitutions are usually modeled after the federal Constitution, but tend to be longer and more detailed and therefore less flexible in the face of changing needs of a changing society.

States raise money through taxes and through the sale of bonds. States face the same problem that a private business does as far as controlling their expenses is concerned, since they do not control the economy. States can borrow money more cheaply than private individuals because the interest on state and municipal bonds is not taxable.

The state and local levels of government are the most important insofar as political activities are concerned. It is at these levels that we find the most elections and therefore the most favorable climate for the development of party politics.

Local governments are created by the states and are subservient to them. In urban local government we find a variety of different systems of organization, while rural government throughout the United States utilizes the county-township system.

The major problem which state and local governments face today is the existence of demands for their services which cross local and state boundaries. In order to meet these challenges it is necessary that local governments, and the states themselves, cooperate in solving them. The general level of intergovernmental cooperation in the United States is quite low, considering the magnitude of the problem; and there is a strong tendency to resort to national action in order to resolve these difficulties. The federal government occasionally intervenes directly, but more commonly uses its superior financial resources to induce state and local cooperation through grant-in-aid systems.

Federal intervention is a possible solution to the growing complexity of American society, but it is a solution which must inevitably diminish that small degree of independence from the federal government which the states still possess.

TWENTY-SEVEN

The Dynamics

of World

Communism

First we shall consider Communist *theory*, or the Communist creed—the articles of faith which Communists believe in and try to persuade others to believe in. Next, we shall examine Communist *promises*, *appeals*, and *techniques*—what Communist parties and Communist leaders advocate and say they will deliver, and how they proceed in non-Communist nations where they are trying to gain a fol-

591

lowing and eventual control of the government. Finally we shall look at Communism *in action*, or what Communists do when they take over a country.

Communism: •   *The evils of ownership.* The first core
The Theory   article of the Communist faith asserts
                   that those who own the means of pro-
                   ducing and distributing goods own and
control everything in the society. These owners (in the demonology of Communism, the "capitalists") buttress and perpetuate their control by shaping and controlling the law, education, the press and radio and TV, the arts, literature, government, standards of taste, and the whole complex of beliefs of a society. Once in control, the capitalists inevitably grow richer and richer, and the mass of the population grows poorer and poorer until they are inevitably reduced to proletariat who have nothing to sell but their labor. Want, misery, disease, personal degradation, and ever greater exploitation in an ever more hostile environment become their daily lot. Unemployment increases and wages fall. This will happen to the working class everywhere in the industrialized non-Communist world —here in the United States, in Canada, Great Britain, Scandinavia, the Benelux nations, France, Germany, Italy, and in Japan.

This talk about the proletariat, exploitation, and widespread poverty probably sounds a bit odd to you. You live in a prosperous age and country in which a three-bedroom "ranch" house with a 40 foot frontage and, of course, a 20- or 30-year mortgage, and a reasonably new car, possibly also complete with mortgage, seem within the reach of every college graduate and of most talented, ambitious high-school graduates. And whom can you name who does not go to high school? Unless you choose to become something unmarketable like a muralist or a sword-maker, your "career" problem is not likely to be how to find a job but rather how, among a range of jobs, to qualify for one which you can live with and find interesting. Make this test yourself. See whether the following description does not fit you and your family and most of your friends. It fits some 70 or 80 per cent of us.

You have never been hungry for more than an hour or two. You have a fairly roomy, warm place to live and are neatly and respectably dressed. You almost always have small cash for your normal needs, say for a haircut or cigarettes, but your family never seems able to save much money. It has to worry about—or at least keep a close eye on—the next month's flurry of bills. And in order to buy anything as expensive as a new car, it has to cut down the amount of money spent for other things and resort

to close economies and tight budgeting, that are as complicated and frequently as painful to think about as major surgery. But *almost* none of
you are fighting off poverty. There are extremes of wealth in America, of
course. The rich drive Mercedes-Benzes or Lincoln Continentals, but
even members of the "proletariat" drive Fords, Chevrolets, or Plymouths.
Machines have replaced the proletariat in our society. Most of us, and
more and more of us, earn our livings in white-collar work, the professions and semi-professions, and service industries. It is not surprising then
that few, if any, of you young people will be emotionally attracted to
Communism.

How does Communist theory fit the rest of the industrialized non-
Communist world? Everywhere in Western Europe the drudgery of hard
labor is diminishing, productivity is increasing, standards of living of ordinary people are rising, and more and more persons are living free of
poverty. In Britain, for example, workmen's wives are beginning to expect
"American kitchens" in their homes; in France, West Germany, and
northern Italy there are now unmistakable signs of mass prosperity—
traffic jams and parking problems. By 1960 in Western Europe private
consumption is expected to have increased 18 per cent over 1956, and by
1980 it is expected to have doubled.[1] In Japan, the only industrialized nation in Asia, standards of living are much lower than they are in the West,
but the Japanese economy is healthy and the masses of the Japanese
people grow less and less needy. Everywhere in the free industrialized
world production, productivity, and industrial innovation are on the increase. And everywhere in the free industrialized world the mass following of the Communist parties is small, or if large, as in France and Italy,
is static and showing signs of decreasing. This core article of the Communist creed is increasingly out of joint with the world it claims to
describe.

But what of the rest of the world outside of the industrialized nations? In North Africa, in Greece and Turkey, in the Arab lands of the
Middle East, in India, Pakistan, Southeast Asia, South Korea—everywhere
along the periphery of Communist power—the task of survival is hard.
And in all these areas people grow more and more aware that the way
of their forefathers is not the only way. These people have heard vaguely
of the wonderful lands of plenty where everybody is rumored to be rich
and fat and where there are motorcars and movies, where no one is ever
hungry and where there are doctors and sickness is not the normal lot of
people. Let us look at a few people in these countries who are questioning the existing system of production and distribution.

In Turkey there is a schoolmaster in a small town. He is a local leader because he can read and write. He has also been trained in the government's rural development institutes in the city, but the backwardness of the villagers he is supposed to be helping makes his tasks seem hopeless and endless. The government officials in the city talk and talk about industry and roads and buildings, but almost all the improvements are made in areas where the rich already enjoy their elegant houses and foreign cars. The system must go. So he teaches the villagers about the coming revolution, when science and planning will wipe out the hated rich and the hated officials, and the leaders of the poor will run things.

In Jordan there is a refugee, one of tens of thousands. He was once a farmer just outside Jerusalem, but he was forced to flee from his land during the war with the Israelis in 1948. Since then he and his wife and nine children have been living on the Jordan government's grain ration, doing nothing but brooding. Most of the refugees hate and blame the Israelis, but he believes that the rich who control the government are responsible; the system is at fault. He has seen the sculptured and sentried palaces of the great landlords and sheiks who live off rents and oil royalties. The cell leader in his cluster of tents, a Communist, has explained that it is the rich, the landlords, who keep him from his lands.

In Calcutta lives a laborer who works 12 hours a day in a tire factory. Three of his sons work at his side. His family lives in a corner of the plant. He earns 20 rupees, less than $6, a month. With his sons' wages the total comes to less than 85 rupees a month. Still, he is not always hungry anymore. His wife carries their eighth child and still nurses son Sita, who is three years old, and the baby, age one. He does not know that his wife's pelvic bones are dissolving in order to provide calcium for the milk she must give. He knows she is sickly, but sickness is not unusual to him. He knows that tonight he must march on Chowringee Road in a Communist party demonstration and hopes it will not last too long because he is tired. He is always tired. The cell leader will give him a placard to carry, and he will carry it because if he were not a Communist he would not have a job in the factory. And there are no other jobs. The job is good. The party got him the job.

In Singapore a Malayan dockworker unloads the boxes, crates, and machinery for the Singapore millionaires' factories. Yesterday he pumped oil into a freighter by hand, back and forth, back and forth, on the wobble pump for 11 hours with only a short rest for his noon meal. To buy his share of rice and vegetables for the family of his uncle, in whose compound his own family lives, he also works evenings in a Chinese restaurant. Singapore is always hot. In the restaurant a number of large panels are hung from the ceiling and connected by a rope. Outside one end of the dining room he pulls the rope which swings the panels so that they stir the humid air. Pull, slack, pull, slack, on the rope to move the six vanes back and forth, back and forth, to make the customers comfortable. One of his sons, half Malay, half Chinese, is in elementary school learning to read and write. At night, if he is not too exhausted to listen, his son tells him of the wonders of the outside world. Last week he recited some of the things he had learned from his Chinese teacher: "I am a good Chinese. I love Mao Tse-tung. China and Russia are Socialist Workers' States." It is wonderful, this learning for his son! And it is more or less what the Communist gang boss at the docks has said. The system is at fault, and some day Communism will end all the hard labor. Perhaps his son will see it in Singapore. There is talk that in not too many years. . . .

So it is in the unindustrialized and underindustrialized lands. Poverty, frustration, sickness and discontent mixed with hope are everywhere. The situation is convenient for the Communist organizer. His words find ready ears. In these lands his theory is attractive. It seems to make sense—and converts.

The inevitability of class struggle and class warfare. Another part of the Communist creed emphasizes that as the rich grow richer and the poor grow poorer, *class struggle* and *class warfare* are inevitable. The rich will use every instrument of power in the nation—police, armies, law courts, churches—to suppress the poor. The poor will eventually rise up in revolution and then the Communist party will lead them against the rich to create a Marxist-Socialist state which will be temporarily led by the Communist party but which will eventually become a classless society because it will be an ownerless society.

"Class struggle" and "class warfare" are alien terms to most Americans. As we saw in Chapter Nine, there are few social or class characteristics which separate Americans from other Americans; some 70 to 80 per cent of us eat about the same kinds of foods, wear the same kinds of clothes, watch the same kinds of television shows, speak the same standard American English, and use about the same table manners. Our system of social stratification is fluid and mobility is general. We are status conscious, of course. Almost everybody wants to "be somebody," and almost everybody can be, locally and temporarily; but few if any of us can become important people permanently. So few achieve this rare pinnacle that we do not have a ruling class. So we go on and on, re-achieving. Mobility has put the emphasis not on hating those higher in the scale but on working to get ahead ourselves or to help our children get ahead.

In other industrialized non-Communist nations the trend is similar. Social and economic class barriers, particularly in Western Europe, are still evident; and the marks of dress, speech, mode of transport, preference in sports, and preference in point of view, still separate the rich from the workers. But these barriers are everywhere being lowered or breached, and the trend there, as in the United States, is toward greater social homogeneity and greater economic leveling down from the top and up from the bottom, and rapidly. The Communist theory of an intensifying class struggle leading to revolution does not fit these nations any more than it fits ours.

The inevitability of depression. A third article of the Communist faith predicts that even though we seem to be prospering at the moment our prosperity must end in unemployment, starvation, riots, and social chaos because capitalism is inevitably bound to the business cycle of boom, overexpansion, and overproduction, followed by bust and economic stagnation. Are the last two decades of prosperity in the United States merely an unusual and lucky break—a variation from our normal lot?

The Communist prediction would have accurately described the United States or Great Britain or France around 1850 or 1890 or 1920. At those times, public and official taboos prevented the government from doing anything about a depression except "toughing it out." But during the great depression of the 1930's, "toughing it out" became intolerable. Too many millions suffered too much. The taboos were abandoned. Since the 1930's government intervention in the economic process is accepted, expected, and demanded. Today, everywhere in the free industrialized world, all major political parties watch the level of employment and the indicators of economic activity closely and are willing to use, and accustomed to using, government fiscal and monetary controls, government spending, and government planning to maintain full or close to full employment. Economists in Communist countries and Communist party leaders have been predicting hopefully ever since 1945 that the Western world economic boom would collapse in depression and unemployment, but so far it hasn't happened. *If*, however, it does happen, then Communist theory will seem much less implausible to many people, and their faith in our and Western Europe's way of running things will be severely shaken. For a man's job is a terribly important buttress to his whole way of life. If the paychecks stop, if there are no other jobs, if he sees his TV set or car or house taken away from him because he cannot meet the payments, if his children must go to school in shabby clothes, then he will grieve—and hate. *If* it happens. But it does not seem to be in the cards. The cycle of extreme boom and bust seems to have been tamed.

The inevitability of war over foreign markets. Communism also stresses that the struggle for foreign markets will inevitably plunge the capitalist states into war. But this prediction does not seem to fit the industrialized world any better than the other prophecies we have examined. There are rivalries between British, French, American, German, and Japanese firms over markets, but it is exceedingly unlikely that these rivalries will lead to war. Everywhere in the world the military power of the non-Communist industrialized nations is being organized and arrayed with but one fear of attack in mind—attack by Communist Russia. The supposed competitors have become partners in a system of collective defense. "Dollar diplomacy" or "gunboat policy"—terms that describe the use of a nation's armed forces to protect its citizens' or commercial firms' economic stakes abroad —have not fitted the facts of international trade since, at the latest, a generation ago. Private investors and government policy-makers now try to adapt to economic conditions and political necessities in foreign countries instead of coercing and exploiting peoples abroad to suit their own interests. War is too cruel, destructive, and expensive an instrument to use to win or maintain markets. Foreign sales are not that important.

The inevitability of imperialism. Communism categorizes all industrialized non-Communist nations as imperialistic and warns that they will inevitably thrust themselves and their armies, propagandists, businessmen, missionaries, diplomats, and other agents upon undeveloped or underdeveloped peoples and colonize them. The industrialized nations must seek colonies, the Communists believe, in order to make certain of a steady supply of raw materials and guaranteed markets in which they can dispose of their surplus manufactured goods at a high profit. This situation, the Communist organ of doom intones, will inevitably lead to violence, uprisings, and wars between the exploited colonial peoples on the one hand and the exploiting industrialized nations on the other.

The kind of colony-grabbing the Communists predict is a thing of the past. What is left but Antarctica, and the moon? But Communism is correct in expecting and predicting that anti-colonialism will continue, both in existing colonies and in countries recently emerged from colonialism to independence. The idea of one country ruling another has been increasingly on the defensive since 1914. The major colonial powers are Western European nations, and these nations have been much weakened militarily since World Wars I and II and therefore are less able to maintain control of their colonies. Colonial peoples almost everywhere are captivated by the magic appeal of national independence. They are becoming increasingly aware of the military weakness of their rulers and in many lands recently have won their independence. Since World War II Great Britain has lost India, Pakistan, Burma, Ceylon and Malaya. The Dutch were forced to give up the Dutch East Indies, now the Republic of Indonesia, in 1949. France was forced to concede independence to Tunisia and Morocco in the 1950's, lost French Indo-China in 1954, and today is fighting against odds to hold Algeria. Colonialism is increasingly hard to defend today, not only to the colonial and ex-colonial peoples but even to the peoples of the home governments. Frenchmen, for example, are sharply divided over the morality of France's efforts to continue to hold North Africa. To more and more people colonialism is becoming immoral, just as slavery, once legal and morally neutral, became immoral in the nineteenth century. Apologists for colonialism increasingly seem to be defending their own personal economic stakes in colonies. The idea is contrary to principles of individual and political freedom for which the colony-holding nations stand.

Communists support and stimulate anti-colonial and nationalist movements. In every world forum, and in every colony or newly free country where there is an anti-colonial movement, Russia and Communist leaders

The Hungarian Revolt, 1956. *In eastern Europe, native Communist governments are maintained in power only by the force of Russian arms.*

urge action against the Western European "imperialists." To the colonial peoples and those recently emerged from colonialism Russia and Communist leaders seem to be on the side of freedom.

The U.S.S.R. and Communism suffer from one weakness in this argument about imperialism and anti-colonialism. The weakness is Russia's de facto empire in eastern Europe where native Communist governments stay in power only because Russian soldiers and tanks support them. Some of these eastern European peoples have recently attempted to win their freedom and throw out the Russian troops and Communists. This happened in East Germany and Poland in 1953, and in Poland and Hungary in late 1956. Every rebellion except the one in Poland in 1956 was suppressed by Russian soldiers and tanks. As Western European prosperity and freedom grow more and more attractive to eastern European peoples, such rebellions may become more frequent. If that happens Russia and Communists everywhere will be embarrassed and may be divided over whether to stay and shoot or grant political freedom and go home, just as Frenchmen and Britons are divided on the issue of colonialism vs. anti-colonialism. Then the Russian advantage of seeming to have taken the righteous side of the argument will diminish.

The inevitability of conflict between Communist and capitalist nations. Communist theory also asserts that conflict between Communist and non-Communist nations is inevitable; that the two systems are antithetical and hence antagonistic; that any agreements between them and us are only temporary truces in a long battle. The Mikoyan variety of "sweet reasonableness" is only for export. Cooperation and mutual interests are assumed to be out of the question; what one gains the other must lose. This vastly increases the difficulties of coexistence, increases mutual suspicion and fear, and makes it more difficult for any people now satellite to the U.S.S.R. to defect and join the United States and its allies. They can scarcely believe the Russians would tolerate defection—and the suppression of rebellions in East Europe indicates Russia would not—or that the United States or Western Europe would tolerate their Communism if they defected.

These things the Communists believe. Beliefs determine how people interpret what they see, hear, and read about. In democratic societies where a political opposition and a free press publish the faults and shortcomings along with the accomplishments and successes of a society and of groups and individuals in the society, Communists can usually find some examples of discrimination and prejudice and inequity. They exploit these examples in their press and through other media to convince un-

committed peoples that such episodes are typical of the conditions in the
Western world, and in doing so reaffirm their beliefs about us. The result
is more than misunderstanding of the West; it is a habit of mind, an inextricably intermixed body of sincerely held errors and deliberately con-
trived falsehoods, and it is exceedingly difficult to alter.[2] Moreover, because they believe that the Western world is moving in certain inevitable
patterns, they organize and work hard to undermine the Western world
as it now is and to bring about the conditions they believe should prevail.

<table>
<tr><td>Communism:
Methods, Promises,
and Appeals</td><td>•</td><td>*The web of government and the goal
of the revolutionist.* Every established
system of government seeks to base its
authority in the consciences and values
of its people. The fundamental beliefs</td></tr>
</table>

and values and ideal behavior patterns are taught to children by their
parents and teachers, and are reaffirmed, reiterated, and reflected throughout their childhood and adult life by mass media and by the public behavior and public utterances of leaders. The basic values are "given" in
each culture, and although the patterns and rules and values differ, they
are constantly reaffirmed and glorified in every society.

Politics differs greatly from revolution. Politics is a struggle between
groups who are seeking office and power to make minor changes. The of-
fice-seekers merely want to replace the office-holders and change some of
their policies; they do not want to bring down the existing order of doing
things. But the Communist revolutionary seeks to undermine and topple
the existing regime and system. He tries to produce a *crisis of conscience*
in masses of people which will cause them to question and to rebel against
the things they have always been taught to believe in and have always
assumed to be right. Further, he seeks to take advantage of such crises.

The technique of agitation. There have been many short-lived revolutionary doctrines—anarchism, syndicalism, Decembrism, and the radical-
ism of the Industrial Workers of the World. Communism survives and
threatens to succeed because of its techniques.

The Communist is a skilled *agitator.* Lenin defined agitation as "maximum exacerbation of existing symbols of loyalty." The Communist party
is watching continuously for signs of stress and trouble in the societies
which it is trying to subvert. When it finds them, it acts to increase trouble
and disorder in order to compel the authorities to use force to restore
order. It does this because the repeated use of force by the government

will turn people against the government, and even more important, against the system of government.

In America in 1948, for example, Henry Wallace was running for the office of president of the United States as candidate of the Progressive party. The Progressive party and Wallace favored a foreign policy of concessions to Russia, and this principle and others attracted American Communists to the Progressive banner. In Columbia, Missouri, a conservative city in a conservative region, the Communists worked hard to get Wallace to come and speak—and they also worked hard to stir up opposition to his appearance. They succeeded in both. When Wallace spoke, Communist agitators in the audience tried to stir up violence by booing and heckling him, and did succeed in making the crowd quite hostile. In Italy in 1949, to cite another example, North Atlantic Treaty Organization military supplies began to arrive from America. The Communist party opposed the shipments and called a strike and mass demonstration against the unloading of the first shiploads of weapons. The Italian port government forbade the demonstration and the Italian police were alerted for trouble. Ignoring police orders, the Communists went ahead with the demonstration, and at one point actually succeeded in blocking the movement of supplies. The police moved in to disperse the demonstrators, a few shots were fired, and a demonstrator was killed. That day and for days following, the Communists again demonstrated by parading the corpse in its coffin as a "victim of police brutality."

In dealing with those who do not share their beliefs and values, Communists are not bound by taboos against killing, lying, and deceit. Ties of friendship and loyalty to the non-Communist nation in which they live do not restrain them. They either regard our standards of morality and virtue as handy tools for the capitalists to use to keep the poor proletariat in its place, or dismiss them as sentimental nonsense. A Communist may behave morally as we understand the word but only for the sake of momentary gain. Because they are unrestrained by moral taboos, Communists can operate ruthlessly and often with the advantage that their actions will not be anticipated. In 1953 India was threatened by famine. From the United States boatloads of wheat were shipped to Bombay, where the grain was transferred to freight cars. Communists swung onto the cars just after the trains pulled out of Bombay and painted "WHEAT, GIFT TO THE PEOPLE OF INDIA FROM THE PEOPLE OF THE SOVIET UNION" on the cars. All the way across India American wheat carried false propaganda credit to the U.S.S.R. Immediately after World War II thousands of packing cases of food and supplies sent to east European nations by the United Nations Relief and Rehabilitation

Administration were repainted and relabeled to give the impression that the U.S.S.R. had donated them. During the negotiations at the end of the Korean War, Communist China charged that America had dropped infected flies on China by airplane to poison the crops and the people. America denied the charge. It is now known that the Communists invented the charge in part for propaganda purposes and in part to goad the Chinese people into a coordinated mass sanitation campaign to clean up China and kill flies and rats and remove garbage heaps. Journalists were present at the site of truce negotiations in Korea, though not at the actual conference tables. Among them was a British Communist. While talking to his press colleagues he kept snatching at flies, popping them into bottles, and saying, "I must take these back to our laboratories to be checked for your bloody germs." He was acting out the Party line. Truth aside, his object was to make more plausible to the other journalists the false charges of germ warfare.

The technique of infiltration. The Communist is also a skilled *infiltrator*. Concealing the fact that he is a Communist, he joins and seeks to rise to positions of authority within organizations or groups that enjoy public sympathy, such as veterans' and civil rights organizations. He also seeks to enter and achieve status in such organizations as the police and armed forces, and the administrative offices which control them, or in labor unions, especially unions whose members operate public utilities, railroads, docks, and shipping. Once entrenched in key spots such as these, the Communist uses his influence to benefit his party.

Very few Communists have ever succeeded in rising to responsible positions in the United States government, and American unions have worked hard to purge Communists from their offices and ranks. But Communist efforts have been more successful in countries where policemen or soldiers receive low wages and where working conditions are wretched and morale is low. Undermining the police and armed forces of a country is a double accomplishment to the Communists: a source of state authority is weakened and captured and substantial supplies of arms fall into Communist hands. In the Chinese Communist uprisings in Canton and Shanghai during the late 1920's, for instance, the police were subverted before the uprisings began. In Indonesia during 1948 and 1949 Communists who were army officers used their units for the Communist party and against the democratic government. In Russia in 1917 the Petrograd garrisons were subverted and joined the Communists. In France in 1946 Communists in the Ministry of the Interior, which controls the police, and their party comrades in the labor unions, were able, by coordinating their actions, to cripple the economy of France for as long as six months.

Communist propaganda techniques. The Communist is also a skilled *propagandist*. To erode and weaken the symbols of authority is not enough to make a revolution; Communists promise substitute solutions and new symbols for people to believe in which they say are "just" and "historically inevitable."

Jobs. The Communist promises that through economic planning the threat of unemployment can be eliminated forever. Long-lasting mass unemployment, as we have seen, no longer appears to be so grave a threat as it once was, but man judges the world not so much by how it is, and will probably be, as by how it *has* been for him. The great depression of the 1930's is still recent enough for millions of persons to remember it vividly in terms of personal failures and personal losses. The Communist's promise of a planned economy and his assurance of secure jobs will appeal less and less in the industrialized nations if prosperity continues and continues and memories of the 1930's grow dimmer and dimmer. But in the underindustrialized world, where unemployment or underemployment are not part of any cycle but the normal lot of millions of people, this Communist promise has a magic appeal about it.

Communist propaganda, like Communist agitation against the established order, is free of the restraints of fair play, good faith, decency, and truth. Communists promise anything. In a recent election in India, for example, Communists told landless village laborers that when the Communists came into power they would give them farms. They asked each to pick out the farm he wanted, then issued receipts which they promised to redeem when they took over the country.

"White is black. Black is white. Night is day—"

603

The promise to abolish the price tag. The Communists also promise to take the dollar sign out of life by doing away not only with unemployment incidental to the business cycle, but with the whole system of ownership, pricing, and marketing. Men, they say, will work and produce, and the state will allocate goods among men according to their abilities and their needs.

How can Communists persuade people to strive and work if with what they can earn they cannot buy or own or enjoy much of anything? We will discuss later what the Communists do where they are in power, but what they promise as a substitute for the pleasures of material things are the *joys of collective ownership.* The farmer in the collective has a stake and share in the whole farm collective, they say. The worker in the nationalized factory has a share in the whole factory because the whole Communist public owns the factory. Does it work? Evidence from Russia and eastern Europe indicates that it does not. Consider the collective housing of most Russian urban workers, for example, where the rooms are family rooms but the kitchens and bathrooms are shared by all. Observer after observer reports that the family rooms are spotless and neat, but the collectively used rooms are the dirtiest in the buildings. Make this test yourself. How often have you gone into a public institution, say a park, and walked into the public washroom and noticed that it was filthy? Did you ever roll up your sleeves, say to yourself, "I have a stake in this!" and clean up the mess? We will see in later pages that in practice collective ownership is simply a change of ownership. But even if collective ownership does not create any new satisfactions, the promise to take the dollar sign out of life forever has enormous appeal.

Special appeals to intellectuals and would-be intellectuals. The Communists promise to order life and society in terms of unspecified "higher" values. This promise has great appeal to intellectuals and would-be intellectuals. *Would-be intellectuals* are people like the obscure clerk in the quality bookstore who is starving to death in a genteel way yet rates himself above the struggle for money, like the perennial candidate for still one more academic degree, like the writer whose manuscripts somehow never get published—the many thousands who have tried and tried and continue to try to be intellectuals and do not make the grade and feel that somehow the system, the environment, "mass tastes," or other vague evils are to blame for their failures. *Intellectuals* are *idea men.* They are people who think and write and speak for a living, who provide the ideas and conceptions a society has of itself and furnish the framework in terms of which the future is discussed and projected.

Being an intellectual has its own frustrations; dealing in ideas and

words one never sees any product. Unlike administrative work, running a
streetcar, cutting or packing steel parts, running tests in a laboratory, or
any of the many, many tasks, from highly skilled to unskilled, which most
of us do for a living, the intellectual works with that most evanescent of
commodities—ideas. He is largely alone; he has no discernible, responsive,
immediate audience. He produces neither products nor decisions. Changing an institution is hard. Trying to change a society is even harder. Even
when his ideas eventually, perhaps decades later, are taken up, they are
seldom traced back to him. Because the intellectual is usually thinking
ahead of most of his audience, many intellectuals feel frustrated by mass
tastes and mass ideas and mass beliefs. And the promise of the Communists to order society in terms of "higher" values seems to appeal to
quite a few intellectuals in every land because their values are also
"higher" values.

Communist theory does not specify clearly what its "higher" values
are, but Marxism makes great pretense to being scientific, and often argues
its case in complex intellectual-sounding language. "Objectivity" is one
of its most used words. Anyone who identifies with Communism and becomes skilled in using its dialectical jargon is able to glory in the supremacy of his intellectual equipment. He feels that *he knows*. Marxism
equips him with a theory which, rather like conversational Freudian
psychology, is never susceptible to proof or disproof, and has a term or
cluster of terms to account for everything. As a leading political scientist,
Harold D. Lasswell, has put it: "Dialectical materialism is the reading of
private preferences into universal history, the elevating of personal aspirations into cosmic necessities, the remolding of the universe in the pattern
of desire, the completion of the crippled self by incorporating the symbol
of the triumphant whole." [3] This explains Communism's appeal to would-be
intellectuals.

Intellectuals seek to effect changes—social, economic, and political
changes. Communism has particular appeal for intellectuals of the political left who have been redesigning society in ink for decades, because
the Communists *have* changed social, economic, and political institutions.
In Russia, and in recent years in other Communist nations adjacent to
Russia, the revolution *is*—it exists. A number of countries have had revolutions—England in 1688, America in 1776, and France in 1789, for example.
But Russia's revolution was in 1917, yesterday so to speak, recent enough
for many proponents of social changes to regard it as a revolution against
what they regard as the problems of their own time.

The claim that Communism is progressive and enlightened. Communism appeals to some intellectuals, especially to those of the political

left, with promises to eliminate social injustices and human backwardness. But more than that, its adherents assert that where Communism is in
power it *has* eliminated them. For example, Communist propaganda insists that in Russia and under Communism there is no religious or racial
or ethnic discrimination. Actually, anti-Semitism and anti-Moslemism are
widespread in Russia. Yet almost no word of this leaks out. All publications and all broadcasts are rigidly controlled to suppress anything critical
of Communist performance. Propaganda beamed abroad denies or con-
ceals Communism's shortcomings and exaggerates its accomplishments.
Russian officials can and do control the impressions which visitors to
Russia receive by leading them on carefully planned tours. If areas within
Russia become discreditable, they are closed to visitors. For example, in
1931 and 1932 Russia experienced a major famine. In its propaganda
abroad Russia and its Communist parties again and again denied there
was any famine. Visitors to Russia at that time were barred from the
famine-ridden areas.

The promise of a short cut to industrialization. Communism promises
efficiency. It promises to do away with what Marx once called "the idiocy
of rural life"—the backbreaking labor of pre-industrial hand agriculture
and hand manufacture. It claims that it is able, through centralized economic planning, to speed up the building of factories and the production
of steel and automobiles and clothing and food and shiny consumer goods.
The Communist tells the poor man that he deserves a better life, and that
Communism is the only fast way to that better life.

Communism has vastly speeded up industrialization in Russia. But
what Communism does accomplish is greatly exaggerated by the Communist parties and Communists everywhere. Everything that is accomplished is claimed as a planned Communist achievement. In America, for
example, if a university adds a new classroom building to its plant the
national government does not point to this is a "mighty proof of America's democratic strength." If a Buick dealer in Iowa enlarges the garage
and maintenance space back of his showroom, the government does not
send out this news over the Voice of America as another proof of American economic superiority. But from Russia and other Communist states
come all claims to all accomplishments, each presented to maximize the
effect. Housing units, for example, are counted and presented not in terms
of apartments or homes but in terms of *meters* of space occupied, so that
the total will seem higher. Statistics and figures are manipulated. If a
canal is dug, a railroad built, an electric line strung, each and all become
Marxist Socialist Achievements. If a Russian team wins a basketball game
the victory becomes a victory for Marxist Socialism. There are even

propaganda phenomena like Socialist Woman Sniper Ludmilla Pawli-
tchenko who shot 137 Germans with Socialist marksmanship during World
War II and was sent on a propaganda showcase tour of the Western World
to describe the process to the Western press with Socialist realism.[4] There
is even Socialist love, which is reported to proceed (officially at any rate)
about like this:

Scene: A stage set as small park. A boy and a girl are seated on a
           bench. Behind them is the director of the play. They are
           rehearsing.
Boy: It is fortunate we can meet. There are so many things to do!
           Tuesday the Young Communist League meeting, tomorrow
           night the Self Criticism Group Executive Committee is meet-
           ing to plan for Thursday night's Worker Evaluation meet-
           ing at the factory—
Girl: (to boy) Have you fulfilled your Work Norm today?
           (to director) How can I speak such a line? I love him!
Director: How can you know you love him if you don't know whether
           he has fulfilled his Work Norm?

The impressive facts of Russian industrialization—a 10 per cent increase annually in recent years—and the repeated and rarely refuted exag-
gerations have a profound appeal in much of the world. While they appeal
to intellectuals of leftist political parties in Europe, they have an even
greater appeal to the intelligentsia of non-Communist underdeveloped
countries in Asia. Where poverty is widespread, as in underdeveloped
non-Communist Asia, there is little in tax money. What little there is
must be carefully used. Everywhere in these lands *industrialization* is
believed to be the key to higher standards of living. The Western European and American economic system of constructing a plant here, making
an investment there, making changes in terms of consumer response, and
so on—in short, the trial-and-error method of largely unplanned economic
development—seems largely unattainable and too slow and too wasteful.
In these lands private enterprise is seldom private and rarely enterprising.
The demand is for government-planned economic growth. The Communist economic system seems to promise the magic of a method that
works in Russia, insofar as they know. In these lands the practical help,
the money and skilled technicians, come from America more often than
from Russia, but despite this the beneficiaries often reserve their admiration for Marxist theory and Communist economic planning.

The appeal of this Communist claim is not likely to diminish unless the free non-Communist industrialized democracies of the world help the underdeveloped nations to build the basic communications and power-producing plant—road networks, key industries, power grids, and occasionally a port or a large dam—to trigger the process of self-sustaining economic growth.

The psychological advantages of Communist propaganda. Communism has still another appeal, especially in underdeveloped nations. Underdeveloped nations are underdeveloped in many ways, including their sophistication about propaganda. Most of their citizens cannot read or write. In India and China, for example, 80 per cent of the people are illiterate; in Indonesia, 65 per cent. In these countries Communist propaganda is etched in black and white; it is direct; it is free of subtleties. It identifies those who it claims are the villains—the rich and the government officials; it identifies those who it claims are the heroes—Communists. It has all the psychological appeal of a fight; and everybody loves or loves to see a fight and everybody can understand a fight. Propaganda in support of democracy as we know it is psychologically pale, complex, and unemotional, in comparison. What is democracy as a process? It is talking, discussing, reasoning, weighing alternatives, making compromises, following parliamentary procedure, counting votes, and slowly edging toward a group decision. Ask yourself which you would rather see or hear about: a good fight (say the biff, bang, socko stuff of Westerns) or a committee meeting on a complicated matter.

The constant hammering against the *status quo,* concentrating on troubles in a society, infiltrating key control organizations such as the police, armed forces, and labor unions, endless propagandizing about the magic of Russian Communist achievements and promises, focusing hatred upon the local symbols of authority—these are the techniques that make it possible for minorities of a few thousand dedicated men, perhaps with only a few hundred guns, to seize power in times of crisis in unstable and poverty-ridden countries.

Is there danger of Communist subversion in America? No. There is danger of espionage and sabotage, but the United States has organizations such as the Federal Bureau of Investigation to root out spies and saboteurs, and there are laws under which to prosecute them. Are the nations of Western Europe in danger? Some, but the threat is diminishing; and if economic prosperity and growth continue the danger will continue to diminish. Is there danger in the underdeveloped nations where unemployment and poverty have always been and continue to be man's lot? Yes. There the danger is great.

Communism's appeal to the marginal man. To what kinds of people does Communism particularly appeal? In *all* countries to intellectuals, especially to those of the political left; to members of oppressed minorities; to social deviants of all types who do not fit into the system. In *underdeveloped* countries it also appeals to those who have known better times and *have lost* a job, lands, or prestige; and to those who have *risen* above the level of mass poverty but are frustrated in their aspirations to rise further; and to those who are dimly *aware* of chances to better their lot but are somehow barred from realizing their hopes. In other words, Communism appeals to people like the Turkish schoolmaster, the refugee in Jordan, the Calcutta factory worker, and the Singapore dockworker. The most fertile ground for the Communist agitator is not static pre-industrial societies but pre-industrial societies that are just beginning to explore, fumblingly, the processes of industrialization, where economic and social changes are beginning to undermine the old established cultures and habits.

The dilemmas confronting the industrialized democracies of Europe and North America are complex. We must "do something" to help trigger economic development and industrialization in the underdeveloped nations of the Middle East, North Africa, Southwest Asia, Southeast Asia, and the Far East. But by the very fact of doing something we begin or speed the shattering of traditional culture and create tensions and troubles that Communism can exploit. The underdeveloped countries—not, as Marx saw it, the industrialized nations—are Communism's principal targets and the industrialized West's greatest challenge.

Communism in Power: The Practices • We have discussed the theory of Communism and the propaganda claims of Soviet Russia abroad. Now we shall see what happens when Communists take over a country. We will take the Soviet Union as our principal example because Communists have been in power there since 1917.

A society on the march. What is a government normally concerned with? First of all, with its security against other nations, but after that, with benefiting its citizens. Whether it is an industrial democracy like the United States or a pre-industrial state such as Ethiopia, it is much concerned with establishing what is accepted as justice and with the system of producing and distributing goods to benefit its citizens. It is interested primarily in the present and the immediate future.

The Soviet Union, on the other hand, resembles an army on the march more than it does a civil society. The citizens are controlled. The Communist party of the Soviet Union controls policy, and the police and armed forces enforce its policies and prevent internal conflicts from developing. The government controls the economic process, deciding what kinds of products will be produced, how much will be produced, who will get them, and who will get credit for producing them. The government controls all interpretations and explanations of what is happening, because it controls all newspapers, magazines, broadcasts, and meetings. Even history, the record of what *has* happened, is rewritten as the government decrees. The government controls all personnel; it is not healthy to resign from a job; wages and work hours per week are decreed, not negotiable.

With such a system of total control it is possible to hold down the standard of living of millions of citizens, even to lower it, by channeling raw materials and production into heavy capital goods industries and into armaments. In other words, instead of consuming steel by producing automobiles for citizens to drive about in, Russia diverts her steel into machines to make more machines, into more steel mills, and into weapons. The object of a Communist nation is the *endless growth* of the state—the economic and military strength of the nation. Ever since the revolution Russians have been forced to get by on a very low standard of living in relation to production, so as to make Russia more powerful in the future. Consumer goods have accounted for only a small portion of total production while the industrial plant has been expanded rapidly. Russia is trying for world supremacy, and the technique is to grow and grow industrially. She will continue to give the United States and our industrialized Western allies a hard race.

Who gets what? But what of the theory of Communism? Does Communism, once in power, eliminate the owners or capitalists? Yes. And what does it substitute? State ownership, or state capitalism. Does state capitalism eliminate the hated rich? It produces a new class of rich, the managerial class who run the government. In every organizational hierarchy in Russia the difference between what those at the top get and what those at the bottom get is great and growing greater. By pushing consumption down and holding it down and by rewarding the bureaucracy ever more handsomely, the system creates, among the mass of its urban workers, the very kind of proletariat it promises to eliminate. It uses the very instruments of worker bargaining—labor unions—to deny the workers the power to bargain and to coerce them into meeting every demand the state makes for more output at lower wages.[5]

Promises and non-fulfillment: jobs, and the price tag. To what extent does Communism fulfill its promises? It promises jobs. Does it eliminate most unemployment? Yes—that is one thing all totalitarian states can do. But, unlike other industrialized societies, Communism provides the jobs but takes away most of the wages. Does Communism take the "dollar sign" out of life? It allocates and distributes goods with only secondary regard for its citizens' needs and wants and does away with the market test of what people want by decreeing what they may have. And what people have had to date is largely the psychological satisfaction of doing without anything much for the sake of future Russia. But more promises are in the air—promises of more consumer goods, promises that soon the Russians will be eating better than Americans.

The claim to be scientific. Communism as a body of social theory that claims to explain man and his behavior is not scientific but pseudo-scientific. It has failed conspicuously to predict the course of events in the non-Communist world. For example, Russian economists have been predicting ever since 1945 that the economic collapse of America and Western Europe was imminent, yet it hasn't happened.

But Communism in power does encourage research in science, especially in applied science. Marxist leaders value science highly; we might even say they worship it. The system of concentrating all authority in the Politburo, the inner executive committee of the Communist party, makes it possible to force students, trained men, money, and materials into channels to speed up scientific research, applications of known science, and scientific training. Examples will show that Russia forces the pace in science faster than non-Communist countries.

(1) Enrollment of students in *technicums,* which are semi-professional schools, mostly scientific or technical, has increased fantastically from 189,000 in 1927 to 1,961,000 in 1957. In institutions of higher education (colleges or universities) the figures rose from 169,000 in 1927 to 1,867,000 in 1957. By way of contrast, in the United States enrollments in equivalent colleges rose from 1,114,000 in 1927 to 2,996,000 in 1957—a higher total today but a much lower rate of increase.[6]

(2) Russian students are required to work more, learn more, and concentrate upon the sciences more than American students. In what corresponds to American junior high schools such core scientific subjects as

physics, chemistry, mathematics, and biology are required. School is held six days a week, 210-213 days a year; in America it is held five days a week, 178-179 days a year. Homework, tests, and oral recitations in Russian schools would be considered rigorous judged by prevailing American standards.

During the past ten years Russia has successfully applied known scientific principles in many fields, and she equals, or excels, the industrialized countries of Western Europe and America in the production of scientific instruments, rocket engineering and the launching of earth satellites, weapons development generally, giant jet airliners, cyclotrons, electronic computers, earth science, and crystallography. And Russia is almost as advanced technically as America and the Western European countries in other fields—metal-working and heavy industry generally, for example. Without doubt, "Russian scientists and technologists . . . are highly competent and productive. They constitute a challenge which we cannot ignore." [7]

There is another advantage inherent in Communism's strong orientation toward applied science. Very often techniques and methods of improving man's lot are ignored because they go against habits or cultural taboos. These cultural lags exist in all societies, but they are most frequently found in the underdeveloped countries. On the island of Java, in Indonesia, for example, millions of peasants still harvest rice with a palm or thumb sickle, stalk by stalk, because they believe that to do it by more efficient methods would make their Rain Goddess angry. In large areas of Southeast Asia there is cultural resistance to vaccination. In Communist-run countries these lags, *except insofar as they exist in the minds of the top rulers,* are abolished by decree. The rulers decide what is "good" for the citizens.

The diminishing advantage of the fact of revolution. The longer the Communist regime continues in power in Russia, the less its "glorious revolutionary beginnings" make sense in terms of the present at home or abroad. The year 1917, though recent, recedes inevitably into history. Within Russia the civil bureaucrats replace the once-zealous revolutionaries. Externally Russia becomes less and less a novelty and more and more a nation in which and from which certain patterns of demands, repressions, and techniques recur. The United States and Western European countries continue to make technical and industrial progress and rapid social adjustments to new techniques by peaceful means. And the whole discussion, idea, and vocabulary of massive social change by revolution becomes less meaningful.

The claim to be progressive and enlightened. Communism claims that it eliminates social injustices. It claims that where it rules unspecified "higher values" are supreme. It claims to improve the lot of the common man. It accomplishes none of these. It does the reverse.

Its successes, the phenomenal growth of the Russian state, can be traced to coercion of the citizenry, common men and intellectuals both. Its successes result, first, from the concentration of authority and the development of a coercive apparatus of control, and secondly, from an internal dynamic cycle unique to Communism in power, an internal cycle of terror, clemency, terror, clemency, ever repeated.

The goaded society. Political scientists identify three primary goals that men in industrial societies tend to pursue more or less simultaneously: income, safety, and respect. The typical modern man wants a little something in his pocket and in his home, physical safety for himself and his own, and a good name.[8] As we saw earlier in the book, man has many and varied goals, but these may be considered primary to politics and government in modern society. In Communist countries these human goals are manipulated in order to keep the people striving. Work and performance norms are set high, but official commands to struggle hard to produce are not enough. Because wages are kept very low and fixed administered prices are prohibitively high, after a time there appear signs of a mass slow-down. People begin longing for a little more consumer goods and a little leisure and fun. When this begins, party zealots begin agitating against "slackers," "Trotskyites," "wreckers," "deviationists," "criminal abusers of state property," and other Communist scapegoats. In a Communist state the vocabulary of abuse and condemnation is vast. If the slowdown has been widespread, and if the state is in special need of stimulating output, there will be more than name-calling by professional agitators. The process will grow and grow. There will be arrests and public trials at which the accused confess all the sins with which they have been charged. Simultaneously, there will be a tightening of limited liberties; writings and public propaganda will follow more closely the line of explanation from the top. Labor unions, youth associations, women's organizations, army unit political indoctrination officers—all such organizations and persons will meet to explain the new crackdown and to exhort their captive audiences of workers, students, youths, women, or soldiers to be ever on their guard against malingerers, doubters, slackers, and counter-revolutionaries. The police will become active and a few deviants will disappear. This process galvanizes everybody into hard-driving action and production soars. But, as the process of terror and accusation and purge goes on and on, it too grows and grows until it begins to resemble a witch hunt which threatens to liquidate too many useful people and to disorganize the populace or a large part of it by sheer fright.

When almost everybody is frightened and over-organized in support of and obedience to the current purge, listlessness reappears. Efficiency and production drop off. Meetings to discuss the newly condemned and to swear loyalty and zeal to the latest decree have begun to supersede normal work. At this moment the time is ripe for a switch in technique from terror to clemency.

The period of clemency or grace goes something like this. The zealots, the accusers, are now accused of "excesses." Clemency is proclaimed from the top, formerly by Stalin himself, now by Khrushchev himself. Some trivial concessions or freedoms are proclaimed, usually in fields remote from political or economic matters, such as literary criticism or archeology. More consumer goods may be promised. The police are quieted down. Procedural rights of citizens in law courts may be reaffirmed. People breathe freely again and regard their neighbors with less suspicion. They praise their rulers for having corrected the errors and excesses of their former advisors who are now in disgrace, and for returning to their former tolerant ideals. Morale again soars, and production increases.

Then, once again, slowly, this situation eventually leads to a new relaxation of effort, a lowering of discipline, and a decline in output. Persons again begin to yearn for more consumer goods, shopworkers again begin to steal a bit of this and that from the plant to sell it or barter it in black markets. Absenteeism increases. The human desires for a little less poverty, a little leisure, and a little dignity are expressing themselves. Then the screws are tightened again and the cycle is begun anew.[9]

This dynamic of terror, clemency, terror, clemency goads the populace into continuous striving and sacrifices. This technique, together with the concentration of authority we have already described, produces a directed and hard-striving society. It produces for the society and its rulers, but thus far at least it has not greatly bettered the lot of the common man. Not only have they not gained appreciably in a material sense, but many have grown old in constant fear of being arrested by the police for something trivial and then charged with some heinous crime against the state such as "criminal abuse of state property." All have been directed, organized, ordered about, and watched. Where is respect or self-respect under such a regime?

And how is the Communist happy land for intellectuals? If they use their intellect in the required directions they are rewarded with high status, adulation, and high income. If, for example, a playwright writes a play that properly reflects the party line it will be performed simultaneously in all the major cities. If a choreographer distorts a ballet into a Marxist-Leninist theme, his work may bring him a Lenin Prize. If a scientist works on some neutral non-political matter such as the conductivity of metals, he may be supported and subsidized lavishly. But let them not tamper with the party line! Let them not "get ideas." Let them not write novels like *Doctor Zhivago*, whose author, Boris Pasternak, gladly accepted the Nobel Prize for Literature in 1958 and then abjectly rejected it, writing in *Pravda* that he had not realized his book (banned in Russia) could be construed as "a work directed against the October Revolution and the founders of the Soviet system."

"Thank you!" "Thank you!" "Thank you!"

Communism creates a hard-striving society, but a society that is *striving toward what?* This brings us to the last promise of Communism, that it is a short cut to industrialization.

The claim of efficiency. A nation under Communism is striving hard toward the goals that its top leaders believe in and determine for it, and by the means they dictate. The system is as efficient as these goals are valid and these means are efficient. If we judge from statistics of industrial growth alone, then these means are efficient indeed.

The industrial potential of Russia and its allies is not as great as that of the West. But the Communist bloc—largely through the tremendous strides in Russia—has been slowly closing the gap. Compared with tiny percentages in the years before World War II, the Communist bloc today produces one-fourth of the world's output of steel, one-third of its coal, one-fifth of its electric power. In Russia alone, steel production has jumped from 4.3 million metric tons in 1927-28 to a projected 59 million metric tons this year. U.S. steel production for 1958 is estimated at 77 million metric tons—or about 50 per cent of capacity.[10]

The last sentence in that paragraph indicates lack of efficiency, waste of potential, in our own economy. Certainly this is one great problem of our type of enterprise, for this figure reflects the recession of 1958. But the Soviet system has its own kind of waste, its own blind spots and errors. They stem largely from the very thing that makes the society efficient in some directions—the total nature of state power.

Such a society risks no delays, encounters no internal opposition, never needs to compromise; it only needs to march. It is controlled and directed. But if the head man makes a mistake, who dares call it to his attention? No one. There is very little adaptability or capacity to correct errors and change policy in such a system. It can be forced to waste resources, to take risks, to accept losses solely because at the top the head man, or the handful of head men who are the Politburo, are in error. The terribly inhuman and costly errors of Stalin have been described in full by Khrushchev himself, but the system's tendency to magnify errors has not changed. For example, Khrushchev believes that corn can be grown in northern Russia where the growing season is short and rainfall negligible. Because Khrushchev is boss, tens of thousands of persons were recruited and moved to a barren part of northern Russia, along with seeds, tractors, construction materials, agricultural gear, livestock, and

The Communist System. *A small, tightly knit power elite rules the Russian state, backed up by a rigid ideology that leaves no room for opposition to official policies.*

other necessary supplies, only to plant and grow corn which did not produce ears of corn but only corn stalks. The growing season was too short,
too cold, and too dry. Farmers from Iowa could have told Khrushchev
in advance that his corn-growing project would fail, for the southernmost
point at which the millions of new acres were planted was about as far
north as St. Paul, Minnesota. Peasants in the Soviet republic of Kazakhstan
could have told Khrushchev the same thing—but didn't, or didn't dare.
And so the nation was ordered to err.

There are similar errors and blind spots in many areas of the economy. Production quotas are centrally controlled and administered and
all activity is directed toward meeting these quotas. This situation leads
to "storming," or an uneconomic rush at the end of each month to schedule easy orders, coerce employees, and delay repairs. The more intense
the "storm" to meet a quota at the end of one month, the longer the
delay for repairs at the beginning of the next month. Storming in one
interdependent industry results in poor supply in another and in more
storming, a kind of business cycle effect of rising and falling effort controlled by the necessity to meet the quotas, because the quota is decreed
to be all important and fixed by the top men.

Since Russia launched the first earth satellite in October of 1957 no
one has seriously questioned her efficiency in applied science. In *pure*
science, however—scientific research that advances the frontiers of human
knowledge and that later, perhaps decades later, may be discovered to
have useful applications—Soviet scientists find that the system is often
a handicap. Stevan Dedijer, a Communist physicist and research director
in Yugoslavia—until he published this report—explains why:

> Secrecy in science and the domination of ideological motives very
> often bring, among other negative consequences ... a flowering of
> pseudoscience and very costly applied research and construction proj-
> ects destined to die stillborn under a veil of secrecy. All such occur-
> rences in the Soviet Union are hidden under the veil of the dictatorship.
> And only after one has had the freedom to investigate and has gotten
> the necessary evidence to integrate over a period of time the loss to
> Soviet research and society incurred because of the lack of open chan-
> nels of communication in actual scientific work or in formulating the
> research policy, and has been able to compare with this the results
> achieved, can one get a true picture of the efficiency of dictatorship in
> developing research. What little evidence is allowed to filter out makes
> one suspect that the waste is considerable.[11]

The Russian lag in pure science is shown quantitatively in the distribution of the world's most honored scientific awards, the Nobel Prizes. An article in the *Bulletin of the Atomic Scientists* in 1957 declared, "None of the greatest advances in pure science—physics, chemistry, or biology— originated in the Soviet Union," and pointed to America's 47 Nobel prizes in these fields as compared to Russia's one award. We must point out here that the 1958 Nobel prize in physics went to three Russian scientists, and may be followed closely by others. But the disproportion in prizes for pure research that has thus far existed indicates, as the article says, "that Soviet education, however well it prepares a future scientist or engineer for competent work in his field in research or industry, is not very conducive to awakening his mind for the unorthodox, fearless, critical thinking, which is required for really epochal discoveries (e.g., evolution, relativity, quantum theory)." [12]

Aside from the recurrent errors inherent in the system, the losses to the society because of things *forbidden* by the top men are probably immeasurable. For example, the field of law has been liberalized since 1955. But it has happened before, and each time the Soviet authorities have discovered that they cannot permit the legal system to develop an independent judiciary, procedural rights, a general presumption of innocence of the accused, and a system of nonpolitical penalties proportionate to offenses without undermining the required absolute obedience to Soviet authorities. And when this was discovered in the past, obedience came first and legal liberties were eliminated. The loss to the system of government is that it has not developed a "rule of law" under which decisions are made impartially and justly. To give another example, psychiatry is dismissed as "bourgeois nonsense" and nobody knows what losses in mentally ill persons Russia suffers from this decision. Social studies are neglected almost completely; the writings of Marx, Lenin, and Khrushchev are regarded as definitive in these fields. Students of geography and communications suffer the handicap of working from maps that lack data on ports, air fields, anchorages, communications patterns, and recently completed economic projects such as large dams. The latest Soviet atlases simply do not print this kind of information because the top men declare it to be of a political nature and hence secret.

Is Communism, then, efficient? It is hard-striving and fast-moving. The system has been effective in forcing applications of known science and in forcing building of heavy industry, but at great cost to the humans whom applications of science and heavy industry are supposed to benefit. It is designed to make people follow directions. March they must and march they do. But freedom, justice, pursuit of knowledge for its own sake—such values dear to the Western world are sacrificed.

To sum up Communism's prospects: (1) It does not threaten to subvert us, nor the other industrialized nations of the world. But it does threaten to subvert and seize control of large parts of the underdeveloped, unindustrialized world. (2) Communist promise and Communist practice are greatly at variance. Communism does not live up to its promises; it is brutally coercive of its own citizens. (3) But, in great part because of its coerciveness, Communist Russia is growing and growing in industrial strength. Industrial strength is potential military strength. Russia's potential military strength and the world-wide race that results from it are the stuff of the next chapter.

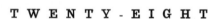

TWENTY-EIGHT

World Politics

In this chapter we shall discuss the conditions
that are necessary for our continued national
survival and prosperity—conditions we cannot
simply take for granted any longer. Our discussion will be cast in terms of what America
is and wants to be and in terms of what the
rest of the world is and wants to be. We are
concerned here with conflicts of groups and
values in a steadily shrinking world.

621

Rules of the Game: •   With the exception of slum and honky-
the Presumption   tonk areas in several of our cities you
of Violence   can go almost anywhere in your coun-
                           try at any hour and feel safe. You come
                           and go every day from home to school
or office, to stores, to friends' homes, and you never worry about your
safety. You feel safe because you know there are policemen to protect
you, and back of the police are the mores and laws that make it socially
taboo and criminal for anyone to molest or rob you. Everybody knows
about the police and courts, and almost everybody obeys the law and
we live quite peacefully together. The police and the courts are part
of the web of government, and an effective part.

Among nations there is no such web. There is no international police
force. There is an international court, in fact there are several, but behind the limited system of international courts there is no system of
law *enforcement.* There are judges, but no sheriffs and no police. This
condition of near anarchy between nations resembles somewhat the state
of frontier society that is recreated in TV westerns. On the frontier
every man carried a gun on his hip and sometimes a rifle on his saddle.
When men quarreled they frequently shot it out. Sometimes they organized groups or gangs to protect or attack one another. The gang
with the most men and guns and daring won, and that ended the dispute.

Each nation, like each frontier farmer, miner, or brigand, wears its
gun on its hip and worries about its skill on the draw. In any dispute
between nations over land, mineral rights, honor, or such matters, there
may be shooting. There is no world police force, no counterpart of the
frontier marshal, to appeal to for protection. The gun on the hip is sometimes fabulously complicated and expensive; the United States, for example, is wearing a $40,000,000,000-a-year sidearm.

The question of capability. If the absence of law enforcement between
nations makes guns and soldiers necessary, why isn't the United States
worried about possibly having to fight, somewhere, sometime, against
every other nation? Why doesn't America consider Yemen, or Belgium,
or Italy, a possible enemy?

There was an equality between men on the frontier; they were
more or less equally well equipped with the same kinds of guns, were
more or less equal in strength, and were more or less equal in ability to
persuade others to join them. Nations differ greatly in what they are able
to do. Yemen, Belgium, or Italy could not possibly threaten the United

States or Russia. They are too tiny. They could not possibly win any dispute by force. Russia and America know they will never be attacked by Yemen, Belgium, or Italy. But turn the situation around. Is the United States, or the Soviet Union, big enough to threaten Yemen, Belgium, or Italy? Yes, and of the three examples of tiny nations we have chosen at random, two, Belgium and Italy, have chosen to ally themselves with the United States in order to have some nation big enough to protect them, if necessary, against the other big nation.

This does not mean that small nations do not arm and threaten each other. It only means that the United States and the U.S.S.R., the two big superpowers, are threatened only by each other. Small nations do occasionally resort to force or threats of force against other small nations in order to settle disputes. Egypt and Israel, for example, threaten and occasionally fight each other. The governments of India and Pakistan spend almost half of their income on arms with which to menace each other. Yugoslavia and Albania, in the area where their borders meet, snarl at each other constantly, and recurrently resort to small-scale shooting.

Basically, these are the facts of world politics. A nation might wage war or threaten another nation. If it has the capacity to win such a war or back up its threat, it could mean the end for the threatened nation. Therefore each nation considers any nation big enough to fight it and maybe defeat it, its potential enemy. Big enough, that is, alone or with its allies.

What is "big enough"? Nations that are big in international matters have large populations, large land areas, and heavily industrialized economies. These resources enable a nation to bear the heavy costs of major international actions. By major international actions we do not necessarily mean military actions. Any kind of international program which affects many of the hundreds of millions of people in the world requires ability to produce for, pay for, and if necessary enforce the program. Without all three of the above characteristics a nation is soon overshadowed and subordinated by more powerful nations. India, for example, has a large area and a huge population but, because it is largely pre-industrial, its freedom of action in world politics is limited to saber rattling against small neighboring adversaries, and to rhetoric and exhortations to the United States and the U.S.S.R. to behave. Rhetoric and exhortations seem to have no effect on nations and nations' leaders. Switzerland, to cite another example, is heavily industrialized but tiny in area and population, and no major problem in international relations in the twentieth century has been much affected by what the Swiss insisted ought to be done.

Why Russia? In Chapter Twenty-seven we discussed Communism. Russia, East Germany, Poland, Czechoslovakia, Bulgaria, Hungary, Rumania, Yugoslavia, North Viet Nam, North Korea, mainland China, and Albania are all Communist-run nations. But if you look at production statistics you will see that of all these countries none but Russia is big. No others have the capacity to threaten the United States. Albania has a population of 1,200,000, less than half that of Los Angeles. Czechoslovakia is smaller in area than Illinois. Mainland China produces less steel per year than Belgium. And, as you would expect, all Communist nations but Yugoslavia are allied with Soviet Russia—their big brother on whom they depend for major protection and major foreign policy leads and decisions. America and its allies worry about and arm themselves against Russia. All the 12 nations we have mentioned are armed with Communism, and, as we have seen in the preceding chapter, this "ism" is a powerful weapon. But only Russia has the "ism" *and* the power to use it on a world-wide scale.

Other "enemies" at other times. At any point in time, whichever nation is big enough to attack and possibly defeat another nation is that nation's "enemy." During most of the nineteenth century America's main antagonist was Great Britain. During the 1930's and 1940's America's principal enemy was Germany, now an ally. During the 1940's we waged war against Japan, also now an ally. The post-war decline in power of our ex-enemies and the economic and military growth of Russia and the expansive tendencies of Communism today have made Russia America's principal opponent. The decline in power of our ex-enemies and our allies and the economic and military growth of America have made us Russia's principal opponent.

**Priorities
and Goals
of Foreign Policy**

• *The human condition.* As we mentioned in the last chapter, political scientists see men in industrial societies as pursuing three goals more or less simultaneously: safety, income, and deference or respect. Ordinarily most persons are safe all the time, but consider how the ordinary person would behave if he were in danger. Suppose as he was walking home someone pushed a gun in his face. Would he surrender his wallet? Yes. Looking at that gun muzzle, with

his hands in the air, would he worry about his dignity and feel compelled to be heroic and struggle hopelessly against an armed robber to
keep his money? No. Safety is more important than money. Consider
again frontier society where men lived with their protection on their hip
and on their saddle. What happened when men who were mining, farming, or tending cattle were suddenly beset by marauding Indians or
armed gangs? Some fled, some stood and fought, but no one went on
farming, mining, or tending his cattle.

Safety first. Nations, unlike people, cannot flee from danger. They may
fight (war); they may display their preparations for and state of readiness to fight if necessary (defense preparations); they may make concessions when they are threatened (appeasement, the counterpart of the
city man who surrenders his wallet or the frontier farmer who lets the
rustlers take his cattle). But the primary concern of any nation is its
safety. A nation will always spend and spend when it thinks its safety
is threatened. The amount it will spend at any moment depends on how
threatened it thinks it is, and groups and leaders within a nation may
differ on which of several things the nation ought to do to guarantee its
safety. They may even disagree so sharply on possible courses of action
and policy that, briefly, the nation may be powerless to act. But when
the threat or assumed threat is obvious, national defense will command
unquestioned priority and money and men will be made available to
the limit of the nation's capability. The United States government, by
no stretch of anybody's imagination a warlike one, has been spending
more than 50 per cent, almost 60 per cent, of its entire income on defense—some $40,000,000,000 a year—year after year. Percentages and
amounts spent on maintaining our reputation and prestige abroad or at
home, or on maintaining our standard of living, are tiny in comparison.
Every new major American foreign policy program is begun in response
to a threat or assumed threat to the nation's security. All the heavy increases in American defense spending and on foreign policy programs are
intended to counteract Russian political or technological successes (which
add areas or skills to their capability) or to meet Russian threats or assumed threats to non-Communist areas.[1]

Money second. Let us go back to our ordinary citizen in an industrial
democracy. When his safety is not involved, why does he join organized
groups and go into politics—for money, or for his ideals and the respect
of others? Politics within a nation, whether on the local, municipal, state,
or national level, is a struggle between interest groups over two things:

who gets what and whose ideas and principles are translated into government policy. Every close student of politics, and not necessarily only American politics, knows that nearly all interest groups are formed and are active in politics to maintain or increase their members' economic stake, that very few are concerned about protecting or improving their members' status, and almost none or only very minor ones exist to further their members' ideals.[2] Touch not the group's sources of income! Money usually has priority over respect and ideals.

Like individuals and groups a nation may sacrifice its economic well-being to safety but not to matters of prestige (respect) or ideals (self respect). One of America's ideals is human welfare and humanitarianism, but the United States spends less than $1,000,000,000 a year on economic development and technical assistance for underdeveloped countries. Security rather than idealism is the factor that prompts foreign aid programs. Consider the matter of tariff reduction. Most nations, whether industrialized or underdeveloped, have in part walled their economy off from other nations' products by networks of tariffs or tariff equivalents such as import quotas, preference systems, and rigged currencies. Nations have long agreed that these tariffs and tariff equivalents should be abolished, and a number of world-wide and regional international conference systems exist for promoting international trade and for removing or lowering barriers to international trade. At these conferences much is said, year after year, about the need for individual nations to face up to economic risks in the interest of world- or region-wide economic ideals of growth and progress. Much is said and written about the need for the industrialized nations to take the lead in cutting import restrictions. Yet nothing happens unless, in detailed negotiations, nations can see that specific trade concessions can be swapped for other specific trade concessions and that there can be mutual economic gain for all bargainers. The limited successes of such international organizations as the International Monetary Fund, the conferences of the signatories to the General Agreement on Trade and Tariffs, the European Payments Union, and the Organization for European Economic Cooperation have stemmed from bargaining and the discovery of mutual economic advantage, not from the nations' dedication to the ideals these organizations represent.

Prestige and democracy abroad. People are egocentric and ethnocentric. Nations reflect these same characteristics in their foreign policy. What do Americans prefer to see established abroad? Multi-party politics, parliamentary or presidential government, preferably with some form of separation of powers and with a liberal amount of local autonomy and local self-government. Americans also prefer decentralized economies, preferably those that encourage private ownership of business. Why? Because this is the American system and Americans like what they have. They understand it and they are used to it. Similarly, the British prefer to see parliamentary democracy and British-type systems of courts and procedures adopted abroad. And Russians and Russia's rulers react enthusiastically to any foreign government that moves in the direction of anti-capitalistic, Communist-oriented structure, ideology, and policies.

In modern industrial nations governments respond, with propaganda and diplomatic support, to regimes abroad which are similar to theirs; that is, which correspond to their ideals. They like to be liked and want to be esteemed and seek to be respected by other nations, and will respond favorably to regimes abroad that respond sympathetically to them; especially if the response does not cost any money and involves no risk to their safety. Examples are numerous at any moment in international politics. The United States identifies strongly with two firmly democratic regimes: Britain and France. Mainland China's government is Communist and her leaders identify strongly with the U.S.S.R., though they are by no means coerced into doing so. In the early 1950's a Communist-oriented regime flared into international prominence in Guatemala. Russia responded to it instantly and sympathetically. Similarly, America welcomed, instantly and enthusiastically, the brief appearance by revolution, until suppressed by Russian tanks, of a socialist but democratic and anti-Communist regime in Hungary in late 1956.

On the other hand, governments are quick to criticize and condemn other countries that deny or reject their ideals. Britain, France, the United States *and* Russia publicly lectured, criticized, and snubbed the Spain of Generalissimo Franco during the period from 1946 to 1953 because Franco's Spain was—and still largely is—neither democratic as we and Western Europe understand the word nor a Socialist People's Democracy in the Marxist-Socialist pattern, but rather is totalitarian and semi-fascist.[3] The United States and Western European democracies have used barrels of ink and months of international radio propaganda time condemning the Communist regimes of Russia's eastern European satellite nations. Similarly, Russian diplomacy and propaganda, since 1945, have condemned every new regime of the non-Communist world because it was the image, more or less, of the Western nations, and quite unlike Russia herself. Yet notice that condemnation of countries and regimes unlike us and praise of countries and regimes like us is rarely carried beyond exhortation and rhetoric. Deplore or praise, yes, but risk bloodshed or more than token amounts of money no—not unless safety is involved.

Why allies? Throughout history wars have been won by the nations with the most friends and allies. A nation's security and prestige are increased if it can call on other nations for help if the need arises. An important part of foreign policy, next in importance to military might, is winning, holding, and helping allies and denying allies or trying to deny allies to your adversary. Back of almost all negotiations between major nations is the implied weight of their economic and potential military capacity. The more allies a nation has the more weight and influence it can exert upon its enemies.

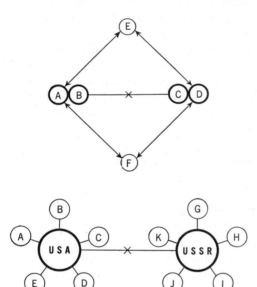

What kind of allies does America seek? It seeks allies that are economically strong, highly industrialized, prosperous, and democratic. A few examples will illustrate this point. Would the United States fight to defend Britain? Yes, indeed! She is strong; after America and Russia she is still the mightiest nation in the world. She is a staunch ally and the United States can be reasonably sure that she will fight with her, wherever and whatever the risk—whether in northern Greece, West Berlin, or South Korea. She is economically strong—a heavily industrialized nation with a highly skilled labor force. She has many friends and influences other nations in America's favor. She is a democracy and very much like us. Would the United States fight for Yugoslavia? We cannot say for certain. Under certain conditions perhaps America would; under other conditions perhaps not. Yugoslavia is opposed to Russia on certain major matters, but

Balance of Power and Bipolarity. *Allies A and B balance allies C and D; both compete for E and F. The U.S.A. with allies A, B, C, D, and E is one pole; the U.S.S.R. with satellites G, H, I, J, and K is the opposing pole.*

the country is largely pre-industrial and not strong militarily, other than quite locally in the South Balkans. Yugoslavia is by no means an ally on whom America could count; rather, she is a prestige item for the United States and the Western European coalition because she is the only Communist nation that has successfully defected from the U.S.S.R. bloc. But Yugoslavia, though anti-Russian in many respects, is a Communist state, and Americans do not like Communist regimes. Would the United States fight for Tibet? No. Tibet is nothing more than a mountain plateau and has no military nor economic potential. She exports only cashmere wool and yak tails—useful only for making expensive sweaters and Santa Claus whiskers. It would be hard to find two peoples in the world less concerned with each other, more unlike each other, and more completely ignorant of each other than Americans and Tibetans. No American politician need ever worry about the Tibetan vote. And Tibet's recent history in world politics illustrates its uselessness as an ally and the West's unconcern about it. In 1950, after 39 years of independence, Tibet was invaded by the armies of Communist China. What did America do? It dispatched a diplomatic note protesting the Chinese invasion and seizure, and that was the end of the matter.

There is one more major need in foreign policy: geographic access to countries close to one's adversary, or military bases abroad. The geographic position of a nation's allies adds to or subtracts from their value. In world politics there is always the possibility of limited resort to force. The destruction is likely to be terrible where it takes place, however localized or brief. Consequently, unlike professional baseball teams, nobody wants to play any home games. The object, if one must fight, is to fight over there and away from here. A nation's most important consideration is its own territory and its own people's safety; next most important, the safety of its principal allies, then the safety of less important allies, and so on to neutrals and uncommitted unimportant countries to the enemy's land and people—from "we" to "they."

The Race • The complicated world-wide race between the superpowers—the United States and the U.S.S.R.—results from the absence of a supranational police force and government, and from each nation's ethnocentrism and its emphasis on its own goals. It is simultaneously a race in *weapons* development and production, in *economic production* and in *applied science* and technology. The whole situation not only adds up to one of the greatest threats to mankind's safety the world has ever known, but also offers the greatest opportunity man has ever had to put scientific knowledge to use for the benefit of mankind everywhere.

The arms race. The Russian superpower is strong and growing stronger. The American superpower warily focuses on its new post-World-War-II enemy and arms itself and its allies to defend themselves if necessary. The Russians, in turn, build up their stockpile of deadly weapons, which alarms the Americans into increasing military appropriations, draft quotas, and arms production. The Russians respond in kind and the race increases in pace.

How many divisions, bases, wings of intercontinental bombers, radar networks, atomic submarines, missiles and anti-missile missiles are enough to guarantee a nation's safety? Each seeks to conceal its precise military strength from the other, and each seeks to exaggerate its military strength in order to make clear to the other that any resort to force will bring at least retaliation and at most devastation. This policy is called "deterrence." Each country, in estimating the other's military strength, works from very inexact information and tends, to be safe, to overestimate its enemy's strength. Each side feels that to be safe it must be stronger militarily than the other. Both cannot be bigger. The race becomes fabulously costly and inconvenient to both camps, but neither can let up.

Involved in the process of defense at any moment in time is each superpower's estimate of its possible enemy's *intentions*. Between powerful nations of somewhat similar institutions, and between nations with strong economic ties, tensions and suspicions lessen slowly over periods of time, and consequently arms burdens can be reduced. The absence of revolutions and wars stabilizes international borders; power shifts originally considered abnormal and almost intolerable slowly come to be accepted as normal; the peoples of rival nations slowly become used to each other's existence and to each other's differing institutions. Then, after these things have slowly taken place, leaders decide that they can safely risk reducing their nation's weapons burdens. Conversely, wars and revolutions upset patterns of expectation in world politics. When one or another big power extends its influence and control and captures or wins new allies it suddenly becomes stronger and this makes its possible enemies nervous and fearful and they build up their armaments. Or, it suddenly becomes weaker, and this makes it nervous and fearful that its possible enemies will attack it, threaten it, or coerce it, and so its leaders increase their armaments.

Recent shifts in power. The international situation in which we find ourselves today derives in part from the shifts and upsets in the military and
political status that had existed in the world prior to World War II. Suddenly, in 1945, Germany and Japan were temporarily eliminated as powerful nations. Britain, France, and the Netherlands, much weakened by the
war, lost their control over large areas in eastern and southern Asia and
in Africa. Russia created or helped create satellite allies in eastern Europe
and in China. America counterexpanded and formed alliances in Western
Europe and non-Communist Asia. Russia responded with a series of coun-
teralliances. So it has gone in recent years. Should the perimeter or border
between Russian-influenced and American-influenced nations be maintained and remain stable for decades, each superpower will slowly grow
used to it, the abnormal will become normal, and each side may risk
reducing the arms load it now carries.

The effects of differences in ideologies. Suspicion and fears between the
two superpowers are greatly increased by differences in ideology. Russia,
for example, stimulates and supports subversion and revolution in some
borderland areas that divide the Russian and American blocs. To Russia
this kind of agitational revolutionary politics *is* politics, and to Russia
what we call national politics is mere ritual. To America and its major
Western European allies Russian policy amounts to revolution and subversion, and is a threat to democratic values. Let us look at another example that illustrates the two-way barriers that separate the opposing
ideological camps. America seeks to encourage United States trade and
investments abroad. Government and private loans, investments, grants,
and gifts to foreign nations have increased tremendously since World
War II. To our political and business leaders this is a good sign and
carries no necessary political connotation or importance. Americans
largely dissociate, for example, another oil refinery abroad from political
connotations. But the Russians and their Communist allies, unlike the
Americans, British, or French, regard foreign holdings, subsidiaries, and
investments as evidence of Western imperialism and justification enough
for their own heavy armament program.

"Gittin' thar fust with the mostest." Surprise and the ability to react or
retaliate swiftly are very important in military and foreign policy. America
defends itself by cantilevering much of its military power to bases abroad
far from its own shores and as close as possible to the enemy. *To the
north,* facing Russia across the Arctic Circle, American defense is closely

coordinated with Canada's; maneuvers, weapons, bases, and even defense production installations are often shared. *To the west* the American defense line stretches out far across the vast Pacific Ocean in a series of bases on small islands and on the territory of allies. Some of these islands are American territory, some are "strategic trusteeships" under the nominal supervision of the United Nations, and some bases are on allied territory in South Korea, Japan, and Formosa. But all are United States military bases that are closer to the possible enemy than our own territory. *To the south* American defense efforts have been negligible and are based on paper compacts such as the Organization of American States of the Latin-American nations and the United States. Russia as yet has made no menacing gestures toward Central or South America and the penguins of Antarctica so far have managed to keep themselves aloof from the international power struggle.[4] *To the east* of us lie the great pawns in the world political struggle, the industrialized nations of Western Europe. In this area American defense rests on its most solidly organized and most expensively supported alliance, the North Atlantic Treaty Organization, and on far more than paper—a network of armed forces and bases and military supply centers. From Britain, France, Germany, Spain, Italy, and southeast Turkey ready forces of the United States and its European allies face the Russians and their eastern European partners.

What looks like defensive operations to America and its allies looks like "armed encirclement" to Russia. Opposite the United States-allied forces, along the whole span of the Eurasian continent from the upper Baltic, through central Europe, across the Black Sea, eastward just north of India, and across the China mainland to Vladivostok in Russia's easternmost province, bristle Russian bombers, missiles, and heavily armed infantry and tank divisions.

The importance of having this year's model. The techniques of military attack and defense change rapidly. Neither superpower wants to risk war, large or small, anywhere, outgunned or outmaneuvered. Each side is busy stockpiling modern weapons and training men to use them. At the same time other men in specialized military units are testing newer, more accurate, more mobile, more deadly weapons. Not yet at the field testing stage are even more accurate and deadly weapons in production or in the blueprint stage. Modern warfare has become so technical and so susceptible to change that today's soldiers have become in great part highly skilled electronic and mechanical technicians. It now takes a year and thousands of dollars to train one!

The difficulty of keeping secrets. Much time, money, and effort goes into trying to stay ahead of the possible enemy in refining the tools and art of war and in keeping each new technical development "secret." The plans, policies, words, or actions of individual leaders can be kept secret, but the race between the United States and the U.S.S.R. is a race in invention, discovery, and innovation. As we saw in Chapter Five, what man can next invent or discover and put to use depends on what stage of technical development he has already achieved. It is a process in which progress comes step by step and few seven-league-boots-sized advances are possible. Both the United States and the U.S.S.R. are at about the same stage of technical development, and if one or the other discovers or invents something that opens up a new avenue in the technological road, in a short time somebody or some group in the other country will figure out the "secret" with a slide rule, paper, and pencil. Invention, as we learned, does not depend on a predestined genius but on the state of the existing culture. America, for example, developed the atomic bomb in 1945 and kept it a secret, but in 1949 Russia duplicated it. In November, 1952, the United States tested the world's first hydrogen bomb; in August, 1953, Russia tested its first hydrogen bomb. Germany developed the jet engine for aircraft late in World War II, but by 1950 both Russia and America had jet fighter aircraft of about equal effectiveness and today both have jet bombers. In October, 1957, the U.S.S.R. launched the world's first space satellite and said nothing about how she did it; but in January, 1958, America launched its first space satellite, too.

Military display and posturing. The object of the race is not to start a war but to prevent one by impressing a possible enemy with your strength. Therefore, whenever one superpower or the other develops some new technique or weapon it tries to let its potential enemy know about it. It publicizes the very things that it simultaneously tries to keep secret. Russia, for example, uses every anniversary of the Red Revolution to display her latest weapons in a vast parade and aerial display in Moscow, and invites representatives from the United States and Western European nations to see how "advanced" her arms are. The United States invites Russians to atomic bomb test explosions. In January, 1953, on the occasion of the inauguration of President Eisenhower, the then-new "atomic cannon" was trundled back and forth conspicuously at this most conspicuous event at the most conspicuous place, Washington, D. C., to impress Russia and our allies with American military might. It is impossible to keep weapons secret from a potential enemy when the object in having them is to impress him by showing them to him. Therefore, Russia and America stay very close to each other in the arms race, one veering a bit ahead in one field, the other outdistancing it a bit in another field, depending on which, among many, each concentrates upon. But neither power dares to fall far behind the other in any major field, and each is able, when it does fall somewhat behind, to benefit from the other's discoveries and catch up rather quickly. Also, the race stimulates both powers to race ever harder for military-technological supremacy, and the pace of the race quickens and quickens. Each superpower races to keep ahead of the other; both rapidly advance in technical capability. The superpowers become SUPERpowers, and by an ever greater margin over other nations.

The economic race. Back of the soldiers and machines of defense are the complicated supply networks and rear-area installations, and back of these are the factories and skills of the population. Every major corporation in the United States is involved in defense production to a degree. The economic planning and production required for defense have created another economy that is separate from the normal economy that turns out consumer goods. In every major industrialized nation (except, as yet, West Germany and Japan) the national government, through its department or ministry of defense, is the nation's biggest single buyer, consumer, stimulator of the economy, and judge of the kinds of goods to be produced.

Each nation watches the total economic production of the other and compares it with its own. Quantitative indicators of total economic strength and capacity such as gross national product, steel capacity, kilowatt-hour output, tons of coal mined, and amount invested in new production facilities are compared, and each increase has prestige value among allies, neutrals, and uncommitted peoples and is presumed to impress one's adversaries. To each the other's economic capacity and growth in this or that sector of its economy is a stimulus to increase its own economic capacity and growth. For example, in steel production Russia stimulates her own people in part by contrasting Russian with American steel output and demanding and promising that Russia will surpass America. In her propaganda abroad Russia does not mention that her steel production is much lower than America's, but she often emphasizes that her rate of increase in steel production is higher than America's. Let us look at another more immediate example. In recent years America has become very concerned with Russia's output of trained technicians in the fields of applied science and engineering. Russia is training more specialists in these fields than we are. Consequently, American officials at the policy level are discussing how to stimulate the study and teaching of the physical sciences, mathematics, and engineering in our high schools and colleges. Not that America needs more engineers and applied scientists than she has for her own economic well-being, but that we must turn out more specialists in these fields to match the Russian figures. We cannot permit Russia to "get ahead."

The race is on in economic development abroad, too. If Indonesia, for example, seeks weapons from the United States and is ignored or refused them, Russia is likely to provide them. If America promises to help pay for and construct a large hydroelectric dam in upper Egypt, so does Russia. If one country builds India a steel mill the other tries to counter it with another steel mill, or with its economic equivalent. But if one superpower has not yet begun offering economic assistance and development in a certain area or country, the other power also tends to ignore that country. Most of the countries and peoples of West Africa, Central Africa, and South Africa, for example, have not yet been caught up in the economic competition between the superpowers, and they receive comparatively little in the way of money, technicians, and goods from either the United States or the U.S.S.R. for economic development. Perhaps these regions also will become competitive targets, but meanwhile the race is on in all other areas and many a road, steel mill, factory, elementary school, antimalaria campaign, and other improvement will result, all to humanity's benefit but mainly because of the race!

The race for scientific and technical leadership. The race is on between the superpowers' laboratories, scientists, and thinkers, too, as well as between their applied scientists and technicians and economists. American prestige and Russian prestige rest in considerable part upon the assumption by their allies that their superpower leads in *ideas*. Recent scientific advances by Russia, such as the sun satellite of January, 1959, have won her much prestige and influence abroad, especially among neutrals and uncommitted peoples. To name a few fields in which human knowledge is being increased by the race: Many research centers in the United States are working on solar energy research—the use of sunlight to run motors, generators, stoves, and other machines. The possibilities of using their scientific findings to gain allies and prestige among the neutral and uncommitted nations that are economically underdeveloped are now being discussed. Almost all these nations are short of sources of energy and many are close to the Equator where sunlight is strong the year round. In uses of radioactive materials for medical diagnoses both Russia and America are experimenting and supplying knowledge and materials to other nations. In the industrial uses of atomic energy both superpowers are experimenting in order to be first to produce inexpensive atomic power plants with almost weightless fuels and to be first to give them away abroad. America has no domestic need for industrial atomic power. It can supply all its energy needs for a hundred years or more by using conventional pre-atomic fuels, and there is no immediate prospect that atomic energy will be able to compete economically with energy produced from coal or oil in the United States. Despite this, because it is competing with Russia for world leadership in science and technology, America is experimenting with and developing industrial atomic power reactors for use not here but abroad.[5] A leader must lead, and must race against other leaders.

Another way to illustrate the race for scientific leadership is to study the statements of political and scientific leaders after each major international scientific conference. A major conference on atomic energy was held in 1956, and reports or comments on the meetings invariably were made in terms of the "score" in the scientific race. The United States is far in the lead in the chemical processing of irradiated fuels; Russia is ahead in using isotopes to control iron and steel quality. Neither power seems to be anywhere near perfecting a fusion type energy reactor. And so on. At this moment newspapers here and abroad are busy trying to guess which superpower will be the first to land a rocket on the moon, which will launch the first manned space vehicle, or which will be the first to develop manned space vehicles capable of altering weather conditions. The race is on in many fields of scientific activity, and government funds flow freely to stimulate and support it.

What if the United States quit the race? What if America suddenly stopped trying to match and surpass the U.S.S.R.? This question, often asked, is like any other completely hypothetical question, such as, for example, "What if Russia were suddenly to become like the United States?" We can only answer questions such as these by assuming that if one miracle can happen then any other miracle can happen. If—other things remaining unchanged—America suddenly quit the world race, the U.S.S.R. would continue to grow more and more powerful. America's allies would be forced to desert her and turn to Russia in the interests of survival. The United States would find itself cut off from trade and raw materials from abroad. It would find itself coerced into making concessions and more concessions to Russia at every turn in the international road. It would lose its present freedom of action, its choice of alternatives, and become, slowly, a satellite of the U.S.S.R., ever threatened by

Russian coercion, with a low standard of living and a gnawing feeling of shame and guilt because it had lost its own self-respect and the respect of the other nations of the world. In short, America would be reduced to a second-rate power and life for Americans would slowly become like life today for citizens of Russian-dominated Poland. At that price the race could be stopped. But American goals being what they are and the United States' capability being what it is, America will *not* quit the race. Nor will Russia.

Problems, Policies, • Having discussed the system and dy-
Instruments, namics of world politics, we will now
and Prospects describe *what* America does or tries to
do in its foreign policy, and *where* and
how. We will also give some idea of
what kind of foreign policy an American citizen can reasonably expect, demand, and support.

Re Russia. American safety requires that the United States and its allies prevent Russia from expanding geographically and taking over any more countries. There are several instruments at hand that can be used to contain Russian expansionism.

(1) Sufficient armed forces are needed to be able to retaliate in case full-scale war breaks out. By being able to retaliate, these forces will deter Russia from starting a third World War at all. These armed forces must also be versatile and mobile enough to meet, on equal terms, any "brush fire wars" that may occur along the periphery of the Soviet-controlled world.

(2) Also essential is diplomatic capacity and willingness to negotiate from positions of strength in order to reach agreements on specific matters where agreement is possible, where concessions can be made or won without basically weakening the United States or strengthening the U.S.S.R. To put this another way, citizens cannot expect that any meeting or series of meetings between president and premier or secretary of state and foreign minister will produce any magic solution to the arms race and to the problems that now divide the free world and the Communist world. Also, citizens cannot demand that their leaders refuse to make concessions and to negotiate with the adversary and still expect any progress toward lessening international tensions and arms burdens. What is needed is a continued willingness and patience to negotiate about specific issues, backed up by military strength which will give meaning to the negotiations.

(3) Lastly, American safety also requires that America continue to run hard in the whole race, to keep up with or somewhat ahead of Russia economically, militarily, and scientifically. The *prospects* are that America will stay in the race. Certainly she has the capacity not only to pace the free world in its contest with the Communist world, but also to add luster to her international image by providing a comfortable and rising standard of living for her own citizens and by helping to provide a rising standard of living for a large part of the rest of the world.

Re Western Europe and Japan. Our policy toward our nominal and actual allies [6] in Western Europe and Japan should stress speed in achieving our goals *and theirs*—providing the margin of military safety they cannot provide, lubricating the economic process a bit here and there to ensure their increasing economic well-being, and winning and maintaining their respect. There are three instruments available for pursuing this policy: (1) special-purpose military forces, (2) special-purpose funds, and (3) a special kind of diplomacy.

(1) Our own and our allies' mutual defense demand that we continue to supply the big expensive weapons that our allies are unable to afford—whether intercontinental bombers, missiles, heavy naval equipment, or the costly research required in the development of new weapons. France, Britain, West Germany, Japan, and others can provide the men to defend themselves, but they cannot afford to spend $10,000,000,000 a year on atomic weapons research. Only the United States Atomic Energy Commission can command amounts that large.

(2) Economically, as we have said elsewhere, Western Europe and Japan are prospering. They need, and they receive, almost no economic aid from the United States. They require only very limited special-purpose loans to grease the wheels of international trade and to help tide them over momentary minor financial crises from time to time. This minor aid can be given through international organizations which already exist, such as the International Monetary Fund, the International Bank of Reconstruction and Development, and the United States Export-Import Bank. By merely increasing its investment in such international revolving funds the United States can help stabilize its allies' currencies and economies and help lessen the risk of economic upset abroad, in just the way that increasing the money deposits in a private bank slightly would enormously lessen its vulnerability to sudden "runs" against it.

In addition to minor financial aid, it is to our own long-run interest to help our industrialized allies to support themselves. To the degree that they prosper they will tend to help us and will require less and less help from us. One major way to increase their prospects of prospering would be to continue to lower our trade barriers. The essence of trade barriers is that they discriminate against foreign products and favor one's own nation's products. In the nineteenth century, when the United States itself was a semi-industrialized country, such a policy, to speed industrialization, made sense. But today it is not to our advantage to restrict imports by high tariffs because we can afford to compete with foreign goods, and we can and do sell a vast volume of goods—billions of dollars' worth every year—abroad. If we do not open our domestic markets to other industrialized nations they will close their domestic markets to us. Moreover, many goods and services become more desirable and more valuable merely by being shipped and sold abroad. In Rome some American dime store items are a novelty; in America very ordinary Japanese dishes are often a delight. Abroad, goods seem different and novel and therefore worth more. There is mutual gain in international trade. Another point is that if America and its industrialized allies trade with each other more and more, they will become more and more interdependent and more and more committed to each other. Trade ties, like other ties, slowly help to form bonds of habit, common understanding, and international community. Tariffs and other trade barriers are often advocated on the grounds that if we buy from ourselves we ensure our prosperity but if we buy from foreign countries we ensure their prosperity at the cost of our own. Actually, barriers to foreign trade only ensure that we will be denied others' goods that they can make and sell less expensively than we, and that they will be denied our goods that we can make and sell less expensively than they. As long as we have goods other nations want to buy —and there are many thousands of industrial products of which Western Europeans and Japanese would buy much more if they could afford to— any dollars which they earn by selling us things will be spent buying our things. The net effect will be the return of our money—not decreased prosperity but increased prosperity. In sum, the industrialized free world will probably continue to prosper slowly, even in the face of American tariff walls if it must. But the industrialized free world *and* America would prosper more, and more rapidly, if American tariffs and tariff equivalents were reduced.

And what about the few areas of Western Europe which are still largely pre-industrial—Spain, southern Italy, Greece, Turkey, and Yugoslavia? These nations require long-term loans and technical assistance in order to industrialize. Their development is to the self-interest of America and industrialized Western Europe, and the capital to develop them is likely to flow jointly from the United States and its industrialized Western

European partners. If we and our allies do not help industrialize these nations, Russia may capture them, for all but Spain are situated close to Russian power and influence.

(3) Our diplomacy should aim at winning and holding our allies' respect by negotiating with them and consulting them on all matters of American policy that affect them. Mutual defense and mutual policy must really be mutual. Joint policy must be jointly hammered out. The decision-making process must be shared through careful diplomacy and multi-lateral conferences.

Re eastern Europe. The eastern European nations are inside the Russian sphere of control, more or less as Britain is within America's. The line of containment, by America of Russia, by Russia of America, runs west of eastern Europe, and the American problem is to get used to this line. Candidates for office in America may talk about and promise the "liberation" of Poland, Czechoslovakia, East Germany, Hungary and the other satellites, but if the satellites are to be freed they will have to free themselves. About the only support we could give them would be moral, for if we made any overt move to pry them loose Russia would fight to hold them, just as America would fight to hold West Germany. A border deline-ates, and usually the wisest thing to do about a new border is to get used to it.

Re Africa. North Africa is made up of countries that only recently have won their independence and of colonies in which people are still strug-gling to free themselves from colonial rule. All, countries or colonies, are barren lands, though explorations for oil in the Sahara Desert may even-tually change this. There are two problems confronting America in this region.

(1) There is the ideological problem. Are we against colonialism or are we indifferent to it? As we noticed in the preceding chapter, the issue of colonialism vs. anti-colonialism is a great and growing one in the world. More than 1,000,000,000 people in the world—the underdeveloped and recently emerged peoples—are intensely anti-colonial. Just as human slavery, once morally neutral, became immoral in the nineteenth century, so colonialism is now considered immoral by many and will increasingly be so considered. America cannot ignore its obligation to decide where it stands. If it remains indifferent to colonialism it will increasingly be judged to be *for* colonialism. How do we decide such an issue? First, our scholars and leaders ascertain and publicize the facts. Is colonial rule benevolent and progressive or is it disgracefully exploitative? To answer

this question we inquire into who gets what, who educates whom, and who respects whom. We look into the long records of colonial rule in terms of the possibilities. The weight of the facts having been ascertained, the next step is to get political leaders in America to bring this question to the attention of Americans in the form of a national issue and a national discussion to be resolved into national moral commitment to one side or the other. There are many side interests mixed up in this issue. In regard to France and her North African possessions, for example, there is the question of compensating Frenchmen for property in North Africa, the need for French managerial talent in running North African economic enterprises, and the necessity to protect Western European minorities' rights against majority rule by non-Europeans, among others. But these can be separately unraveled and the problems solved once the United States makes up its mind where it stands on the larger issue. The issue cannot be avoided much longer. Once the United States has decided where it stands, its influence will be exerted through diplomatic channels and at international conferences, and the U.S.S.R. will no longer have the ideological advantage of seeming to be righteous in this matter and making us appear to be reactionary.[7]

(2) The second problem is to help the peoples of North Africa to make their lands a little less barren, to help them to wrest a better living from what soil they have. Solving this problem requires money and technicians and is complicated by a cluster of minor problems such as finding well sites, bringing in cement and wood for construction, turning cement into dams, introducing chemical fertilizers, and all the while restricting ourselves to giving advice and help and keeping hands off the actual reins of control.

Central and South Africa are still largely pre-political or sub-political, and for the next decade or two America can probably afford to continue to have no foreign policy with respect to these areas.

Re the Middle East, Southwest Asia, and Southeast Asia. The countries of these areas have already won their independence, but in some of them the political situation is far from stable. America faces the same problem in this area as she does in North Africa—how to provide money and technicians to help people lift themselves out of poverty. We must also keep in mind that these countries all lie along the rimland of Soviet power, and the prospects that some of them might be attracted to or captured by Communism are far from dim. This situation causes America to view them as "targets of Soviet aggression," and the Soviet press and periodicals make it clear that their strategic proximity to Russia causes

Russia to view them as "targets of American imperialism." Both Russia and America regard these countries as pawns. But *they do not think of themselves as pawns*. It is a rare Indian, Pakistani, Thai, Indonesian, or Burmese leader who is convinced or can be convinced of "the necessity to contain Russia," or of the necessity to reject America. The problem for America is to get used to the neutralist point of view. These people are much more concerned with the problem of survival than they are with American imperialism. The choice in Asia is clear. We can help these countries to industrialize or stand by and watch them sink into grinding poverty, social chaos, and then one by one fall prey to Communism. But here, too, the main problem is complicated by other problems. The United States, in its own interest, must help them in terms which they consider help; it cannot wring promises of support against Communism from them in return for our help, for they will not commit themselves to either Russia or America in the sense that Communist China leans to the U.S.S.R. and Britain commits herself to the United States. Nor will they barter armed divisions for United States wheat or money. America must grow accustomed to offering economic and technical assistance to these nations without attaching any "strings."

Re the Far East. In East Asia *mainland China* has been Communist since 1949, and no amount of political or diplomatic rhetoric seems likely to make her slip the ties that bind her to the Communist bloc. Our defensive perimeter lies outside mainland China. South Korea, Japan, Formosa, the Philippines, South Viet Nam, Cambodia, Laos, Burma, Thailand, and Malaya must be defended and the military *status quo* preserved, as it is in Europe. This can be done by maintaining United States military units in or very near these countries, ready and able to help defend them if necessary, and by assisting them with arms and with training programs to develop their own military forces. In addition to maintaining this posture of military strength, we must maintain a willingness to negotiate with Russia about specific limited issues where agreements can be made without basically weakening the United States vis-à-vis Russia in the area. We need a combination of (1) an umbrella of American military power over the most threatened countries (South Korea, Formosa, South Viet Nam); (2) a program to stimulate and support the international trade of the area, especially the trade of the one developed country, Japan; and (3) everywhere but in Japan we must formulate a flexible program to supply economic development funds and skilled technicians to make the recipients of our aid showcases for the rest of the world to see and judge us by.

Re Latin America. Latin America is far from any possible line of fire in any peripheral war between Russia and America and their respective allies, and therefore there is nothing much that we need to do for her or with her, militarily. Economically, our trade with Latin America grows steadily more important. Half of America would never survive the morning without Latin-American coffee. Without her mineral ores a good part of our defense industry would be forced to slow down. But America is not completely dependent on Latin America, nor is Latin America completely dependent on America. Rather, the pattern is one of increasing economic interdependence and is largely outside the world race between the United States and the U.S.S.R.

America's long-run foreign policy. It is hazardous to make long-range predictions about the course of world politics. The projections in this chapter are all made in terms of the next 10 to 20 years. At this point in time and for as far ahead as we can see, the primary loyalties of people, aside from

Into whose hands?

family ties, are to their nations. They are not likely to forsake their national loyalties and to throw their support to ideas for a world government or any other kind of supranational organization. Exhortations to call a convention of mankind, to form a world or Western World or Atlantic government, to embrace world pacifism, become citizens of the world, and so on, attract negligible audiences and produce negligible responses. People continue to behave as citizens of nations. For a long time to come nations will endure as the chief political units of the world, pursuing their own separate goals and interests.

Yet slowly, over generations broken by occasional wars, small and large, nations have evolved international codes and institutions that regulate their dealings with one another to the mutual convenience and benefit of all or most. Consider international politics a few hundred years ago:

> When Justin II sent ambassadors to negotiate with the Seljuk Turks they were first subjected to purification for the purpose of exorcising all harmful influence. The tribal wizards danced around them in a frenzy of ecstasy, burning incense, beating tambourines and endeavouring by all known magic to mitigate the dangers of infection. Envoys to the Tartar Khans were also obliged to pass through fire before they could be allowed into the presence, and even the gifts which they had brought with them were similarly sterilized. So late as the fifteenth century the Republic of Venice threatened with banishment, or even death, those Venetians who held intercourse with any member of a foreign legation.[8]

Such taboos against foreigners were once common. Today about a million Americans go abroad each year as tourists; foreign students by the tens of thousands are in America; some 150 raw materials are being imported constantly into the United States, all without bloodshed or chaos under remarkably orderly international rules. In these peaceful exchanges of persons, things, and ideas there is at least some trace of world community.

Although security and allies are imperatives of American foreign policy in the present and for the short-run future, the United States also has a more farsighted aim: to shore up what world community does exist and build further upon it. We can do this in two ways. First, we can depoliticize international matters whenever possible. That is, the rules, systems, and bodies of custom that do exist to settle disputes between nations—international law, arbitration, commissions of inquiry, and international economic agencies—can be appealed to, supported, and followed or obeyed, to the limit consistent with security, whether other countries follow our lead or not. Secondly, we can share the political decision-making process with as many other nations as possible, and explain and justify our political decisions as widely as possible among other nations. This can best be done through existing international organizations and especially—foreign policy exigencies at any moment permitting [9]—through the United Nations.

America and the United Nations. The United Nations is, regrettably, only a decision-suggesting instrument in major international matters. That is, it can investigate, ascertain facts, examine possible courses of action, discuss alternatives, and tell America, Russia, Britain, or Egypt, what it should do. But that is all it can do. It has no men, no guns, and almost no money, and so cannot itself *do* anything much; nor can it compel any nation to do anything—except by censuring them if they do not. But our 80-some fellow nations can, to the degree that America takes foreign policy matters to the U.N. for discussion and examination, force America to examine problems and policies and actions in terms of a broader range of possibilities and in terms of many more points of view. Specific programs—e.g., most technical assistance—can be channeled from the United States through the United Nations to the beneficiary nations rather than bilaterally from the United States to the receiving nations.[10] We should follow the same policy of sharing our views with our allies in regional organizations, for example, N.A.T.O. or S.E.A.T.O.

There is another aspect to sharing the decision-making process. We can let other nations' citizens, leaders, and political groups run their own affairs and keep out of disputes *within* nations. The United States is competing with Russia in extending economic aid to the underdeveloped nations. The United States is involved in mutual defense pacts with other nations. Incidental to mutual defense, we are inevitably a factor in some of their most important domestic matters—budgeting, financing, and taxing, for example. We have seen in the preceding chapter that the very process of internal economic change may disrupt old established cultures. Economic change renders obsolete traditional ways of doing things and behaving, and may create periods of social chaos and strife. What is America to do if strife occurs or threatens to occur? If landlords take to slaughtering or suppressing insurgent peasants, or peasants take to slaughtering or threatening reactionary landlords, we should keep our hands *off*. Why? For two reasons. First, we are certain to know very little about internal affairs in these countries, and so could not hope to prescribe very realistic or workable solutions to their problems. American preferences for due process or for land ownership patterns that prevail in Iowa or the Ohio Valley would probably be completely alien to an underdeveloped country in Southeast Asia, for example. Second, the object of foreign policy is to win friends and influence peoples and to avoid making enemies. Meddling in intimate political matters is certain to cost us friends and make us enemies. American foreign policy must not attempt to make over other lands in our image nor to control the outcome of their internal dissensions, even when they are or seem likely to become quite explosive.

The American mirror image abroad. Our success in containing and deterring our potential enemies and winning and holding our friends varies and will continue to vary directly with our success in solving our own major domestic problems—in putting our ideals into democratic practice, and in maintaining a prosperous and equalitarian economic system. There are things which can be done in the field of international relations to improve other peoples' image of us. Among these are larger appropriations for such organizations as the United States Information Agency, many more exchanges of persons between our nation and others, and greater publicity even for such largely ceremonial utterances as the speech the American ambassador to France makes on Bastille Day. But much more important is what we *do*. America is an open society and foreign newsmen, friendly or hostile, can see and report us as we are. Some of our senior diplomats believe that although foreign leaders credit America with technical near-omnipotence, they look at social lags and political malorganization in the United States and wonder whether we are really masters of our own fate.[11]

Trends in World Politics • *Decline in the use of force between great and small nations.* Between nations which are near equals, whether superpowers such as the United States and the U.S.S.R. or small powers such as Egypt and Israel, force has always been and continues to be the ultimate sanction at the international conference table. But against smaller peoples force is waning as an instrument of national policy. The possession of superior weapons is no longer a prime factor in American relations with, for example, Saudi-Arabia or Chile. Mexico no longer need fear that if the United States disapproves of its government's actions it will land the marines to change things. The latest trial of the old traditional methods by Great Britain and France against Egypt in late 1956 ended in ignominious disaster.

Earlier, and as recently as 40 years ago, the situation was different. Germany could take the Shantung Peninsula as England took Hong Kong, as the United States took Panama, and as all the major European powers sliced up Africa. Persia, Haiti, and other small countries that had been coerced by the great powers complained, but their complaints were barely audible in the press and were disregarded in international diplomatic circles. As the use of force against them has decreased, small nations have come to play a greater role in world politics. The Western World speaks time and again of no alternatives to peace; and tiny states with few resources and no ability to sustain military operations are able to achieve important international changes by the threat to, so to speak, commit suicide—by daring to risk their very existence against mighty adversaries. Irresponsibility has become a political weapon. This adds to the irrationality of world politics. It also somewhat diminishes its bipolarity. The prospect is that smaller nations will have a larger voice—or rather choruses of discordant voices—in major world affairs. Their voices are also considerably magnified in the principal world forum of opinion, the United Nations; for in the U.N. the basis of representation is one state: one vote, and mighty Russia and tiny Yemen are equal—in voting power. This means a kind of "representation without taxation" or power to vote and decree action without responsibility for carrying the action out.

Trends within the U.S.S.R. Russia, as we have said, makes the United States fearful because of her economic and military capability, and part of this is due to her astonishing rates of economic growth. But a number of signs indicate that the Russian pace of industrialization may soon slow down. The Russian leaders are hard pressed to lessen Russia's investments in heavy industry—the fields of industry that mean even greater capacity to produce for and support war, the fields that make the United States and West Europe particularly suspicious—and to divert more of Russia's investment money to related but less alarming fields of production like housing, transportation, and agriculture. Needs for large investments in agriculture are particularly pressing.

In addition, Russia faces a growing labor shortage. During the First and Second Five-Year plans it was possible to transfer millions of workers from farms to factories, but no spare rural population any longer exists.

In addition, the tendency increases for the political controllers of the system (the party members) to merge with the actual managers of the system (the middle layers of the administrative hierarchy). Revolutionaries are becoming bureaucrats, as we remarked in the preceding chapter.

When it is difficult to tell the would-be whippers from those to be whipped, the lash is likely to fall less often and less heavily. This overlap between the political drivers of the state and the economic decision-makers is likely to mean a slow-down on the part of the managers. It is likely to mean organizational confusion while the regime experiments with changes in controls, in planning techniques, and seeks means other than the lash of Party denunciation and rewards other than money and Party status to goad its managerial group on. In fact numerous experiments along these lines are now going on in the U.S.S.R. under the eye of Premier Khrushchev—an engineer as well as First Secretary of the C.P.S.U. These trends all indicate that the pace of heavy industrialization in Russia may well be slowing down. If so, America and the rest of the free world soon may be able to breathe a bit easier.

Signs of a shift in the race. Increased competition in economic development. The underdeveloped nations are beginning to expect and demand that the United States or the U.S.S.R. make money and resources available to them for economic development and industrialization. They are beginning to claim it as a right. As yet neither the United States nor the U.S.S.R. recognizes any such right. They do not admit that this is necessarily their burden. Russia, however, is becoming increasingly involved and is putting up more and more money for technical assistance and economic development outside her power sphere, especially in the Middle East, Southwest Asia, and Southeast Asia. From 1954 to 1956 she committed approximately $1,000,000,000 to these areas—a larger sum than the United States dispensed over the same period. Clearly if the U.S.S.R. is accelerating its foreign aid program, the United States will have to do so too. This development may mean less emphasis on armaments in the future—a welcome prospect and much safer.

The growing risk of accidental war. Atomic weapons with a staggering destructive capacity are becoming common "hardware" in the arsenals of the superpowers and their major allies. At first the United States had a monopoly in the production of atomic weapons, but the Russians soon learned the secret, then the British, and finally the French. Soon Japan and West Germany will be in production. As production increases and manufacturing techniques are refined, costs go down. Eventually it seems likely that obsolete atomic weapons will be distributed to more and more countries under the various military aid programs. And in the more distant future, rocket-powered missiles with atomic warheads will probably go to the armed forces of Egypt, Argentina, Thailand, Korea, Albania, and other nations. The prospect for the world is a long-run trend toward slowly increasing military stability between the superpowers. But clouding this otherwise hopeful picture is the danger that war could be set off by a rash decision of an Argentine or Egyptian general to press this or that button and blow up cities or render whole provinces radioactive, in what was intended to be a local retaliatory action or at worst a localized war. The warning time on atomic missiles is close to zero—a matter of minutes between continents! Defense against them is close to impossible. If a nation *thinks* it has been attacked the time to investigate and make inquiries is not likely to be available. The pressure to retaliate with its missiles may be too great to resist.

The population problem. In Africa, southern Europe, the Middle East, Southwest Asia, Southeast Asia, the Far East, and most of Latin America, the problem of economic improvement is compounded by rapid increases in population. The birth rates in all underdeveloped areas are high; until recently death rates also were high. But these death rates have fallen in recent years and are still falling rapidly because of spectacular advances in public health, medicine, and preventive sanitation. The result, as we saw in Chapter Eight, is a "population explosion." Every year there are millions of additional people in these lands, where most people are underprivileged already. By the time Egypt completes the Aswan Dam and considerably increases the amount of her arable soil, the population will have grown so much that the Egyptian standard of living will be no higher than it is today. In India there are 10,000,000 more people seeking jobs every year. In China the population increases every year by 15 to 20,000,-000. Although production goes up population seems to go up almost as fast and in many countries actually faster, so that despite increased output, standards of living continue to fall.

It is possible for an underdeveloped country to push its output and gain on the ever-growing demands of the ever-rising population. Mexico and a few other underdeveloped countries are doing it. But if the rise of population could somehow be checked, the climb would be much less difficult. The possibility of cheap chemical fertility depressants which can be taken orally with complete safety now exists. They are still in the laboratory testing stage in America but have been tried in field tests in Puerto Rico—and they work, promising that through their mass use birth rates could be leveled off. Even those most firmly opposed to contraception on religious grounds see the dangers of the population explosions now occurring in the world and are seeking solutions consistent with their beliefs. If this explosion can be curbed in some fashion that does not violate cultural values, the burdens of the superpowers in the growing race to develop the underdeveloped nations will slowly lessen.

The prospect of vastly greater mastery of the environment. The problem of eliminating poverty in the underdeveloped nations is not likely to go unsolved for want of technical knowledge. Unless the world destroys itself by war, technological progress will continue, vastly accelerated by the race between the superpowers. Russia and America are both moving technically closer to mastery over nature.[12]

These six trends indicate that slowly, over the fairly long run, we stand an increasing chance of seeing world politics become less bi-polarized around the United States and the U.S.S.R., of seeing the world race shift somewhat from military to economic competition, of seeing large areas of the world begin to dig their way out of grinding, seemingly hopeless poverty, and of seeing Russia and the United States and their respective blocs of allies grow somewhat less uneasy about each other. Running counter to these trends is the growing risk of accidental war and the growing risk of greater irrationality in world politics because of the irresponsibility and increasing influence of small recently independent nations.

**How Do We   •   You often hear people ask, How will
Ever Win?   America win the race with Russia? We
                    won't. But neither will we lose it. For-
                    eign policy problems are not like head-
aches. You can't take something for them and get rid of them. They are like the problem of earning a living—always with you. The thing we must do is keep moving in the right *directions* toward our goals, and keep the future open, to preserve for our children and our children's children freedom of action to solve their problems themselves in terms of the kind of world they want to live in.

Appendix

Notes

Chapter One

1 William James, *Principles of Psychology*, Vol II (New York: Holt, 1890), pp. 640-641, as quoted by Howard Becker, *Through Values to Social Interpretation* (Durham, North Carolina: Duke University Press, 1950), p. 294.

2 C. West Churchman and Russell L. Ackoff, *Methods of Inquiry: An Introduction to Philosophy and Scientific Method* (St. Louis: Educational Publishers, 1950), p. 10.

3 *Ibid.*

4 Leslie A. White, *The Science of Culture* (New York: Farrar, Strauss, 1949), Chapter 1.

5 Attributed to Julian Huxley by Herbert L. Searles, *Logic and Scientific Methods* (New York: Ronald, 1948), p. 126.

6 Harry Elmer Barnes, *A History of Historical Writing* (Norman, Okla.: University of Oklahoma Press, 1938).

7 White, *The Science of Culture*, p. 66.

8 *Ibid.*, pp. 68-69.

9 George A. Lundberg, *Social Research: A Study in Methods of Gathering Data* (New York: Longmans, Green, 1929), p. 6.

10 Ernest Greenwood, *Experimental Sociology: A Study in Method* (New York: King's Crown, 1945), p. 28.

11 Emory S. Bogardus, *Sociology* (New York: Macmillan, 1949), p. 546.

Chapter Two

[1] This account is based on David B. Stout, *San Blas Cuna Acculturation: An Introduction* (New York: The Viking Fund, Publications in Anthropology, No. 9, 1947). Consulted as a supplementary reference was Fred McKim, *San Blas, An Account of the Cuna Indians of Panama* (Göteborg, Sweden: Etnografiska Museet, Etnologiska Studier, No. 15, 1947).

Chapter Three

[1] Arthur C. Clarke, "Where's Everybody?" *Harpers*, November, 1957, pp. 73-77.

[2] Alfred R. Lindesmith and Anselm L. Strauss, *Social Psychology*, Rev. ed. (New York: Dryden, 1956), pp. 275-276. We may note here that even in the lower animals much behavior is the result of early and rapid learning.

[3] Kingsley Davis, *Human Society* (New York: Macmillan, 1949), pp. 204-208.

[4] *Ibid.*, p. 205.

[5] Ralph L. Beals and Harry Hoijer, *An Introduction to Anthropology* (New York: Macmillan, 1953), p. 539.

[6] These four paragraphs are based on Melville J. Herskovits, *Man and His Works* (New York: Knopf, 1948), pp. 153-165.

[7] Ralph Linton, *The Study of Man* (New York: D. Appleton-Century, 1936), p. 310.

[8] Ralph Linton, *The Cultural Background of Personality* (New York: D. Appleton-Century, 1945), p. 29.

[9] Horatio H. Newman, *Multiple Human Births* (New York: Doubleday, 1940), pp. 189-199.

[10] Lindesmith and Strauss, *Social Psychology*, p. 53.

[11] *Ibid.*, pp. 54-55.

[12] Ralph Ross and Ernest Van den Haag, *The Fabric of Society* (New York: Harcourt-Brace, 1957), p. 304.

[13] Edward Sapir, *Language*, Vol. 5 (Charlottesville, Va.: Linguistic Society of America, 1929), p. 209.

[14] Richard and Patricia Waterman, field notes, 1952-1953.

Chapter Four

[1] Davis, *Human Society*, p. 76.

[2] Robert Bierstedt, *The Social Order* (New York: McGraw-Hill, 1957), p. 299.

[3] Davis, *Human Society*, p. 72.

Chapter Five

[1] Bierstedt, *The Social Order*, p. 151.

[2] Davis, *Human Society*, p. 143.

[3] By permission of the Macmillan Company from J. S. Slotkin, *Social Anthropology* (New York: Macmillan, 1950), p. 62.

[4] By permission of the Macmillan Company from R. M. MacIver, *The Web of Government* (New York: Macmillan, 1949), p. 4.

[5] *Ibid.,* pp. 5, 39.

[6] R. M. MacIver and Charles H. Page, *Society: An Introductory Analysis* (New York: Rinehart, 1949), p. 152.

[7] A. L. Kroeber, *Anthropology* (New York: Harcourt-Brace, 1948), p. 294.

[8] *Ibid.*

[9] William F. Ogburn, *Social Change* (New York: Huebsch, 1922), pp. 90-102.

[10] Stuart Chase, *The Proper Study of Mankind* (New York: Harper, 1956), p. 131.

[11] Robert Lowie, *Culture and Ethnology* (New York: McMurrie, 1917), p. 78.

[12] Linton, *The Study of Man,* pp. 292-293.

[13] William F. Ogburn, "Cultural Lag as Theory," *Sociology and Social Research,* Vol. 41, January, 1957, pp. 167-174.

Chapter Six

[1] Ralph Linton, "One Hundred Per Cent American," *The American Mercury,* Vol. XL, pp. 427-429.

[2] Herskovits, *Man and His Works,* pp. 69-70.

[3] *Ibid.,* p. 75.

[4] Clyde Kluckhohn, *Mirror for Man* (New York: McGraw-Hill, 1949), p. 41.

[5] Ruth Benedict, *Patterns of Culture* (New York: Penguin Books, 1946), p. 33.

[6] Chase, *The Proper Study of Mankind,* p. 65.

[7] *Ibid.,* p. 66.

Chapter Seven

[1] Arnold Green, *Sociology: An Analysis of Life in Modern Society,* 2nd ed. (New York: McGraw-Hill, 1956), p. 42.

[2] *Ibid.,* p. 250.

[3] *Ibid.*

[4] Scott Greer, *Social Organization* (Garden City, N. Y.: Doubleday Short Studies in Sociology, 1955), p. 39.

[5] Davis, *Human Society,* p. 294.

[6] MacIver, *The Web of Government,* p. 222.

[7] Robert Redfield, "The Folk Society," *American Journal of Sociology,* January, 1947, pp. 293-308.

[8] *Ibid.*

[9] Peter Blau, *Bureaucracy in Modern Society* (New York: Random House, 1956), p. 14.

[10] *Ibid.,* p. 106.

[11] Logan Wilson and William L. Kolb, *Sociological Analysis* (New York: Harcourt-Brace, 1949), p. 681.

[12] Green, *Sociology: An Analysis of Life in Modern Society,* p. 59.

[13] *Ibid.,* p. 50.

[14] Norman F. Washburne, *Interpreting Social Change in America* (Garden City, N. Y.: Doubleday, 1954), p. 12.

[15] *Ibid.,* p. 21.

[16] Ralph H. Turner and Lewis M. Killian, *Collective Behavior* (Englewood Cliffs, N. J.: Prentice-Hall, 1957), p. 4.

[17] Louis Wirth, "Consensus and Mass Communication," *American Sociological Review,* Vol. 13, February, 1948, pp. 1-15.

[18] *Ibid.*

[19] *Ibid.*

[20] Turner and Killian, *Collective Behavior,* p. 308.

[21] *Ibid.,* p. 529.

Chapter Eight

[1] Kingsley Davis, "Analysis of the Population Explosion," *New York Times Magazine,* September 22, 1957, pp. 15 ff.

[2] Karl Sax, *The Population Explosion,* Foreign Policy Association, Headline Series, No. 120, 1956.

[3] Dennis H. Wrong, *Population* (New York: Random House, 1956), p. 25.

[4] Kingsley Davis, "The Political Impact of New Population Trends," *Foreign Affairs,* Vol. 36, No. 2, January, 1958, pp. 293-301.

[5] Sax, *The Population Explosion,* p. 2.

[6] See Christopher Rand, *The Puerto Ricans* (New York: Oxford University Press, 1958).

[7] Robert C. Cook, ed., *World Migration, 1946-1955,* Population Bulletin XIII, Population Reference Bureau, Inc., August, 1957.

[8] Louis Wirth, "Urbanism as a Way of Life," *American Journal of Sociology,* July, 1938, p. 8.

[9] William E. Cole, *Urban Society* (Boston: Houghton Mifflin, 1958), p. 28.

[10] *Ibid.,* p. 32.

[11] *Ibid.,* p. 56.

[12] Donald J. Bogue, *Population Growth in Standard Metropolitan Areas, 1900-1950,* (Washington, D. C.: United States Housing and Home Finance Agency, Division of Housing Research, December, 1953).

[13] *Ibid.*

[14] Frederick Lewis Allen, "The Big Change in Suburbia," *Harpers,* June, 1954, pp. 21-28.

[15] August Heckscher, "The Next Two Decades: Coming Changes in American Life," address presented at the opening session of the Twelfth National Conference on Higher Education, Chicago, March 3, 1957.

[16] Mel Ravitz, "Urban Sociology," unpublished manuscript, Wayne State University, January, 1957.

[17] United States Bureau of the Census, *Statistical Abstract of the United States,* 78th ed., Washington, D. C., 1957, p. 47.

[18] Adolph S. Tomars, "Rural Survivals in American Urban Life," *Rural Sociology,* December, 1943, pp. 378-386.

[19] Robert Cooley Angell, "The Moral Integration of American Cities," *American Journal of Sociology,* Vol. LVII, Part 2, July, 1951, pp. 1-140.

[20] Robin Williams, *American Society: A Sociological Interpretation* (New York: Knopf, 1951), p. 470.

[21] MacIver and Page, *Society: An Introductory Analysis*, p. 11.

[22] Cole, *Urban Society*, p. 256.

[23] Allen, "The Big Change in Suburbia," pp. 21-28.

[24] George C. Homans, *The Human Group* (New York: Harcourt-Brace, 1950), pp. 466-467.

[25] Heckscher, "The Next Two Decades: Coming Changes in American Life."

Chapter Nine

[1] Davis, *Human Society*, p. 367.

[2] Kurt B. Mayer, *Class and Society* (Garden City, N. Y.: Doubleday, 1955), pp. 14-16.

[3] *Ibid.*, pp. 16-19.

[4] *Ibid.*, p. 8.

[5] Green, *Sociology: An Analysis of Life in Modern Society*, p. 219.

[6] Paul Samuelson, *Economics: An Introductory Analysis*, 4th ed. (New York, McGraw-Hill, 1958), p. 61.

[7] Based on 1950 census as reported in *Statistical Abstract of the United States*, 1952, p. 186; 1 per cent not reported.

[8] Mayer, *Class and Society*, p. 40.

[9] Kenneth MacLeish and Kimball Young, *Landaff, New Hampshire* (Washington, D. C., Bureau of Agricultural Economics, 1942).

[10] August B. Hollingshead, *Elmtown's Youth* (New York: Wiley, 1949).

[11] See W. Lloyd Warner and Paul S. Lunt, *The Social Life of a Modern Community* (New Haven: Yale University Press, 1941); W. Lloyd Warner, Marchia Meeker, and Kenneth Eells, *Social Class in America* (Chicago: Science Research Associates, 1949).

[12] Williams, *American Society: A Sociological Interpretation*, p. 122.

[13] Albert J. Mayer and Philip Hauser, "Class Differentials in Expectation of Life at Birth," *La Revue de l'Institut International de Statistique*, Vol. 18, No. 200, 1950, reprinted in Reinhard Bendix and Seymour M. Lipset, *Class, Status, and Power* (Glencoe, Ill.: The Free Press, 1953), pp. 281-284.

[14] Green, *Sociology, An Analysis of Life in Modern Society*, p. 202.

[15] Warner, Meeker, and Eells, *Social Class in America*, p. 21.

[16] Green, *Sociology: An Analysis of Life in Modern Society*, pp. 212-216.

[17] Mayer, *Class and Society*, p. 70.

[18] Neal Gross, "Social Class Identification in the Urban Community," *American Sociological Review*, Vol. 18, No. 399, August, 1953.

Chapter Ten

[1] *Statistical Abstract of the United States*, 1957, pp. 50-51.

[2] Brewton Berry, *Race and Ethnic Relations* (Boston: Houghton Mifflin, 1958), p. 49.

[3] This discussion follows Otto Klineberg, *Social Psychology* (New York: Holt, 1954), pp. 300-304.

[4] Copyright, 1949, by Richard Rodgers and Oscar Hammerstein, 2nd. Reprinted by permission.

[5] *Statistical Abstract of the United States,* 1957, p. 315.

[6] *Ibid.,* p. 313.

[7] *Ibid.*

[8] Arnold Rose, *The Roots of Prejudice* (Paris: UNESCO, 1951).

[9] *My Several Worlds* (New York: John Day, 1954).

[10] John Biesanz, "Cultural and Economic Factors in Panamanian Race Relations," *American Sociological Review,* Vol. XIV, No. 6, December, 1949, pp. 772-779.

[11] Kenesaw M. Landis, *Segregation in Washington, A Report of the National Committee on Segregation in the Nation's Capital,* Chicago, 1948, p. 54.

[12] Gunnar Myrdal, *An American Dilemma: The Negro Problem and American Democracy* (New York: Harper, 1944), pp. 60-61.

[13] See Lloyd Allen Cook, *College Programs in Intergroup Relations* (Washington, D. C.: The American Council on Education, 1950); and *Intergroup Relations in Teacher Education,* 1951, volumes 1 and 2 of the College Study in Intergroup Relations.

[14] Research Branch, Information and Education Division, Hdqtrs., ETO Report, *ETO-82,* June, 1945.

[15] Gordon W. Allport, "Resolving Intergroup Tensions, An Appraisal of Methods," in Lloyd Allen Cook, ed., *Toward Better Human Relations* (Detroit: Wayne State University Press, 1952), p. 51.

[16] *Ibid.,* p. 71.

Chapter Eleven

[1] Gordon W. Allport, *Personality: A Psychological Interpretation* (New York: Holt, 1937), p. 193.

[2] Lindesmith and Strauss, *Social Psychology,* p. 559.

[3] John B. Watson, *Behaviorism* (New York, Norton, 1930), p. 82.

[4] Lindesmith and Strauss, *Social Psychology,* p. 509.

[5] George H. Mead, *Mind, Self, and Society* (Chicago: University of Chicago Press, 1934), pp. 135 ff.

[6] To Alvin Rose, Wayne State University social psychologist, we express thanks for his interpretation of Mead's theory.

[7] Charles Horton Cooley, *Human Nature and the Social Order* (New York: Scribners, 1903), pp. 151-153.

[8] Hubert Bonner, *Social Psychology* (New York: American Book, 1953), pp. 130-131.

[9] Margaret Ribble, *The Rights of Infants* (New York: Columbia University Press, 1944).

[10] Margaret Mead, *Sex and Temperament in Three Primitive Societies* (New York, Mentor Books, 1950), p. 158.

[11] Lindesmith and Strauss, *Social Psychology,* p. 509.

[12] *Ibid.,* p. 303.

[13] *Ibid.,* p. 310.

[14] *Ibid.,* p. 86.

[15] Jerome S. Bruner, "Social Psychology and Perception," in Eleanor E. Maccoby, *et al.*, eds., *Readings in Social Psychology,* 3rd ed. (New York: Holt, 1958), pp. 85-94.

[16] Roger W. Brown and Eric H. Lenneberg, "Studies in Linguistic Relativity," in Maccoby, *et al.*, eds., *Readings in Social Psychology,* p. 17.

[17] Lindesmith and Strauss, *Social Psychology,* p. 116.

[18] Harvey Warren Zorbaugh, *The Gold Coast and the Slum* (Chicago: University of Chicago Press, 1929), p. 86.

[19] Green, *Sociology: An Analysis of Life in Modern Society,* p. 149.

[20] *Ibid.,* pp. 138-139.

[21] David Riesman, *The Lonely Crowd: A Study of the Changing American Character* (New York: Doubleday-Anchor, 1955), p. 338.

Chapter Twelve

[1] Green, *Sociology: An Analysis of Life in Modern Society,* p. 346.

[2] *Ibid.*

[3] Bierstedt, *The Social Order,* p. 346.

[4] *Ibid.,* p. 359.

[5] *Ibid.,* p. 362.

[6] Robert Lowie, *Social Organization* (New York: Rinehart, 1948), pp. 119-121.

[7] Ralph Linton, "The Natural History of the Family," in Ruth Anshen, *The Family: Its Function and Destiny* (New York: Harper, 1949), pp. 18-38.

[8] *Statistical Abstract of the United States,* 1957, pp. 208-209.

[9] *Ibid.,* p. 41.

[10] *Ibid.*

[11] Francis E. Merrill (with H. Wentworth Eldredge), *Society and Culture: An Introduction to Sociology* (Englewood Cliffs, N. J.: Prentice-Hall, 1957), p. 383.

[12] "The Death of the Hired Man," in *The Complete Poems of Robert Frost* (New York: Holt, 1949), pp. 49-55.

[13] Ernest W. Burgess and Harvey J. Locke, *The Family, From Institution to Companionship,* 2nd ed. (New York: American Book, 1953), p. 25.

[14] Mayer, *Class and Society,* p. 50.

[15] Francis E. Merrill, *Courtship and Marriage: A Study of Social Relationships* (New York: Sloane, 1949), p. 34.

[16] *Ibid.*

[17] Hollingshead, *Elmtown's Youth.*

[18] Willard Waller, "The Rating and Dating Complex," *American Sociological Review,* Vol. 2, 1937, pp. 727-734.

[19] Robert F. Winch, *The Modern Family* (New York: Holt, 1952), p. 436.

[20] Clifford Kirkpatrick and Theodore Caplow, "Courtship in a Group of Minnesota Students," *The American Journal of Sociology,* Vol. 51, pp. 114-125. Reprinted in Judson T. Landis and Mary G. Landis, eds., *Readings in Marriage and the Family* (Englewood Cliffs, N. J.: Prentice-Hall, 1952), pp. 79-90.

[21] Ernest W. Burgess and Leonard S. Cottrell, *Predicting Success or Failure in Marriage* (Englewood Cliffs, N. J.: Prentice-Hall, 1939); and Lewis M. Terman, *Psychological Factors in Marital Happiness* (New York: McGraw-Hill, 1938).

[22] Judson T. Landis, "Length of Time Required to Achieve Adjustment in Marriage," *American Sociological Review,* Vol. 11, 1946, p. 668.

[23] Clifford Kirkpatrick, "Inconsistency in Marriage Roles and Marriage Conflict," *The International Journal of Ethics,* Vol. XLVI, 1936, pp. 444-460. Reprinted in Landis and Landis, eds., *Readings in Marriage and the Family,* pp. 386-392.

[24] *Ibid.*

[25] Della D. Cyrus, "What's Wrong With the Family?" *The Atlantic Monthly,* Vol. 178, 1946, pp. 67-73; and "Why Mothers Fail," *The Atlantic Monthly,* Vol. 179, 1947, pp. 57-60. Excerpted in Landis and Landis, eds., *Readings in Marriage and the Family,* under the title, "Problems of the Modern Homemaker-Mother," pp. 392-402.

[26] Green, *Sociology: An Analysis of Life in Modern Society,* pp. 377-379.

[27] Mayer, *Class and Society,* pp. 48-49.

[28] Sidonie M. Gruenberg and Hilda Sidney Krutch, *The Many Lives of Modern Woman* (New York: Doubleday, 1952).

[29] Willard Waller and Reuben Hill, *The Family* (New York: Dryden, 1951), p. 460.

[30] Judson T. Landis and Mary G. Landis, *Building a Successful Marriage,* 3rd ed. (Englewood Cliffs, N. J.: Prentice-Hall, 1958), pp. 6-7.

[31] Paul W. Alexander, "A Therapeutic Approach to the Problem of Divorce," *University of Illinois Law Forum,* 1949, pp. 105-108, 168-172. Reprinted in Landis and Landis, *Readings in Marriage and the Family,* pp. 360-374.

[32] By permission from *Marriage and the Family* by Ray E. Baber. Copyright, 1953. McGraw Hill, p. 527.

[33] Linton, "The Natural History of the Family," p. 38.

Chapter Thirteen

[1] Lloyd Allen Cook, *Community Backgrounds of Education* (New York: McGraw-Hill, 1938), p. 4.

[2] Williams, *American Society: A Sociological Interpretation,* p. 286.

[3] Margaret Mead, "Our Educational Emphasis in Primitive Perspective," *American Journal of Sociology,* Vol. 48, 1943, pp. 633-639.

[4] James B. Conant, "Education in the Western World," *The Atlantic Monthly,* November, 1957, pp. 73-77.

[5] *Detroit News,* May 10, 1957.

[6] Hollingshead, *Elmtown's Youth.*

[7] For one such teacher's story see Charles G. Spiegler, "A Teacher's Report on a Tough School," *New York Times Magazine,* November 24, 1957, p. 25.

[8] Alvin C. Eurich, "Russia's New Schooling," *The Atlantic Monthly,* April, 1958, pp. 55-58.

[9] Although 113,565 children were enrolled in special classes for the mentally retarded in 1952-53, only 22,916 were in classes for the mentally gifted—of whom there are theoretically as many in the population.

[10] Study by H. H. Remmers, cited in John R. Cunning, "If We Are to Catch up in Science," *New York Times Magazine,* November 10, 1957, p. 92.

[11] *Detroit Free Press,* August 13, 1957.

[12] Robert J. Havighurst and Bernice L. Neugarten, *Society and Education* (Boston: Allyn and Bacon, 1957), p. 185.

[13] Lloyd Allen Cook and Elaine Forsyth Cook, *Sociological Approach to Education* (New York: McGraw-Hill, 1950), pp. 321-322. This classic social science experiment, which for lack of space is not detailed here, provides an example of controlled scientific experimentation in group relations.

[14] Laurence Wylie, "Bringing up Children—French Way, Our Way," *New York Times Magazine,* June 30, 1957, pp. 9 ff.

[15] Eurich, "Russia's New Schooling."

[16] William Wattenberg, *et al.,* "Social Origins of Teachers and American Education," in Lindley J. Stiles, ed., *The Teacher's Role in American Society,* John Dewey Society, Fourteenth Yearbook, Chapter 5.

[17] Havighurst and Neugarten, *Society and Education,* p. 363. Based on five-level social structure.

[18] Mary Herrick, "The Annual Salary Story," *The American Teacher,* February, 1958, p. 7.

[19] Havighurst and Neugarten, *Society and Education,* Chapter 17.

[20] L. K. Frank, *Child Study Magazine,* Vol. 29, 1952, p. 4.

[21] Harvard Committee, *General Education in a Free Society* (Cambridge, Mass.: Harvard University Press, 1945).

[22] Havighurst and Neugarten, *Society and Education,* p. 331.

[23] William H. Kilpatrick and Arthur Bestor, "Progressive Education: A Debate," *New York Times Magazine,* September 8, 1957.

[24] C. R. Carpenter, paper presented at the Twelfth National Conference on Higher Education, Chicago, March 4, 1957.

[25] Herbert Blumer, *Movies and Conduct* (New York: Macmillan, 1933), pp. 196-197.

[26] John Dewey, "Education and Social Change," *Social Frontier,* Vol. 3, May, 1937, pp. 235-237. By permission of the John Dewey Society.

[27] Zechariah Chafee, Jr., "The Freedom to Think," *The Atlantic Monthly,* January, 1955, pp. 27-33.

Chapter Fourteen

[1] *Yearbook of American Churches,* 1958, p. 258.

[2] Includes some religious bodies that are "Protestant" only in the sense that they grew out of the Christian tradition, yet are not Roman Catholic.

[3] *Encyclopaedia Britannica Book of the Year,* 1958, p. 162.

[4] These estimates, which are often obviously inflated and overlapping, are useful primarily for gross comparisons.

[5] See, for example, Louis Bultena, "Church Membership and Church Attendance in Madison, Wisconsin," *American Sociological Review,* Vol. 14, June, 1949, pp. 384-389; Vattel Elbert Daniel, "Ritual and Stratification in Chicago Negro Churches," *American Sociological Review,* Vol. 7, June, 1942, pp. 352-361; W. R. Goldschmidt, "Class Denominalization in Rural California Churches," *American Journal of Sociology,* Vol. 49, January, 1944, pp. 348-355.

6 Arthur Huff Fauset, *Black Gods of the Metropolis* (Philadelphia: University of Pennsylvania Press, Publications of the Philadelphia Anthropological Society, Vol. 3, 1944), p. 26.

7 Wilson D. Wallis, *Messiahs: Their Role in Civilization* (Washington, D. C.: Public Affairs Press, 1943).

8 Hollingshead, *Elmtown's Youth.*

9 James Westfall Thompson and Edgar Nathaniel Johnson, *An Introduction to Medieval Europe, 300-1500* (New York: Norton, 1937), pp. 49-52.

10 Edmund W. Sinnott, *Science and Religion: A Necessary Partnership* (The Hazen Pamphlets, 1950), pp. 49-52.

11 Dorothy Thompson, "The Banishment of Anxiety," *Ladies Home Journal,* July, 1957, p. 14.

12 The descriptive term "Cult of Reassurance" was coined by the late Paul Hutchinson in his article "Have We a New Religion?" *Life,* Vol. 38, April 11, 1955, pp. 138-158. Hutchinson also suggested that the popular Norman Vincent Peale should be regarded as the "high priest" of the cult.

13 Although it may seem strange to call "The American Way of Life" a religion, it does have that quality of sacredness—notice how often it is written in capital letters and spoken with a tremor in the voice—mentioned in the definition at the beginning of this chapter. For a discussion of Communism as a secular religion see Maude Fiero, "Religion as a Social Institution," in John and Mavis Biesanz, *Modern Society,* 1st ed. (Englewood Cliffs, N. J.: Prentice-Hall, 1954), p. 278.

14 Liston Pope, *Millhands and Preachers* (New Haven: Yale University Press, 1942), pp. 89-90.

15 J. Milton Yinger, "Present Status of the Sociology of Religion," *Journal of Religion,* Vol. 21, July, 1951, p. 207.

16 James B. Christensen, "The Tigari Cult of West Africa," *Papers of the Michigan Academy of Science, Arts, and Letters,* Vol. 39, 1953, pp. 389-398.

17 W. Edgar Vinacke, Jan Eindhoven, and James Engle, "Religious Attitudes of Students at the University of Hawaii," *The Journal of Psychology,* Vol. 28, 1949, pp. 161-179.

18 Frederick A. Shippey, *Protestantism in Indianapolis* (Indianapolis: The Church Federation of Indianapolis, 1946), p. 34.

19 Max Weber, *The Protestant Ethic and the Spirit of Capitalism,* Talcott Parsons, trans. (London: Allen and Unwin, 1930).

Chapter Fifteen

1 We are grateful to economist Leonard Weiss for substantial help on this chapter.

2 Mead, *Sex and Temperament in Three Primitive Societies,* pp. 25-27.

3 Labor includes all the productive efforts of humans whether employed by others or working for themselves. Land refers to all the resources provided by nature, including soil, topography, climate, minerals, waterways, and location. Capital embraces all the means of production made by man—buildings, machinery, stocks of raw materials, fuel, finished or semi-finished products, improvements on the land, manmade waterways, roads, planted forests, and so forth. It does not include stocks and bonds, doctor bills, life insurance policies, or bank deposits. Enterprise refers to planning, risk-bearing, and decision-making, and is often listed as a fourth factor of

production. The general terms for payments to the factors of production are wages (for labor), rents (for land), interest (on capital), and profits (for enterprise).

[4] Herskovits, *Man and His Works,* Chapter 17. See also the same author's *The Economic Life of Primitive Peoples* (New York: Knopf, 1940).

[5] With our great modern storehouse of knowledge and machines, present-day division of labor is infinitely more rewarding than it once was. It makes possible more efficient production by (a) making use of special talents, (b) minimizing the training necessary for a particular amount of production while providing maximum training for each person in his particular skill, (c) eliminating lost time in moving from job to job, and (d) reducing the tools necessary to perform a complete productive process since each specialist need not duplicate the tools of other specialists.

Chapter Sixteen

[1] More fully, *An Inquiry into the Nature and Causes of the Wealth of Nations.*

[2] *Ibid.,* Modern Library Edition (New York: Random House, 1937), p. 651.

[3] *Ibid.,* p. 423.

[4] Quoted by D. H. Robertson, "The Economic Outlook," *The Economic Journal,* Vol. LVII, December, 1947, p. 429.

[5] *Wealth of Nations,* p. 98.

[6] Because he feared too much money would be issued.

[7] Or, in President Eisenhower's phrasing, the federal government "should perform an essential task only when it cannot otherwise be adequately performed; and . . . in performing that task, . . . should not impair the self-respect, freedom, and incentive of the individual." (State of the Union Address, January, 1955.)

Chapter Seventeen

[1] The manner in which expansion of output through the introduction of machinery can stimulate still further expansion may be illustrated in the following way. Suppose a shoe manufacturer buys one machine that will cut leather for 1,000 pairs a day, another that will stitch the soles of 750 pairs a day, and a third that will nail shoes together at the rate of 500 pairs a day. If he stops there, one or more of the machines will be idle a good part of the time. To get full value for his money, he must produce not 1,000 but 3,000 pairs each day by installing three cutters, four stitchers, and six nailers. See George W. Stocking and Myron W. Watkins, *Monopoly and Free Enterprise* (New York: The Twentieth Century Fund, 1951), pp. 57-58.

[2] William H. Husband and James C. Dockery, *Modern Corporation Finance* (Homewood, Ill.: Irwin, 1947), p. 20.

[3] *Statistical Abstract of the United States,* 1957, p. 488.

[4] David Lynch, *The Concentration of Economic Power* (New York: Columbia University Press, 1946), p. 117.

[5] *Statistical Abstract of the United States,* 1957, p. 488.

[6] Lynch, *The Concentration of Economic Power,* p. 117.

[7] Federal Trade Commission, *Report on Corporate Mergers and Acquisitions, Summary,* May, 1955, p. 2.

[8] Stocking and Watkins, *Monopoly and Free Enterprise,* pp. 142-143.

Chapter Eighteen

[1] Arthur M. Schlesinger in the *Washington Post,* January 1, 1950, as quoted by J. B. S. Hardman and Maurice F. Neufield, *The House of Labor: Internal Operations of American Unions* (Englewood Cliffs, N. J.: Prentice-Hall, 1951), p. 52.

[2] Reliable figures concerning world trade union membership are almost impossible to secure. The figure here given includes both Communist and non-Communist unions.

[3] Samuel E. Morison and Henry S. Commager, *The Growth of the American Republic,* 4th ed., Vol. 2 (New York: Oxford University Press, 1950), p. 153.

[4] A.F. of L., Report of Proceedings, 1936, p. 41; Florence Peterson, *American Labor Unions: What They Are and How They Work* (New York: Harper, 1952), p. 62.

[5] Attributed to Adolph Strasser by Morison and Commager, *The Growth of the American Republic,* Vol. 2, p. 158.

[6] Arnold Beichman, "The I.C.F.T.U.—Its Aims and Achievements," in Jack Schuyler, ed., *International Labor Directory and Handbook* (New York: Praeger, 1955), pp. 14-17.

[7] See Fritz Roethlisberger and William J. Dickson, *Management and Worker: An Account of a Research Program conducted by the Western Electric Company, Hawthorne Works, Chicago* (Cambridge, Mass.: Harvard University Press, 1939).

[8] Burleigh B. Gardner, *Human Relations in Industry* (Homewood, Ill.: Irwin, 1945), pp. 7-8.

[9] Osgood Nichols and T. R. Carskadon, *Can Labor and Management Work Together?* Public Affairs Pamphlet No. 151 (New York: The Public Affairs Committee, 1949), p. 8.

[10] *Ibid.,* p. 15.

[11] Clyde E. Dankert, *Contemporary Unionism in the United States* (Englewood Cliffs, N. J.: Prentice-Hall, 1948), pp. 466-467.

[12] Sumner H. Slichter, *Trade Unions in a Free Society* (Cambridge, Mass.: Harvard University Press, 1948), p. 5.

[13] Irving Howe and B. J. Widick, *The UAW and Walter Reuther* (New York: Random House, 1949), p. 200.

[14] See C. Wright Mills, *The New Men of Power: America's Labor Leaders* (New York: Harcourt-Brace, 1948).

[15] Kermit Eby, "What Labor Needs," *The Progressive,* Vol. 22, No. 4, April, 1958, p. 30.

Chapter Nineteen

[1] Dr. Julia J. Henderson, Director of the Social Welfare Division of the UN, quoted in the *New York Times,* November 20, 1952.

[2] *Statistical Abstract of the United States,* 1957, p. 307.

[3] Sylvia Porter, "Middle-Income Market Growing," *Detroit Free Press,* June 3, 1958.

[4] Roger Babson in *Commercial and Financial Chronicle,* October 9, 1952.

[5] Lewis D. Stillwell, "The Consumer," in Robert E. Riegel, ed., *An Introduction to the Social Sciences,* Vol. 1 (New York: Appleton-Century, 1941), p. 434.

[6] *Ibid.,* pp. 420-421.

[7] LeBaron R. Foster, *Credit for Consumers*, Public Affairs Pamphlet No. 5, Rev. ed. (New York: The Public Affairs Committee, 1950), p. 12.

[8] *Ibid.*

[9] John Ise, *Economics*, Rev. ed. (New York: Harper, 1950), p. 309.

[10] Vance Packard, *The Hidden Persuaders* (New York: David McKay, 1957), p. 240.

[11] Ise, *Economics*, Rev. ed., p. 308.

[12] *Consumer Reports*, April, 1953, p. 142.

Chapter Twenty-one

[1] Frank P. Chambers, C. P. Harris, and Charles C. Bayley, *This Age of Conflict* (New York: Harcourt-Brace, 1950), pp. 164-165.

Chapter Twenty-two

[1] MacIver, *The Web of Government*, pp. 31-38.

[2] G. Lowell Field, *Controlling Group Clashes: The Institutions of Political Power* (Dubuque, Iowa: William C. Brown, 1952), p. 2.

[3] Davis, *Human Society*, p. 481.

[4] Herman C. Beyle, "Government and Politics as Social Control," in William Mosher, ed., *Introduction to Responsible Citizenship* (New York: Holt, 1941), p. 203.

[5] A. D. Lindsay, *The Modern Democratic State* (New York: Oxford University Press, 1947), p. 206.

[6] For a clear and competent discussion of the nature of social institutions see Harry Elmer Barnes, *Social Institutions* (Englewood Cliffs, N. J.: Prentice-Hall, 1947), pp. 29-31.

[7] See J. O. Hertzler, *Social Institutions* (Lincoln, Nebraska: University of Nebraska Press, 1946), pp. 114-116.

[8] MacIver, *The Web of Government*, pp. 32-33.

[9] Francis Coker, *Recent Political Thought* (New York: Appleton-Century, 1934), pp. 21-22.

[10] James J. Maguire, "The Anatomy of Natural Rights," *The Newman Review*, Vol. 1, May, 1950, pp. 4-5.

[11] For purposes of our discussion we are using "civil liberties" and "civil rights" as if they were synonymous phrases.

[12] John Stuart Mill, *On Liberty* (London: Watts, 1929), pp. 12-21.

[13] *Ibid.*, pp. 19-20.

[14] *Abrams* v. *United States*, 250 U.S. 624 (1924).

[15] Henry Steele Commager, *Freedom, Loyalty, Dissent* (New York: Oxford University Press, 1954), p. 18.

[16] Zechariah Chafee, Jr., *Free Speech in the United States* (Cambridge, Mass.: Harvard University Press, 1941), p. 564.

[17] Robert L. Hale, *Freedom Through Law: Public Control of Private Governing Power* (New York: Columbia University Press, 1952), p. 1.

[18] Merle Fainsod, *How Russia Is Ruled* (Cambridge: Harvard University Press, 1953), p. 320.

[19] For a more detailed analysis of Soviet Communism see Chapter Twenty-seven.

[20] *Schwimmer* v. *United States,* 279 U.S. 653 (1929).

[21] *Declaration of Human Rights,* Article 30.

[22] *Schenck* v. *United States,* 249 U.S. 47 (1919).

[23] Sidney Hook, *Heresy, Yes—Conspiracy, No!* (New York: John Day, 1953), p. 22.

[24] For further elaboration of this generalization see Chapter Twenty-seven.

[25] Norman Thomas, *The Test of Freedom* (New York: Norton, 1954), p. 49.

[26] *Communism, Conformity, and Civil Liberties: A Cross Section of the Nation Speaks Its Mind* (New York: Doubleday, 1955).

[27] *Ibid.,* p. 13.

[28] *Ibid.,* p. 87.

[29] *Ibid.,* pp. 28, 32, 40.

[30] *Ibid.,* pp. 107, 130, 155.

Chapter Twenty-three

[1] Alexander Heard, *Money and Politics* (New York: The Public Affairs Committee, 1956).

[2] Bernard R. Berelson, Paul F. Lazarsfeld, and William N. McPhee, *Voting* (Chicago: University of Chicago Press, 1954).

Chapter Twenty-four

[1] *Time,* July 29, 1957, p. 10.

[2] D. W. Brogan, *Politics in America* (New York: Harper, 1954), p. 268.

[3] Clinton Rossiter, *The American Presidency* (New York: New American Library, 1956), pp. 10-29.

[4] Sidney Hyman, "To Remove the Causes of Executive Strain," *New York Times Magazine,* October 16, 1955, p. 72.

[5] Rossiter, *The American Presidency,* p. 15.

[6] Harlan Cleveland, "Survival in the Bureaucratic Jungle," *The Reporter,* April 5, 1956, p. 30.

[7] *Ibid.,* p. 32.

[8] John Friedman, "Planning, Programs, and Social Welfare," *Diogenes,* Spring, 1957, p. 105.

[9] Frances Perkins, *The Roosevelt I Knew* (New York: Viking, 1946), p. 377.

[10] Gallup Poll, *Detroit Free Press,* July 18, 1957, p. 22.

[11] Harold J. Laski, *The American Presidency: An Interpretation* (New York: Harper, 1940), p. 7.

[12] Woodrow Wilson, *Congressional Government,* 15th ed. (Boston: Houghton, Mifflin, 1913), p. 45.

[13] *Ibid.,* pp. 52-53.

[14] Brogan, *Politics in America,* p. 312.

[15] William S. White, *Citadel* (New York: Harper, 1954), pp. 49-50.

[16] Brogan, *Politics in America,* p. 323.

[17] White, *Citadel*, pp. 180-181.

[18] *Ibid.*, pp. 111-116.

[19] *New York Times*, May 6, 1949, pp. 1, 6.

[20] *Manchester Guardian*, May 7, 1949, p. 8.

[21] *New York Times*, August 3, 1957, p. 1.

[22] White, *Citadel*, pp. 245-249.

[23] Select Committee on Lobbying Activities, *Interim Report*, 81st Congress, 2nd Session, House of Representatives, p. 31.

[24] *Ibid.*, p. 9.

[25] *Ibid.*, p. 67.

[26] Dean Acheson, *A Citizen Looks at Congress* (New York: Harper, 1957), p. 32.

Chapter Twenty-five

[1] Quoted in Charles Howard McIlwain, *Constitutionalism Ancient and Modern* (Ithaca, N. Y.: Cornell University Press, 1940), p. 4.

[2] Edward M. Sait, *Government and Politics of France* (Yonkers-on-the-Hudson, N. Y.: World Book, 1920), p. 17.

[3] A. H. Kelly and W. A. Harbison, *The American Constitution* (New York: Norton, 1948), p. 163.

[4] Brogan, *Politics in America*, p. 33.

[5] *Ibid.*, pp. 32-35.

[6] In addition to the constitutional courts Congress has created such legislative courts as the Court of Military Appeals, the Customs Court, the Court of Customs and Patent Appeals, and territorial courts.

[7] Speech by Judge Leonard Hall, *St. Louis Post Dispatch*, February 6, 1958, pp. 1, 6.

[8] Quoted in Brogan, *Politics in America*, pp. 390-391.

[9] *United States* v. *Butler*, 297 U.S. 1.

[10] *New York Times*, December 4, 1957, pp. 1, 34.

[11] Quoted in James M. Burns and Jack W. Peltason, *Government by the People*, 3rd ed. (Englewood Cliffs, N. J.: Prentice-Hall, 1957), p. 538.

[12] James Bryce, *The American Commonwealth*, Vol. 1 (New York: Macmillan, 1931), p. 274.

[13] Fred V. Cahill, Jr., *Judicial Legislation* (New York: Ronald, 1952), p. 3.

[14] *New York Times*, July 27, 1957, p. 6.

[15] Robert H. Jackson, *The American Supreme Court in the American System of Government* (Cambridge, Mass.: Harvard University Press, 1955), pp. 82-83.

Chapter Twenty-seven

[1] O.E.E.C. Eighth Report, Vol. II, *Europe in 1960* and *The Western European Markets, 1957* (New York: J. Walter Thompson, Co., 1957).

[2] George F. Kennan, "The Soviet Mind and World Realities," *The Listener*, London, November 21, 1957.

[3] "The Strategy of Revolutionary and War Propaganda," in Quincy Wright, ed., *Public Opinion and World Politics* (Chicago: University of Chicago Press, 1933).

[4] The terms, including the capitalizations, are from the Soviet press. Taken from Arthur Koestler, *The Yogi and the Commissar* (London: Jonathan Cape, 1945), p. 145.

[5] Milovan Djilas, *The New Class* (New York: Praeger, 1957). On debasement of unionism see François Fetjo, "Trade Unionism in Eastern Europe: The Conflict between Working-class Ties and the Single Party," *International Affairs*, Vol. 33, October, 1957.

[6] *Education in the U.S.S.R.* Report of a two-year study by the United States Office of Education, November 10, 1957.

[7] *Second Interim Report*, The President's Committee on Scientists and Engineers (Washington, D. C.: United States Government Printing Office, November, 1957).

[8] The primacy of these goals is generally established and accepted by political scientists. See, for example, Harold D. Lasswell, *The Analysis of Political Behavior* (New York: Oxford University Press, 1948).

[9] See O. Utis, "Generalissimo Stalin and the Art of Government," *Foreign Affairs*, Vol. 30, January, 1952, pp. 197-214; and Isaiah Berlin, "The Silence in Russian Culture," *Foreign Affairs*, Vol. 36, October, 1957, pp. 1-24.

[10] The *New York Times*, March 30, 1958.

[11] Stevan Dedijer, "Research and Freedom in Underdeveloped Countries," *Bulletin of the Atomic Scientists*, Vol. 13, September, 1957, pp. 238-242.

[12] Eugene Rabinowitch, "After Missiles and Satellites, What?" *Bulletin of the Atomic Scientists*, Vol. 13, December, 1957, pp. 346-350.

Chapter Twenty-eight

[1] The biggest single United States economic aid program, the Marshall Plan to aid Western Europe, totaled about $5,000,000,000 a year and was motivated by the fear that Western Europe, particularly France and Italy, would be captured by Russia and Communism. United States aid to Asia, in the mid-1950's the biggest single recipient area, flows predominantly to the threatened countries of South Korea, Nationalist China on Formosa, and South Viet Nam.

[2] See any major writer in the field, e.g., David B. Truman, *The Governmental Process* (New York: Knopf, 1953) or V. O. Key, *Politics, Parties, and Pressure Groups*, 3rd ed. (New York: Crowell, 1955).

[3] The Spanish dictatorship became ideologically tolerable to America only when the need for air and naval bases on Spain—matters of security—overrode ideological considerations.

[4] Certain exceptions should perhaps be explained. Obsolete defense installations are occasionally found along the Atlantic Coast of Latin America and in the Caribbean, remnants of defenses against former enemies (Britain in the nineteenth century and German submarines and naval raiders as recently as World War II). An occasional base exists for tracking test missiles, but none of these installations are active defense bases, nor do any amount to anything significant in terms of American or Allied manpower, money, or weapon power.

[5] Jack Usher Mowll, "The Economic Geography of Nuclear Power," *Annals*, Association of American Geographers, Vol. 47, June, 1947; Bernhart C. Bechoefer and Eric Stein, "Atoms for Peace: The New International Atomic Energy Agency," *Michigan Law Review*, Vol. 55, April, 1957; K. D. Nichols, "Progress in Atomic Power," *Military Engineer*, Vol. XLIX, March-April, 1947; John Jay Hopkins, "Atomic

Power Will Guide the Future," *Systems,* Vol. XXI, March-April, 1957; Clark Crand Vogel, "International Bilateral Agreements for Cooperation in Atomic Energy," *George Washington Law Review,* Vol. 25, April, 1957.

[6] Examples of nominal allies are Sweden and Switzerland; examples of actual allies are Britain, France, West Germany, and other members of alliances with the United States.

[7] See the preceding chapter and Lorna Hahn, "Last Chance in North Africa," *Foreign Affairs,* Vol. 36, January, 1958, pp. 302-314.

[8] Harold Nicholson, *Diplomacy,* 2nd ed. (London: Oxford University Press, 1950).

[9] Every close student of foreign policy is aware that much of American foreign policy tends to be made at the moment of and by the circumstances of the crisis of the moment, and allows only limited possibilities for immediate action. The "cable" makes much of the policy, so to speak. See, for example, Joseph Alsop and Robert Kintner, *American White Paper* (New York: Simon and Schuster, 1940).

[10] There is not space here to describe the United Nations' possibilities and handicaps. The interested reader is referred to *Everyman's United Nations: A Ready Reference to the Structure, Functions, and Work of the United Nations and Its Related Agencies* (New York: United Nations Department of Public Information, 1955) for the organizational picture, and to Werner Levi, *Fundamentals of World Organization* (Minneapolis: University of Minnesota Press, 1950) for the political difficulties.

[11] George F. Kennan, Stafford Little Lectures, 1956.

[12] Robert Jungk, *Tomorrow Is Already Here* (New York: Simon and Schuster, 1954). For the technical possibilities in food production see Sir George Thomson, "The New Industrial Revolution," *Bulletin of the Atomic Scientists,* Vol. 13, January, 1957.

Other Works
to Read

Chapter One

Beard, Charles A., *The Nature of the Social Sciences* (New York: Scribner, 1934). Offers a provocative introduction to the whole social science field. It contains several challenging sections on science and social science.

Gee, William, *Social Science Research Methods* (New York: Appleton-Century-Crofts, 1950). A useful if not especially original general introduction to social science methodology.

Lundberg, George A., *Social Research*, Rev. ed. (New York: Longmans, Green, 1942). A classic work on social science investigation.

Standen, Anthony, *Science Is a Sacred Cow* (New York: Dutton, 1950). Written by a chemist. A clever antidote to science worship.

White, Leslie A., *The Science of Culture* (New York: Farrar, Straus, 1949). Includes many interesting observations concerning the nature of science and the possibility of developing a more mature social science.

Chapter Two

McKim, Fred, *San Blas: An Account of the Cuna Indians of Panama* (Göteborg, Sweden: Etnografiska Museet, Etnologiska Studier, No. 15, 1947). Very readable.

669

Stout, David B., *San Blas Cuna Acculturation: An Introduction* (New York: The Viking Fund, Publications in Anthropology, No. 9, 1947). Perhaps the best single study of the Cuna.

Chapter Three

Benedict, Ruth, *Patterns of Culture* (New York: Pelican Books, 1946). This fascinating comparison of three cultures offers voluminous proof of the variability of culture and an interpretation of it.

Kluckhohn, Clyde, *Mirror for Man* (New York: McGraw-Hill, 1949). This book on "the relation of anthropology to modern life" is written for the layman by a noted anthropologist. Highly readable and stimulating.

Linton, Ralph, *The Study of Man* (New York: Appleton-Century, 1936). A classic textbook on culture.

Mead, Margaret, *Sex and Temperament in Three Primitive Societies* (New York: Mentor Books, 1950). Extremely interesting accounts of the values and behavior patterns of three tribes, which though living in the same general area present striking personality and cultural contrasts.

Chapter Four

Benedict, Ruth, *The Chrysanthemum and the Sword* (Boston: Houghton, Mifflin, 1946). Shows how culture serves as social control by setting patterns of behavior for the Japanese.

Davis, Kingsley, *Human Society* (New York: Macmillan, 1949). Chapter 3, "Social Norms," is an excellent discussion of culture as social control. For the serious student.

Frank, Lawrence K., *Nature and Human Nature* (New Brunswick, N. J.: Rutgers University Press, 1951). Difficult but thought-provoking reading.

Sumner, William Graham, *Folkways* (Boston: Ginn, 1906). This classic account of folkways, mores, and law is still interesting, though some of the author's viewpoints have been modified by recent social science research.

Chapter Five

Allen, Francis R., and others, *Technology and Social Change* (New York: Appleton-Century-Crofts, 1957). As the title indicates, this book deals with the impact of technological change on society and culture.

Allen, Frederick Lewis, *The Big Change* (New York: Harper, 1952). This book, written for the layman, notes many changes in American folkways, mores, and values since 1900.

Buck, Pearl S., *My Several Worlds* (New York: John Day, 1954). The autobiography of the famous novelist's early life in China is a fascinating account of cultural contact.

Commager, Henry Steele, ed., *America in Perspective* (New York: Random House, 1947). A collection of comments by foreign observers of the American scene over several hundred years.

———, *The American Mind* (New Haven: Yale University Press, 1950). An examination of American ideas, beliefs and values.

Lerner, Max, *America as a Civilization* (New York: Simon and Schuster, 1957). This volume, although not a text in sociology, utilizes sociological concepts among many other perspectives on American culture and social organization.

Linton, Ralph, *The Study of Man*. Chapters 17-21 deal with cultural content and cultural change.

Williams, Robin M., Jr., *American Society: A Sociological Interpretation* (New York: Knopf, 1951). Chapter 11 is an excellent discussion of American values. The entire book is very helpful for the serious student.

Chapter Six

Barzini, Luigi, Jr., *Americans Are Alone in the World* (New York: Random House, 1953). According to one reviewer, this "intelligent and observant outsider is able to find in the activities of the [American] daily routine characteristics and revealing features of which those involved are frequently unaware."

Gorer, Geoffrey, *The American People: A Study in National Character* (New York: Norton, 1948). An interesting exercise in "seeing ourselves as some see us," though we may not agree with many of this English anthropologist's interpretations.

Kluckhohn, Clyde, *Mirror for Man*. Written in clear and simple style especially for the purpose of explaining what an understanding of the culture concept can contribute to modern society. Especially valuable in counteracting ethnocentrism are chapters 1, 2, 9, and 10.

West, James, *Plainville, U.S.A.* (New York: Columbia University Press, 1945). Chapter 3 discusses the ethnocentric attitudes found in a Midwestern town.

Chapter Seven

Green, Arnold, *Sociology: An Analysis of Life in Modern Society*, 2nd ed. (New York: McGraw-Hill, 1956). Chapters 3 and 4 are especially pertinent as supplementary readings on social interaction and social organization.

Greer, Scott, *Social Organization* (Garden City, New York: Doubleday Short Studies in Sociology, 1955). An excellent brief discussion of social organization.

Redfield, Robert, "The Folk Society," *American Journal of Sociology,* January, 1947, pp. 293-308. A classic description of the folk society.

Turner, Ralph H., and Lewis M. Killian, *Collective Behavior* (Englewood Cliffs, N. J.: Prentice-Hall, 1957). A comprehensive and authoritative text on collective behavior.

Chapter Eight

Alegría, Ciro, *Broad and Alien Is the World* (New York: Farrar, Straus, and Young, 1941). Prizewinning novel depicting the impact of secondary groups upon a tightly-knit, tradition-ruled Indian farm village in Peru.

Cole, William E., *Urban Society* (Boston: Houghton, Mifflin, 1958). An excellent readable text on urban sociology.

Davis, Kingsley, "Analysis of the Population Explosion," *New York Times Magazine,* September 22, 1957, pp. 15 ff.

———, "The Political Impact of New Population Trends," *Foreign Affairs,* Vol. 36, No. 2 (January, 1958), pp. 293-301. These articles by a leading demographer examine the significance of recent trends in world population.

Fisher, Robert Moore, ed., *The Metropolis in Modern Life* (Garden City, N. Y.: Doubleday, 1955). This book of readings examines the impact of the urban trend on social institutions.

The editors of *Fortune, The Exploding Metropolis* (New York: Doubleday-Anchor, 1958). The contributors to this stimulating volume believe that the big, tense, heterogeneous city should be preserved. The book deals with the problems of migration to the suburbs, urban transit, city administration, slums, and the planning of downtown areas, among other topics.

Miner, Horace, *St. Denis: A French Canadian Parish* (Chicago: The University of Chicago Press, 1939). Excellent study of the values and relationships of a peasant society.

Rand, Christopher, *The Puerto Ricans* (New York: Oxford University Press, 1958). Examines the causes of the recent influx of Puerto Ricans into New York City, what it is doing to their way of life, and what it is doing to the city. The book is based on a series of articles that appeared originally in the *New Yorker*.

Sax, Karl, *The Population Explosion*, Foreign Policy Association, Headline Series, No. 120, 1956. A brief and simply written treatment of recent population trends.

Wirth, Louis, "Urbanism as a Way of Life," *American Journal of Sociology*, July, 1938. A classic statement on the meaning of the urban trend.

Chapter Nine

Baber, Bernard, *Social Stratification* (New York: Harcourt-Brace, 1957). An authoritative text.

Bendix, Reinhard, and Seymour M. Lipset, *Class, Status, and Power* (Glencoe, Ill.: The Free Press, 1953). Readings on social stratification in the United States and other countries.

Lewis, Sinclair, *Babbitt* (New York: Harcourt-Brace, 1922). Well-known portrait of a middle-class American businessman.

Mayer, Kurt, *Class and Society* (Garden City, N. Y.: Doubleday, 1955). An excellent short study of social class.

Ryan, Bryce, *Caste in Modern Ceylon* (New Brunswick, N. J.: Rutgers University Press, 1953). Authoritative and detailed study of a complex and persistent problem.

Warner, W. Lloyd, and Paul S. Lunt, *The Social Life of a Modern Community* (New Haven: Yale University Press, 1941). Describes research methods and the cultural life of Newburyport, Massachusetts. Chapter 7, "Profiles from Yankee City," will be especially interesting to the beginning student.

Williams, Robin M., Jr., *American Society, A Sociological Interpretation*. Chapter 5, "Social Stratification in the United States," is a thought-provoking analysis that refers to the most important studies of social class in America.

Chapter Ten

Allport, Gordon W., *A B C's of Scapegoating*, Rev. ed. (Anti-Defamation League of B'nai B'rith, 1948). A clear analysis of psychological factors in race relations.

Barron, Milton L., ed., *American Minorities: A Textbook of Readings in Intergroup Relations* (New York: Knopf, 1957). An excellent collection of readings on race, religion, and nationality.

Benedict, Ruth, and others, *The Races of Mankind*, 2nd Rev. ed. (New York: Public Affairs Pamphlet No. 85, 1951). Like most Public Affairs Pamphlets, this is easy and interesting reading on an important subject.

Berry, Brewton, *Race and Ethnic Relations* (Boston: Houghton, Mifflin, 1958). A detached, scientific, but readable treatment of this timely and emotion-charged subject.

Kluckhohn, Clyde, *Mirror for Man*. Chapter 5, "Race: A Modern Myth," is written in the same clear and lively style as the rest of the book.

Myrdal, Gunnar, *An American Dilemma: The Negro Problem and Modern Democracy* (New York: Harper, 1944). This voluminous and valuable study was made by a team of scholars.

Chapter Eleven

Hall, Calvin S., and Garner Lindzey, *Theories of Personality* (New York: Wiley, 1957). A fuller discussion of the theories we have mentioned as well as others.

Lindesmith, Alfred R., and Anselm L. Strauss, *Social Psychology*, Rev. ed. (New York: Dryden, 1956). A social psychology text expounding the symbolic interactionist viewpoint.

Linton, Ralph, *The Cultural Background of Personality* (New York: D. Appleton-Century, 1945). An excellent assessment of the relationship among culture, society, and personality.

Mead, Margaret, *Growing Up in New Guinea* (New York: Morrow, 1930). A readable and interesting account of how the Manus tribe brings up its children and how the methods of socialization are related to the culture and personalities of the Manus.

Newman, Horatio H., "How Differences in Environment Affected Separated One-Egg Twins," in Edgar A. Schuler, Duane L. Gibson, Maude L. Fiero, and Wilbur B. Brookover, eds., *Outside Readings in Sociology* (New York: Crowell, 1952), pp. 49-57.

Chapter Twelve

Baber, Ray E., *Marriage and the Family*, 2nd ed. (New York: McGraw-Hill, 1953). An excellent text.

Beers, Howard W., "A Portrait of the Farm Family in Central New York State," in Schuler, Gibson, Fiero, Brookover, eds., *Outside Readings in Sociology*, pp. 599-612. Affords excellent perspective for consideration of the modern family.

Burgess, Ernest W., and Leonard S. Cottrell, *Predicting Success or Failure in Marriage* (Englewood Cliffs, N. J.: Prentice-Hall, 1939). A pioneer and still very valuable study in this field.

Burgess, Ernest W., and Harvey J. Locke, *The Family, from Institution to Companionship*, 2nd ed. (New York: American Book, 1953). An authoritative volume.

Landis, Judson T., and Mary C. Landis, *Building a Successful Marriage*, 3rd ed. (Englewood Cliffs, N. J.: Prentice-Hall, 1958). Presents in readable form scientific knowledge about mate selection, courtship, and the adjustment problems of marriage. Authoritative and useful.

————, *Readings in Marriage and the Family* (Englewood Cliffs, N. J.: Prentice-Hall, 1952). An excellent collection of materials from a variety of sources.

Queen, Stuart A., and John B. Adams, *The Family in Various Cultures* (Chicago: Lippincott, 1952). This survey of 11 family systems affords excellent cultural and historical perspective.

Yang, Martin C., "Intrafamilial Memberships in a Farm Village of Shantung Province, China," in Schuler, Gibson, Fiero, and Brookover, eds., *Outside Readings in Sociology*, pp. 569-581. Family roles are related to the form and function of the Chinese family.

Chapter Thirteen

Cook, Lloyd Allen, and Elaine Forsyth Cook, *Sociological Approach to Education* (New York: McGraw-Hill, 1950). A study of American community life as it bears upon all aspects of school practices.

Havighurst, Robert J., and Bernice L. Neugarten, *Society and Education* (Boston: Allyn and Bacon, 1957). An analysis of the role played by the school in interpreting and transmitting the values of society to children.

Hollingshead, A. B., *Elmtown's Youth* (New York: Wiley, 1949). Excellent social class analysis of the youth and schools in one community.

Kirkpatrick, William H., and Arthur Bestor, "Progressive Education: A Debate," *New York Times Magazine*, September 8, 1957. A defender of our educational system and a persistent critic present their views.

Chapter Fourteen

Everett, John, *Religion in Human Experience* (New York: Holt, 1950). A unique comparative study with emphasis on religious differences, particularly those in Hinduism, Buddhism, Christianity, and Judaism.

Goode, William J., *Religion Among the Primitives* (Glencoe, Illinois: The Free Press, 1951). A functional approach to religion, using as its vehicle a minute description of religion in five nonliterate societies.

Hoult, Thomas Ford, *The Sociology of Religion* (New York: Dryden, 1958). A functional analysis of religion in general, with special emphasis on religio-social interaction patterns.

Nottingham, Elizabeth K., *Religion and Society* (Garden City, N. Y.: Doubleday Short Studies in Sociology, 1954). A lengthy pamphlet with a sociological point of view.

Sellin, Thorsten, ed., "Organized Religion in the United States," *The Annals of the American Academy of Political and Social Science*, Vol. 256, entire issue, March, 1948.

Chapter Fifteen

Bunzel, Ruth, "The Economic Organization of Primitive Peoples," in Franz Boas and others, *General Anthropology* (Boston: Heath, 1938), pp. 327-408. A careful analysis. For the serious student.

Herskovits, Melville J., *The Economic Life of Primitive Peoples*, 2nd ed. (New York: Knopf, 1953). Scholarly text by a noted anthropologist. For the serious student.

Richards, A. I., *Land, Labour and Diet in Northern Rhodesia* (London: Oxford University Press, 1939). Details how one group (but there are many others) spends most of its waking time thinking about and working for something that occupies only a fraction of our own time—food.

Slotkin, James S., *Social Anthropology* (New York: Macmillan, 1950). Although many chapters can be read with profit in connection with *Modern Society*, Chapter 11, "Types of Economy," is especially good at this point, for it provides overwhelming evidence from various cultures that economics does not abound with rigid "laws."

Chapter Sixteen

Chandler, Lester V., *A Preface to Economics* (New York: Harper, 1947). A readable analysis of the laissez-faire economy.

de Schweinitz, Karl, Jr., and Kenneth W. Thompson, *Man and Modern Society* (New York: Holt, 1953). See especially de Schweinitz's lucid anaylsis of the price system (Chapter 3); also Part II, "Industrial Society and the Problem of Choice."

Ise, John, *Economics*, Rev. ed. (New York: Harper, 1950). See Part VII, "The Other Isms," and Part VIII, "An Appraisal of Capitalism." A balanced and objective treatment.

Samuelson, Paul A., *Economics: An Introductory Analysis*, 3rd ed. (New York: McGraw-Hill, 1958). Chapters 3 and 38 describe the chief economic systems.

Chapter Seventeen

Galbraith, John Kenneth, *American Capitalism* (Boston: Houghton, Mifflin, 1952). Develops the theory of countervailing power in American economic life.

Lilienthal, David E., *Big Business—A New Era* (New York: Harper, 1953). An interesting evaluation of the problem of bigness by a prominent public figure.

Stocking, George W., and Myron W. Watkins, *Monopoly and Free Enterprise* (New York: The Twentieth Century Fund, 1951). Comprehensive, scholarly, and very readable.

Whyte, William H., *The Organization Man* (New York: Simon and Schuster, 1956). A challenging examination of American organization life.

Chapter Eighteen

Barbash, Jack, *The Practice of Unionism* (New York: Harper, 1956). Emphasizes the way in which unions function on a day-to-day basis.

Daniels, Walter M., ed. *The American Labor Movement* (New York: H. W. Wilson, 1958). Contains much useful and recent information on American unionism.

Daugherty, Carroll R., and John R. Parrish, *The Labor Problems of American Society* (Boston: Houghton, Mifflin, 1952). A good text on industrial relations.

Dulles, Foster Rhea, *Labor in American Life, A History* (New York: Crowell, 1955). The best recent history of the American labor movement.

Hardman, J. B. S., and Maurice F. Neufeld, *The House of Labor: Internal Operations of American Unions* (Englewood Cliffs, N. J.: Prentice-Hall, 1951). Provides important insights into the internal workings of American labor unions.

Mills, C. Wright, *The New Men of Power, America's Labor Leaders* (New York: Harcourt-Brace, 1948). Offers many keen insights into contemporary labor leaders and the bureaucratic structure within which they operate.

Peterson, Florence, *American Labor Unions: What They Are and How They Work* (New York: Harper, 1952). A brief but authoritative general work on American trade unions.

Schultz, George P., and John R. Coleman, *Labor Problems: Cases and Readings* (New York: McGraw-Hill, 1953). A very readable and original text on labor relations.

Chapter Nineteen

Campbell, Persia, *The Consumer Interest: A Study in Consumer Economics* (New York: Harper, 1949). Readable and valuable.

Ise, John, *Economics*. See Chapter 21, an analysis of the problems of consumption by an able economist. For the serious student.

Packard, Vance, *The Hidden Persuaders* (New York: David McKay, 1957). A best-selling exposition of the attempts of advertisers to exploit the findings of social science and psychology in regard to motivation.

Public Affairs Pamphlets (New York: The Public Affairs Committee). Many of these pamphlets, which are well-written by experts, deal with the consumer and his problems.

Troelstrup, Arch W., *Consumer Problems* (New York: McGraw-Hill, 1952). Practical guide to consumer problems.

Chapter Twenty

American Assembly, *United States Agriculture: Perspectives and Prospects* (New York: Graduate School of Business, Columbia University, 1955). This volume consists of research reports and background papers on American agriculture.

Benedict, Murray, *Can We Solve the Farm Problem?* (New York: The Twentieth Century Fund, 1956). This volume is a comprehensive survey of agricultural problems with specific proposals for their solution.

Benson, Ezra, *Farmers At The Crossroads* (New York: Devin-Adair, 1956). This book, by the Secretary of Agriculture, is an exposition of problems and solutions as he sees them.

Davis, John, and Kenneth Hinshaw, *Farmer in a Business Suit* (New York: Simon and Schuster, 1957). This volume emphasizes farm efficiency and the solution of farm problems through application of proven business practices.

McLaughlin, Kathleen, *New Life In Old Lands* (New York: Dodd, Mead, 1955). This is a highly favorable report on the technical assistance work of the UN, told in terms of individual human-interest stories.

Staley, Eugene, *The Future of Underdeveloped Countries* (New York: Harper, 1954). This is a symposium of expert opinion, published for the Council on Foreign Relations. Communist and democratic approaches are contrasted.

Chapter Twenty-one

American Assembly, *International Stability and Progress: United States Interests and Instruments* (New York: Graduate School of Business, Columbia University, 1957). This report contains sections on the economic development of Asia and the role of American aid.

Burns, Arthur F., *Prosperity Without Inflation* (New York: Fordham University Press, 1958). The former economic adviser to President Eisenhower charts a government program to control business cycles.

Galbraith, John Kenneth, *The Great Crash, 1929* (Boston: Houghton, Mifflin, 1955). This analysis of the great depression is offered by a "liberal" economist who favors vigorous government action to prevent economic calamities.

Jacoby, Neil H., *Can Prosperity Be Sustained?* (New York: Holt, 1956). The author believes that the business cycle can be tamed through reform of existing laws and institutions.

Kiplinger, W. M., and staff, *Boom and Inflation* (New York: Simon and Schuster, 1958). This book is designed as a guide for the average citizen who is faced with the fluctuations of the business cycle. Kiplinger believes that the long-range trend is inflationary.

Myrdal, Gunnar, *An International Economy: Problems and Prospects* (New York: Harper, 1956). An analysis of international economic problems that is notable for its scope and breadth of vision.

Randall, Clarence B., *Foreign Economic Policy for the United States* (Chicago: University of Chicago Press, 1955). A businessman speaks out for freer international trade.

Wernette, John Philip, *The Future of American Prosperity* (New York: Macmillan, 1955). The author believes that if government and business work together harmoniously we can avoid future depressions.

Chapter Twenty-two

Hook, Sidney, *Heresy, Yes—Conspiracy No!* (New York: John Day, 1953). A heretic with a keenly analytical mind clarifies the issues that lie behind many of our contemporary civil liberty problems.

Lipson, Leslie, *The Great Issues of Politics* (Englewood Cliffs, N. J.: Prentice-Hall, 1954). A provocative and sophisticated analysis of the nature of politics and government.

MacIver, Robert M., *The Web of Government* (New York: Macmillan, 1947). A classic discussion of government by an eminent political scientist and sociologist.

Smith, T. V., and Eduard C. Lindeman, *The Democratic Way of Life* (New York: New American Library, 1951). An important commentary on the nature of a democratic society.

Stouffer, Samuel A., *Communism, Conformity, and Civil Liberties* (New York, Doubleday, 1955). The best available statistical study of American opinion on civil liberty issues.

Chapter Twenty-three

Berelson, B., P. Lazarsfeld, and W. McPhee, *Voting* (Chicago: University of Chicago Press, 1954). The best description and analysis of the voting process in the United States.

Katz, E., and P. Lazarsfeld, *Personal Influence* (Glencoe, Ill.: The Free Press, 1955). How people make up their minds about soap, movies, and politics.

Key, V. O., Jr., *Politics, Parties and Pressure Groups*, 2nd ed. (New York: Crowell, 1947). A classic description of the national political processes.

O'Connor, E., *The Last Hurrah* (New York: Bantam Books, 1957). A great novel about the life and death of a big-city boss.

Truman, D., *The Governmental Process* (New York: Knopf, 1951). Covers the same topic as Key's book but is far more theoretical and analytic.

Chapter Twenty-four

Acheson, Dean, *A Citizen Looks At Congress* (New York: Harper, 1957). A former Secretary of State thoughtfully comments on some of the basic problems in legislative-executive relations.

Bailey, Stephen K., and Howard D. Samuel, *Congress at Work* (New York: Holt, 1952). One of the best studies to appear in recent years.

Brownlow, Louis, *The President and the Presidency* (Chicago: Public Administration Service, 1949). An easy to read and penetrating account of the presidency by a distinguished student of American government.

Burns, James MacGregor, *Congress On Trial* (New York: Harper, 1949). A stimulating analysis of Congress as a political institution.

Corwin, E. S., and L. W. Koenig, *The Presidency Today* (New York: New York University Press, 1956). A topnotch book dealing with the development of the presidency and its present status.

Hyman, Sidney, *The American Presidency* (New York: Harper, 1954). A good survey of the presidency both as a constitutional office and as a political process. Chapter 4, "The President as an Artist" is especially pertinent.

Laski, H. J., *The American Presidency: An Interpretation* (New York: Harper, 1940). A provocative study of the presidency.

Lee, Raymond, James Burkhart and Van Shaw, *Contemporary Social Issues* (New York: Crowell, 1955). Problem 8, pp. 184-218, presents various views on the strength of the office of the president.

Rossiter, Clinton, *The American Presidency* (New York: New American Library, 1956). This is probably the most perceptive analysis of the presidency as a political institution. Interesting, incisive, and stimulating.

Smith, T. V., *The Legislative Way of Life* (Chicago: University of Chicago Press, 1940). A defense of the legislature by an ex-congressman, ex-state legislator, philosopher, and political scientist.

White, William Smith, *Citadel, The Story of the United States Senate* (New York: Harper, 1957). An excellent analysis of the Senate as a political institution.

Wilson, Woodrow, *Congressional Government* (New York: Meridian Books, 1956). Although written over 70 years ago, this book remains the most quoted commentary on Congress.

Young, Roland, *This Is Congress* (New York: Knopf, 1943). A comprehensive and careful study.

Chapter Twenty-five

Cahill, Fred V., Jr., *Judicial Legislation* (New York: Ronald, 1952). A re-examination of the traditional operation of the Supreme Court, which stresses the legislative functions of the judiciary.

Cahn, Edmond, ed., *Supreme Court and Supreme Law* (Bloomington, Ind.: Indiana University Press, 1954). A provocative selection of articles evaluating and analyzing the Court.

Cardozo, Benjamin N., *The Nature of the Judicial Process* (New Haven, Conn.: Yale University Press, 1921). This volume, by the former Supreme Court justice, is one of the most revealing descriptions of the judicial process ever written.

Corwin, Edward S., *The Constitution and What It Means Today* (Princeton, N. J.: Princeton University Press, 1920). Points up the difference between the Constitution as a document and the Constitution as an instrument.

Jackson, Robert S., *The Supreme Court in the American System of Government* (Cambridge, Mass.: Harvard University Press, 1955). Chapter III, "The Supreme Court as a Political Institution," is excellent.

McIlwain, Charles Howard, *Constitutionalism Ancient and Modern* (Ithaca, N. Y.: Cornell University Press, 1940). One of the best studies on constitutionalism.

Schwartz, Bernard, *The Supreme Court: Constitutional Revolution in Retrospect* (New York: Ronald, 1957). Illustrates the changing role of the Supreme Court.

Chapter Twenty-six

Bailey, Stephen K., "A Structured Interaction Pattern for Harpsichord and Kazoo," *Public Administration Review,* Summer, 1954. An hilarious day in the life of a mayor.

Key, V. O., Jr., *American State Politics: An Introduction* (New York: Knopf, 1956). A general description of the organization and practices of political parties and pressure groups at the state level.

La Palombara, Joseph L., *Guide to Michigan Politics* (New York: Citizenship Clearing House, 1955). A good description of political organization in a state.

Neuberger, Richard L., *Adventures in Politics: We Go to the Legislature* (New York: Oxford University Press, 1954). The adventures of a very literate state legislator, now United States Senator from Oregon, and his state legislator wife.

Schlesinger, Joseph, *How They Became Governor* (East Lansing, Mich.: Michigan State University Governmental Research Bureau, 1957). Describes and analyzes the pre-political and political careers of a sample of American state governors.

Steffens, Lincoln, *The Shame of the Cities* (New York: McClure, Phillips, 1904). The classic "muckraker's" description of city government at the turn of the century.

Chapter Twenty-seven

Bauer, Raymond A., Alex Inkeles, and Clyde Kluckhohn, *How the Soviet System Works* (Cambridge, Mass.: Harvard University Press, 1956). Probably the best single volume on the U.S.S.R. and what motivates its citizens.

de Jouvenal, Bertrand, "On the Character of the Soviet Economy," *Bulletin of the Atomic Scientists,* Vol. XIII, November, 1957. This article offers evidence that the Soviet economy is repeating all the mistakes the English and Americans made during the early years of the Industrial Revolution, despite almost a century of ceaseless criticism of "early capitalism" and its social welfare problems.

Djilas, Milovan, *The New Class* (New York: Praeger, 1957). Like Koestler's, *The Yogi and the Commissar,* this work describes the real beneficiaries of Communist revolutions—the new bureaucratic class.

Kennan, George F., "The Soviet Mind and World Realities," *The Listener,* London, November 21, 1957. America's senior Russian diplomat and former Ambassador to the U.S.S.R. describes the state of mind and bias of the Soviet rulers and how they interpret America.

Khrushchev, Nikita, *The Crimes of the Stalin Era,* speeches to the Twentieth Congress of the Communist party of the Soviet Union, February 22-24, 1956. Annotated by Boris I. Nicolaevsky. Pamphlet published by *The New Leader.* A detailed account of the inhumanities ordered committed by Stalin until his death in 1953. Overwhelming evidence that the U.S.S.R. system does not limit the power of its top leaders.

Koestler, Arthur, *The Yogi and the Commissar* (London: Jonathan Cape, 1945). An excellent discussion of the shift of the U.S.S.R. from once revolutionary theory to entrenched bureaucracy that distorts theory for its own purposes.

Russian Institute of Columbia University, *The Anti-Stalin Campaign and International Communism* (London: Oxford University Press, 1956). An account of the reactions to Khrushchev's revelations about Stalin among Communist parties outside Russia.

Seton-Watson, Hugh, *From Lenin to Malenkov* (New York: Praeger, 1953). This book traces the theory of Communism as practiced in Russia from the time of Lenin to 1955.

Chapter Twenty-eight

Asher, R. E., *The United Nations and the Promotion of the General Welfare* (Washington, D. C.: The Brookings Institution, 1957). An account of what the U.N. has managed to do in economic technical assistance despite the vagaries of world politics.

Barghoorn, Frederick C., *The Soviet Image of the United States* (New York: Harcourt-Brace, 1950). Like Kennan's article listed under Chapter Twenty-seven this book deals with the distorted picture the Russian people and leaders have of the United States.

Bowles, Chester, "The 'Brown Man's Burden' Analyzed," The *New York Times Magazine*, September 5, 1954. A former United States ambassador to India explains the "holier than thou" attitude of the Indians and other Asian leaders toward America and the West.

Davis, Kingsley, "The Political Impact of New Population Trends," *Foreign Affairs*, Vol. 36, January, 1958. This article describes the seeming hopelessness—assuming no unanticipated breakthrough—of efforts to aid the underdeveloped countries, unless something is done to help them check their rising populations.

International Stability and Progress, background papers and final report of the Eleventh American Assembly, May 2-5, 1957 (New York: The American Assembly, Graduate School of Business, Columbia University, 1958). An examination of the trends in world politics, especially the factors affecting the growth and foreign policies of the United States and the U.S.S.R.

Jungk, Robert, *Tomorrow Is Already Here* (New York: Simon and Schuster, 1954). Describes the overlay of defense economy and defense society in the United States and presents alarming evidence of the growth of a garrison state in this country.

Kissinger, Henry A., *Nuclear Weapons and Foreign Policy* (New York: Harper, 1957). A timely book that discusses the relationship between military force and the will to use it, if necessary, with diplomacy. Also explains what the United States should be doing to make its diplomatic policies more effective.

Levi, Werner, *Fundamentals of World Organization* (Minneapolis: University of Minnesota Press, 1950). A discussion of the major political obstacles that prevent the formation of an effective United Nations.

Marshall, Charles B., *The Limits of Foreign Policy* (New York: Holt, 1954). The handicaps that shackle United States foreign-policy makers—the fact that most of any situation is unalterable, that most actions must be carried out quickly, and so forth.

Wright, Quincy, *Problems of Stability and Progress in International Relations* (Berkeley: University of California Press, 1954). An overview of world politics with emphasis on the seemingly diminishing prospects of maintaining world peace and progress, by one of our leading scholars of international relations.

Some Points
to Discuss
and Study Aids

Chapter One

1. Why isn't science highly regarded in all societies?

2. How can scientific investigation be distinguished from non-scientific investigation?

3. How do you account for the fact that the chemist, for example, enjoys more prestige in contemporary American society than does the sociologist?

4. Distinguish between the scientific spirit and the scientific method.

5. How would you qualify the suggestion that science is an "organized body of knowledge"?

6. What is the greatest obstacle to the achievement of a more mature and exact social science?

7. Why is the scientific method not very appropriate for studying events that occur only once?

8. How would you justify the integrated approach to the social sciences?

9. How are qualitative and quantitative analysis interrelated?

10. What relationship does a natural law have to the natural world?

681

Study Aid

Psychologists tell us that meaningful study requires that we read against the relevant background of our experiences. This guiding principle is also the basis of a "contest for understanding" which you can wage with yourself and with others throughout your study of this book. These are the steps in this contest:

(1) Before reading a chapter, convert the topic headings into questions. For instance, the first heading in Chapter One would become "What is the scientific method?" (2) Record, or have the teacher or your roommate record, the main points in your answers about the topics. (3) Now read the chapter, checking your answers about the topics with the statements in the book. (4) See if you can find out the cause of your omissions and errors.

How did you make out in this "contest for understanding"—30 per cent, 40 per cent? Did your class know half or more of the topics? Perhaps your success has demonstrated the value of exploring for answers—*before* you read and *while* you read.

Chapter Two

1. Before reading further, set down your reactions to the San Blas Cuna way of life. What did you think of the way they look? Their marriage customs? Their government? Their interpretation of the universe and their place in it? Their ways of dealing with sickness? Their puberty ceremonies? What things do you find shocking? Surprising? Queer? Admirable? Ridiculous? Superstitious? Wise? Sensible? Natural? Right? Wrong? Moral? Immoral? Beautiful? Ugly? Disgusting? Pleasing? Save your notes to refer to after you have read the next four chapters.

Study Aid

This chapter requires you to master many new ideas in a short time. One of the most effective ways to do this is to make a kind of floor plan of the chapter, so that you can readily distinguish and remember the major and minor points and recall their position and importance in relation to each other and to the total plan. Here is one way to construct such a "floor plan."

Open your large, loose-leaf notebook so that you have two blank pages in front of you. Put the chapter number and title at the top of the left-hand page. Determine how many *topic headings* there are in the chapter and the proportionate amount of space devoted to each topic, then place the headings on the two pages of your notebook, spaced accordingly. Consider the introduction to Chapter Two as a separate topic. Number each heading sequentially, perhaps with a Roman numeral.

Next, determine the number of *main points* under each topic. Express each point in a one-line sentence, which should be indented one inch from the left edge of its topic heading. Assign a capital letter in alphabetical sequence to the main points under each topic heading—beginning each time with "A."

Frequently, the main point of a paragraph is expressed in its opening or topic sentence. For example, the second topic in Chapter II, "The People," which follows the introduction, might consist of three main points—"A. Cunas are unusual among American Indians. B. Cunas are a distinct physical type. C. Specific practices regulate personal habits and apparel."

The first two main points, taken from topic sentences, represent one paragraph each. "C" is a composite statement representing the main idea common to three paragraphs. In this case, the *sub-points* under "C" might well be designated: "1. Male apparel, 2. Female apparel, 3. Personal cleanliness." A sub-point should be indented one inch from the left edge of its main point.

Proceed in this fashion to fill in the balance of points and sub-points. When you have completed your two-page plan of the chapters familiarize yourself with its over-all appearance and the order of the major and minor points, then have someone test your ability to recall the pattern and its parts.

Chapter Three

1. What biological and social factors make man "The only animal with culture"?

2. "Human nature is the same all over the world." In the light of the discussion of the uniformity and variability of culture, how would you qualify this statement?

3. Of what sub-cultures are you a member? What beliefs and customs do you share as a result of this membership?

4. Is culture everything people do? Try to think of some things you do that are not culturally patterned.

5. Drawing on your own experience, analyze the relation between your increasing command of language and your participation in American culture.

6. Explain why culture is a concept or an abstraction, not a tangible reality.

Study Aid

You will encounter many new concepts and technical terms in this chapter. Fortunately, the authors have already placed the important conceptual terms—and frequently their definitions—in italics. However, to complete your mastery of this type of situation you need a simple code system, which you can mark in your book, that will tell you at a glance the essential information about a concept and its relation to other ideas in the chapter.

To illustrate, the word "society," defined in the first paragraph of this chapter, is a fundamental concept—i.e., we must know what the word means in order to understand the science of sociology and the orientation of this book. So, in the margin beside the sentence describing this concept, we place three short lines parallel to the side of the page and underline the word or write it in the margin. In the second paragraph we follow the same procedure to call our attention to the concept of "culture."

However, in the third paragraph we encounter terms which designate two categories of societies—urban and nonliterate. We underline these words, but place only two short parallel lines in the margin beside the sentences in which they occur. Then we number the underlined terms so that we can tell at a glance how many categories there are.

The opening sentence in the fourth paragraph defines the science of anthropology, a definition that is highly relevant to this chapter. So proceed as we did with the terms we encountered in the first and second paragraphs. Or, we may underline the definition or paraphrase or condense it accurately.

In like manner proceed to mark the rest of the pages of this chapter, developing your own code system as you go along so that you can remember and think clearly about the new concepts you have learned. In order to be certain that you understand these terms, compile a list of them and ask someone to check your spelling and definition of them.

Chapter Four

1. What fears do you have that a San Blas Cuna Indian would share? What fears does he have that you lack? What do you fear that he does not?

2. Social control is essential to individual freedom. Discuss.

3. Which of the following behaviors violate the folkways? Which violate the mores? (1) Giving classified material to alien spies; (2) Going to church without a necktie; (3) Getting a Mexican divorce and marrying someone else at once; (4) A woman smoking a cigar; (5) Eating peas with a knife; (6) A man staying home with the children while his wife works.

4. Reconcile the following statements: "Those laws that are most firmly grounded in the mores are the most effective." "Law can initiate social reform." Prove that these statements are not contradictory.

5. Are there mores in our culture that have not been enacted into law? Are there laws that have no inherent relationship to the mores?

6. How does San Blas Cuna culture serve as a device for social control without formal laws?

7. Why are informal techniques of social control insufficient in modern society?

8. Distinguish between San Blas Cuna folkways and mores.

9. Analyze the institution of education in terms of (1) a cluster of folkways, mores, and laws; and (2) in terms of its concept and structure.

Study Aid

How efficiently are you reading this book? Here's a way to find out: (a) Determine the exact number of minutes it takes you to read a chapter. (b) Determine the number of words in the chapter—there are approximately 500 per full page. (c) Then divide (b) by (a) to find your reading rate. (d) Measure the level of your receptive comprehension by determining the percentage of "objective" questions you can answer from the series of questions that accompany this chapter. (e) Measure the level of your reflective comprehension by determining the percentage of "discussion" questions that you can answer from the series of questions that accompany this chapter.

For college freshmen, an average efficient reading rate for this book would be 250 words per minute (about two minutes per full page), with at least 75 per cent comprehension. If you are below this average, you will be especially interested in the Study Aid for the next chapter.

Chapter Five

1. Construct a scale of your personal values, using the values listed as dominant in our culture. Add any other values that you hold. How do these values determine your goals? Your daily schedule? To what extent do they differ from your parents' values?

2. Analyze the elements of symbol, ritual, and ceremony in your routine day. In your observance of the Sabbath and holidays. In what ways do they affect your emotions?

3. In the light of our discussion of invention, would it have been possible to have kept the atomic bomb a secret indefinitely?

4. What people in our society are most likely to change culture by their introduction of individual peculiarities? Relate this question to fashions, language, and the like.

5. Discuss the effect of television on our culture in terms of (1) resistance by interests viewing it as competitive, and (2) its influence on recreation patterns, language, and other aspects of our culture.

6. Why is there a lack of understanding between generations during a period of rapid cultural change?

7. What social inventions have been proposed and strongly resisted in recent years? Who advocates them? Who opposes them? Why?

8. Why did early automobiles resemble horse-drawn buggies?

9. Was penicillin discovered or invented? Account for its rapid diffusion.

Study Aid

Ten ways to improve your reading of this book: (1) Read for a purpose (see "contest for understanding" in the Study Aid for Chapter 1). (2) Read by thought units, not word by word. (3) To read by thought units, focus on the middle of from three to five words at a time and thus read a whole thought unit in one fixed glance. (4) Your eyes should jump from thought unit to thought unit, making about three fixations a line. (5) While you read do not move your lips or pronounce the words to yourself. (6) Identify the principal ideas quickly and relate the other ideas to them. (7) Improve your vocabulary as you go so that new words will not confuse or delay you. (8) Take advantage of introductory and summary paragraphs, topic sentences, italics, topic headings, and so on, which will help you to understand as you read. (9) Read critically; ask yourself about the validity and reliability of the material. (10) Continually force yourself to read faster, while maintaining a high level of comprehension.

Chapter Six

1. Refer back to your impressions of San Blas Cuna culture. Have they changed as you read the subsequent chapters on culture? How would you analyze the change in your attitude in terms of ethnocentrism and cultural relativity?

2. How does Ralph Linton's sketch of the morning routine of the 100 per cent American illustrate the importance of cultural diffusion?

3. What would a map of the U.S. look like if drawn by an ethnocentric inhabitant of your home town?

4. With what "we-groups" do you identify yourself? What advantages do you derive from this feeling of belonging? Does cultural relativity mean that you must abandon your loyalties?

5. Which of these types of "we-group" feeling do you consider harmful? Which add interest to life without being particularly dangerous? (1) Family loyalty, (2) Neighborhood pride, (3) Racist beliefs, (4) School spirit, (5) California vs. Florida, (6) Nationalism, (7) Patriotism, (8) An immigrant's pride in the old country.

6. Read one of the suggested books on America by a foreigner and analyze your reactions and his observations in terms of ethnocentrism.

7. Do you consider progress in other countries to be synonymous with their adoption of American culture?

8. Reconcile these statements: "Ethnocentrism is inevitable." "Cultural relativity is essential to harmonious living in a multi-group society."

Study Aid

This chapter raises the novel question: *How can I really find out about the ethnocentric beliefs and practices of some of the groups to which I belong— fraternity, sorority, "independent" club, college, church, hometown, country, and so forth?*

One answer is provided by *documentary investigation*—i.e., by going to the original sources and letting them speak for themselves. This project is made doubly effective and exciting if the investigation can be tape-recorded and played back to the entire class.

These are the requirements for the project, which can probably be met best by working in small teams of four to six people: (1) a scientific or, at least, objective attitude toward the people and ideas being studied; (2) a clear-cut statement of objectives with an over-all plan and timetable for achieving them; (3) reliable interviewees, who will provide representative samples of each group's range and types of ethnocentrism; (4) a basic pattern for conducting and reporting interviews—who, when, where, why and what; (5) well-planned questions designed to provoke frank statements because the speaker has confidence in the interviewer; (6) adequate time for each team to edit interviews and prepare appropriate introductions, "bridges," summaries, and conclusions.

Chapter Seven

1. Are the following social groups? (1) The population of Chicago, (2) Members of a social science class, (3) American females age 30, (4) The Smith family next door, (5) Passengers on the same bus, (6) Children playing in the back yard.

2. What social processes are paramount in a football game?

3. Some social scientists find it useful to distinguish between helpfulness and cooperation and between competition and rivalry. Discuss these distinctions in terms of other people and groups.

4. What elements of competition besides those mentioned in this chapter would you guess are present in San Blas Cuna society?

5. Why does assimilation of immigrants often take three generations?

6. Would cooperation or competition be more likely to prevail in a society where most statuses are ascribed? Where they are achieved?

7. Analyze a typical day or week in terms of the roles you played.

8. How does your use of the mass media provide you and your acquaintances with common cultural understandings?

9. To what publics, crowds, and audiences have you belonged within the last year? How did your roles differ in the various groups?

10. Is our cultural belief in competition unlimited? What reasons can you give for your answer?

Study Aid

Again, here is a chapter that introduces you to many new concepts and terms. By annotating (see the Study Aid for Chapter Three) this material you should be able to pick out at a glance the essential information about a concept and its relation to other ideas in the chapter. However, with the additional aid of the following group procedure, you will achieve a more meaningful mastery of these new and complex ideas.

The question of "how to relate these new concepts to meaningful experiences common to the members of our class," is divided among small committees or "buzz" groups of four to six members. Each such group will find these steps useful in working as a committee: (1) Get acquainted—know the others in your group. (2) Select a chairman to encourage everyone to speak. (3) Select a secretary-spokesman to record the statements of committee members and to report their findings to the class.

Then, after the question for each group has been stated by your instructor (1) make certain that each member understands the question; (2) take a minute of silence for each person to screen out his best idea; (3) have each person state his best idea *before* there is any discussion; (4) make certain that the committee spokesman has recorded each best idea; and (5) decide within each committee which recorded idea they would like to present first to the whole class for its consideration.

Chapter Eight

1. Relate fluctuations in fertility and mortality to: scientific and technical progress, changing values, the urban trend, and international relations.

2. Does your city fit the "concentric zone" pattern that social scientists have perceived in Chicago? If not, try to account for its ecology.

3. How do you account for the existence of enclaves? Is it rational? Is it selfish? Is it ethnocentric?

4. Is the growth of suburbs a reversal or a continuation of the urban trend? Discuss.

5. What urban influences reach most American farmers?

6. Cite examples of concentration, dispersion, segregation, invasion, and succession in the city with which you are most familiar.

7. Is the slum a natural and inevitable phase in the growth of the city?

8. Discuss the reasons for having a unified governmental set up for metropolitan districts rather than the present arrangement of central cities surrounded by politically independent suburbs and satellite cities. What obstacles would such a plan encounter?

9. Does San Blas Cuna society fit the picture of the "ideal" folk society in every respect?

10. Why is loneliness a common complaint of urban-dwellers in spite of the presence of great numbers of people in cities?

11. Compare the methods of social control in primary and secondary groups.

12. How can a multi-group society hold together if there is no agreement on sacred values?

13. What efforts do you see to produce a feeling of belonging in the city and to banish emotional isolation? What problems are such efforts ultimately aimed at alleviating?

Study Aid

Up to this point your study in *Modern Society* has consisted largely of examining a series of tableaux of different aspects of culture and society. In this chapter, however, a moving picture of the dynamic, fluid nature of your society emerges. This situation is filled with implications for your future. Since you have now gained some basic knowledge and understanding of your culture and your society, perhaps it is time to put your new abilities and information to work on a mid-term paper about the future—your own and your society's. The following outline is intended to be merely suggestive of content and general structure.

(Title)
   "Urbanization, My Vocation, and My Society"

(Thesis)
   To analyze some of the probable effects of our shifting population and changing society upon my vocational choice.

(Introduction)
   What is my present vocational inclination or choice?
      A. Name and current status of vocation
      B. Brief description of vocation today

(Body)
    I. What do personal factors indicate as a choice of vocation?
        A. My capabilities
        B. My interests
        C. My beliefs
        D. My values
        E. Other personal factors
   II. How are the factors of urbanization likely to affect my vocational choice?
        A. Accelerating rate of urbanization
           1. Effect upon future need for vocation
           2. Effect upon future role of vocation
           3. Effect upon future required level of competence
        B. Extent of changes wrought by urbanization
           1. Geographic—increasingly world-wide
           2. Economic—higher standard of living
           3. Psychological—tempo, tensions, conflicts
        C. Uneven rate and extent of change
           1. Disruptive, distorted progress
           2. Conflict between old and new ways
           3. Variation in need for, and role of, vocation
        D. Greater heterogeneity
           Effect upon personal and vocational interests, beliefs, and values
        E. Greater physical and social mobility
           Effect upon personal and vocational interests, beliefs, and values
        F. Secondary contacts strengthened; primary contacts weakened
           Effect upon personal and vocational interests, beliefs, and values
        G. Private freedom increased; public freedom decreased
           Effect upon personal and vocational interests, beliefs, and values
        H. Increasing secularization
           Effect upon personal and vocational interests, beliefs, and values
(Conclusion)
    I. This is a summary of the probable effects of urbanization upon my vocational choice
        A. Probable future need, role, and status of vocation
        B. Probable effect upon personal factors of vocational choice
           1. My capabilities
           2. My interests
           3. My beliefs
           4. My values
           5. Other factors
   II. This summary leads to this conclusion about the choice of my future vocation
        A. Same as my original inclination or choice
        B. Modified from my original inclination or choice
        C. A complete change from my original inclination or choice

Chapter Nine

1. Does stratification impress you as a deliberately and rationally planned method of getting society's job done? What are the evidences that it is not?

2. Frederick Lewis Allen in *The Big Change* said, "We Americans are all middle class." Discuss.

3. Why is it so difficult to analyze the American class structure?

4. What elements of caste are present in the situation of the American Negro? What elements are unlike those in a true caste system?

5. Where would you place the following in our social class system? George Apley of Marquand's novel? Ma Joad of *The Grapes of Wrath*? A "typical" movie actress? The president of a bank in a town of 8,000 people? A Texas millionaire? The Mayo brothers? Dr. Ralph Bunche? Your milkman? A street-car conductor? The owner of a neighborhood grocery store?

6. From your experience in your own community, could you construct a class-structure chart using the phrases with which each class describes itself and others?

7. A class may or may not be a social group in any one community. Discuss.

8. Why is wealth alone not an adequate criterion of social status?

Study Aid

This chapter may be the first of several that mount stumbling blocks to your ability to think critically as you study. For example, you may find it very difficult to deal objectively and logically with such long-standing, erroneous beliefs as "America is a classless society."

Now, see if this two-fold practice will help you to think critically and objectively as you study this book. First, convert the topic headings of this chapter into questions, as we described in the Study Aid for Chapter One. Second, check your answers with the following ten-point test of critical thinking:

(1) Are there grounds for this belief or conclusion?
(2) If not, how valid is the assumption?
(3) If there are grounds, are they based largely on opinion or on fact?
(4) Is the supporting evidence relevant, verifiable, valid?
(5) Is there enough valid evidence to support this belief and is it sufficiently representative?
(6) Has the negative evidence been given due consideration?
(7) Has the selection of evidence been slanted through omission or over-emphasis?
(8) Is the belief largely a rationalization—i.e., a self-justification based on a "good" reason rather than a valid reason?
(9) Have emotion-laden terms distorted the belief?
(10) Have the names (symbols) for persons and things been confused with the realities they stand for? (Saying that a person is a middle-class citizen, for example, does not make him one.)

Chapter Ten

1. Why is there so much confusion in the use of the word "race?"

2. Why do Americans exhibit more prejudice toward Negroes than toward Indians?

3. What are the difficulties in the way of establishing a national policy in regard to intergroup relations?

4. Is it instinctive for human beings to like people similar to themselves and to hate people who are different?

5. What can an individual do to combat prejudice and discrimination?

6. What headway has been made in recent years toward alleviating our minority-group problems?

7. "Race is a fact, like sex." Discuss, pro and con.

8. "Racial differences are not important." In what sense is this statement true? In what sense is it not true?

9. To what extent is race discrimination grounded in our mores? To what extent does it violate our mores?

10. Why are race riots more frequent in the North than in the South? Why have lynchings occurred more often in the South than in the North?

11. Evaluate the progress of desegregation in transportation, housing, and schools as regards what has been said in preceding chapters about (1) collective behavior and public opinion, (2) cultural change, (3) social stratification, and (4) natural areas of cities and the ecological processes.

Study Aid

After studying this chapter see if you can identify a problem situation involving intergroup tensions on your campus, in your dormitory, fraternity, on the athletic field, in the local community, or in your home town.

If you expect to ease tensions or develop realistic solutions to your problem situation, you will have to operate in terms of human beings and their attitudes, beliefs and feelings. This means, among other things, that you will need to: (1) consider the nature and causes of the problem from different viewpoints, (2) sense how it feels to be the various persons involved in the situation, and (3) explore or try out possible solutions to the specific situation. The group technique that is designed to deal with situations in this fashion is called *role-playing*.

Before you undertake this procedure, however, these conditions should prevail in your class: a sense of individual inner-security and of a comfortable, democratic group in action; an active, common concern for the problem area; and sufficient individual and group motivation to work out solutions to the problem through self-disciplined discussion and action.

After these conditions are established, proceed according to the following steps:

(1) Decide on a statement of the problem situation and the characters involved.

(2) List the different ways of handling the situation.

(3) Determine the leader and the observer for the role-playing situation.

(4) Under the guidance of the leader select a specific scene in the problem situation on which to test the solution, and select the role-playing participants.

(5) Act out the scene, remembering to (a) watch for clues and cues that indicate how the situation might better be handled; (b) try out different ways of handling the scene; and (c) have the characters express their inner-thoughts aloud as asides.

(6) With the help of the observer, your class should discuss and evaluate the clues, cues, and possible solutions.

(7) The conclusions, recommendations, and suggestions of the class for easing tensions and/or solving your problem situation should be recorded for all to see. If necessary, the entire process should be repeated until it is possible to record results that are satisfactory to the entire class.

Chapter Eleven

1. Some students of human behavior find a very definite relationship between methods of toilet-training, weaning, feeding, and baby care in general and the basic cultural personality type. Discuss.

2. H. Warren Dunham and Robert E. L. Faris found the highest rate of mental disorders in Chicago in the rooming-house districts, in the area of homeless men, in deteriorated Negro areas, and in immigrant slums. Explain why.

3. "The solid facts of life are the facts of the imagination." Discuss.

4. How do the definitions of sex roles of the Arapesh, Mundugumor, and Tchambuli differ from our own? How are they similar?

5. "A person's character is his generalized other." Discuss.

6. Give examples of the use of defense mechanisms from literature, movies, or personal experience.

7. Discuss the advantages and disadvantages of marginality in terms of ethnocentrism, emotional security, a stable and satisfying self-conception, and compatibility of roles and values.

8. Discuss our attitudes toward mental illness as an example of cultural lag.

9. "There are no problem children, only problem parents." Discuss.

10. How is lack of cultural integration reflected in personal disorganization?

11. "His grandfather and father before him were drunkards; naturally he's an alcoholic. It runs in the family." Discuss.

12. In regard to freedom and control, how does the symbolic interactionist theory differ from determinist theories?

13. To what extent might your parents or grandparents be inner-directed personalities? Do you consider yourself inner-directed, other-directed, or autonomous?

Study Aid

For the third time you encounter a chapter that introduces you to a number of new concepts and terms. Let us combine some of the study aids we have already learned to help us master these new and complex ideas.

First, identify those terms that are new to you or about which you are uncertain by waging the "contest for understanding" (See the Study Aid for Chapter One). Second, use the study aid set forth for Chapter Seven—annotate the book for material relevant to the terms you have selected and then assign different terms to several small committees or discussion groups who will investigate the meaning of the terms in light of their own backgrounds and experience. Each committee then reports its findings to the whole class for further consideration and evaluation.

Chapter Twelve

1. How have the criteria of success in marriage changed? Why have they changed?

2. Although they work well among the Yoruba, why do polygamous marriages work out poorly in those sects in our society that have tried them?

3. Recalling the discussion of personality in the preceding chapter, account for the "back to grandma" trend in child-rearing.

4. Although in rural America there was little place for the unmarried adult, the marriage rate is now higher than it was in 1900. How do you account for this change?

5. Discuss the socializing function of dating in terms of the self-conception.

6. From your experience would you say that dating is a clearly defined institution or one that is still being defined?

7. Why is the rate of failure high in hasty marriages, very young marriages, and wartime marriages?

8. What relationship is there between the changing function of marriage and the changed attitude toward broken engagements?

9. Discuss our treatment of the aged in terms of cultural lag.

10. Explain why divorce is a more severe crisis than death in terms of the self-conception and in terms of the social definition of the situation.

11. What does the current confusion in regard to feminine roles mean for the personality organization of many women in modern society?

12. Discuss the problems of adolescence in terms of role confusion.

13. Do you think rivalry and conflict between brothers and sisters is "natural" and inevitable? Relate sibling rivalry and conflict to such cultural values as competition and affection and to changes in the functions of the family.

Study Aid

How do your beliefs about dating, engagements, mate-selection, and husband-wife-child relationships compare with those of your classmates? Do your beliefs about American family life change as you study and learn more about it? Here's a way to find out:

(1) *Before* reading this chapter or discussing it with your classmates, write down very briefly your most important beliefs about the different stages in American family life as indicated by the main headings listed in the table of contents.

(2) Your instructor will then collect these initial statements and use them as guides for setting up intra-group, and then intra-class, discussions about different beliefs concerning the various stages of American family life.

(3) At the end of the study and discussion periods, your instructor will return your initial written statements for you to re-examine, re-emphasize, elaborate, or change.

Chapter Thirteen

1. Relate the changes in American education to the principles of cultural change listed in Chapter Five, and to the trend toward an associational society described in Chapter Eight.

2. What is the role of schools—ideally and actually—in socialization, in the teaching of perception, in motivation, in the development of a healthy self-conception?

3. Analyze several of your elementary and high-school teachers in terms of role performance.

4. Describe as clearly as you can the sub-culture of schools and colleges you have attended.

5. What is the function of education in your own hopes for social mobility? How is your attendance at a particular college and your choice of a future career related to your class status?

6. To what social categories do you as a student belong? To what social groups?

Study Aid

How do your beliefs about education compare with those of your classmates and other Americans? As a student of social science, how *scientifically* can you examine and evaluate your beliefs?

Before reading this chapter or discussing it with your classmates, write down very briefly your most important beliefs about education. Using these statements as the basis for grouping, your instructor will divide the class into small teams of four to six members who hold similar beliefs. Intra-group discussion should serve the two-fold purpose of critically examining the bases of each individual's beliefs and preparing a panel-type report to the entire class.

Among themselves, each group might consider such questions as: Just where did I get my present beliefs about education? Why do I accept them? What satisfactions do I get from holding such beliefs? For their panel reports each group may wish to assign to individuals such questions as: What are our particular beliefs about education? What action should issue from such beliefs? Who should take this action—parents, students, teachers, administrators, local government officials? When and how should such action be undertaken? Class discussion with each panel should be aimed at clarifying and validating both the evidence and the reasoning behind each report and recommendation for action.

At the end of the time assigned to considering this subject, your instructor will return to you your initial statement of beliefs on this subject. Re-examine it, and write down anything you think should be re-emphasized, added, or changed.

Chapter Fourteen

1. This chapter views religion as a natural rather than as a supernatural phenomenon. What are some of the possible limitations of the "naturalistic" point of view?

2. Compare the sociological view of religion with what you may know about the psychological view.

3. What do you think of the assertion that religion is bound to disappear as science becomes more prominent?

4. What different consequences might result from defining religion in terms of what it is rather than in terms of what it does?

5. Using general American values as your frame of reference, name some of the positive functions of different types of religion. Name some of the negative functions.

Study Aid

Can you distinguish between your ideas *about* an institution and the beliefs you have acquired largely as a *result of* that institution? This chapter provides a valuable opportunity for you to make this distinction between your role as a student of social science and your role as a member of an institution.

Proceed as you did in the first step in the Study Aid for Chapter Thirteen. But, in addition, jot down a brief statement of your personal religious creed. In your small group discussion, add these questions to those suggested in Chapter Thirteen: In the past, have I ever had different ideas about the role of religion as a social institution? Have I ever held religious convictions different from my present creed, which may range from agnosticism to orthodoxy? If so, what caused me to become dissatisfied with my earlier ideas and/or convictions?

For panel reports individuals may be assigned such questions as: What are our ideas about the role of religion as an institution? What are our religious beliefs and practices? How and to what extent do our creeds and practices satisfy our ideas of the role of religion in our society? How could our creeds and practices more effectively satisfy our ideas about the role of religion in our society?

At the end of the discussion your instructor again will return your initial statement to you. Re-examine it and then write down anything you think should be re-emphasized, added, or changed.

Chapter Fifteen

1. List some of the ways in which the economic system is interwoven and "integrated" with other aspects of a culture.

2. Some young women expect to work for a living for only a short time before they marry and settle down. Would such a person benefit from a knowledge of economics?

3. What are the basic economic problems faced by any society?

4. Are the following economic wants: (1) a college degree, (2) a beautiful church, (3) a golf game, (4) a clean and orderly home, (5) a pretty complexion, (6) well-pressed trousers?

5. Give examples of production that our society encourages, tolerates, and forbids.

6. Discuss the proposition that modern society is attempting to regain some of the economic values of nonliterate societies that were lost during the early decades of the Industrial Revolution.

7. Discuss the advantages and disadvantages of the division of labor.

8. Write down what you consider to be the chief features of the American economic system, including beliefs and practices. Refer again to your notes after reading the next two chapters.

9. What are the four chief uses of money? Give an example of how you or your parents have employed money for each of these uses.

10. Why does money serve less well as a store of value than as a measure of value?

Study Aid

Our beliefs about institutions can change. It is usually not easy for us to change such basic ideas, however, even though their continuance may be harmful. Let us try out a method that will help us cast overboard mistaken or false beliefs.

First, to establish a point of departure, follow the procedure outlined in the preceding study aids and set down your most important beliefs about the American economic system. Second, study this chapter, annotating it (as you did for Chapter Three) so that you will have some understanding of new economic concepts and terminology. Third, within your small discussion groups, composed this time of students with *divergent* beliefs, let each member report on: (1) a belief he formerly held about how goods and services are produced and distributed; (2) the contrary evidence that existed at the time he held the belief; (3) the reasons he overlooked or ignored such evidence; and (4) the new needs that prompted a positive response to the contrary evidence.

Fourth, having demonstrated that beliefs are not fixed facts but opinions that can change, let each member of the group state one of his current beliefs about the American economic system and then, with the help of other members of his group, attempt to state the evidence contrary to his belief. Finally, aided by his group, each member should try to determine the needs and circumstances that might induce him to change his belief.

At the end of the time assigned, follow the preceding study aid practice and re-examine your original statement of economic beliefs. Revise it in terms of whatever needs to be re-emphasized, added, or changed.

Chapter Sixteen

1. What are the weaknesses of the theory that private gain is public benefit?

2. Are there any distinctions between the economic logic of socialism and the economic logic of laissez faire?

3. What are the chief functions of a central planning board in a socialist economy?

4. In what way is it misleading to speak of a laissez-faire economy as "unplanned?"

5. Why do societies usually increase the area of the planned economy in war years and decrease the area in time of peace?

6. Has our country been tending more toward a laissez-faire economy or toward a planned economy during the present century? Why?

7. Is one type of economy more "democratic" than another? Why or why not?

8. Why is no large society either entirely laissez faire or entirely planned?

Study Aid

You are the first full-fledged citizens of the Atomic-Space Age—this new world in which it may soon be possible to travel through space; employ atomic and solar energy to distill sea water and work automated homes, offices, factories and stores; utilize instantaneous, two-way audio-visual electronic communication anywhere, and so on. This means that far-reaching changes are already taking place in your way of life—including the economic system that undergirds it.

How well will the new economy serve you? Will it make you happier, or will it be your master? These matters are important to you, so let us try to anticipate and plan for the future now.

Using the information and insights you have gained from reading this chapter and from library research and imaginative reasoning, let us see what our present economic systems may be like 25 years from now. Here's how this projective technique might work with an example for which we know the answers. Consider the deer and the buffalo in the United States 200 years ago and today with respect to (a) their economic role and ownership, (b) their care, and (c) the means and basis of their distribution.

Or, take an example from the future. How might an independent solar heating system for the home in 1985 affect present-day concepts of natural gas, petroleum, and coal resources with respect to (a) their economic role and ownership, (b) converting processes, and (c) the basis and means for distributing the utilities derived from these natural resources?

Now to proceed with the study project. Divide the responsibilities for the following operations among the members of a project team or the entire class. The operations may be applied to all three systems described in this chapter or confined to a mixed economy.

(1) Largely on the basis of information found in this chapter, list the main characteristics of the organizational pattern for (a) the ownership of natural resources and raw materials, (b) converting natural resources and processing raw materials, and (c) distributing processed materials and the utilities derived from natural resources.

(2) On the basis of library research and open-minded reflection, list the major changes you anticipate within the next 25 years in (a) the substance and ownership of natural resources and raw materials, (b) the conversion of natural resources and the processing of raw materials, and (c) the means and the basis for distributing processed material and utilities derived from natural resources.

(3) Using further research and imaginative reasoning, decide how the preceding changes are most likely to affect our present concepts of (a) the economic role and ownership of natural resources and raw materials, (b) the conversion of natural resources and processing of raw materials into finished products, and (c) the basis and means of distributing finished products and the utilities derived from natural resources.

Without a doubt, this project will prove to be difficult and complex. But these very questions will be, or are being, asked; and the future belongs to those who will be the first to answer them wisely.

Chapter Seventeen

1. Show how the development of power machinery affected price competition.

2. Why has the laissez-faire theory been particularly strong in the United States? In what ways has the development of large-scale business organization modified that theory?

3. Business units often have sought to expand to a size greater than that warranted by the economies of large-scale operation. Discuss the reasons why.

4. What have been the advantages to the consumer of business concentration? What have been the disadvantages?

5. Discuss the differences between price competition and monopolistic competition.

6. What are the advantages of the corporation over the single proprietorship and partnership in an era of large-scale business operation?

7. Discuss some of the advantages of horizontal, vertical, and lateral expansion of business units.

8. Explain the seeming contradiction in the statement that large modern corporations are widely owned but narrowly controlled.

9. What are the qualities cultivated by a young man who embarks upon a career as an executive in a large corporation? How do these qualities differ from those cultivated by a man who starts out in a small business of his own?

10. In what ways has the growth of the giant corporation affected the belief pattern of the American community as a whole?

11. What have been the causes of government's attempts to regulate the size and activities of corporations? Discuss the reasons for the success or failure of various types of regulation.

12. Why is it unlikely that the United States will go as far as the United Kingdom in government ownership and operation of business? Do you believe that the factors that so far have held the United States back will become stronger or weaker in the future?

Study Aid

The continued trend toward the giant corporation and monopolistic competition which Chapter Seventeen reveals makes some of our popular beliefs about the prevalence of a laissez-faire economy in this country appear quite unrealistic. To help us realize more clearly the implications of such contemporary facts of economic life let us assume that certain business enterprises have expanded into monopolistic situations. Attempts at moral suasion by local groups have proved ineffective to halt the movement toward monopoly, and representatives of the administrative and judicial branches of the federal government have been asked to sit in as consultants on a meeting with the heads of the businesses concerned and with local and national political leaders to try to resolve the situations. Their discussions will reveal the nature and extent of social control that political parties and the government may exercise in such situations.

Specifically, (1) a nation-wide vegetable processing corporation is about to purchase the final block of farm land necessary to establish vertical control over the market; (2) a regional restaurant chain threatens to acquire the last remaining, independent eating establishment in the area; (3) a giant food store chain is about to force its last competitor to sell out or close its doors; or (4) a news and advertising monopoly is imminent because a powerful national newspaper chain is about to acquire ownership of the sole remaining newspaper and radio-television station in the area.

To play the different roles assigned at the meeting, the student will be required to carry out extensive research in the library and to consult with available authorities on the interpretation of various regulations such as the Sherman Act, the Clayton Act, and the rulings of the Federal Trade Commission and the Federal Communications Commission.

Chapter Eighteen

1. How is the development of the organized labor movement related to the development of the factory system?

2. Why did organized labor experience so marked a growth in prestige and power during the 1930's?

3. What was the nature of the obstacles that confronted the early organizers of American labor?

4. In what respects were the C.I.O. and the A.F. of L. alike and in what respects were they different?

5. What evidence is there to indicate that factories possess systems of social stratification?

6. On what grounds can the social regulation of organized labor be justified?

7. How do you account for the fact that violence in labor disputes has been considerably reduced during recent years?

8. Would it be socially desirable to eliminate all conflict between labor and management in contemporary American society?

9. Distinguish between arbitration, mediation, and compulsory arbitration.

10. List the probable effects of automation upon industrial relations in the United States.

Study Aid

The dynamic role that labor plays in American society might become personally more meaningful to you if you were to role-play certain characteristic problem situations involving the American laborer. The following two suggestions are situations of this type.

(1) Representatives from two groups of workers in a large manufacturing corporation are having a hearing before the National Labor Relations Board. They are asking the Board to call and to supervise an election at the various plants of the corporation to determine which group shall represent all the workers in their dealings with the corporation—especially in collective bargaining negotiations. One group of workers was organized by the A.F.L.-C.I.O. and the other group was organized by the corporation as a company union. The hearing is complicated by allegations from both sides that the civil liberties of the workers are being violated by their opponents in denying to the workers freedom of speech and assembly.

(2) Representatives from labor and from owner-management have accepted an invitation to appear before the House of Representatives Committee on Labor and Education. They have been asked to testify whether, in the interest of public welfare, it is desirable and/or necessary to develop legislation that would regulate the rate and the way in which automation is introduced into American industry. The testimony from these two groups, which include the National Association of Manufacturers, the United States Chamber of Commerce, and the A.F.L.-C.I.O., is enlivened by charges and countercharges that those called to testify have been using the occasion to distort the basic issues through the public press instead of concentrating on informing the legislators. In preparing this situation you may find it helpful to refer to Chapter 24.

Chapter Nineteen

1. Why need the United States be concerned about extreme poverty and inequality elsewhere in the world?

2. Try to reconcile these two statements: "The dollar votes of consumers determine what shall be produced." "Goods are produced first, then buyers are sought."

3. Discuss the proposition that advertising is essential to our present economic system.

4. Cite further examples of how advertising plays upon hidden motivations.

5. How would you answer Vance Packard's questions about the morality of "the hidden persuaders"?

6. Do you rely on brand names for standards? Do you shift brands easily?

7. Why is conspicuous consumption more associated with urban than with rural society?

8. What elements of our belief system work against rational buying, cooperative buying, and consumer organization?

9. With what elements of our traditional belief system do installment buying and borrowing conflict? Does their widespread use indicate a change in our values?

10. What "social inventions" have arisen to strengthen the consumer's position?

Study Aid

This chapter reveals that, as an American consumer, you are a member of a group that is practically unorganized, the poorest informed about the knowledge essential to its role, and almost indifferent to its rights and responsibilities. Both as a study aid and as an attempt to stimulate a more lasting concern for, and understanding of, your role as a member of this largest of all economic groupings, the two following role-playing situations are proposed.

(1) Representatives from a group of organized consumers and from the state retail merchants association are appearing before the state trade commission. The consumer group is presenting a petition for incorporation as a consumers' retail cooperative store and the merchants' group is opposing the granting of a charter of incorporation on the grounds that the consumer group does not meet the necessary qualifications for incorporation and that such a consumer operation would be in violation of "sound" fair-trade practices.

(2) Representatives of a national consumers' reporting service are opposing a national association of advertisers and a giant drug corporation in successive hearings before the Federal Food and Drug Administration, the Federal Trade Commission and the Senate Committee on Public Welfare and Labor. The two commissions are investigating possible violation of federal laws under their respective administrations and the Senate committee is seeking to determine whether or not additional legislation is needed to protect the public welfare. These hearings have been provoked by the sensational ad-

vertising and distribution of a new food-drug of questionable health and food value.

The hearing has been complicated by a decision to broadcast the sessions by radio and television. The broadcasts are being conducted in the public interest, although charges have been made that the advertisers and the drug firm are trying to use the hearings to promote the sale of their product.

Chapter Twenty

1. In what sense is the technological revolution in agriculture a result of mechanical invention? Soil chemistry? Improved breeding? Electricity?

2. Why has farm population declined? What connection exists between the rising Negro population in northern cities and farm technology?

3. What conflicting evidence do we have regarding the disappearance of the family farm?

4. Why does the price of beef vary more than the price of steel?

5. Should the United States fix its sights on a world market for farm products?

6. Why do falling prices often bring increased production of farm goods?

7. How many farmers do we need? Would you classify as "expendable" the 2.7 million farmers who produce less than $2,500 a year?

8. Who is responsible for the wide gap between at-the-farm and consumer prices?

9. Do you believe that farmers will eventually be able to fix the price of their products through cooperative effort? Is this desirable?

10. Should government encourage the movement toward farm consolidation?

11. How does the soil bank differ from acreage restriction programs?

12. What factors that produce farm surpluses in the United States are absent in underdeveloped countries?

Study Aid

Given: A problem situation in which the United States farmer and the United States economy are swamped with vast food and fiber surpluses, while two-thirds of the world goes undernourished and ill clad.

Proposal: Because of the world-wide economic implications of the situation a world-wide conference under the United Nations is convened.

Specific Suggestions: (1) Role-play a joint meeting of the U. N. Economic and Social Council and the FAO (Food and Agriculture Organization) to consider this problem under the chairmanship of the U. N. Secretary-General. (2) Students select the countries they wish to represent, being sure to provide for especially well-prepared and vigorous discussion from countries that "have not" and from countries that "have." (3) Working in small delegation teams, students prepare for the joint meeting by doing library research and by consulting the U. N. and other sources of qualified experts in order to: (a) distinguish the real problem from its symptoms, (b) gather appropriate data, (c) list possible solutions, and (d) evaluate these proposed solutions in light of both short- and long-range effects on intranational and international markets, economies, and standards of living.

Chapter Twenty-one

1. Define the underconsumption-overinvestment theory of depressions. Among what American groups is this theory popular?

2. What relationship allegedly exists between consumer purchasing power and inflation?

3. What weapons does the Federal Reserve Board have for curbing inflation? Which do you believe are the most effective?

4. What tax policies should be adopted during depressions? In inflationary periods?

5. What advantages are claimed for government spending programs as a depression cure? What are the disadvantages?

6. What explanation of the business cycle is offered by Communists?

7. In what ways is foreign trade related to the American economy?

8. Define gross national product. What are the three major categories into which it is divided?

9. What is the effect of inflation on those who are heavily indebted? On retired people living on pensions?

10. Discuss Keynesian economic theory. What difficulty may Keynesian policy encounter in a democracy?

11. Why can modern inflationary pressures continue in the face of unemployment and unused factory capacity?

12. Describe the work of the various agencies that are extending aid to underdeveloped countries. In what manner is the United States affiliated with them?

Study Aid

Several pitfalls to understanding may open up before us as we approach the much-talked-about subject of this chapter. However, by combining three study aids we already have used we may be able to avoid these pitfalls.

First, before reading this chapter, wage the "contest for understanding" as you did in following the Study Aid for Chapter One.

Second, get as much documentary information as you can about a prosperity boom and a serious depression from your parents and older relatives. Record their most striking impressions and conclusions, as you did in using the Study Aid for Chapter Six.

Third, evaluate as critically as you can the information you have gathered on this subject by applying the tests of critical thinking that are included in the Study Aid for Chapter Nine.

Chapter Twenty-two

1. What is the justification for viewing government as part of the cultural environment?

2. In what ways is the institution of government unique among social institutions?

3. Distinguish between moral control and political control.

4. Make a list of the ways in which the practices of American society do not coincide with the American democratic myth.

5. How do you account for the high degree of governmental stability the United States and Great Britain have enjoyed for so many years?

6. Is it necessary to accept the theory of natural rights in order to justify a belief in civil liberty?

7. Why were civil liberty problems easier to resolve in Jefferson's day than in our own?

8. Can the maintenance of civil liberties be justified on practical grounds?

9. Distinguish between substantive and procedural rights.

10. "A written constitution is the keystone of democratic government." Comment.

Study Aid

Is the rise of "big government" incompatible with personal freedom? This problem is one of the most important and difficult you will have to deal with in your lifetime.

Let us cut our intellectual teeth on this problem by selecting a tough situation —one involving a basic freedom, such as set forth in the Bill of Rights—and by using one of the keenest tools of social science—the case study team.

The first step involves locating an apparent denial of civil liberties that is of concern to you and to four or five of your classmates, or to the entire class, if you all wish to work on the same case. Such a situation might be found in a school, a home, a community, a country, or a religious, business, or professional organization.

Next, divide the following investigatory responsibilities among each case study team (maximum of six members) so that no more than two members are working on a task:

(1) Prepare as brief and accurate a description of the situation and relevant events as possible. Note carefully the sources of your information and their reliability.

(2) Prepare a list of the stated objectives or aims of the contending parties. Note carefully the exact source of such statements.

(3) Prepare a list of what you believe are the motivating drives—social, economic, psychological, political, and so on—of each of the parties in this situation. Note the major premises and the specific evidence upon which your inferences are based.

(4) List the major assumptions each party appears to be making about the

other and about the total situation. Note carefully the premises and evidence upon which your conclusions are based.

(5) Secure a copy of the laws or legal requirements which are alleged to be, or appear to be, involved in this situation. Find out what you can about judicial rulings covering similar situations.

After these two steps have been completed, each case study team listens to and evaluates the report of its own members. Specifically, each team first evaluates reports (1) and (2) for completeness, accuracy, and reliability. Report (3) is checked for the validity of the premises and evidence on which the conclusions are based. In light of this examination, the most likely motivations or needs in this situation are selected. These needs are then compared with the stated objectives of the respective parties to determine whether the attainment of these objectives is likely to satisfy the apparent needs. If so, this conclusion should be noted; if not, the team should determine what objectives, in its opinion, would probably satisfy the basic needs of the party in question.

Report (4) is next evaluated for its accuracy in determining the major assumptions. The most likely assumptions are then compared with the information and conclusions obtained from evaluating the first three reports in order to determine which assumptions of the contending parties appear to be sound and which seem to be unsound.

In light of the foregoing conclusions and the information presented in Report (5), each team then determines: (a) the pattern of action it would recommend as most likely to bring about a better understanding and maintenance of civil liberties in the situation, and (b) the individuals and factors within the situation through which such remedial action might be taken.

The fourth and final step in this procedure calls for each team to report very briefly to the entire class on its case findings and to deliver its recommendations concerning the most appropriate and effective action to be taken and through which agents or means.

Chapter Twenty-three

1. What is the relationship between campaigns and voting? What is the purpose of a campaign?

2. Which organizations in our society are most concerned with political issues? How do they make their concern felt?

3. How does the electoral college determine the choice of presidential candidates?

4. What relationship exists between the type of election and the number of political parties in the system?

5. To what extent does our present political system depend on an alert, informed electorate?

Study Aid

You will probably find that this chapter says some disturbing things about our American political system and political behavior. Here is a way to test the truth of these implications and to provide the basis for a constructive response to your findings.

Together with several of your classmates make a list of a number of the political issues that are currently highly controversial—state or federal government aid to education or health, United States foreign policy toward China or Russia, and so on. Then poll your classmates and yourself to find out how you stand on these questions.

Next, prepare a list of your closest associates—father, mother, other relatives, friends at home, at college, in your church, or on your job. As accurately as possible indicate what you understand or believe their position to be on each political issue on your list.

Now compile a list of writers and radio and television commentators who present contrasting viewpoints on the political issues you have listed. Which ones have you and your closest associates been following most closely? After paying close attention for several days to what these speakers and writers say or omit saying about these issues, classify each commentator in terms of whether your response to him and/or his remarks is generally favorable or unfavorable.

Finally, prepare a statement for presentation to your class which (1) summarizes your findings in this personal investigation, (2) sets forth your explanation for the results, and (3) comments critically (see the Study Aid for Chapter Nine) on your need and ability to consider objectively the statements of speakers and writers holding viewpoints that differ from your own.

Chapter Twenty-four

1. In his classic study, *The American Commonwealth,* Lord Bryce has a chapter on "Why Great Men Are Not Chosen President." Name the presidents you would classify as great, near-great, and failures and explain your selections. Bryce first published his book in 1893. Do you think he would arrive at the same conclusions if he were writing on the American presidency today?

2. Comment on the proposition, "The greatest single change in the American system of government since 1789 has occurred in the role of the president."

3. Professor Herman Finer notes that the presidency is "an impossible burden." After reading the varied roles the president is called upon to exercise, would you agree or disagree with this commentary?

4. How do the activities of the president as "Chief Legislator" relate to the principle of the separation of powers?

5. Enumerate some of the merits of the presidential press conference. Is there any danger in raising complex and crucial questions in view of the fact that most answers must be given "off-the-cuff" and unstudied?

6. What are some of the obvious difficulties which would result if Congress and not the president conducted the foreign affairs of the nation?

7. In what ways are administrative agencies increasingly affecting the lives of individual citizens?

8. Is there any basis for the contention that we are moving into an era of presidential government? Cite three effective limits on presidential power.

9. Is the office of the president equal to the job? What suggestions would you make for strengthening the office?

10. Precisely what mental images occur to you when you hear the word "congressman"? Does the "picture in your mind" have more favorable or more unfavorable associations?

11. Mention some of the conflicting interest groups and controversial points of view existing in the present United States Congress.

12. It is sometimes argued that it is better to kill a poor law than to pass a good law. Discuss.

13. Evaluate the respective positions of the president and the Congress today. Which of the two institutions appears to be in the ascendency?

14. Senator Robert LaFollette once said that any measure lost through the filibuster deserved to be lost. Discuss.

15. Why is it virtually impossible to understand the operation of the United States Congress without first understanding the congressional committee system?

16. In what ways does Congress exercise judicial and executive power?

17. In his speech to the Electors of Bristol, Edmund Burke argued that a representative should not carry out every wish of his constituents but should, instead, retain his unbiased opinion, mature judgment, and enlightened conscience. Comment.

18. Discuss the proposition, "Every man is a lobbyist."

19. Will the admission of Alaska as a state increase or decrease the conservative orientation of Congress? Discuss.

Study Aid

This chapter points up the relationships between the Legislative and the Executive branches of your government, especially in the matter of developing and enforcing the legal basis for dealing with, or solving, problems that confront the nation. One of the most effective ways for you to increase your understanding of this process is to undertake a research paper that focuses upon an important national problem, which you expect will require action by the Congress and the President.

After observing the American scene for a few days through the mass media select one of the problem areas that interests you most and then proceed with this 4-step formula: (1) Identify the problem. (2) Determine the causes. (3) Develop possible solutions. (4) Test out the proposed solutions.

Be careful with Step (1). If your statement of the problem can be answered by a "yes" or "no," or by a simple statement of fact, you have hold of a question but not a problem. A problem is a much more complex matter than a simple question, though it is usually stated in question form—"How Can We Eliminate Graft in Government?" or "What Would Be the Most Efficient and Democratic Way to Produce and Control Atomic Power for Peaceful Purposes?"

A symptom should not be confused with its problem. Pain and fever are usually symptoms of an ailment—a medical problem. But it could prove fatal to treat the symptom as if it were the problem. You probably are considering a symptom and not the problem if a test run of your proposed solution doesn't seriously reduce or eliminate the cause.

The identification of the problem also requires that you be clear about its nature and why it is a problem. Answering these questions then should help complete the identification: *Who* or *what* is being harmed or damaged? Just *how* are they or it being harmed? What is the *extent* of the damage? What is the *present trend*—is the situation more or less serious than in the past? Just how are *you affected* by this situation now, and how are you likely to be affected by it in the future?

In Step (2) you collect all the relevant information you can, seeking to get valid data as nearly firsthand as possible. Some causes will suggest themselves from the data, but most of them will probably be advanced in the course of your investigation of oral and written sources of information.

Step (3) especially calls for an open mind and imaginative thinking. As you let your mind roam freely and frequently over the causes and other collected data, jot down every possible solution that occurs to you or to anyone else working with you on the problem. Of course, you will probably run across some proposed solutions in the course of your investigation of spoken and written channels.

Step (4) requires that you evaluate the proposed solutions as objectively as possible, being careful to suspend judgment and to avoid picking out the solution you have secretly favored all along. Your criteria for testing your solutions may well include its suitability, feasibility, and acceptability.

A research team of as many as four students might undertake this type of project, each student being responsible for a major part of the problem-solving procedure, as well as sharing in the preparation of the final research paper.

Chapter Twenty-five

1. If you were given a choice, would you prefer to live under a government of laws or a government of men?

2. How has it been possible for the American Constitution, an eighteenth-century document, to remain vital and dynamic?

3. Harry S. Truman recently said, ". . . people who believe in special privilege are enclosing the . . . Constitution . . . into a mummy as dead as some old pharaoh of Egypt." Do you agree with his statement?

4. Americans generally regard the Supreme Court's power of judicial review as one of the cornerstones of the American system. Yet of all the republics to adopt the American model, few, if any, have followed our practice of judicial review. How would you explain this situation?

5. Approximately 36 states elect their top judges at the polls, and in 4 other states the highest judges are elected by the state legislature. Would you be in favor of electing United States Supreme Court justices?

6. It has been charged that the Supreme Court pays more attention to

sociology and ideological considerations than it does to the fundamental interpretation of the Constitution. Is this charge valid?

7. Should the interpretation of the law be based upon fundamental principles or the needs of the day? How would Oliver Wendell Holmes feel about this question?

8. Cite some cases in American history in which the Supreme Court was under attack.

9. Do you think civil liberties would have fared as well as they have in the United States without the Supreme Court to protect them?

Study Aid

A chapter so richly filled with the drama of the courtroom and the stuff that forms a major part of the living political heritage of America invites you to role-play the United States Supreme Court in action. The following procedure is suggested.

Since the justices of the Supreme Court are appointed, perhaps your teacher or classroom president might select the nine members and designate the chief justice. If the class is large, possibly two or three different courts could be appointed. Next, the opposing legal teams of four to six members should be set up to prepare the briefs and plead the cases.

In order to insure maximum benefit for all concerned, the various major functions of the Supreme Court should be represented in the different scenes that are role-played. The following case situations suggest how these functions might be brought out. First, the constitutionality of a new federal law might be tested, such as excluding the so-called subversive-loyalty cases from the jurisdiction of the Supreme Court; or the Bricker Amendment, which would restrict the treaty-making powers of the president, might be examined in the same light. A second case might involve alleged violations of a long-established interstate commerce regulation by a large, national corporation. A third type of case could concern the alleged unconstitutionality of a state "right-to-work law," or a state law that apparently attempts to circumvent the Supreme Court ruling regarding desegregation in the public schools of the nation. A fourth and final case might involve an individual and the alleged violation of his civil liberties—such as whether his freedom of speech is infringed by a special "non-disloyalty oath" that is required by a federal agency of all its employees—or possibly an alleged violation of freedom of the press through discriminatory and punitive action taken by a federal agency against a newspaper that published "classified" information, which it believed was vital for the public to know at once.

Chapter Twenty-six

1. What are the most important differences between the state and federal constitutions?

2. How do the governors of our states compare to the president in their ability to act as effective chief executives?

3. In what ways do the financial problems of our states and cities differ from those of the national government?

4. What are the major problems of municipal finance in the United States today?

5. Federalism has had profound effects on intergovernmental cooperation. What are some of the more important effects?

6. Contrast the relations between the states and the federal government with those between the states and local governments. Compare "home rule" with "state's rights."

Study Aid

Your study of state and local government can be considerably enriched by bringing representatives of these governmental units and of the state political parties into your classroom either in person or by means of tape-recorded interviews. Responsibility for planning such a presentation can be assigned to one large committee or divided up among several program committees comprising the entire class. In either case these procedures will probably have to be considered.

(1) Make a list of the officials and political leaders you would like to invite, such as the mayor and/or city manager, an alderman or councilman, a magistrate or judge, and leaders of the state political parties. (2) Prepare specific questions to be submitted in advance to these officials. These questions might include such aspects of official matters as: (a) By what procedure is your official or party position filled? (b) What is the nature of your specific area of responsibility? (c) Describe a "typical" day of official or party activities. (d) What is the extent of your authority and the limits of your jurisdiction? (e) What are the official relationships, if any, among the various offices represented?

The presentation might take the form of a panel report followed by impromptu questions from the class. If the officials you would like to invite cannot be present in person, then the students responsible for a particular tape interview might be expected to introduce that interview and lead the follow-up discussion.

Chapter Twenty-seven

1. Why do Communist predictions of what will happen in industrialized Western European countries seem to be faulty?

2. What differences are there between politics as the Communist practices it and politics as the Western world office-seeker or party worker practices it? How does each react to the other's politics?

3. Is colonial imperialism likely? If not, why do the Communists seem to be on the morally right side of the argument about colonialism?

4. Distinguish between Communist agitation and Communist propaganda.

5. How does Communism manage to support its claim that it is progressive and enlightened?

6. Explain what we mean when we speak of Communist Russia as a goaded society? How is the cycle of terror, clemency, followed again by terror, then clemency, used? What procedure is followed in each half of the cycle, and with what general effects?

7. Why do Communist predictions of what will happen in the under-developed countries of Asia seem plausible to many Asian peoples?

8. To what kinds of persons, in what kinds of countries, does Communism appeal?

9. What basic advantages does Communist propaganda have over democratic propaganda?

10. What do the Communists mean when they promise to "take the dollar sign out of life"? How do the Communists say that they will accomplish this? To what degree do they succeed when they are in power?

Study Aid

See Study Aid for Chapter Twenty-eight.

Chapter Twenty-eight

1. What factors enable one nation to exert power and influence over other nations?

2. Why does America spend so much money every year on defense? Why is it impossible for a nation to produce all the weapons and defense installations it needs at one time—more or less the way a person buys a house or a suit when he needs one.

3. How does America describe N.A.T.O.? How does N.A.T.O. look to the U.S.S.R.?

4. Why do America and Russia compete in making loans and grants to underdeveloped countries?

5. How does Japan differ from the rest of non-Communist East Asia as a problem in American foreign policy?

6. What can the United Nations do and what can the United Nations *not* do to affect United States foreign policy?

7. Why is Latin America largely outside world politics?

8. Why does it seem likely that, slowly, over many years, we will see world politics become less bipolarized around the U.S. and the U.S.S.R.?

9. Why does a medium-sized nation such as France or Britain want allies? What reasons are more important than others?

10. Why is it difficult to keep defense secrets?

Study Aid

Given: Official presumption by national governments that foreign policy and peace are geared to an arms race in which more than half the national income of the major powers is devoted to this non-productive end; meanwhile, international tensions and the dangers of world suicide appear to be increasing.

Proposal: Since official commitments and pronouncements prevent governments from realistically re-considering their arms race policies, the peoples of the world, through their non-governmental agencies, have decided to call a world disarmament peace conference.

Specific Suggestions: (1) Role-play such a conference called by the major religious, service club, public welfare, professional, business, labor, women's club, educational and scientific organizations of the world. (2) Students select the organizations and countries they wish to represent, after learning about the disarmament and peace platforms of these organizations from their parents, local and regional offices, and by library research. (3) Students work in both national and international delegation groups to prepare for the conference. Preparation should include a thoughtful study of Chapters 27 and 28 with their suggestions for further readings, extensive library research, and additional consultation with the offices of the organizations they represent.

These investigations, which should lead to specific recommendations to the conference, might include: (a) challenging the basic assumptions about the future and about human nature upon which the arms race policy rests; (b) inquiring into the economic necessity for an arms race—i.e., in order to maintain prosperity under a "peacetime" economy; (c) making a careful distinction between publicized symptoms and fundamental causes of this problem situation; (d) a thoroughly factual inquiry into the question of atomic fall-out and human survival; and (e) a program of workable alternatives to an arms race policy.

Films

Film Producers Referred to in Listings

Reference Mark	Company and Address
(AF)	Association Films, Inc., 347 Madison Avenue, New York 10, New York.
(ADL)	Anti-Defamation League of the B'Nai B'rith, 212 Fifth Avenue, New York 10, New York.
(B&F)	Broadcast & Film Commission, 220 Fifth Avenue, New York, New York.
(Christ)	Christophers, The Christophers, 18 East 48th Street, New York 17, New York.
(Barr)	Arthur Barr Productions, 1265 Bresee Avenue, Pasadena, California.
(Cont)	Contemporary Films, Inc., 13 East 37th Street, New York 16, New York.
(Coronet)	Coronet Films, Coronet Building, Chicago 1, Illinois.
(EBF)	Encyclopaedia Britannica Films, Inc., 1150 Wilmette Avenue, Wilmette, Illinois.
(FN)	Films of the Nation, 62 West 45th Street, New York, New York.
(FP)	Film Publishers, Inc., 25 Broad Street, New York 4, New York.
(IF)	International Film Foundation, 1 East 42nd Street, New York 17, New York.
(IFB)	International Film Bureau, 57 East Jackson Boulevard, Chicago 4, Illinois.
(Ind)	Audio-Visual Center, Indiana University, Bloomington, Indiana.
(Mus)	Museum of Modern Art, 11 West 53rd Street, New York 19, New York.
(McG-H)	McGraw-Hill Book Co., Text-Film Dept., 330 West 42nd Street, New York 36, New York.
(NEA)	National Education Association, 1201 16th St., N.W., Washington 6, D.C.
(NFB)	National Film Board of Canada, 1270 Avenue of the Americas, New York 20, New York.

(PSU)   Pennsylvania State University, Psychological Cinema Register, University Park, Pennsylvania.

(PFC)   Princeton Film Center, Carter Road, Princeton, New Jersey.

(SUI)   State University of Iowa, Bureau of Audio-Visual Instruction, Iowa City, Iowa.

(TI)   Transfilm Inc., 35 West 45th Street, New York 36, New York.

(TFC)   Teaching Film Custodians, 25 West 43rd Street, New York 36, New York.

(UWF)   United World Films Inc., 1445 Park Avenue, New York 29, New York.

(USA)   United States Department of Agriculture, Washington, D.C.

(YAF)   Young America Films, McGraw-Hill Book Co., Text-Film Dept., 330 West 42nd Street, New York 36, New York.

Chapter One

Using the Scientific Method, 11 min, b&w or color, sd. (Coronet) Beginning with the definition of an everyday problem, this film shows the steps involved in the scientific method, from the collection of information, formation of a hypothesis, and the experimental testing of the hypothesis to the retesting of results obtained.

Science and Superstition, 11 min, b&w or color, sd. (Coronet) In a clever classroom situation, pupils use the scientific method to prove that superstitions about the ground hog, rabbit's foot, and so on, are inaccurate. Basing their conclusions on research and experimental evidence, they learn to use the scientific method.

What Is Science? 11 min, b&w or color, sd. (Coronet) Describes the "scientific method," which begins with curiosity, then involves observation, hypothesizing, and testing of the hypothesis, and finally, the formulation of a conclusion.

Why Study Science? 11 min, b&w, sd. (YAF) A discussion of why the study of science is important to the student now and in later life.

Broader Concept of Method (Pt. I), 13 min, b&w, sd. (McG-H) The teacher-dominated, lesson-hearing recitation, and effects of this method on students are contrasted in this part of the film with the informal group discussion type of class sessions, in which students share in planning their work.

Broader Concept of Method (Pt. II), 19 min, b&w, sd. (McG-H) In this part of the film students are shown learning to work together, organizing themselves into functional groups, making and carrying out plans for investigation, and presenting their findings and recommendations in a final report.

Chapter Two

Polynesian Culture, 21 min, color, sd. (Barr) This is the story of a people of the Pacific, a region of increasing importance in the modern world. The film portrays the basic pattern of an ancient way of life as it still exists in the villages of American Samoa, and reveals the Samoans as a self-sufficient people utilizing the products of their isolated island world to meet their daily needs.

Life of a Primitive People (Africa), 13½ min, b&w or color, sd. (Coronet) The simple way of life of a non-literate tribe of people in Africa today closely parallels the existence of man in prehistoric times.

Remnants of a Race, 18 min, color, sd. (EBF) In the great waterless Kalahari desert (Bechuanaland, South Africa) the Bushman exists precariously, relentlessly hunting for food. Evidence of his sketching and painting appear on the ostrich-egg utensils he uses.

Lobola, 26 min, b&w, sd. (Cont) A rare documentary film that illustrates some of the social problems confronting millions of South African natives. The film offers glimpses of the daily life in a primitive tribal village and portrays the social contrasts between life there and in large cities.

Chapter Three

Belonging to the Group, 16 min, b&w, sd. (EBF) The need for people to respect and accept one another in a free society, the vital role of groups in the community, and the importance of the "feeling of belonging" are all illustrated in this film.

Man and His Culture, 15 min, b&w, sd. (EBF) This offering considers the things most cultures have in common, the ways in which cultures are transmitted from one generation to the next, and the ways in which cultures change.

Our Inheritance from the Past, 11 min, b&w or color, sd. (Coronet) A presentation of the contributions of the past to our modern life, which creates a better understanding and appreciation of historic advances. The film establishes the fact that our modern world is actually a product of the past by focusing on past civilizations and their accomplishments.

The Way of the Navaho, 21 min, b&w, sd. (YAF) A penetrating documentary study of life among the Navaho Indians of the American Southwest, of the impact of modern life upon them and of their struggle to resolve the conflicting problems arising from the clash of old and new cultures.

Chapters Four and Five

Law and Social Controls, 11 min, b&w or color. (Coronet) The three broad areas of social control—customs, moral codes, laws—are examined in this film, and some of the levels of law—local, state, and national—are described.

We Do It Because, 7 min, b&w, sd. (TFC) This film presents theories on the origins of various social customs such as shaking hands, tipping the hat, toasting in wine, the wedding ring and wedding veil, kissing the bride, why table knives have round ends, and why we launch ships with a bottle of wine.

Ancient World Inheritance, 11 min, b&w or color, sd. (Coronet) A tour of a great museum affords us glimpses of the ancient civilizations which gave us our money, our alphabet, and even the beginnings of modern industry. The film stresses the contributions of a primitive culture and their effect on our culture.

Double Heritage, 11 min, b&w, sd. (IFB) Between the St. Lawrence and the United States border is a settlement of English- and French-speaking people, among whom tolerance and amity are traditional. This story of a mixed people's forbearance and understanding is an example to the nation and the world.

Chapter Six

America, the Beautiful, 20 min, color, sd. (TFC) This film is a moving pageant of the wild beauty, the farms, cities, industries and people of our mighty land. It carries the message of pride in our heritage and of responsibility to keep America strong and beautiful.

Made in U.S.A., 10 min, b&w, sd. (IBF) Our dependence on foreign sources for raw materials is illustrated in this film via a humorous incident in which each part of an automobile made from imported materials disappears until practically nothing is left of the machine.

One People, 11 min, color, sd. (ADL) This film tells the story of the contribution made to American life by groups representing every nationality on earth. The various ethnic groups who came to the United States are described, and in chronicling the background of our culture, the film makes the point that our country's greatness stems from its mixture of nationalities, races, and religions.

Chapter Seven

Cooperation, Competition, Conflict, 9 min, b&w, sd. (McG-H) This film demonstrates how the three fundamental social processes—competition, conflict, and cooperation—operate to make society function.

The Social Process, 20 min, b&w, sd. (EBF) To understand and deal with the problems of a free society, this film recommends we have a systematic way of describing and analyzing societies, thereby making it possible to evaluate and measure the extent to which those societies are moving toward democratic goals.

Iran—Between Two Worlds, 15 min, color, sd. (EBF) This study of Iran today shows the effect that Western thought and technical development have had on surviving elements of ancient Persian culture.

Beginning of Conscience, 16 min, b&w, sd. (McG-H) The social conscience which James Bryce, the adult, manifests is traced back in this film to his socialization as a child. The conscience he gradually develops in childhood by experiencing such social sanctions as force, exclusion and ridicule, later functions almost automatically in adulthood to make him a social being.

Journey from Etsn, 30 min, b&w, sd. (NFB) A story of village life on the coast of Ghana, revealing something of the character and aspirations of the people of this new independent member of the commonwealth of nations. A gentle interpretation of how a people are making the transition from the old to the new, without destroying the good things of the past.

Chapter Eight

Food and People (An Introduction to the World's Food Problems), 25 min, b&w, sd. (EBF) This film raises two basic questions: Can our world ever become one of plenty? Is a world of plenty really worth working for? Ways of increasing food production and of improving world-wide facilities for the distribution of foods are emphasized.

The Living City, 25 min, b&w, sd. (EBF) In this film we see the necessity for urban redevelopment in a cross-section of American cities. It stresses the importance of making the best possible use of available land and other facilities to serve the growing needs of business, industry, transportation, and everyday urban living.

Cities—How They Grow, 11 min, b&w, sd. (EBF) This film covers the natural influences affecting the location and growth of cities—harbors, water courses, raw materials, and climate—and traces the gradual growth of cities from trading centers to modern metropolitan areas. Outlines current trends in city development, and points out advantages of decentralization and careful city planning.

Cities—Why They Grow, 11 min, b&w, sd. (Coronet) This picture is concerned with the economic factors that give rise to the growth of cities. Departing from the statistical approach that is usually used in detailing problems that arise from the growth of cities, the film concentrates on observing what the workers of a city do in order to establish why the city grew.

The City, 30 min, b&w, sd. (Mus) A survey of the problem of planning community living in America, embodying the views of the American Institute of Planners, this film contrasts the turmoil of the planless city with the color and spaciousness of the small planned community.

Chapter Nine

Social Classes in America, 16 min, b&w, sd. (McG-H) This film shows some significant contrasts in the lives of three boys who come from three different social classes. It relates the ascribed, or inherited, status of each boy to the wealth, occupation, residential address, and social status of his parents and shows how graduation from the public high school marks the beginning of their increasingly different lives.

The House I Live In, 11 min, b&w, sd. (YAF) Frank Sinatra stars in a dramatic plea for racial and religious tolerance, emphasizing that America is a nation "made up of a hundred different kinds of people."

New India's People, 26 min, b&w, sd. (McG-H) This film describes the important segments of the Indian population that are determining the nation's future—the Maharajahs, a tiny, politically unimportant but fabulously wealthy group; the Untouchables, 60 million strong, who have benefited from the new government in terms of educational and social advancement although their living standard remains about the same; the Brahmins, India's intellectual leaders; and the Parsees, leaders in Indian commerce and industry.

One Tenth of Our Nation, 26 min, b&w, sd. (IFB) An authentic picture of the education of Negro children in the rural South. This film tells a moving story of the struggle for education from one-room shacks to high schools and colleges.

Chapter Ten

Boundary Lines, 10 min, color, sd. (McG-H) This animated film shows that once the impulse to draw such boundary lines becomes ingrained, the fear and prejudice developed can produce concentration camps and other subversions of freedom. The film stresses the need for education to counteract the effects of intolerance.

Race Relations (Fisk University) (From the Search Series), 27 min, b&w, sd. (YAF) The citizens of Baltimore report their progress in learning to live together despite the tensions engendered by racial, social, and religious differences.

Common Fallacies about Group Differences, 15 min, b&w, sd. (McG-H) This film analyzes seven common notions about races, heredity, and group differences in the light of known scientific evidence and shows in what way they are all fallacious. By so doing, it firmly establishes such facts as: there is no "French," "Italian," or other race; and group differences in behavior are the result of cultural influences, not heredity.

High Wall, 32 min, b&w, sd. (McG-H) An analysis of the kind of background that fosters bigotry and other anti-social attitudes. This film is for those interested in the real emotional and mental attitudes behind intolerance.

Americans All, 16 min, b&w, sd. (McG-H) In a gripping and objective presentation, interracial and interreligious hatreds are exposed as menaces to American democracy. Included is an analysis of a plan that any forward-looking community can adopt to fight intolerance.

Chapter Eleven

Development of Individual Differences, 13 min, b&w, sd. (McG-H) No two individuals are alike. Differences result from both heredity and environment. This film reviews and illustrates what is known and generally accepted about the relative influence of those two factors.

Out of Darkness, 55 min, b&w, sd. (McG-H) The story of a young woman admitted to California's Metropolitan State Hospital, mute, withdrawn, her eyes blank and disregarding of the world about her. For two and a half months a concealed camera recorded her psychiatric sessions with Dr. Louis Cholden in his slow struggle to reach a human being who is submerged in indifference, until the dramatic moment when she finally smiles and speaks her first word.

Heredity and Environment, 11 min, b&w, or color. (Coronet) Audiences learn that heredity influences certain basic capabilities, and environment determines the extent and direction of our use of those capabilities. An accurate overview of cultural inheritances, genetics, environmental influences, and their interrelationships.

Personality and Emotions, 13 min, b&w, sd. (EBF) This film is designed for junior college and college audiences studying personality development and mental health. It presents an overview of the development of emotions from infancy through early childhood, and implies that emotional maturity is a desirable goal in the development of personality.

Mental Illness (Tulane University) (The Search Series), 27 min, b&w, sd. (YAF) A two-part report on progress in psychiatry and research on the human brain, presenting the newest theories on mental illness.

Chapter Twelve

Our Changing Family Life, 22 min, b&w, sd. (McG-H) A farm family in 1880 is shown as a closely integrated unit—economically, culturally, and emotionally. Members of the three generations live under one roof according to a well-established pattern. Religion and recreation, in addition to the sharing of work, are important elements in holding the family together as an institution. Since 1880, industrial expansion, the growth of cities, and the political and economic emancipation of women have radically changed the traditional pattern of family life.

Family Affair, 31 min, b&w, sd. (TFC) This film depicts a critical chapter in the life of the Cooper family—exposing a boy's flight from home, a husband's decision to leave his wife, a mother's inability to understand those she most loves, and a daughter's bitter resentment of her parents.

Making a Decision in the Family, 8 min, b&w, sd. (McG-H) When a teen-ager declares her preference for going to a gathering of her friends rather than to a family party on the same evening, she runs into a flat refusal from her parents. The parents' insistence on having their decision followed causes a clash of wills. The question of how the parents might have better handled the situation is left up to the audience.

Family Circles, 31 min, b&w, sd. (McG-H) Following an excellent general discussion of the family as it used to be and as it is today, this film presents several cases of children, showing how their home life affects their school life. Emphasis is placed on the need for wholehearted cooperation between home and school.

Marriage and Divorce, 18 min, b&w, sd. (McG-H) No ceremony more deeply symbolizes the hope of man and woman than that of marriage. Yet one out of every three American marriages is headed for trouble. This film is a frank survey of the problem and what should be done about it.

Marriage Today, 22 min, b&w, sd. (McG-H) Two couples are the protagonists in this film, two couples who have made their marriages work by clearly analyzing their mutual aims and cooperating in achieving them.

When Should I Marry? 19 min, b&w, sd. (McG-H) A young couple, eager to marry but urged by their parents to delay, ask a minister's advice. He describes the experiences of two other couples who married at an early age. From this description, he is able to summarize some practical points that should be of help to all young people who are puzzling over the question of when to marry.

This Charming Couple, 19 min, b&w, sd. (McG-H) This film focuses on a frequent cause of broken marriages—false ideals of "romantic" love. We follow the courtship of two young people who refuse to evaluate each other's good qualities and shortcomings. Because they are in love with "love" and not with each other, their marriage is doomed to fail.

Choosing Your Marriage Partner, 13 min, b&w, and color, sd. (Coronet) In this film a young man is trying to decide which of two girls to marry. He is advised to consider such factors as emotional maturity, family background, philosophy of life, and harmony of personalities before making his choice.

Chapter Thirteen

Design of American Public Education, 16 min, b&w, sd. (McG-H) This film explains the organization of the American democratic school system as opposed to an authoritarian system and offers a philosophy of education that has as its primary aim the development of responsible citizens in a democratic society.

Who Will Teach Your Child? 24 min, b&w, sd. (McG-H) This film raises important issues on the subject of teacher education and suggests where some of the answers may be found. It asks, "how can we attract teachers into a career, train them, and persuade them to remain in the profession?"

School House in the Red, 40 min, color, sd. (EBF) The story of a one-room country school, the children who learn in it, and the parents of the district who support it. The film tells of the controversy that arises when the parents have to decide whether to continue to maintain the old school, with its many limitations, or send the children to a modern school in town.

Not by Chance, 28 min, b&w, sd. (NEA) Mayburn's work as an artistic teacher is revealed as a complex and demanding profession, which requires a very special kind of preparation. Donna, a prospective teacher of high-school science, is then introduced. In a sound program of undergraduate teacher education we see her acquiring the knowledge, the understanding of children, and the special skills that all good teachers must have.

School Facilities (Harvard University) (The Search Series) 27 min, b&w, sd. (YAF) Harvard specialists explain how they survey a community to determine its school status and needs.

Experimental Studies in Social Climates of Groups, 33 min, b&w, sd. (SUI) Part I— Democratic, autocratic, and laissez-faire atmosphere; Part II—Transitions of social atmospheres, (a) from autocracy to democracy, (b) from democracy to autocracy, and (c) from laissez faire to democracy.

Chapter Fourteen

We Hold These Truths, 28 min, b&w, sd. (B&F) A young Negro soldier, about to embark for Korea, finds slums and racial segregation in Washington, D.C., and New York City, and wonders if we have a right to call ourselves a "Christian Nation." He finds that the church is vitally interested in these problems.

More for Peace, 44 min, b&w, sd. (B&F) A drama of one man's search for Christian ideals in a troubled world. A veteran of the Korean War upon returning home is disillusioned about the working of democracy and the effectiveness of the Christian church. Through a series of experiences in his own local church, he finds an answer to the problems that have been troubling him.

Major Religions of the World (Development and Rituals), 19 min, b&w, sd. (EBF) This film presents an objective survey of the origins, rituals, and symbols of the major religions of the world today—Hinduism, Buddhism, Judaism, Christianity, and Islam. It is designed to help inspire an appreciation for, and a tolerance of, the religions of others.

One God, 37 min, b&w, sd. (AF) In this interfaith film, based on Mary Fitch's book, *One God,* the audience watches the rituals and ceremonies of the Jew, the Roman Catholic, and the Protestant. Great stress is placed on the important place freedom of worship has always played in the development of this country.

Chapter Fifteen

The Basic Elements of Production, 30 min, b&w, sd. (EBF) This film presents a graphic definition of each of the four basic elements that enter into the production of goods and services—natural resources, labor, capital, and management; shows what each of these elements contributes to the production process; and demonstrates how in our economy the increasing use of capital has contributed to the attainment of higher production levels than man has ever achieved before.

Productivity—Key to Plenty, 21 min, b&w, sd. (EBF) An explanation of how America has attained the world's highest standard of living because we have developed and learned to use machines—machines which, in turn, have enabled us to achieve a tremendous capacity for production. Included is a warning that continued prosperity depends on our uninterrupted technological progress and on the full use of our basic productive resources.

What Is Business? 11 min, b&w or color, sd. (Coronet) This comprehensive film takes the audience around the world of commerce to see how familiar services and goods are produced and distributed to satisfy consumer demand in our profit-motivated economic system.

What Is Money? 11 min, b&w or color, sd. (Coronet) This journey of a five-dollar bill through many transactions shows how money functions as a standard of value, standard for future payment, storehouse of value, and convenient medium of exchange for goods and services. The film traces our monetary systems from the days of primitive barter and shows how checks serve as a substitute for money.

Chapter Sixteen

Backfire, 15 min, b&w, sd. (PFC) An economics teacher poses the question to his pupils and neighbors: "Should men receive rewards in proportion to their investment in enterprise or was Karl Marx right in his theory of 'from each according to his ability, to each according to his need'?"

The Law of Demand and Supply, 11 min, b&w or color, sd. (Coronet) This film illustrates how the law of demand and supply affects business and stimulates discussion of the many economic factors to which this law may be applied.

Capitalism, 11 min, b&w or color, sd. (Coronet) Examined in this film are some important aspects of the capitalistic system—private property, profit, competition, freedom of contract, and free enterprise. A high-school radio forum provides an opportunity for the audience to listen to the conflicting opinions of several people, each of whom tries to tell what our system means to him.

Two Views on Socialism, 16 min, b&w or color, sd. (Coronet) In this film the aims of socialism and charges leveled by Socialists against capitalism are presented to stimulate discussion in the classroom. Standard of living, freedom of choice, and individual opportunity are compared in a capitalistic society and in a socialist society.

Chapter Seventeen

Competition and Big Business, 22 min, color, sd. (EBF) Based on an objective analysis of the relationship of big business to competition, this film defines big business in its proper perspective alongside other forms of enterprise. It analyzes the effect of big business on such problems as monopoly, entry into the market, and technological progress.

Other People's Property, 11 min, b&w, sd. (YAF) A dramatic situation designed to stimulate discussion on the problem of respect for property and the moral responsibility for protecting public property.

Big Enterprise in a Competitive System, 44 min, color, sd. (EBF) What place has big business—the giant industrial corporations—in a competitive private enterprise system? This film covers three aspects of big business: (1) How has big business affected the balance of competitive opportunities for risk-takers and employees? (2) To what extent has the position of industrial giants become immune from the challenge of competitors? (3) What chances are there for vigorous competition in those industries where a few big companies share the bulk of the output?

What Is a Corporation? 11 min, b&w or color, sd. (Coronet) The principal forms of business ownership—single proprietorship, partnership, and corporation—are thoroughly discussed in this film. The concept of business ownership is introduced and the advantages and disadvantages of each type are illustrated.

Internal Organization, 10 min, b&w, sd. (McG-H) This film illustrates the fundamental purposes behind business organization and explains basic organizational principles. It takes up such problems as delegation of authority, division of labor, and assignment of responsibility, and shows types of organization that can be adapted to the needs of any enterprise.

Chapter Eighteen

The Age of Specialization, 13 min, b&w, sd. (McG-H) In a country store in 1900, a farmer, shoemaker, store-owner, and country doctor speculate about changes the new century will bring in their occupations. The film then goes on to describe the subsequent technological changes in production, communications, and transportation which have caused radical economic changes, spawned increased specialization, and created new skills. The contrast between what each of these four men did in 1900 and what the multitude of new specialists and machines do today is vividly drawn.

The Structure of Unions, 11 min, b&w, sd. (McG-H) The organization of modern labor unions is examined in this cartoon film. Examples are given to illustrate the functioning of a union at its various levels from the union local to the national labor congress.

Grievance, 30 min, b&w, sd. (McG-H) This film illustrates the orderly processing of a grievance through several stages of negotiation between union and management, showing how the rights of a worker with a genuine grievance are protected under the union contract.

Local 100, 32 min, b&w, sd. (McG-H) The story of how Local 100 was formed, with the help of an organizer from union headquarters. The film also illustrates how collective bargaining methods obtained a better contract for the members.

Strike in Town, 28 min, b&w, sd. (McG-H) What happens in a town when its biggest industry is threatened with a strike? This film presents such a situation, dramatically describing the disagreements within families, the reactions of public opinion, and the strike preparations. Point-by-point descriptions of labor-management negotiations are included.

Bargaining Collectively, 11 min, b&w, sd. (TFC) Set in the period of the 1930's, this film presents arguments of labor and management for and against union recognition, as a committee of workers meets with plant directors to settle a strike.

Chapter Nineteen

Changing American Market, 17 min, color, sd. (TI) Facts, figures, and conclusions of 12 articles published in *Fortune* in 1953 and 1954 are presented in this film, which reports recent changes and predicts future developments in the American market.

The Importance of Selling, 20 min, b&w, sd. (EBF) This film describes the role of selling in our society, emphasizing the relationship between selling and other aspects of the business organization. It points up services provided by salesmen to business and to the consumer, describes the structure of typical sales organizations, and shows the duties of sales executives, following a product to its ultimate sale to the consumer.

Consumer Protection, 11 min, b&w or color, sd. (Coronet) The Whites, who buy on the basis of price and appearance alone, often make foolish purchases. But the Kings, who take advantage of information available from both government and private consumer services, are adequately protected in their buying and enjoy an improved standard of living.

Wise Buying, 11 min, b&w or color, sd. (Coronet) Important factors like seasonal changes, quantity purchases, and product labels are discussed in this film. The effects of wise buying—more, better, and necessary goods for less—prove that a person can raise his standard of living by buying wisely.

Distributing America's Goods, 11 min, b&w, sd. (EBF) This film utilizes animated drawings and natural photography to explain the cost of distributing America's goods. It considers distribution costs of the producer, wholesaler, retailer, and transporter in showing how 59 cents out of each purchase dollar goes to pay for costs of distribution.

Chapter Twenty

Science and Agriculture, 11 min, b&w, sd. (EBF) This film presents the soybean as an example of the ever-increasing importance of science and technology in agriculture. It describes how science strives, through research, to increase productivity and to find new industrial uses for farm products.

Our Soil Resources (Formation and Conservation), 11 min, b&w, sd. (EBF) A graphic explanation of how soil is formed by the physical and chemical disintegration of rock and by the decomposition of plant and animal matter. The film points out the world's four soil groups and defines their geographical limits in the United States, describes how man, through poor farming methods, has depleted the soil, and explains techniques for restoring fertility to worn-out land and curbing erosion.

The Agriculture Story, 13 min, color, sd. (USA) The major theme of this film is the unfolding story of how American agriculture has become the most efficient in world history. It dramatizes the importance of the forces of nature, the gifts of science and research, and the achievements of the American farmer and American machines, all working in a free economy.

Chapter Twenty-One

Inflation, 21 min, b&w or color, sd. (EBF) Inflation is defined, its causes and effects are revealed, and measures for its prevention are suggested in this film. We learn that a war or defense crisis can bring about inflation by increasing the supply of money and decreasing the supply of goods and that the remedies for inflation are measures which reduce the amount of money in circulation and at the same time increase productivity.

Federal Reserve System, 23 min, b&w, sd. (EBF) This film graphically explains the purpose and functions of the Federal Reserve System and shows how the system, growing naturally out of a national need, was devised to meet certain economic conditions. It covers the period from the money panic of 1907 through World War II, emphasizing historical high spots in the system's development as well as important contributions made to its founding and operation by several national leaders.

Round Trip: The U.S.A. in World Trade, 19 min, b&w, sd. (EBF) An American auto worker, a southern farmer, a housewife, a British machinist, a French laborer, and a Mexican farmer give their views on world trade. The film documents the importance and extent of world trade, emphasizing its significance to the United States and points up the effects of tariffs and how nations are planning to bring about more satisfactory trade arrangements.

Understanding the Dollar, 11 min, b&w or color, sd. (Coronet) We examine in this film various types of income, discover the essential purposes of money as a medium of exchange, and analyze factors which affect the real value of the dollar. Exactly how the changing value of a dollar affects the lives of people with various sources of income is clearly shown.

Protective Tariff vs. Free Trade, 26 min, b&w, sd. (McG-H) Watches are used in this film to dramatize the complex problems and issues involved in tariffs. The controversy over America's recently increased tariff on imported watch works vividly illustrates the difficulties involved in weighing the national interest and reciprocal trade relationships against the welfare of domestic industries.

Dollar Dance, 5 min, b&w, sd. (NFB) An amusing fantasy in which a dollar sign "$" sings and dances through a series of adventures portraying the evils of inflation and its prevention.

Chapter Twenty-Two

Defining Democracy, 18 min, b&w, sd. (EBF) Combining dramatic scenes with animation, this film compares the signs that distinguish a democratic community—shared respect and shared power—with the signs of despotism—restricted respect and concentrated power. The conditions that favor the growth of democracy are compared with the conditions that encourage despotism—economic balance and enlightenment as opposed to slanted economic distribution and controlled information.

Government Is Your Business, 30 min, b&w, sd. (Christ) This is the story of a young college graduate who enters politics against the wishes of his parents and fiancée. Running against a corrupt city machine, he finds himself confused about the issues. The climax is reached when he challenges the corrupt, machine-backed candidate.

Public Opinion in Our Democracy, 10 min, b&w or color, sd. (Coronet) This film explains the importance of public opinion in our society—the attitudes that American citizens hold toward major issues in political and social life. It shows that one man's vote *does* count and that everyone must express his opinion lest the minority point of view rule.

Social Change in Democracy, 30 min, b&w, sd. (UWF) This film has been prepared by the United States Army for use in occupied areas, but it is also available for American audiences. It portrays students in a high-school social studies class discussing the difference between conditions in a democracy and in a totalitarian state.

Chapter Twenty-Three

Meaning of Elections, 11 min, b&w and color, sd. (Coronet) This film dramatizes the concepts of equality, the relationship of the elected official to his constituency, the importance of voting, the operation of election machinery, and the necessity for people to strive continually to improve their electoral systems.

Political Parties, 18 min, b&w, sd. (EBF) Emphasizing that political parties provide the means by which citizens act together to choose public officials and to further programs that express their own interests, this film points out that parties are as important when they are in opposition as when they are in power. It stresses that political parties can exist only where citizens can express their opinions and act on them.

Presidential Elections, 15 min, b&w, sd. (EBF) The most significant event in American political life, the election of a president, is described in this film. Dynamic and graphic charts and a wealth of photographic material describe recent campaigns. The structure and strategy of campaign organizations and the major political moves involved in the nomination and election of a president, are analyzed.

Pressure Groups, 22 min, b&w, sd. (EBF) This film defines pressure groups and shows that when democratically used, they are an important instrument for decision-making in a democracy. Methods used by democratic pressure groups to promote legislation are illustrated and contrasted with the underhanded and behind-the-scenes methods employed by undemocratic groups.

Chapter Twenty-Four

Federal Government: The Plan of Organization, 13½ min, b&w and color, sd. (Coronet) Structure and functions of the federal government are presented in this film and the primary divisions of responsibility in government are outlined. The reasons for these divisions and the problems that arise from the many quasi-legislative and quasi-judicial boards and agencies also are illustrated.

How We Elect Our Representatives, 11 min, b&w and color, sd. (Coronet) This film describes registration procedure, the primary election, the campaign, voting, and the counting of the ballots, and shows that the functional basis of our democracy is the electoral system.

Conduct of Congressional Investigations, 26 min, b&w, sd. (McG-H) Congressional committees, their function, purpose, and the legal conduct of their investigations are analyzed in this film. The two types of congressional committees and their respective roles are described. All the major moral and political aspects of the committees are inspected. The film suggests wise and advantageous changes in the committees' rules and regulations.

The President, 17 min, b&w, sd. (EBF) This film dramatizes the major historical events by which the present power and influence of the presidency were established. It also surveys the scope and responsibilities of today's chief executive, showing how the office has grown as a result of the actions of strong presidents in times of crisis.

The Congress, 20 min, b&w, sd. (EBF) This film is a dramatic demonstration of the powers and duties of the Congress. It illustrates how law-making process begins with citizens at home concerned with a vital issue. This issue—a community's need for a flood-control program—is traced from the action of a local committee to the campaign of a congressman, through debate in a congressional committee, to final action on the Senate floor. With the president's signature, a locally-inspired bill becomes the law of the land. Scenes of actual congressional committees at work illustrate the scope of congressional authority.

Chapter Twenty-Five

The Constitution Series, Three parts, app. 60 min ea, b&w, sd. (McG-H) Here is the dramatic story of the creation and continued growth of the document that guides the destiny of this country, the Constitution. The three films of the series are narrated not through a fictional script, but in the actual words of the figures who played important parts in the Constitution's development and history. In the role of commentator is the noted American lawyer, Joseph N. Welch.

One Nation
    Part 1: The Constitution Is Drafted
    Part 2: The States Adopt the Constitution
One Nation Indivisible
    Part 1: The States Challenge Federal Powers (1790-1849)
    Part 2: Slavery and Secession (1850-1865)
With Liberty and Justice for All
    Part 1: Supreme Court Decisions on Civilian Trial, Racial Equality, and Individual Belief
    Part 2: Supreme Court Decisions on Reforms, Religious Belief, and Fair Trial

The Supreme Court, 18 min, b&w, sd. (EBF) This film discusses the history and function of the Supreme Court and relates how, under the guidance of Chief Justice John Marshall, the Court gained recognition of its power to determine the constitutionality of federal and state laws. It describes ways in which Court decisions bear on the welfare of all citizens and indicates the procedures by which these decisions are made.

. .*Our Living Constitution,* 11 min, b&w and color, sd. (Coronet) This film illustrates the importance of the Constitution in our everyday life in guaranteeing the rights and freedoms of the individual, protecting the interests of the people, and growing to meet the needs of the times. There is a clear explanation of the basic structure of the Constitution and how it changes by acts of Congress, custom, and usage while retaining its original principles.

The Supreme Court, 11 min, b&w and color, sd. (Coronet) As we follow a case from inception, through the lower courts to the Supreme Court, we learn the relationship between the Court and the "plain citizen." We see the Supreme Court as the guardian of constitutional rights and learn about its function, powers, and jurisdiction.

Chapter Twenty-Six

Centralization and Decentralization, 18 min, b&w, sd. (EBF) A review of the problems created by the gradual transfer of decision-making from local communities to centralized bodies operating at state and national levels. The film points out that citizens today face the need of preserving local freedom and initiative and at the same time of centralizing control wherever necessary and suggests that the proper way is to preserve a balance between local and central authority.

The Legislative Process, 28 min, color, sd. (Ind) Using the General Assembly of Indiana as an example of a state legislature in action, the film presents detailed information about the various steps through which bills must pass to become laws.

Chapter Twenty-Seven

Russia, 24 min, color, sd. (IF) The historic background of Russia starting about 1905 and carrying through to modern Russia today is the main theme of this film.

Rare scenes on collective farms and other interesting aspects of Russia are included as well as a contrast between Russia under the tzars and the Russia of today.

Communism (One of the pre-military orientation series), 11 min, b&w, sd. (Coronet) Why is communism a threat to our values and our way of life? What methods are we employing to withstand the danger of communism? Such questions are considered in this film.

What Price Freedom? 40 min, b&w or color, sd. (B&F) A dramatic motion picture of courage and intrigue behind the Iron Curtain in East Berlin, based on an actual incident. It defines a crucial triangle, as dynamic as today's headlines. At one point of the triangle is the vigor and freedom of democracy—perhaps too readily accepted and insufficiently appreciated.

Chapter Twenty-Eight

World Balance of Power, 18 min, b&w, sd. (EBF) A discussion of the principles of world balance of power as the foundation of national independence and international peace in the modern world. The film suggests that in the present international crisis new aggressions and wars can be prevented if all nations adhere to the balance of power principle.

Nationalism, 20 min, b&w, sd. (EBF) This film defines nationalism and traces its growth as one of the most powerful forces in the modern world. The three phases of nationalism are explained, nationalism as a force both for progress and regress in the modern world is described, and constructive approaches to the problems of world peace are emphasized.

Planning Our Foreign Policy, 21 min, b&w, sd. (EBF) (Problems of the Middle East) In this film we see the procedure by which a working-level government committee concerned with United States foreign policy in the Middle East analyzes the problems it faces. Problems are broken down into their economic, military, political and psychological components and various alternatives are considered.

Pattern of Peace, 22 min, b&w, sd. (TI) Officially approved and recommended by the United Nations Film Board, this film explains the functions of the United Nations, and by charts, animation, and a clear commentary describes how the organization is set up and what the purpose of each department is.

One World or None, 11 min, b&w, sd. (FP) This film outlines the relative effectiveness of weapons of war, and points out that atomic power must be channeled into constructive rather than destructive uses if the human race is to survive.

Beginning or the End? 30 min, b&w, sd. (TFC) Adapted from the feature picture of the same title, this film reviews the early concern of scientists involved in atomic energy research, the realization of the political implications of the A-bomb, the work at Oak Ridge, and the part played by Roosevelt, Churchill, Bush, Groves, and Truman in the development and use of the bomb.

Peoples Charter, 20 min, b&w, sd. (IFB) This film relates the organization of the United Nations at San Francisco, and describes the first meeting of the U. N. Assembly, with statements by various U. N. leaders.

Illustrations

Index

N1